AESTHETICS EXPOSED

MASTERING SKIN CARE IN A MEDICAL SETTING AND BEYOND

TERRI A. WOJAK, LE

Aesthetics Exposed:
Mastering Skin Care in a Medical Setting and Beyond

ISBN-10: 1937235483
ISBN-13: 978-1937235482
ISBN-13 (Kindle): 978-1937235505

Copyright 2014, by Allured Publishing Corporation, dba Allured Business Media, and Terri A. Wojak. All Rights Reserved.

Editorial

Editor:	Brian W. Budzynski
Indexer:	Brenda Kozlowski
Interior and Cover Design:	Bryan Crowe and Lisa Hede
Page Layout:	Bryan Crowe

Administration

Director of Marketing and Business Manager:	Linda Schmitt
Sales and Brand Specialist:	Marie Kuta
Audience Database Specialist:	Anita Singh

Neither this book nor any part may be reproduced or transmitted in any form by any means, electronic or mechanical, including photocopying, microfilming, and recording, or by any information storage retrieval system, without permission in writing from the publisher.

NOTICE

To the best of our knowledge the information in this book is accurate. However, in a time of rapid change, it is difficult to ensure that all information provided is entirely accurate and up-to-date. Therefore, the author and the publisher accept no responsibility for any inaccuracies or omissions and specifically disclaim any liability, loss, or risk, personal or otherwise, which is incurred as a consequence, directly or indirectly, of the use and/or application of any of the contents of this book. Mention of trade names or commercial products does not constitute endorsement or recommendation for use by the publisher.

an imprint of Alluredbooks
336 Gundersen Drive, Suite A, Carol Stream, IL 60188 USA
Tel: 630-653-2155 Fax: 630-653-2192
www.Alluredbooks.com
E-mail: books@allured.com

845 N. Michigan Ave., Suite 925W
Chicago, IL 60611
Tel: 312-440-9740
www.trueuesthetics.com

Table of Contents

Prefatory Note   i

Part 1   *Aesthetics & Cosmetic Medicine: The Framework*
1. Cosmetic Medicine Meets Skin Care   3
2. The Legalities of Aesthetics in a Medical Setting   13
3. OSHA: Safety Regulations   19
4. HIPAA: The Privacy Act   25

Part 2   *The Aesthetic Consultation*
5. The Science of Beauty   37
6. The Client Experience   43
7. Effective Consultation Techniques   59
8. Skin Condition Analysis   67

Part 3   *Aesthetically Challenging Skin Concerns*
9. Acne   93
10. Rosacea   109
11. Hyperpigmentation   117
12. Aging Skin   129

Part 4   *Professional Skin Care Treatments*
13. Chemical Exfoliation: AHAs, BHA, TCA, & Jessner's   153
14. Microdermabrasion   173
15. Dermaplaning   181
16. Micro-needling   187

Part 5   *Laser and Light Therapy*
17. Laser Safety Regulations and Considerations   207
18. Light Physics   219
19. Visible Light Lasers and Intense Pulsed Light (IPL)   229
20. Laser Resurfacing: Ablative, Non-ablative, & Fractionated   247

Part 6 Complementing Medical Procedures with Skin Care

21	Neurotoxins	273
22	Soft Tissue Fillers	285
23	Facial Cosmetic Surgery	299
24	Pre- and Post-Surgical Treatment: MLD and Camouflage Makeup	311

Part 7 Innovative Skin Rejuvenation Techniques

25	Five Steps to Making a SMART Purchase	333
26	Devices: From Tightening to Rejuvenation, From Medical to Spa	339
27	Effective Formulations and Breakthrough Ingredients	359
28	Focusing on the Eyes	381

Part 8 The Road to Success: Skin to Win

29	Landing Your Dream Job	395
30	Easy and Efficient Business Building	403
31	Retail: Educating vs. Selling	407
32	Tools for Client Retention	417

Appendices

A	Medical Terminology, Recognizing Instruments Used in Aesthetic Medicine, and Anatomy & Skin Physiology	429
B	Standard Operating Procedures (SOPs)	441
C	Intake Forms, Consents, and Checklists (including Fitzpatrick Charting)	449
D	Documentation Practices	461

Glossary	467
Review Question Answer Key	491
Author Bio & Acknowledgments	535
Index	539

PREFATORY NOTE

Aesthetics vs. Esthetics: A Distinction

Throughout this book you will see the spelling for (a)esthetics varies between *aesthetics* and *esthetics*. These words are often used interchangeably in the cosmetic industry; however, they do have different meanings, and this difference is important to your complete understanding of *Aesthetics Exposed*.

Aesthetics is about the nature of art dealing with beauty. This term is commonly used when dealing with cosmetic medicine.

Estheticians are licensed professionals who practice skin care or *esthetics* to improve the appearance of the outer layers of the skin. Estheticians are likely trained on basic anatomy of the skin, facials, hair removal, exfoliation treatments, and makeup application. There are now more schools that offer extended curriculums that go above and beyond the basics.

The distinction between these terms is important for the following reasons, linked to the respective terms' application within this book:

Esthetics will be used when discussing treatments performed by estheticians dealing with the outermost layer of the epidermis. Aesthetics will be used when describing beauty, as well as treatments performed in cosmetic medicine.

You may also see the words *patient* and *client* used at different points, as well. Patient is the term used when speaking of someone receiving a medical service. Client is used when one is receiving a service in general such as a facial, massage, or haircut.

PART 1

Aesthetics & Cosmetic Medicine: The Framework

AESTHETICS EXPOSED
MASTERING SKIN CARE IN A MEDICAL SETTING AND BEYOND

CHAPTER 1

Cosmetic Medicine Meets Skin Care

In this Chapter:
- The Aesthetics Industry
- Skin Care Meets Cosmetic Medicine
- Benefits of Combining Skin Care and Medicine
- Benefits to Practice
- Importance of Professionalism

The Aesthetics Industry

The skin care industry is constantly growing, resulting in more career options for the esthetician. According to the Bureau of Labor Statistics, "Employment of skin care specialists is expected to grow 25 percent from 2010 to 2020, faster than the average for all occupations."[1] This growth is led by the increased awareness that skin care is an important adjunct to cosmetic medicine. In recent years, not only are dermatologists and plastic surgeons offering cosmetic services, but family practice physicians, ob/gyns and even dentists have jumped on the cosmetic bandwagon.

There has been some controversy regarding *cosmetic* skin care in medical settings such as dermatology, cosmetic surgery, or anything in between. The old way of thinking for some, notably those in the medical community, was that medicine and cosmetics were separate entities and should be kept that way. With physicians already addressing conditions of the skin and offering medical treatments for cosmetic enhancements, skeptics were asking the question of why one would need to see an esthetician. It had become somewhat of a battle wherein the majority of physicians thought that non-prescription topical skin care was unnecessary. What would "cosmetics" do for patients that prescriptive medicine would not?

One reason underlying this separation included the unfortunate fact that some skin care professionals, including estheticians and sales representatives, make false claims about cosmetic treatments. Moreover, there were also instances where estheticians gave advice against what was recommended by a physician—which is beyond the scope of practice for any non-medical provider and can cause serious complications.

Medical professionals are meant to *treat* conditions or abnormalities, whereas estheticians are meant to *cosmetically enhance* the skin. When this combination of treatment is implemented correctly, all involved win, and the client obtains the best results while the health of the skin is maintained. The medical practice has increased patient satisfaction, thereby producing higher retention rates and referrals, and the esthetician is inevitably credentialed by the physician.

> Medical professionals are meant to *treat* conditions or abnormalities, whereas estheticians are meant to *cosmetically enhance* the skin.

Among the cosmetic services available today, the largest increase has been in nonsurgical procedures. In the last eight years alone, the number of these services has increased more than 680%.[2] Two of these procedures, microdermabrasion and chemical peels, are most commonly performed by estheticians. This clearly indicates the increased value of adding skin care to the medical practice. This demand has prompted a large number of physicians to introduce cosmetic procedures, esthetic treatments, and skin care products.

According to recent information from the American Society for Aesthetic Plastic Surgery,[3] nonsurgical procedures accounted for 83% of the total number of procedures performed, representing 39% of total expenditures. The top five minimally invasive procedures by number of cases reported are shown in the following chart:

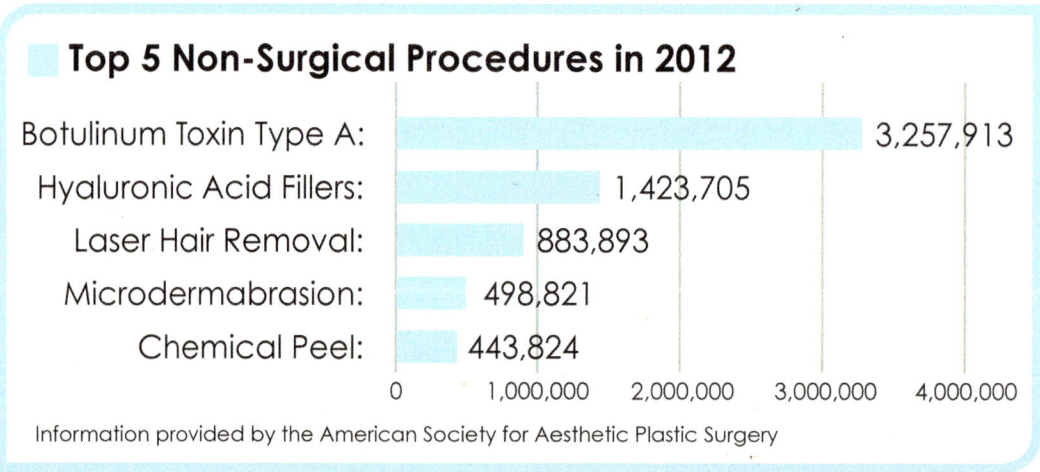

Top 5 Non-Surgical Procedures in 2012

Botulinum Toxin Type A:	3,257,913
Hyaluronic Acid Fillers:	1,423,705
Laser Hair Removal:	883,893
Microdermabrasion:	498,821
Chemical Peel:	443,824

Information provided by the American Society for Aesthetic Plastic Surgery

Cosmetic Medicine Meets Skin Care

SCENARIO: Safe Skin Care & Medicine

What could happen:
Provider: "We cannot perform microneedling while you are on blood thinners."
Client: "But that is the treatment I came in for; I was really excited to try it."
Provider: "If you discontinue your blood thinners, I can do the procedure next week."

The problem: The esthetician suggested she stop recommended treatment from her physician. The medication could be used for a serious medical condition. Only a physician can tell a client to discontinue a medication. Even if it were a prescribed topical agent for aging, such as Retin-A, an esthetician cannot interfere with a client's medical treatment or the recommendations of her physician.

What should happen:
Provider: "We cannot perform microneedling if you are on blood thinners."
Client: "But that is the treatment I came in for; I was really excited to try it."
Provider: "I'm sorry for any inconvenience, but your health comes first. We have plenty of great treatments that will provide you results without putting you in harm's way. Let me tell you more about the blended TCA peels we offer." ... or ... "Consult with your physician as to whether or not (however temporary) it's advisable to come off those blood thinners for this procedure. And if not, there are many other treatments that your skin type is a candidate for that can bring about the same results you're looking for."

Skin Care Meets Cosmetic Medicine

Treatments performed in a medical setting often differ from those commonly performed in a salon or day spa. In a spa environment, facial treatments are frequently focused on relaxation and maintaining healthy skin, whereas the medical setting focuses on results-driven products and services. Chemical peels, microdermabrasion, and dermaplaning are some of the most common treatments performed.

It has become increasingly obvious that skin care ultimately complements cosmetic medicine. The easiest way for an aesthetic practice to implement skin care is to hire an esthetician, though the issue remains that there is currently no specialized license for estheticians to work in a medical practice. This can be confusing, as many estheticians use the title "medical esthetician." At one time, this title was used loosely to define those with advanced training for a medical setting, or for those already working under the direction of a physician. Now that regulations are becoming more stringent, some state departments threaten inactivating licensure for improper labeling of an esthetician's title. This does not mean that an esthetician is unable to work successfully in a medical practice; however, they must always remain within their professional scope of practice, which varies from state to state.

SCENARIO: Knowledge of Medical Procedures

A client comes into a spa for a microdermabrasion. It's an impromptu, spur-of-the-moment decision. During the consultation she admits that she had a laser treatment two weeks prior.

What could happen:
Provider: "Do you know what type of laser treatment was performed?"
Client: "Well, they said it was noninvasive, and my skin healed within a week."
Provider: "Great, let's get started then."

What could go wrong:
If the client had an ablative resurfacing treatment, the skin would still be in its healing phase and microdermabrasion could cause severe trauma to the skin and interrupt the healing cycle, thus causing damage to the skin.

What should happen:
Provider: "Do you know what type of laser treatment was performed?"
Client: "Well, they said it was noninvasive, and my skin healed within a week."
Provider: "What treatment did you get the laser for? And how was the healing process? Was there any bleeding, redness, or swelling?"
Client: "There was minor bleeding the first day, followed by redness and stinging for about five days."
Provider: "It sounds as though you may have had an ablative resurfacing procedure. Microdermabrasion would not be the best option for you today. We do, however, have an amazing facial that is great post-laser; it will add vital nutrients to the outer layers of skin to promote healing and provide an immediate glow."
Client: "That sounds great!"

Many physicians and estheticians alike think that additional education is not necessary for an esthetician employed in the medical field since there is no licensing to be a "medical esthetician." With the surge in cosmetic medicine, it has become increasingly important for *all* estheticians to have at least a basic understanding of medical procedures that they may come in contact with in order to treat clients safely. Advanced training for medical settings should not imply that estheticians have the skills to perform medical procedures; rather, it is quite the opposite, as a professional training center should inform the licensed estheticians or cosmetologists of what they are able and unable to do to enhance and maintain results.

> Advanced training for medical settings should not imply that estheticians have the skills to perform medical procedures; rather, it is quite the opposite, as a professional training center should inform the licensed estheticians or cosmetologists of what they are able and unable to do to enhance and maintain results.

Although basic training on cosmetic medicine is necessary for all skin care professionals, there is further education needed for those actually working alongside a physician. Training for work in a medical setting must consist of standard regulations governing patient health and privacy, including the Occupational Safety and Health Administration (OSHA) and Health Insurance Portability and Accountability Act (HIPAA), which will be addressed in Chapters 3 and 4, respectively. Employers are ultimately responsible for ensuring these regulations are met; however, it is best to have a good understanding of them before entering the medical field. It is also important that each provider has knowledge of every procedure being performed throughout the workplace, regardless of whether they are performing it themselves. This connection throughout the office ensures safety, optimal results, and consistency throughout the practice. **Knowing the indications, contraindications, possible complications, and what the patient will experience during each treatment helps to determine safe and effective skin care protocols and recommendations.**

In recent years, it has become more common for medical professionals including medical assistants (MAs), registered nurses (RNs), nurse practitioners (NPs), physician assistants (PAs), and even physicians to become more involved in learning and/or performing skin care treatments. This is certainly a positive step for the aesthetic industry. As stated earlier, it has been somewhat difficult in the past for medical providers to see the benefit in skin care. There are several treatments for skin rejuvenation that can be performed by an esthetician to a certain level, but if a more aggressive treatment is necessary, a medical professional must be involved (e.g., medium-depth chemical peels and micro-needling).

The medical provider mindset is quite different from that of an esthetician. Regardless of specialty, physicians invest many years of training with the strictest of protocols. Due to this stringent educational format, physicians are inclined to default to a "clinical" bedside manner and are focused on the root of the problem and developing a solution. In contrast, the esthetician's base training is far more limited and focuses on superficial skin treatments and recommendations. Overall, estheticians tend to cater to the emotional side of the patient and serve as an "ambassador" for the medical staff. To have a successful aesthetic practice, all staff members should work as a team with the end result being the client's well-being. A collaborative effort between the two provides patients with the best of both worlds.

Benefits of Combining Skin Care and Medicine

When skin care is implemented properly, the benefits are endless. Offering patients safe and effective products that support procedures will not only enhance and maintain results, but it will also keep them coming back. There are several medical procedures that are enhanced with skin care, which is a topic much of this book will address. Product use is especially important following invasive treatments (e.g. deep laser resurfacing), and this is where the provider drives home that message and/or monitors the patient's compliance with post-care protocols, which the physician sets in place. Otherwise, if the skin is not cared for properly when the client leaves the office, adverse reactions including infections, discoloration, and even scarring may occur.

Overall, the importance of maintaining healthy skin has become more popular than trying to fix skin that has already been damaged. Healthy skin often repairs itself faster, reducing the chance of side effects and providing better results. This will make patients happy and provide added value. **The skin care provider is typically booked more time with the patient to go over a pre- and post-treatment plan to optimize results. Patients appreciate the extra attention and having access to another provider for support while working toward end results.**

Benefits to Practice

With the number of aesthetic providers increasing daily, cultivating client relationships is important, and multiple connections with staff builds loyalty and trust in the practice.

Cosmetic Medicine Meets Skin Care

SCENARIO: Benefits of Multiple Providers

Rita comes in to see Dr. Glass for filler in her nasolabial folds, after which she will not need another treatment for at least nine months.

Rita's friend Sue goes to Dr. Smith, whose office is just up the road and who Sue says "does an amazing job." Dr. Smith, says Sue, presently has a special going on where new patients get half-off their treatments, and Sue thinks it would be fun for her and Rita to go together.

Rita's decision in this matter—to go or not to go—clearly depends on her relationship with Dr. Glass, but it would be hard to turn down Sue's friendly suggestion, not to mention the discount offered by Dr. Smith's office, if Rita had only seen Dr. Glass once or twice before.

Now, picture this same scenario with Rita coming in to Dr. Glass's office on a monthly basis to receive skin care services. Rita has now built a relationship with the physician and his staff where she receives her facials, products, and cosmetic medical treatments. She is comfortable communicating with Dr. Glass and his staff, and feels they ensure she has the best outcomes. Rita will now be more likely to pass on Sue's offer and stay loyal to the practice that cares for all of her needs.

The best way to introduce a skin care professional to patients is to have him/her assist the physician during the work day. This has dual benefits, as it helps the physician see more patients and gives the skin care provider experience from the patient's point of view. The esthetician can perform an initial skin care consultation while prepping the patient's skin prior to their appointment. During the treatment, the esthetician can provide comfort to the patient and assist the physician as needed. Assistance may include holding pressure on an area that may be bruised, or applying post-treatment products. At the end of a procedure, the esthetician can educate the patient on how to properly care for their skin in affected and unaffected areas in order to obtain the best results from the treatment received.

> The skin care provider can perform an initial consultation while prepping the patient's skin prior to their appointment.

The physician's time is the most valuable asset of a practice, and having assistance can free time to see more patients. The skin care provider can also make the most of free time by preparing the treatment room, escorting patients back to their appointed room, and taking photos. Relationships are built through multiple interactions, and this provides the skin care provider a chance to build a relationship with the patient.

> Relationships are built through multiple interactions, and this affords the skin care provider a chance to build a relationship with the patient.

The Importance of Professionalism

To succeed in the aesthetic industry, maintaining the highest level of professionalism is crucial. There are core professional ethics that must be followed—and the most important is to always do what is best for the client. This does not mean what is best for the client's *skin*, but what is best for the client's *well-being*. Choosing the best treatment for the client's well-being is a trait to be learned that will prove beneficial to your career, and serve you well on a client by client basis. Skin care is often taken more seriously in a medical setting. Physicians typically support clinically proven services and products; therefore, esthetic treatments and product offerings become validated in the client's mind by their presence in a medical setting. Clients also tend to think of physician recommendations for skin care in a context similar to a "prescription." Those working in a medical setting are held to higher standards than those employed at a spa due to medical regulations and standards of care. Good bedside manner is essential in a medical setting, because patients may present with additional needs. This is especially important in light of the fact that invasive procedures can be distressing for some patients.

> There is benefit to everyone involved when each professional understands their scope of practice and plays a role in the client's *well-being*.

Regulations for estheticians in a medical setting vary from state to state; unfortunately, no matter the region, regulations are uniformly unclear, which has made it difficult to know where the esthetician ends and the medical provider begins. Recent advancements in education and strides made by industry organizations working toward clearly defined roles have led to medical providers and estheticians working together for a standard of care. There is benefit to everyone involved when each professional understands their scope of practice and plays a role in the client's *well-being*.

References
1. *www.bls.gov/ooh/personal-care-and-service/skincare-specialists.htm#tab-6* (accessed Apr 15, 2014)
2. *www.plasticsurgery.org/Documents/news-resources/statistics/2012-Plastic-Surgery-Statistics/Cosmetic-Procedure-Trends-2012.pdf* (accessed Apr 15, 2014)
3. *www.surgery.org/sites/default/files/2012-top5.pdf* (accessed Apr 15, 2014)

CHAPTER 2

The Legalities of Aesthetics in a Medical Setting

by Alex R. Thiersch, JD* & Renee E. Coover, JD

When I became a lawyer close to 15 years ago, there was no such thing as a "medical spa." Botox, laser hair removal, fillers—these procedures were just becoming known and being offered almost exclusively by physicians. No one could foresee how, in just a few short years, the term "medical spa" would not only emerge, but explode into a billion-dollar industry. Even though we are only recently recovering from a devastating recession, revenue from aesthetic procedures has continued to steadily increase.

It is important to note this explosion in the number of med spas and aesthetic treatments has brought increased scrutiny from medical boards and governing authorities. The med spa industry now faces increased regulation, and violation of local laws results in substantial fines, suspension, and even criminal prosecution. The risk for getting in trouble while operating a med spa has never been higher, especially now that non-physicians and non-medical professionals are entering the arena.

As a lawyer focusing almost exclusively on med spa-related matters, I get calls every day asking the same basic questions. I am continually amazed at how many industry professionals are unaware of the basic legal guidelines that govern the industry. No matter what profession or level of education—I've dealt with physicians, surgeons, nurses, estheticians, and even other health care lawyers—hardly anyone is properly educated on what they are and are not permitted to do in the medical aesthetic industry. And since **ignorance of the law is never an excuse**, it is high time that the industry starts focusing on educating itself.

There are a number of legal issues that affect medical professionals in med spas.

---

*Alex R. Thiersch is a partner at Thiersch & Associates, a Chicago based law firm, and founder of the American Med Spa Association (AmSpa), an association dedicated to educating the medical spa industry on the rules and regulations affecting it. This chapter was contributed graciously at the author's request.

But before we dive in, a major, super-important disclaimer: *The laws are different everywhere, so it is essential that practitioners discuss these issues with their local attorneys. Nothing in this article should be construed as legal advice. Without discussing your situation in person, it is impossible to make a determination as to your legal needs. These are generalities only.*

Supervision

First and foremost, it is crucial to know what med spa services require physician supervision in your particular state and what constitutes an adequate amount of supervision. In Illinois, for example, all medical treatments, including Botox and laser hair removal, require physician supervision.

Although it is difficult to make generalities regarding supervision, the fact remains that the treatments we are discussing here (neurotoxins, fillers, and laser treatments) are generally considered *medical* treatments. As such, these treatments must be supervised by *medical* professionals. I cannot tell you how many times clients have come to me after being investigated, because lasers were being fired without a medical professional in sight. There are very few places in the industrialized world (I can't, in fact, think of any offhand) where you can receive medical treatment by a non-medical professional. Thus, at a minimum, medical supervision is required on-site for the practice to be compliant. If a physician is not on-site, a nurse, nurse practitioner or other medical professional should be, and the physician should be available by phone.

Delegation

Supervision goes hand in hand with delegation. The medical aesthetic industry is different from most other medical practices because many of the treatments are not performed by physicians. Botox and fillers are often performed by nurses or physician assistants (PAs), and laser treatments are performed by laser technicians. Consequently, non-physicians are often left to perform treatments without proper supervision, and physicians often leave their practices in the hands of others without procedures in place to ensure proper supervision.

Although a physician may delegate initial patient consults and medical treatments to nurse practitioners (NPs) and PAs, the physician must be involved and available to patients should an emergency occur. **Remember that ultimately, physicians are responsible for each patient that walks through the door of a medical practice; simply put: the physician's license is on the line.** Some states have additional oversight requirements as well. In Illinois, a medical professional must be on-site at the med spa at all times when medical procedures and treatments are performed. This means that if a physician owner only has one other employee and that individual is a non-medical professional, the physician must be on-site at all times to provide supervision.

Corporate Practice of Medicine

The "corporate practice of medicine" is a sticky concept that often comes up in my legal practice, and many med spa professionals are unaware of this crucial rule that governs the practice in several states. In essence, this doctrine states that only physicians may practice medicine. Non-physicians (1) may not practice medicine, and (2) may not own a business or corporation that practices medicine. In other words, the practice of medicine is the sole domain of physicians and physician-owned corporations, therefore only physicians and physician-owned corporations may own med spas. **The policy behind this rule is that physicians, and only physicians, should practice medicine and be in charge of medical care.**

This has become a significant issue as the industry has gotten bigger. Non-physicians, seeing the potential for large returns, have begun opening laser centers and med spas. While this is allowed in some jurisdictions (the state of Florida being one), in most states this is a HUGE no-no. In Illinois, where I practice, for instance, the state boards have prosecuted many med spas because the ownership structure is improper. In order to run a medical facility in Illinois, the business must be owned solely by physicians.

This becomes problematic when physicians and non-physicians wish to partner in a med spa. In many jurisdictions, this is not allowed due to the corporate practice of medicine doctrine. In these jurisdictions, the medical company must be owned only by physicians, with no lay people allowed in the ownership structure whatsoever.

Unauthorized Practice of Medicine

Here's a quick question: Let's say you are a physician who owns a med spa that performs laser hair removal. You are properly staffed with nurses, laser techs, and estheticians. One day while you are away from the spa, a woman comes in off the street and asks for laser hair removal. Your nurse, who has performed hundreds of these treatments, does a thorough history and physical exam and then delegates the procedure to a very qualified laser technician. The procedure goes smoothly and additional treatments are scheduled. The woman goes on her way as a satisfied customer. All is well, right?

Not quite. Your nurse and laser technician have very likely just engaged in the unauthorized practice of medicine, and if you knowingly allowed this to happen, you, the physician, just aided and abetted in the unauthorized practice of medicine. All three of you could very well face suspension and a hefty fine.

So, what's the problem? The patient, after all, was examined by a qualified medical professional, treatment was delegated to a qualified laser tech, and the patient was happy. The issue here is that medical treatment was performed without the patient ever being examined by a physician (or a proper delegate like a PA). Remember, medical treatment is the domain of physicians. While treatment can be delegated to nurses or other professionals as discussed above, such delegation must originate from the physician, and that can happen only after a physician-patient relationship is established. In many states, this means a face-to-face consult with the physician.

This issue is particularly problematic in the med spa industry as physicians are not always present and the medical procedures are not, medically speaking, overly complicated. But med spas are still medical facilities and, as such, all rules applicable to medical facilities apply. This means that an exam from a physician or nurse practitioner is necessary before any medical treatment is performed. (Note that in some jurisdictions, physician's assistants may perform initial consults as well).

Fee Splitting

I'm often surprised at how many practitioners are unaware of the prohibition against fee splitting. It's been around forever, and the laws in many jurisdictions haven't changed for some time. The rule is simple: Physicians may not split medical fees with anyone other than physicians. Or put differently, non-physicians may not split medical revenue with physicians. This means that when a fee is paid for an aesthetic medical treatment, that fee must be paid directly to the physician or physician-owned corporation only, and no part of that fee can be split with a non-physician.

In the med spa setting, this problem often manifests itself in one of two ways: first, a nurse, laser technician, or other professional is paid a commission on the amount of revenue he or she generates (i.e. 10% of all revenue generated from Botox or laser hair removal); or second, non-physicians (including patients) are paid referral fees for bringing in new patients. Both of these practices, depending on the jurisdiction, may constitute fee-splitting.

The prohibition against fee-splitting stems from policymakers' belief that allowing non-physicians to share in medical revenue has the potential to affect patient care. **Physicians should be motivated by healing, not volume, the thinking goes, and so paying others for referring business is inherently unethical.** Accordingly, if you're paying your employees a commission for the medical treatments they are performing, or if you receive commissions for medical treatments, proceed with caution as you might be guilty of illegal fee-splitting. To play the game safely while simultaneously appeasing your med spa employees, it is best to use a pre-set bonus structure based on employee performance to avoid fee-splitting concerns.

Social Media and Advertising

Technology and social media have driven businesses, big and small, to use the Internet as a tool to provide information to their clients. Med spas are no exception. Many of my med spa clients use social media—websites, Facebook, LinkedIn, and even Twitter—to market their services and attract new patients. And with the recent uptick in the number of med spas, competition is forcing them to stand apart to get noticed by prospective clients. Several med spa clients have asked for my opinion on advertising their med spa services using daily deal sites like Groupon to get ahead of competitors by offering their services at a discount. Although in Illinois, where I practice, Groupon has been deemed legal by the state regulatory authorities, not every state agrees. **Since Groupon receives a percentage of the total revenue, instead of a flat fee, from the med spa's patient treatments, some states consider this a form of fee-splitting.** And while this form of advertising may be lucrative at first, many of my med spa clients have later regretted the decision to offer a Groupon because of disgruntled clients, negative reviews, and loss of profits.

Furthermore, never forget that medical spas are medical facilities, and they are therefore governed by the same rules as physicians. **There are strict prohibitions on certain statements that can be made in advertisements and on websites, and patient confidentiality must be strictly guarded.** Patient testimonials, for instance, are inherently risky as many state boards deem them to be unreliable and misleading. Also, clients often inadvertently violate HIPAA through seemingly innocuous posts or tweets due to the explosion of social media. A very common mistake being made by med spas is the failure to create and maintain a website, Facebook page, or LinkedIn account that accurately reflects and realistically represents the business structure and ownership of the med spa. This can easily put the med spa in jeopardy of being flagged by state regulators for false or misleading advertising, risking the business's and the medical staff's licenses.

So, remember—although it is important to keep current with technology trends to stay competitive in the marketplace, you have to be extra careful that your med spa marketing and advertising practices are compliant with your state's laws.

PAs, NPs, and RNs

As the shortage of physicians increases across the country, the role of registered nurses (RNs), nurse practitioners (NPs), and physician assistants (PAs) is rapidly expanding. In most states, RNs and PAs are prohibited from practicing autonomously from physicians. NPs, on the other hand, can practice separately from physicians in several different areas. For example, at Walgreens, Walmart and other big retailers, NP-run care clinics are becoming very popular and no physicians are involved.

Check with your state's regulatory board to find out exactly what you are allowed to do as an RN, NP, or PA.

The Role of Estheticians

One question I am asked over and over by estheticians across the country is, "What can I legally do in a medical aesthetic setting?" Of course, the answer to this really depends on which state you are in, but generally, estheticians are allowed to engage only in the practice of massaging, cleansing, exfoliating, stimulating, and beautifying the skin in a superficial mode. This means that (at least in most states) estheticians cannot perform any treatments or procedures that constitute the practice of medicine, like Botox, laser hair removal, and laser skin rejuvenation. Specifically, estheticians are prohibited (in most states) from using any techniques, products, or practices intended to affect the living layers of the skin. Estheticians are also prohibited from rendering advice on what is appropriate medical treatment for diseases of the skin. **While physicians may delegate the performance of medical procedures to almost anyone in their employ, that person must be experienced and trained to perform medical treatments. Estheticians, by definition, are not medical practitioners, and thus they may not perform medical treatments.**

> The term "medical esthetician" has become popular in the industry, but this term is a misnomer. Commonly misused, this term denotes that the esthetician is able to perform medical treatments, which is not the case. To avoid confusion, estheticians should use the term "esthetician in a medical spa" when referring to themselves or advertising their services to clients.

The term "medical esthetician" has become popular in the industry, but this term is a misnomer. Commonly misused, this term denotes that the esthetician is able to perform medical treatments, which is not the case. To avoid confusion, estheticians should use the term "esthetician in a medical spa" when referring to themselves or advertising their services to clients.

On the other hand, laser technicians are authorized to perform laser, hair, and skin treatments in most states. Thus, estheticians who desire to expand their area of practice can become trained and certified as laser technicians (and use the proper laser technician title when treating patients) in order to perform laser treatments.

In Conclusion...

Medical spas and laser centers are becoming bigger targets for law enforcement. Lawsuits and prosecutions are on the rise. As the industry grows, scrutiny and oversight will grow with it. I have only scratched the surface of the many rules and regulations that apply to medical aesthetic practices, and it is crucial that practitioners get the guidance they need from a qualified health care attorney. And I would be remiss if I failed to refer back to the super-important caveat that different jurisdictions have different laws, and some jurisdictions are stricter than others. Please check with your local attorney and proceed with care.

CHAPTER 3

OSHA: Safety Regulations

In this Chapter:
- What is OSHA?
- Bloodborne Pathogens, HBV, and HIV
- What Employers Must Do to Protect Employees
- How to Prevent Accidents and Avoid Exposure

The Occupational Safety and Health Administration (OSHA) was created by the United States Congress in 1970. Its mission is to prevent work-related injuries, illnesses, and deaths by issuing and enforcing regulations for workplace safety and health. Regulations regarding bloodborne pathogens were developed in 1991 to further protect employees who are exposed to potentially infectious materials, including human immunodeficiency virus (HIV), hepatitis B (HBV), and hepatitis C.

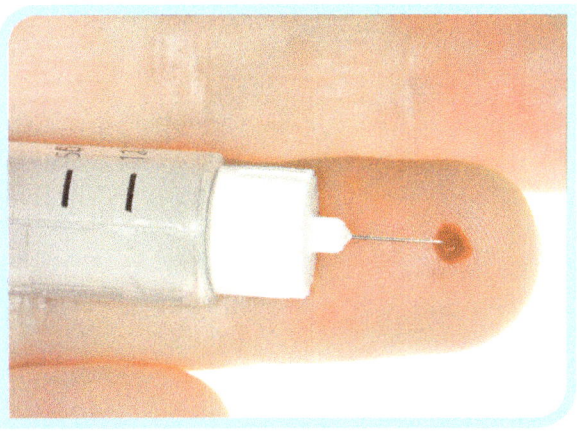

All employees whose performance of regular duties introduces the possibility of coming in contact with potentially infectious material must carry a certificate of training and have it renewed yearly. Many medical offices that work with estheticians have a separate area for spa-like services. That does not mean there is no chance of coming in contact with bloodborne pathogens. In a medical setting, support staff,

> Estheticians, regardless of the place of employment, should not intentionally go past the epidermis, which would greatly increase the chance of the client's skin bleeding.

including estheticians, will likely be in treatment rooms throughout the day. An esthetician may be asked to speak to a client about skin care while they are waiting for their procedure, or to lend a helping hand in a clinic room. Working in a medical environment, regardless of position, poses an increased risk of coming in contact with potentially infectious material.

The following information is derived from both the US Department of Labor's website on OSHA regulations, and my own personal experience working in a medical office.

Bloodborne Pathogens

Bloodborne pathogens[1] are infectious materials in blood that can cause diseases (e.g., hepatitis B and C and human immunodeficiency virus [HIV]) in humans. Employees who have the potential to be exposed, even if the odds of exposure are small, must be aware of OSHA regulations and take precautionary measures. Anyone exposed to these pathogens is at risk of serious illness, or even death. **What is commonly known as the "Universal Precaution Law," all blood and human tissue should be considered infectious and a biohazard.**

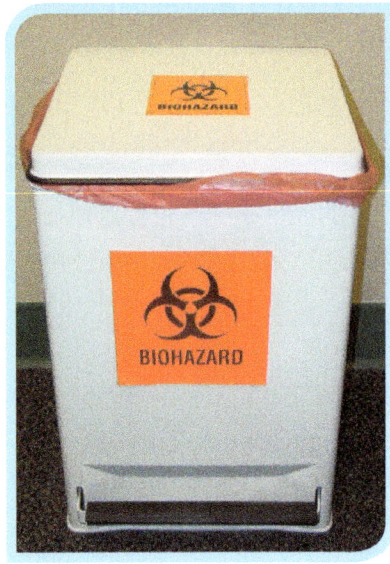

Biohazard waste container   All materials with blood must be disposed of properly.

What is HBV?

Hepatitis B virus (HBV) is a potentially life-threatening bloodborne pathogen that can cause liver disease and death. It can be transmitted through semen, blood, saliva, and urine. The Centers for Disease Control and Prevention estimates that HBV infections have declined by approximately 82% since 1991. This decline is due to the routine vaccination of children and the availability of vaccine to health care workers.

Vaccination: OSHA standards require employers to offer the three-injection vaccination series free to any employee who may be exposed to blood or other potentially infectious materials during their employment. The vaccination must be offered within 10 days of the employee's start date.

HBV vaccination is a noninfectious, yeast-based vaccine given as three separate injections. After the first injection, the second is given within a month, and the third is given six months after the first dose. It is important for the individual to receive all three injections.

What is HIV?

Human immunodeficiency virus (HIV) is a condition in which the immune system fails and can lead to life-threatening diseases. It is transmitted through blood, semen, vaginal fluid, and breast milk. There have been no reported cases of infection from sweat, saliva, tears, food, or casual contact. There is no vaccine yet available that can prevent HIV. The virus eventually evolves into what is known as acquired immunodeficiency syndrome, or AIDS, though, at present, medical advancements can forestall this evolution for periods extending years, and sometimes decades.

Hepatitis C

Hepatitis C is a liver disease that results from infection with the hepatitis C virus.[2] It can range in severity from a mild illness lasting a few weeks to a serious, lifelong illness. Hepatitis C is usually spread when blood from a person infected with the hepatitis C virus enters the body of someone who is not infected.

Hepatitis C can be either "acute" or "chronic." Acute hepatitis C virus infection is a short-term illness that occurs within the first six months following initial exposure to the hepatitis C virus. For most people, acute infection leads to chronic infection. Chronic hepatitis C is a serious disease than can result in long-term health problems, or even death.

There is no vaccine for hepatitis C. The best way to prevent hepatitis C is by avoiding behaviors that can spread the disease, notably injection drug use.

What Employers Must Do to Protect Employees
- Establish a written plan to eliminate or minimize employee exposures; this plan must be updated *annually*, and it is advised that OSHA regulations be made an explicit part of any plan.
    - The plan must also reflect technological changes (e.g., sharps disposal, new needle devices).
- Provide information and training to employees at the start of employment and every year thereafter.
- When regulatory changes occur, it is mandatory for employers to stay up-to-date and pass the information on to the rest of the staff.
- Use devices that isolate or remove bloodborne pathogen hazards from the workplace.

- OSHA-approved sharps disposal containers must be present in any area in which treatment occurs or in which needles are stored, and safer medical devices such as self-sheathing needles, sharps engineered with sharp injury protection, and needleless systems should be investigated and adopted, if available.
- Disposable sharps containers must be placed at eye level and maintained upright to keep liquids and sharps inside.
- Personal protective equipment such as gloves, gowns, and masks must be provided to all employees. Wearing gloves, gowns, masks, lab coats, face shields, and eye protection can significantly reduce health risks for workers exposed to blood and other potentially infectious materials.
- HBV vaccinations must be made available to all employees with any risk of occupational exposure to bloodborne pathogens within 10 days of assignment.
- If an accident were to occur, the employer must provide free post-exposure follow-up to any worker who experiences an exposure incident and maintain a sharps injury log to track any incidents.
- Sharps containers must be clearly marked to warn patients/staff of its sharp and hazardous contents.

Standard Operating Procedures (SOPs) must be on file for every treatment or service performed in the office. Enforcing safe work practices will reduce the risk of unexpected exposure. SOPs for a medical setting should include appropriate procedures for hand-washing, sharps disposal, lab specimen packaging, laundry handling, and contaminated material cleaning. It is equally important to have SOPs for each individual treatment from sanitation to treatment to post-procedure care. (Sample SOPs are shown in Appendix B.)

How to Prevent Accidents
Employee Responsibilities:
- Protect themselves from direct exposure to blood and bodily fluids, using their best judgment along with the recognized policies.
- Wear gloves for any procedure where there is a possibility of contact with blood or other bodily fluids.
- Discard gloves after contact with any patient; hands should be washed immediately.
- Place visibly contaminated waste products in red biohazard bins for appropriate disposal; gloves must be worn when handling these items.
- Properly dispose of infectious waste in infectious waste containers labeled with a biohazard symbol.

OSHA: Safety Regulations

Safe Handling of Needles:
- All providers will wear vinyl/latex gloves when handling needles.
- Providers who handle needles will be sure to implement newer, safer needle types as they become available. (This goes along with maintaining an up-to-date list of business operation policies in conjunction with OSHA regulations.)
- Manipulation of needles and/or recapping of contaminated needles will be prohibited unless medically necessary or if no alternative option is available.
- Sharps will be properly disposed of in OSHA-compliant sharps containers that are:
  - Leak-proof, puncture-resistant, closable, and labeled with a biohazard sticker.
  - Not be tampered with or opened by any employees.
  - Near any area where sharps are present and able to be replaced before becoming overfilled.
  - Sharps containers will be sealed shut or placed in a biohazard bag if leaking.

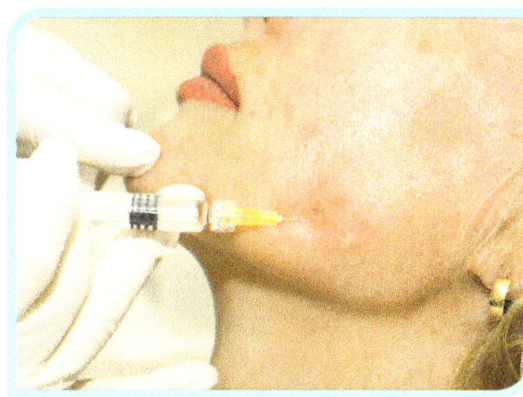

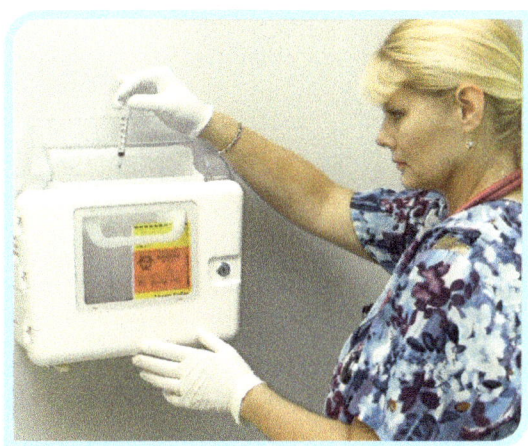

Proper sharps disposal

Sanitary Work Environment:
- All employees will keep the office clean and in sanitary conditions at all times
- Rooms will be sanitized following every individual patient appointment to prevent transmission of infection. This rule applies to skin care treatment rooms as well.
- All equipment and work surfaces will be wiped down and decontaminated after any contact with blood or other potentially infectious material, after any procedure if there is visible contamination, and at the end of the clinic work day.
  - Disinfectant will pass OSHA regulations and be cleared by the US Food and Drug Administration (FDA) as sufficient for decontamination of blood and other potentially infectious materials.
  - Disinfectant will be effective against HIV and HBV.

- All employees will use personal protection devices when handling disinfectant.
- Any object that has been contaminated with blood must be disposed of in the proper biohazard waste containers.

Personal Protective Equipment (PPE):
- PPE will be readily available and worn by all employees when in contact with blood or other potentially infectious material.
- Gloves will be worn at all times when in contact with blood, other potentially infectious material, mucous membranes, non-intact skin or contaminated items/surfaces.
- Masks/Eye protection will be worn at all times when in contact with splashing, spraying, or splattering of blood or other potentially infectious material, as well as with aerosolized droplets of blood or other potentially infectious material.

How to Handle an Exposure

The most common exposure incident is a needle stick, but any specific contact with blood or other potentially infectious materials to any mucous membranes or non-intact skin is considered an exposure incident and must be reported in the injury log. If an employee were stuck by a needle or other sharp or were to get blood or other potentially infectious materials in their eyes, nose, mouth, or on broken skin, the exposed area should be immediately flooded with water and any wound should be cleaned with soap and water or a skin disinfectant. The incident should be immediately brought to the employer, medical attention should be sought, and it must be reported right away. This will help prevent the chance of spreading potential infections to others.

Working in a medical office increases potential risks, and caution must be taken. To ensure all employees' safety, these guidelines must be met. It is in each staff member's best interest to ensure that their employer is following these regulations and has a set plan in place. There are several proactive steps the employees can take to prevent accidents as well. **Personal care should be taken to reduce the chance of infection through common lesions including acne, dry cuticles, cat scratches, or scrapes that can spread bloodborne pathogens.** Each employee must take responsibility for cleanliness and sanitation to ensure a safe work environment.

For a full list of OSHA regulations, visit *www.OSHA.gov*.

References
1. *www.osha.gov/SLTC/bloodbornepathogens* (accessed Apr 15, 2014)
2. *www.cdc.gov/hepatitis/C/index.htm* (accessed Apr 15, 2014)

CHAPTER 4

HIPAA: The Privacy Act

In this Chapter:
- What HIPPA Is and Why it Matters
- General Guidelines
- HIPPA Violations & Potential Penalties

The Health Insurance Portability and Accountability Act (HIPAA) was enacted by the United States Congress in 1996. It outlines federal standards created to protect patients' medical records and other health information. Any employee that has access to health information must abide by these regulations. The rules laid out by these provisions are administered through the Department of Health and Human Services.

HIPAA's privacy rule protects all "protected health information," or PHI, in any form including visual media, electronic, paper, or oral. This includes any individual's physical or mental health condition, the provision of health care, and information of or relating to payments for the provision of health care. **Any health information that specifically identifies a given individual, such as name, address, birth date, or Social Security number, is strictly protected.** Those working in a medical environment, including anyone with access to patient information, must adhere to these rules.

Text messaging and/or emailing clients from personal devices, notably smartphones, puts the provider in direct risk of violation. **All communication with patients must be done over an encrypted source to ensure no one else can see it.** It seems simple enough to book an appointment by text message or answer emails out of the office, but think of it this way—if a provider/employee has patient information on their personal devices and someone not associated with the practice has access to this information, even via theft of the devices, the employee can and likely will be held liable.

Another common source of potential HIPAA violation is *before and after pictures*. These pictures *should* be obtained for each patient who undergoes a procedure, because they are important for comprehensive medical records. They can also be a great source for education and marketing, provided the individual patient consents to their use for purposes other than record-completion. The use of patient pictures should not be taken lightly. Many people would be embarrassed if anyone were to see pictures of them without makeup; on the other hand, some enjoy showing off their results, regardless of what the *before* picture looks like. Patients must consent to having their photos taken, and it must be clearly stated on the consent form what the pictures will be used for. Even if pictures leave out the client's eyes or face, the photographed area could have distinguishing factors (tattoos, birthmarks, or even a unique facial structure) and one could be held liable for releasing them. The language of a patient consent form must be exact, even if it seems unnecessary to render in simple language the full intent of what the patient is agreeing to. **Remember: client rights are absolute, and are to never be taken lightly; to do so can have potentially damaging repercussions on practice and provider alike.**

What follows is a brief summary of regulations that need to be taken into account when considering employment in a medical setting. Further information is sourceable at: *www.hhs.gov*.

SCENARIO: Patient Calls

What could happen:
Provider: "Hi, may I speak to Barbara, please?"
Patient's Husband: "She isn't in at the moment, can I take a message?"
Provider: "Sure, this is Mary calling from Dr. Johnson's office regarding her Botox treatment and upcoming facial. Have her give me a call back at 555-555-5555."

What should happen:
Provider: "Hi, may I speak to Barbara, please?"
Patient's Husband: "She isn't in at the moment, can I take a message?"
Provider: "No, thank you. I will try back again later."

Why is this difference important? Because Barbara's appointment and the specifics of her treatment are *Barbara's*, not her husband's and not anyone else's who may live under the same roof or share the same telephone line. It would be easy enough to assume that a patient's spouse would be a safe person to leave information about an appointment with, but the old adage about the word *assume* applies as well to this scenario as to any other.

If a patient's voicemail is reached, only leave a detailed message if the patient mentions his or her name on the voicemail greeting. Otherwise, just leave a generalized message from the patient's doctor's office requesting a call back.

General Guidelines for following HIPAA

- Patients and clients must be referred to by their first name only. This can be awkward when addressing older people, but if they are told the reasons for doing so, they usually understand. Patients appreciate a practice that is conscientious about confidentiality. This rule also applies to telephone calls and voicemail. It sounds fairly simple, but can be difficult to adapt one's self to, especially for someone new to medical practice where the rules are more stringent regarding client protection.
- All patient files must be kept in a secure location at all times, including when they are in use by staff. Files must not be left in view of anyone other than an employee authorized to view these documents. During the day, **a good practice is to place all files face down**. Likewise, it is important that all files are returned to their specified secured area at the close of business.
- All information about a client, including their name, is confidential and may not be disclosed to *anyone*. Patients requesting their own medical information must sign a release form. This can be hard when treating friends or family members. It may not seem like a big deal, but if a client asks if their neighbor has been in recently and the provider says yes, that is a violation.

SCENARIO: Treating Friends/Family

What could happen:
Client: "You know my friend Jennifer? She told me she saw you last week for a chemical peel and it was amazing! Can I have the same treatment?"
Provider: "Glad to hear Jen had great results. She had a TCA peel. Let's do the same treatment for you!"

What should happen:
Client: "You know my friend Jennifer? She told me she saw you last week for a chemical peel and it was amazing! Can I have the same treatment?"
Provider: "We have several great treatments, and chemical peels are a good option. Let me take a look at your skin and see what kind of treatment would be appropriate for you today."

In the second scenario, the provider dismissed the statement that invited specification of the "friend's" treatment, so as to not cause any argument or interference. If the provider were to say "I can't tell you," the client may get offended. But in some cases that is the only way to get around it if the question recurs.

- Discretion is also very important in an environment where patients are receiving treatments they may not want others to know about. Never talk about the specific treatments of others in front of patients in the office, e.g., "Hi Sue, we are ready for your chemical peel and Botox." Instead you can simply say "Hi Sue, are you ready to come back?"
- It is a violation of a patient's privacy to acknowledge them outside of the office. If a client speaks to you first, then you may speak to them, but you should not initiate the conversation.

SCENARIO: Out of Office Encounters

What could happen:
You are walking down the aisle at the grocery store and see a client of yours. You tap her on the shoulder to say hello and you chat for a while.

What should happen:
If you see a patient, it is best to conduct yourself as if you do not know them unless they acknowledge you.

Why does this even matter, you may be asking. Medical professionals, including those staff members who are not licensed physicians but work in a medical setting, such as estheticians, carry with them the definition of their vocation everywhere they go.

Example: The client could be at a store with someone they do not want knowing about their aesthetic procedures. Were the esthetician, also at the same store, to introduce herself, this may cause the other party to ask questions about how you know one another, causing immediate and unnecessary discomfort to the client.

So … what happens in the event of a violation of HIPAA regulations?

If any of the HIPAA regulations are broken, there are penalties. The penalties for non-compliance can range from $100 per violation to a $1.5 million fine and up to 10 years in prison under criminal law with intent to sell or transfer information. Remember, law is not about what is known but what can be proven. Intent lies on the law's side, which is to say it errs toward the federal regulatory bodies and their statutes. In order to work in a medical setting, one must be ready and willing to adhere to the breadth of HIPAA, without compromise.

In Part 2, we will be looking at client consultation. You've read the framework. It is now time to begin applying this information to the practical operation of skin care in a medical setting.

Part 1: Review Questions

1) The job of an esthetician in a medical setting is to:

    a) Perform medical treatments

    b) Treat medical conditions of the skin

    c) Cosmetically enhance the skin

    d) Take clients from the physician

2) What are the two most common procedures performed by skin care professionals in a medical setting?

    a) Chemical peels and microdermabrasion

    b) Facials and massages

    c) Ultrasound treatments and dermaplaning

    d) Lymphatic drainage massage and facials

3) What are some of the benefits of working with a physician?

    a) Products, procedures, equipment will have scientific validity

    b) The ability to build a strong clientele

    c) You can give medical advice

    d) Answers a and b

4) How can an esthetician help a client to maintain their skin after medical procedures?

    a) Educating them on the importance of using the proper products

    b) Perform medical treatments for the physician

    c) Enhance treatments by applying a deep chemical peel the day of procedure

    d) The esthetician cannot help a client after medical procedures

5) What is the best way to introduce skin care treatments and products to patients?

    a) Ask the patient if they would like a consultation

    b) Cleanse the patient's skin before their medical service

    c) Have the physician come in to sell products after the appointment

    d) Cold call all of the patients of the medical practice

6) What is the most valuable asset of a practice?

   a) Medical supplies
   b) Medical rooms
   c) The spa
   d) The physician's time

7) Product use is especially important following invasive treatments (e.g., deep laser resurfacing). If the skin is not cared for properly following deep laser resurfacing treatments which adverse reactions can occur?

   a) Infections
   b) Discoloration
   c) Scarring
   d) All of the above

8) What does OSHA stand for?

   a) Occupational Safety and Health Administration
   b) Occupational Safety and HIV Administration
   c) Occupational Sharps and Health Administration
   d) Occupational Safety and Hepatitis Administration

9) What are bloodborne pathogens?

   a) Blood
   b) Uncapped needles
   c) Bleach solutions
   d) Infectious materials in blood that can cause diseases

10) What type of vaccination should be available from the employer to all employees within ten days of employment?

    a) HIV
    b) Hepatitis A
    c) Hepatitis B
    d) Hepatitis C

Review Questions

11) How can the employee prevent an accident from a cut or a stick?

   a) Recap needles
   b) Clean work areas thoroughly with bleach
   c) Wear gloves
   d) Dispose of sharps immediately

12) Who should supply all personal protective equipment?

   a) Employees
   b) Employers
   c) OSHA
   d) Patients

13) What does HIPAA stand for?

   a) Health Insurance Portability and Accountability Act
   b) Health Insurance Preventability and Accountability Act
   c) Health Insurance Portability and Auditing Act
   d) Health Insurance Preventability and Auditing Act

14) What does HIPAA protect?

   a) It protects the practice from insurance fraud
   b) It protects employee records
   c) It protects patients' medical records and other health information
   d) It protects physicians' records and other health information

15) Is it appropriate to call a person by their full name in front of others?

   a) No, patients and clients may be referred to by their first name only
   b) Yes, it is more professional
   c) Only with new clients
   d) Only on regular clients

16) When using a patient's file, where is it acceptable to place that file?

   a) All patient files must be kept in a secure location
   b) Files should not be left any place where anyone other than an employee can see the names on them
   c) A good rule of thumb is to place all files face down
   d) All of the above

17) If you see a patient outside of your office, should you say hello to them?

   a) Yes, as long as you're friendly
   b) If the client speaks to you first then you may speak to them
   c) You must never speak to them outside the office
   d) Yes, as long as you're the first to speak

18) Who may own and operate a medical spa in most states?

   a) A physician
   b) A physician partnered with an esthetician
   c) Anyone with a business license
   d) A medical esthetician partnered with a physician

19) The prohibition against fee-splitting stems from:

   a) Lawsuits from injured clients
   b) The belief that allowing non-physicians to share in medical revenue could affect client care
   c) It is unethical to pay others for referring business to physicians, who should be concerned more with healing than with revenue
   d) Both b and c

20) Which treatments are estheticians allowed to perform in medical spas in all states?

   a) Neurotoxin and fillers
   b) Superficial treatments
   c) Laser skin rejuvenation
   d) Micro-needling

Review Questions

21) How can social media be a detriment in medical spa advertising?
    a) Facebook is for a younger generation than those going to a medical spa
    b) Clients may inadvertently violate HIPAA via posts or tweets
    c) Anyone can see the treatments offered at the medical spa
    d) None of the above

22) With the increased popularity of medical spas, what are some issues that have arisen?
    a) Decreased regulation
    b) Criminal prosecution
    c) Fewer violations of local laws
    d) Lack of suspension due to negligence

23) In most states, if a physician is not on-site who may substitute in his or her place?
    a) A trained medical esthetician
    b) A laser technician
    c) A medical assistant
    d) Another medical professional as long as the physician is available by phone

24) Who can benefit from incorporating skin care and cosmetic medicine?
    a) The patient
    b) The practice
    c) The physician
    d) All of the above

25) Who in the practice is ultimately responsible for patient care?
    a) The practice manager
    b) The physician
    c) The insurance company
    d) Whoever provided the service

PART 2

The Aesthetic Consultation

AESTHETICS EXPOSED
MASTERING SKIN CARE IN A MEDICAL SETTING AND BEYOND

CHAPTER 5

The Science of Beauty*

In this Chapter:
- Beauty as a Form of Communication
- The Power of the First Impression
- The Meaning of Beauty

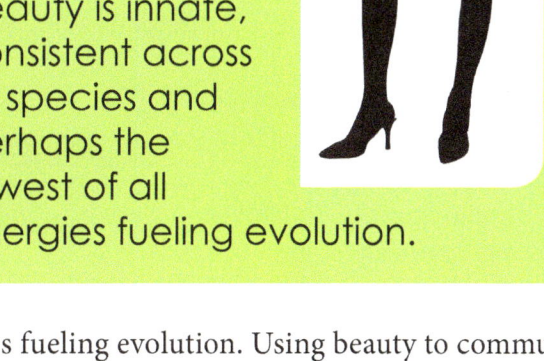

Beauty relates to all that we do, especially in the aesthetics industry. There is so much more that goes to into *treating* a client than one might think. **The most important thing is to make the clients feel better, as opposed to making them look better.** The language of beauty is innate, consistent across all species and perhaps the rawest of all energies fueling evolution. Using beauty to communicate a message matters. We may not like to admit it, but we all know and depend on it.

> The language of beauty is innate, consistent across all species and perhaps the rawest of all energies fueling evolution.

Common scenario: After a long day at work, you and your friends decide to meet for a drink. You are just about to finish your cocktail when you see him walk into the room. He's tall and handsome with a chiseled jaw, deep-set eyes and a full head of hair. He confidently settles in at the bar, purposely unfastens the top button of his form-fitting designer suit and takes a sip of his martini. That's when he notices you and shoots you a playful smile. Your heart flutters as you play coy, avert your eyes and resume conversation with your friends. Knowing that he is watching, you get up and seductively make your way across the bar for another drink. As you sashay across the floor, you feel his eyes scanning your hips and moving up to your lips and eyes. As you sit down and fluidly cross your legs, you casually flip your head, allowing your hair to be tossed through the air. You gently turn your chin downward and direct your gaze towards his eyes. He gets the message and rises from his seat to move toward you. While you were imagining that scene, real encounters very similar

---

*This chapter has been adapted from portions of Dr. Steven Dayan's self-published book, *Subliminally Exposed*.

to it were happening all over the world, from a trendy club in Chicago to a dive bar in Berlin. Eyes met, hearts raced, and potential mates were found.

The above scenario is but one example of how one's physicality sends clear and distinct signals to others. An equally important parade of similar events occurs when interviewing for a job or encountering one's in-laws for the first time. **Regardless of the situation, the impression we make is lasting and consequential.** Nature is big on efficiency, especially when it comes to human beings sizing up each other. It seems obvious that impressions would be based on physical traits, but it actually goes deeper than that, much deeper. The ability to instantly sense danger, likability, or aggressiveness in others has been hard-wired within the most primitive depth of our brains for tens of thousands of years. This wiring follows our most basic neural pathways; I have discovered surprisingly simple actions that significantly alter the impression people project to others and how that impression changes the responses they receive. For example, something as simple as greeting someone with a smile can greatly affect the way that person responds to you. Project one type of signal, get one type of response. Project a different, more "attractive" signal, get a more positive reaction. It's that basic. It's that quick. And it's that effective. There are several other actions we can take to better relate with individual personality traits that we will go over in detail in Chapter 6.

With that in mind, let's revisit the above chance encounter, but this time through the eyes of an evolutionary psychologist. First, as the well-dressed stranger studies the woman's walk, posture, and how she carries herself, he is picking up certain clues regarding her fertility from the set of her breasts, buttocks, and hips. He notices her full lips, a powerful signal to suggest ovulation. Unblemished skin tips him off to her youngish age and underlying health. As she sits down and gently tosses her hair over her shoulder, she releases pleasant and genetically unique odors into the environment—a calling signal that seeps into his primitive brain. At that same subconscious level, he reads her lowered chin as a sign of her diminutive position, which indicates her need for assistance (vulnerability—another mark of youth). Altogether, those signals sum up that she's an ideal prospective mate. Meanwhile, the woman is processing the man's signals that exude confidence and masculinity. His chiseled jaw suggests high levels of testosterone (she instinctively knows this) and his tall, handsome demeanor imply that he has good genes. His suit jacket accentuates his physical prowess by emphasizing his overall level of fitness and forces her to notice that his upper torso is larger than his waist, indicating that he is strong and likely to be a good protector. All of these qualities combine to form a favorable impression that he is resourceful, both physically and emotionally. Then his eyes meet hers, piercing, direct and forceful. She may not realize it, but her brows are elevating and expanding and her pupils are maximally dilated, sure signs that she is interested. As the man confidently walks up to her, his breathing rate increases in order to better inhale her pheromones. Her nose is also in the air testing for his smell to see if he is a genetic match. Everything about the random encounter is serving a greater purpose—to signal the loud and clear message, "I have great genes!"

Where you end up in life may depend entirely on one chance encounter and the impression you make.

This is the complicated yet lightning-fast process illustrating the power of beauty as the most primitive form of communication, an unconscious program running full-speed. Where you end up in life may depend entirely on one chance encounter and the impression you make. I would bet that if we polled people on the street about their definition of beauty a few might click off some favorite traits like nice eyes, broad shoulders, or long hair, but most would hide behind the politically correct answer that beauty is found on the inside. They may believe that, which is wonderful, but they also know that deep down they can't help but be attracted to certain characteristics and repelled by others.

Harnessing the Power of the First Impression

Many of the human instincts that developed to help our species survive are incompatible with modern standards of behavior. We're taught to restrain ourselves against our instincts. This leads to the inner conflicts that Sigmund Freud, a neurologist known for developing the theories behind psychoanalysis, wrote about. We

Aesthetic concerns should be received with patience and positivity.

can use the power of our instincts to our advantage, too. **Once we know how to send out irresistibly positive/attractive signals, whether we're seeking a partner or trying to convince someone that we're the best person for the job, we can gain better understanding and more control of our lives.** When we make a step toward improving our attractiveness signal by getting a hairstyle and makeup that are perfectly appropriate for our facial structure, for example, we can expect more positive responses from others based not only on our physical appearance, but also on the energy surge we gain from our ramped-up self-esteem. Those enhancements are simple yet powerful adjustments that send positive signals in order to stimulate a positive response in the other person. A potential date may want to connect or a new employer may recruit us further into the fold. Yet, if we go overboard with impression "enhancements," we can ignite the opposite response by tipping off someone's subconscious mind that we're trying to hide something, like bad genes, poor health, or even deceit. It is the reason that women who wear excessive makeup are negatively perceived and that the balding man's comb-over is considered highly unattractive. It is more beneficial to employ minor enhancement to what you already have than to try to be what you are not. Taking charge of the impression you project is easier than you think, thanks in part to the connection between the mind and our physiology. The mind has the ability to change the chemistry and other physical functioning of the body; in medicine and science, we call this the placebo effect. This effect can be as strong as many of our modern-day medical interventions, and we can learn to harness, hone, and maximize our ability to use the mind to alter our first impression. When it comes to cosmetic alterations, whether a new fashion sense, hairstyle, or a wrinkle removal treatment, the placebo effect is likely to be as important as the products, procedure, or treatment a person receives.

It is more beneficial to employ minor enhancement to what you already have than to try to be what you are not.

The key is using both the mind and the intervention synergistically. If a middle-aged adult wants to look more youthful and seeks out assistance to remove forehead wrinkles, one can't realistically make the wrinkles go away by just telling her to visualize them gone and hoping the placebo effect works. That would be too simplistic. But after providing neuromodulator, filler, or skin care, a medical provider may reduce the wrinkles and prevent her brow from fully emoting anger. Studies show that once a person views her face with fewer wrinkles and is less efficient at  emoting anger, she likely will feel better, thereby setting off a cascade of physiological and biochemical events that result in projecting a more youthful impression. With minimal interventions—hairstyles, posture, clothing styles, makeup—we can all increase the amount of likeability, friendliness, or power we project. This, too, can be achieved without much effort, but it does require some insight. Once this particular insight into our instinctual responses is revealed and understood, it becomes so blatantly obvious you will recognize signs and evidence of people engaging in it everywhere you look.

Throughout the breadth of human existence, many social and political systems have been tried and tested, from democratic republics to tyrannical regimes. The morals and ethics of mating, marriage, and child-rearing have also varied widely based on the social, cultural, and political factors of the times. However, evolution doesn't take these external forces into account. **Nature's only concern is the survival of the fittest—from nurturing healthy bodies to nudging us toward mates that have the best odds of carrying on our genes.** That may sound rather simplistic, but it's true. And to work *with* the foundations of our most basic drives instead of being unaware of or denying them is to give yourself a tremendous advantage in achieving what you want in life.

Whether you believe this system was instituted by intelligent design or by nature alone, the prevailing theory of evolution is one of natural selection. And it is within this primitive system that human development can most easily be explained, including the workings of beauty, attraction, and the first impression. I invite you to put any preconceived political, religious, or cultural notions aside as you explore the science behind our behavior. If you are adamant that you don't care about how you look or that our concept of beauty is constructed by the media instead of our biology, I invite you to keep an open mind, too.

The truth is we're all, to some degree, concerned with the impression we make, even if the presentation of that concern is limited to brushing our hair or making sure our socks match. To understand those drives is the first step in working them to your advantage. I repeat: *To work with the foundations of our most basic drives instead of being unaware of or denying them is to give yourself a tremendous advantage in achieving what you want in life.* This knowledge is the key to your success and is a solid basis for the practice of aesthetics. Knowing this secret is the ideal point at which to proceed.

CHAPTER 6

The Client Experience

In this Chapter:
- The Secret about Cosmetic Care
- The Cosmetic Client
- Relating to Specific Personality Types

The Secret about Cosmetic Care

The big secret about cosmetic care, not to be underestimated, is that in order to make clients happy one must practice treatments and seek to obtain results that lead to the client *feeling* as good, or better, than they *look*. These two seemingly different criteria may not always occur together; however, they occur enough to consider the importance of their impact on your clients' satisfaction. Furthermore, they bear a cause-and-effect relationship to one another as evidenced by a scientific study suggesting that although physical appearance is important to an individual, it is the way this person feels about him- or herself that can trump the effect of their perceived physical appearance.[1] In many studies, women who *believed* that they were viewed as attractive were more animated and more confident than those who were physically more attractive with a lower sense of self-esteem.[2] Therefore, evidence supports the conclusion that physical appearance and attractiveness matters only if they are accompanied by concurrent feelings of self-esteem and self-worth. As the saying goes, *beauty is in the eye of the beholder*.

The aesthetic provider must consider every possible reason the client may want a procedure. The majority of clients come in to improve a part of themselves that will make them feel more attractive, and the possibility of a related psychological issue should not be ruled out. Many people are dissatisfied with something about themselves, such as the size of their nose, the amount of wrinkles on their face, dry skin, or freckles. The aesthetic provider's job is to understand this issue and respect it. Many of us frequently assess clients receiving cosmetic treatments objectively; however, practicing more subjective assessments will take into account the client's emotional state and provide a higher probability of client satisfaction. Essentially, countless clients may obsess upon something that the average eye would never pick up on, but it is important to make them feel listened to and do your best to functionally address their needs, no matter how negligible their concern may appear to you.

SCENARIO: Focusing on the Client's Concerns

What could happen:
Client: "I am concerned with my acne."
Provider: "You don't have acne; let's address the fine lines around your eyes instead."
Upset Client: "I didn't realize my eyes were that bad. I really came in today to clear up my skin."

    This puts a bad taste in the client's mouth. She came in for a particular service to make her feel better and the skin care provider has completely discounted it. In the end, the client does not get what she wanted, and this could leave the client feeling worse than she did when she arrived.

What should happen:
Client: "I am concerned with my acne."
Provider: "You have gorgeous skin. I do see that you have a small breakout on your left cheek. We will definitely address that."
Client: "That's great! These breakouts have been bothering me for a while."
Provider: "Do you have any other concerns with your skin that I can help you with?"
Happy Client: "Is there anything you can recommend for my eyes as well?"

As a cosmetic provider, it is essential not only to make the person *look* better, but to also bolster their self-esteem so they actually *feel* better. Likewise, it is essential to stress their positive features. *Remember: Listen to your clients… Be attentive to their needs…. Help them reach their goals.*

The Cosmetic Client

People who seek cosmetic procedures are not necessarily wealthy, vain, or self-centered. Physical appearance and the visage of self-worth are too intertwined to assume any given person is acting on purely aesthetic impulses. The truth of the matter is that countless people are interested in cosmetic procedures these days, even those that might surprise you. People in all walks of life are concerned with the way they look and have one thing in common—the desire to enhance a part of themselves they find important.

Fortunately, most clients are realistic, well-informed, and are a pleasure to work with. But occasionally you may have dissatisfied clients due to miscommunication or unrealistic expectations. Being attentive and relating to clients with strong personalities is vital for success. Your natural inclination may be to walk away and dismiss the unhappy client; however, it is crucial that you do not do this. It is best to address a client's issue head-on, and there are appropriate ways to do so.

Unrealistic expectations are the most common cause of dissatisfaction. Communication is an important aspect of all successful relationships, and this includes relationships with clients and co-workers, as well as friends and family. The aesthetic provider must first *listen*, and then give essential and true information regarding the client's individual concerns. It can be difficult to send the right message while some cosmetics tout advertisements for "Botox in a bottle" or when competitors allude to a facial treatment that gives a "non-surgical facelift." It is in your and your client's best interest to provide dependable information on all recommendations. A simple rule of thumb would be to always under-promise and over-deliver. (For example, if you believe the client will have a significant reduction in pigmentation after four chemical peels, say it will likely take six to eight. You err to the side of caution, and if success comes in fewer treatments the client will be most satisfied with your services.)

If a client is not satisfied with their outcome, it is important to listen intently to their concerns

> A simple rule of thumb would be to always under-promise and over-deliver.

> **Dissatisfied Clients Can Damage the Credibility of You and the Practice.***
>
> A dissatisfied customer will tell between 9-15 people about their experience. Around 13% of dissatisfied customers tell more than 20 people.
>
> – White House Office of Consumer Affairs
>
> *http://returnonbehavior.com/2010/10/50-facts-about-customer-experience-for-2011/

and give a solution to help resolve the issue. It is critical for the provider and the practice that the client leaves satisfied. It's an old adage, but it's true: "The customer is always right." Whatever the problem, it is the provider's responsibility to fix it. It is not always best to offer free services, as this can be perceived as an admission of guilt, and the disappointed client may exploit this. However, on occasion it may be the only way to make a client feel cared for. Use this option judiciously, while recognizing that the situation may turn into a lingering problem. A displeased client can do more to ruin a reputation than poor advertising ever could. Keep the clients that you have happy and continued success will be abundant.

Common Personality Types

There are some common personality types to look for in clients that will help you to better address client needs. Learning to communicate with others is the key to building and maintaining strong relationships, which directly or indirectly reflect all aspects of life. The best way to address a strong personality is to relate to and validate it. Consider the word "DAVE" not as a name, but as an acronym for Detect, Acknowledge, Validate, and Empathize. In the face of a difficult client, apply "DAVE" and see if it works. This methodology applies in equal measure to each of the client personality types to follow.

"Satisfied Sally"

"Sally" is the ideal client. She likely is scheduled on a regular basis and views her visit as an escape. She is always pleased with the outcome of her treatments since she has an easy-going personality. It is still important to let "Sally" know how greatly appreciated she is. Although you cannot directly reward her for a referral, due to fee-splitting, let her know she is appreciated in other ways. VIP status is a good way to do this. Try not to take money away from the business by continually offering discounts. Instead, provide a random add-on to a treatment. A great option is to offer a rejuvenation treatment for the neck, décolleté, or hands. This typically doesn't take a lot of time and gives the client an opportunity to try new treatments. "Sally" is likely to be a life-long client resulting in multiple referrals.

The Client Experience

Relating to "Sally":
- Make sure she feels welcomed, relaxed, and appreciated.
- Occasionally, give her an add-on treatment or a sample product.
- Send cards on special occasions such as birthdays, anniversary, and holidays.
- Call her personally with any schedule changes or updates including specials she may be interested in.
- Do not take advantage of the fact that she will likely try anything you recommend.

> **Remember:** Treating the spirit is as important as treating the skin.

SCENARIO: Consultation with "Sally"

Sally comes in for her monthly facial.

What could happen:
Provider: "Do you have any concerns with your skin you want to address today?"
Sally: "I really want to relax today, but whatever you suggest is fine."
Provider: "OK, I understand you wanted to relax, but I really think a chemical peel would be best to address your fine lines."

What should happen:
Provider: "Do you have any concerns with your skin you want to address today?"
Sally: "I really want to relax today, but whatever you suggest is fine."
Provider: "OK, I understand you want to relax, so let's do a hydrating facial that includes plenty of facial massage. Is there anything else you would like me to address today?"

This allows the client to express if she is concerned with fine lines or anything else. If she is, another treatment can be added to the facial, or you could set up an additional appointment for two weeks later for something stronger.

"Esthetic Shopper Sharon"
This client has been considering treatment for the last year or so, and she has been to five of your competitors on a type of "information-gathering expedition." While flattering you, she is now ready and wants to hear your opinion. When she is just about to commit to a service, she needs to check something and promises to get back to you the next day. She may come in for repeated consultations without committing to an actual service. Charging for consultations is a good way of eliminating this type of client in most cases.

Let her make the final decision. If she immediately undergoes a cosmetic treatment, she may have second thoughts or regrets afterwards. The number one way to destroy your career is to have a displeased client discussing you in a negative way—especially a "Sharon" who may be holding a grudge.

Relating to "Sharon":
- Give her all the necessary information and let her make the final decision.
- Show your own before and after pictures of services she is considering.
- After the first consultation, provide her with detailed information that she can take with her.
- Don't aggressively talk her into getting treatments.
- Do not let her take advantage of your time; this client may look for recommended products or services at discounted rates on the Internet.

SCENARIO: Consultation with "Sharon"

"Sharon" comes in for a consultation to see which products are best for her skin type.

What could happen:
Provider: "Good morning, what brings you in today?"
Sharon: "I just had a few questions regarding products."
Provider: "Great, is there something in particular you wanted to address, or were you focused more on preventative treatments?"

Sharon: "I was hoping you could take a look at my skin and tell me what I need."
Provider: "Ok, let me go over some of the products we have."
Sharon: "I have more research to do, can you please write down all of the products you recommend for me?"
Provider: "Of course, hope to see you soon."

What should happen:
Provider: "Good morning, what brings you in today?"
Sharon: "I just had a few questions regarding products."
Provider: "Great, is there something in particular you wanted to address, or were you focused more on preventative treatments?"
Sharon: "I was hoping you could take a look at my skin and tell me what I need."
Provider: "Ok, let me go over some of the products we have."
Sharon: "I have more research to do, can you please write down all of the products you recommend for me?"
Provider: "Let me write down the basics, and I will give you a sample of the antioxidant serum to take with you; if you like it, you can bring the sample bottle back for $10 off your first purchase."

This *should happen* exchange invites "Sharon" to return with the promise of a discount and a product line she may find attractive and useful—without the esthetician doing her homework for her.

"Know-it-all Nancy"

This client has researched the Internet exhaustively and has read many articles on cosmetic procedures. She will explain what she wants done and why (i.e., she saw it on a talk show and is convinced it is the best treatment). She will look puzzled if you tell her that something else may be more beneficial. Her information may be outdated, incomplete, or, in most cases, just not right for her particular skin type and concerns. This client comes in not so much for your expert opinion and diagnostic skills, but for your technical services. Realize that if you give her the treatment she wants and it fails to meet her expectations, she may fault you. On the other hand, if you provide a different treatment and it fails to meet her expectations, she may also fault you.

Relating to "Nancy":
- Try to understand her ultimate goal, and then explain how to best achieve it.
- Calmly explain the pros and cons of each treatment with detailed specifics.
- Educate the client on her particular skin concerns.
- Let the client make the final decision, unless the particular treatment she wants may be harmful.

SCENARIO: Consultation with "Nancy"

"Nancy" comes in for micro-needling to reduce fine lines, but is presenting with inflamed stage 2 papulopustular rosacea. She saw on TV how her favorite celebrity had micro-needling done and professed how much she loved it. "Nancy" wants that same feeling.

What could happen:
Provider: "You're looking for a treatment to reduce fine lines is that correct?"
Nancy: "Yes, and I want the micro-needling. I have read all about it, and I saw Kim K. on television saying how she'd had it done and how much she loved it, and I'm so excited!"
Provider: "Micro-needling is a great treatment and I would love to treat you with it; however, we need to take the proper steps to ensure you are getting the best possible outcomes. Have you ever had a superficial chemical peel?"
Nancy: "No, I don't want chemicals on my skin. I am very sensitive, and I have rosacea."
Provider: "All right, we can do the micro-needling, but there is a chance of more redness and inflammation following the procedure."

What should happen:
Provider: "You're looking for a treatment to reduce fine lines is that correct?"
Nancy: "Yes, and I want the micro-needling. I have read all about it, and I saw Kim K. on television saying how she'd had it done and how much she loved it, and I'm so excited!"

> Provider: "Micro-needling is a great treatment and I would love to treat you with it; however, we need to take the proper steps to ensure you are getting the best possible outcomes. Have you ever had a superficial chemical peel?"
> Nancy: "No, I don't want chemicals on my skin. I am very sensitive, and I have rosacea."
> Provider: "I understand the term chemical peel can be scary, but we have a peel that was actually developed with your condition in mind. I have used this treatment on many clients with skin issues similar to your own with terrific success. Let me show you some before and after pictures of how this particular peel has worked on others with similar skin conditions. Unfortunately, we cannot do the micro-needling today since your skin is inflamed, but we can work on controlling the inflammation. We can schedule the micro-needling for next month."
> Nancy: "All right, that sounds great."

"Bitter Betty"

"Betty" has spent thousands of dollars on treatments and products from other providers, and she has been unsuccessful in obtaining the results she wants. This is common in those suffering from acne or hyperpigmentation. She is skeptical and believes that all cosmetic providers are simply out to get her money. Before proceeding with treatment, check to make sure that her expectations are realistic; if they are unrealistic, it is better not to treat her. If expectations can be achieved, explain each recommendation as it pertains to her concerns. You must make a positive impression on "Betty" to gain her trust. Educating this client on her skin condition will prove beneficial. Some providers explain the treatments available but fail to take the time to give detailed information on why the condition is occurring in the first place.

Relating to "Betty":
- Explain all potential outcomes of the recommended treatment, including possible side effects.
- Provide a treatment that will show an immediate result but is not over-priced.
- Refrain from selling multiple products and additional services on the first visit.
- When recommending products, provide samples so that she can see the difference without investing more money.
- A follow-up phone call will ensure that you ultimately care about the outcome of her treatment and are committed to her well-being.

SCENARIO: Consultation with "Betty"

A female client, 28 years old with grade III acne, comes in to the medical office requesting Isotretinoin. She has tried "everything" in the past (facials, glycolic peels, antibiotics, and a commonly used skin care line based on benzoyl peroxide). She is upset about spending so much time and money and just wants to get on Isotretinoin, regardless of the potential side effects.

What could happen:
Provider: "I understand you have tried many things in the past, and being that your acne is still persistent, when the physician comes in we will discuss putting you on the medication you requested. Did you also want to talk about products to improve results?"
Betty: "No, I was told that the medication will clear my acne completely, so I don't want to spend the additional money."
Provider: "I understand."

What should happen:
Provider: "I'm sorry that you haven't had any luck with the methods that you tried. I understand you want to go straight for the medication, but I think with the right home care and in-office treatments we could see beneficial results."
Betty: "I am nervous to invest more money for treatments that may not help."
Provider: "Let me go over in detail what is happening beneath the skin and how the recommended treatments can help. We can then discuss options with the physician and work together to develop the best plan to get you the results you are looking for."

"Passive-Aggressive Patty"
This is the client who comes in and seems compliant with the recommendations made. She signs all consent forms and appears to be the model client, a pleasure to treat. Unfortunately, this person doesn't always follow after-treatment recommendations. A prime example is her compliance with wearing sunscreen. "Patty" does not bother wearing sunscreen, because she feels better with the look of a tan. Tanning gives people immediate gratification with regard to the look of their skin, and although they want to be compliant with the provider's post-treatment protocols, it can be somewhat of an addiction. If "Patty" receives an exfoliation treatment and goes  in the sun immediately after, her skin will most likely get worse. She may be nice in person while discussing her concerns, but she might speak negatively of you on the Internet or to others. It is hard to see this type of client coming, because they are deceptively nice and overly attentive in person.

How to Relate to "Patty":
- Reiterate all possible side effects of the treatment.
- Be explicit as to how this client should care for her skin at home following treatment.
- If unsure, show her pictures of adverse effects that occurred from non-compliance; this may make the client more serious about post-care instructions.
- Make sure all consent forms are signed, including post-care instructions and give the client a copy.
- Take before and after pictures and document everything.

SCENARIO: Consultation with "Patty"

"Patty" comes in for a follow-up appointment following a chemical peel and is presenting with red, inflamed skin that is sensitive to the touch. You notice that the skin on her arms and shoulders is significantly tanned.

What could happen:
Provider: "I see that you have had some trouble since our last appointment."

continued on next page

Patty: "Yes, my skin is very painful and I am dissatisfied with the effects of this treatment."
Provider: "Did you follow your post-care instructions as outlined?"
Patty: "As best I could, but there are only so many hours in the day, and I have a very busy life."
Provider: "I understand. Let's see if we can correct the issue you are having with your skin."

What should happen:
Provider: "I see that you have had some trouble since our last appointment."
Patty: "Yes, my skin is very painful and I am dissatisfied with the effects of this treatment."
Provider: "Did you follow your post-care instructions as outlined?"
Patty: "As best I could, but there are only so many hours in the day, and I have a very busy life."
Provider: "Post-care instructions are designed to give you the best results, but also to protect you from harm. Tanning, for example, can cause a severe reaction, like the one you are experiencing now, when combined with the service you received last time."
Patty: "I didn't realize that."
Provider: "Before we discuss what treatment will help alleviate your present issues, I feel we should go over post-care protocols step-by-step, in order to avoid this circumstance in the future. Without strict adherence to post-care routines, your skin will pay a terrible price."

"Too-Friendly Fran"
Who doesn't want friendly clients? We all do, of course; however, you should see a red flag if that friendliness is overdone (i.e., if it feels/seems like a performance). Those who repeatedly tell you how privileged they feel to be your client and send multiple gifts can be concerning. This client may try to befriend providers and other staff members for her own personal gain. If you don't maintain a healthy and professional relationship with "Fran," she will expect discounts and personal favors. Be friendly, but always bring conversations back to the reasons for her visit. Never give clients personal information about yourself, respectfully decline invitations to go out with them socially, and always maintain boundaries regarding phone calls and e-mails.

Relating to "Fran":
- Be sure to document in her chart all gifts, cards, and phone calls. Remember, an ounce of prevention is better than a pound of regret.
- Of course, be friendly and appreciative of their kindness, but simply decline any offer that takes the relationship outside the practice setting in a polite manner.
- Do not start discounting services because she is always bringing you gifts and referring clients. This is the start of a vicious unending cycle of multiple expectations.

SCENARIO: Interaction with "Fran"

Client comes in for her normal visit and invites you to a party.

What could happen:
Fran: "I wanted to invite you to my holiday party. It's this Saturday and I will not take no for an answer."
Provider: "Will there be any cute guys there for you to set me up with?"
Client: "Of course, my brother is single and would be great for you."
   This scenario seems farfetched, but it is meant to illustrate just how potentially problematic personal involvement with a client can become. If the provider was to go to the party and did not like her brother, it could upset the client, resulting in her not coming back, thereby damaging the esthetician's business.

What should happen:
Fran: "I wanted to invite you to my holiday party. It's this Saturday and I will not take no for an answer"
Provider: "That sounds like a lot of fun! I really appreciate the offer, but I am over-committed for the weekend already."
Fran: "There'll be plenty of single guys to meet and chat with."

continued on next page

> Provider: "Thank you just the same. Let's do dermaplaning today. Your skin will look amazing and your makeup will go on smoothly. I think you'll really love the results."
> Client: "That sounds great."

"Wendy Wants-It-All"
This client often comes in and says she wants (or needs) every treatment that you offer. You need to be very sensitive to clients who want it all, because they could potentially have a medical condition resulting from a distorted body image, commonly known as Body Dysmorphic Disorder (BDD). This is a very serious psychiatric condition that needs to be handled by a medical professional. Clients with BDD are extremely critical of their physique, despite the fact there may not be any noticeable disfigurement or defect. Regretfully, just about every cosmetic provider has treated

or experienced such a client without knowing it, as the signs of BDD do not always present in the same or most notable manner. This client may have had multiple procedures by other cosmetic providers wherein they were never satisfied with the results of the treatments. **BDD sufferers often fixate on their nose, skin, and weight, and may frequently examine themselves in the mirror or avoid mirrors altogether.** There are patient questionnaires available to physicians that can be used to better identify BDD sufferers. (Note: Since "Wendy" presents a distinct medical issue outside the scope of the esthetician's role in a medical setting, the "scenario" on which to depend is simple referral to a medical professional.)

How to Relate to "Wendy":
- If you believe the client has BDD, do not treat him or her. Immediately refer them to the appropriate medical personnel.
- If the client is just excited about treatment and is overzealous to try things, ask him or her to focus on two concerns to start with.
- Listen to your instincts or "gut feeling." If you intuitively feel uncomfortable treating someone, proceed appropriately.

Signs of Body Dysmorphic Disorder

1. Having anxiety or stress about their looks
2. Picking at their skin or hair
3. Frequently looking in the mirror (or avoiding it altogether)
4. Coming back to the office for more and more procedures
5. No treatment ever being good enough
6. Seeing multiple physicians for cosmetic procedures

No Matter Who Your Client Is …

Consultation is the key to defining the best treatment for your client. Ask questions and listen carefully to your clients' responses. This is by far the best tool for satisfying your clients' desires. **If you get the best clinical outcome from the procedure, but your client is dissatisfied then you have failed to achieve your primary objective, which is client satisfaction.** You may have missed something in the consultation before making your recommendation. Conversely, if your outcome is a little less than you would have liked, but the client is thrilled with the result then you have succeeded in your consultation and in performing your job. The client is happy, and this is the secret to success.

References
1. E Diener et al, Physical attractiveness and subjective well-being, *J Pers Soc Psychol*, 69 120-129 (1995).
2. M Snyder et al, Social perception and interpersonal behavior: On the self-fulfilling nature of interpersonal stereotypes, *J Personal Soc Psychol*, 35 656-66 (1977).

CHAPTER 7

Effective Consultation Techniques

In this Chapter:
- The Successful Client Consultation
- Past Treatments
- Discussing Client Lifestyles
- Product Use
- Medical Conditions

> The first and most essential question to ask every client is, "What are your concerns with your skin?"

The Purpose of a Successful Client Consultation

The most important part of any aesthetic appointment, regardless of treatment, is the consultation. Without a thorough consultation, you may not be providing the best treatment for the client's *well-being*. As discussed in earlier chapters, the client's motives are most important; therefore, the first and most essential question to ask every client is, "What are your concerns with your skin?" or "What can I help you with today?" Such an open-ended question lays the groundwork for willing communication about treatments and products that will best help your client look and feel better. **Too often a consultation and skin analysis starts with the provider discussing what they see wrong with the client's appearance.** This approach, while prescriptive, is also *restrictive*. If a condition is not a concern for the client, then it should not be a concern of the provider, unless that condition is clearly and potentially unsafe.

The reason for the client's visit is just a starting point. It gets him or her through the

> An initial consultation should take at least 45 minutes.

door, and what happens on *your side of it* depends, in large part, on your first point of face-to-face contact. An initial consultation should take at least 45 minutes. Going over the client's intake form along with important questions is necessary, as this will ensure safe and consistent results. The consultation is about the client giving information, and it is also an opportunity for the provider to educate the client thoroughly as to the scope and purpose of the recommended treatments for the client's respective concerns. For example, if a chemical peel is recommended, the client must be aware that visible peeling may occur, but it is not necessary for results. This discussion prior to treatment is necessary in order to avoid any confusion post-treatment. If physical peeling does not occur, a client may feel as though the treatment didn't work when in actuality the cells are at a microscopic level and may visibly peel or not peel for a variety of reasons. (The minutiae of this example will be discussed in depth in Part 4 on Professional Skin Care Treatments). Another necessary discussion to have prior to treatment is immediate post-treatment instructions, because they are crucial to maintaining treatment results. A client may choose to avoid certain treatments if they have plans that will result in non-compliance with post-care. **Make certain that the client has realistic expectations of how the recommended treatment can help, and this will result in happy clients.**

Past Treatments

After discussing initial concerns and gathering information as to what has brought the client to your office, you should inquire about treatments and products the client has tried in the past. Of these, were there any that proved beneficial? Or, on the other hand, that showed no improvement at all or were detrimental to their skin? This will help you accurately gauge the direction in which to steer your recommendation for treatment. For example, if someone has had several glycolic peels and did not see any improvements, it would be wise to choose another method of exfoliation.

The time frame of past treatments is also important. **It is crucial to be aware of when the client's last treatment took place in order to know whether or not she has allowed the skin an appropriate amount of time to heal.** Furthermore, gaining an understanding of what the client's behavior toward treatments has been in the past, such as how much time she *usually* lets pass before seeking subsequent treatment, will aid you in gauging the overall state of their skin and assist you in determining the reasons behind a past treatment's failure or success. There are several treatments often performed by medical professionals that require a certain amount of healing time. For example, microdermabrasion could cause severe complications if performed within a few weeks of an ablative laser treatment, although the technique can be safely used to enhance the effects of a non-ablative laser treatment as early as one week post-treatment. If the client has not received treatments in the past then it is best to start out with mild recommendations in order to watch for skin sensitivity and reactions.

Lifestyle Discussions

Not only do you need to understand your client's desires, but their lifestyle and schedule is important to know as well. The average person in our society leads a very busy life. The idea of the straight 9-to-5 is pretty much a thing of the recent past. **You will need to consider the time it will take your client to recover from the treatments you recommend or any adverse effects the treatments might have.** Is the client amenable if some physical peeling should occur following a treatment? Will the client follow post-treatment instructions, including avoiding excess heat in the days immediately following treatment, staying out of the sun, and using the recommended products? If the client is extremely active (exercises vigorously daily), they may not want to change their daily schedule, and this could cause complications following certain procedures. Perhaps their job does not allow for time off on short notice or appearing in the workplace in any condition other than perfectly normal. On the other hand, the client may be willing to change their lifestyle to some degree for a couple of days in order to gain the best possible results for their skin. Although a chemical peel may offer the best outcome, a quick and lower-impact 30-minute microdermabrasion might be all the client wants.

Another lifestyle consideration is the client's regard to overall health—we're talking full body health, including diet and possible negative habits. **Not only does health affect the appearance of the skin, the body's largest organ, but an unhealthy lifestyle could alter outcomes of certain treatments.** This must be discussed with the client during the consultation prior to performing any treatment. The extent of visible damage from smoking or other unhealthy habits may not be apparent right away, but eventually the lack of oxygen, decrease in nutrients, and increase in free radicals can wreak havoc on the skin. Clients must understand that they may not get typical results from treatments due to lack of oxygen and a longer post-care healing process. For this reason, certain medical procedures, such as cosmetic surgery, are not performed unless the client has quit smoking for at least two weeks prior to the procedure. **You must be sensitive to the client's lifestyle, but also be direct and unequivocal about the realities of how certain behaviors, such as smoking, will affect their expectations of aesthetic results.**

Stress and diet are also related to the function of the skin. Stress can have an indirect relation to skin conditions including acne, rosacea, and psoriasis. Therefore, it would follow that increased stress can affect the outcome of treatments as well. Post-care treatments can include a stress relief aspect, although not necessarily in conjunction with post-care product offerings; however, suggestions of an avenue of stress relief to aid the healing process and enrich the sense of well-being can be incorporated into product recommendations.

As far as diet is concerned, it is not the esthetician's place to give nutritional advice; however, the client should be aware that treatment results are often seen quicker and with a higher probability of satisfaction when a healthy lifestyle is maintained including a balanced diet, regular exercise, and stress management.

Product Use

The client's skin care regimen must be discussed before choosing a course of action to improve skin conditions. First and foremost, is the client wearing sunscreen on a regular basis? If a client refuses to use sunscreen as a part of their daily routine, then any treatment that requires avoiding sun exposure should not be performed. Similarly, if a client is using a harsh soap without an included or subsequently applied moisturizer, this becomes a concern for post-treatment compliance. Using only soap or water on the skin will often incur improper barrier function, which could result in overly sensitized, dry skin. **For those clients who are not used to caring for their skin at home, it is better to start with rebalancing skin care products and hydrating facials before proceeding to more advanced treatments.**

If a client is currently on a home skin care routine, ensure that the products are compatible with in-office treatments. There are certain ingredients, including vitamin A derivatives, alpha hydroxy acids (AHAs), and cortisone, that must be discontinued before specific treatments. **Knowing the complexity of the client's routine will also give you some understanding as to what he/she will do at home for maintenance.** If all the client uses is a basic cleanser, recommending a six-step routine may be overwhelming for them. On the other hand, some feel they have better results using multiple products, including weekly masks and regular exfoliation. The provider must ask comprehensive questions about product use in order to make the smartest choices for the client's well-being, choices tailored to individual need.

Medical Conditions

This is a sensitive but crucial aspect of the client consultation. The client intake form—of which an annotated example is included both in this chapter and in the book's concluding appendices (Appendix C)—should include several medical history questions. Two of the most important medical conditions to be aware of are pregnancy and breast-feeding. There are several treatments and even home care products that are contraindicated due to the unknown side effects on the fetus or child. Other medical conditions can have adverse effects on the skin, including dryness, irritation, and poor wound healing. Sensitivity, dehydration, and inflammation can all show up on the skin due to medical conditions and certain medications being taken to treat them. In this case, any treatment that can create a wound response (i.e., deeper chemical peels) should be avoided. See the section on **Skin Sensitizing Conditions** as a means of quick reference.

Skin Sensitizing Medications

Please note: It is important to get medical clearance for any unknown medications or if there is uncertainty.

Blood Thinners
Blood thinners present a bleeding, bruising or petechial risk; dermaplaning, microdermabrasion, micro-needling and ablative lasers should be avoided.
Examples include: *warfarin, coumadin, ibuprofen, aspirin, Plavix, Pletal, Prevacid, vitamin E (which is a natural blood thinner)*

Wound Healing
Anti-inflammatory drugs such as steroids and non-steroidal anti-inflammatory drugs (NSAIDs) may reduce the inflammatory response necessary to prepare the wound bed for granulation. Care should be taken with treatments to create a wound response, i.e., radio frequency, ablative lasers, and deep micro-needling.
Examples include: *ibuprofen, Naproxen, Ketorolac, aspirin, hydrocodone, magnesium salicylate, Suprofen, oxycodone, Fenoprofen, acetaminophen, and pseudoephedrine*

Acne Medications
Since these medications are drying, the skin becomes more sensitive as a result. Care should be taken with all aesthetic treatments, notably chemical peels, microdermabrasion, dermaplaning, micro-needling, lasers, and energy-based devices. Topical products are typically discontinued for at least three days before treatment; however, with Isotretinoin (formerly known as Accutane) treatments should not be performed for at least six months.
Examples include: *EpiDuo, Tazorac, Trentinoin, Renova, Atralin, Retin-A, Differin, Avage, Clindamycin, Doxycycline, Accutane, and Ziana*

Photo-sensitizing Agents
(There is a fuller list of these agents in Appendix A.)
These agents can cause minor to severe reactions to any light-based therapies or from exposure to the sun. All lasers, intense pulsed light (IPL), and LED must be avoided, in most cases for two weeks following the last dose of medication or with the treating physician's clearance.
Examples include: *tetracyclines, sulfonamides, terconazole, diphenhydramine, quinines, 5-fluorouracil, thiazides, Tretinoin, Isotretinoin, and chlorpromazine*

(Circle One)   Miss. Ms. Mrs. Mr. Dr.   Date_____

First Name: _____ Middle Initial: _____ Last Name: _____

Address: _____

City: _____ State: _____ Zip: _____

Home Telephone: (_____)_____ *Mobile: (_____)_____

Work Telephone: (_____)_____ Occupation: _____
[Could affect skin condition or treatment choice]

Date of Birth: _____ Age: _____ What is your hereditary background? _____
[Helps determine Fitzpatrick type]

*Email Address: _____ @ _____

How would you describe your skin?
☐ Oily   ☐ Sensitive   ☐ Dry   ☐ Normal   ☐ Combination

[Helps you gain a sense of how they view their skin and compare it to your findings]

If yes, please explain: _____ _____

Have you received any of the following procedures?
☐ Chemical Peel   ☐ Facial Ultrasound   ☐ Eyelash/Eyebrow Tinting
☐ Microdermabrasion   ☐ Facial   ☐ Waxing
☐ Dermaplaning   ☐ Laser Hair Removal   ☐ Skin Care Products

Other: _____

[Gaining feedback on the client's past experiences with previous treatments will help determine current course of action]

Have you used any of the following topical/oral medications?
☐ Accutane®   ☐ Differin®   ☐ Retin-A®   ☐ Avage®
☐ Renova®   ☐ Tazarac®   ☐ Trentinoin   ☐ EpiDuo®
☐ Hydroquinone   ☐ Topical Antibiotics ☐ Alpha Hydroxy Acids   ☐ Ziana®

Other: _____

[The use of certain products can sensitize the skin and/or be contraindicated for specific treatments]

Current Medications (Include Birth Control and Over The Counter)		Current Herbal Supplements and Vitamins	
1.	5.	1.	5.
2.			6.
3.			7.
4.	8.	4.	8.

[Certain medications are contraindicated to treatments or ingredients. Get physician clearance if there is any question]

Habits:	Never	Frequency Of Use	# Of Years	Date Late Used
Tobacco		packs/day		
Alcohol		beverages/day		
Caffeine		glasses/day		
Drugs Used:				

[Lifestyle may affect different aspects of the skin]

Allergies (Food, Latex or Medications) ☐ Yes ☐ No **if yes, please list:**

[Avoid allergic reactions by ensuring that you are not using any product ingredient that the client has had a negative reaction to]

Distinguish ALLERGY (shock, hives, & swelling) from ADVERSE REACTION (nausea & upset stomach)

MEDICAL HISTORY

Have you ever had any of the following conditions?

Condition			Note
Acne	☐ Yes	☐ No	*Determine stage before deciding proper treatment*
Arthritis	☐ Yes	☐ No	*Use caution in massage*
Diabetes	☐ Yes	☐ No	*Be aware of the lack of wound response*
Severe Headache/Migraine	☐ Yes	☐ No	*Fragrance, light therapy may trigger*
Cold Sores/Fever Blisters	☐ Yes	☐ No	*Certain treatments may cause an outbreak*
Seizures	☐ Yes	☐ No	*Light therapies must be avoided*
Cancer	☐ Yes	☐ No	*Skin sensitivity and wound-healing impaired*
Heart Conditions	☐ Yes	☐ No	*Products containing phenol should not be used*
Pacemaker/Metal Implants	☐ Yes	☐ No	*Avoid Radio Frequency/Electrotherapies*
Hepatitis	☐ Yes	☐ No	*Avoid causing a wound response*
Skin Disorder (i.e. Dermatitis)	☐ Yes	☐ No	*If present, don't treat refer to physician*
Hypertrophic scaring (i.e. Keloids)	☐ Yes	☐ No	*Aggressive treatments should be avoided*
Bleeding Disorder (i.e. Anemia)	☐ Yes	☐ No	*Avoid treatments where blood may be drawn*
HIV/AIDS	☐ Yes	☐ No	*Avoid causing a wound response*
Thyroid Disease	☐ Yes	☐ No	*Avoid causing a wound response*
Lupus	☐ Yes	☐ No	*Avoid causing a wound response*

REVIEW OF SYSTEMS

How much water do you consume daily?   *Regular water consumption helps keep the skin hydrated*

How much caffeine do you consume daily?   *Regular caffeine consumption can dehydrate the skin*

Do you currently have a sunburn/windburn or red face? ☐ Yes ☐ No *Best not to treat for 24 hours*

Are you in the habit of using tanning booths? ☐ Yes ☐ No *Tanning is not safe and only facials should be done*

Are you pregnant or breast feeding? ☐ Yes ☐ No *Beware of contraindications*

Do you wear contact lenses or eyeglasses? ☐ Yes ☐ No *Contacts need to be removed for some treatments*

Do you have intolerance to heat or cold? ☐ Yes ☐ No *Good insight to help predict treatment sensitivities*

Do you have any other medical concerns that have not been covered in this form? ☐ Yes ☐ No

If yes, please explain:
_____

Do you understand that every procedure/ operation is followed by a period of healing before the tissue returns to normal and the final result is apparent? ☐ Yes ☐ No

> This is important and should be laid out specifically in individual consents per procedure

Do you understand that the objective of any cosmetic procedure is an improvement not perfection? ☐ Yes ☐ No

_____   _____
Patient Signature   **Date**

_____   _____
Parent/Guardian Signature (If Under the Age of 18 Years)   **Date**

> Any treatment delegated by a medical professional must be noted

Healthcare Provider Signature   **Date**

Furthermore, it is important to know the client's health history in the event that an emergency should occur. A thorough history of symptoms or medical complications (i.e. light-headedness, passing out, and/or flushing) should be collected. Questioning about allergies should not be taken lightly, as allergic reactions can result in serious health concerns and even anaphylactic shock. Clients will not always think to tell you about internal allergies such as those related to food and medication when receiving a treatment. If you recommend a treatment or product that contains common allergen-producing ingredients, ask the client about each ingredient before proceeding with the treatment or use of product.

> Questioning about allergies should not be taken lightly, as allergic reactions can result in serious health concerns and even anaphylactic shock.

The client consultation should not be taken lightly. It is, even though the information being collected is of a professional, objective nature, a remarkably *personal* interaction. **The aesthetic provider should consider always that the client is making him/herself vulnerable, and commensurate sensitivity to this fact is required at all times.**

Following the consultation process, a thorough skin analysis is the next step to providing the best treatment for the client. This will be further discussed in the next chapter, along with skin conditions the skin care professional will commonly come up against.

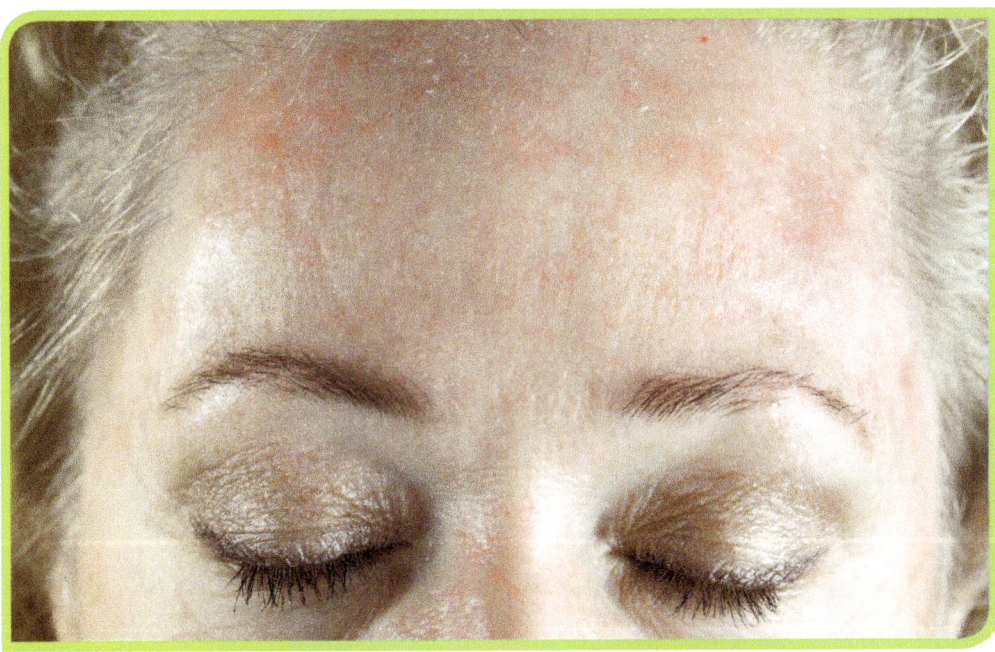

An example of allergic skin reaction.

CHAPTER 8

Skin Condition Analysis

In this Chapter:
- Identifying Skin Types
- Real vs. Perceived Skin Age
- The Fitzpatrick Scale
- Observing Skin Chracteristics

Performing a skin condition analysis should immediately follow the client consultation and result in a continued discussion to determine the best course of action for the client. A thorough skin analysis will allow you to see any underlying conditions that may be hidden by makeup or otherwise not visible to the naked eye. **It is common for clients to be unaware of present skin conditions or even hide them in order to receive a stronger treatment.** There are several potentially dangerous skin conditions that should be recognized by the skin care provider so they can refer the client to the correct medical professional; this point is important because some clients may have skin conditions they are entirely unaware of, including but not limited to rosacea, cold sores, fungal infections, warts, and even cancerous lesions.

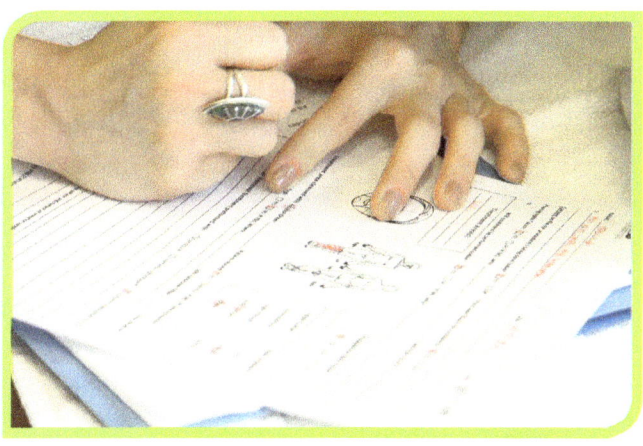

Documentation
During skin analysis, it is essential to document *all* findings. The best way to do this is to take standardized pictures. **Pictures should be taken at each visit for visible documentation.** This will protect you and the practice from any misconstrued outcomes from clients. For instance, if a client tries to blame you for a pigmented spot or other lesion, the pictures could be used to show the client that it was already there. Similarly, if a client states he/she is not seeing visible results, it is beneficial to be able to show the changes. A client may not see the difference in the state of their skin as a result of ongoing treatment simply because they are looking in the mirror every single day, and change is gradual. Having pictures to show improvement will

help keep clients satisfied and ensure them that your recommendations are being applied successfully. **Tracking changes for each client prior to treatment could not only lead to recognizing potentially dangerous lesions but also ensure that the client is obtaining her desired results.** (Appendix B contains standard operating procedures for photo-documentation.)

Besides visible documentation, written documentation standards must be met. In a medical practice, if it is not written down, it never happened. SOAP notes are used to record the Subjective, Objective, Assessment, and Plan. *Subjective* is what the client complains of; for example: "I have deep wrinkles on my forehead and my skin tone is uneven." *Objective* is the physical exam; for example: "Pigmented spots on cheeks after pregnancy and mild dynamic horizontal forehead rhytides are observed." *Assessment* is the diagnosis; for example: "30-year-old female presenting with signs of facial aging and melasma." *Plan* is the treatment; for example: "Even application of skin lightening product AM and PM for two weeks; Jessner's peel in two weeks following skin lightening prep, and 30 units of Botox in glabella and crow's feet." A detailed sample SOAP note can be found in Appendix D.

Skin Types

Skin type and skin condition vary from client to client, and it is important to distinguish each type and condition in order to provide the best solutions for each individual client. Establishing the client's skin type is a good starting point, but it should never be the only consideration. Just as each person is a unique human being, each person's skin, despite any categorical presentations or manifestations, is commensurately unique. As stated in Chapter 7, the first thing to address is the client's concerns and most often that will be a skin condition. (Part 3 on *Aesthetically Challenging Skin Conditions* will provide details of the top four aesthetic complaints: acne, aging, pigmentation, and rosacea.)

Determining skin type is basically the first step toward more individualized assessment. Skin types are broken down into the following loose categories:

Normal
- Client typically has no complaints.
- Skin is a healthy color, with soft, fine texture, and small pores.

Oily
- Client complains of oil coming through makeup, clogged pores, breakouts.
- Visible oil on the skin, enlarged pores, thick skin (congested, prone to breakouts).

Dry
- Client complains of dry skin, regardless of product use, fine lines, wrinkles.
- Fine lines and/or wrinkles are visible; sagging, thin skin that is often rough to the touch.

Sensitive
- Client complains of visible capillaries; skin is dehydrated and inflames easily.
- This skin is warm to the touch, flaky, and shows signs of erythema (redness).

Combination
- Client complains of oily congestion, likely in T-zone, along with dry patches.
- Comedones (small white or dark bumps) are visible in the T-zone, and skin is rough to the touch in certain areas.

Real and Perceived Skin Age

Chronological age plays a role in choosing the right treatment for safe and effective results. As we age, expected cellular turnover and collagen production dramatically slows down, particularly if the skin has been neglected or exposed to harsh conditions. The concept of cellular turnover is based on the amount of time that it takes for the new cells being produced in the deep layer of the epidermis to travel to the superficial layer of the skin and slough off. Many skin rejuvenation methods are meant to create a mild *wound response* in the skin to restore or speed up cellular turnover and stimulate collagen production. If the skin lacks the ability to properly respond to the wound, the seemingly beneficial treatment quickly becomes harmful. For this reason, it is recommended to start out with mild treatments to ensure timely healing and desired results before building up to more aggressive treatments. It is a *wound response* we are looking for, not a *wound*.

> It is a *wound response* we are looking for, not a *wound*.

While the client's real age is more obviously important to treatment selection, their perceived age plays an equally essential role. Perceived age is directly correlated to how well the skin has been cared

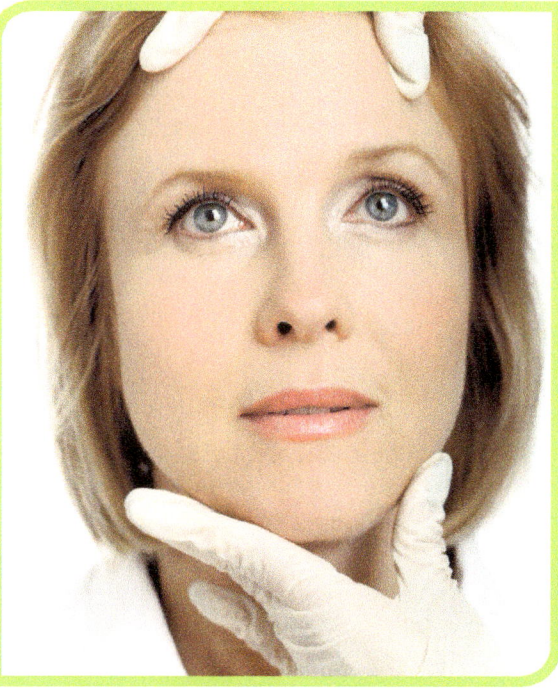

Properly cared for skin affects a persons perceived age versus their real age.

for over the years. As a result, there are often 50-year-olds who look like they are 35, and 30-year-old clients who appear to be nearly twice their real age; hence, the importance of taking both real and perceived ages into account.

The perceived age of a person is commonly referred to as their "photo-age." The **Glogau Wrinkle Scale** is commonly used in the medical community to quantify the degree of photoaging, or the result of premature damage to skin due to ultraviolet (UV) exposure. This system was developed by Dr. Richard Glogau[1] in 1996, and breaks down as follows:

Group Classification Description	Typical Age	Skin Characteristics	
Type I **Mild** **No wrinkles**	Age 28 to 35	Early photoaging Mild pigment changes No keratosis Minimal wrinkles	
Type II **Moderate** **Wrinkles while face is in motion**	Age 35 to 50	Early to moderate photoaging Appearance of smile lines Visible brown age spots (pigmentation) Pores may be more prominent Keratosis palpable, not visible	
Type III **Advanced** **Wrinkles while face is at rest**	Age 50 to 65	Advanced photoaging Wrinkles at rest Prominent pigmentation Visible blood vessels Visible Keratosis	
Type IV **Severe/** **Pervasive** **Wrinkles**	Age 60 and up	Prior skin malignancies Severe photoaging Yellow-gray skin color Wrinkles throughout	

The Fitzpatrick Scale

An in-depth knowledge of the Fitzpatrick Scale is quintessential to any aesthetic treatment. The scale qualifies skin types on a scale of I–VI on the basis of amount of pigment, with a skin type I being the lightest. Many aesthetic treatments function on the basis of creating some type of inflammatory response to the skin, and any stimulation poses a risk for those with higher Fitzpatrick types (IV–VI).

Fitzpatrick skin types IV–VI have the greatest chance of developing hyperpigmentation, hypopigmentation, or even potential scarring. The skin is programmed to adapt to its surroundings and invoke responses to potential threats, if necessary. Inflammation is the broadest of the threats and presents itself in routine actions such as sun exposure, picking, aggressive rubbing, and treatments with the intent of stimulating the skin. The body's automatic response is to increase melanin production in the skin when an invasion is sensed, whether intended or not. In higher Fitzpatrick types, the melanocytes (skin cells that produce pigment in response to hormonal triggers or inflammation) at baseline are innately more active than those in lower Fitzpatrick types. Stemming from primitive times, those with darker skin tones typically inhabited areas closer to the equator, thus receiving an increased amount of sun exposure. Accordingly, their skin adapted to become thicker and darker as a form of protection. Today, the world has become one big melting pot and people of all different skin types live in every area imaginable. It is for this reason that it is vital to assess (via simply asking outright) a client's ethnic background; don't only rely on visual analysis. **Even those who are very fair-skinned, but have a heritage of darker-skinned decent can trigger melanocytes to overproduce pigment when stimulated.** When in doubt, always classify the skin as darker for safety when starting treatment. Refer to the Fitzgerald Skin Type Worksheet that I use in my role as education director of True U Laser (Appendix C) for an example of what kind of questionnaire you ought to employ in your practice. (The formation of pigment will be discussed in depth in Chapter 11.)

Fitzpatrick Classification Method

The Fitzpatrick scale is based on skin response to sun exposure. It determines the patient's potential to tan or burn.

Type I:	White (always burns, never tans); commonly of Irish/ Scottish descent; blond/red hair and green eyes	

Type II:	White (usually burns, difficult tanning); commonly of Eastern European descent; blond hair and green/hazel/blue eyes	
Type III:	White (sometimes burns, good tan); commonly of Western European or Asian* descent; blond/brown hair and blue/brown eyes	
Type IV:	Olive (rarely burns, easy tan); commonly of Latino, Middle Eastern, or Hispanic descent; brown hair and brown eyes	
Type V:	Brown (very rarely burns, easy tan); commonly of East or West Indian descent; brown/black hair and brown eyes	
Type VI:	Black (very rarely burns, very easy tan); commonly African-American descent; black hair and brown or black eyes	

*Always treat Asian skin as type IV at first, as complications can arise without applying caution.

Skin Characteristics Under Observation

Texture

Looking and touching the skin to assess texture helps determine the course of action to take with products and treatments. Dry or rough patches present for a variety of reasons, and it may be necessary for a patient to alter or enhance their home care regimen or add a regular exfoliation product to their regimen in order to achieve a smoother result. **Texture is not only raised or uneven impressions in the skin, but can also include the appearance of large pores or fine lines and wrinkles.** Using a thorough hands-on approach is also helpful in discovering what may be going on beneath the surface of the skin. Whiteheads, keratosis, and keratin buildup can often be felt but not always seen.

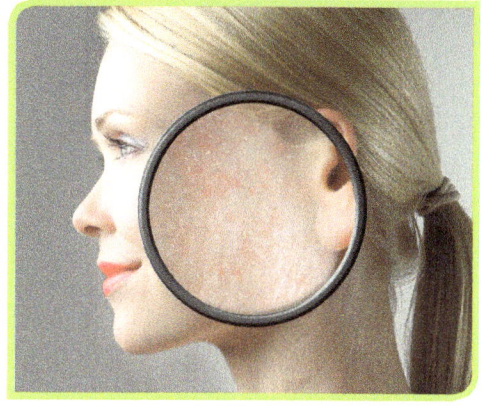

Hydration

Dehydrated skin can easily be mistaken for dry skin, but they are *not* the same thing. **While dry skin is a result of a lack of oil, dehydrated skin lacks overall moisture and can be seen in all skin types and conditions.** Symptoms of dehydrated skin include itching, flaking, tightness, and a dull appearance. A balanced skin care regimen including hydrating agents, like hyaluronic acid or glycerin, helps in most cases. Lifestyle and diet also play a role in appearance of the skin; drinking eight glasses of water per day and cutting down on caffeinated drinks helps the skin stay moist.

Dehydrated skin

Look for visible oil coming through makeup before removing it. Ask what time the client cleansed her skin that day. If cleansing was done an hour or less beforehand and the makeup is broken up and shiny, then you will know to degrease the skin more effectively and use oil-absorbing products.

Sebum Levels
The overall sebum content is assessed by palpating the skin, in addition to asking thorough questions of the patient. Assessment is thus a combination of verbal and practical measures. Such questions include what time the client's makeup was applied before coming into the appointment, what type of product was applied (e.g., moisturizer, sunscreen, toner), and then assessing the visible oil present on the skin surface. This will aid in determining both the type and strength of treatment to perform. This will be further addressed in subsequent chapters along with chemical peeling, but as a rule of thumb, those with oilier skin can often handle a more aggressive peel or may need to be degreased differently than drier skin types. Conversely, skin with less sebum tends to react more intensely to chemical exfoliation; therefore, care must be taken when deciding the strength.

How thick is the skin? One may immediately look as though they have thick skin, but it is important to pinch the skin lightly at several spots to check. This will also help determine peel strength, and depth for micro-needling procedures and microdermabrasion settings. **Those with thinner skin will likely see visible signs of aging sooner than those with thick skin. On the other hand, thicker skin often experiences more oil and typically leads to acne.** Many treatment protocols are dependent on the color of the client's skin, amount of sebaceous activity, and the condition being treated. An important aspect of skin evaluation should also be how thick or thin the skin is, both overall and in specific areas. For instance, the skin around the eyes is very thin, about 0.5 mm, therefore the same products and treatments used on the rest of the face, which bears a thickness of around 1.5 mm, would cause a much different reaction than around the eyes. This is especially important with exfoliating treatments and micro-needling; if the treatment goes past the intended area, it can cause more harm than good.

Steps for Analysis	
Look at the skin under traditional room lighting	Look for visible oil, dry patches, lesions, surface irregularities, pigmentation
Look under a magnifying lamp	Visible lesions, texture, oil content, dehydration, pigmentation
Cleanse the skin	Feel for texture, palpable lesions, skin density, and temperature (Note: warmth can be a sign of inflammation)

Look at the skin under a Wood's lamp	White fluorescence = thick stratum corneum
	Purple = dehydration
	Orange, yellow, or pink = excess of sebum
	White spots = dead cells
	Bluish white = normal healthy skin
	Brown = uneven pigmentation
	Pigmentation that is present in regular light and becomes LESS visible under a Wood's lamp is *most likely* dermal melasma
	Pigment that shows up darker under a Wood's lamp than under traditional light is *likely* epidermal, although it can be a mixture of both
Look at the skin under a magnifying lamp once again	Look at any areas that were seen under the Wood's lamp but were only visible under the black light
	Double check for areas that felt questionable while cleansing

Inflammation

If a patient presents with any existing inflammation in the skin, there are a plethora of treatments that should be avoided. Anything aggressive, including but not limited to microdermabrasion, aggressive chemical peels, micro-needling, radio frequency, or ultrasound, has the ability to trigger chronic inflammation.

Acute inflammation is good and will trigger a" wound response"; chronic inflammation is bad and can create a "wound."

Lesions

The presence of any lesions or irregularities on the skin needs to be addressed before any treatments are performed. The severity of a lesion varies tremendously, and can be as benign as a broken capillary or acne pustule or as serious as an indication of cancer. Hence, a thorough understanding of lesions can actually save a person's life. **It is important for all aesthetic providers to recognize anything that can be potentially dangerous and remain within their scope of practice by referring the client to a qualified physician.** If anything looks dangerous, infectious, or unknown, it is important to avoid treatment until a diagnosis is reached. Lesions have the potential to be cold sores, which resemble pimples, fungal infections that could present like a dry patch, or be an indication of other serious health conditions.

Lesions are defined as any abnormality involving any tissue or organ due to any disease or any injury. Yes, this definition is incredibly broad in nature. Determining the type of lesion is the first step a physician takes in diagnosing a skin disorder. Awareness of the shapes, margins, arrangement, and distribution of lesions is also important.

Primary Lesions		
Papule	Solid, palpable lesion Less than 10 mm in diameter Examples: *warts, elevated nevi, a pimple before it becomes a pustule*	
Nodule	Solid, palpable lesion More than 10 mm in diameter Example: *lipoma*	
Macule	Flat, non-palpable lesion Less than 10 mm in diameter Example: *freckle*	
Patch	Flat, non-palpable lesion More than 10 mm in diameter Example: *vitiligo, melasma*	
Plaque	Plateau like lesion 10 mm in diameter Example: *psoriasis*	
Vesicle	Circumscribed, elevated lesion containing fluid Less than 5 mm Examples: *herpes simplex, herpes zoster, chickenpox*	
Bulla	Circumscribed, elevated lesion containing fluid More than 5 mm Examples: *blisters, 2nd degree burns*	

Skin Condition Analysis

Wheal	Transient, elevated lesion caused by local edema, usually disappears in hours Examples: *bite, hive*	
Pustule	A raised lesion filled with pus Less than 10mm Example: *acne, impetigo*	

Secondary Lesions		
Crust	Hard, rough surface formed by dried sebum, exudate, blood, or necrotic skin Example: *scab*	
Scale	Heaped up piles of horny epithelium with a dry appearance Example: *dandruff, psoriasis*	
Ulcer	Depressed lesion of epidermis and upper papillary layer Example: *abrasion produced by scratching or scraping*	
Scar	Slightly raised or depressed mark on skin after injury or lesion has healed (hardened tissue) Example: *keloid, hypertrophic*	

Note: Precancerous and cancerous lesions are detailed in Chapter 11.

Aesthetic Skin Conditions
Sebaceous Hyperplasia
Enlarged sebaceous glands most commonly seen on the forehead and cheeks. They are yellowish bumps with a depression in the middle. No treatment is necessary; these are largely cosmetic. Cause is unknown.
- Treatments include: Electrocautery, ablative lasers, and Isotretinoin in extreme cases. Retinols may slow down occurrence, but it often recurs after discontinued use.

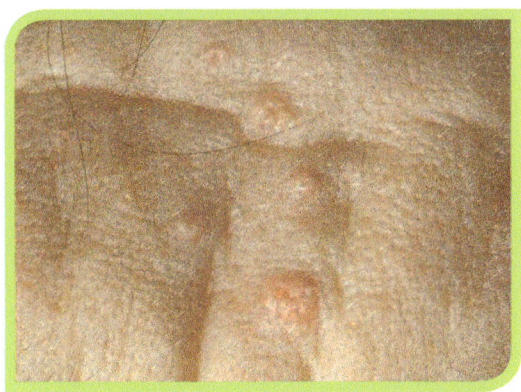

Syringomas
Very small papules that have the same color as normal skin or have a yellowish color; these are harmless sweat duct tumors. These are commonly mistaken for milia. To differentiate, milia are very white, pearly, and almost perfectly round.
- Treatments include: CO_2 laser, electrocautery, surgical removal.

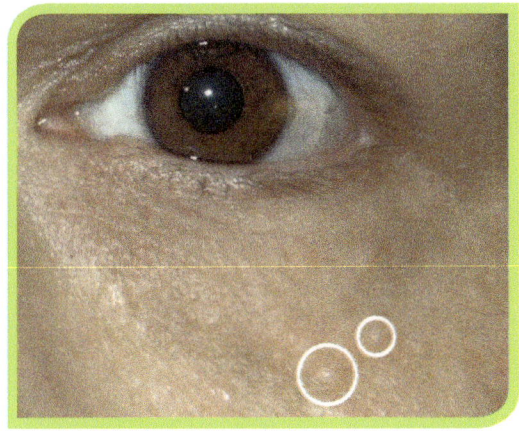

Milia
Small white cysts caused by a buildup of keratin. White, raised papules with a pearly appearance. Milia often derives from trauma to the skin including laser resurfacing.
- Treatments include: Removal with a lancet is most common. Products to stimulate cell turnover including retinoids, AHAs, and BHA are helpful. Chemical peels and laser resurfacing can be done as well.

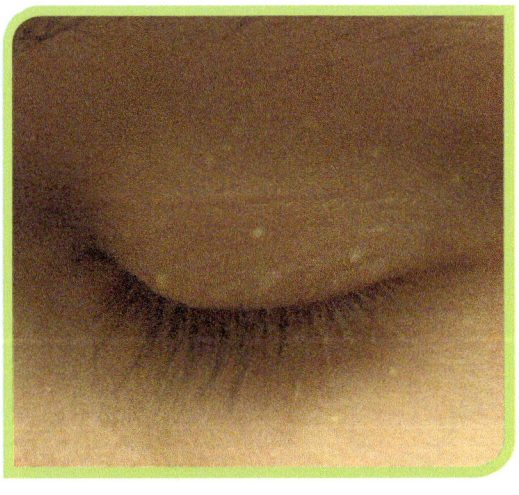

Skin Condition Analysis

Xanthelasmas
Yellow soft bumps found around the eyes; they often occur with medical conditions resulting from lipid disorders. Due to this cause, they are often called *cholesterol deposits*. These should be treated by medical professionals only.
- Treatments include: If caused from lipid disorder, healthy lifestyle changes. TCA, ablative laser, excision and electrocautery are also used.

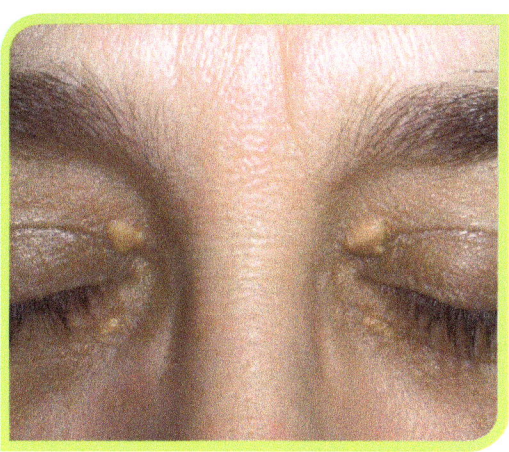

Vascular Disorders
Port Wine Stain
A vascular formation of dermal blood vessels that is present at birth. They may become softer over time, but rarely disappear. Port Wine Stains are most commonly seen on the face, but can occur anywhere and can become blue or purple with age.
- Treatments include: Laser treatments are commonly used, but it is not guaranteed to be removed

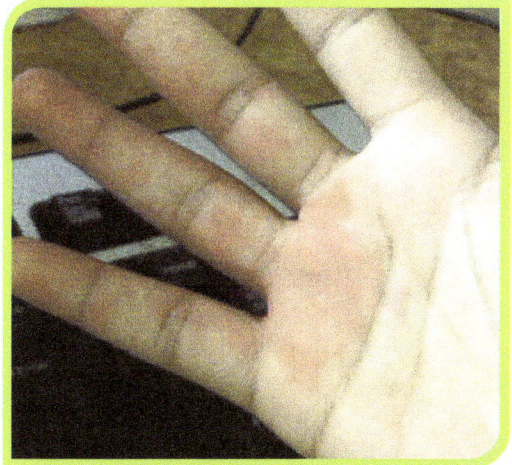

Venous Lakes
Small, dark blue papules resulting from a dilated cavity, lined with a single layer of flattened skin cells and a thin wall of fibrous tissue filled with red blood cells.
- Treatments include: electrocautery or laser

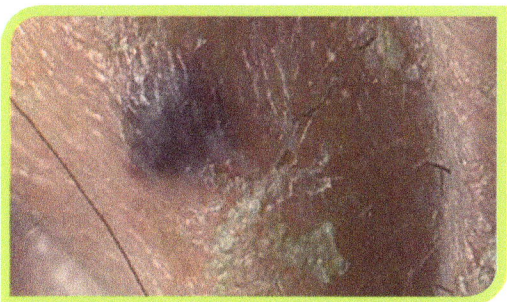

Cherry Angioma
Common bright red papules found mainly on the trunk. They consist of numerous dilated capillaries, lined by endothelial cells.
- Treatments include: electro-coagulation or lasers, although larger lesions may need to be excised.

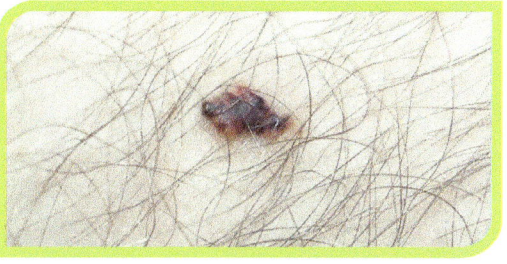

Infections of Hair Follicles

Folliculitis
This is an infection of the upper part of the hair follicle that is often confused with acne, due to the presence of red-ringed papules or pustules. May be caused by shaving, plucking, waxing, occlusion, and climates with high humidity.
- Treatments include: Commonly treated with antibiotics from physician.

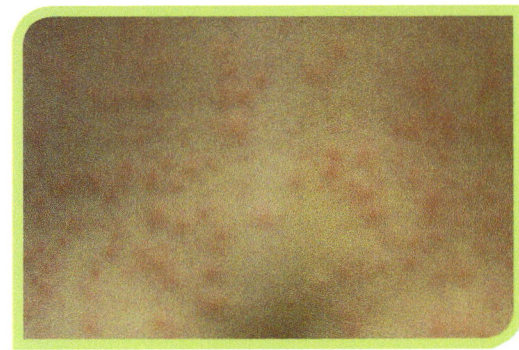

Pityrosporum follicultis
Usually occurs on the back and upper arms. Looks very similar to bacterial folliculitis. A physician will likely perform a skin scraping and/or biopsy to determine if the papules or pustules contain yeast.
- Treatments include: Commonly treated with antifungal medications and topical agents like ketoconazole cream or shampoo.

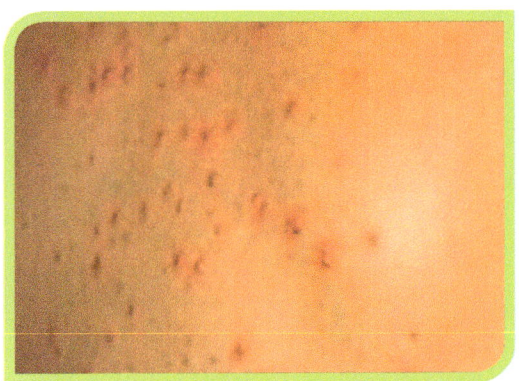

Pseudofolliculitis barbae
This is mostly seen on the facial area of African-American males. It is an infection of the hair follicle, caused by curly hair turning inward.
- Treatments include: This can be treated with alpha hydroxy acids, salicylic acid, and laser hair removal. Some providers use electrolysis, but it is not as effective because the treatment uses a straight needle in a curly hair follicle.

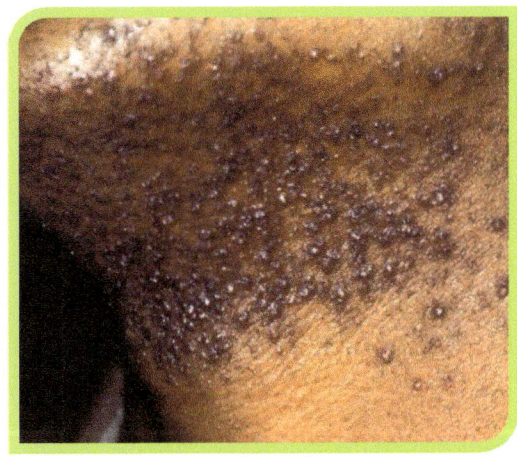

Skin Condition Analysis

Keratosis pilaris
Characterized by small follicular papules, due to a buildup of dead skin in hair follicles. It most commonly occurs on the upper arms, legs and back.
- Treatments include: Gentle cleansers, fragrance-free moisturizers, AHAs, and retinoids are commonly used as home care. Microdermabrasion, chemical peels, IPL, and resurfacing lasers can be used in the office to speed results.

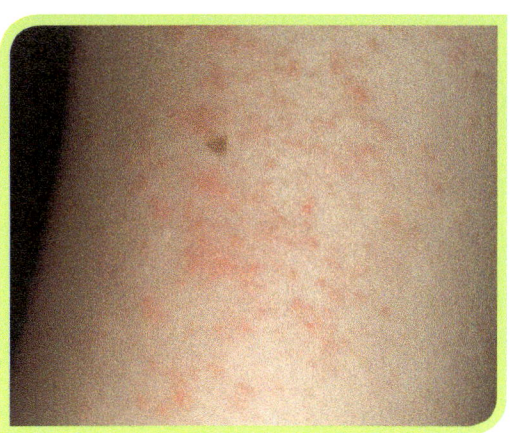

Inflammatory Disorders
Contact Dermatitis
This can be an acute or chronic inflammatory reaction. Irritant contact dermatitis is caused by a chemical irritant (not an allergen) on the skin. Allergic contact dermatitis is caused by an allergic type IV hypersensitivity reaction, or by an allergen. The patient will usually have itching and burning in the area, along with erythema and plaques.
- Treatments include: Determined by physician; often concern topical or internal steroids, or antihistamines.

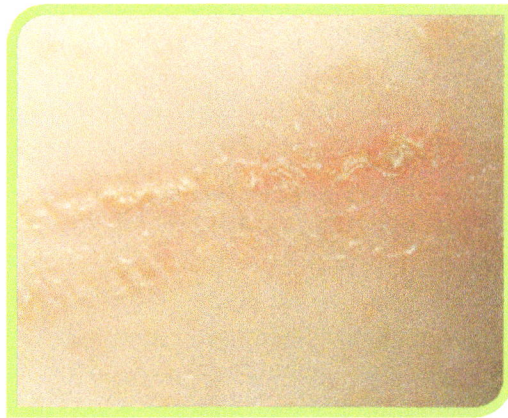

Atopic Dermatitis
A chronic relapsing skin disorder that starts in childhood. It is a hypersensitivity reaction and is characterized by papules and plaques, with or without scales and usually associated with edema.
- Treatments are usually antihistamines, topical corticosteroids and topical emollients. UVB can also be helpful.

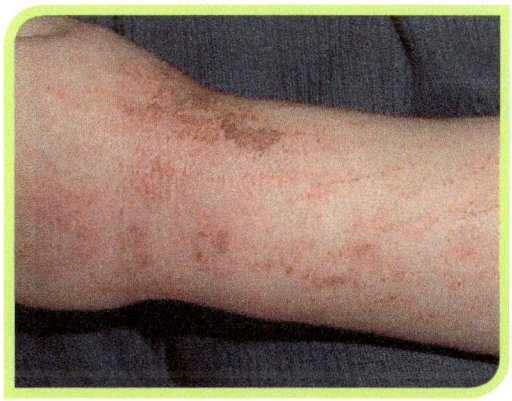

Seborrheic Dermatitis

Caused by overproduction of the sebaceous glands and *Pityrosporum* yeast. It is characterized by redness and scaling and can be exacerbated by bacteria.

- Treatments include: Shampoos used for dandruff conditions are often recommended, as well as salicylic acid, coal tar, and sulfur. UV radiation may also be helpful, but for more severe cases a steroid is used.

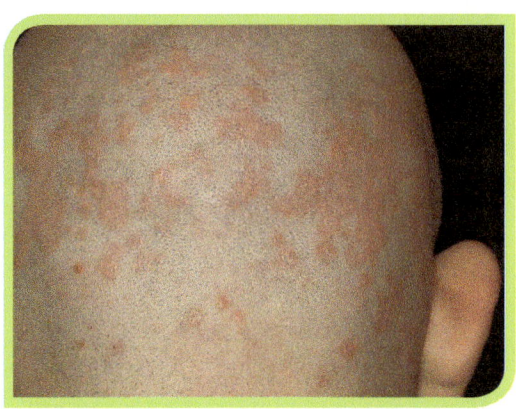

Psoriasis

It is a chronic inflammatory scaling condition of the skin, characterized by papules and plaques with distinct margins and loosely adherent silvery scales. Most commonly found on the scalp, elbows, and knees, but can be found anywhere on the body. There is a genetic predisposition for this disorder.

- Treatments include: In mild cases topical steroids and vitamin D can be helpful. In more severe cases, systemic steroids may be used. Topical retinoids and chemical exfoliation treatments are beneficial as well.

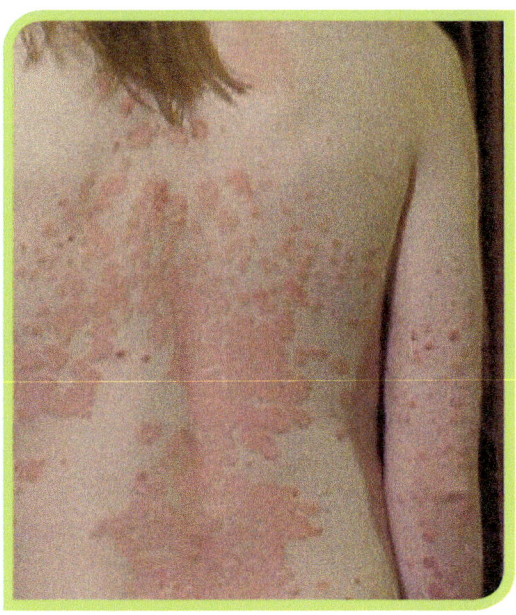

Sebaceous Gland Disorder
Seborrheic Keratoses

These lesions have a rough brown to black, "stuck-on" appearance. They are benign growths on the skin that look similar to warts, commonly found on the scalp.

- Treatments include: No treatment is necessary but cryogenic therapy or physical removal can be used

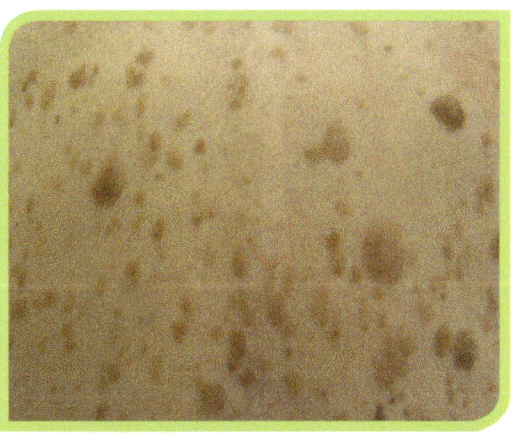

Infections

Tinea corporus (Ringworm)
A fungal infection of the skin, characterized a red scaly ring.
- Treatments include: Topical antifungal treatments are used as treatment.

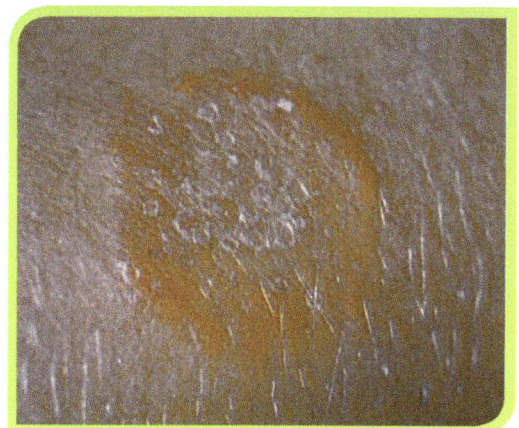

Impetigo
It is a highly contagious bacterial infection of the skin. Symptoms are small blisters that become crusty.
- Treatments include: Skin lesions must be kept clean and treated with oral and local antibiotics

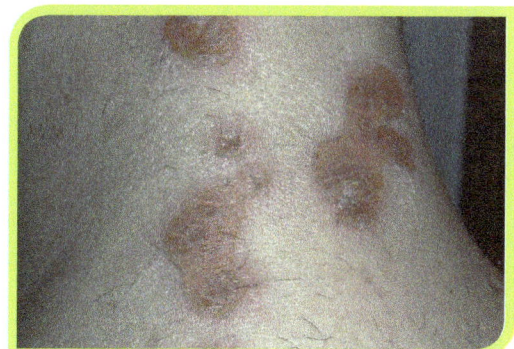

Warts
Caused by viral infections of the skin. Symptoms are rough, hard, elevated, rounded surfaces on the skin.
- Treatments include: Warts can be removed by electrocautery, salicylic acid, or liquid nitrogen.

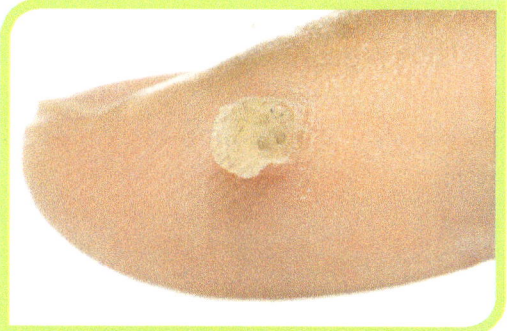

Scars
Keloid Scars are raised fibrous tissue that may have claw-like extensions. What differentiates a keloid scar from otherwise scarred skin is its ability to grow beyond the wounded area. This makes it very difficult to treat. When stimulated, the scar may become worse.
- Treatments include: Can be treated by physicians with ablative lasers, steroids, or micro-needling.

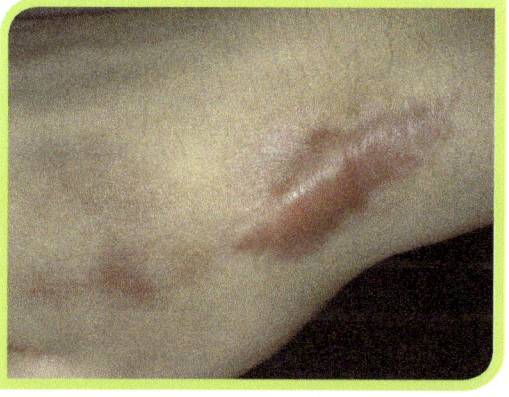

Hypertrophic Scars consist of raised fibrous tissue but tend to soften and flatten over time.

- Treatments include: Can be treated by physicians with ablative lasers, steroids, or micro-needling.

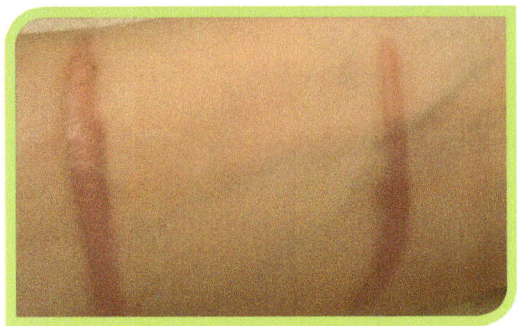

Atrophic scars are indented from loss of support structure, often caused from acne, picking, and trauma to the skin. There are a few variations of atrophic scarring: "Ice pick," which is characterized by a deep hole in the skin that looks like it was made by an ice pick; "rolling," which has a wave-like look; and "box car," which is characterized by round or oval depressions with steep vertical sides.

- Treatments include: ablative lasers, steroids, micro-needling, chemical peels, and retinoids.

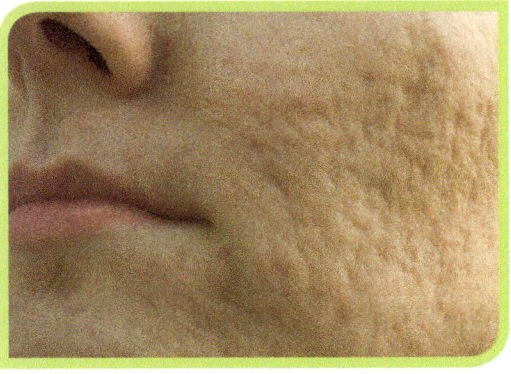

This information is just a starting point for recognizing skin conditions. It is the job of the aesthetic provider to ensure their clients are being treated safely. Dermatology is extremely difficult due to the multiple skin conditions that can occur and the varying visual aspects of each; no two lesions are the same, just as no two people are the same. My recommendation would be to choose a skin condition for each week that you want to learn more about, have it set on a calendar. For each skin condition you will dedicate a certain amount of time looking at pictures online as well as researching causes and treatments. This often leads to researching those particular treatments or ingredients in products that may be helpful. To really understand the skin, education should be sought out on a continual basis.

Knowledge is powerful and is always beneficial to you and, ultimately, to your clients.

References

1. *www.sfderm.com/wrinklescale.html* (accessed Jan 17, 2014)

Part 2: Review Questions

1) Which of the following is most important when treating clients?

    a) Making the client relaxed

    b) Making the client feel better

    c) Making the client look better

    d) Making the client spend money

2) Which male trait suggests a high level of testosterone?

    a) A long neck

    b) Full lips

    c) Small ears

    d) A chiseled jaw

3) What happens to a woman's eyes when she is attracted to someone?

    a) They flutter

    b) She blinks a lot

    c) Her pupils dilate

    d) All of the above

4) What trait, along with physical appearance, can anticipate more positive responses from others?

    a) The energy we gain from self-esteem

    b) The color choices we wear on a daily basis

    c) The vehicle we choose to drive

    d) None of the above

5) Studies show that once a person views his or her face with fewer wrinkles they are less efficient in emoting anger but *will feel more* anger.

    a) True

    b) False

6) Cosmetic enhancements should be

   a) Simple and powerful
   b) Extravagant and noticeable
   c) Subtle and unique
   d) Obvious and extreme

7) The morals and ethics of mating, marriage, and child-rearing have varied widely based on what factor?

   a) Social status
   b) Culture
   c) Political status
   d) All of the above

8) What are first impressions based on?

   a) Appearance
   b) Self-esteem
   c) Personality
   d) Financial status

9) During a client consultation, what is the most important thing the provider should do?

   a) Tell the client what he/she thinks would be best for them
   b) Tell the client about procedures that they have had done themselves
   c) Understand what the client wants and support their decisions
   d) Sell as many services as possible

10) What should you do with a dissatisfied client?

    a) Dismiss the unhappy client
    b) Address the client's issue head-on
    c) Admit that you are guilty
    d) Avoid the client at all costs

Review Questions

11) What can the provider do for a "Satisfied Sally" to let her know she is appreciated?

   a) Discount the price on all services
   b) Give free products with each treatment
   c) Provide an add-on treatment once in a while
   d) Nothing, she is privileged to be your client

12) Who gets cosmetic procedures?

   a) People who have a lot of money
   b) People with Body Dysmorphic Disorder
   c) People who are overly concerned with their appearance
   d) People from all walks of life

13) Which patient personality type likely comes in knowing the procedure she wants?

   a) Satisfied Sally
   b) Esthetic Shopper Sharon
   c) Know-It-All Nancy
   d) Passive-Aggressive Patty

14) What are some of the signs to look for with Body Dysmorhpic Disorder?

   a) Having anxiety or stress about their looks
   b) Picking at the skin or hair
   c) Frequently looking in the mirror
   d) All of the above

15) What is the first and most essential question to ask every client during the initial consultation, before the treatment?

   a) What are your concerns with your skin?
   b) What treatments have you had in the past?
   c) Do you have any vacations coming up?
   d) Is your skin sensitive?

16) What is the minimum length of time the *initial* consultation should take?

   a) 10 minutes
   b) 25 minutes
   c) 45 minutes
   d) 1 hour

17) What information is important to gather from the client during the initial consultation?

   a) Allergies or past allergic reactions
   b) The client's lifestyle and product use
   c) Any medical conditions the client may have
   d) All of the above

18) From information gathered during the initial consultation, which client would the esthetician more likely *not* recommend a chemical peel for?

   a) A client getting family pictures taken a few days post-treatment
   b) A client who has arranged to have a week off from work post-treatment
   c) A client who received a chemical peel in the past and liked the results
   d) A client who wants results for pigmentation

19) Why is it important to know what home skin care products the client is currently using?

   a) To ensure the client's products are compatible with in-office treatments
   b) To ensure the client will only use products bought from your office
   c) To ensure the client discontinues the use of antioxidants for five days before a peeling treatment
   d) To help determine how much money the client is willing to spend on services

20) Why is providing medical history information on an intake form crucial?

   a) To help the esthetician find out as much personal information about the client as possible
   b) To ensure there are no contraindications to recommended treatments
   c) To help better educate the esthetician on competing techniques
   d) To recommend medical treatments for medical conditions if it will help the client's skin

21) Why is it important to know the past treatments a client has received?

   a) To help determine what has and has not worked for the client in the past
   b) To ensure enough time has passed since the last treatment
   c) To discuss why treatments you offer are better
   d) All of the above

22) When cleansing the skin during analysis what should the technician be feeling for?

   a) Whiteheads
   b) Keratin buildup
   c) Keratosis
   d) All of the above

23) When looking under a Wood's lamp at pigmentation and the pigment appears *lighter,* what is that a sign of?

   a) Infection
   b) Dermal melasma
   c) Scarring
   d) Dry skin

24) When skin is inflamed, which treatments are to be avoided?

   a) Microdermabrasion
   b) Ultrasound
   c) Radio frequency
   d) All of the above

25) Which of the commonly seen skin lesions is caused by an enlarged sebaceous gland?

   a) Milia
   b) Syringoma
   c) Xanthelasma
   d) Sebaceous hyperplasia

PART 3

Aesthetically Challenging Skin Conditions

AESTHETICS EXPOSED
MASTERING SKIN CARE IN A MEDICAL SETTING AND BEYOND

CHAPTER 9

Acne

In this Chapter:
- Brief Overview
- The Four Grades of Acne
- The Psychological Effects of Acne
- Causes of Acne and Lifestyle Triggers
- Treatment, Practice, and Prevention
- Educating the Client

Acne is the most common skin condition to affect the majority of the population to some extent at some point in their lives. In the United States alone, 40–50 million people have acne.[1] Although acne is more prevalent in teenagers, many adults become affected as well. In healthy skin, just enough sebum is produced to protect and moisturize the skin and can be washed away with proper cleansing. However, hormonal fluctuation, stress, illness, poor health and certain medications can all directly or indirectly affect acne formation. These medical conditions and lifestyle choices can trigger or halt the amount of sebum produced, the desquamation of dead skin cells, and/or the ability to fight bacteria—all of which are culprits in acne formation. Although the aforementioned conditions cause an increase in acne breakouts, there may be a hereditary component as well.

Pathogenesis of Acne
- When dead skin and sebum build up beneath the skin's surface, it is referred to as a closed-comedone, or *whitehead*.
- If the pore is open on the surface, oxidation occurs, causing the plug to turn black, which is referred to as an open-comedone, or *blackhead*.
- The combination of excess sebum and dead skin cells makes a breeding ground for *Propionibacterium acnes* (*P. acnes*) bacteria. This bacteria is always present in the skin, but flourishes in this moist environment, causing inflammatory signals that form papules and pustules.

- Following the presence of bacteria, immune triggers are released, resulting in inflammation. This accumulation of activities can lead to red, hot, painful and pus-filled acne lesions. In severe cases, large cysts form under the skin's surface which can lead to permanent "ice-pick" scarring (as previously mentioned in Chapter 8).

Acne is most commonly broken up into four grades, of which a simple bullet breakdown appears on the opposite page. Grades I and II are considered acne simplex and have little to no inflammation. Grades III and IV, or acne vulgaris, are associated with visible inflammation.

Grade I is the mildest form of acne, consisting of comedones, blackheads, and whiteheads. This type of acne is often treated successfully with topical products and esthetic treatments. Grade II acne commonly has a large presence of comedones, along with occasional papules and pustules. Grade III acne consists of inflamed papules and pustules, along with blackheads and whiteheads. Grade IV acne is a severe form of acne in which the person affected will likely have a combination of blackheads, whiteheads, papules, pustules, and nodules or cysts. It is often accompanied by severe inflammation that may become very red and even purplish. Examples are **shown**.

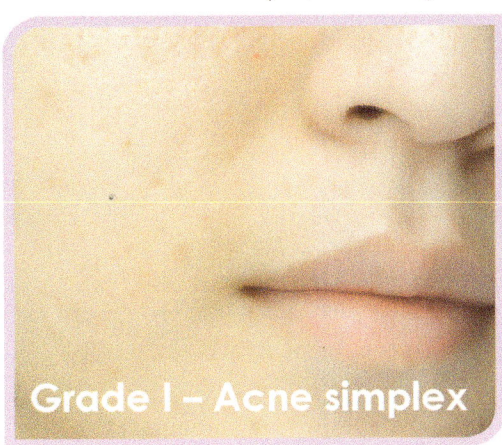
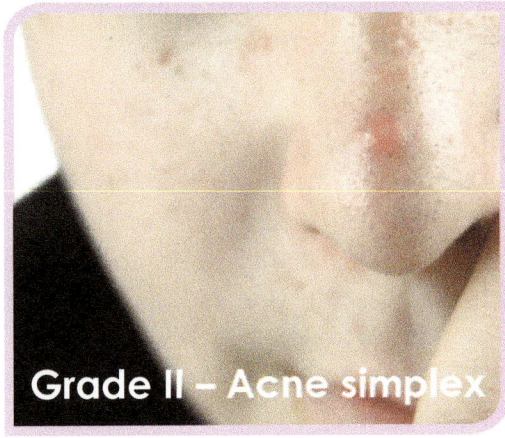
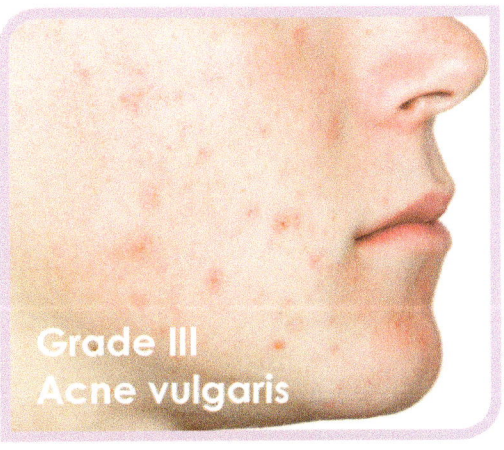
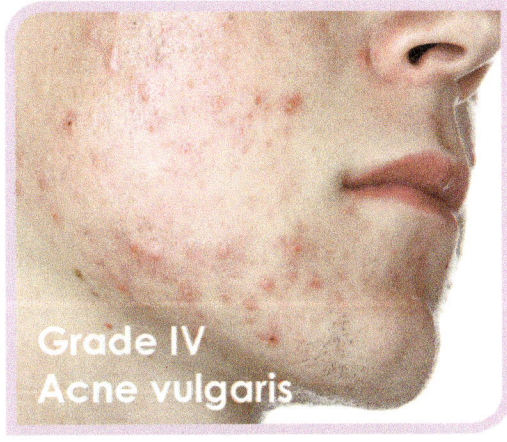

Four Grades of Acne

Acne Simplex—Grades I and II

■ *Common Causes*
- Improper product/cosmetic use
- Dry or dehydrated epidermis
- Asphyxiated skin (common in smokers)
- Lack of circulation
- Slowed cellular turnover
- Overproduction of sebum

■ *Common Treatments*
- Facial with manual extractions
- Alpha hydroxy acid peels for drier skin
- Beta hydroxy acid peels for oilier skin
- Microdermabrasion
- Dermaplaning
- Micro-needling
- Oxygen treatments
- Non-ablative resurfacing lasers

■ *Beneficial Ingredients**
- Salicylic acid, AHAs (glycolic/lactic)
- Papaya enzyme
- Beaded mechanical exfoliants
- Retinol
- Hyaluronic acid
- Niacinamide
- Bakuchiol[2]

Acne Vulgaris—Grades III and IV

■ *Common Causes*
- Hormone fluctuations
- Overstimulation of the skin
- Medical conditions, typically hormonal
- Medications
- Occlusion or pressure
- Accumulation of bacteria
    - Unsanitary environments, clothing, makeup brushes, etc.

■ *Common Treatments for Grade III Acne include:*
- Calming facial *without* extractions
- Alpha hydroxy acid peels for drier skin

* Ingredients will be discussed in depth in Chapter 27.

- Beta hydroxy acid peels for oilier skin
- Oxygen treatments, depending on the level of inflammation
- Jessner's peel for oilier skin, non-sensitized
- Blended TCA peels for drier skin
- Laser/Light therapies
- Blue LED
- Medication: Internal/topical antibiotics, Isotretinoin

■ **Beneficial Ingredients**
- Benzoyl peroxide
- Bakuchiol
- Salicylic acid
- Lactic acid
- Niacinamide
- Sulfur
- Hyaluronic acid
- Retinol
- Tea tree oil
- Green tea
- Azelaic acid

■ **Common Treatments for Grade IV Acne include:**
- Physician must make recommendations; treatments are commonly oral medications combined with topical products based on reducing inflammation and killing bacteria; when inflammation is reduced, the use of laser therapy.

The Psychological Effects of Acne

Acne not only causes visible effects, but renders very definite psychological effects, as well. This is another reason that gentle bedside manner is essential for medical providers and estheticians alike. Teenagers are plagued with acne at a time in their lives when their outward appearance most greatly affects how they feel about themselves, critically impacting their developing self-esteem. Over 80% of teenagers between the ages 13 and 18 are affected by acne at some point.[3] During this phase of development, puberty-dependent sex hormones are released at high levels and the oil glands are particularly sensitive to these hormones. The relative commonness of this condition in no way detracts from the profound affect it can have on a person's self-image and self-esteem.

Causes of Acne

Acne ultimately occurs due to an overproduction of sebum triggered by androgens. This excess sebum, comprised of fat and epithelial debris, blocks the follicle opening, which creates a perfect breeding ground for bacteria. Bacteria flourishes and triggers inflammation, which further prompts an immune response with the ability to result in swollen and painful acne lesions.

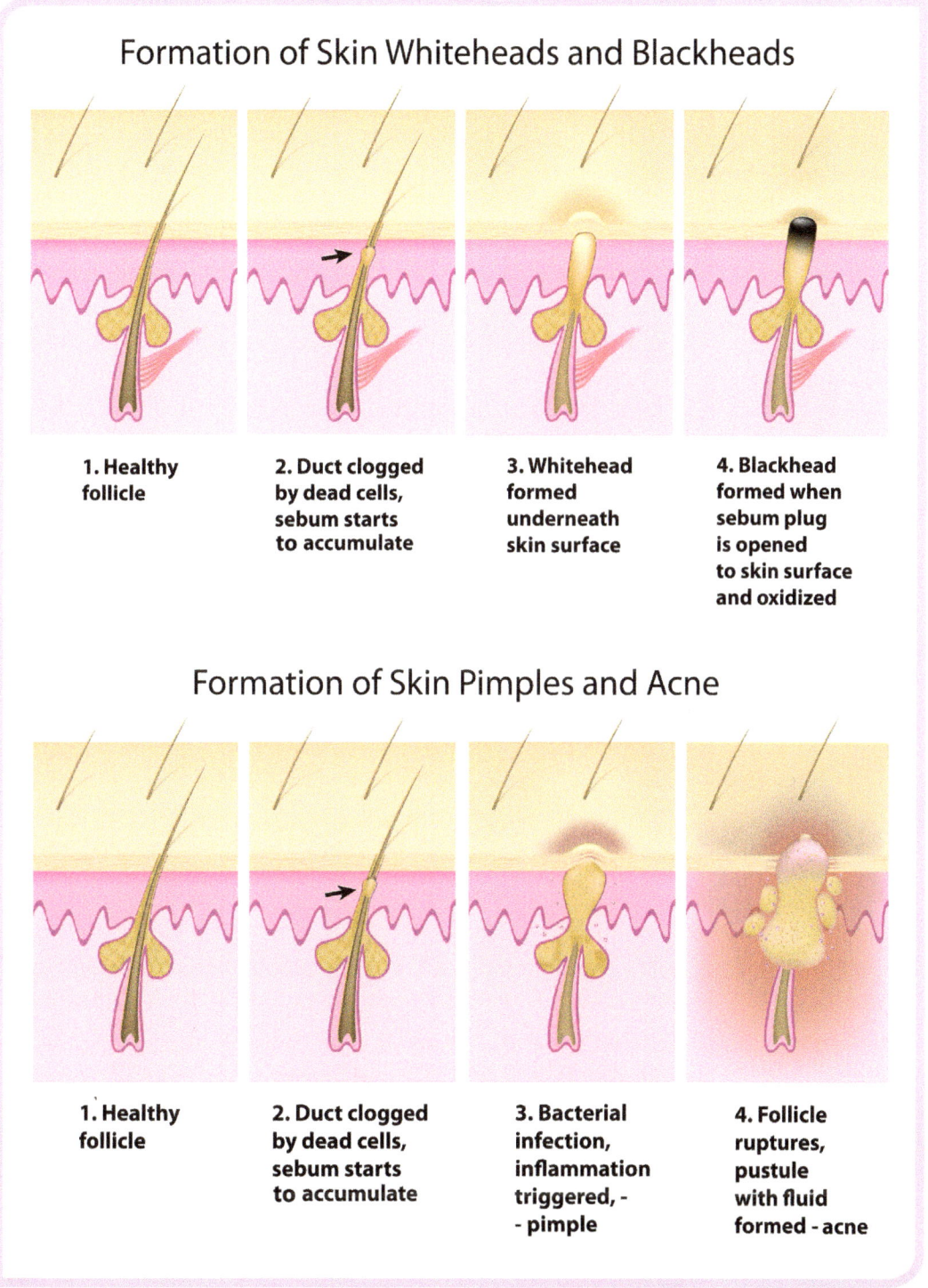

Androgens are hormones responsible for the development of the male reproductive system and secondary male sexual characteristics such as voice depth and facial hair. Testosterone belongs to the class of androgens and is normally produced by the testes in large quantities in men. Testosterone also occurs in women, but in far smaller quantities. As a side effect of testosterone, both sexes can experience an increase in oil production and frequent acne breakouts.

Adults who never experienced acne in their teens tend to unrealistically believe that they have escaped it altogether. However, women, notably, are often surprised to find themselves in their 30s or 40s experiencing burdensome breakouts. Acne during these decades most commonly presents around the chin and jaw line. It has been reported that 80% of adult women report persistent acne, and 53% of women older than 33 years have premenstrual acne flare-ups.[4] For women, fluctuations in hormone levels during the menstrual cycle and menopause may also affect acne breakouts. Acne seems to be generally less common in men after age 25, but can still occur. Many women notice that their acne breakouts are less severe when they are taking birth control pills. This is because birth control pills cause testosterone levels to drop. Naturally occurring high levels of testosterone or polycystic ovarian syndrome can both can lead to increased bouts of acne, and medical recommendations should be sought. *Polycystic ovarian syndrome* is a condition characterized by the accumulation of numerous cysts (fluid-filled sacs) on the ovaries leading to chronic anovulation (absent ovulation) and other metabolic disturbances. One of the most prevalent side effects of polycystic ovarian syndrome is hyperandrogenism, the excessive production of androgens, particularly testosterone, by the ovaries. This accounts for male hair-growth patterns and acne in women with this condition.

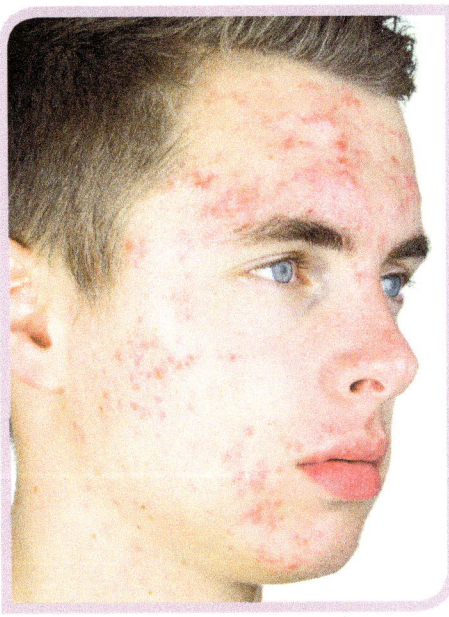

Severe Acne
To treat acne effectively, the underlying causes must first be addressed. Once breakouts are relatively under control, it is essential that the client remain on a stable skin care regimen that maintains a good balance of oil and hydration so that breakouts do not occur. This regimen may vary depending on the season, and for women, the point in their menstrual cycle.

Lifestyle Triggers

Diet: There is no scientific evidence proving that acne is caused by eating a particular food; the commonplace fear exemplified by "I ate a potato chip, and now I have a pimple" is just that, a fear. (Unless you account for potato chip grease-smeared fingers touching your facial skin, then that's a different story.) Although specific foods may not directly affect acne, lifestyle including diet can play a role in the improvement of acne conditions, as overall health impacts skin quality in general. A healthy lifestyle, particularly with regard to diet, will provide the best results when treating skin conditions from the inside out. If foods high in fat, sugar, and dairy trigger inflammation in general, then it may have a direct correlation to the body's largest organ, the skin. There has been speculation about the overconsumption of dairy as a contributor to acne. A positive association between the intake of skim milk and acne has been found. This finding suggests that skim milk contains hormonal constituents and, in sufficient quantities, can have biological effects.[5]

Although a certain food may not directly cause acne, allergies to food can cause a facial rash that looks similar to an acne breakout and should be evaluated by a medical professional. Just as many general health conditions can at least be improved or stabilized with a healthy diet, so can skin conditions. It is not the diet itself that rids the skin of acne, but replenishing with essential nutrients allows the body to fight off potential complications.

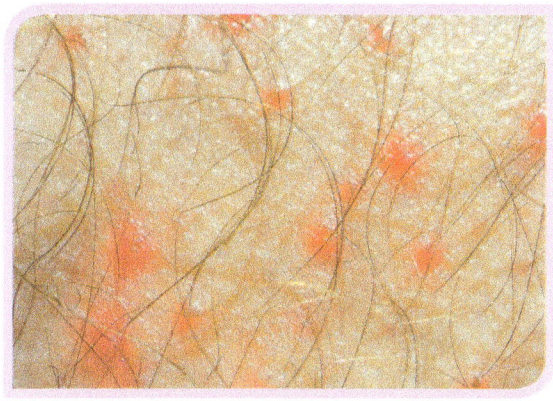

Food allergies can cause an acne-like reaction.

Stress is another condition that can have an indirect effect on the formation of acne. Stress increases the levels of steroids in the body and can cause fluctuations with sex hormones again triggering excess sebum production. It can be helpful for one, noticing that his or her condition is becoming more prevalent during stressful times, to take proactive measures by learning methods of relaxation. There is little prescriptive methodology here, as what constitutes stress relief differs person to person, but the usual suspects include choice of music, yoga, meditation, exercise, reading a book, or simply closing off from the attentions of the digital world altogether. This, along with a healthy diet, can help manage the effects that stress can cause on the body.

Other contributing factors for acne include occlusion or pressure on the skin, misuse of cosmetic products, unsanitary environments, medications including steroids, and any health condition related to the skin or to the application or ingestion of medications with potential or known side effects.

TREATMENT, PRACTICE, AND PREVENTION
Recommending Products

Clients may experience acne breakouts from simply using the wrong products or by neglecting their skin care at home. Using the correct products on the skin can make a world of difference for some acne sufferers. **Clients fighting acne often erroneously believe that the more they dry out their skin, the better their chance of eliminating acne.** Quite the contrary; drying out the skin too much sends a response to the body to produce more oil to combat the dryness. This ultimately results in more breakouts due to the increase in oil and dry, irritated epidermis.

Salicylic acid is often considered the gold standard for exfoliation of skin with acne. Products containing salicylic acid in the 2–5% range are often offered over-the-counter (OTC). Salicylic acid is a lipid-soluble ingredient known for its ability to decongest clogged pores by attracting to oil-filled areas. An effective exfoliation product will continually shed the buildup of dead skin, releasing clogged oil in the follicles. Salicylic acid may be used with other beneficial ingredients as well; e.g., a combination of salicylic and azelaic acids work well together to reduce acne.

> **Retinoids** are vitamin A derivatives that include retinol, retinyl palmitate, and retinaldehyde, which are commonly used in cosmeceuticals, and Tretinoin, Adalpene, Tazarotene and Isotretinoin. The differences and uses for each will be discussed in detail in Part 7.

Retinol-based OTC products have come a long way in the treatment of skin conditions without the increased risk of potential side effects associated with prescription strength retinoids. Retinoids in general are used to stimulate cell renewal. Prescription strength products contain stronger derivatives of vitamin A, which can produce a more profound chance of sensitivities. As damaged cells are moving toward the surface at a rapid rate, the skin may become sensitive and begin to peel. There have been many retinol-based products available over the counter that did not provide significant results, but like anything else, as research continues to evolve, newer generation retinols allow for a reduced risk of side effects while delivering results. Retinoid products have the additional benefit of reducing the appearance of aging skin, which makes them a top choice for those with adult acne. It is important to educate on the importance of sunscreen when recommending any retinoid, because the skin will be more vulnerable to the sun. Because retinoids are stimulating, the initial reaction often increases sebaceous activity due to the cellular turnover. This overproduction of sebum may take six to eight weeks to normalize. Therefore, it generally takes up to two months before a significant improvement can be seen, but once the goal is reached, results tend to be continuous. Products should prove effective and safe through clinical studies before being recommended to clients.

Clients with overly sensitized skin, pregnant women, and those who are breast-feeding should not use products containing retinoids because they can enter the bloodstream and harm an unborn fetus or be transmitted via breast milk.

Benzoyl peroxide (BPO) is an effective topical agent used to fight off bacteria associated with acne. *P. acnes* is an anaerobic bacteria, which means it is unable to survive in an oxygen-rich environment. Benzoyl peroxide products reduce acne by effectively delivering oxygen to affected areas, thus controlling the presence of *P. acnes* bacteria in the skin. Cleansers, serums, and moisturizers with BPO are usually in strengths of 2.5% to 10%. Although benzoyl peroxide is extremely beneficial when used correctly, side effects including dry skin, sensitivity, and hyperpigmentation in darker skin types can occur when overused. Additionally, the use of BPO for extended periods of time can eventually dry the skin so much that after initial clearing of acne the condition comes back even worse than before. As with all treatments, it is important to remember not to overdo a good thing. It is all about balance.

Recommended Treatments

Cleansing facials and superficial chemical peels can increase the effectiveness of treatment and speed results when implemented properly. Cleansing facials including steam and extractions are beneficial for cases of acne simplex (Grades I and II). There are opposing thoughts to performing facials with extractions on Grade III and IV acne, as overstimulation can worsen the inflammation associated with acne vulgaris, leading to more breakouts. **The recommendation of most skin care professionals is not to extract and stimulate inflamed skin, but rather to calm the inflammation and fight bacteria.** When inflammation is present there is a higher risk of complications with extractions, including spread of bacteria, post-inflammatory hyperpigmentation, and scarring. Extractions (**pictured**) should only be performed by trained professionals. Clients may try to repeat the process at home, as it seems easy enough but even when working on comedones the skin can be bruised, torn, or even scarred.

Heat, steam, massage and other methods to increase circulation are beneficial for Grades I and II, but should not be used on inflammation, including Grades III and IV acne.

Chemical peels, both salicylic and glycolic, show definite results for comedonal and inflammatory acne.[6] These superficial peels are used to stimulate cellular turnover,

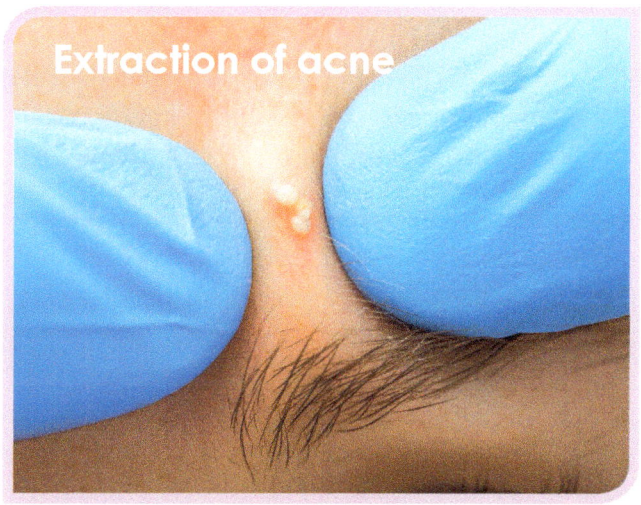

reducing the buildup of dead skin in the follicles. By regulating cell turnover this can cause an effect on regulating sebum production. Salicylic acid is more commonly used due to its lipid-soluble properties and ability to kill bacteria. The ingredient is actually an aspirin derivative that gives an added anti-inflammatory benefit. As a chemical peel, salicylic acid is most commonly used in 20–30% formulations. Alpha hydroxy acid peels also provide results, but are more effective on dry, dehydrated, or sensitized skin. Alpha hydroxy acid peels, most often glycolic or lactic, are commonly used in 30–70% formulations.

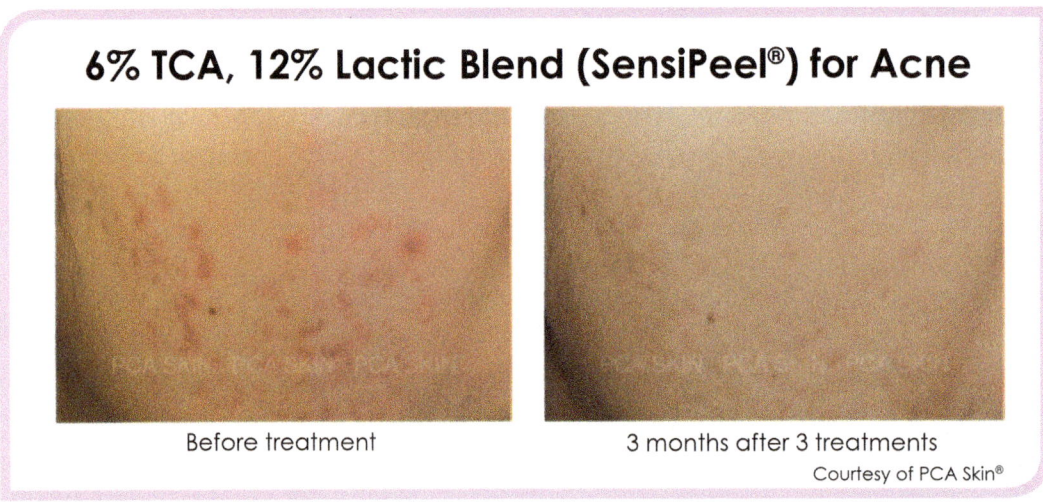

6% TCA, 12% Lactic Blend (SensiPeel®) for Acne

Before treatment — 3 months after 3 treatments

Courtesy of PCA Skin®

If superficial peels aren't producing effects, deeper peels including Jessner's or TCA may be the next step. Jessner's peels are more commonly used for those with thick, oily skin; they contain salicylic acid, lactic acid, and resorcinol (a keratolytic agent) in an alcohol base. Low-percentage TCA peels are common for inflamed acne with notable sensitivities, because they typically don't contain alcohol. Many clients see progressive results during treatments, but a series of six peels is recommended for dramatic results. Treatments should be spaced three to four weeks apart and post-care instructions, including product use, must be given.

Minimizing the underlying causes of acne will prove most effective for treatment. It is essential to target the three main acne-causing culprits—*P. acnes* bacteria, dead skin accumulation, and excess oil—for optimal results.

Medical Treatment Recommendations

If topical treatments are not effective, the use of oral medications is usually considered. Remember this type of treatment falls under the purview of the medical professional, but knowledge thereof is necessary for the skin care provider to safely complement medical recommendations. Generally, this tends to not be a first-choice therapy, because adverse effects (e.g., yeast infections, stomach upset, and increased sensitivity to the sun) may outweigh the benefits. For most people, acne will resolve quickly after introducing an oral antibiotic regimen. ***Minocycline*** and ***doxycycline*** currently appear to be the best option for acne;[7] however, as with any antibiotic, continued use produces resistant bacteria, thus rendering the antibiotic ineffective. This is commonly seen with erythromycin, which was often a first choice for antibiotic treatment in the past.

Isotretinoin (most commonly known by the trade name Accutane) is a powerful drug that is recommended by physicians to treat patients with severe, persistent acne. Although it is only taken for six to eight weeks, the results can last a lifetime. This medication is an internal form of vitamin A used to reduce sebum production by shrinking sebaceous glands. There are several negative side effects that can occur with the use of this drug; therefore, the bad must be weighed against the good. The entire body often becomes severely dry—not just the skin but the mucous membranes as well. The lips, mouth, and eyes are often the most troubling sites to the patient. Although it seems minor, the extent of dryness can cause cracked skin and open wounds, both of which can be painful and lead to infection. This drying out of the skin also significantly reduces the wound healing process, making it a contraindication to many skin treatments. In most cases, treatments should not be performed for at least six months after the medication is discontinued; for more invasive procedures, the treating physician may recommend waiting one to two years, in order to reduce the chance of side effects.

There are also significant adverse effects associated with the use of Isotretinoin including serious birth defects if taken by a mother during pregnancy. This is such a large issue that a female patient must have two negative pregnancy tests and consent to using birth control pills before a prescription for Isotretinoin will be given. There have also been reports of increased rates of depression and suicidal behaviors in people taking Isotretinoin; this data is, however, inconclusive. (As discussed earlier, severe psychological effects can occur from those suffering with acne.) The number of other possible side effects ranging from drowsiness, muscle pain, and osteoporosis, to bone damage and even liver disease can be alarming, but some patients are so focused on ridding their skin of acne that they are willing to risk these conditions. In fact, many patients seeking a physician for help with severe acne will ask for this medication specifically when they feel that all other efforts have been exhausted.

As vitamin A derived medications, of which Isotretinoin is itself derived, are effective for acne, so are topical vitamin A products or retinoids. Due to the associated side effects of Isotretinoin, physicians are more apt to recommend topical prescription retinoids. Retin A, discovered by notable dermatologist Albert Kligman, was the first retinoid product to gain FDA approval for acne treatment. Renova, Differin, Tazorac are a few of the most commonly used prescription retinoids that have shown great success for acne. As previously discussed, vitamin A-based products are known as *skin normalizers*, meaning they have been shown to promote healthy cell growth and proliferation of old cells.

For women suffering from hormonal breakouts, physicians may recommend a medication called **Spironolactone** to limit the amount of androgens produced by the body. This medication is particularly helpful in women with naturally occurring high levels of testosterone or those with polycystic ovarian syndrome. Certain birth control pills have also shown positive results for controlling hormonal breakouts. Spironolactone is an effective treatment for polycystic ovarian syndrome. Spironolactone is furthermore beneficial in reducing the swelling and water retention caused by various medical conditions, such as heart, liver, or kidney disease. It also blocks the release of excess hormones, including testosterone, which is how it helps acne. Although Spironolactone provides temporary relief, it is not considered a "cure" for acne; if treatment is discontinued, hormone production goes back up almost immediately. Moreover, Spironolactone can negatively affect a male fetus, due to its effect on androgen hormones, and therefore *must not* be given to pregnant women or women trying to become pregnant. Patients on Spironolactone must be monitored closely by a physician to ensure blood pressure and potassium levels are within normal ranges.

Women trying to control hormonal breakouts may try birth control pills before taking the step to Spironolactone. Although birth control pills can trigger acne breakouts, they can also help to reduce them. Any hormone fluctuation could throw off the balance of estrogens and androgens, resulting in more or less oil, depending on the skin of the individual.

Light-based Therapies

Multiple lasers and light-based devices are now US Food and Drug Administration-approved to treat acne.

There has been much excitement about the use of light-based therapies for improving acne. Laser light in the blue to red spectrum is effective at killing *P. acnes* bacteria while also decreasing the inflammation associated with acne.[8] Laser light works by activating a protein (porphyrins) that when activated destroys the walls of *P. acnes* as well as the surrounding inflamed cells. Injury is limited to only the acne lesions, and the normal skin is not affected. Porphyrins are highly absorbed by light at, or close to, 410 nm, which is in the blue light spectrum, although other wavelengths are still effective to varying degree. Lasers alone, or lasers used in combination with a topically applied solution (called *photodynamic therapy*), are highly successful in-office medical treatments for acne.

> Laser light works by activating a protein (porphyrins) that when released destroys the walls of *P. acnes* as well as the surrounding inflamed acne cells.

Photodynamic therapy: Photodynamic therapy (PDT) is a combination of a topically applied drug used to photo-sensitize the area where light will be applied. It has proven to be a good treatment for those with severe acne breakouts who want a significant improvement and can afford a few days' downtime. One treatment can significantly decrease acne lesions for up to two and a half months, and after multiple treatments, results can last up to five months.[9] Treatments should be separated by one calendar month in order to avoid unnecessary complications. A series of three to five treatments is often recommended. (See Part 5 for further discussion.)

Steroid Injections

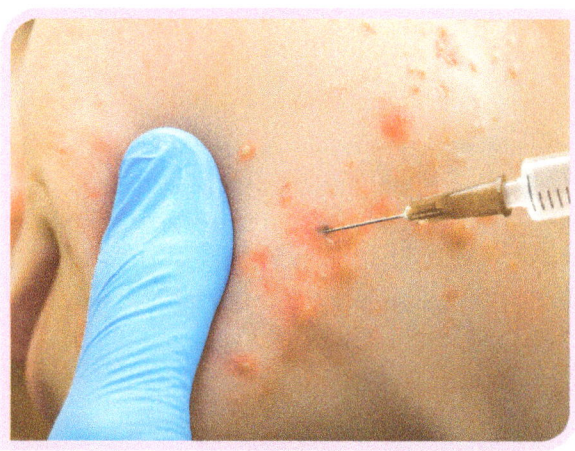

Anyone who needs immediate relief from a large acneic lesion may look into getting a steroid injection. The steroid shot can be injected by a physician directly into the acne lesion. There is mild discomfort; however, most people are willing to receive the shot because they know that the lesion will likely dissipate by the following morning. There is a small possibility with this treatment of local fat necrosis, which is when local fat cells are killed, resulting in a depression in the area where the injection was done. Usually, it is only temporary, and the skin eventually fills in. Sometimes, though, it can leave a permanent atrophic scar in the skin and may cause a permanent blanching of the skin, resulting in a white spot. Using a low concentration of steroid coupled with proper injection technique by the physician can make the occurrence of these complications rare. Having said that, this treatment is typically recommended as a last resort.

Educating the Client

To achieve the best results in treating acne of any grade, treatments that include chemical exfoliation, cleansing facials, and product recommendations should be introduced. Products recommended should include a cleanser appropriate for the client's skin type, an exfoliant to stimulate cellular turnover, antibacterial agents to reduce bacteria, antioxidants, and a physical sunscreen. In the case of excessively oily skin, sebum-controlling ingredients should be used as well. If a client chooses not to use recommended products, results will be limited and this is something they will need to understand. Educating clients on other ways to keep breakouts to a minimum is essential to begin a regimen. What follows are tips you can communicate to your clients that are helpful in getting acne under control.

- Cleanse the skin twice a day.
    - Some clients believe that if they do not wear makeup, then cleansing is not necessary. The excess oil accumulated during the day, as well bacteria that can come from environmental factors, can contribute to acne.
- Change pillow cases regularly.

- White cotton with no fabric softener, changed daily, is best. Fabric softener and dyes can both be irritants that trigger inflammation.
- Reduce friction or pressure on areas prone to breakouts.
  - Not using the hands to prop up the face when sitting or speaking or using the telephone; also, cease rubbing, touching or picking breakouts.
- Be aware of body breakouts.
  - Similar to pillow cases, white cotton materials without fabric softeners should be used. Showering after workouts can also help cut down on the presence of acne.
- Protection from sun exposure.
  - Some may argue that sun dries up breakouts; they should be educated on the residual effects of drying out the skin and the dangers of UV exposure. Many medications for acne are also photo-sensitizing, which can result in severe damage and scarring.
- Refrain from smoking.
  - Smoking can asphyxiate the skin, resulting in lack of circulation leading to breakouts. Grade II acne is common in smokers.
- Be cautious with makeup.
  - Mineral makeup is best. Avoid heavy makeup products and those that contain talc.
- Don't pick. Period.
  - As discussed, picking leads to a spread of infection and potential scarring.
- Don't over-dry the skin. A moisturizer is needed for balance.
  - Over-drying the skin can trigger an increased production of oil. Without moisture, the skin will not function properly.
- Reduce stress.
  - Look into methods of reducing stress, such as those suggested earlier in this chapter.
- Reduce the intake of dairy.
  - There is speculation that a diet high in dairy could lead to acne breakouts, especially in women.

Because acne is so common; all skin care professionals should have an in-depth understanding of how and why it occurs. Targeting all elements of acne is best; reducing excess sebum, controlling bacteria, reducing the buildup of keratinized cells, protecting from inflammation—each of these aspects of acne maintenance and treatment are crucial. Although the factors associated with acne remain constant, response to treatment tends to be unique. Several treatments and product combinations may be tested before finding the best solution for each individual. If the provider and client work as a team, breakouts can be kept under control.

References

1. *www.aad.org* (accessed Jan 21, 2014)
2. RK Chaudhuri and F Marchio, Bakuchiol in the management of acne-affected skin, *Cosm Toil*, 126 (7) 502 (2011).
3. S Purdy and D DeBerker, Acne is the most common skin disease of adolescence, affecting over 80% of teenagers (aged 13-18 years) at some point, *Clin Evid* (online), 1714 (2008).
4. S Stoll et al, The effect of the menstrual cycle on acne, *J Am Acad Dermatol*, 45 957-960 (2001).
5. CA Adebamowo et al, Milk consumption and acne in teenaged boys, *J Am Acad Dermatol*, 2008; 58 (5) 787-93 (2008).
6. Amy Forman Taub, Procedural treatments for Acne vulgaris, *Dermatol Surg*, 33 1005-10026 (2007).
7. JJ Leyden and JQ Del Russo, Oral antibiotic therapy for acne vulgaris, *J Clin Aesthet Dermatol*, 4(2), 40-47 (2011).
8. E Shnitkind et al, Anti-inflammatory properties of narrow-band blue light, *J Drugs Dermatol*, 5 605-610 (2006).
9. W Hongcharu et al, Topical ALA-photodynamic therapy for the treatment of Acne vulgaris, *J Invest Dermatol*, 115 183-192 (2000).

CHAPTER 10

Rosacea

In this Chapter:
- Clinical Characteristics and the Stages of Rosacea
- Common Causes of Rosacea
- Rosacea Treatments
- Skin Care Recommendations

The word *rosacea* is derived from the Latin word *rosaceus*, meaning *rosy*. Rosacea is a vascular disorder of the skin characterized by flushing, erythema, and telangiectasia. The visual side effects are typically prominent on the central face, namely the nose, cheeks, eyelids, and forehead. The exact cause is unknown, but several theories have been posited on what may trigger the vessel dilation, resulting in flushing and redness. A 2002 article published by leading experts classified rosacea into four subtypes: *erythematotelangiectactic*, *papulopustular*, *phymatous*, and *ocular*.[1] Other clinical considerations in rosacea include glandular and granulomatous rosacea, represented by nodularities that can lead to scarring but not necessarily associated with flushing. Currently there is no cure for rosacea, making the goal for treatment to control and alleviate symptoms.

    The one thing that all forms of rosacea have in common is chronic poor vascular hemostasis leading to leaky vessels, pooling of blood, delayed removal of inflammatory mediators, and a prolonged perivascular inflammation. Inflammation is a common denominator in rosacea and when prolonged leads to tissue hypertrophy and fibroplasias, the mechanism behind rhinophyma. The origin of the inflammation in rosacea is debatable, and controversy surrounds the theory of a perifollicular inflammatory process that is aggravated by microbial organisms. The bacteria *Propionibacterium acnes* and démodéx mites have been causatively linked to rosacea with evidence that antibiotics targeting these organisms have proven helpful in treating symptoms of rosacea, but these organisms are also found in high concentration in those without rosacea.[1] However, a neurogenic (dysfunctional facial nerves) component may also be related to the inflammation associated with rosacea. A neurogenic origin to the inflammatory, as well as vascular, component of rosacea can be well supported. Therefore, as elucidated by Schwab et al., drugs that affect neurovascular and neuroimmune communication may be advantageous in the treatment of rosacea.[2]

Clinical Characteristics and the Stages of Rosacea

The primary symptoms of rosacea include redness, flushing, and telangiectasia (small, dilated blood vessels near the surface of the skin), yet the severity of these symptoms varies from person to person. Rosacea is most often associated with people of Celtic or Scandinavian ancestry. People between ages 30 and 60 are most commonly affected. Rosacea is uncommon in those of African descent; it has what is referred to as an *inverse relationship* with increased epidermal pigmentation,[3] meaning that the more pigment (color) one has in their skin, the less likely they are to get rosacea. Accordingly, rosacea is less visible in people with darker skin, as it is has a light pink tinge which may make it harder to recognize. The clinical features are present in periods of inflammation and remission. The spectrum of clinical findings can vary widely, depending on the stage. There are four stages ranging from mild to severe involving the skin; in stage four, the eyes are likewise affected. Rosacea doesn't necessarily need to occur in the order of stages, described and pictured below, although most of the time it does.

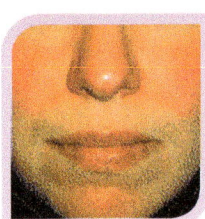

Stage 1 (erythematotelangiectatic rosacea)

Erythematotelangiectatic type rosacea (ETR), noted by flushing that persists for longer than ten minutes, can be brought on by different triggers, from emotional stress to foods to topical products.[4] It often is associated with burning and stinging.

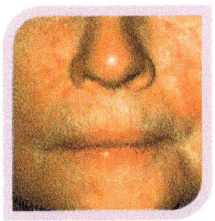

Stage 2 (papulopustular rosacea)

Papulopustular rosacea (PPR) is the classical rosacea characterized by a red central portion of the face with small papules that may be surrounded by pinpoint pustules. Flushing occurs, but is not as marked as in ETR. Persistent or episodic inflammation is commonly seen and the inflammation may lead to chronic edema and fibrous changes to the skin. There is usually stinging and burning of the skin involved. The pores may become larger in this stage and have a somewhat rough-textured appearance. It can be hard to differentiate between this type of rosacea and acne; one way to differentiate is the lack of comedones present in papulopustular rosacea.

It can be hard to differentiate between Stage 2 rosacea and acne; one way to differentiate is the lack of comedones present in papulopustular rosacea.

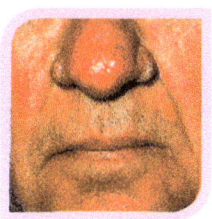

Stage 3 (phymatous rosacea)

Phymatous rosacea is characterized with marked skin thickening and irregular surface nodularities leading to rhinophyma (nose), gnathophyma (chin), and metophyma (forehead). This is often seen in middle-aged men. There is also pronounced redness and telangiectasia in this stage.

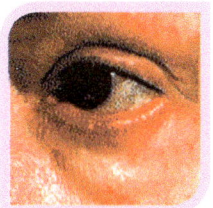

Stage 4 (ocular rosacea)

Occular rosacea has the presence of red, watery, swollen eyes along with the characteristics of other stages. The patient usually experiences burning, stinging, and even blurred vision in the eyes.

Potential Causes of Rosacea[6]

Vascular disorder: Vascular endothelial growth factor, or VEGF, plays a role in the growth of blood vessels and is more profound in those with rosacea.

Microorganisms: Certain bacteria, fungus and demodex mites are seen in those with rosacea in much higher amounts. It is unknown if these are a possible cause or effect of the condition.

Immune Response: Peptides known as cathelicidins are part of the immune response to protect against bacteria, viruses, and fungi. High levels of cathelicidins are present in rosacea and with *H. pylori*, a bacteria that has been linked in some studies to rosacea.

Genetic disorder: As rosacea is common in certain hereditary backgrounds, it is supposed that genetics may play a role.

Environment: There is also speculation that environmental factors including sun exposure and stress may not only be rosacea triggers but also a cause.

In patients with rosacea, 20–58% will develop into stage 4 rosacea with ocular symptoms that may occur in combination with skin symptoms.[5] The eye findings include a foreign-body sensation, telangiectasia, blepharitis (inflammation of the eyelids), keratitis (inflammation of the cornea), conjunctivitis (inflammation or redness of the lining of the white part of the eye and the underside of the eyelid), meibomian gland dysfunction (dysfunction of the sebaceous glands in the corners of the eyelids), and irregularity of the lid margin.

As mentioned, there is currently no cure for rosacea, so treatment is based on symptom management. Providing education on what is occurring beneath the skin, and why, gives the patient a head-start in learning to control symptoms. The patient must first learn to recognize what triggers their condition in order to avoid its potential to flare up, and ultimately to avoid inflammation. This may include lifestyle changes, such as reducing sun exposure, eliminating spicy food and alcohol from diets, controlling stress, and using non-irritating products.

> The patient must learn to recognize what triggers their condition in order to avoid its potential to flare up, and ultimately to avoid inflammation.

Rosacea Triggers
- Sun exposure
- Extremes of hot and cold
- Stress
- Alcohol consumption
- Spicy foods
- Humidity
- Wind
- Irritating products/cosmetics
- Medications

Skin Care Recommendations

Emphasis should be placed on using the right products. The use of physical sunscreen is particularly important to help prevent further damage to the skin. Rosacea patients are extremely sensitive to topical agents and many chemical sunscreens can be irritating. Physical sunscreen reflects UV rays, whereas chemical sunscreen absorbs the light and turns it into heat. Although the skin is protected from the damaging effects of UV exposure, the heat absorbed can still trigger inflammation. Zinc oxide is often the sunscreen of choice due its natural anti-inflammatory properties. Care must be used with makeup as well; mineral-based makeup is recommended due to its anti-inflammatory and sun-protective qualities.

Humectants and occlusive agents used to moisturize the skin are essential for those plagued by rosacea. There is evidence that shows decreased barrier function resulting in transepidermal water loss (TEWL), which is the loss of moisture through the outer layers of skin. Hyaluronic acid, urea, and glycerine are some of the most commonly used humectants in skin care products. These ingredients are hydrophilic, thus rehydrating the skin by attracting water. While the skin absorbs this additional moisture, it should be occluded to avoid losing moisture through the impaired barrier. Common occlusive agents that are beneficial for rosacea are silicones, shea butter, niacinamide, and zinc oxide.

> Common occlusive agents that are beneficial for rosacea are silicones, shea butter, niacinamide, and zinc oxide.

Controlling inflammation and associated redness is difficult with topical products alone, but there are ingredients that are beneficial. Bisabolol, vitamin B5, aloe vera, and aldavine, composed of red and brown algae, are beneficial for sensitized skin types, including rosacea. Vitamin K oxide may also be used to reduce redness by activating coagulation factors.

For optimal results, the client should also use an antioxidant and mild exfoliant to increase cellular turnover. Antioxidants provide added protection from external factors, thereby shielding the skin from inflammation caused by free radicals. Vitamin C in the form of L-ascorbic acid and vitamin E are examples of topical antioxidants commonly used in products for rosacea. (Chapter 27 lists many more.) To increase cell turnover, products containing low percentages of lactic acid, enzymes, and salicylic acid are gentle enough even for rosacea use.

> The last thing a rosacea patient needs is more inflammation in the skin. For this reason, steam, facial massage, ultrasound, radio frequency and other treatments that create excessive heat or stimulation in the skin should be avoided.

Skin care treatments perfomed in-office are beneficial when implemented correctly. Many esthetic treatments are stimulating and the last thing a rosacea patient needs is more inflammation brought to the sensitized skin. For this reason, steam, facial massage, ultrasound, radio frequency and other treatments that create heat or stimulation in the skin should be avoided. There are opposing thoughts as to the safe use of chemical peels for rosacea clients; this may be the result of inexperienced providers using over-aggressive techniques. Progressive peeling of the skin with the right product can provide profound results. A mild lactic acid peel at a concentration of 20–30% is good to start for dry, overly sensitized skin. Lactic acid is gentle and has hydrating properties making it beneficial for over-reactive skin seen in rosacea patients. For those with thicker skin along with papules and pustules, salicylic peels are well received due to their antiseptic and anti-inflammatory properties. Although product selection is important, as many salicylic peels are in an alcohol base and may cause more irritation, one specific formulation with 6% TCA, 12% lactic acid, and anti-inflammatory agents has shown extraordinary results in my experience. Severe cases of rosacea that are highly inflamed should be seen by a physician before any recommendations are given by the skin care provider.

6% TCA, 12% Lactic Blend (SensiPeel®) Stage 2

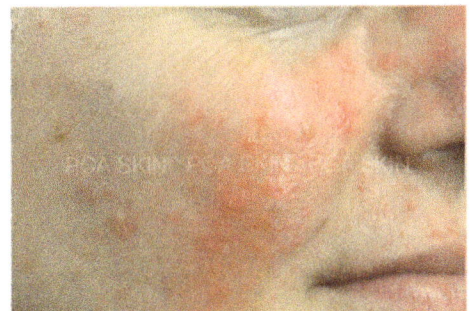
Before treatment

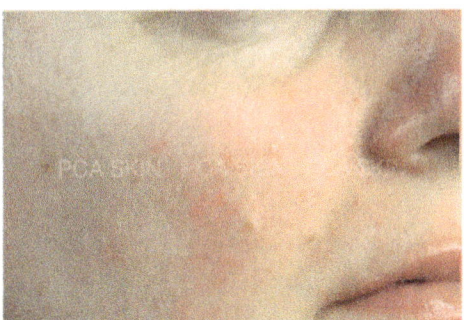
3 months after 1 treatment
Courtesy of PCA Skin®

If skin care and trigger avoidance is not enough, topical antibiotics are typically recommended by a physician to relieve inflammatory lesions. If the disease is resistant or if symptoms of nodular rosacea or ocular symptoms occur, oral antibiotics may be used in combination with topical therapies. Oral antibiotics that have shown to be useful are tetracycline, erythromycin, and minocycline. These antibiotics are used to limit the growth of bacteria but also have the added benefit of anti-inflammatory properties. As these medications are commonly used to fight bacteria in acne, in rosacea it is speculated that they work by reducing inflammation.[7]

Metronidazole is an antifungal that can be used with or without oral antibiotics to decrease lesion counts by as much as 60%. Other topical agents frequently recommended include azelaic acid, sulfacetamide, clindamycin, erythromycin and benzoyl peroxide. These agents should be used for at least four to six weeks before results are assessed.

When symptoms of rosacea persist, topical retinoids may be considered, such as tretinoin cream or retinol-based OTC formulations. It is recommended that rosacea patients slowly build up a tolerance to a retinoid product, because slight irritation will likely be experienced at first due to its chemical exfoliating properties. Treatment with retinoids should start with application at bedtime two to three times per week until the skin becomes accustomed to it, and then gradually increasing the frequency to nightly. Some clients may not need to increase, as a couple of times per week may be sufficient to provide results, especially for those with sensitive skin.

Lasers and light therapy have been used with great success in the reduction of redness, flushing, and telangiectasia associated with rosacea.[8] These lasers have filters that bracket the visible light spectrum, so the emitted light energy is absorbed superficially in the epidermis and dermis.

Vascular lesions contain oxyhemoglobin, which is responsible for the red coloring. Specific lasers target oxyhemoglobin to heat up the vessel walls, causing them to collapse. After the vessels collapse, they are then removed by the body's lymphatic system.

When treating rosacea with lasers or intense pulsed light (IPL), individual red lesions may be treated; however, the treatment often includes the entire area in order to even out skin tone. Patients may appear slightly red or flushed after treatment. Improvement from flushing and the deep redness of rosacea can be expected within a week. To attain stable control of the rosacea, most patients receive a series of three treatments spaced three to four weeks apart. This seems to provide a plateau in symptoms for several months in most patients, after which time patients may return for maintenance treatment as needed.

LED light therapy in the red spectrum can also be used to alleviate the side effects of rosacea. As lasers and IPL can dissipate vascular lesions almost immediately, LED often takes several continued treatments to see visible improvement, but there are devices that can be sold for home use, making it easier for the client to receive repeated treatments.

Dermabrasion and ablative lasers seem to be the best options for treating rhinophyma and other areas of thickened skin associated with Stage III rosacea. Dermabrasion is a treatment that removes the upper layers of skin using a wire brush or diamond wheel. Ablative lasers remove the upper layer of skin thermally as opposed to mechanically. Both treatments can be painful; therefore, in most cases, the patient is given a local anesthetic and pain medications. (More information on ablative laser treatments is available in Chapter 20). When phymatous rosacea is treated, the patient must be clear that the skin growths may come back—for some it is months; for others, years—but there are also cases of continued success.

A new innovation in the treatment for rosacea is the use of intradermal botulinum toxin injection to the affected areas (**pictured**). Botulinum toxin type A supports a mechanism of action that reduces facial and neck flushing. Onabotulinum toxin A as a potential modality for treating flushing was described by Yuratis and Jacobs,[9] who noted a decrease in facial flushing and extremely

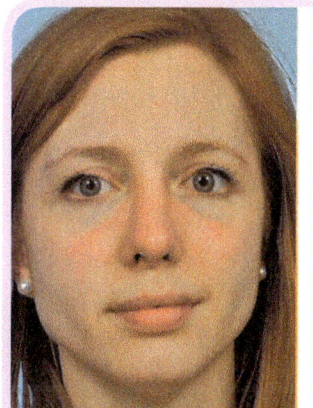
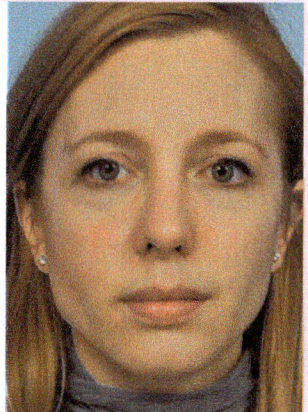

Botulinum Toxin Treatment for Rosacea

satisfying results two weeks following treatment into the cheek of a 26-year-old male.

Although there is no cure for rosacea, treatments to control symptoms have come a long way and are more constantly being discovered. The hardest part for clients seems to be avoiding triggers—which include everyday instances such as temperature changes, eating hot foods or drinking hot liquids, and exposure to sunlight. Rosacea can be frustrating for the client and aesthetic provider alike, since any improvement can be reversed when an outbreak occurs. It is important for the client to know that treatment is a joint effort between you and them, and if symptoms recur, there are a multitude of treatments available to help.

References
1. GH Crawford et al, Rosacea: I. Etiology, pathogenesis, and subtype classification, *J Am Academy Dermatol*, 51(3) 327-341 (2004).
2. VD Schwab et al, Neurovascular and neuroimmune aspects in the pathophysiology of rosacea, *J Invest Derm Symp P*, 15(1) 53-62 (2011).
3. JK McDonnell and KJ Tomecki, Rosacea: An update, *Cleve Clin J Med*, 67 587-590 (2000).
4. J Wilkin et al, Standard grading system for rosacea: Report of the National Rosacea Society Expert Committee on the classification and staging of rosacea, *J Am Academy Dermatol*, 50(6) 907-912 (2004).
5. MJ Quarterman et al, Ocular rosacea: Signs, symptoms, and tear studies before and after treatment with doxycycline, *Arch Dermatol*, 133 49-54 (1997).
6. E Lazaridou et al, The potential role of microorganisms in the development of rosacea, *J Deutsch Dermatol Ges*, 9 21 (2011).
7. B Berman, Update on rosacea and anti-inflammatory-dose doxycycline, *Drugs Today*, 43(1) 27-34 (2007).
8. A Benjamin et al, Use of the KTP laser in the treatment of rosacea and solar lentigines, *Facial Plast Surg*, 20 77-83 (2004).
9. M Yuraitis and CI Jacob, Botulinum toxin for the treatment of facial flushing, *Dermatologic Surg*, 30(1) 102-104 (2004).

CHAPTER 11

Hyperpigmentation

In this Chapter:

- Clinical Characteristics of Hyperpigmentation
- Melasma
- Actinic keratoses
- Solar lentigines / freckles (well-defined)
- Recognizing Cancerous Lesions
- Treatment Options

Clinical Characteristics of Hyperpigmentation

Hyperpigmentation is a discoloration of the skin that shows up as brown spots or patches and is caused by various elements such as inflammation, hormonal response, and sun exposure. These inflammatory instances trigger a process known as *melanogenesis*, which is responsible for producing melanin as a means of protecting the skin. Hyperpigmentation manifests in several ways. Melasma, sometimes referred to as chloasma or pregnancy mask, shows up as dense areas of pigment in the central third of the face. Sun-induced pigmentation is more sporadic and presents as spotty discoloration commonly on areas of excessive sun exposure including the bridge of the nose, cheeks, and forehead, while post-inflammatory hyperpigmentation (PIH) develops from physical trauma to the skin and is associated with inflammation.

The process of melanogenesis is complex. When inflammation occurs, melanocytes (cells that lie in the basal cell layer of the epidermis and are responsible for producing melanin) are activated. Although the number of melanocytes in each individual is similar, those with darker skin types are highly reactive and easily stimulated by hormonal triggers or inflammation. The melanocytes produce pigment through a complicated process involving tyrosinase, a copper-containing enzyme involved in producing melanin from tyrosine via oxidation, similar to what happens when an apple turns brown after exposure to the oxygen in the air. The pigment produced through oxidation is then packaged into melanosomes, organelles involved in storing and transporting melanin. The dendrites (arms) of the melanocyte cell then carry the melanosomes to keratinocytes in order to protect them against possible damage, most commonly UV light. Ingredients that interrupt this process are used in skin lightening products, commonly those that stop the action of tyrosinase to form pigment. These products work best when multiple ingredients are used to stop various steps of the melanogenesis process.

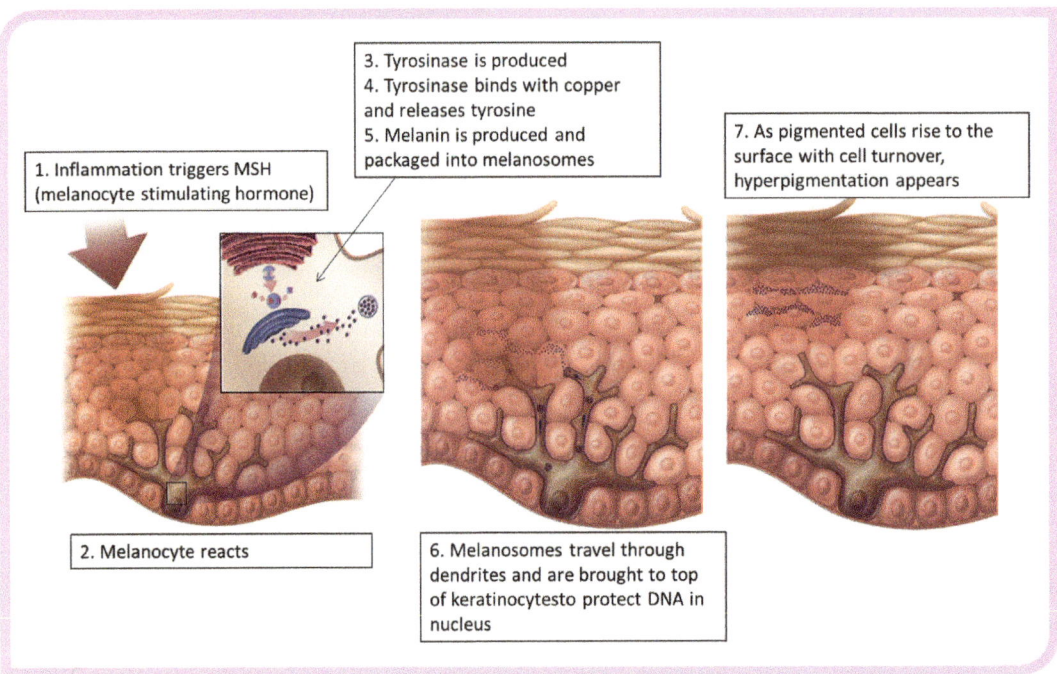

Melasma: Melasma is a skin condition causing a dark facial skin to present in the central third of the face, most commonly seen in women with darker skin types, Fitzpatrick IV, V, or VI. (Refer back to Part 1 for a look at the Fitzpatrick Scale.) Pregnancy, oral contraceptives, and hormone replacement therapy can all play a role in the development of this stubborn discoloration. It is also prevalent in men and women of Native American descent (on the forearms) and those of German/Russian Jewish descent (on the face, as pictured). Ultraviolet exposure stimulates an increase in the levels of melanin present in all cases of melasma.

There are three categories of melasma commonly used to determine possible treatment outcomes: *epidermal*, *dermal* and *mixed*.

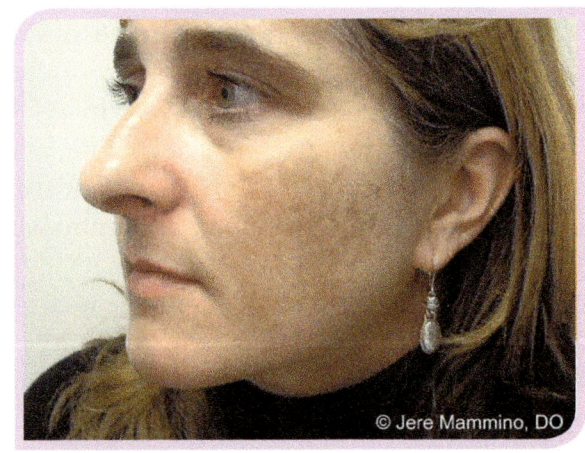

Melasma

It should be noted that there are opposing views as to what constitutes dermal melasma. Most aesthetic providers use a Wood's lamp to determine if pigment is deeper in the skin or more superficial. As stated earlier, superficial pigmentation fluoresces under UV light, while deeper or dermal pigmentation tends to disappear.

Epidermal melasma is most common and should be the target for any melasma treatment, as the melanocytes lie in the basal cell layer of the epidermis; with natural cell progression, pigmented keratinocytes move up to the superficial layers of skin.

Dermal melasma is caused from the production of melanin that is more rapid than cell turnover, leading to the pigment forming in the dermis of the skin.

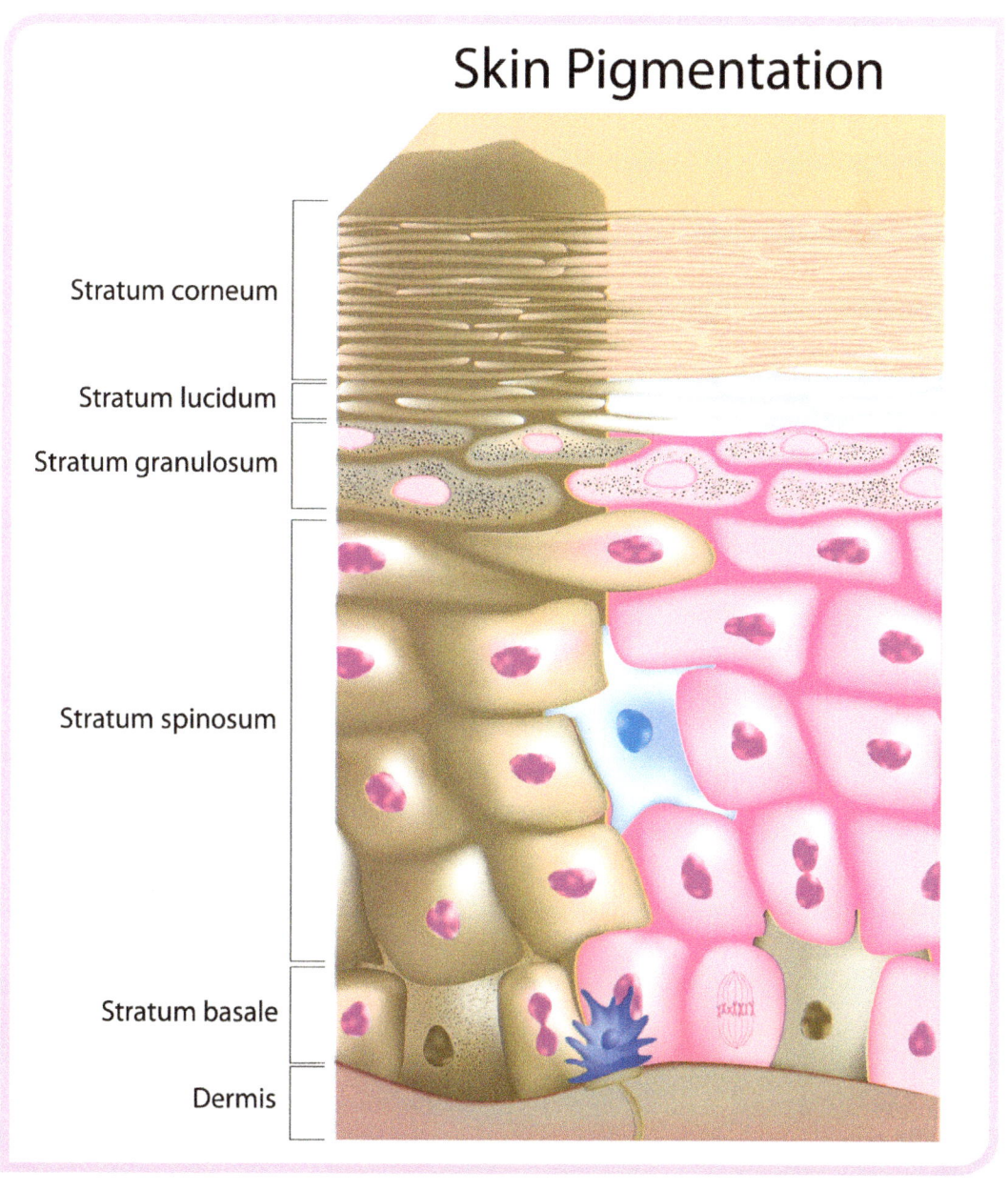

Melanophages are cells in the papillary layer of the dermis that ingest melanin and are what is commonly seen as dermal melasma.[1] This is difficult to treat and patient expectations must be managed accordingly, as some patients, regardless of treatment, see little to no improvement.

Mixed melasma is hard to determine as the pigment may show up darker under the Wood's lamp, giving hope that treatments will likely be effective, but there may be underlying dermal pigment as well.

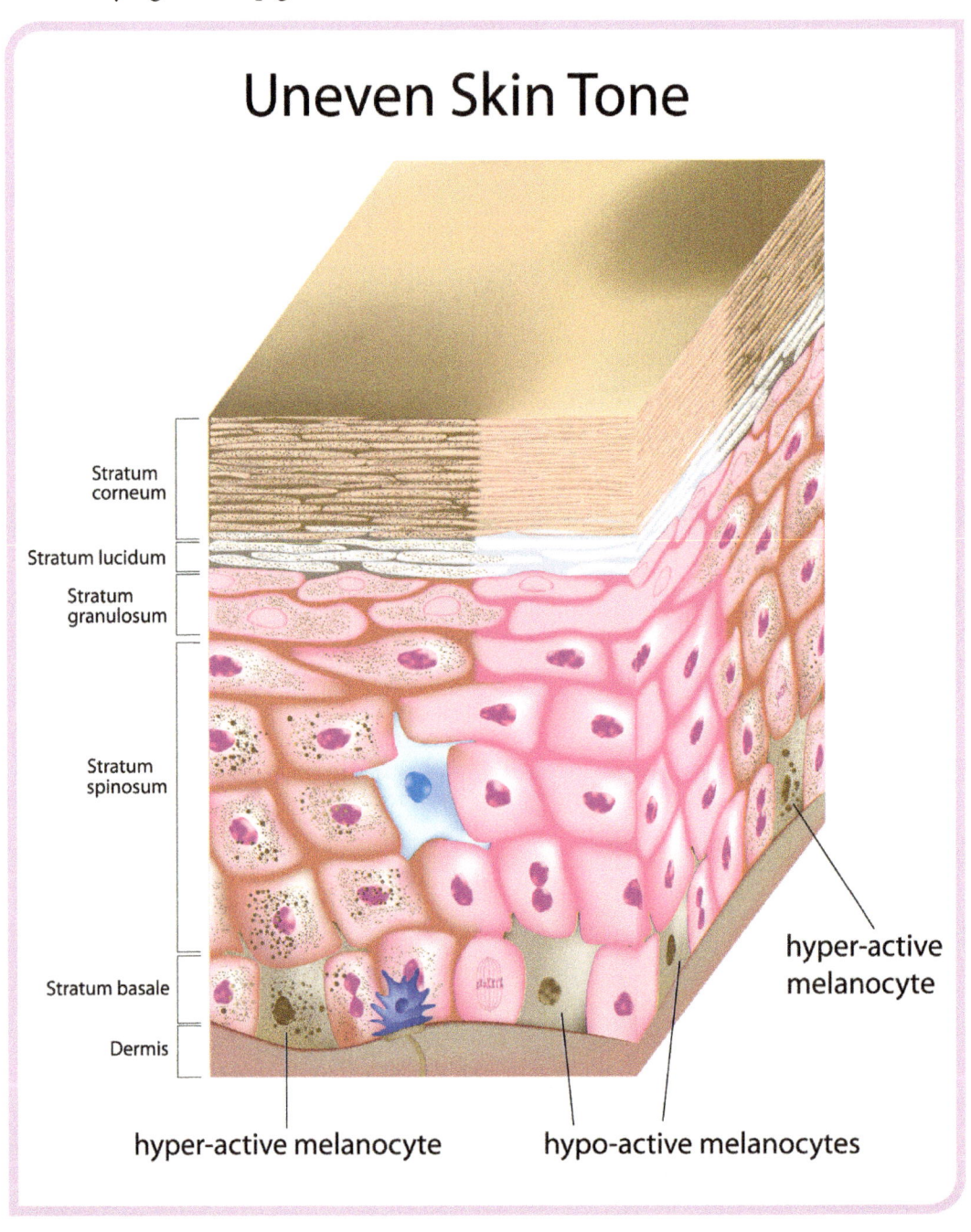

Hyperpigmentation

There is also a fourth kind of pigment that is undetermined due to the lack of contrast in darker skin types. As stated in the skin analysis chapter, the Wood's lamp is most commonly used to try to differentiate the type of pigment; however, this not an end-all, be-all. It is up to the treating physician to determine the course of action. As with any treatment, realistic expectations must be discussed before recommendations are given.

Although melasma may resolve after pregnancy or with the discontinued use of hormone therapy, it can also be permanent. There are several treatments for pigment related skin conditions, but when dealing with melasma, it is even more critical to understate possible outcomes. It is not uncommon for those with severe cases of melasma to try several treatments and only demonstrate slight improvement, if any. Pigment lightening agents are recommended, but work best in conjunction with in-office treatments. Traditionally, laser treatments provide the best option for the treatment of sun-induced or post-inflammatory pigmentation; however, there are opposing thoughts on whether lasers improve melasma or actually cause the condition to come back worse than before. This is because any inflammation can trigger this chain reaction of pigment production.

Solar lentigines, also known as *old age spots* or *liver spots*, appear as flat, oval, evenly pigmented macules (a simple dermatologic lesion) in areas of chronic sun exposure. They are the focus of highly active melanocytes that result in an area of hyperpigmentation. Solar lentigines, or freckles, are among the most common benign lesions of the skin. The most commonly affected areas are the face, the backs of the hands, shoulders, and back. These lesions may vary from light to dark brown, but are fairly uniform in color within the individual lesion. UV-induced pigment is

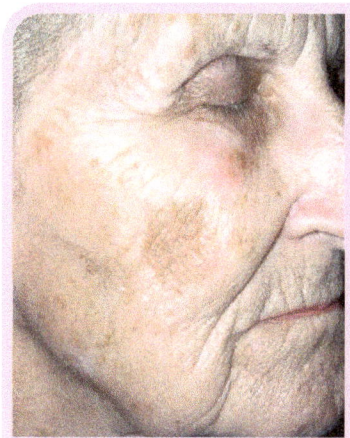
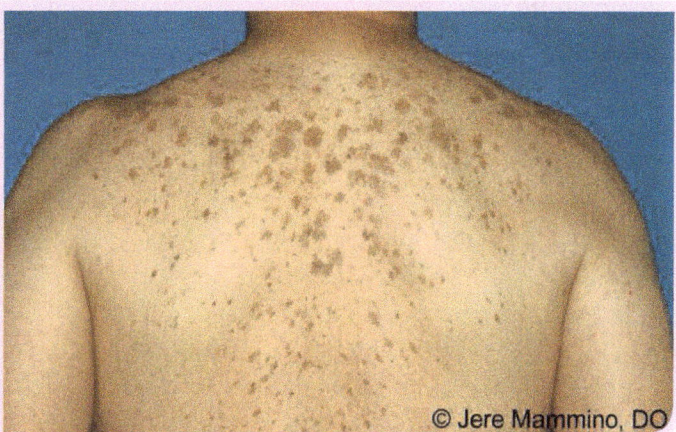

© Jere Mammino, DO

No treatment is necessary for solar lentigines. However, if cosmetic removal is desired, treatments include topical agents such as a freezing with liquid nitrogen, skin lightening products, laser treatments, and chemical peels.

made up of keratinocytes with dense pigment, produced by active melanocytes. The features of solar lentigines are mostly limited to the epidermis, and although there is a great deal of melanin in the epidermis, the number of melanocytes does not change with skin that falls into Fitzpatrick grades I through VI.

No treatment is necessary for solar lentigines; however, if cosmetic removal is desired, treatments include topical agents such as a freezing with liquid nitrogen, applying skin lightening products on a continual basis, laser treatments, and chemical peels are often used.

Post-inflammatory hyperpigmentation, or PIH, can be caused by any cutaneous inflammation or trauma to the skin. Like other forms of pigmentation, it is more prevalent in darker skin types, those of African-American, Hispanic, Latino, Asian, Native American, or Pacific Islander heritage, as well as those of Middle Eastern descent. Mechanical injuries, including rubbing or picking, can prompt pigment formation. Inflammation is already associated with most acne lesions, making them highly susceptible to a more severe response. Other injuries include scratching or rubbing; this can be seen under the nose of those with allergies that scratch or rub to alleviate itching. Another common area for PIH is the area under the breasts where bras fit snuggly. The friction caused from the tight strap causes a line of pigment to form beneath it.

Medications can also darken lesions, including certain antibiotics and anti-cancer drugs. Just as the sun can darken melasma and solar letigines, this is also the case for PIH. Trauma to the skin such as deep wounds or burns also create this pigment. It is important to note that this is why caution must be used with aesthetic treatments such as lasers and chemical peels, especially in darker skin types. PIH occurs at the site of injury and may show some mild red or purple discoloration. It can be treated with the same methods used on other forms of pigmentation; however, being particularly careful and attentive to skin reactions is necessary. This will be discussed throughout the book according to treatment type as well.

Actinic keratoses, also known as solar keratoses or AKs, are precancerous lesions. These raised lesions are usually pink or brown and often have a white scale on the top. They are rough to the touch and the size is usually between two and six millimeters. They are present in areas of excessive sun exposure, such as the face (as pictured), neck, scalp, and hands. Since these are precancerous lesions, the patient, the skin care provider, and the physician should

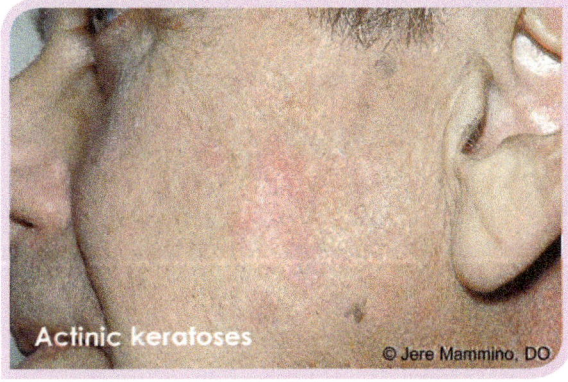
Actinic keratoses © Jere Mammino, DO

all monitor the area closely and remain aware of any changes occurring in color, shape, and size. Physicians may treat actinic keratoses by cutting them out or freezing them with liquid nitrogen, which causes them to slough off. There is also topical fluorouracil (prescribed by a physician) which inhibits the replication of cells. This product will cause the lesion to become red and inflamed and then fall off, typically in two to four weeks. Photodynamic therapy, discussed in the acne section and more thoroughly in Part 5's look at Lasers and Light Therapy, is an FDA approved procedure used to photosensitize actinic keratoses before targeting them with a light source to remove them.

> It is of the utmost importance that an esthetician never diagnose or give medical advice.

SCENARIO: Addressing Lesions

Client comes in for her monthly facial. During the preliminary skin analysis, the esthetician notices that a mole has changed on the client's skin; it looks bigger than before and now has uneven borders.

What could happen:
Esthetician: "Wow, have you seen how big his mole has become? It looks a cancerous lesion to me. You need to see a dermatologist right away."

What should happen:
Esthetician: "Have you noticed any changes to this mole on the right cheek?"
Client: "No, but now I'm nervous, is it cancer?"
Esthetician: "I didn't mean to worry you, but I do see a slight change, and with any change I would recommend you get it checked out by a dermatologist to be safe. Can I recommend one to you?"

Recognizing Cancerous Lesions

It is well known that cancer is on the rise, and skin cancer is the second most common form of all reported cancer cases.[2] The skin analysis is the perfect time to take a look at the client's skin and check for anything questionable. Seeing clients on a regular basis and tracking the skin closely can lead to saving lives. There have been many instances, in my experience, where skin care professionals have saved lives by noticing changes in the appearance of lesions on a client's skin. If there is anything questionable on the skin that the skin care professional suspects could be cancerous, the client should be referred to a physician.

Basal Cell Carcinoma

This is the most common type of skin cancer. It typically appears as a small raised bump with a pearly appearance. The center may begin to erode, and there is usually the presence of telangiectasia surrounding the lesion. Most commonly seen on skin types I and II and on areas of the skin that have received excessive sun exposure. It may spread to the skin around the cancer, but rarely spreads to other parts of the body. These can be easily treated by surgical removal performed by a dermatologist or surgeon.

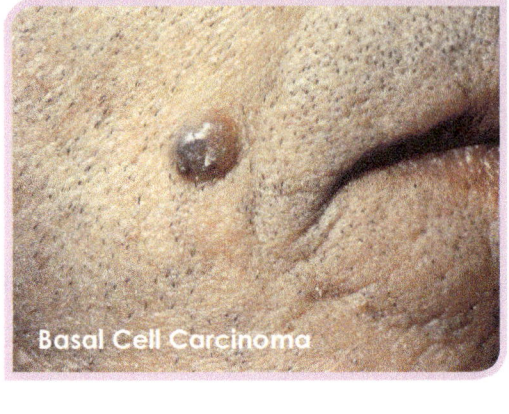

Squamous Cell Carcinoma

These are often seen on areas of the body that have been exposed to excessive sun, but can also be caused by other factors, such as exposure to chemical carcinogens. They often appear as a firm nodule or ulceration of the skin that does not heal. It can spread to lymph nodes in the area.

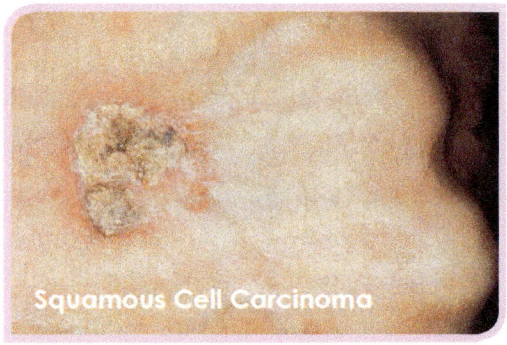

Melanoma

Melanoma is a malignant skin cancer that arises from the melanocytes in the skin. They typically present as pigmented lesions in the skin with an irregular shape, irregular border, and multiple colors. Melanoma is the most harmful of all the skin cancers, because it has a high chance of spreading to other areas in the body.

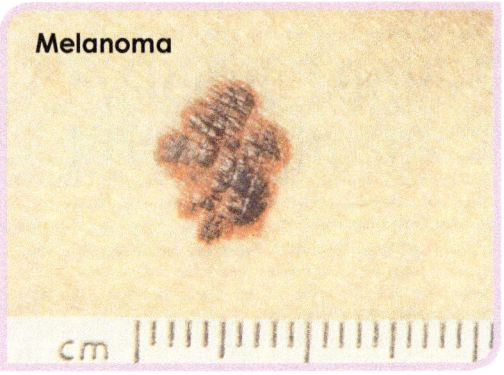

Melanomas can be cured when identified and treated early, but they can also be deadly. All skin care providers should educate their clients on the **ABC's rule** so they can observe changes in skin lesions such as moles on a regular basis as well:

- **A**symmetry—when both sides of a mole or lesion don't look the same
- **B**order—the edges are blurry or jagged
- **C**olor—the area becomes darker than before; if the color spreads or disappears; or multiple colors appear
- **D**iameter—when a mole is larger than one quarter-inch in diameter
- **E**levation—when a mole is raised above the skin and has a rough surface

Hyperpigmentation

Other changes to watch for:
- A mole that bleeds
- A mole that grows fast
- A scaly or crusted growth on the skin
- A mole that itches

> Only physicians should treat any potentially cancerous lesion.

Treatment Options for Pigmentation

The following is a short list of some common pigment lightening ingredients that the esthetician can ascribe for use in product selection (see Chapter 27 for more):

- Hydroquinone
- Kojic Acid
- Bearberry/Arbutin
- Licorice root
- Emblica
- Rumex extracts
- Phytic acid
- Retinoids
- Lactic acid
- L-asorbic acid

Major Risk Factors for Melanoma

M oles: atypical moles, more than 10 on various areas of the body

R ed hair and freckling

I nability to tan

S unburn: severe before age 14

K indred: family history of melanoma

The best outcomes for pigmentation occur from a combination of treatments. First and foremost, sun protection is key for attaining results. If a client is not willing to protect their skin from the sun, it is best *not* to treat them. The pigment will likely get worse if sun exposure were to occur during the course of treatments. In conjunction with sunscreen, skin lighteners should be

> If a client is not willing to protect their skin from the sun, it is best *not* to treat them.

used continuously throughout treatments, and in the case of melasma perpetually in order to prevent reoccurrence. Hydroquinone is still commonly sought out by clients and providers as the go-to product for skin lightening. Although there has been some controversy as to its safety,[3] its efficacy holds true. Nonethless, err to the side of caution when recommending products with this ingredient.

The use of prescription strength hydroquinone (4%) can result in lightening of solar pigmentation as well as melasma, but the results usually takes six to eight weeks. The concentration and duration of therapy are usually limited by what adverse effects occur, usually consisting of irritation, depigmentation, and ochronosis (a bluish-black discoloration).[4] Patients should only use hydroquinone for two to three months at a time, maximum, and then take two months off, repeating the process until the desired outcome is reached.

There are many skin-lightening agents that have been shown to produce improvements, but they work best when paired with in-office treatments to enhance the results. These products are most often used by clients to reduce further pigmentation. Products containing retinoids are also effective and work synergistically with pigment lighteners. Retinoids stabilize melanin production, reducing the rate of pigment to the base skin color for that person. Furthermore, exfoliating darkened skin using vitamin A products has shown favorable results in lightening facial solar lentigines.

Phenol and physician-level trichloroacetic (TCA) acid peels (25–35%) have been used to treat hyperpigmentation. However, the adverse effects include darkening of the pigmented area, hypopigmentation, scarring, persistent erythema, and with phenol, cardiac arrhythmias (irregular heartbeats)—all of which has made these treatments fall out of favor. This is why milder, *progressive* peeling treatments as opposed to *aggressive* peeling treatments are more commonly used. However, these treatments take time, and clients may need several treatments performed in conjunction with skin-lightening agents, as aforementioned, to obtain results.

For those with darker, more reactive skin, alpha hydroxy peels are commonly used at two-week intervals for a series of approximately six to 10 treatments, the most common being lactic acid peels at ~30–40% due to their pigment lightening and exfoliating properties. This ensures that clients are at low risk for adverse reactions, while still obtaining results. For lower Fitzpatrick skin types (I–III) that can tolerate a stronger treatment, a Jessner's peel is often recommended. Jessner's peels should be spaced four weeks apart, due to the deeper penetration into the skin, starting with a total series of three to four treatments.

If the patient is sensitive to chemical peeling treatments, microdermabrasion, dermaplaning, or microneedling may be used, although the results are not as significant.

Light therapy, including lasers, can also be used to treat pigmented lesions. The wide range of treatment options stems from the broad absorption spectrum of melanin, as will be discussed in Part 5. Lasers have specific targets and a common target used in aesthetic applications is pigment.

Modified and Enhanced Jessner's for sun-induced pigmentation

Before treatment

2 weeks after treatment

Courtesy of PCA Skin®

Not all Fitzpatrick skin types can tolerate certain light therapy devices. The more pigment that the tissue surrounding the treatment area contains, the harder it will be to target the pigment being treated. This can cause epidermal injury, resulting in adverse reactions such as burns, worsened hyperpigmentation, and hypopigmentation.

Lower Fitzpatrick types may have more options in terms of suitable lasers, but the importance of a proper consultation is the same no matter the Fitzpatrick type. Contraindications for a laser treatment must be investigated and proper post-treatment care is just as important to discuss if the patient is to achieve long-lasting results. The patient also must be advised on what to expect following treatment: the lesion may change in color, erythema may be present, and results should not be expected immediately.[5]

Following each laser treatment, the pigmented area may appear ash-like, with a circumferential area of redness. Over the subsequent week, the lesion transiently becomes darker and ultimately fades. Occasionally, the lesion will slough off in the second week. Subsequent treatments are spaced three to four weeks apart and may be necessary depending on the density of the lesion, the surrounding skin, and treatment settings. Most people are satisfied after three treatments, and results continue to improve over the next three months.

> The skin care provider's role is important in the treatment of pigmentation because combination treatments seem to be most effective.

The skin care provider's role is important in the treatment of pigmentation because combination treatments seem to be most effective. Laser treatments can be alternated with chemical peels or microdermabrasion at two-week intervals. This is especially beneficial because with laser treatments, the pigment most often gets darker before it lightens; a superficial peel, dermaplaning, or microdermabrasion can speed up the process of sloughing off the excess pigment on the epidermis. Recommending skin care products is of the utmost importance during the full term of treatment, because, once again, at-home regimens must be cultivated to aid in exacerbating the very best in-office treatment results. Poor regimens can lead to poor or diminished results.

References
1. HY Kang and J-P Ortonne, What should be considered in treatment of melasma, *Ann Dermatol*, 22(4) 373–378 (2010).
2. *www.skincancer.org*, accessed Jan 24, 2014.
3. D Howard, Hydroquinone: Is the cure worse than the problem? *Skin Inc*, 4 (2009), accessed at: *www.skininc.com/skinscience/ingredients/41973632.html*, posted Mar 27, 2009 (accessed on Apr 15, 2014).
4. R Charlín et al, Hydroquinone-induced exogenous ochronosis: a report of four cases and usefulness of dermoscopy, *Intl J Dermatol*, 47(1) 19-23 (2008).
5. M Haedersdal and HC Wulf, Pigmentation-dependent side effects to copper vapor laser and argon laser treatment, *Lasers Surg Med*, 16 351-358 (1995).

CHAPTER 12

Aging Skin

In this Chapter:
- Healthy Skin
- Intrinsic vs. Extrinsic Aging
- UV Effects & Lifestyle Effects on Skin Aging
- Presentation of Aging Skin
- Cellular Processes with Skin Aging
- Chronological Aging Treatment Recommendations

Aging is both inevitable and continuous. The ultimate goal for most people is to do so gracefully. As previously discussed, focus should be shifted away from artificial methods of "youthfulness" towards healthy aging and prevention, which, to an extent, is in the client's control. Unfortunately, it is all too common to see both women and men who are overdone with filler and look simply pulled too tight. These overzealous attempts to turn back the clock do not reverse aging, but rather, conversely, show a sense of insecurity by portraying an unnatural "plastic" look. At some point, embracing imperfections promotes confidence and draws attraction back to one's self for the right reasons. Knowing the factors associated with aging skin and how they produce damaging effects is essential in learning to prevent and/or manage it.

Healthy Skin
The makeup of human skin is complex and its health is dependent on several contributing factors. An overview of the components present in healthy skin will help determine how these external events produce aging. The skin is made up of three main layers: the epidermis on the surface, the dermis in the middle, and the subcutaneous beneath.

The *epidermis* is essential for protection of both the layers beneath it and the internal portions of the body as a whole. It functions best when regular cellular turnover takes place, the natural moisturizing factor (NMF) or lipid barrier, which are extant in each skin cell as a biologic method surrounding the cell and insuring skin hydration, is intact, and pigment is regulated. The *dermis* is composed of blood vessels, nerve fibers, sebaceous glands, sudoriferous glands, and the extracellular matrix (ECM). The ECM gives support and structure to the skin. The main components of this environment are collagen, elastin, glycosaminoglycans (GAGs), and fibronectin. The *subcutaneous* layer is made up of adipose cells, blood, nerves, and lymph supply. The fatty layer provides a protective cushion for the skin, but loses substance over time, which can present as "sagging" skin.

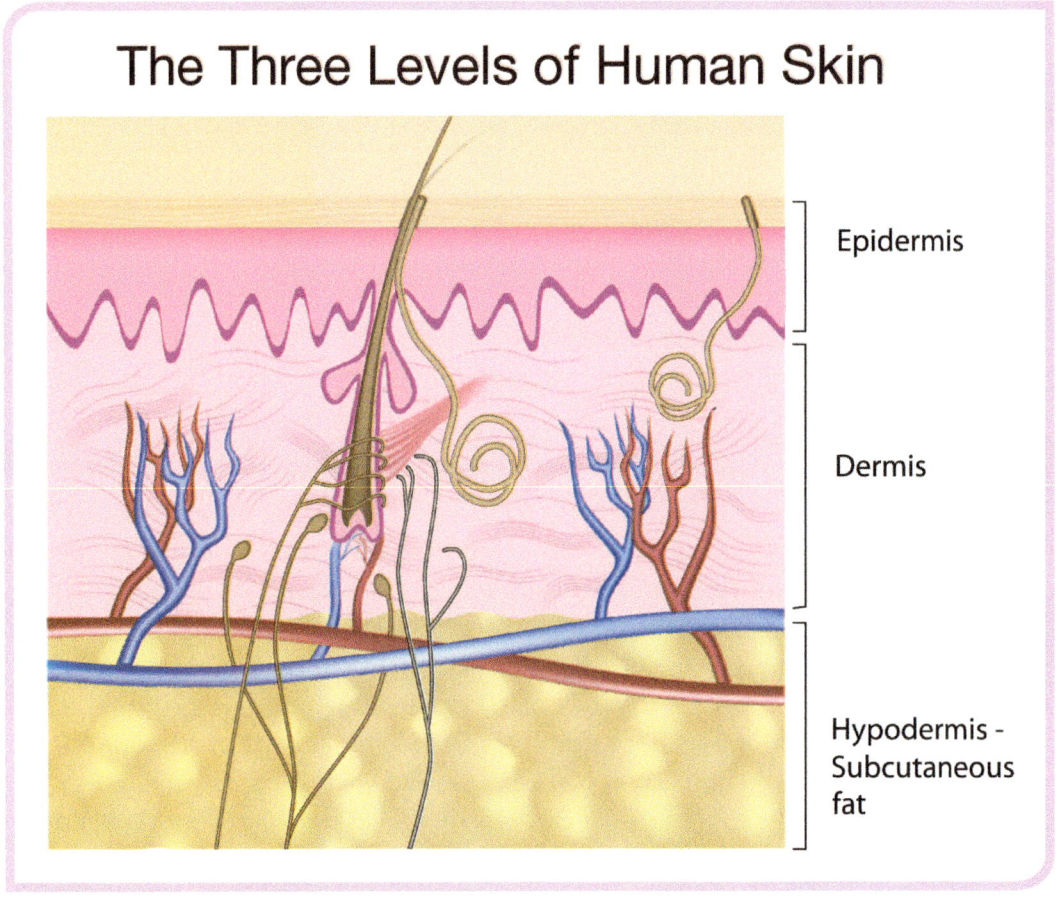

Intrinsic vs. Extrinsic Aging
There are two primary factors that cause aging—*intrinsic* and *extrinsic*.

Intrinsic aging is related to how the skin changes due to the passage of time, regardless of environmental factors. Genetics play a large role in this process and cannot be altered, as they are the essential building blocks of who we are. Genetics can be related to the loss of subcutaneous fat and the reduction of collagen and elastin. Physiology is a part of the intrinsic aging process, as well. It describes the way an individual's body carries out everyday functions. This can be as simple as expression lines from smiling and loss of elasticity from gravity. If intrinsic aging were to occur without exposure to external elements, the skin would still lose volume due to the reduction in subcutaneous fat. Loss of structure from collagen and elastin and the effects of gravity would result in loose or sagging skin. Fine lines would appear in areas of facial expression, as would deeper wrinkles, which are often associated with external aging. However, the skin would remain smooth without keratosis, pigmented lesions, hypopigmentation, telangiectasia, and damaged collagen and elastin leading to deeper, more pronounced wrinkles.

What Contributes to Skin Aging? Extrinsic vs. Intrinsic Culprits

Intrinsic:
- Passage of time, regardless of environment
- Physiology
- Genetics
- Heredity

Extrinsic (accounting for ~ 85% of aging):
- Sun exposure
- Pollution / ozone
- Stress
- Unhealthy diet / alcohol consumption
- Smoking

ALL of these extrinsic factors can trigger inflammation, as it is the body's natural defense against invaders including bacteria, viruses, and injury. But unlike intrinsic factors, these CAN be controlled.

This does not mean that if a client insists her mother smoked cigarettes and sunbathed on a regular basis and yet still has beautiful skin that she will have beautiful skin herself when she reaches her mother's age. The reason for this is that approximately 85% of the changes we see in our skin come from external factors or extrinsic aging. Smoking, lifestyle choices, ozone depletion, diet, and water intake—all of these are factors that are, individually, enough to make a significant difference in whether a client will have the same skin conditions as another member of her family or not. Although there are a multitude of environmental influencers and aggressors, the most common, ultraviolet radiation from direct sunlight, has the ability to harm or breakdown body tissues, as evidenced in the adjacent **image** of a truck driver who has experienced skin degradation on the side of his face that was consistently exposed to sunlight. Ultraviolet radiation, whether produced by the sun or artificially (tanning beds, etc.), is not only the most prevalent, but also the most dangerous extrinsic factor, due to the speed with which it can irreversibly harm the skin layers. This light energy is broken down into three portions of the UV spectrum: UVC, UVB, and UVA rays, as differentiated by the portions' respective range on the solar spectrum (**shown**).

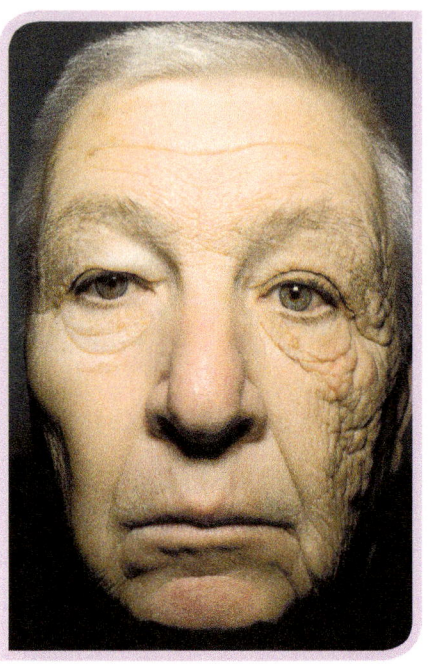

UVC does not reach the earth's surface; it is consumed by the ozone layer before entering the atmosphere. UVB rays are known as the "burning" rays. A portion of UVB radiation is absorbed by the ozone layer, but much of this solar energy reaches the earth's surface and can be dangerous. UVB can penetrate the superficial layers of skin and is responsible for sunburns, which is one of the leading contributors to sun-induced pigmentation and damage to the skin cells leading to skin cancer. UVA, or "aging" rays, are the least dangerous portion of UV radiation, but ultimately cause the most damage, and can lead to cancer, as they are up to 100 times more prevalent than UVB. UVA can penetrate glass and clouds, but most people falsely believe the skin is safe unless they are outside on a sunny day.

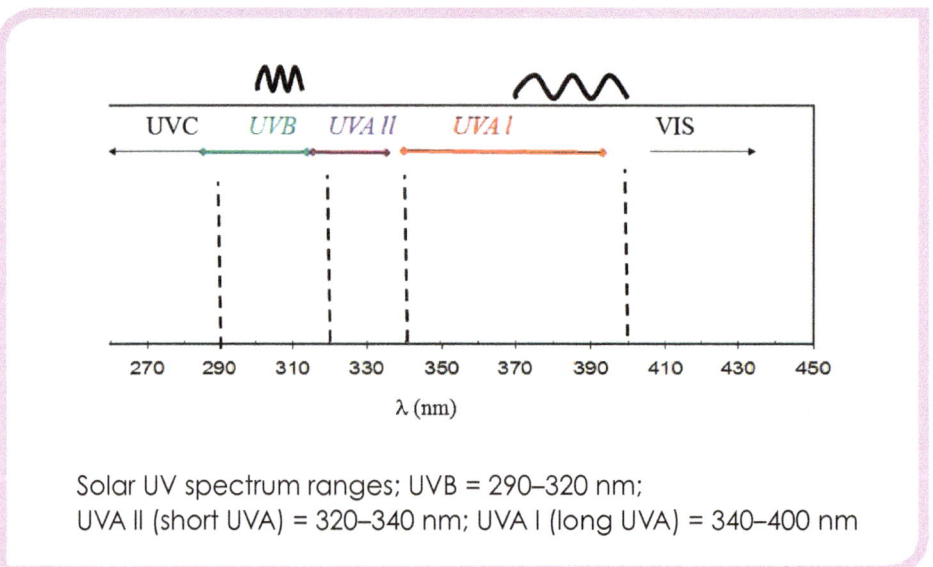

Solar UV spectrum ranges; UVB = 290–320 nm; UVA II (short UVA) = 320–340 nm; UVA I (long UVA) = 340–400 nm

Used with the permission of Patricia Aikens from her chapter titled "Formulation of Sunscreens in the United States," in the book, *Apply Topically* (C&T Books 2013).

These rays can penetrate thin clothing and reach the deeper layers of skin, eventually breaking down the structure of a healthy dermis.

UV Effects on Aging Skin

Some of the UV light that reaches the skin is reflected by skin cells and oil—this is yet another reason it is important to maintain balance in the skin and not strip it of oil. Light that is not reflected enters the epidermis, where some of it is absorbed by melanin. Fitzpatrick skin types I–III have little absorption due to the low amount of melanin present, while types IV–VI will absorb more UV initially. UV that is not absorbed may affect protein, DNA, and other structures of the epidermis, or potentially continue into the dermis. This also creates damage to Langerhans cells, the skin's microbial antigen processing cells, which greatly affects the immune system and can lead to skin cancer. UV rays that enter the dermis can then be absorbed by dermal components including collagen, elastin, and GAGs, leading to accelerated damage of skin structure.

A Little UV Exposure Education …

Explain that UV exposure is the #1 contributor to aging and there is not much one can do aesthetically without the client's compliance. Many think the effects of sun exposure are only dangerous when laying out in the sun in the summertime. For these clients, use simple formulas; for example: If a person were exposed to sunlight without sunscreen for only four minutes per day for 10 years, the skin would be exposed to more than 243 hours of damaging UV rays with no protection. Recommend antioxidants and sunscreen first and foremost. Assure the client that if she sticks to a regimen without excessive sun exposure, a retinol can be added, as well as more aggressive treatments such as peels and lasers. If the client will not use sunscreen, a potent antioxidant serum can help prevent some UV damage.

Lifestyle Effects on the Skin

Smoking

A person's overall health is also part of the extrinsic factors that affect the appearance of the skin. For instance, it is well known that smoking is bad for your health and can lead to cancer. It's written on the labels of cigarette packets; it is the reason you no longer see advertisements for cigarettes on television and limited ads in magazines and on websites. But the effects of smoking on the skin are not as well understood as those of the lungs and heart. As with all organs of the body (of which the skin is the largest), oxygen is essential to properly function. Smoking decreases the amount of oxygen available for the body's systems to function properly, while simultaneously substituting carbon monoxide in place of the deprived oxygen. Cigarette smoke is not only a complex mixture of numerous chemicals with carcinogenic and toxic potential, but also contains stable free radicals, reactive oxygen species (ROS), and gaseous free radical species.[1] This leads to asphyxiation, a dramatic slowdown of cellular turnover and circulation in the skin, resulting in a dry, dull, gray appearance. The slowed cellular turnover and decrease in oxygen can also cause acne, most commonly Grade II acne, which primarily consists of closed comedones. Cigarette smoke also triggers the production of matrix metalloproteinases (MMPs), enzymes responsible for breakdown of collagen and elastin.

Diet
There has been much speculation on the relation of diet to the appearance of the skin. It only makes sense that the largest organ of the body would present what is happening inside. Those with diets high in fat, sugar, and complex carbohydrates experience increased blood sugar levels rapidly after each meal, which makes for a short energy boost but soon follows with a rapid and potentially dangerous fall in blood sugar levels. This rapid drop results in fatigue and hunger. So what happens? More fat, more sugar, more carbs to make up for what it feels like has been lost. This vicious cycle is unhealthy and leads to long-term inflammation and cell injury. Excess sugar in the body can over time negatively affect many organs, including the skin. A diet heavy in sugar ultimately affects the aging of skin and can make one look older. Excess sugar may also affect collagen fibers though a process called *glycation*, which causes the skin to yellow and look older.[2] Excessive alcohol consumption can likewise trigger this process, and lead to dehydration of the skin and the inability to maintain expected cellular turnover.

Stress and Sleep

Stress is another factor that can affect the skin. The "fight or flight" response releases adrenaline which reduces blood flow resulting in a dull, tired appearance. Although there is not a lot of scientific evidence that sleep directly affects the appearance of the skin, if reserved energy is used up by the body to maintain alertness, then resources are diverted from the skin and other systems. Mood clearly is negatively affected by sleep deprivation, and sleep deprivation leads to stress. Stress also releases the body's levels of the hormone cortisol, which, similar to diet, increases blood sugar levels in the body, resulting in glycation.

Methods of stress relief have whole body implications. Advising clients to explore avenues such as exercise, yoga, or meditation can result in happier, calmer clients whose treatment results are more successful.

Cellular Processes with Aging Skin

Advanced Glycation End-Products (AGEs)[2]

Glycation is the result of a sugar molecule, such as glucose, binding to a fat or protein without the controlling action of an enzyme. Although glycation occurs naturally, this process is heightened when a person introduces excess sugar into their system. With aging, this process forms advanced glycation end-products, or AGEs, which cause cross-linking of fibers, including collagen and elastin, to become stiff and immobile, leading to the visible signs of aging. AGEs also form a complex called Receptor-AGE (RAGE) that contributes to inflammation and increased formation of free radicals, further damaging the skin.

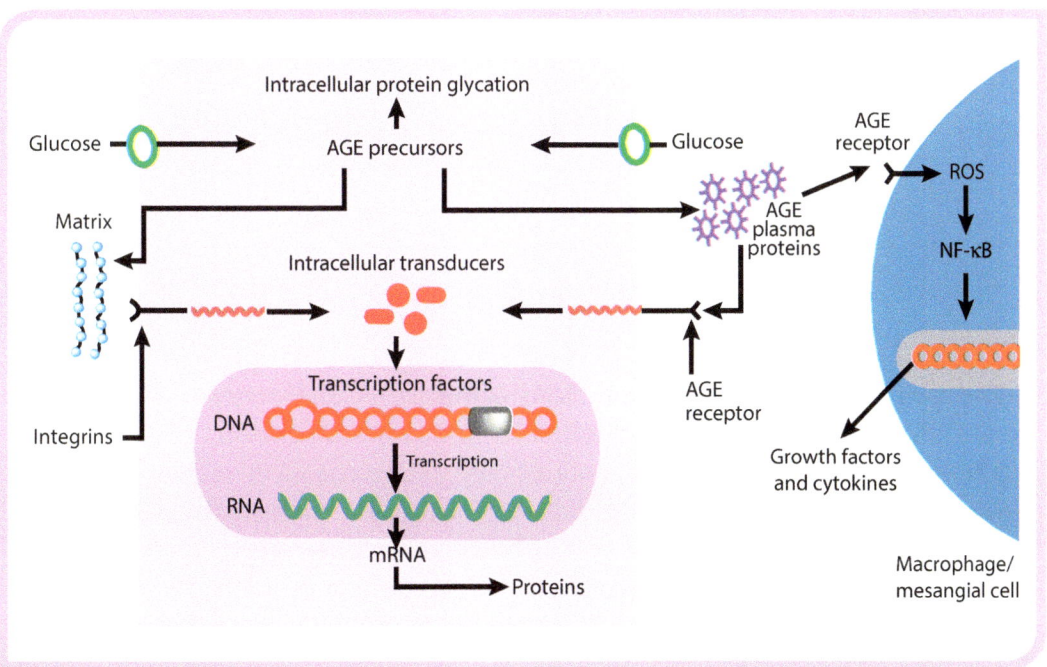

> ## How Do We Combat AGEs?
> - Reduce consumption of foods that contribute to glycation
> - Regular exercise
> - Have a diet based on foods with a low glycemic index
> - Use of antioxidant supplements
> - Topical ingredients, including EGCG from green tea, resveratrol, retinols, aminoguanadine, bakuchiol, blueberry extract, and gota kula (centella asiatica)

Reactive Oxygen Species (ROS)

Reactive oxygen species, or ROS, a type of free radical, are probably the most discussed contributing factor to aging skin. Free radicals are atoms, molecules, or ions with unpaired electrons that are highly reactive and cause cell damage. ROS are free radicals containing oxygen. As these molecules are necessary for cellular communication, an increase causes oxidative stress which creates damage to DNA in cells, proteins, and enzymes. ROS can also produce inflammation, resulting in cross-linking of collagen and elastin. It is well known that free radicals are harmful to cells, and the use of antioxidants internally is necessary. Many don't realize the importance of applying topical antioxidants to protect the superficial layers of skin. Aesthetic professionals must make clients aware of the potential benefits of topically applied antioxidants.

> ## Combating ROS
> - Reduce external factors that can trigger free radicals, namely sun exposure, smoking, alcohol use, unhealthy diet and stress.
> - Topically applied antioxidants, including vitamin C and E.
> - Sunscreen, sunscreen, sunscreen.
> - Glutathione, polyphenols, and uric acid

MMPs

There has been a lot of focus on the effects of matrix metalloproteinase (MMPs) on aging skin. MMPs are necessary enzymes in human skin that aid in the breakdown and removal of damaged proteins. For instance, collagenase is an enzyme that breaks down damaged collagen so the body can replace it with healthy collagen, a process known as neocollagenesis. As most of the body works under the theory of checks and balances, overproduction of MMPs can be harmful to proteins. MMPs are heightened by extrinsic factors and eventually these enzymes break down healthy collagen and elastin.

Controlling MMPs: Matrix metalloproteinase inhibitors, or *MMPIs*, are ingredients that stabilize the production of the enzymes. Limited unhealthy environmental exposure, sunscreen, and antioxidants including resveratrol, EGCG, vitamins C and E, and glycine soja have been shown to help control the overproduction of MMPs.

> Inflammation is a contributor to every skin condition from acne to aging. There are several internal processes that occur which can lead to the appearance of aged skin. With the increased popularity of cosmetic medicine and vast advancements in the aesthetic industry as a whole, it is vital for all providers to understand what is happening beneath the surface of the skin.

Telomeres

Telomeres are caps at the end of chromosomes that are responsible for protecting the gene sequence that resides at the end of the chromosome. In doing so, they help protect DNA, which is used as a blueprint for cell replication. The telomeres serve to allow the chromosomes to shorten each time replication occurs. They shorten until eventually they are no longer capable of dividing. As cell division is essential for maintaining healthy skin, when this process no longer occurs it leads to aging.

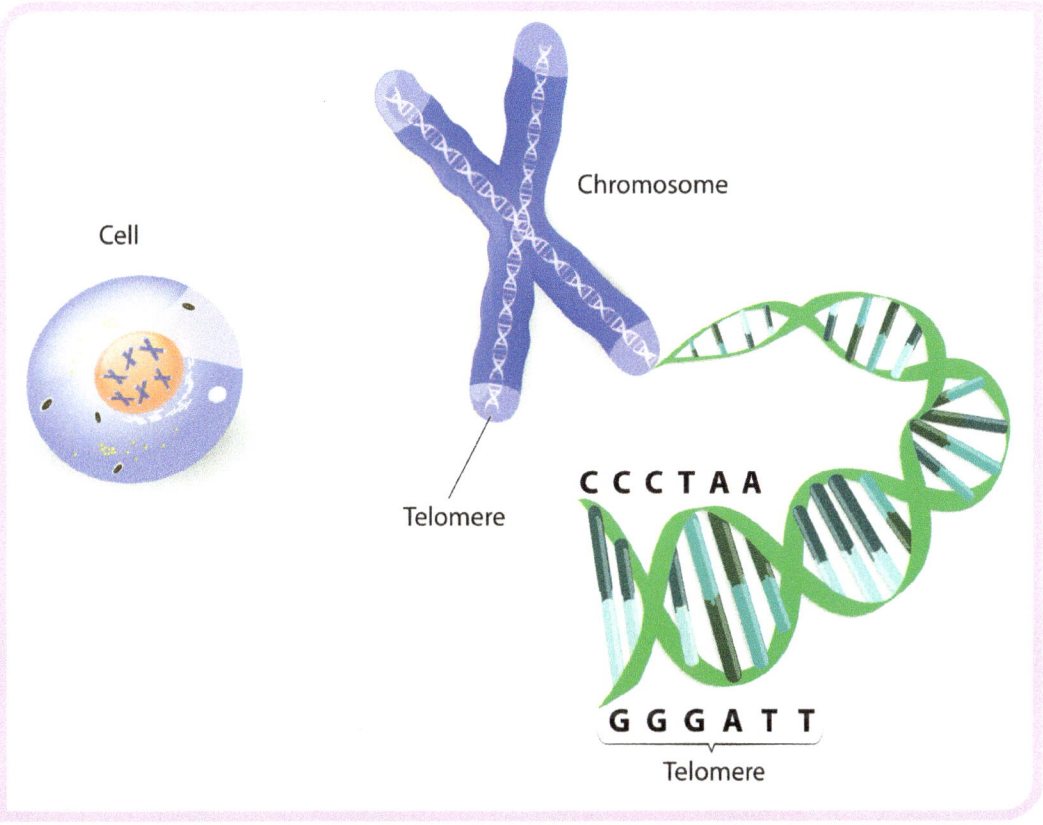

Presentations of Aging Skin

As the skin ages, the loss of subcutaneous fat, and decrease in collagen and elastin brought on by intrinsic and extrinsic factors cause the skin to sag. It is estimated that adult skin loses approximately 1% of its dermal collagen content on an annual basis due to increased collagen degradation and decreased collagen synthesis.[5]

The visible signs of skin aging manifest individually, yet these signs are categorical and include the following:

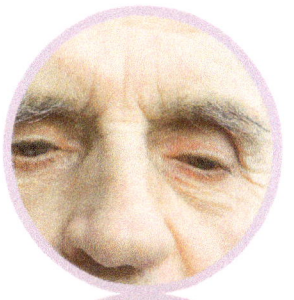

- **Visible color changes**
  - Appearance of discolorations with definite edges, or lentigines
  - Development of sallow yellow color
  - Loss of pink glow
  - Gradual appearance of telangiectasia

- **Skin texture**
  - Loss of palpable smoothness
  - Progression of keratoses
  - Fine lines, followed by deeper folds and wrinkles
  - Loss of subcutaneous fat around the mouth, temples, and brows
  - Epidermal thinning
  - Lower eyelid skin becomes more transparent

- **Functional changes**
  - Loss of elasticity
  - Gravitational effects
  - Increase in sensitivity
  - Decrease in barrier function
  - Transepidermal water loss (TEWL)

Damaged cells have the innate ability to self-destruct, a process called apoptosis. This is an important function of cells that protect the body from replicating damaged proteins, leading to potential disease including cancer. Imagine then, what would result if this cycle were interrupted? By controlling the length of the telomeres, there is a theory[3] that the body would not age as it does with the shortened telomeres that are no longer capable of replicating.

In 1961, Lenhard Hayflick discovered that the degradation of telomeric DNA causes a stage at which the cell can no longer divide.[4] In other words, as the cell divides, telomeres shorten until they become too short. At this point, cells achieve replicative senescence and are unable to divide further, thereby leading to the various changes that are associated with aging.

The enzyme telomerase is known to lengthen or replace telomeres in DNA that have been lost due to age. Therefore, a theory was developed that using this enzyme would significantly halt the aging process. However, by not allowing the telomeres to shorten, damaged cells can continue to replicate, thus disrupting apoptosis which could lead to the overproduction of unhealthy cells that lead to cancer. In the future, there could be more substantial studies and scientific research that will lead to a safe anti-aging cure through telomerase. As of now, it seems as though lifestyle changes including healthy diet, exercise, and stress reduction are a safe way to prevent the shortening of telomeres and prolong the cycle of cell replication leading to a more youthful body.

Combating Lifestyle Effects on Skin

Well, there's the obvious—quit smoking, reduce stress, eat healthy, exercise, get plenty of sleep, and stay out of the sun.

"Good fats" are shown to improve the appearance of the skin. These include monounsaturated fats like those found in olives, olive oil, peanuts, almonds, and avocados, and polyunsaturated fats like those found in corn, soybeans, and fish. Some fish, namely salmon, also contain high amounts of polyunsaturated omega 3 fatty acids. Omega 3 fats are not naturally produced in the body and can only be acquired via diet. Omega 6 fats are also found in nature and are important for healthy metabolic function. Omega 6 is found in soy and various oils, including sunflower, cottonseed, canola, peanut, grape seed, and corn oils. Food rich in omega 3 and omega 6 help maintain moisture levels in the skin, leading to a more youthful appearance.

Eating foods high in cholesterol, an essential component to skin that appears healthy, was at one time thought to be dangerous and could lead to heart disease. It was previously believed that a person should eat a diet low in cholesterol, excluding high cholesterol foods such as eggs and shellfish. However, it is now recognized that although high cholesterol levels may affect the heart, the amount of cholesterol a person consumes has less of an effect on internal cholesterol levels than does the body's own production of cholesterol. In fact, genetic predisposition has the greatest impact on cholesterol levels.[6]

> With all of the factors that contribute to the production of free radicals, it is more important than ever to maintain a diet high in antioxidants.

With all of the factors that contribute to the production of free radicals, it is more important than ever to maintain a diet high in antioxidants. Many studies have shown the health-protecting benefits of fighting off oxidative stress with antioxidants. The best known antioxidant is vitamin E. Vitamin E can help the body fight against heart disease and inflammation, but it is also an important protector of the skin. By increasing vitamin E levels in the body, it is theorized that the skin will not sustain as much damage and will repair injured cells at a faster rate. Vitamin E is also thought to improve the general appearance of the skin. Researchers have found that taking 400 international units (IU) of vitamin E orally will increase the concentration of vitamin E in the skin.[7]

Vitamin C is also a potent antioxidant and a necessary contributor to collagen synthesis and wound healing. A balanced diet is enough to maintain healthy levels of vitamin C for collagen production; therefore taking additional vitamin C orally doesn't seem to have a direct effect on reversing the appearance of fine lines and wrinkles. On the contrary, vitamin C as a topical serum has shown some impressive results with regard to protecting the skin, reducing inflammation and promoting collagen production.[8] It is essential that it be delivered to the skin in the right form. As a topical product, vitamin C formulated in the form of L-ascorbic acid must be at a low pH with a stabilizer, otherwise it may lose its potency quickly due to oxidation. Other nutritional supplements such as lycopene, which is found in tomatoes, resveratrol, which is found in certain kinds of berries (e.g., blueberries), minerals such as zinc, and botanicals such as green tea are also beneficial in reducing inflammation and reserving structures of the skin.[9]

Along with diet and nutrition, the benefits of exercise are undeniable. Regular exercise produces a significant improvement in cognitive function and mood, increasing the ability to handle stress. Its cardiovascular benefits are well known, as is its role in preventing muscle injury. Improved oxygen intake is vital for all body systems. Exercise can also decrease blood pressure and bad cholesterol levels, as well as assist in regulating metabolism.

Treatment Recommendations Based on Chronologic Age

Late-teens to Mid-twenties (18–26)
Focus on prevention and maintaining healthy skin.
Any lines at this stage are usually inherited, and acne may be present.
Products containing antioxidants (vitamin C, E, resveratrol) are crucial.
Cleansers with enzymes, AHAs or BHAs.
Moisturizer use dependent on skin type.
Broad spectrum sunscreen is crucial.

Treatments may include:
- Monthly maintenance facials
- Enzymatic exfoliation
- Superficial peels (lactic, salicylic)
- Mechanical exfoliation (microdermabrasion, dermaplaning)
- Oxygen treatments

Mid-twenties to Mid-thirties (27–36)
Focus on prevention.
Fine lines around mouth and eyes.
Some photo-damage is visible.
Hormonal breakouts are possible.
Recommend products containing:
- AHAs, BHAs or enzymes
- Antioxidants (vitamins C & E, resveratrol)
- Peptides; stem cells
- Moisturizers
- Retinol
- Broad spectrum sunscreen

Treatments may include:
- Hydrating Facials
- Superficial micro-needling
- Superficial to medium-depth peels
- Mechanical exfoliation (microdermabrasion, dermaplaning)
- Oxygen treatments
- Neurotoxin
- Tissue fillers
- Laser treatments

Mid-thirties to Mid-forties (37–46)
Less oil production.
Eye area loses tone.
Wrinkles deepen.
Pigmentation from sun damage will surface.
Recommend products containing:
- Ingredients for cellular turnover: retinols, AHAs, BHA
- Pigment lighteners: hydroquinone, kojic acid, licorice root, phytic acid
- Collagen stimulators: peptides, stem cells, growth factors
- Antioxidants (vitamins C & E, resveratrol)
- Moisturizer
- Broad spectrum sunscreen

Treatments may include:
- Neurotoxin
- Filler
- Superficial exfoliation: dermaplaning
- Medium-depth chemical peels
- Skin tightening treatments
- Laser treatments (ablative and non-ablative)
- Cosmetic surgery, usually blepharoplasty

Mid-forties to Mid-fifties (47–56)
Wrinkles around eyes and nose.
Face, chin and neck begin to sag.
Skin loses plumpness and tone.
Skin becomes drier.
Actinic keratosis may appear.
Recommend products containing:
- Antioxidants (vitamins C & E, resveratrol)
- Ingredients for cellular turnover: retinols, AHAs, BHAs
- Pigment lighteners: HQ, kojic acid, licorice root, phytic acid
- Collagen stimulators: peptides, stem cells, growth factors
- Moisturizers with occlusive agents
- Broad spectrum sunscreen

Treatments may include:
- Neurotoxin
- Filler
- Superficial exfoliation: dermaplaning
- Medium-depth chemical peels
- Skin tightening treatments
- Laser treatments (ablative and non-ablative)
- Cosmetic surgery procedures, usually blepharoplasty or or rhytidectomy

Mid-fifties and Beyond (57 and older)
Nasolabial folds deepen dramatically.
Neck sags.
Wrinkles are more prevalent.
Dryness and sensitivity of the skin are prevalent.
Recommend products containing:
- Ingredients for cellular turnover: retinols, AHAs, BHAs
- Pigment lighteners: HQ, kojic acid, licorice root, phytic acid
- Collagen stimulators: peptides, stem cells, growth factors
- Moisturizer with occlusive agents
- Broad spectrum sunscreen

Treatments may include:
- Neurotoxin
- Filler
- Laser treatments (ablative and non-ablative)
- Cosmetic surgery, usually blepharoplasty or rhytidectomy
- Skin tightening treatments
- Chemical peels

One Final Thought ...

Today, there is a movement called *age management medicine*. Physicians who are proponents of this movement argue that the goal is not to make you live longer but to make you live healthier. Traditional medicine teaches us that eating a balanced meal will provide our bodies with all the vitamins and minerals necessary for good health. Some concepts such as supplementation with oral antioxidants and fish oils have been thought of as radical. But today, antioxidant therapy is known to reduce inflammation and even to reverse some of the damage of heart disease. While evidence is mounting that nutritional supplementation is beneficial to a person's health, it is not clear how much and to what extent they help. Invariably, nutrition will continue to be an increasingly important component for preventing and treating disease and a major and necessary aspect of improving the appearance of one's skin.

References
1. A Valavanidis et al, Tobacco smoke: Involvement of reactive oxygen species and stable free radicals in mechanisms of oxidative damage, carcinogenesis and synergistic effects with other respirable particles, *Intl J Environ Res Public Health*, 6 (2), 445–462 (2009).

2. P Gkogkolou and M Böhm, Advanced glycation end products: Key players in skin aging? *Dermatoendocrinol*, 4 (3), 259–270 (2012).
3. MA Shammas, Telomeres, lifestyle, cancer, and aging, *Curr Opin Clin Nutr Metab Care*, 14 (1), 28–34 (2011).
4. L Hayflick and PS Moorhead, The serial cultivation of human diploid cell strains, *Exp Cell Res*, 25 (3), 585-621 (1961).
5. J Chung et al, Why does the skin age? in: DS Rigel et al, eds, *Intrinsic Aging, Photoaging and their Pathophysiology*, New York: Marcel Dekker (2004) pp 13.
6. K Rahman, Studies on free radicals, antioxidants, and co-factors, *Clin Interv Aging*, 2 (2), 219–236 (2007).
7. Z Draelos, *Procedures in Cosmetic Dermatology Series: Cosmeceuticals*, Philadelphia: Saunders (2005) pp 59.
8. BV Nusgens, Topically applied vitamin C enhances the mRNA level of collagens I and III, their processing enzymes and tissue inhibitor of matrix metalloproteinase 1 in the human dermis, *J Invest Dermatol*, 116(6), 853-9 (2011).
9. H Hendricks et al, Metabolism, mood and cognition in aging: The importance of lifestyle and dietary intervention, *Neurobiol Aging*, 26 (suppl 1), 1-5 (2005).

Part 3: Review Questions

1) What is acne?

    a) A chronic inflammatory disorder of the capillaries
    b) A chronic inflammatory disorder of the sebaceous glands
    c) A chronic inflammatory disorder of the suderiferous glands
    d) A chronic inflammatory disorder of the skin cells.

2) Which treatment is beneficial for inflamed papules and pustules?

    a) Extractions
    b) Salicylic acid peel
    c) Micro-needling
    d) Microdermabrasion

3) Who is affected by acne?

    a) Teenagers going through puberty
    b) Women going through menopause
    c) Those that don't care for the skin
    d) Virtually everyone at some point in their life

4) What factors can contribute to acne?

    a) Excess sebum
    b) Buildup of dead skin cells
    c) *Propionibacterium acne*
    d) All of the above

5) Which oral medication used to treat acne can cause severe side effects including extremely dry skin, poor wound healing and depression, and needs to be monitored closely?

    a) Minocycline
    b) Spironolactone
    c) Isotretinoin (Accutane)
    d) Aminolevulonic acid

6) What treatment can be used to treat a large painful acneic lesion to reduce inflammation quickly?

   a) Botox injections
   b) Restylane injections
   c) Steroid injection
   d) Photodynamic therapy

7) Which would be the best treatment option for rosacea on a client whose main concern is redness?

   a) Intense Pulsed Light (IPL)
   b) Lactic acid peel
   c) Dermaplaning
   d) Topical antibiotics

8) What is the main characteristic difference between acne vulgaris and papulopustular rosacea?

   a) There is a lack of pustules with rosacea
   b) There is a lack of comedones with rosacea
   c) There is a lack of cysts with rosacea
   d) There is a lack of nodules with rosacea

9) Which medication or treatment is proven to cure rosacea?

   a) Ablative laser treatment
   b) Accutane
   c) Antibiotics
   d) Rosacea is not curable

10) Who is rhinophyma most prevalent in?

    a) Middle-aged men
    b) Middle-aged women
    c) Teenage boys
    d) The elderly

Review Questions

11) What is the beneficial key ingredient someone with rosacea should look for in a sunscreen?

   a) Avobenzone
   b) Benzoyl Peroxide
   c) Titianium dioxide
   d) Zinc Oxide

12) What are some topical medications used to treat rosacea?

   a) Metronidazole
   b) Sulfacetamide
   c) Clindamycin
   d) All of the above

13) _____ should be avoided during facial treatments on a client with rosacea?

   a) Steam
   b) Facial massage
   c) Ultrasound
   d) All the above

14) What condition of rosacea does ablative laser or dermabrasion treat?

   a) Redness
   b) Capillaries
   c) Telangiectasias
   d) Rhinophyma

15) What is the cause of solar lentigines?

   a) Overexposure to the sun
   b) Inflammation or skin trauma
   c) Hormones
   d) Acne

16) What are solar lentigines?

   a) Old age spots or liver spots
   b) Flat, oval, evenly pigmented macules in areas of chronic sun exposure
   c) Common benign lesions of the skin
   d) All of the above

17) What is melasma most often caused from?

   a) Aggressive picking of the skin
   b) Birth control and hormone replacement therapy
   c) Harsh product use on the skin
   d) Infection in the body

18) What are treatment options for solar lentigines?

   a) Freezing with liquid nitrogen
   b) Hydroquinone topical agent
   c) Chemical peels
   d) All of the above

19) The loss of subcutaneous fat, resulting in volume loss, can be caused by which type of aging?

   a) Intrinsic aging
   b) Extrinsic aging
   c) Both intrinsic and extrinsic aging
   d) The skin does not lose subcutaneous fat during aging

20) Which two skin care treatments can be performed 7–10 days following non-ablative laser treatments to reduce superficial pigmentation?

   a) Dermaplaning and microdermabrasion
   b) Ultrasound and phenol peels
   c) Lymphatic drainage massage and dermabrasion
   d) Phenol peels and lasers

21) What types of supplements are known to reduce inflammation and even to reverse some of the damage of heart disease?

   a) Antioxidants
   b) Minerals
   c) Vitamin B5
   d) Vitamin B12

22) Which layer of the skin is mostly affected by extrinsic aging?

   a) Dermis
   b) Epidermis
   c) Both A and B
   d) Subcutaneous

23) Extrinsic aging is also called?

   a) Slow aging
   b) Photoaging
   c) Out of town aging
   d) Lipo aggressive-aging

24) A diet rich in sugar ultimately affects the aging of skin and can actually make you look older. Excess sugar can also affect collagen fibers. What is this process called?

   a) Glycation
   b) Collaganese
   c) Elastosis
   d) Wrinkles

25) What does AGE, relating to glycation stand for?

   a) Advanced Genetics Energy Systems
   b) The intrinsic aging factor index
   c) Abnormal Glycation End Products
   d) Advanced Glycation End Products

PART 4

Professional Skin Care Treatments

AESTHETICS EXPOSED
MASTERING SKIN CARE IN A MEDICAL SETTING AND BEYOND

CHAPTER 13

Chemical Exfoliation: AHAs, BHA, TCA, & Jessner's

In this Chapter:
- Chemical Peels: From Past to Present
- Indications and Contraindications for Chemical Peels
- Alpha Hydroxy Acid Peels
- Beta Hydroxy Acid Peels
- Jessner's Peels
- Trichloroacetic Acid (TCA) Peels
- Treatment Expectations
- Protocols including Post-treatment Care

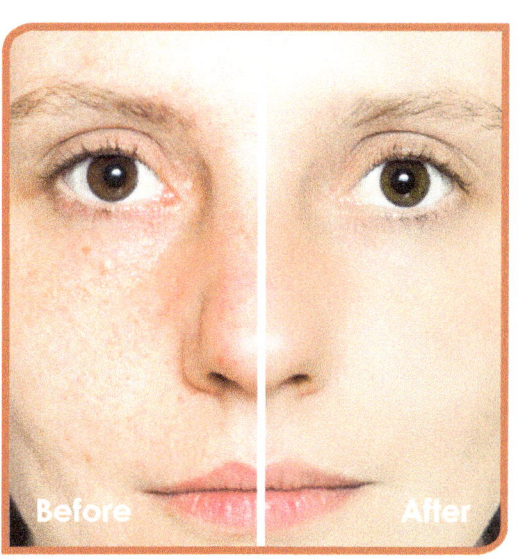

Chemical Peels: From Past to Present

The use of exfoliation methods to improve the appearance of skin dates back to the ancient Egyptians. The cosmetic benefits of alpha hydroxy acids were discovered when sour milk, containing lactic acid, was used in baths to soften the skin. Several other methods using everything from mineral scrubs to chemicals have been used in different cultures to treat the skin.[1] Turks used fire to singe the skin in an attempt at superficial exfoliation. In the mid-1800s, the use of aggressive exfoliation methods was introduced to treat various skin conditions. These sometimes extreme methods were successful, but at an expense; the more aggressive the treatment, the higher the risk of side effects and complications. Today, we see a surge in mild to moderate chemical peeling techniques as providers and clients gear more toward *progressive* treatments as opposed to *aggressive*.

The terms "chemical peel" and "acid" can make clients apprehensive. Despite negative connotations associated with these terms, the truth is there are several different methods of chemical peeling that range from very superficial to deep. To avoid confusion or alarm with clients,

> The terms "chemical peel" and "acid" can make clients apprehensive.

153

the terms "chemical exfoliation" or "resurfacing treatment" are more consistently employed when promoting superficial chemical peels.

It is well known that peels exfoliate the outer layers of skin, but an equally important function of exfoliation is to create a *controlled wound response*. When skin responds to acute inflammation, it stimulates the growth of new cells, including epithelial cells, endothelial cells, and fibroblasts, resulting in a healthier appearance. Cellular turnover is a natural process during which dead skin cells are released from the stratum corneum of the epidermis and are replaced with new cells from the basal layer of the epidermis, where cells are replicated. In healthy skin, cells turn over approximately every 28 days until a person reaches age 30, after

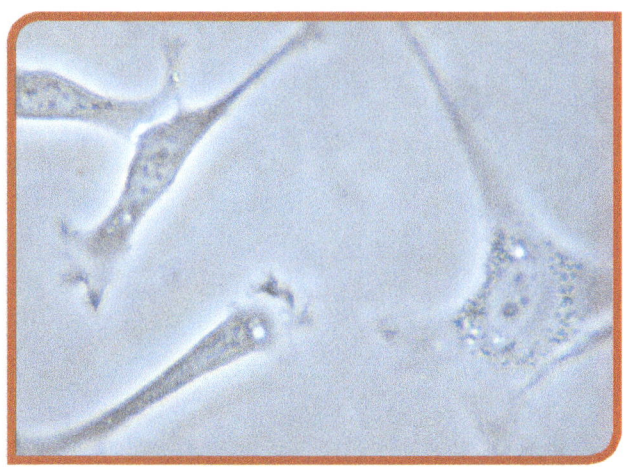

Fibroblasts are cells responsible for collagen production.

Stimulating the rate of skin exfoliation in a controlled manner can reduce superficial imperfections while simultaneously building healthier skin structure.

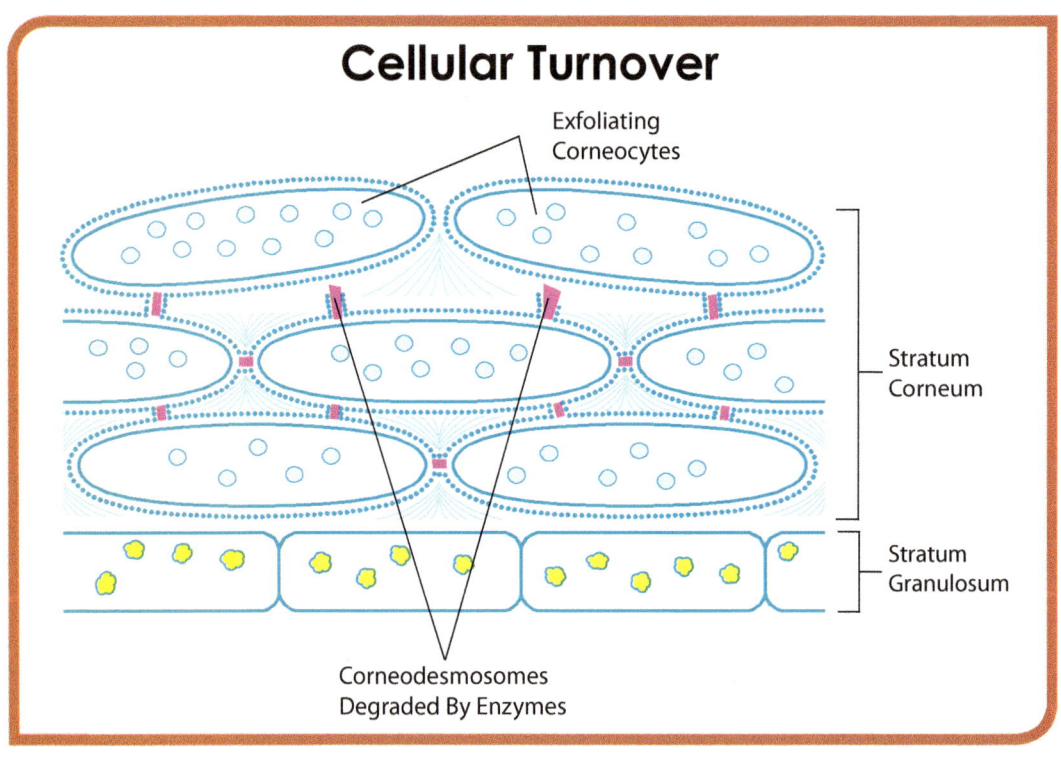

Peel Depths and Possible Combinations

NOTE: This is a general chart, peel strengths can be altered by pH, application technique, and prepping method used.

SUPERFICIAL PEELS

Combinations can be made with very superficial peels, it is only recommended to combine two of the modalities in one treatment unless specific advanced protocols are provided by the manufacturer or medical director. These can also be added to a facial without the use of steam; the timing to add extractions with the peel is below.

Depth	Layer of Skin	Chemical Peel	Extractions
Very Superficial	Stratum corneum	Microdermabrasion	After
Very Superficial	Stratum corneum	Dermaplaning	After
`Superficial	Stratum corneum	AHA up to 30%	After
Very Superficial	Stratum corneum	BHA up to 20%	Before
Very Superficial	Stratum corneum	Retinol 10%	Before

The following superficial peels cannot be combined in general protocols but can be boosted with a retinol product to stimulate cell turnover providing a slightly deeper exfoliation.

Depth	Layer of Skin	Chemical Peel	Booster
Superficial	Epidermis	AHA 30% to 50%	10% Retinol
Superficial	Epidermis	BHA 20% to 30%	10% Retinol
Superficial	Epidermis	TCA up to 10%	10% Retinol
Superficial	Epidermis	Modified Jessner's up to 2 Layers	10% Retinol

MEDIUM TO DEEP PEELS

Medium and Deep peels are MEDICAL only and may be combined by physicians for more aggressive customized techniques. These peels should only be performed by medical professionals.

Depth	Layer of Skin	Chemical Peel	
Medium	Papillary dermis	AHA 50% to 70%	
Medium	Papillary dermis	TCA 15% to 40%	
Medium	Papillary dermis	Jessner's multiple layers	
Depth	Layer of Skin	Chemical Peel	
Deep	Reticular dermis	Phenol	
Deep	Reticular dermis	Baker's Gordon	

which this natural exfoliation process decreases at an estimated rate of about 10 days every decade.[2] This decrease in the skin's natural exfoliation can contribute to fine lines, wrinkles, acne, and a dull, dry appearance. Stimulating the rate of skin exfoliation in a controlled manner can reduce superficial imperfections while simultaneously building healthier skin structure.

> Levels of peeling vary, but most are categorized as either superficial peeling, which affects the outer layers of the epidermis, medium-depth peeling that can affect the papillary layer of the dermis, or deep peeling, which can reach the reticular layer of the dermis.

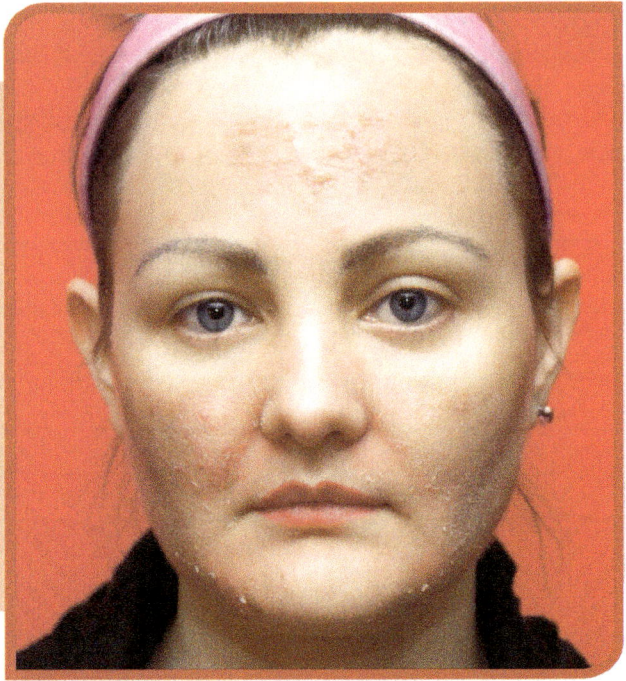

Peeling skin following medium-depth treatment.

Percentages and pH differ greatly depending on the peeling agent being used; for example, a 10% TCA peel is stronger than a 40% lactic acid peel due to its chemical structure.[3] Low pH, under a 2.0, has the potential to induce crusting and necrosis.

In most states, estheticians can only perform superficial exfoliation treatments, as they can cosmetically enhance the skin's appearance. Medical professionals, as determined by individual state regulations, can perform more aggressive treatments.

Superficial peels are the only peels that should be done by estheticians who are not under the direct supervision of a physician. These include alpha hydroxy acids (up to 30%, pH 3.0), beta hydroxy acids (20%, pH 3.0), modified Jessner's peels, and low percentage TCA peels. (See sidebar on **Understanding pH**.) For optimal results, superficial peels are most commonly done in a series of four to six treatments spaced three weeks apart, although if the skin is sensitive it is recommended to wait four weeks between treatments. These mild exfoliants are a great way to introduce clients to peeling treatments because they have little-to-no downtime associated with them, they work well on those with highly sensitive skin, and they are a safer choice for higher Fitzpatrick types. In a survey comparing microdermabrasion and chemical peels (using a 20% glycolic acid peel), those who received both treatments reported that microdermabrasion was more enjoyable and caused less facial redness than did

Chemical Exfoliation: AHAs, BHAs, TCA, Jessner's

chemical peels, but that glycolic peels were more effective in improving the appearance of the skin.[4]

There are many things to consider when deciding to treat a client with a chemical peel, including the type of peel you will use, its percentage, and its pH.

> Superficial peels are the only peels that should be done by estheticians who are not under the direct supervision of a physician.

The concentration of the peel depends on the percentage of acid in the solution; the greater this percentage, the stronger the acid concentration. Similarly, chemicals with a lower pH are more acidic and can cause greater injury to the skin.

What to be Aware of with All Peels
- Never pour the acid around the client's face
- Protect the client's eyes for additional safety
- Check labels to ensure the right peel is being used
- Test patch for sensitivities
- Occlude sensitive areas of skin including the border of the lips, inner and outer canthus of the eye, and the corners of the nose

Prepping the Skin for Peels
- The use of a mild keratolytic agent, such as glycolic acid (5% to 10%) or salicylic acid (2% to 5%), or mild retinols can increase the effectiveness of the peel. These should be discontinued three days prior to the peel to decrease the chance of side effects.
- Skin lightening agents should be used for a minimum of two weeks for those suffering from hyperpigmentation as well as darker skin types (Fitzpatrick IV–VI) to reduce the risk of PIH.
- The skin should be properly protected and hydrated; the use of a regular antioxidant, moisturizer, and sunscreen will provide optimal results.
- Products containing vitamin A should be discontinued three days before the treatment and not reinstated until the skin has completely healed from the peeling process (typically five days).

Alpha Hydroxy Acid Peels
There are six alpha hydroxy acids (AHAs) used in skin care: *glycolic*, derived from sugar cane; *lactic*, from sour milk; *malic*, from apples; *tartaric*, from grapes; *mandelic*, from bitter almonds; and *citric*, from fruit. There are many theories as to how alpha hydroxy acids work; however, the most widely accepted is that they dissolve corneocyte

Understanding pH

- pH stands for Power of Hydrogen
- pH is important to understand for product reaction
- The lower the pH, the more acidic the product
- More acidic = more active; product amount can remain the same, but lower the acid level

Concentration of hydrogen ions compared to distilled water		Examples of solutions at this pH	
10,000,000	pH = 0	Battery acid, strong hydrofluroric acid	
1,000,000	pH = 1	Hydrochloric acid secreted by stomach lining	
100,000	pH = 2	Lemon juice, gastric acid, vinegar	Chemical Peels
10,000	pH = 3	Grapefruit, orange juice, soda	
1,000	pH = 4	Tomato juice, acid rain	
100	pH = 5	Soft drinking water, black coffee	Skin
10	pH = 6	Urine, saliva	
1	pH = 7	"Pure" water	Neutral
1/10	pH = 8	Seawater	
1/100	pH = 9	Baking soda	
1/1,000	pH = 10	Great Salt Lake, milk of magnesia	Neutralizing Solutions
1/10,000	pH = 11	Ammonia solution	
1/100,000	pH = 12	Soapy water	
1/1,000,000	pH = 13	Bleach, oven cleaner	
1/10,000,000	pH = 14	Liquid drain cleaner	

adhesions in the granular layer of the epidermis, resulting in exfoliation.[5] These adhesions, called desmosomes, are "hair-like" protein structures that anchor cells to each other. Breaking apart these bonds is necessary for exfoliation. Low percentage AHAs are commonly used in salon and spa settings due to the relatively low risk of adverse reactions provided they are performed properly.

Glycolic acid is the most commonly used AHA because of its small molecular size, which gives it a greater ability to penetrate the epidermis. The percentage (amount of acid in the product) for AHA peels typically ranges from 30% to 70% with a pH range of 2.0–3.5, although there are variations. Clients generally like the appearance of their skin following glycolic peels, although results may not be as significant as with other peeling agents.

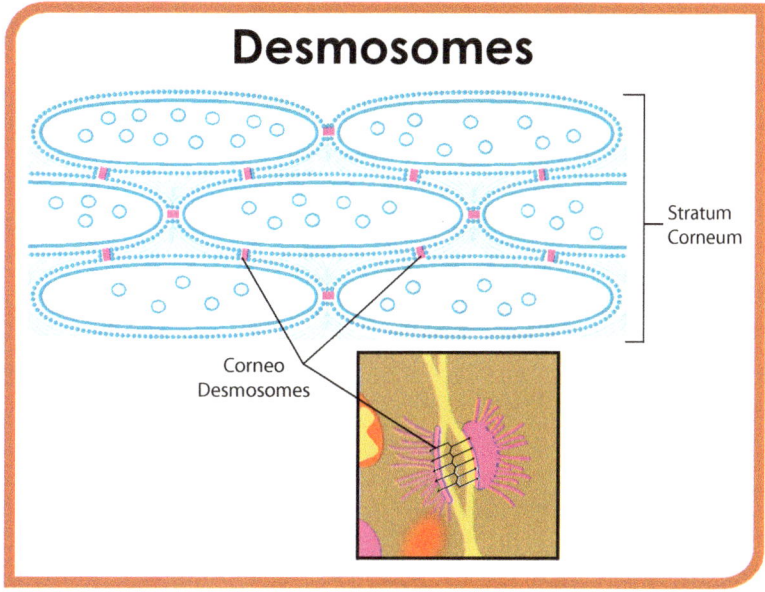

Multiple clinical studies have shown improvements in the appearance of the skin with the use of glycolic acid. It has also been shown to strengthen collagen, expanding its benefits for the skin.[6]

Lactic acid has properties similar to glycolic acid regarding its method of exfoliation; they are both water-soluble and dissolve bonds between keratinized cells. Lactic acid is commonly used on clients with more sensitive skin conditions, including rosacea, due to its larger molecular size, which makes it gentler than the smaller glycolic molecule. **The added benefits of skin lightening and hydrating properties make lactic acid one of the most widely used exfoliants on the market, not only for in-office peels, but also in products for home use.**

Malic acid, *citric acid*, *mandelic acid*, and *tartaric acid* are also water-soluble ingredients with exfoliation properties. These acids are typically not used as stand-alone peeling agents, because they are often milder compared to glycolic acid and lactic acid, and seem to provide the most benefit when used in blends. The use of these acids is more often seen in product formulations and blended chemical peels.

> Take the knowledge about treatment options, do your own research, and form your own opinion on what is best for you and your clients.

Alpha Hydroxy Acid Protocol

Indications for Treatment
- Acne grades I and II
- Uneven skin texture
- Superficial keratoses
- Superficial pigmentation
- Fine lines, wrinkles

Contraindications to Treatment
- Pregnant or lactating/nursing
- Current antibiotic use, topical or oral/internal
- Isotretinoin use within six months
- Open wounds or cold sores
- Poor wound healing response (cancer, diabetics, autoimmune disorders)

What a Client Should Expect
- Itching or tingling sensation during treatment
- Sensitivity or redness for up to four days
- Mild peeling (if any) on the forehead, nose and chin

Protocol

Note: This is a general protocol for alpha hydroxy acid peels. Always follow the manufacturer's instructions.

1. Review the client's history form and have him/her sign a consent form, including possible adverse effects and post-treatment care (see sample in Appendix C).

2. Thoroughly explain each step of the treatment, including the importance of keeping the eyes closed and providing feedback regarding skin sensation, i.e. "I will be asking how your skin feels on a scale of one to 10; one is barely anything at all, 10 would be an extreme burning sensation."

3. Prepare supplies including a timer and a hand-held fan to minimize discomfort.

4. Cleanse the skin thoroughly with a gel cleanser, repeat if necessary.

5. Degrease the skin with alcohol, acetone, or specified prepping solution to remove excess oils and allow for a more even application.

6. Any sensitized areas of the skin—such as the corners of the eyes, the lip border, and under the nostrils—must be covered with an occlusive agent, such as Vaseline, Aquaphor, or any petrolatum-based product.

7. Prepare the appropriate neutralizing solution, keeping it close at hand. Since AHAs are timed peels and increase in strength the longer they are left on, a timer must be set for the appropriate time according to the manufacturer's instructions, typically between one and 10 minutes.

8. Let the client know they will experience an itchy or tingling sensation. Start applying the peel with a twice folded 4 x 4 gauze, beginning at the forehead according to the diagram as pictured.

9. Ask the client to rate the peeling sensation based on the scale of 1 to 10 as discussed prior to the treatment. If the patient is extremely uncomfortable, 7 or above, neutralize the peel immediately. Remember to fan the client's skin if they are uncomfortable.

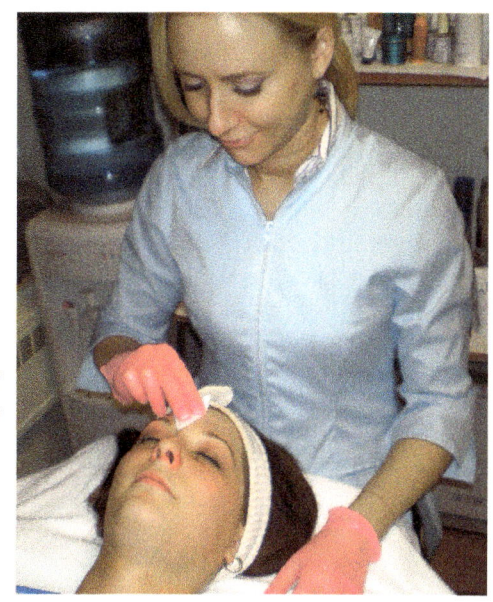

10. Once the peel has been applied, if the sensation is under a 4, you may massage it in circular motions with a 2 × 2 gauze or cotton square for added penetration on areas that need more aggressive peeling (for example, on pigmented lesions and areas of pitted scarring).

11. Once the peel has set for the indicated time, let the client know that you will be removing the peel and the sensation may increase before

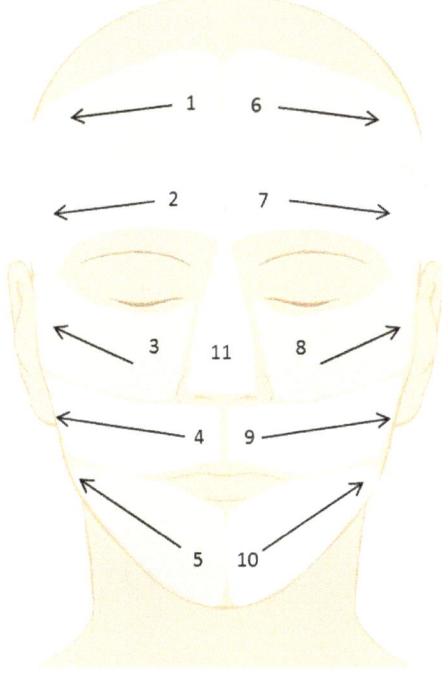

Steps for applying an AHA peel.

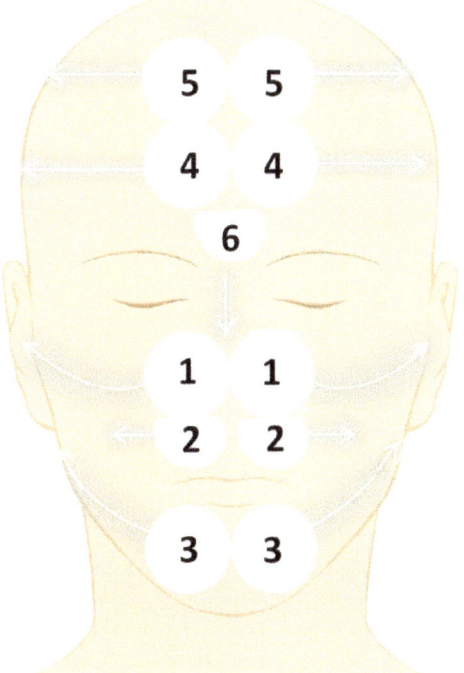

Steps for neutralizing an AHA peel.

subsiding. This is a chemical reaction from heightening the pH from an acid to a base; for this reason, it is important to remove the peel quickly and methodically, starting on sensitive areas like the upper lip and corners of the nose.

12. Quickly remove the peel with cotton pads (gauze is too rough at this step, as the skin may be sensitized) saturated with neutralizing solution, going over the area as many times as necessary until the stinging or itching sensation subsides. Note: If the client still feels some sensation after neutralizing the skin several times, ask if it feels like the product is still active or if it feels similar to a mild sunburn. If it feels like a mild sunburn, it is likely just the aftereffects of the peel.
13. Follow with cool water, again on cotton instead of gauze, until the client is comfortable and all of the tingling has subsided.
14. At this time, topical products will penetrate more effectively. Apply an antioxidant serum, a corrective product according to the client's concerns, a hydrating product, and a zinc-oxide based sunscreen.
15. Educate the client on proper skin care and give specific post-treatment care instructions with a written copy to take home.

Post-Treatment Instructions

- Excessive sun should be avoided, and an SPF 30 sunscreen should be worn every day for a minimum of two weeks following the peel.
- If there is a concern of hyperpigmentation, a pigment lightening product should be applied twice a day for a minimum of two weeks following the peel via a serum or moisturizer. Examples of pigment lighteners include hydroquinone, kojic acid, lactic acid, emblica, licorice root, rumex, arbutin, azelaic acid, and L-ascorbic acid.
- Extra moisture should be added to prevent excess dryness or irritation.
- The client should refrain from activities that will cause excess heat in the skin (aerobic exercise, steam baths, hot showers and saunas) for at least 48 hours following the treatment. The excess heat can lead to sweat blisters or pigmentation.

Tip

If using AHAs with extractions, it is recommended to do extractions after. The AHAs will help loosen clogged pores for easier removal. Extractions with beta hydroxy acids are done before, due to the lipophilic nature of salicylic acid; it is best to remove the built up sebum first, allowing the salicylic to penetrate the follicle more effectively to exfoliate the surrounding cells.

It is important to educate the client that peeling isn't necessary for results; skin cells are at a microscopic level. Peeling should be thought of as a side effect that can occur. Additionally, clients should keep the skin hydrated during the healing process as the skin heals better in a moist environment.

Factors that Affect How Skin Reacts to Peeling Treatments

1. The percentage of acid in the product
2. The pH of the product
3. The amount of time left on the skin (for timed peels)
4. The number of layers applied to the area (for layered peels)
5. The amount of product applied to a given surface area
6. The condition of the skin before treatment
7. Product use by the client
8. Client's post-care compliance
9. Prepping solution/treatment used

Beta Hydroxy Acid Peels

Salicylic acid is a beta hydroxy acid (BHA) widely known for its use as a superficial peeling agent with the ability to reduce acne. Salicylic acid can be synthetically produced or derived naturally from the bark of the willow tree and is chemically similar to the main component of aspirin (acetylsalicylic acid). Salicylic acid is lipid-soluble product (attracted to oil) and has anti-inflammatory properties which makes it a top choice for oily, acneic skin. Salicylic acid is also used for the treatment of superficial pigmentation, warts, keratosis pilaris, psoriasis, and calluses. Most salicylic acid formulations are safe for darker Fitzpatrick skin types, since they work on the superficial layers of skin, reducing the chance of post-inflammtory hyperpigmentation. Salicylic acid is also used as a prepping solution by physicians to degrease the skin before medium to deep peeling treatments. Degreasing, or removing lipids from the surface, will increase the aggressiveness of chemical peels by reducing the oil barrier. Salicylic acid peels are usually used in concentrations of 20% to 30% with a pH of less than 3.0. Salicylic acid takes some time to work on the skin, which is why it is typically left on for optimal results.

Salicyclic acid treatments cannot be done on those allergic to aspirin, as it can cause a similar allergic reaction. In high doses it can also cause dizziness, nausea, or ringing in the ears. Be sure and ask about any allergies before treatment.

Note: A general protocol for BHA, as well as Modified Jessner's and superficial TCA peels appears at the end of this chapter.

Indications for Treatment
- Acne grades I, II, and III
- Open and closed comedones
- Uneven skin texture
- Superficial pigmentation
- Pseudofolliculitis barbae (razor bumps)

Contraindications to Treatment
- Allergies to aspirin or salicylic acids
- Pregnancy or nursing/lactating
- Current use of topical antibiotics
- Accutane use within the last six months
- Open cold sores, wounds, or other infections
- Poor wound healing response
- Autoimmune disease

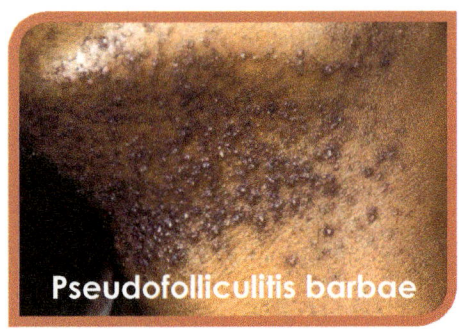

Pseudofolliculitis barbae

What a Client Should Expect
- Tingling or burning sensation during treatment (although superficial, this acid tends to sting)
- Sensitivity or redness for up to four days
- Tight or dry feeling
- Mild peeling (if any) on the forehead, nose and chin or around acne breakouts

Post-treatment Care Instructions
- Excessive sun should be avoided and an SPF 30 sunscreen should be worn every day for a minimum of two weeks after the peel.
- If there is concern of hyperpigmentation, a pigment lightener should be applied twice a day for a minimum of two weeks, via a serum or moisturizer.
- Extra moisture should be added to prevent dryness or irritation.
- The client should refrain from activities that will cause excess heat in the skin such as aerobic exercise, steam baths, hot showers, and saunas for at least 48 hours following treatment.

> When treating the neck or décolleté always "think half." Timed peels should be left on half the time; layered peels, half the amount of layers done on the face.

Modified Jessner's Peel

A traditional Jessner's peel is a combination of 14% resorcinol, 14% salicylic acid, and 14% lactic acid in an alcohol base. Jessner's, developed by Dr. Max Jessner, has been safely used for skin rejuvenation for more than a decade. Many of the formulas used today are *modified* Jessner's peels because they have been slightly altered. The

Chemical Exfoliation: AHAs, BHAs, TCA, Jessner's

Jessner's peel was originally developed to reduce the effects of using only resorcinol (a keratolytic agent that has antibacterial properties) on the skin. The Jessner's peel is most commonly used for combination to oily skin that shows some degree of photo-damage. Sensitive, dry skin types, including those with rosacea, should not receive a Jessner's peel due to the high alcohol content.

Depending on the formulation and the number of layers applied, a modified Jessner's peel can be used superficially by estheticians or as a medium-depth peel by physicians. Jessner's are self-neutralizing peels that are applied in layers. The more layers of the peel that are applied, the stronger the effect will be. This makes it extremely important to follow manufacturer instructions for individual levels of training. This peel is most effective for hyperpigmentation, acne, and oily conditions. It also can be used as a prepping solution by physicians to increase the effectiveness of other peels, including TCA (which will be discussed next).

Note: A general protocol for Modified Jessner's, as well as BHA and superficial TCA peels appears at the end of this chapter.

Indications for Treatment
- Acne grades I, II, and III
- Open and closed comedones
- Uneven skin texture
- Superficial keratoses
- Superficial pigmentation
- Photo-damage

Contraindications to Treatment
- Allergies to aspirin or salicylic acids
- Pregnant or nursing/lactating
- Current use of topical antibiotics
- Accutane use within the last six months
- Prone to cold sores (A medical professional may provide the client with anti-virals to reduce the chance of an outbreak.)
- Medical conditions that cause poor wound healing
- Higher Fitzpatrick types (dependent on formulation)

What the Client Should Expect
- Tingling or burning sensation during treatment
- Sensitivity or redness up to five days
- Tightening and dryness of the skin
- Peeling commonly occurs three to five days following treatment

Post-treatment Care Instructions
- The peel should be left on the skin for at least six hours for best results.

- Excessive sun should be avoided and an SPF 30 sunscreen should be worn every day for a minimum of two weeks following the peel.
- The client must not pick or pull at loose peeling skin; it could result in hyperpigmentation or scarring. Large pieces of peeling skin may be trimmed with manicure scissors.
- Extra moisturizing agents should be added for the next five days to prevent excess dryness or irritation.
- The client should refrain from activities that will cause excess heat in the skin such as aerobic exercise, steam baths, hot showers, and saunas for at least 48 hours following the treatment.

The Three Levels of Blanching

Frosting and **blanching** are two commonly used terms in the skin care industry for whitening of the skin. The whitening in some cases is due to the product leaving a visible "frost" on the skin; this is common with salicylic acid. A more prominent whitening of the skin is often indicative of blanching or tissue coagulating. Medical professionals will often use higher strength peels to achieve blanching on the entire skin, creating a more intense wound response and tightening of the skin. Estheticians should never reach this level of peeling as it is beyond their scope of practice.

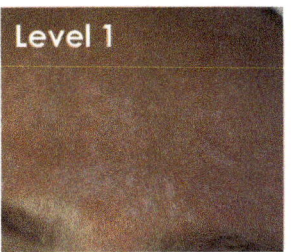

- **Level 1** blanching produces a light white frost that affects only the upper layers of the epidermis.

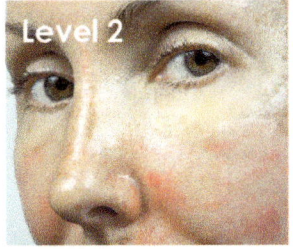

- **Level 2** blanching produces a white coat and erythema (redness of the skin signaling inflammation) that affects the entire epidermis.

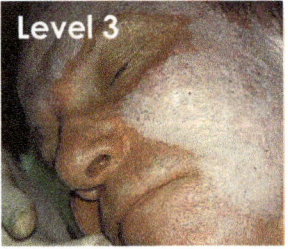

- **Level 3** blanching produces a solid white enamel frosting with no red background. This is the frosting seen most often with medium-deep peels; healing time with this level is usually seven to 10 days.

Trichloroacetic Acid (TCA) Peels

Trichloroacetic acid (TCA) was originally used as a medium-depth chemical peeling treatment by medical professionals. TCA is a synthetic acid shown to be safe for use on the skin as a peeling agent with no systemic effects. TCA is an agent that coagulates skin protein. It should be used with caution, as it has the ability to penetrate the dermis. If it is used incorrectly, it can cause a bacterial infection, a herpes simplex breakout, pigment abnormalities, and scarring. This peel should not be used on Fitzpatrick types V or VI, and there is a risk of hyperpigmentation and scarring in persons with skin type IV. TCA is available in concentrations of up to 50%; however, the most commonly used concentrations range from 10% to 30%. TCA is available to estheticians in concentrations ranging from 7% to 12%. As with stronger peels, TCA peels should be used with caution and only under the direction of a physician. Depending on the number of layers applied, even lower strengths may be harmful and will produce frosting of the skin (see **The Three Levels of Blanching**).

Note: A general protocol that covers superficial TCA, as well as BHA and Modified Jessner's immediately follows this section.

Indications for Treatment
- Photo-damaged skin
- Hyperpigmentation including actinic keratoses (a warty lesion, often premalignant, occurring on sun-exposed skin of the face or hands, especially of light-skinned persons)
- Acne grades I, II, and III
- Acne scarring
- Fine lines, wrinkles, and laxity

Contraindications to Treatment
- Pregnancy or nursing/lactating
- Current use of topical or internal antibiotics
- Accutane use within the last year
- Open cold sores
- Unusual tendency to scar
- Cancer
- Autoimmune disease
- Fitzpatrick skin types V or VI for medical-grade
- Smokers will not have as good of a result because the skin will be asphyxiated

What the Client Should Expect
- Tingling or burning sensation during treatment
- Sensitivity or redness up to five days
- Tightening and dryness of the skin
- Peeling commonly occurs three to five days following the treatment

Protocol General Protocol for Salicylic (BHA), Modified Jessner's, and superficial TCA

Note: The difference between these protocols and AHA, are that these peels are *most often* layered and left on the skin, whereas AHAs are timed and neutralized.

1. Review the client's history form and have him/her sign a consent form, including possible adverse effects and post-treatment care (sample in Appendix C).

2. Thoroughly explain each step of the treatment, including the importance of keeping the eyes closed and providing feedback regarding skin sensation; i.e. "I will be asking how your skin feels on a scale of one to 10; one is barely anything at all, 10 would be an extreme burning sensation."

3. Prepare supplies including a timer and a hand-held fan to minimize discomfort.

4. Cleanse the skin thoroughly with a gel cleanser, repeat if necessary.

5. Degrease the skin with alcohol, acetone, or specified prepping solution to remove excess oils and allow for a more even application. **Note**: *This can alter the effects of the peel, if there are concerns of sensitivity this step can be skipped; if more aggressive peeling is sought, acetone may be used.*

6. Any sensitized areas of the skin, including the corners of the eyes, the lip border, and under the nostrils, must be covered with an occlusive agent, such as Vaseline, Aquaphor, or any petrolatum-based product. Let the client know they will experience a stinging or warm sensation.

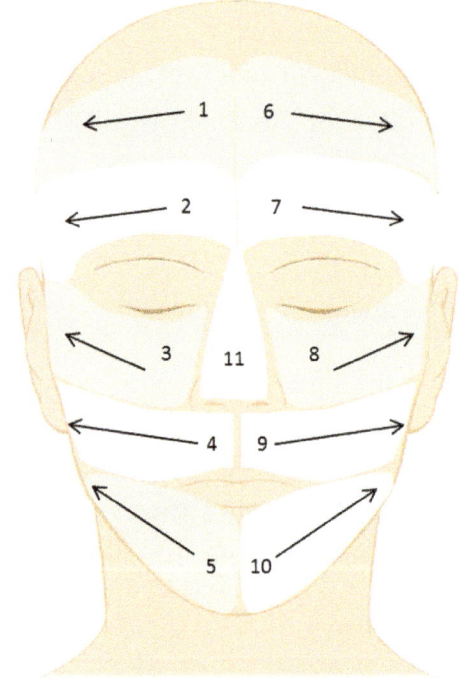

Chemical Exfoliation: AHAs. BHAs, TCA, Jessner's

Start applying the peel with a 2 × 2 gauze or cotton pad beginning at the forehead according to the diagram as shown. **Note:** Since the strength of these peels is heightened as they are layered, they must be applied evenly, opposed to AHAs where timing determines strength. Ask the client to rate the peeling sensation based on the scale of 1 to 10 as discussed prior to the treatment. If the patient is extremely uncomfortable, 5 or above, no additional layers should be applied. Remember to fan clients' skin if they are uncomfortable. *Note: Salicylic acid should not be fanned unless necessary as it can decrease the effectiveness of the peel. The number of layers per peel differs according to the acids used, the percentages, and pH level; it is extremely important to follow individual manufacturer instructions on the maximum number of layers.*

7. Once the peel has set for the indicated time *and* the client's skin sensation has reduced to a 2 or below, additional layers may be applied. **Note:** *Each additional layer should start on the opposite side of the face, as the first layer will have more product on it.*

8. Once the appropriate number of layers is applied, topical products will penetrate more effectively. Apply an antioxidant serum, a corrective product according to the client's concerns, a hydrating product, and a zinc-oxide based sunscreen.

9. Educate the client on proper skin care and give specific post-treatment care instructions with a written copy to take home.

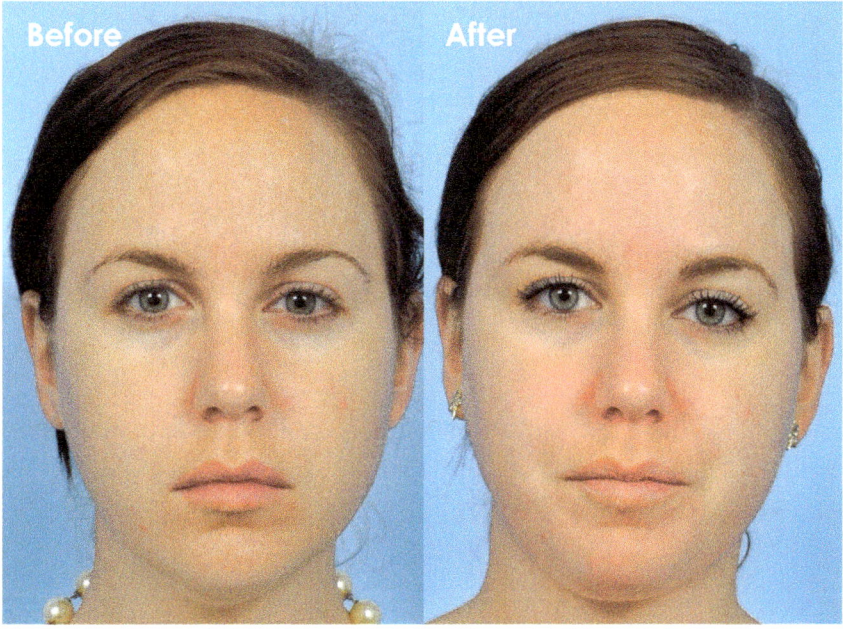

Before and 10 days after one treatment with a 15% TCA peel.

Post-treatment Care Instructions
- The peel should be left on the skin for at least six hours for best results.
- Excessive sun should be avoided and an SPF 30 sunscreen should be worn every day for a minimum of two weeks following the peel.
- The client must not pick or pull at loose, peeling skin; it could result in hyperpigmentation or scarring. If there are large pieces of peeling skin, it may be trimmed with manicure scissors.
- Extra moisturizing agents should be added for the next five days to prevent excess dryness or irritation.
- The client should refrain from activities that will cause excess heat in the skin such as aerobic exercise, steam baths, hot showers and saunas for at least 48 hours following the treatment.

Deep Peels Performed by Medical Professionals

Deep chemical peeling agents, including phenol and Baker's Gordon, can produce dramatic results for reducing the appearance of photo-damage, wrinkles, large pores and acne scarring in some patients. These aggressive peels that extend down to the reticular layer of the dermis are rarely used due to the higher incidence of adverse effects associated with them and the availability of other options. Chemical peels at this level have a much higher chance of causing infections, severe hyperpigmentation, hypopigmentation, and even scarring.[7] Phenol, one agent used for deep peeling, may cause significant toxicity, as it is absorbed through the skin, metabolized by the liver, and excreted through the kidneys.[8] Phenol is extremely uncomfortable and requires the patient to be under local or general anesthesia. The downtime associated with a phenol peel is generally two weeks followed by two to three months of severe redness and sensitivity. Deep peels are rarely used anymore; they are now often a last resort for patients with extreme scarring on the skin.

References
1. HJ Brody et al, A history of chemical peeling, *Dermatologic Surgery*, 26 (5), 405–409 (2000).
2. MA Farage et al, Characteristics of the aging skin, *Adv Wound Care (New Rochelle)*, 2(1), 5–10 (2013).
3. FF Becker et al, A histological comparison of 50% and 70% glycolic acid peels using solutions with various pHs, *Dermatol Surg*, 22 (5), 463-5 (1996).
4. M Alam et al, Glycolic acid peels compared to microdermabrasion: A right-left controlled trial of efficacy and patient satisfaction, *Dermatol Surg*, 28(6), 475-9 (2002).
5. EJ Van Scott and RJ Yu, Alpha hydroxy acids: Procedures for use in clinical practice, *Cutis*, 43, 222-228 (1989).
6. SJ Kim et al, Increased in vivo collagen synthesis and in vitro cell proliferative

effect of glycolic acid, *Dermatol Surg*, 24 (10), 1054-1058 (1998).

7. MI Rendon et al, Evidence and considerations in the application of chemical peels in skin disorders and aesthetic resurfacing, *J Clin Aesthet Dermatol*, 3(7), 32–43 (2010).

8. AH Hall and BH Rumack, eds, *CCIS*, Volume 160, accessed at: *http://toxnet.nlm.nih.gov/cgi-bin/sis/search/a?dbs+hsdb:@term+@DOCNO+113*, on Feb 11, 2014; original publication data as follows: CL Corey, Facial chemical peels, Baylor College of Medicine website, *www.bcm.edu/oto/grand/11_10_05.htm*, website now inactive.

CHAPTER 14

Microdermabrasion

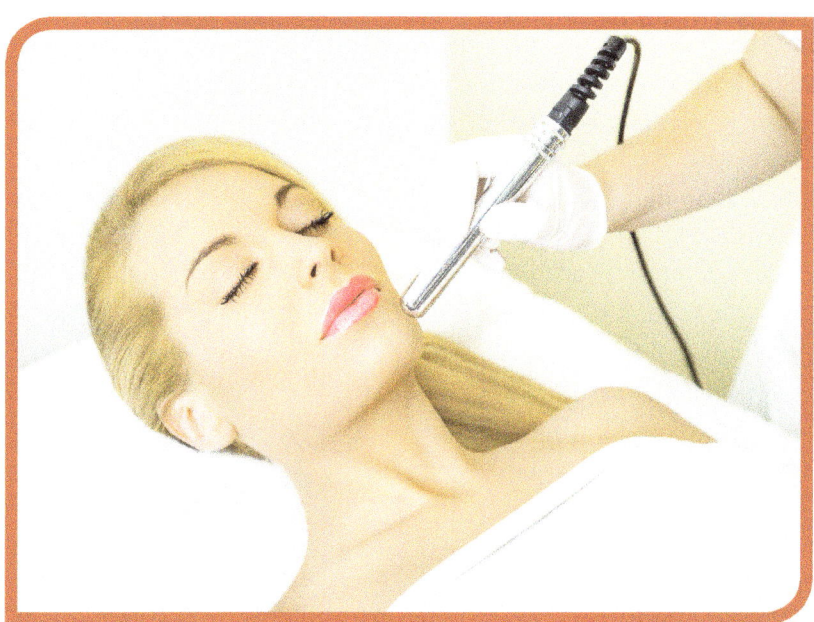

In This Chapter:
- What is Microdermabrasion?
- Indications and Contraindications
- Treatment Expectations
- Treatment Protocol
- Factors Affecting Results

What is Microdermabrasion?

The term *microdermabrasion* refers to a technology using suction and a rough surface to exfoliate the superficial keratinized layers of skin. It was developed in Italy in the mid-1980s, achieving wide popularity in Europe before being introduced in the United States in the mid-1990s. It is one of the top five non-surgical cosmetic procedures being performed in a medical office.

A microdermabrasion treatment involves a trained technician mechanically exfoliating the skin through a hand piece. These devices most commonly use abrasive particles such as aluminum oxide crystals, sodium bicarbonate salts, or a micronized diamond-tip as the

Micronized diamond-tip

method of exfoliation. As the hand piece is gently glided over the skin, the particles or diamond-tip are directed on the outermost layers of the skin. At the same time, the crystals and detached keratinized cells are drawn into a waste container of the machine via suction. This combination of exfoliation and suction creates a mild stimulating response in the skin, similar to that of superficial chemical peeling methods.

Aluminum oxide crystals were the first to be used with microdermabrasion. Aluminum oxide is the second hardest material—second only to diamond. Aluminum oxide is an inert substance, meaning that it will not cause any chemical reaction, including allergies; care should be taken around the eyes due to the chance of eye irritation. Sodium bicarbonate is an organic form of crystals used for microdermabrasion. This organic alternative's advantages are that the crystals are fine and polished, and their alkaline nature can help to reduce acne. Sodium bicarbonate may not be as effective for those needing a more aggressive treatment, but can be used closer to the eyes than aluminum oxide crystals and are easily removed with water.

> **Tip:**
> If a client has a sensitivity to a product though not to touch, the use of microdermabrasion should be a first option for superficial exfoliation. On the other hand, if the client is sensitive to touch, but not product, an AHA or salicylic acid peel may be better.

Diamond-tip microdermabrasion was developed in 1999. There are different grades that can be used, from very fine for sensitive skin to coarse for thicker skin types. Eliminating the use of crystals has advantages and disadvantages. The advantages are that it removes the worry of inhaling crystals, there is no residue left on the skin, there are no concerns about harming the eyes, and the procedure has lower overall costs because you do not have to replenish the crystals. The disadvantages of the diamond-tip technique include higher initial investment and an increased risk of contamination if proper sanitizing methods are not followed.

As new technology is constantly arising, the use of "wet microdermabrasion" devices has been gaining popularity. These devices employ a diamond tip to *resurface* the skin while simultaneously delivering topical products to the superficial layers of the skin. Many of these topical products include hyaluronic acid to hydrate and soften the skin; others include skin lightening agents, antioxidants, and even mild chemical exfoliants. The idea of applying products to the skin while exfoliating for better penetration is great; however, if the ultimate purpose of the microdermabrasion treatment is to exfoliate, it makes sense that if the skin were dry, a deeper exfoliation would occur. Newer devices have the ability to work as either dry or wet, providing multiple options for the user. The use of simultaneous hydrating products allows for a more comfortable, gentle procedure for those clients too sensitive for more aggressive treatments using the rough tip alone.

The variety of devices and means of exfoliation can make it difficult to choose which method to use. As each of these methods has their pros and cons, it is up to the technician to decide which is best for them and their clients. When choosing a device, research several distributors. A good rule to follow when choosing any device is to examine at least three companies. Make sure the company offers a warranty. Call other customers for feedback on customer service, and find out the cost of consumables including maintenance on the device.

Indications for Treatment

While results vary among individuals, microdermabrasion has been reported to improve the appearance of the skin. This widely used exfoliation method softens fine lines, reduces superficial skin discoloration, evens the texture of the skin, provides the skin with a healthy glow, and can improve non-inflammatory acne conditions. Microdermabrasion should not be promoted to remove deep wrinkles, acne scars or dermal pigmentation, as it is not intended to reach the dermis. (Chapter 8 on Skin Analysis discusses how you can check for dermal pigmentation.) Although some clients do see improvement in these conditions with multiple treatments, it should not be overstated. The treatment of dermal conditions often requires deep resurfacing and should be conducted under the guidance of a medical professional. The laws surrounding who can legally perform microdermabrasion treatments vary from state to state. In most states, licensed estheticians can exfoliate and stimulate the superficial epidermis, which describes the use of microdermabrasion. As with all treatments, it is important to check individual state regulations to see requirements. Additionally, microdermabrasion should never be used for inflamed skin conditions including grade III or IV acne, rosacea, eczema, and psoriasis. Microdermabrasion can exacerbate these conditions and cause further inflammation.

Indications
- Fine lines and wrinkles
- Superficial skin discoloration
- Uneven textured skin
- Non-inflamed acne conditions
- Stimulate circulation

Alternative Indications
- Keratosis pilaris (**pictured**)
- Body resurfacing (hands, elbows, back, décolleté, knees)
- Preparing the skin for topical treatments
- Before a superficial chemical peel to increase effectiveness
- To remove crusted pigmentation seven to 10 days after non-ablative laser treatments

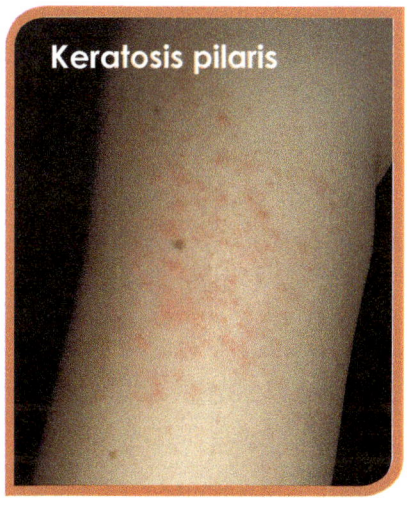
Keratosis pilaris

Contraindications include but are not limited to:
- Vitamin A products or alpha hydroxy acids (If these are being used, they should be discontinued 24 hours before treatment.)
- Isotretinoin use within six months
- Cold sores or open wounds on the skin
- Pregnancy (for devices using crystals)
- Inflamed acne (grades III and IV)
- Rosacea
- Presence of burns, rashes, or infection
- Broken capillaries

Treatment Expectations

During a microdermabrasion treatment, the client should be seated in a reclining chair or on a facial bed under soft lights, with the eyes covered for protection. Depending on the particular method being used (i.e. diamond-tip), keeping the eyes closed may be adequate. The client may feel a rough scrubbing sensation as the hand piece moves over the face. Microdermabrasion is not painful. In fact, when compared with superficial chemical peels, many clients say that microdermabrasion is more comfortable. A physician may choose to do a more aggressive microdermabrasion treatment, by going over the face several times on a high setting. This can go to a deeper level and lead to pinpoint bleeding. However, a treatment performed outside a medical setting should never reach this level.

A microdermabrasion treatment can be completed in less than 30 minutes. Treatments are commonly done in a series, from as few as three treatments to as many as 12. While a series will show greater improvement on the appearance of certain skin conditions including fine lines, discoloration, and large pores, it is important to remember that even one treatment can be beneficial. The number and timing of treatments depends on the patient's skin type, skin condition, and schedule. For best results, it is recommended that treatments be done at least two weeks apart so that there is sufficient time for the stratum corneum to heal.

A superficial microdermabrasion should not require downtime if it is performed correctly. Following the treatment, the client's face should feel refreshed and a healthy glow can be expected. Although the face may be slightly pink, clients can return to work immediately, and makeup may be applied instantly following treatment. Microdermabrasion is designed to rejuvenate and refresh the skin without an extended recovery period. Without question, these advantages are what makes it one of the most popular "lunch-time procedures."

Post-treatment Expectations

Microdermabrasion removes a portion of the skin's protective barrier (the stratum corneum), leaving the skin more vulnerable to external factors. Following treatment, a client may be more sensitive to topical products including makeup, botanicals, fragrances, acids, and preservatives. It is therefore essential to know what products the client is using before performing the procedure. Sun exposure, extremes in temperature, and aggressive topical products should be avoided for at least 48 hours following the treatment. Medical professionals may choose to use a medium or deep chemical peel after microdermabrasion, or even use it as preparation for certain laser treatments including intense pulsed light (IPL) and mild laser resurfacing.

Factors Affecting Microdermabrasion Results
- The type of machine used
- The type of crystals or coarseness of diamond tip
- The level of crystal flow
- The amount of suction used
- Speed of the application by the technician
- The number of passes done on the skin
- The condition of the client's skin before the treatment

Microdermabrasion Machine

A microdermabrasion machine with individual settings for crystal and diamond technology treatments.

Image of Megapeel EX courtesy of DermaMed Solutions and *Skin Inc*.

Protocol

1. Review the client intake form and look for any contraindications to treatment.
2. Consult with the client, answering any questions and providing detailed information about the treatment.
3. Reiterate to the client that the skin may be a little sensitive following the treatment.
4. Have the client sign a consent form that states all possible complications.
5. Cleanse the skin thoroughly with a gel cleanser.
6. Degrease the skin using alcohol or acetone; this will result in a more effective exfoliation. (If the client's skin is too sensitive for degreasing, skip this step.)
7. Set the levels of suction and crystal flow (or the level of the diamond-tip) according to the manufacturer's instructions for the client's skin type and conditions.
8. Test the device to ensure it is working properly; you can do this by testing it on your arm prior to applying the sanitized tip to avoid cross-contamination.
9. Apply a properly sanitized tip to the hand piece before each treatment.
10. While holding the skin taut with your non-dominant hand, use your prominent hand to move the hand piece gently across the skin.

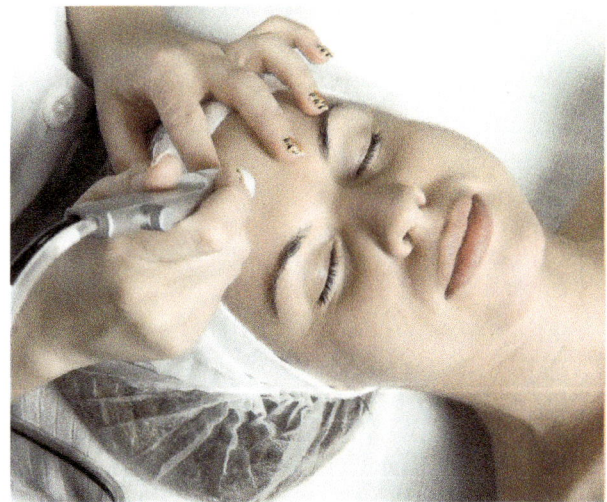

11. Following a consistent pattern that uses vertical and horizontal movements in

each section will ensure safe, predictable results. (An optional pattern is shown in the chart, pictured.) Beginning technicians tend to use smaller sections and shorter strokes for more control, while experienced technicians tend to use longer movements on larger sections.

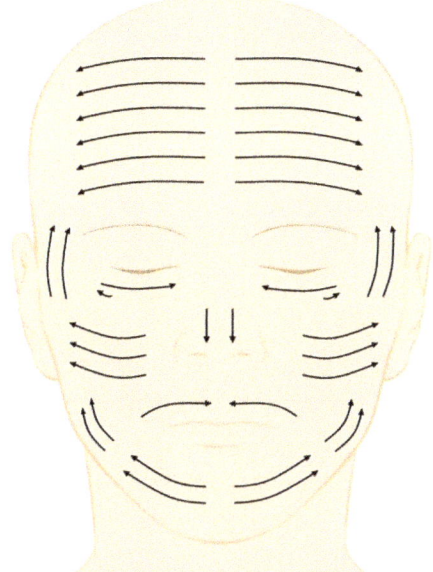
1st Pass (horizontal)

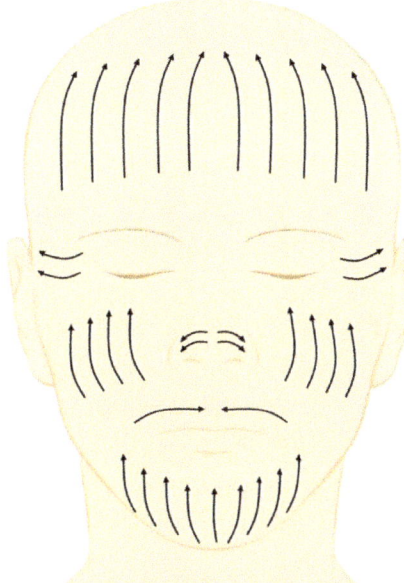
2nd Pass (vertical)

12. You may at this point, using your discretion, go over any pigmented areas, larger pores, scarring, or uneven texture.
13. If another treatment is being performed, use extra caution. The skin may be more sensitive to topical treatments and products.
14. Following treatment, apply an antioxidant serum, a moisturizer, and broad-spectrum sunscreen.
15. Go over post-treatment instructions making particular note of avoiding excess sun exposure and the use of an SPF 30 for at least two weeks.
16. Educate the client on the importance of home care to enhance and maintain results.
17. Follow OSHA regulations for disposing of crystals and properly sanitizing the machine.

Tips for Safe, Effective Treatment

- Perform a patch test on a hidden area before beginning the treatment.
- Cover the client's eyes with goggles or eye protectors while using crystal methods.
- The hand piece should be perpendicular to the skin, with no gaps between it and the surface of the skin.
- The hand piece should be always be moving when in contact with the skin.
- The skin must be held taut at all times.
- When breaking suction make sure to "feather-off" the face, as opposed to lifting it quickly.
- The hand piece should be glided gently without applying any pressure.
- Adjust the suction for sensitive areas of the face: i.e. settings for under the eyes and neck should be reduced to half of what was used on the rest of the face.
- Work in an even pattern, going over every area vertically and horizontally.
- Overlap stripes slightly to avoid leaving marks on the skin.
- NEVER go over the eyelids. Some companies claim it safe, but it is unnecessary and can be damaging. The skin on the eyelids is much different than that of other areas; the lack of support structure alone should indicate that using suction on this area would not be beneficial.
- Follow OSHA guidelines for disposal of used crystals.
- Follow maintenance instructions to ensure consistent, safe results.

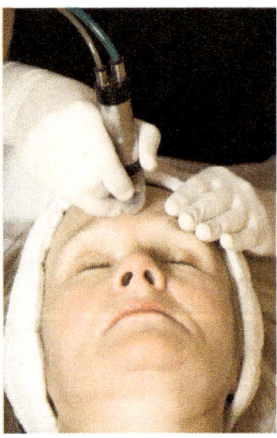
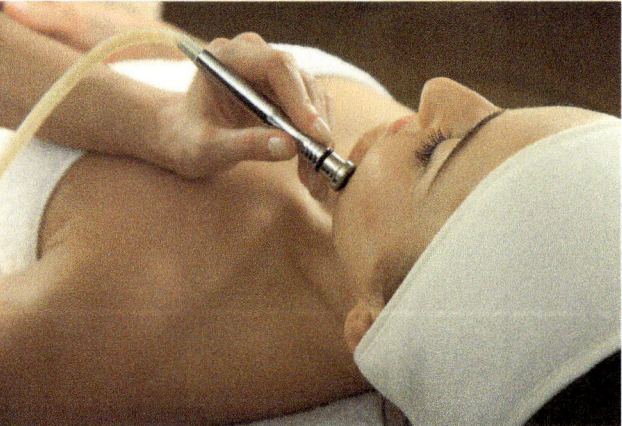

CHAPTER 15

Dermaplaning

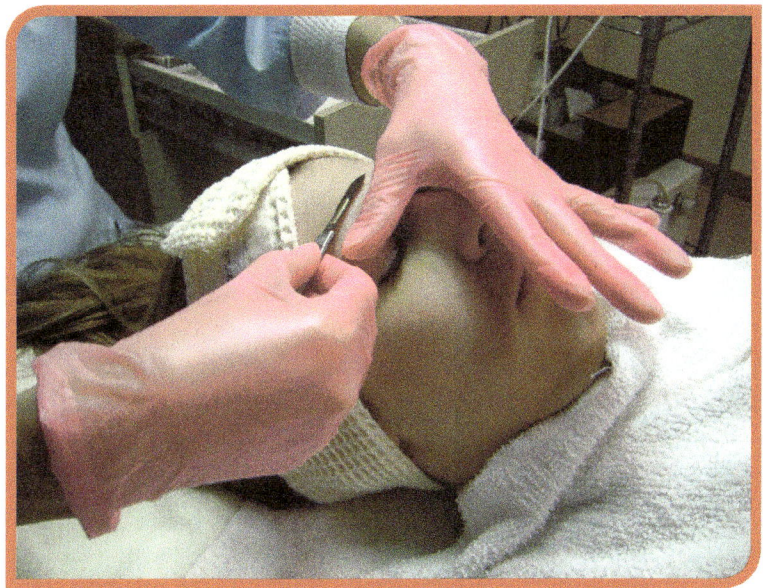

In this Chapter:
- What is Dermaplaning?
- The Procedure
- What the Client Can Expect
- Cautions and Contraindications

What is Dermaplaning?

Dermaplaning is a simple and safe procedure for exfoliating the epidermis and ridding the skin of fine vellus hair ("peach fuzz"). Although this procedure has been used for many years, it is still a unique service that few skin care professionals offer. One reason is that regulations on estheticians performing this treatment vary from state to state and some licensing boards make answers unclear by couching their respective regulations in vague, inconclusive language. Estheticians are allowed to work on the non-living superficial layers of the epidermis in most states; however, dermaplaning utilizes a scalpel, which is considered a medical instrument. It is important for the provider to use their best judgment when answers are unclear. It is the opinion of most professionals that dermaplaning should only be performed under the direction of a physician.

When patients hear the word *dermaplaning,* they may associate the term with the procedure known as *dermabrasion,* and wouldn't even consider it as a treatment. Dermabrasion, unlike dermaplaning, is a medical procedure in which the skin is abraded down to the dermis using a whisk-like device. Dermaplaning, on the other hand, is a superficial technique that requires a scalpel to perform a simple "shaving" of the skin with a precise, delicate touch by the provider.

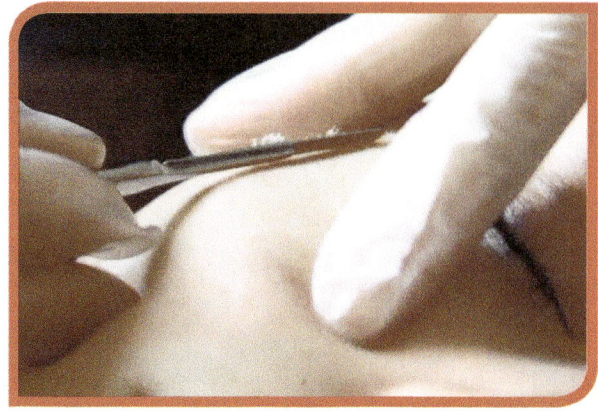

Dermaplaning provides an immediate result with a low chance of adverse effects when the technician is properly trained and practices safe measures. This treatment is gaining popularity among cosmetic medical providers, as it is a great treatment on its own and also can be used to compliment certain medical treatments. Indications for treatment include a dry or dehydrated epidermis, fine lines, wrinkles, grades I or II acne, and the presence of vellus hair. It can also be used to superficially remove dead skin, allowing products to penetrate more effectively, as well as between certain laser and light therapies to remove raised areas of superficial pigmentation. This is also a great treatment to offer clients who are pregnant or nursing and are looking for a more effective exfoliation method while they cannot use exfoliating acids due to the risk of certain chemicals being absorbed into the bloodstream. **Clients who have an excess amount of vellus hair particularly favor dermaplaning for the smooth texture that results after the hair removal.** This hair can also trap dead skin cells and oils in the follicles, resulting in clogged pores; thus removing the hair yields clearer looking skin.

Superficial pigment post-laser.

Although merely an old wives' tale, many patients are concerned that the hair will grow back heavier and darker following a dermaplaning procedure. You can calm your client's fears, and tell them that as long as the hair is superficial vellus hair, it will grow back at the same rate and texture as before the treatment. **It is important to warn the client that when the hair initially grows back it may feel blunt at first, but this should not be confused with "thicker" hair growth.**

Removing superficial keratinized cells on the epidermis has the additional benefit of allowing products to penetrate more effectively. It is most commonly used to prepare the skin for superficial chemical peels or before performing a cleansing facial.

Physicians also recommend dermaplaning in preparation for medical procedures including micro-needling, laser treatments, and medium-depth chemical peels.

Indications
- Vellus hair removal
- Acne grades I or II
- Dry or dehydrated epidermis
- Preparing the skin for topical treatments
- Before a superficial chemical peel to increase effectiveness
- To remove crusted pigmentation 7 to 10 days after non-ablative laser treatments

Contraindications include but are not limited to:
- Blood thinners
- Uncontrolled diabetes
- Terminal hair growth
- Cold sores or open wounds on the skin
- Inflamed acne (grades III or IV)
- Inflamed rosacea
- Presence of burns, rashes, or infection

What the Client Can Expect

There is no downtime associated with this procedure, unless of course a superficial scratch adversely appears. Clients can expect a smooth, glowing appearance and a nice canvas for the application of makeup. The patient should be educated about the importance of using sunscreen, because the skin may be more sensitized in the days following treatment. Dermaplaning is most commonly performed on a monthly basis, but can be done as often as every two weeks. Clients see the best results when using a customized daily skin care regimen to address any underlying concerns.

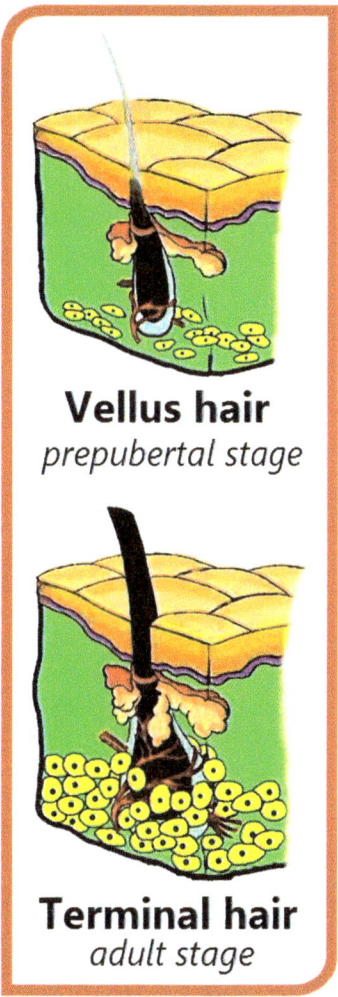

Vellus hair
prepubertal stage

Terminal hair
adult stage

Supplies Needed:
- Cleanser
- Degreaser (alcohol; acetone)
- Tissue
- Scalpel
- No.10 blade (it is recommended to use the blunt edge)
- Blade remover
- Moisturizer
- Sunscreen

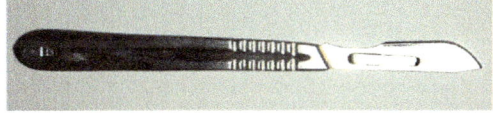

Protocol

1. Consult with the patient. Inform him/her about the details of the procedure, making note that, although unlikely, there is a chance that they may obtain a superficial scrape or nick on the skin.
2. Have the patient sign a consent form that states they are fully aware of the possibilities of complications.
3. Clean the patient's skin thoroughly. Using a cleanser with mild keratolytic properties, such as beta- or alpha hydroxy acids, will loosen dead skin and allow for a deeper exfoliation.
4. If the skin is not sensitive, acetone or alcohol may be used to enhance the depth of treatment.
5. Prepare the scalpel by carefully applying a No. 10 blade according to manufacturer instructions.
6. Make sure the client's skin is *completely dry*. Blot with facial tissues or fan the skin. If the skin has any moisture on it, there is more of a chance of nicking the skin, and the treatment will not be as effective.
7. Before beginning treatment, make it clear to the client that they must keep still during the procedure. Tell them to let you know if they feel they are going to sneeze or need to make any other sudden movements, such as satisfying a facial itch.
8. Developing a pattern, such as starting at one side of the face and finishing at the other, will help ensure that all areas are covered (see left- and right-hand diagrams).
9. Holding a 2-3 inch section taut and starting at the forehead, perform a back-sweeping motion to gain control before lightly abrading the surface in an upward motion with the blade at a 45-degree angle using precise, controlled movements.
10. After the entire area has been treated, place a hydrating moisturizer and sunscreen on the skin to finish the treatment.

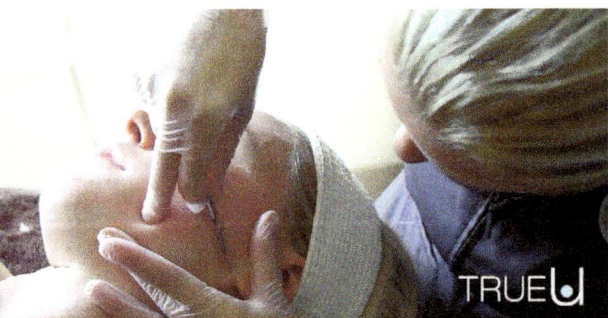

11. If another treatment is going to be performed, ensure that you use extra caution: The peel will penetrate more deeply after the superficial layers have been removed.

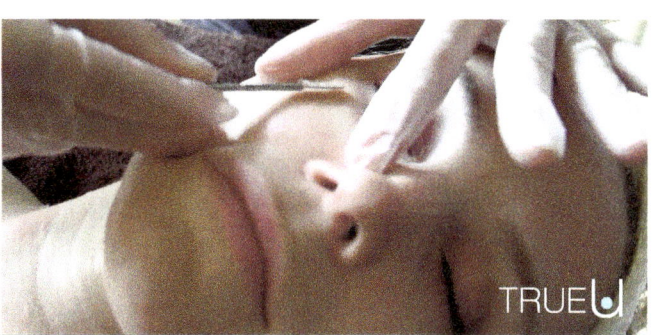

Dermaplaning - Left hand

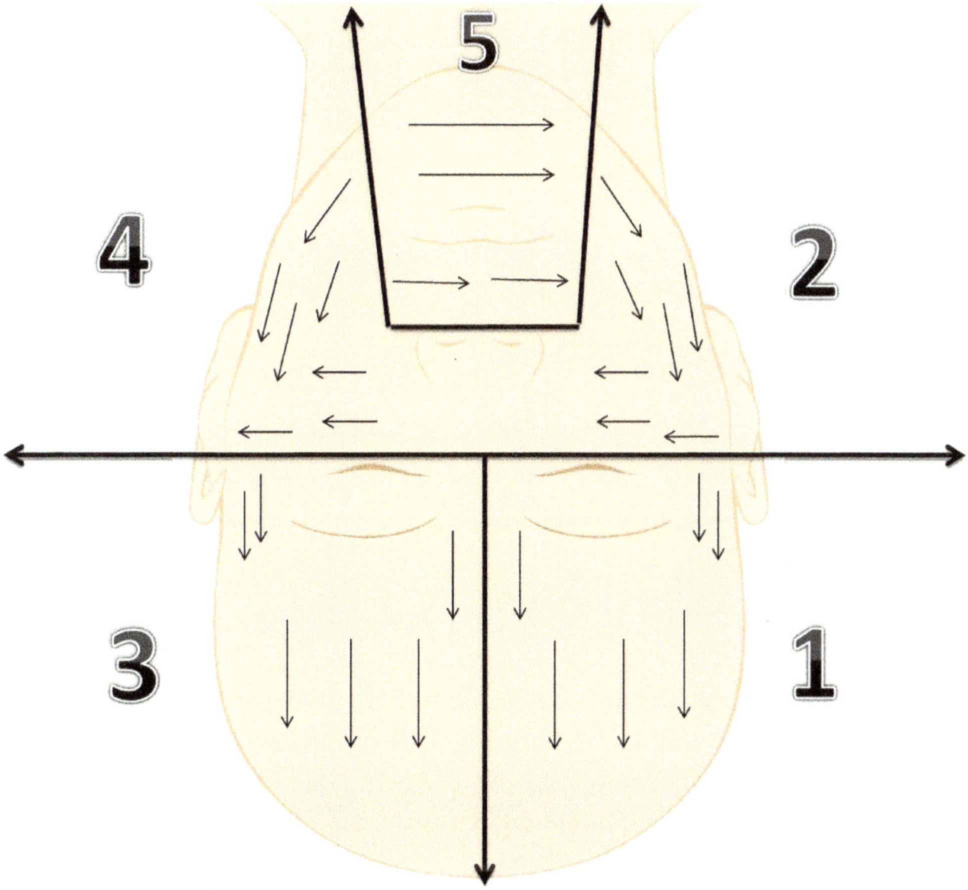

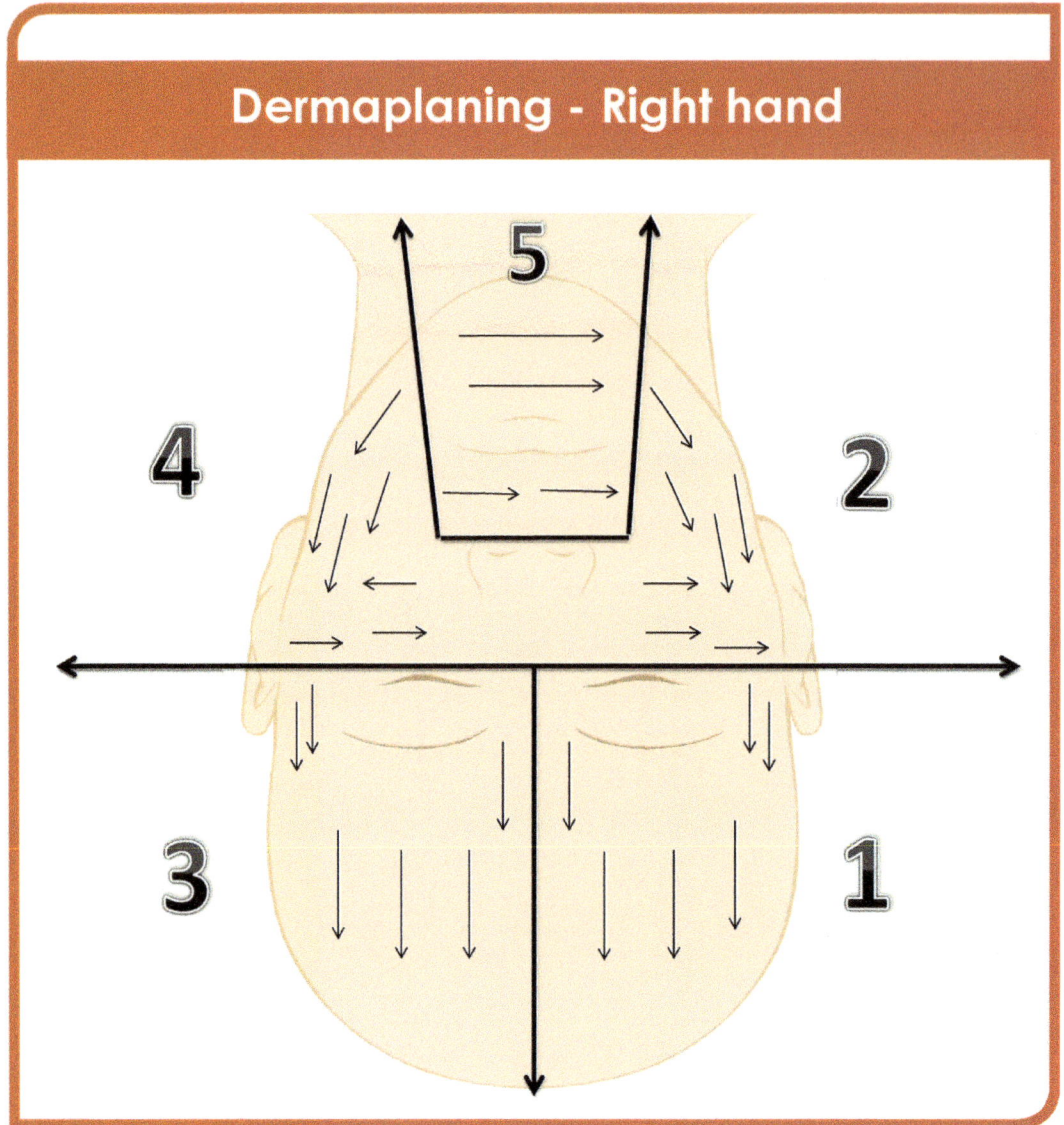

Dermaplaning Cautions and Contraindications

Dermaplaning should not be performed on clients who are on blood thinners; if there were a mishap that caused bleeding, even if due to a superficial cut or scrape, it could be difficult to control. The same goes for uncontrolled diabetes. In cases such as these, were something to happen the body does not have the ability to heal a facial wound quickly. It is furthermore important to avoid raised lesions on the skin; therefore, the treatment should not be performed on those with numerous lesions that can get in the way. Inflamed acne is another condition in which dermaplaning should not be performed; apart from the raised lesions, it could cause a more severe breakout. In oily skin types, think of the hair as a wick that carries excess sebum out of the follicle.

CHAPTER 16

Micro-needling

In this Chapter:
- History of Micro-needling
- Indications and Contraindications
- Devices Used for Needling
- Non-medical Treatment Protocol
- The Stages of Wound Healing

A Brief History of Micro-needling

Micro-needling, commonly called collagen induction therapy or CIT, is quickly becoming one of the most sought-after methods for skin rejuvenation. Micro-needling is a procedure used to create a controlled wound response without abrading the epidermis. As discussed earlier, *controlled wound response* means to stimulate a wound response to improve the appearance of the skin. The motivation for the wound response is to essentially thicken the skin. Dr. Des Fernandes, the pioneer of collagen induction therapy,[1] stated, if we are trying to thicken the skin then why are we removing the superficial layers? It was a question and challenge both, and as aesthetic treatments have evolved, the use of fractional modalities have become favored by many providers due to the reduction in downtime and lowered chance of complications.

Skin needling for skin rejuvenation was originally discovered by Dr. Orentreich in 1995 with the use of 18–20 gauge single needles to reduce the depressions in scars and deep wrinkles.[2] This individual needling technique showed great improvement for these lesions but also showed rejuvenation in the surrounding skin. In 1996, Dr. Fernandes developed a stamp-like device to cover a larger area by inserting multiple needles at a time.[1] In 1997 Dr. Andre Camirand published his experience using a tattoo gun without ink on hypochromic scars. Like Dr. Orentriech, Camirand also discovered improvements in the appearance of the skin around the treated scars.[3]

The first dermal roller, released in 2004 by a German inventor named Horst Lieble, was called (simply enough) the *Dermaroller*, and it led to the development of percutaneous collagen induction therapy by Dr. Fernandes. Other companies soon followed, boosting micro-needling's status as one of the most popular skin rejuvenation techniques.

The premise of micro-needling is similar to that of other methods aimed at skin rejuvenation by triggering a wound response, namely fractionated devices that are targeting specific portions of the skin. The idea behind treating portions of the skin is to leave support skin for the growth of new, healthy tissue and allow for a quicker healing time along with improved results. Human skin is amazingly resilient yet complex in its methods of protection and repair; in order to create a wound response, there are several things to take into consideration including skin type, skin conditions, Fitzpatrick skin type, and skin density, among others. It is known that no two people have the same exact skin, and this is why there are a variety of techniques available for overall skin rejuvenation. Many clients and providers alike think that the more aggressive the treatment, the better the result; this is not always the case. There is definitely a place for stronger treatments, but dependent on the skin type, a superficial treatment can provide great benefit without increased risks. The key word is *controlled,* when the objective is to create a controlled wound response. Of course, there are things out of one's control, which is why it is important to state plainly, beforehand, any and all possible side effects and complications with any procedure. The goal in skin rejuvenation is to stimulate the skin just enough to trigger a mild wound-healing, resulting in increased growth factors and collagen stimulation. If the skin does not have the ability to heal, the treatment could be ineffective or, worse, create an actual wound. This is yet another reason that a thorough consultation and skin analysis are essential; certain medical conditions, environmental factors, and skin conditions can cause an impaired wound response.

> Many clients and providers alike think that the more aggressive the treatment, the better the result; this is not always the case.

> The goal is to create a wound response, not a wound.

There are several methods for skin needling available, including stamps, rollers, and automated devices. The stamps are not as frequently used but can be more cost-effective as they are simply made of a plastic handle with needles on the end. The rollers have a higher price point, for the simple reason that more goes into making them and they can average 200 needles per device. The rolling method seems to be the most commonly used, due to its easy accessibility to providers and clients alike, although new modalities are constantly being developed. As the roller showed great improvement in the appearance of the skin, companies have found ways to make the treatment safer and more effective. The most recent development is the use of an automated needling device or

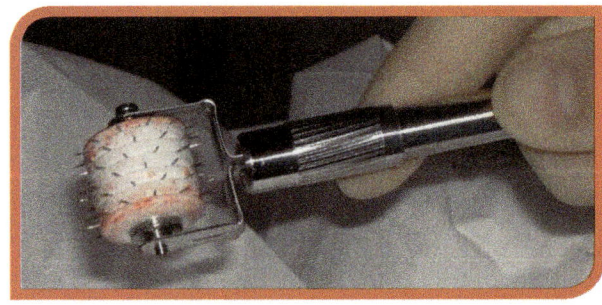
Needling stamp device

a "pen." Automated needling is aimed at providing the user with more consistent needling, using vertical insertion to reduce the risk of tears in the skin. Needling devices have other benefits as well, including ease of use with an ergonomically comfortable device and the ability to alter the needle depth during treatment. This new technology is changing the scary thought of a provider using a drum-like rolling device aggressively over the skin (some say it resembles a meat tenderizer). The rollers can be painful, produce excessive bleeding on the skin, and leave the skin with prolonged erythema. The automated needling is performed in a controlled manner making side effects less probable and results more profound, as shown in the following before and after examples.

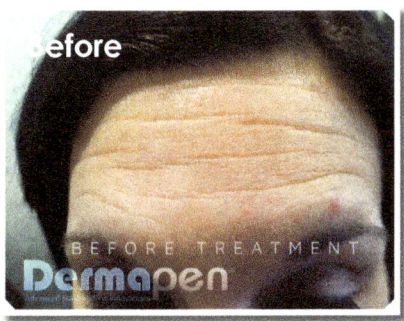
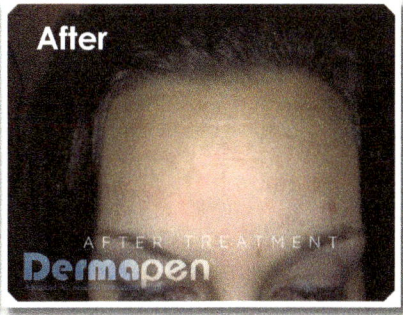

Wound Healing Stages

■ *Inflammatory Stage: up to four days after injury*
Injury causes platelet release to clot bleeding. Immune cells are introduced to fight off potential bacteria. The use of hydrating agents, antioxidants and sun protection is vital.

■ *Proliferative Phase: up to 42 days after injury*
Angiogenesis aids in the formation of blood vessels and oxygen supply. Growth factors are released from fibroblasts, keratinocytes, and monocytes. The use of hydrating agents, antioxidants, and sun protection is still necessary. Stem cells, peptides, or growth factors can likewise be introduced.

■ *Remodeling Phase: up to two years*
Skin tissue remodels itself in an organized fashion. Vascular lesions mature. Collagen III (younger, fresh collagen present in wound healing) turns into Collagen I (tougher, longer-lasting collagen), and the skin is tightened. The use of home care products including antioxidants, sunscreens, and moisturizers will help continue to enhance and maintain results.

As with most cosmetic treatments available today, micro-needling treatments can be performed at grades that range from superficial to deep, depending on several factors. Needle depths typically range from 0.2 mm, which only affects the epidermis, to 3.0 mm, which can reach the reticular dermis. The gauge or width of the needle is another important factor; ranges are typically between 18 gauge and 34 gauge, most commonly 30 to 34 gauges are used. (Note: the larger the number, the more narrow the needle). Additionally, the amount of punctures per square centimeter (cm^2) can make the treatment more conservative or aggressive. This can be altered by the number of passes, as well as the speed on specific automated devices. Regardless of the device, needles should never be reused. Used needles must be disposed of according to OSHA regulations. This point is yet another advantage to using automated needling devices—rolling devices are typically a higher cost per treatment, since the entire device must be disposed of following use. Needling devices may have an initial higher cost, but the tips are disposable, cutting down on long-term costs.

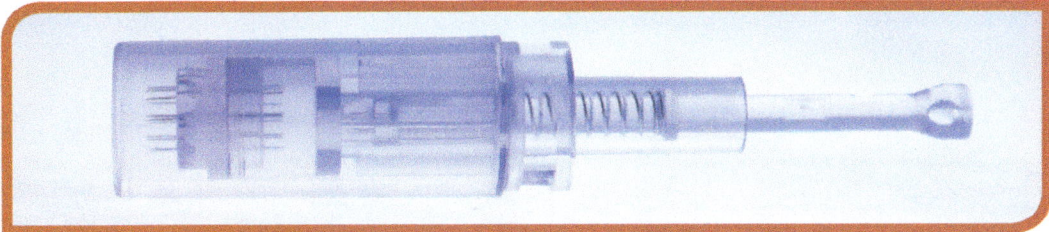

Tip for micro-needling device

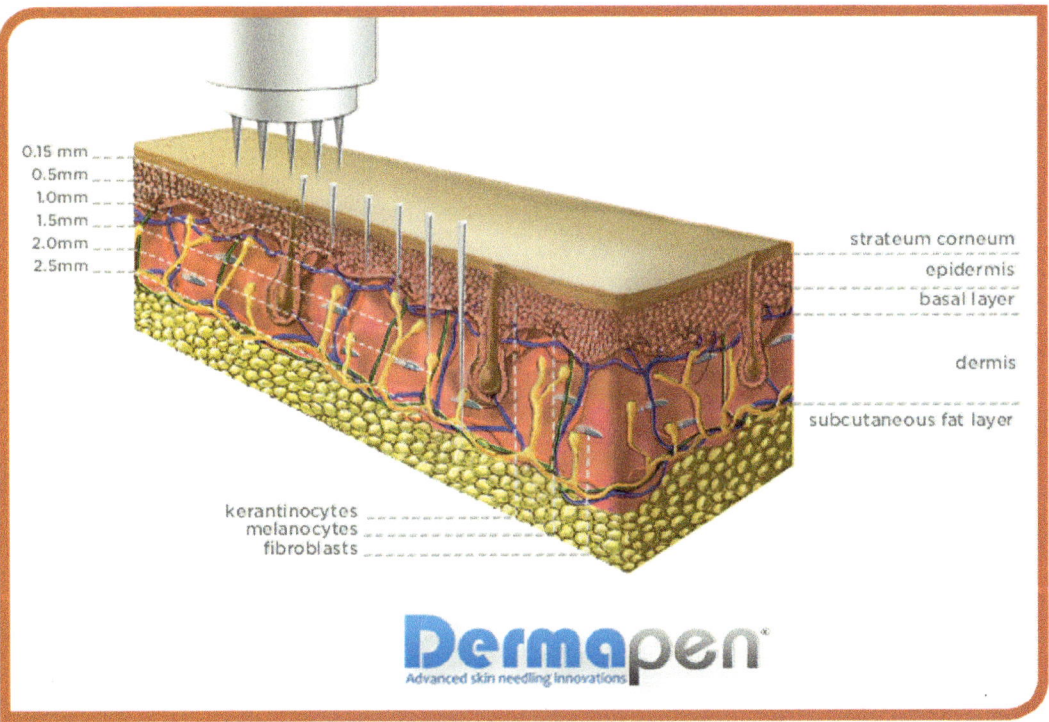

Targeted areas by needle depth

Piercing the skin not only stimulates the growth of vital skin components, but also forms micro-channels through the epidermis that allow topical products to penetrate more effectively. Micro-needling can be related to aerating a lawn, whereby puncturing holes in the ground provides pathways for fertilizer to enter. Studies show that micro-channels can remain open for up to one hour. Since the skin heals better in a moist environment, it is important to apply hydrating products containing hyaluronic acid following treatment. Hyaluronic acid is a natural substance that supports vital skin proteins including collagen and elastin. It is used topically as a humectant to hydrate the skin by attracting water to the area where it is applied. It is equally important to avoid topical products that can cause sensitivities including those with exfoliating agents, micronized particles, and botanical ingredients that may have a high reaction rate. Makeup would also qualify in this case as a product that could cause sensitivities or non-inflamed cases of rosacea.

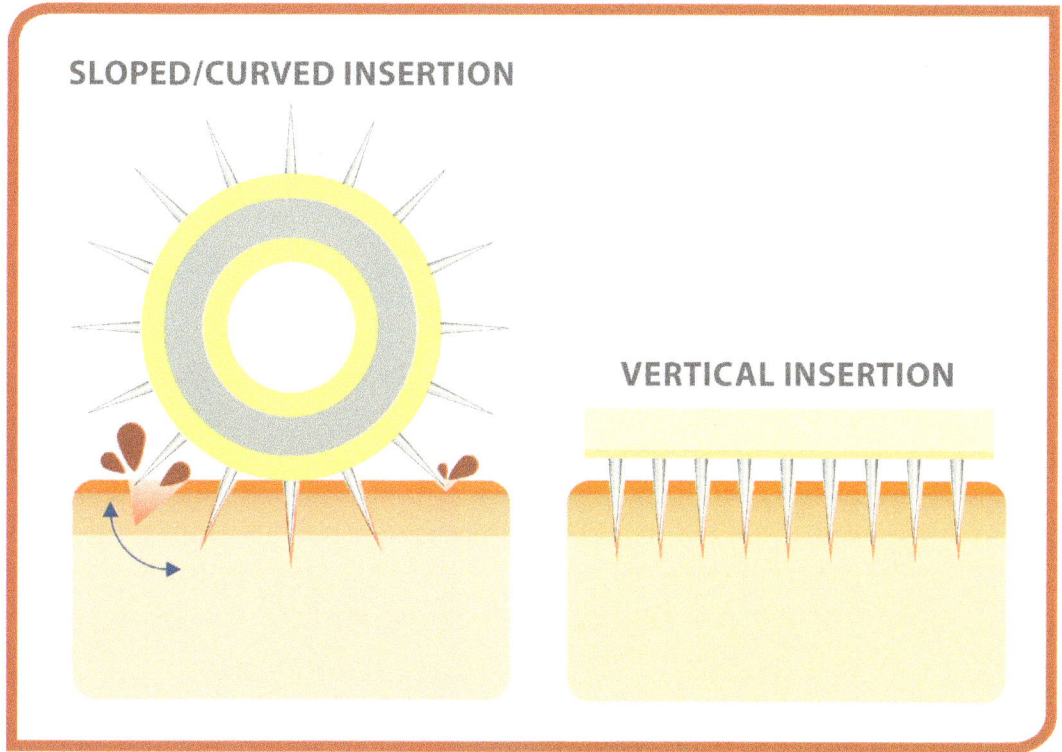

Micro-needling can be used on almost all skin types and conditions. It is most commonly used for fine lines, wrinkles, acne scarring, stretch marks, and even non-inflamed rosacea. Clients suffering from rosacea are often too sensitive to receive other mechanical rejuvenation techniques. Micro-needling at a lower depth (up to 0.5 mm) is beneficial since it does not physically remove the surface skin, but still stimulates growth factors to increase platelets and strengthen vessel walls. Physicians frequently use micro-needling with longer needles for the treatment of more pronounced wrinkles or scarring, and prior to medical procedures that include the use of PRP (Platelet Rich Plasma). PRP is a method of skin rejuvenation in which a licensed medical professional draws the patient's blood, uses a device to separate the plasma, and reapplies the serum topically to rejuvenate the skin. This treatment is sometimes called the "vampire" facial.

FDA Approved Indications:
- Fine lines and wrinkles
- General dermabrasion
- Acne scarring
- Scars
- Tattoo removal

Other Indications:
- Stretch marks
- Alopecia

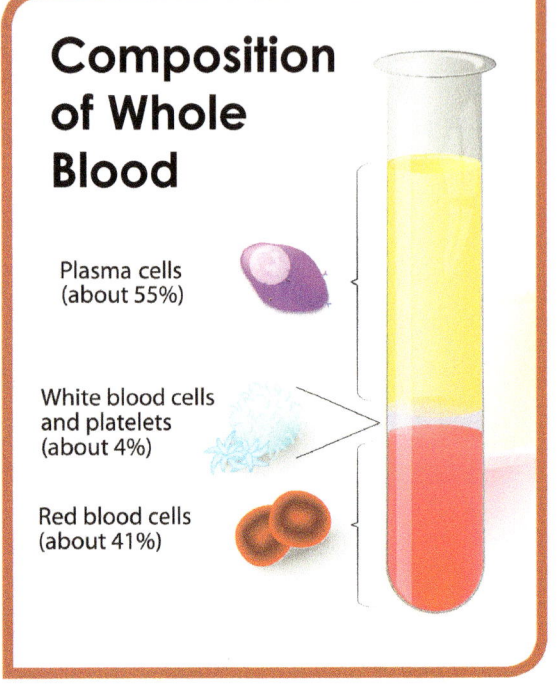

Contraindications:
- Acne grades III or IV (Needling should not be done on actively inflamed, acneic areas of the skin.)
- Papulopustular rosacea (though the procedure is safe for vascular rosacea)
- Presence of cold sores or other infections (if prone, antivirals should be recommended)
- Accutane use within six months of potential treatment
- Medical conditions that can alter the wound response (e.g., diabetes, cancer, auto-immune disorder)

Differences Between Needling & Lasers

The major difference between micro-needling and fractionated lasers is that lasers create heat, which can result in thermal damage, whereas needling does not. Fractionated lasers are considered safe for skin rejuvenation when used properly as directed by a medical professional.

A second difference is that micro-needling causes damaged cells to go into apoptosis (programmed or natural cell death), to then be eliminated from the body. Lasers destroy all cells in the heated area causing necrosis (premature cell death).

Micro-needling

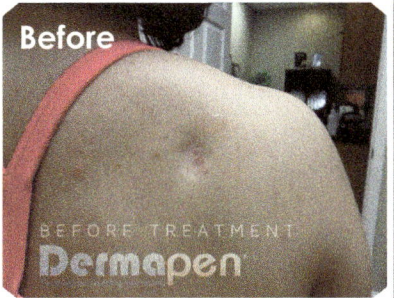
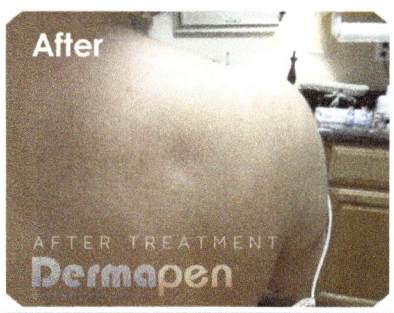

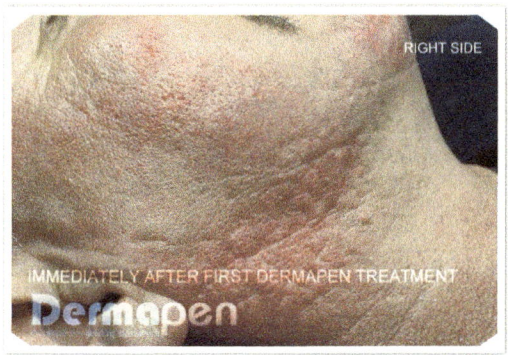
Immediately after first dermapen treatment

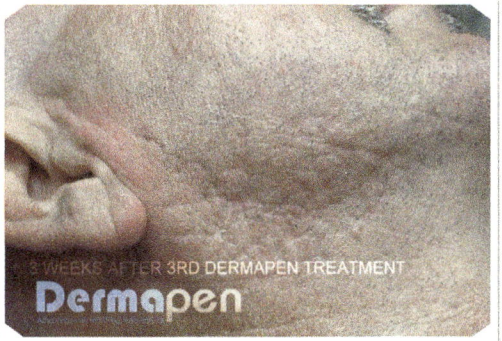
3 weeks after third dermapen treatment

Needle depths at 0.2–0.3 mm are epidermal and often used by estheticians and clients.

Needle depths of 0.5–3.0 mm are used by medical professionals. Many states prohibit the esthetician from puncturing the skin in any way; this includes all micro-needling regardless of needle length.

Some states allow estheticians to use needle depths up to 1.0 mm but it is important to check individual state regulations.

Micro-needling at a lower depth (up to 0.5 mm) is beneficial for rosacea, since it does not physically remove the surface skin, but still stimulates growth factors to increase platelet growth factors and strengthen vessel walls.

- Use of anti-coagulants (Remember: Never recommend that a client stop any medical treatment in order to receive an esthetic treatment.)
- Pregnancy or nursing
- History of allergies; a histamine response is possible on the skin's surface, though a physician can prescribe anti-histamines
- Keloids (These cases become physician-only.)

Regardless of the condition being treated; it is recommended to wait four to six weeks between treatments. It is best not to re-trigger a wound response during remodeling that occurs in the fibroplastic stage of healing (five to 20 days post-treatment).

Pre-treatment Considerations

Topical retinoids should be discontinued for three days prior to planned treatment in order to avoid any potential negative reaction. Moreover, clients who are prone to cold sores must be pre-treated by a physician; otherwise, stimulation in the skin may trigger a viral breakout. There can be no sun exposure, and certainly no evidence of sunburn, for 48 hours prior to the scheduled treatment.

If the client has used isotretinoin, the waiting period is significantly longer—at least six months after last use; otherwise, wound healing response will be poor. For those clients with Fitzpatrick skin types IV, V, or VI, pigmentation may get darker before it gets lighter, therefore the use of pigment lightening agents beforehand is recommended for optimal results.

What to Avoid:
- Neurotoxin treatment for 48 hours prior to needling.
- Soft-tissue fillers for two weeks prior to needling.
- Non-ablative laser and light therapy treatments for at least two weeks prior to and post-treatment.
- Ablative resurfacing procedures for at least three months post-needling.
- Makeup application for at least 12 hours following treatment.
- Retinoids for 72 hours prior to and post-treatment.

A series of three to six treatments is typically recommended, depending on the severity of conditions. Treatments should be spaced four to six weeks apart, so as to not interrupt the collagen regeneration process. It is important the client know that results may not be seen until three months following the first treatment but can continue to improve over a year. Remember: Always under-promise and over-deliver, especially when dealing with acne scarring and stretch marks, which may take several treatments before there is visible improvement.

Factors Affecting Micro-needling Results:
- The type of device used

- The type of needle employed; stainless steel should be used
- The length of the needles
- The pressure used by the provider with the hand piece
- Gauge (width) of the needle
- The number of passes performed
- With automated devices, the speed, which average anywhere from 200 to more than 1,000 holes per second
- The client's skin type and condition
- Pre- and post-treatment care

Overall, micro-needling is a great technique to improve the appearance of the skin. It is important that providers have a good understanding of how the skin responds to wounds to better understand the skin rejuvenation process. A thorough hands-on training with the specific device being used must be completed prior to use to ensure client safety.

Post-treatment Expectations

Day 1: Erythema and red appearance depends on how aggressive the treatment was.

Day 2: Red or pink hue similar to a mild sunburn and swelling may be more noticeable.

Day 3: Swelling subsides; the skin may be pink or have begun returning to its normal color.

References

1. D Fernandes, Minimally invasive percutaneous collagen induction, *Oral Maxillofac Surg Clin North Am*, 17, 51–63 (2005).
2. DS Orentreich and N Orentreich, Subcutaneous incisionless (subsicion) surgery for the correction of depressed scars and wrinkles, *Dermatol Surg*, 21 (6), 543-9 (1995)
3. A Camirand and J Doucet, Needle dermabrasion, *Aesthet Plast Surg*, 21, 48–51 (1997).

Non-medical Treatment Protocol

1. Review the client intake form with the client and look for any contraindications to treatment.
2. Consult with the client, answering any questions and providing detailed information about the treatment as stated above.
3. Reiterate to the client that they must remain still during the treatment.
4. Have the client sign a consent form that clearly states possible complications.
5. Cleanse the skin thoroughly with an antibacterial cleanser.
6. *Optional:* A topical anesthetic product, applied according to individual instructions, and removed thoroughly after the allotted time.
7. Prep the skin with an antibacterial, antimicrobial product.
8. Disinfect the device according to OSHA instructions; disposables should not be opened prior to use. Hand pieces, cords, and any other equipment must be thoroughly cleansed with a hospital-grade disinfectant.
9. Apply the appropriate topical product (according to manufacturer instructions.)
10. The device is glided over the skin without using pressure in a specific pattern. Most protocols promote three passes in opposing directions per area. Note: Needle depths can be altered during treatment to safely treat all areas of the face or body.
11. The needle is disposed of according to OSHA regulations in a sharps container.
12. An active topical product may be applied at this time to target specific skin conditions. (**Always** follow individual device and product protocols to ensure safety.)
13. Topical zinc oxide should be applied for sun protection. It is extremely important not to apply chemical sunscreens or micronized zinc oxide. Micronized particles may enter micro-channels and cause complications.
14. Go over post-treatment instructions including avoiding excess sun exposure for at least two weeks. Make it clear to the client that the use of an SPF 30 for two weeks post-needling is *mandatory*, and make it known that optimal results are seen when using proper skin care products at home.

Directional Chart

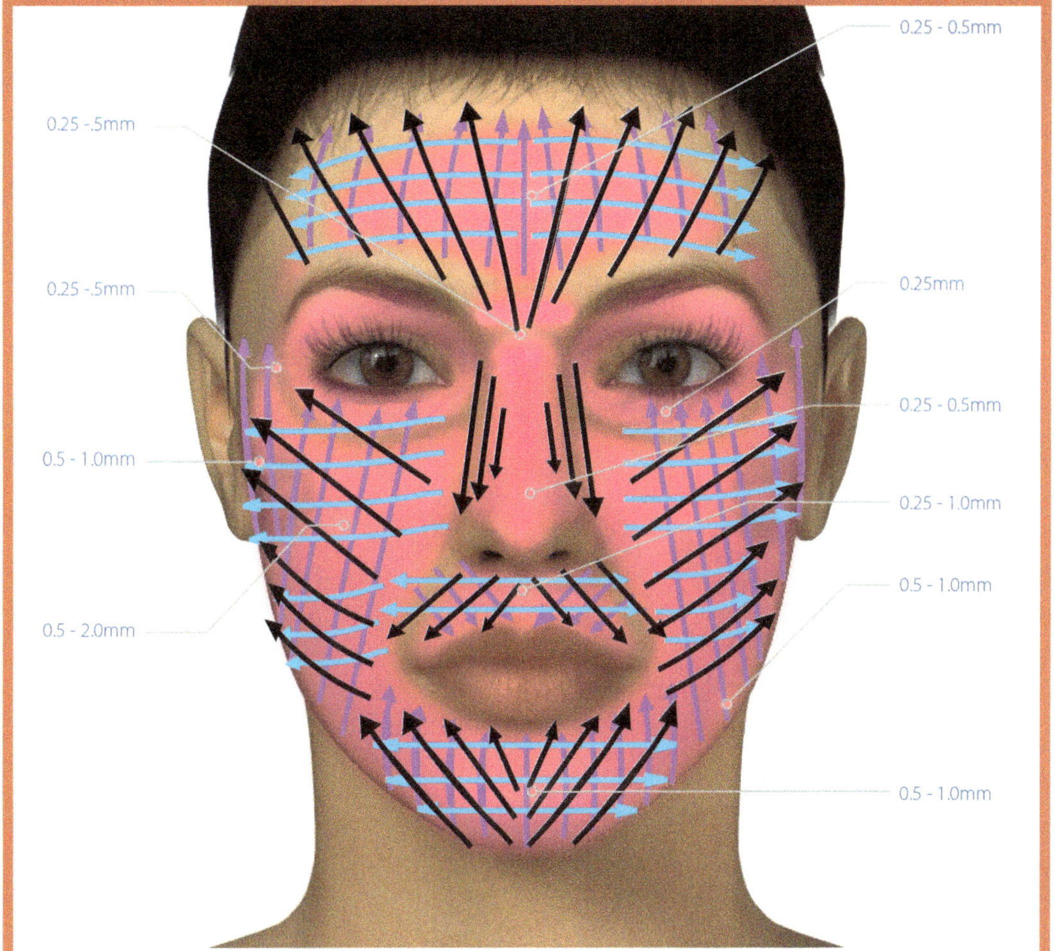

0.25 - .5mm
0.25 - .5mm
0.25 - .5mm
0.5 - 1.0mm
0.5 - 2.0mm
0.25 - 0.5mm
0.25mm
0.25 - 0.5mm
0.25 - 1.0mm
0.5 - 1.0mm
0.5 - 1.0mm

First Pass Purple Treat using the "stiping technique" and follow the direction bottom to top. Start at the bottom of the movement and treat with upward strokes.

Second Pass Blue Making constant contact, start medially and work laterally from inside toward the outer face. Pickup the tip from the face at the end of the outer face and then repeat starting from the inside to the outer face. This creates a "striping" movement which follows protocol.

Third Pass Black Outward and upward (when treating nose and upper lip on third pass use downward strokes as indicated in diagram above).

© 2013 Needlelogics, LLC
All Rights Reserved • needlelogics.com

Part 4 Review Questions

1) What is *not* one of the benefits of chemical peels?

   a) To refine fine lines
   b) To lighten hyperpigmentation
   c) To exfoliate dead skin cells
   d) To add volume to the skin

2) Which factor will affect the results of a chemical peel?

   a) The percentage of acid in the product
   b) The pH
   c) The amount of acid applied to the skin
   d) All of the above

3) Which peeling treatment needs to be neutralized following the proper application?

   a) Glycolic acid
   b) Salicylic acid
   c) Jessner's peel
   d) TCA peel

4) What is the most commonly used alpha hydroxyl acid (AHA) for people with sensitive skin?

   a) Glycolic acid
   b) Lactic acid
   c) Malic acid
   d) Tartaric acid

5) Which chemical peel is often the first choice for oily and acne skin types?

   a) Glycolic acid
   b) Lactic acid
   c) Salicylic acid
   d) TCA

6) If a client is allergic to aspirin, which chemical peels should not be used?

   a) Glycolic acid, lactic acid
   b) Salicylic acid, Jessner's
   c) Jessner's, TCA
   d) No chemical peels can be used

7) What are some of the post-care instructions given to a client after a peeling treatment?

   a) Avoid excess sun exposure, don't moisturize the skin for three to five days until the peeling has subsided
   b) Avoid activities that cause excess heat in the skin, refrain from using skin lightening agents for two weeks
   c) Avoid excess sun exposure, keep skin well hydrated with a suitable moisturizer
   d) Keep the skin well hydrated, apply heat to the skin every couple of hours for three to five days

8) Describe microdermabrasion.

   a) A technique that involves mechanically exfoliating the upper layers of dead skin cells through a hand piece using suction
   b) A technique that involves mechanically exfoliating the upper layers of dead skin cells with an ablative rotary device
   c) A technique that involves vacuuming layers of dead skin cells through a hand piece
   d) A technique that involves exfoliating the living layers of skin through a hand piece with crystals

9) What are some factors that affect the results of microdermabrasion?

   a) The type of machine used
   b) The condition of the client's skin before the treatment
   c) The flow of crystals and suction strength used
   d) All of the above

Review Questions

10) Which area of the skin should not be treated with microdermabrasion?

   a) Eyelids
   b) Hands
   c) Neck
   d) Nose

11) What is an alternate use for microdermabrasion in a medical setting?

   a) To replace the client's moisturizer
   b) To replace the client's exfoliator
   c) To remove crusted pigmentation seven to 10 days after non-ablative laser treatments
   d) To remove crusted pigmentation one to two days after ablative laser treatments

12) What is a contraindication to microdermabrasion?

   a) Superficial pigmentation
   b) Presence of blackheads and whiteheads
   c) Inflamed acne grades III and IV
   d) The use of antioxidants and pigment lightening products

13) When deciding on the type of microdermabrasion to be used, it is important to know:

   a) The cost of consumables
   b) The warranty on the device
   c) OSHA regulations for sanitation
   d) All of the above

14) Define dermaplaning.

   a) Using a scalpel to deeply exfoliate the epidermal layers of the skin down to the dermis
   b) Using a scalpel to gently abrade the epidermis using light feathering strokes
   c) Using a whisk-like device to gently abrade the epidermal layers of the skin down to the dermis
   d) Using a whisk-like device to gently abrade the surface of the epidermis using light feathering strokes

15) Which of the following does dermaplaning *not* accomplish?

   a) Removes unwanted vellus facial hair
   b) Lightly exfoliates the skin
   c) Allows other products or treatments to penetrate more effectively
   d) Removes pigmented lesions

16) What is the downtime associated with this dermaplaning?

   a) Two days
   b) One week
   c) Two weeks
   d) There is no downtime

17) When performing dermaplaning, at what angle should the blade be held?

   a) 30° angle
   b) 45° angle
   c) 65° angle
   d) 90° angle

18) Which of the following is a contraindication for dermaplaning?

   a) Fine, vellus hair
   b) Rough surface skin
   c) Inflamed acne
   d) Rosacea

19) What is another name for micro-needling?

   a) Microdermabrasion
   b) Collagen Induction Therapy
   c) Ablative Resurfacing
   d) Epidermal Growth Factor

20) What is not an indication for needling?

    a) Fine lines and wrinkles
    b) Acne scarring
    c) Inflamed acne
    d) Stretch marks

21) Micro-channels on the skin formed by micro-needling stay open for an average of _____.

    a) 10-15 seconds
    b) 10-15 minutes
    c) 1 hour
    d) 12 hours

22) How many days, on average, does it take following micro-needling for swelling and redness to subside?

    a) 1 day
    b) 3 days
    c) 1 week
    d) 3 months

23) What stage of wound healing can continue for up to two years?

    a) Inflammatory stage
    b) Proliferative stage
    c) Fibroplastic stage
    d) Maturative stage

24) Which method of micro-needling allows for different treatment depths during a single treatment?

    a) Stamping
    b) Rolling
    c) Automated Needing Device
    d) The depth cannot be changed during treatment regardless of device

25) Which of the following factors affect the results of micro-needling?
    a) The client's skin condition prior to treatment
    b) The needle gauge
    c) Post-treatment care
    d) All of the above

PART 5

Laser and Light Therapy

AESTHETICS EXPOSED
MASTERING SKIN CARE IN A MEDICAL SETTING AND BEYOND

CHAPTER 17

Laser Safety Regulations and Considerations

In this Chapter:
- OSHA Regulations
- Eye Protection
- Laser Classifications (ANSI)
- Pre-treatment Considerations
- General Contraindications
- General Safety Guidelines

Laser safety regulations cannot be taken lightly. Regulations may be difficult to keep up with but they are put in place for a reason. The high energy light used in lasers can cause severe damage to the skin and eyes, even resulting in blindness. These unfortunate risks can be greatly reduced when safety measures are enforced and diligently followed. It is the responsibility of the laser owner, the certified laser safety officer, and each provider to maintain all standards set forth by the regulating agencies whose oversight governs the state and/or country in which laser services are being performed.

Laser Safety Regulators

There are several agencies involved in the management of safe laser use.

The American National Standards Institute (ANSI) is a non-profit organization that oversees guidelines for safe laser use throughout the United States. *ANSI Z136.3* is the original book developed in the early 1970s to regulate the laser industry. Within this volume, ANSI established four classifications (some of which include sub-classifications) of lasers as regards hazard prevention, shown in the sidebar labeled **ANSI Classifications of Laser Safety**.

> As noted in Chapter 2's discussion of legalities concerning practice within medical settings, the laws regarding laser and light therapy use vary from state to state. These regulations are strict and not following them could result in the loss of professional license.

The Center for Devices and Radiological Health (CDRH) is the branch of the

US Food and Drug Administration (FDA) responsible for radiation safety. The CDHR must approve physical devices, including those using lasers and light therapy, before they come to market.

The Occupational Safety and Health Administration (OSHA), as discussed in Chapter 3, regulates safe work environments, which includes the laser safety measures that are outlined below.

ANSI Classifications of Laser Safety*

1, *indicating* no damaging radiation levels under normal conditions

1M, *indicating* it is not known to cause damage unless optical aids are used

2, *indicating* low power lasers or systems considered safe due to the human aversion response, defined as a human's natural response to light which triggers blinking in 0.25 seconds of recognition of a light source. This only works for light in the visible light spectrum. Protective eyewear should be worn, regardless.

2M, *indicating* it is not known to be hazardous unless being viewed with optical aids.

3R, *indicating* low power lasers that need control measures including protective eyewear and no direct or specular reflection.

3B, *indicating* medium powered lasers which are dangerous if aimed at the eye. Eye protection is required, but there is no fire hazard.

4, *indicating* high powered lasers. Direct, specular, and diffuse reflection can all produce hazards to the eyes or skin. Fire hazards can also occur.

*A comprehensive accounting of these standards can be obtained from ANSI or its secretariat and publisher, The Laser Institute of America.

Certified Laser Safety Officer: In any environment where Class 3R, 3B, or 4 lasers are being utilized, a certified laser safety officer (CLSO) is required on-site. This would be a qualified staff member who has received CLSO certification, commonly taken online. The CLSO is in charge of making sure all safety measures are put in place, all documentation is current, upkeep or maintenance to devices is completed and done so thoroughly, standard operating procedures are in place, and that each staff member with the ability to be exposed to laser radiation be trained and follow regulatory safety measures. This is an immense responsibility that requires diligent managerial ability. Ongoing obligations include staying up-to-date on regulations, precise record keeping, and frequent evaluations of safety practices. All laser devices housed in the practice must be initially evaluated for the Nominal Hazard Zone (NHZ), the distance around the light beam that could be hazardous, and the laser safety classification must be confirmed. The CLSO also has to approve eyewear for each device and always be on the lookout for other safety measures that can be put in place. Laser safety training must be completed and kept current by all providers and documented by the CLSO. It is considered best practice to conduct laser safety training on a yearly basis.

Eye Safety / Possible Eye Injuries from Light Therapy

The biggest safety concern when it comes to the use of lasers is the damage that emitted light can cause to the eyes. Eye injuries can differ significantly; an injury can be immediate or take years to present its damage. The injury can be a small blind spot to a complete loss of vision; the effects are often related to the type of light one is exposed to and the exposure time. The retina, the portion of the eye responsible for sending images to the brain, can be damaged with exposure in wavelengths of 400–1400 nm. The cornea, the transparent covering of the eye, is more likely to be damaged over time with shorter or longer wavelengths. The damage, again, can be immediate or show up years later.

Protective eyewear

The use of protective eyewear is mandated for all Class 3 and 4 laser usage. It seems an easy task to make sure providers and patient's eyes are protected but there is much more to consider. The required eyewear is specific to the wavelength being emitted by the laser; this means that there may be different goggles needed for each individual laser treatment. Each pair of goggles must be directly imprinted with the wavelengths covered and the optical density. The optical density is the measure of radiation permitted to pass through a filter; it is calculated by the potential fraction of the beam that could possibly be let through the eyewear. For example, an optical density of 4, means that 1/10,000th of the emitted light can pass through the lens. This can be difficult to understand, and it is the responsibility of each laser manufacturer to provide practitioners with the safety requirements pertaining to their device.

These calculations are used in determining safety measures for each individual device. There are simple calculations regarding the light source used, but there is more to take into consideration. The MPE and/or NHZ can change according to pulse width, spot size, and energy produced. MPE, or Maximum Permissible Exposure, is the minimum amount of time that the skin or eyes can be exposed without biological damage. NHZ, as previously defined, is the distance around the light beam that could be hazardous.

Protective eyewear with side shields

All goggles worn by providers must have side shields on them (**pictured**) to protect from light entering the eye area peripherally. Patient's eyes must also be completely protected; therefore, if the face is being treated the use of goggles that completely surround the eyes, or laser-safe tape, is mandatory; the elastic bands on this type of eyewear must also fit snugly. Prior to each treatment, eyewear must also be inspected for any damage, such as cracks, holes, scratches, or discoloration. If there is any damage to the eyewear, it cannot be used and must be replaced. There should always be backup goggles to prevent patient cancellations. Goggles tend to be somewhat fragile and if dropped, usually crack. The cancellation or unnecessary rescheduling of an appointment due to a lack of foresight on the part of the provider can betray a lack of professionalism and preparation, and cause the patient to second-guess their choice of your services.

SCENARIO: Always Have a Backup

A patient comes in for a laser hair reduction treatment and is upset since you are running late and she has already been waiting 30 minutes. As you enter the room, you notice there is a hairline crack in the goggles which have been selected as appropriate for the laser hair removal device being used for the patient's treatment. There is, however, another set of goggles in the room, but the imprint showing the wavelengths that these goggles cover has worn off.

In this scenario, an already perturbed patient now finds both

> you and the medical setting to be disorganized and ill-prepared. She will immediately wonder what kind of treatment she can come to expect from you, and whether you are even capable of providing a safe and proper treatment.
>
> Avoiding this situation is as simple as checking goggles before and after each use and having backup safety eyewear that is clearly marked and ready for immediate use.

Environment

Lasers are highly reactive devices; therefore, the conditions of the laser treatment room must be, like the operation of the laser devices themselves, mandated as well. Lasers produce a directed beam, and regardless of how cautious the provider, mishaps can occur, causing the light to be directed, reflected, or scattered in the wrong direction. It should be fairly common sense not to leave flammable materials out during a laser procedure, but the treatment room should be checked for them nonetheless. Many laser protocols require the use of alcohol to prep the skin, and it would be easy for the bottle to be left out inadvertently while the provider continues with the treatment protocol. All flammable materials in the room must be labeled according to stated OSHA regulations. The CLSO is responsible for putting safety protocols in place, which if followed directly decrease potential hazards. (An example SOP can be found in Appendix B.) Since light can be reflected, reflective materials such as mirrors or glass-faced light fixtures, either on the walls or overhead, should not be placed in any treatment room housing a laser device. A less obvious risk is reflective jewelry on the patient or provider. Remember that diffused light can still cause injury. To cut down this risk, providers should make it a habit to not wear large pieces of jewelry of any kind in the clinic. These precautions are crucial in the event that a laser is inadvertently misdirected and the beam bounces off a surface, becoming aimed at an unintended target and potentially causing significant or severe damage.

A warning sign must be placed on the outer side of the treatment room door that states "Danger: Visible and/or invisible laser radiation, avoid eye or skin exposure to

OSHA Label for Flammable Materials

direct or scattered radiation." The warning sign should only be visible when the laser is in use. If it is always on the door, other staff members will not know if a device is actually in use or not within the room, and thus whether or not the room is available or approachable. Signage is essential to avoid the unnecessary risk of someone walking into a treatment room without protection in the midst of the treatment. The door should always remain closed during treatment but not locked, in the rare event that something catches fire and escape is required. Due to the ability of light to penetrate glass, windows must be covered with flame retardant material of the appropriate ocular density.

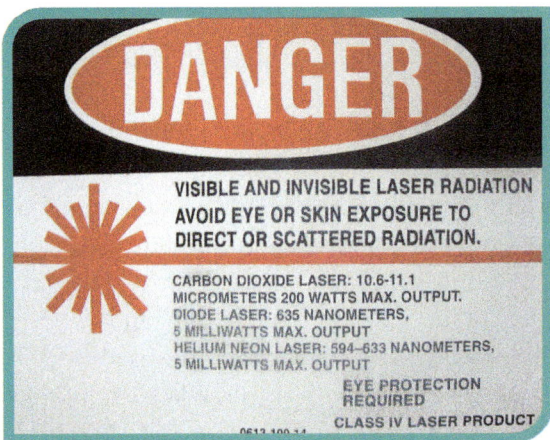

Ablative lasers, which vaporize tissue, also require the use of personal protective equipment, including face masks. Although face masks are required to be worn by anyone in the treatment room, the room must also have adequate ventilation to reduce any toxic contaminants or potentially hazardous fumes from being inhaled. A plume evacuator, or vacuum device to reduce debris, must also be used to reduce the amount of laser-generated air contaminants (LGAC) that result from ablative laser treatments such as CO_2.

The laser hand piece must be cleaned with a solution containing at least 70% alcohol and a germicidal or a disinfectant solution approved for use by OSHA. Hands and gloves must remain sanitary for all providers and assistants who are in contact with the patient. If a device requires the use of conducting gel, the gel must be clear.

Preventing mishaps: A laser should never be turned on until all electrical wires and systems associated with the laser device are checked. The key must be taken out of the device between treatments and locked away when not in use, especially overnight. If anyone had access to the device and mistakenly or deliberately turned it on, and something happened (short-circuit, fire, burnout, etc.), the site (i.e., the clinic or provider) would be liable. Any time the provider needs to adjust the location of the laser or reposition to another area, the hand piece must be placed on standby mode and made secure in the holder. While operating the device, the hand piece should

Laser Safety Regulations and Considerations

be pointed towards the ground and one should never look into the hand piece's distal end. It is also mandatory to place a safety belt around the wrist area that is attached to the laser hand piece in the event that it was to become loose from the provider's hand. Finally, a fire extinguisher, with an up-to-date safety status, must be kept in each treatment room, and all staff must have been trained on how to operate it in the event of an emergency.

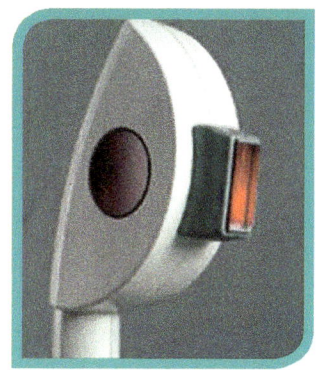
Distal end of laser hand piece

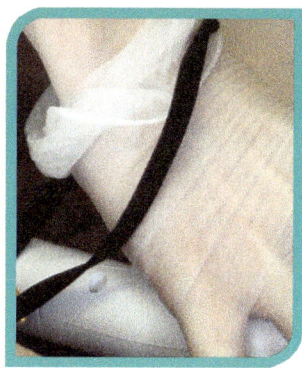
Safety belt for laser hand piece

Electrical and fire safety training exists within the medical setting to keep employees and patients safe. Immediate discard and replacement of any damaged or frayed electrical or extension cords is required and must be noted. If at any time the machine is acting out of character for what the provider deems to be normal, treatment immediately must be stopped and the manufacturer is to be contacted.

General Safety Guidelines for Laser Treatments

What follows is an example series of safety guidelines, broken down into three categories: Contraindications to Treatment, Supplies, and Checklist of Precautions. The reader should bear in mind that each laser device type has its own contraindications; as treatments vary, so may the standards associated with them.

Contraindications to Treatment:

Accutane: A patient should not receive laser treatment if he/she has taken Accutane within six months of proposed treatment.

Tattoos: Do not apply laser treatment close to tattooed areas unless the tattoo itself is your target chromophore. The skin could become severely burned in the area when using a wavelength and/or energy not intended for tattoo removal.

History of photosensitivity: The use of any type of laser light could cause an immediate reaction.

Pregnancy or breast feeding: The effects of laser application to women who are pregnant or nursing are yet unknown, and therefore treatment is unadvisable.

Photosensitizing medications: Any of the medications listed in Appendix C denote a contraindication to treatment, as coupling their use with laser treatment could result in rash, burns, or even scarring.

HSV 1&2: Do not treat if active lesions are present, or if the patients has a history of frequent HSV 1&2 lesions. The patient should begin prophylaxis prior to treatment as prescribed by physician.

Medical conditions that require complex treatments or treatments that affect the entire body, notably the auto-immune system: These include, but are not limited to HIV/AIDS, cancer, untreated or undertreated diabetes, and hepatitis.

Poorly controlled medical conditions: These patients should be carefully evaluated by their physician for medical clearance. The skin must be in a state to heal itself; if the skin shows an inability in this regard, or if the patient displays notable health issues, she should be referred to a physican before any treatment consideration.

Active skin infection/wounds: Lasers are stimulating and thus could spread infection to other areas of the skin, or beneath the skin's surface in the case of more deeply penetrating treatment types.

Keloid or hypertrophic scarring: Treating a patient with keloids should only take place at the physician's discretion, because stimulated keloid scars could come back worse than initially presented.

Implanted medical devices: Laser energy could complicate these devices' ability to function.

Do not treat recently tanned skin, including skin applied with self-tanners: Because most light therapies are attracted to color, this could result in burns.

Skin cancer: Any possible cancerous lesions must be avoided and the patient referred to her physician. Raised moles, birthmarks or other suspicious lesions are also contraindicated.

Epilepsy: Pulsed light in particular can trigger a seizure or comparable physical reaction.

Pacemaker: Have the patient consult with his/her physician first and obtain written clearance for treatment.

Supplies:

Clear ultrasound gel: Many lasers require the use of a conductive gel for comfort and ease of treatment.

Tongue depressors: To remove and apply products in a sanitary manner.

Non-woven gauze pads: To cleanse the window of the laser without leaving cotton behind, as well as to cleanse the skin in that area to be treated.

Alcohol: To thoroughly cleanse the patient's skin after makeup removal. To cleanse the hand piece of the laser.

Paper towels: For quick clean-up if something were to spill.

Patient drapes or towels: To protect the patient's clothing and/or hair and to cover areas of the body that may cause the patient discomfort to have exposed.

Hair wrap: To protect excess hair from getting in the treatment area.

Disposable Gloves: All aesthetic procedures require the use of gloves.

Disposable razors: Patients should be shaved prior to their appointment for laser hair reduction, but there are times when an area may have been missed or required redress.

Laser Safety Regulations and Considerations

Cold compresses: To alleviate discomfort in the case that the patient feels excessive heat following the treatment.

Sunscreen with at least SPF 30: Following laser and light therapy procedures, the skin is more susceptible to damage from the sun, thus sunscreen application is necessary.

Eye protection for employees and patients: As discussed, this is of the utmost importance. Protective eyewear is required, as is the full array of eyewear needed for each laser type used in treatments offered by the practice.

Degreasing cleanser: To remove makeup, lotions, fragrance, and deodorant from treatment areas before disinfecting the areas with alcohol.

Disposable filtration masks: In the case of both ablative and non-ablative laser procedures that may generate contaminants, providers should be properly equipped.

Plume evacuator: For ablative laser treatments it is necessary to remove laser-generated air contaminants (LGAC).

Checklist of Precautions:

Laser Eyewear Protection
- Must be based on specific wavelengths.
- Glasses or goggles of sufficient **optical density**; most OD 4–8 level of reduction for laser beam, i.e. $10^4 = 10{,}000$ allows $1/10{,}000$ of the beam through the eyewear.
- Must have side shields to protect from peripheral injury and impact.
- Sanitize goggles before and after each use according to the manufacture procedure for cleaning.
- Must be inspected for cracks, holes, scratches, discoloration, or other damage before and after each procedure.
- Patient goggles with elastic band must fit snugly.

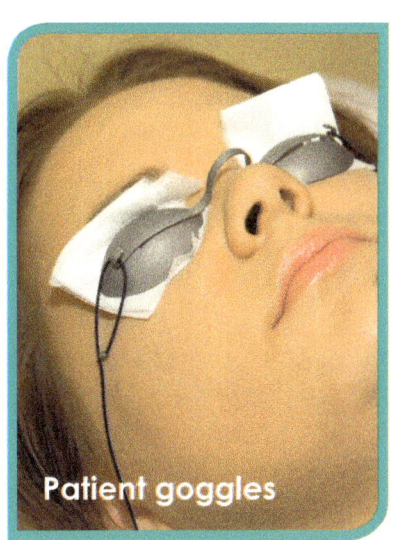
Patient goggles

Treatment Room Setup
- No flammable materials left visible in the room.
- No reflective materials such as fancy glass vases, chandeliers, or mirrors should be present.
- Metal implements should be put away, never left out on countertops.
- Windows must be covered with flame retardant material of the appropriate ocular density.
- Adequate ventilation should be installed to reduce any toxic contaminants or potentially hazardous fumes.
- For ablative procedures, a plume evacuator to remove laser-generated air contaminants (LGAC) is required, as are filtration masks.

- A fire extinguisher is to be kept near treatment rooms during procedures.

During Treatment
- A sign stating *Danger: visible and/or invisible laser radiation, avoid eye or skin exposures to direct or scattered radiation* must be put on the treatment room door before laser use.
- The door to the laser room should be closed during treatment but never locked.
- The laser hand piece must be cleaned according to manufacturer instructions.
- Technician and patient both should remove any reflective jewelry.
- Hands must be sanitized before the procedure and gloves are mandatory.
- The laser hand piece must be held securely; if the device has a safety belt that connects the hand piece to the wrist, it should be used for extra protection.
- A test patch should be done on each area being treated, waiting the appropriate amount for that area's skin color to register an accurate result.
- While working with lasers on different parts of the body, the technician must place the laser machine on standby mode when moving from one side of the treated area of the body to the other. Also reevaluate the area, as skin color and targets can change dependent on the area in question.
- When operating the laser, the hand piece should be pointed towards the ground and the technician should never look into the distal end of the hand piece.

Patch Test

Prior to each laser treatment, a patch test should be done to ensure safe and effective results. It is without question that busy practices and patients would like to shorten treatment times; however, the extra time taken to guarantee safety is essential to success. Patch tests are necessary with laser treatments because there can be a delayed response in skin reaction, especially with darker skin types. An understanding of pigmentation response triggered from any inflammation shows that the application of heat can produce worsened pigmentation, hypopigmentation, or even scarring. *It is important to always follow manufacturer instructions first, as certain lasers may have longer wait times following a patch test.* A patch test must be done in an area that is the same color and has as much sun exposure as the area that is to be treated. If treating the face, the test can be done above the jawline in front of the ear. Some protocols

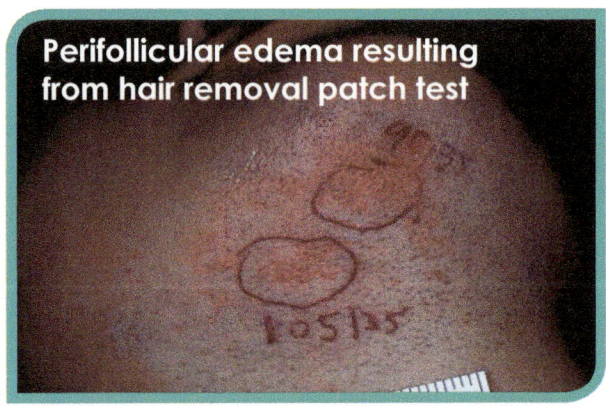
Perifollicular edema resulting from hair removal patch test

call for this test to be performed in an inconspicuous area; however, that area may react differently due to its incongruent amount of sun exposure, skin thickness, or skin color. With lighter skin types, namely Fitzpatrick types I through III, it is often recommended to do one pulse in the treatment area and wait five to 10 minutes for the skin reaction. When treating darker skin types, it is best to do a test spot 24 hours before treatment, due to the increased chance of post-inflammatory hyperpigmentation. After the allotted time, the patient's skin reaction and tolerance should be observed. It is good to have *mild* erythema and perifollicular edema (inflammation of the hair follicle) in the case of laser hair reduction. Reactions including prolonged redness, pigmentation, excessive swelling, itching or blistering can occur if the settings are not correct for that patient.

In My Professional Experience

Laser safety is, of course, of the utmost importance. Laser sales people unfortunately tend to prioritize the sale first, and safety concerns second. Such is the nature of sales. Consequently, these medical devices often get into the wrong hands. I have been working with lasers for about 11 years and training estheticians on how to handle them for eight of those. In that time I have amassed a wide range of experiences as to the right and wrong way to apply laser treatments in both a business setting and a classroom atmosphere. It is extremely disheartening when a student who is working with lasers on a daily basis attends one of my training sessions and does not even know the basics of laser safety or treatment parameters.

When I first started working with lasers, my educator (representative) taught me to follow a chart and choose settings accordingly. As I am always into learning as much as I can, I asked many questions as to why. "Why do we choose this amount of joules? What are joules? What does pulse width mean?" and so forth. I was told that I was looking too much into it and all I needed to do was follow the chart that was given to me. So I did as I was told and brought in family members for practice. As I treated my sister's entire body for laser hair removal, staying within the range provided on the chart, I finally reached the back of her thighs. She started crying out that it was burning. I said, "Well it looks fine, and I am at the right setting so just bear with me. We are almost done." She called that night in extreme pain; she had third-degree burns on the back of her thighs and had to sit in a bath tub full of ice to ease the discomfort. The physician I was working for at the time had to treat her with topical steroids. This happened right before summer and prevented my sister from being able to expose her

Continued on the next page

thighs at all. She had black "burn-like" marks up and down the entire surface of her thighs, which later turned to hypopigmented areas. Hypopigmentation, the loss of color due to damage of the melanocytes, does not, in most cases, reproduce pigment.

The reason this complication occurred is because I was not properly educated. I am not blaming the trainer, rather I blame myself for knowing I wasn't properly educated. I knew only that I needed to press the laser against the skin, being careful to have it in full contact, and to press the button to activate the device. The fact is, I had no idea why I was choosing these settings, other than because the chart I was instructed to follow indicated a specific setting for my sister's skin color and hair texture. Moreover, I was never told that either I or patient needed to wear safety goggles. Quite the opposite; I was told they were not easy to see out of. As long as we (the patient and I) blinked during pulses that would be fine.

Lasers are considered medical devices and there are reported cases of blinding from improper protection during treatments. But even more common are burns, and not just small burns, but severe burns that lead to lifelong pigment changes and scars. Many don't think of the severe psychological implications this can cause. As accidents can occur, I was able to see the other side by being closely involved in the process. I received calls nightly from my sister crying that she would be scarred for life, and she was severely depressed. The psychological impact of this on both of us may be implied. **From my own experience, if something does not seem right or if proper education on a product or device is not given, do not use it until it is fully understood.** Learn from my mistake; it is worth it to wait. If you are going to be working with lasers, please ensure you feel comfortable with the knowledge received and that you strictly follow safety protocols. Remember: you alone are responsible for your own education.

CHAPTER 18

Light Physics

In this Chapter:
- A Brief History of Light Energy
- The Electromagnetic Spectrum
- Visible vs. Non-visible Light
- Laser Components

A Brief History of Light Energy

In the 17th century, when the nature of light particles was being debated, it is almost certain that no one was considering the cosmetic effects that would come hundreds of years later. As light was studied, it could not be agreed upon whether what constituted "light" was a wave or a particle. While working on his theories of gravity, Issac Newton sparred with his rival, Robert Hooke, whom at the time published a theory of light.[1] Newton proposed that light consisted of particles, while Hooke was convinced light acted like a wave. In 1917, Albert Einstein introduced the theory of stimulated emission of radiation. His theory postulated that a photon, when released from an excited electron, could stimulate a subsequent photon release from the excited electron.[2] In other words, Einstein supported the particle theory. Eventually, the field of quantum mechanics settled the debate in the 20th century, proving that light has the ability to act as both a particle and a wave. This information often goes ignored, but what it truly means has critical implications on the study of laser technology.

Modern day usage of light has broadly expanded the range of medical treatments. Everything from laser resurfacing to surgery has exploited the multifunctional abilities of light. Preceding the modern day laser, the "maser" was a device that produced coherent electromagnetic waves through amplification via stimulated emission. The maser, or **M**icrowave **A**mplification by **S**timulated **E**mission of **R**adiation, was developed in 1954 by Jim Gordon and Charles Townes. Building upon similar microwave mechanics, the maser demonstrated a means to not only urge excited particles to further excite additional ones, but to emit energy via a straight uniform beam, which was the first time this was done.[3] This was influential to Dr. Leon Goldman. Dr. Goldman, who is now considered the father of laser medicine, was the first to utilize the Ruby laser on a patient in 1961, in Cincinnati, Ohio.[4] The creation of this laser spurred the development of the lasers that are today being employed for various medical and industrial functions.

> ## So... what does LASER stand for?
>
> It is an acronym for **L**ight **A**mplification by **S**timulated **E**mission of **R**adiation.
>
> - **Light**—potential to be visible or invisible dependent upon wavelength
> - **Amplification**—increased energy
> - **Stimulated**—to excite
> - **Emission**—molecular process in which energy is released
> - **Radiation**—energy in the form of electromagnetic waves

The Electromagnetic Spectrum

Entire doctoral programs are devoted to understanding how light energy operates with regard to wavelength, but for our purposes only a general understanding of the process is needed. Light is divided into the categories of *visible* and *non-visible*, which together comprise a portion of the electromagnetic spectrum (**pictured**).

The electromagnetic spectrum is the range of all possible frequencies of electromagnetic radiation. When used as a descriptive, it refers to the characteristic distri-

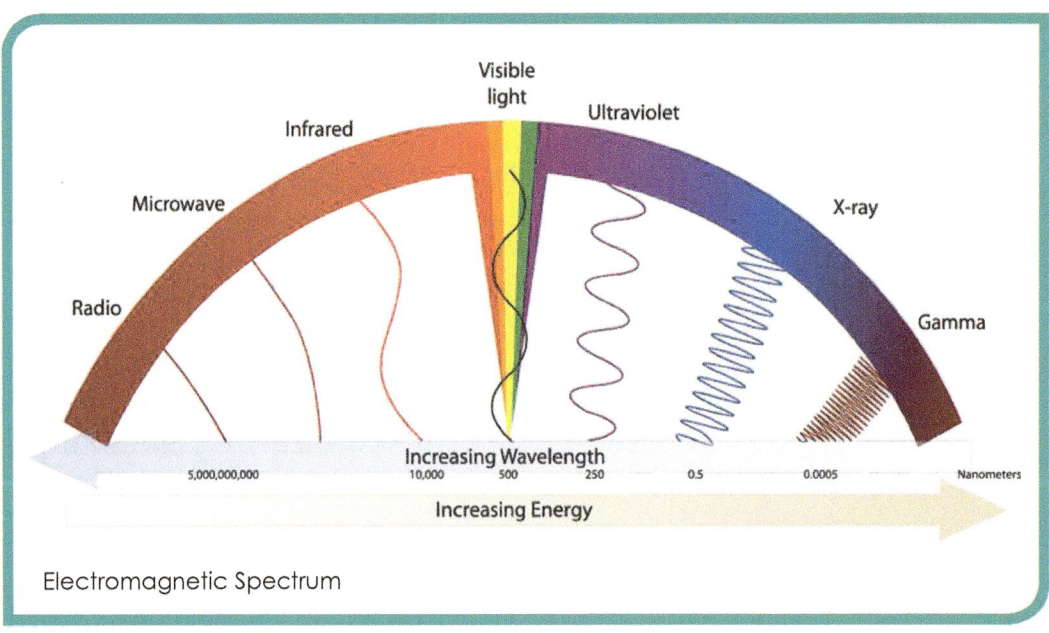

Electromagnetic Spectrum

bution of electromagnetic radiation emitted or absorbed by a particular object.

Light is measured in wavelengths. One wavelength is defined as the distance from the crest of one wave to the crest of the next. They are measured in nanometers (nm), one-billionth of a meter. Wavelengths range from zero to infinity. Visible light falls between the 400 nm range of violet light with shorter wavelengths to the range of 700 nm for red light with a longer wavelength. Short wavelengths have higher frequencies because more repetitions can occur from one crest to the next. Accordingly, it makes sense that the longer the wavelength, the lower the frequency of the light. While the amplitude of a wave measures its height and change over a single

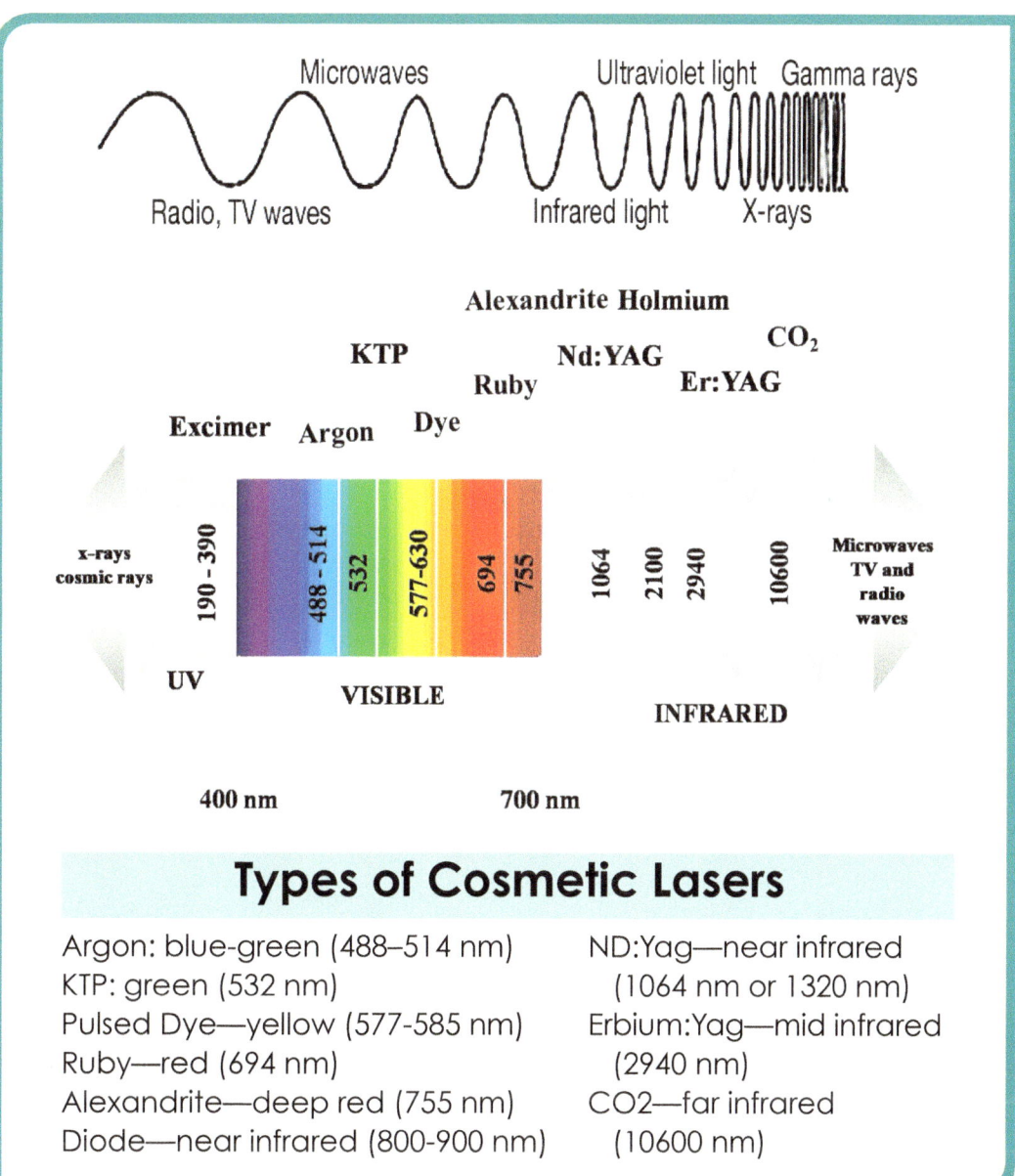

Types of Cosmetic Lasers

Argon: blue-green (488–514 nm)
KTP: green (532 nm)
Pulsed Dye—yellow (577-585 nm)
Ruby—red (694 nm)
Alexandrite—deep red (755 nm)
Diode—near infrared (800-900 nm)

ND:Yag—near infrared
(1064 nm or 1320 nm)
Erbium:Yag—mid infrared
(2940 nm)
CO2—far infrared
(10600 nm)

period of time, the frequency translates to the number of wavelengths per second.

The entire electromagnetic spectrum ranges from gamma rays (the shortest wavelengths) all the way to radio waves (the longest wavelengths), and as previously mentioned, visible light falls in between.

Radiation across the electromagnetic spectrum is ultimately divided into two categories, *ionizing* and *non-ionizing*. Non-ionizing radiation has enough energy to move atoms in a molecule around or vibrate them, but not enough energy to remove any electrons. Having very long wavelengths and low frequencies, non-ionizing radiation is found in audio, microwave, visible, and UV portions of the spectrum. On the other hand, ionizing radiation has enough energy to remove the electrons that are bound tightly to atoms. When this occurs, ions are created, as the previously neutral molecule is left with a slightly positive charge due to the loss of the electron. The electron is then floating freely with a slight negative charge. This is what people typically think of as "radiation" in terms of going after cancer cells or the by-products of electrical processes. Overexposure to UV radiation, as well as X-ray and gamma ray radiation, has the potential to cause harm.

Gamma rays are incredibly energetic and have the highest frequencies. These types of rays are typically associated with nuclear reactions and lightening. In a medical setting, gamma rays have been used in the development of gamma knives which are used in the removal of brain tumors. Gamma rays are able to travel through very dense material, but have several limitations in the medical field because they are unpredictable and have not been studied in many long-term tests.

X-rays fall next on the electromagnetic spectrum, which means they are the second smallest in size. They are about the size of an atom (0.3–20.0 nm) and can see through tissues in the body. Although exposure to such rays must be limited due to their ionizing nature, these rays are necessary for the diagnosis and treatment of myriad known medical conditions.

Ultraviolet (UV) rays are just outside of the spectrum of visible light,

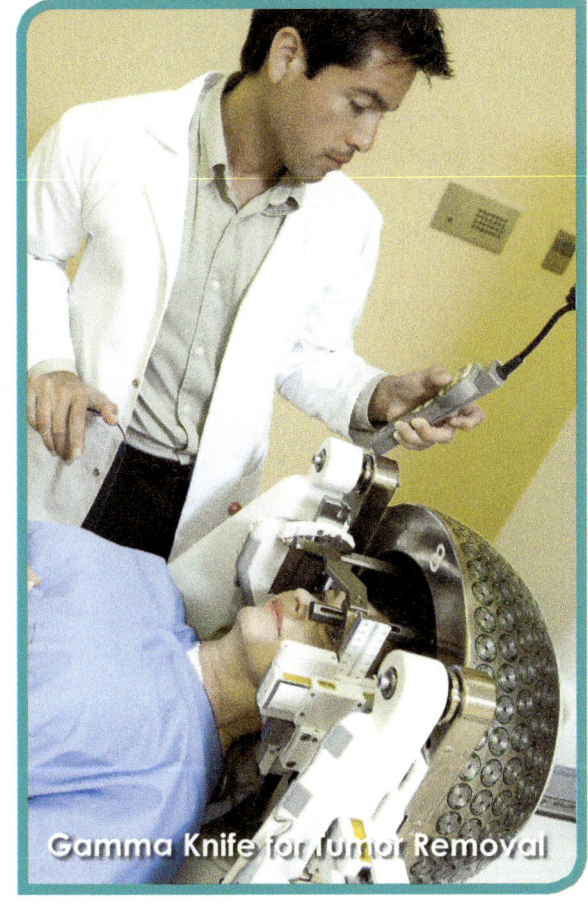
Gamma Knife for Tumor Removal

making them invisible. They have shorter wavelengths, ranging from 10–400 nm or about the size of a virus. Mostly derived from the damaging rays of the sun, UV rays are composed of a great deal of detrimental energy. Due to the fact that their wavelengths are shorter than those of visible light rays, they are unable to penetrate deeply into the skin, and are therefore mostly absorbed into the superficial layers. However, this makes them particularly dangerous because they cause the greatest damage to the skin. Not only do UV rays result in sunburns, they are able to alter a cell's DNA, the nucleic acid blueprint that houses the cell's genetic information. When a cell's DNA becomes compromised, it has the potential to continuously replicate additional damaged cells without regulation, which may lead to the creation of pre-cancerous lesions and eventually skin cancer. Due to the fact that UVC rays are the shortest of ultraviolet rays, they are often referred to as the "cancer causing rays." UVC rays are unable to reach the earth, but are present in fluorescent and ambient lighting. UVB rays, often called the "burning rays," are responsible for the erythema associated with excess sun exposure. UVA rays, known as "aging rays," penetrate deeper, causing more damage to the dermal layers, associating them with visible signs of aging such as wrinkles and sun spots. It should be noted that UVA rays have the ability to penetrate glass, and although they are often believed to be not as dangerous as UVB or UVC rays, they have just as high a potential to cause skin damage and potentially skin cancer.

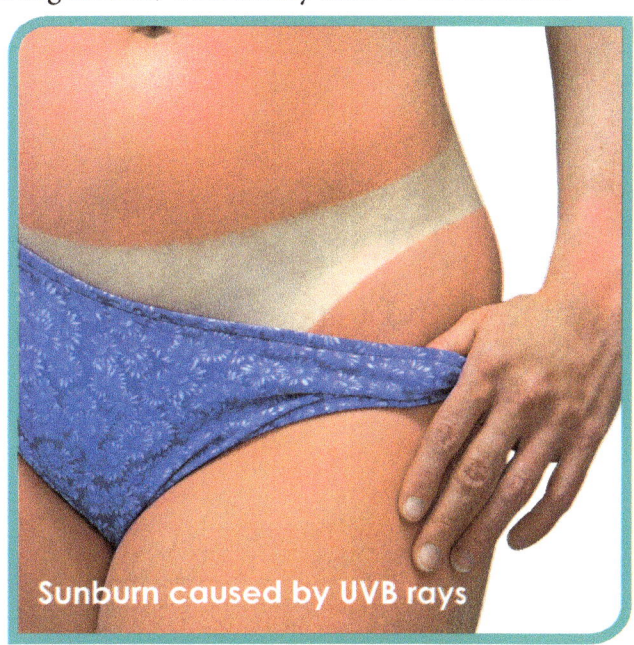

Sunburn caused by UVB rays

As previously stated, visible light falls in the range of 400–700 nm on the spectrum. Visible light is a combination of colors that are blended together. This phenomenon is best

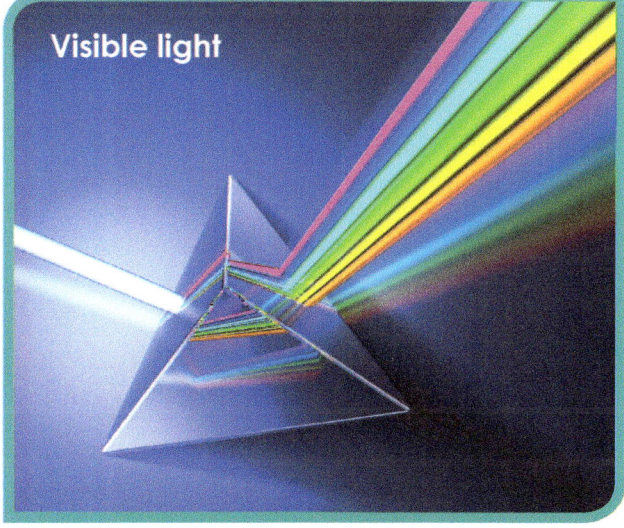

Visible light

exemplified when light is shown through a prism or similarly when a rainbow forms after rain. Whether the medium is a prism or a raindrop, light is broken into each of its most basic components and the individual colors have the ability to be seen. The visible light spectrum is broken down into red, orange, yellow, green, blue, indigo, and violet; remember the acronym ROY G. BIV. Each color has a corresponding wavelength ranging from violet (400 nm) to red (700 nm). Pure white light is a combination of all the colors in the visible light spectrum.

Infrared (IR) light is broken down into *near infrared*, found between 750–2,000 nm; *mid infrared*, found between 2,000–5,000 nm; and *far infrared*, found between 5,000–15,000 nm. These have longer wavelengths than visible light and begin following the minimal red end of the visible light spectrum. IR light has had a wide array of use in cosmetics, as it is a fairly benign treatment. People have used it for purposes ranging from skin tightening and cellulite reduction to addressing occurrences of acne and rosacea.

Finally, there are microwaves and radio waves. While microwaves are about the size of a water molecule, radio waves can be as large as a building or even a mountain. Radio waves are the least powerful or damaging, which is a good thing, because they are constantly sending signals all around us as one of greater society's most used and reliable methods of global communication.

Laser Components

Understanding the wide array of energy usage requires a working knowledge of laser mechanics. As previously mentioned, light can maneuver as a particle or as a wave. For the most part, light is conceptualized in its most general forms such as the sun, light bulbs, traffic lights, etc. All light is produced as electrons and releases energy in the form of photons once they reach an excited state. Lasers are unique in that while conventional light photons are released randomly, laser light is highly organized so that each emitted photon follows a pre-determined course. Additionally, regular light itself is projected without any specific direction, whereas laser light is projected as a compact beam with definite direction.

Laser lights are considered monochromatic because they are comprised of only one wavelength or color on the light spectrum. This is accomplished by using a specific lasing medium, which can be a gas, metal, solid, or liquid (see sidebar).

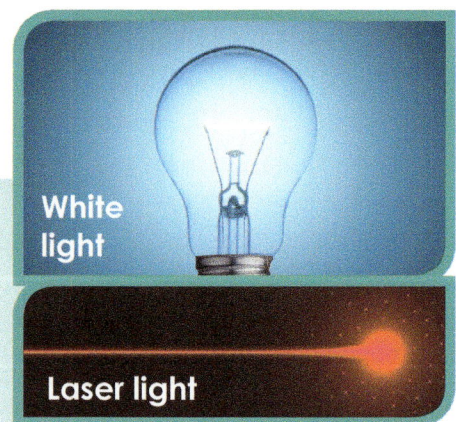

> White light itself is projected without any specific direction, whereas laser light is projected as a compact beam with definite direction.

Light Physics

Laser Mediums	
Gas:	CO_2, Argon, Krypton
Metal:	Diode
Solid Crystals:	Nd YAG, Holmium YAG, Erbium YAG, Ruby, KTP
Liquid:	Dye (v-beam)

The lasing medium determines the wavelength or color of light to be emitted. A flash tube is used in conjunction with the lasing medium and two opposing mirrors. One of the mirrors is 100% reflective and the other is partially reflective (95–98%). A power supply is then required for the laser to produce all of this energy. As the flash tube fires, these mirrors emit energy by bouncing electrons between one another in order to create photons. These photons run parallel to the rod, which means they will bounce back and forth off of the mirrors and stimulate emission in other atoms. This process results in amplification, which is the production of trillions upon trillions of photons of the same wavelength and direction. There is a small opening at the end of the partially reflective mirror which allows the monochromatic light to leave the tube as a laser beam.

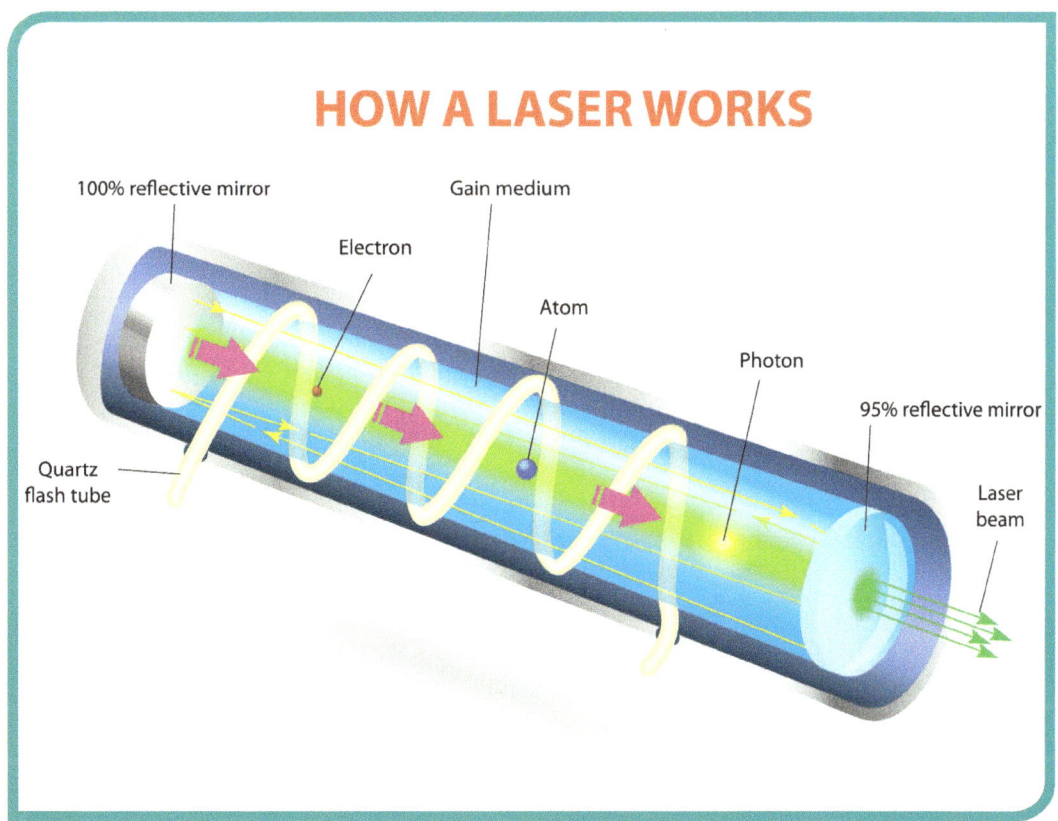

Learning the physics of electromagnetic energy is essential to providing safe, effective results. The type of light modality or wavelength to be used is the first consideration. The energy produced is directed to specific targets or *chromophores*, which are chemical groups capable of selective light absorption. Common chromophores for aesthetic laser treatments are melanin, oxyhemoglobin (proteins in red blood cells), ink (for tattoo removal), and water. Once the laser hits the target, it must be absorbed to retain heat and cause a reaction, using *selective photothermolysis*, which is the delivery of an amount of heat that will destroy the intended target without damaging the surrounding tissues, as the goal.[5] The wavelength-specific light must be absorbed to the target chromophore to be effective. The depth of the target must also be considered, as each wavelength has a specific distance that its energy is focused.

The next step is to take into account the aforementioned selective photothermolysis, which is based on choosing the right fluence (amount of energy to be delivered) along with the right pulse width (time to deliver the energy) and spot size (diameter). (See the sidebar on **Treatment Settings** for additional detail.) Determining the thermal relaxation time (the time in which the chromophore loses about half of the

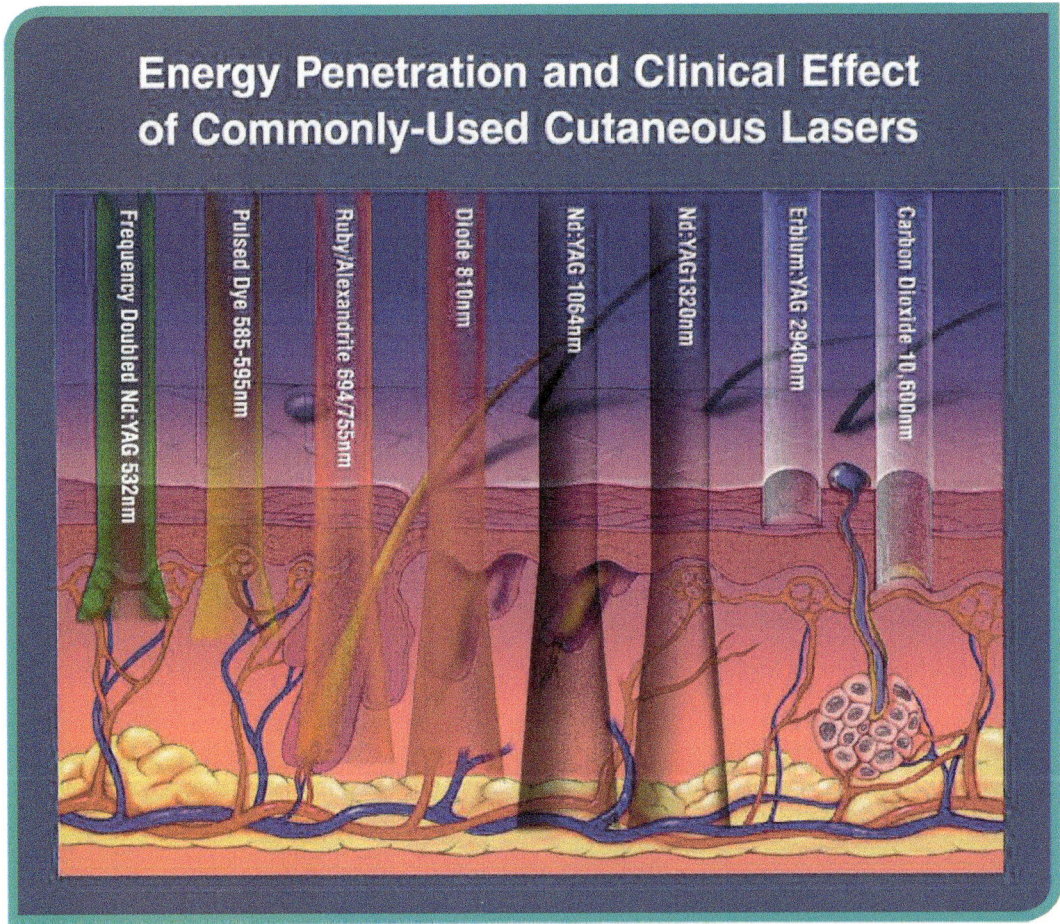

heat absorbed) is necessary to choose the right settings. Thermal relaxation time, or TRT, is a measure used in laser treatment by which to determine how long it takes the target chromophore to lose 50% of the heat it absorbs. This can be tricky; it is important to have a pulse duration that is shorter than the TRT of the target but longer than that of the epidermis, otherwise superficial burns could occur. Controlling TRT is crucial to yielding results and maintaining safety.

To illustrate, consider the cooling time of a cup of coffee versus that of a pot of coffee. It would take the pot of coffee much longer to cool off than the cup, because the pot has more substance by which to absorb and hold onto heat. The same goes for target chromophores. A very small target, such as a broken capillary, would lose heat quickly compared to a thick dense hair. Therefore, the smaller target would need a shorter pulse duration, while the larger or denser target would need a longer one.

Treatment Settings

Joule: A measure of energy emitted (J)

Fluence: Energy delivered per centimeter squared (J/cm^2)

Pulse width or pulse duration: The measure of *time* specified to deliver energy. The pulse width is most commonly measured in milliseconds (ms), although some new technologies use faster pulse widths measured in nanoseconds and even picoseconds.

> Millisecond, *equal to* 1/1 thousandth of a second
> Microsecond, *equal to* 1/1 millionth of a second
> Nanosecond, *equal to* 1/1 billionth of a second
> Picosecond, *equal to* 1/1 trillionth of a second

NOTE: Pulse duration does not change the amount of energy delivered, but can change the impact or chance of inflammation by delivering the same amount of energy at a different rate.

Spot Size: The radius of the beam

Light Energy Effects:

Photo-thermal, *meaning* use of a light source to heat up and destroy a target

Photo-chemical, *meaning* use of a light to activate a chemical to destroy a target

Photo-mechanical, *meaning* use of a light energy to mechanically breakdown a target

These terms and concepts will be useful in the next sections when relating to specific treatments. Now that safety measures and physics are defined, the next chapters will take a more focused look at the use of laser and light therapies on skin concerns commonly seen in an aesthetic practice.

References
1. J Lohne, Hooke versus Newton, *Centaurus*, 7 (1), 6-52 (1960).
2. DE McCumber, Einstein relations connecting broadband emission and absorption spectra, *Physical Rev*, 136 (4A), A954 (1964).
3. C Townes, *The Creative and Unpredictable Interaction of Science and Technology*, Netherlands: Springer (2008).
4. RR Anderson, Dermatologic history of the ruby laser: The long story of short pulses, *Arch Dermatol*, 139 (1), 70-74 (2003).
5. RR Anderson and JA Parrish, Selective photothermolysis: Precise microsurgery by selective absorption of pulsed radiation, *Science*, 220, 524–527 (1983).

CHAPTER 19

Visible Light Lasers and Intense Pulsed Light (IPL)

In this Chapter:
- Defining Non-ablative
- Lasers vs. IPL: What are the Differences?
- Indications for Treatment Application
- A Look at VLL & IPL Use, indication by indication
    - Reducing fine lines and wrinkles
    - Hyperpigmentation
    - Reduction of vascular lesions
    - Hair reduction
    - Tattoo removal

Defining Non-ablative

Non-ablative is defined as treatment that does not remove the superficial layers of the skin. This can be somewhat confusing, as there are non-ablative lasers that still effectively perform resurfacing by heating up portions of the superficial layers of the skin. These lasers will be discussed thoroughly in the next chapter, as several different devices comprise this category, capable of a range of resurfacing from light to deep. In this chapter, we will focus on *non-ablative, non-resurfacing* light therapy, meaning that the heat is directed to the deeper layers of skin, leaving the epidermis intact. All targets of energy are beneath the skin's surface. This category will be comprised of *intense pulsed light, visible light lasers*, and *near infrared lasers*.

> *Non-ablative* is defined as treatment that does not remove the superficial layers of the skin.

Visible light lasers and near infrared lasers target specific wavelengths between 400 nm and 1,064 nm. As explained in Chapter 18, each wavelength has unique properties that attract different chromophores. The most common targets for this type of light energy in aesthetic medicine are melanin and oxyhemoglobin, although they can be used to target *P. acnes* bacteria, stimulate collagen, and remove tattoos.

> Laser or light therapy can also increase a target's metabolism or be used as a tool to stimulate or activate a target. Specific medications can be applied to the skin, which lie dormant until a light source is used to activate them. This is called *photodynamic therapy* and has use in treating common skin conditions such as acne and actinic keratosis.

In the previous chapter, the wavelength spectrum was organized by laser type, through which the specific wavelengths that attract different components of the skin could be observed. The argon laser, for example, produces wavelengths in the blue-green spectrum and absorbs melanin and oxyhemoglobin in blood. Argon lasers are often used to treat skin disorders such as hemangiomas, superficial spider veins, and rosacea. Potassium titanyl phosphate (KTP) lasers emit green wavelengths whose energy is selectively absorbed by the melanin that causes pigmentation, as well as superficial vascular lesions. This laser is used to treat conditions such as sunspots, broken capillaries, rosacea, and keratosis, and has even been researched in the treatment of acne vulgaris.[2] Pulsed dye lasers produce yellow wavelengths which are delivered in short flashes. This light is absorbed by the hemoglobin in the blood and produces damage with heat. Accordingly, these lasers are often used in the treatment of vascular lesions such as port wine stains and hemangiomas, as well as hypertrophic scarring. Finally, Ruby lasers, which produce a red beam of light at a wavelength of 694 nm, were initially used for hair reduction upon first development, until more advanced applications were conceived. The Ruby laser was commonly used for reducing pigmentation and is currently used in high energy rapid pulses, to remove tattoos and dark pigmentation.

The Alexandrite (755 nm) and Diode (800–900 nm) lasers are past the visible light spectrum in the near infrared portion of the spectrum. These two wavelengths are most commonly used for hair removal due to their ability to target pigment with a longer wavelength that reaches the follicle base. The Nd:YAG (1064 nm) laser, also in the infrared spectrum, is capable of treating many skin concerns because it targets both blood and pigment. More common uses for the 1064 nm wavelength are hair removal for darker skin types, deeper vessels like varicose veins, and collagen stimulation. The Nd:YAG laser penetrates deep into the dermis, making it a superior treatment for stimulating collagen production. Also, the longer wavelength decreases the chance of post-inflammatory hyperpigmentation, which makes it safer for hair removal on higher Fitzpatrick types.

> The Nd:YAG laser penetrates deep into the dermis, making it a superior treatment for stimulating collagen production. Also, the longer wavelength decreases the chance of post-inflammatory hyperpigmentation, which makes it safer for hair removal on higher Fitzpatrick types.

Below is a brief reduplication of the wavelength range of visible and infrared light—this time segregated by respective sub-categories, based on light type:

Visible Light and Near Infrared Lasers and Their Targets
- Argon: blue-green (488–514 nm) melanin, blood
- KTP: green (532 nm) melanin, blood
- Pulsed Dye: yellow (577–585 nm) blood
- Ruby: Deep red (694 nm) melanin
- Alexandrite: near infrared (755 nm) melanin, blood
- Diode: near infrared (800–900 nm) melanin, blood
- Nd:YAG: near infrared (1,064 nm) melanin, blood

Mid-Infrared to Far Infrared Lasers and Their Targets
- Erbium:Yag mid infrared (2,940 nm) water
- CO_2 : far infrared (10,600 nm) water

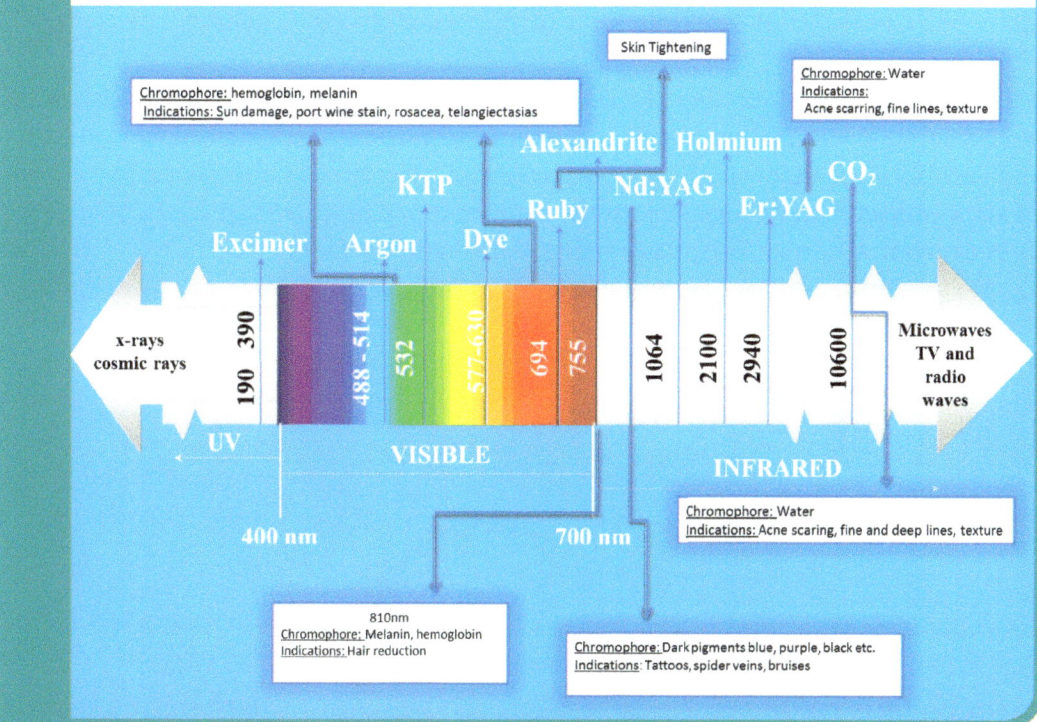

IPL: Undoubtedly the most requested, yet misunderstood non-ablative light therapy treatment is *intense pulsed light,* or *IPL.* As opposed to lasers that are directed at one specific wavelength, IPL targets multiple wavelengths of the electromagnetic spectrum. IPL is commonly called *photo-rejuvenation* since the multiple wavelengths can target various chromophores with a single setting. One might ask, why use a laser if IPL targets multiple wavelengths? The answer is that IPL can be used for many of the same conditions as lasers, but delivers less energy to each specific wavelength or target. Picture a flashlight pointed at the wall compared to a laser pointer, the flashlight would be similar to IPL where it covers a larger area but there is not a specific point to where the light is directed; the light in the laser pointer is focused at one specific target, but only covers a small area. For example, the use of IPL for hair reduction is not as effective as near-infrared lasers since the follicle needs focused heat, although it still can be an option. On the other hand, a patient that has areas of pigmentation, telangiectasia, flushing associated with rosacea, and loss of collagen would be better off getting IPL opposed to visible light laser treatments, since it will target multiple conditions with one modality. That is not to say that lasers cannot treat multiple conditions, but they are more focused at one target area.

A misunderstanding tends to arise from the perceived notion that *IPL* is synonymous with *laser*; for a quick and simple explanation of what discriminates one from the other, see **Lasers vs. IPL: What Are the Differences?**

IPL is most commonly used to reduce hyperpigmentation, diminish red blood vessels, and subsequently improve the appearance of the skin quickly with no down time.[3] IPL can also stimulate collagen with the heat it produces, although consensus opinion insists that longer wavelengths and ablative lasers are more effective for this indication. (Chapter 20 will look further at the differences between ablative and non-ablative lasers.) Other conditions treated with IPL include hair reduction, sun damage, flushing associated with rosacea, poikiloderma (characterized by vascular lesions and red/brown pigmentation), acne, and telangiectasia. IPL can be performed on the face, décolleté, arms, hands, and back.

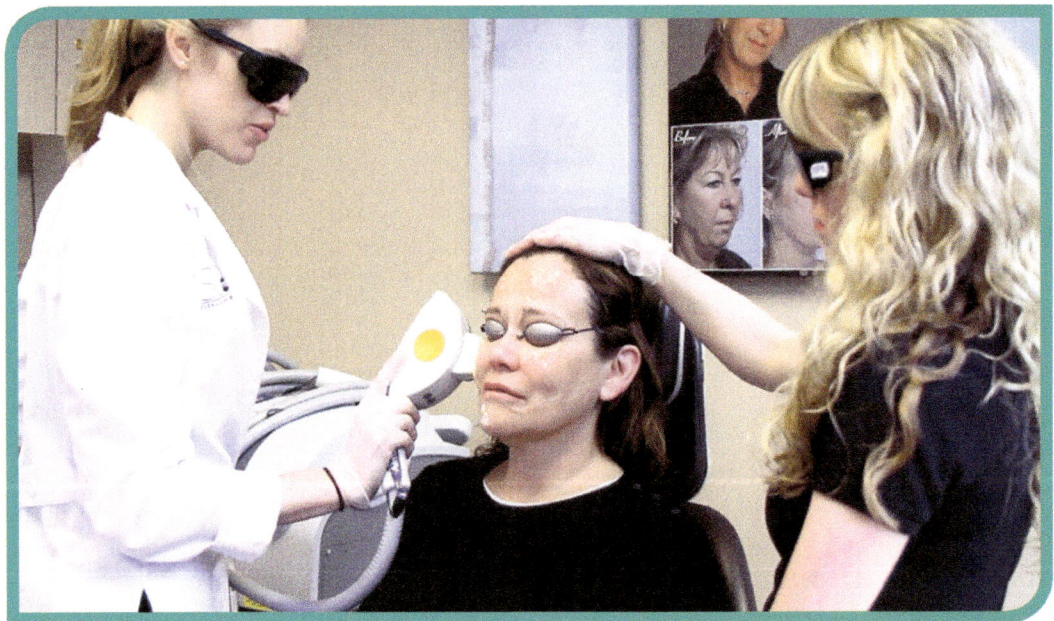

Intense Pulsed Light (IPL) Treatment

Lasers vs. IPL: What Are the Differences?

There are three main differences between IPL and lasers:

1. Laser is monochromatic, directed at one wavelength/color, whereas IPL hits multiple wavelengths or colors of the light spectrum.

2. The laser light is coherent, meaning that all the light waves are in phase (peak together). IPL, having multiple wavelengths, cannot be in phase. It is, instead, scattered.

3. Laser beams are parallel to each other, meaning that along a distance there is minimal loss of energy; they can be focused and delivered through an optic fiber. IPL light, like ordinary lamp light, is divergent, meaning that the longer the distance to the target, the less energy density per area. In other words, distance causes it to become unfocused.

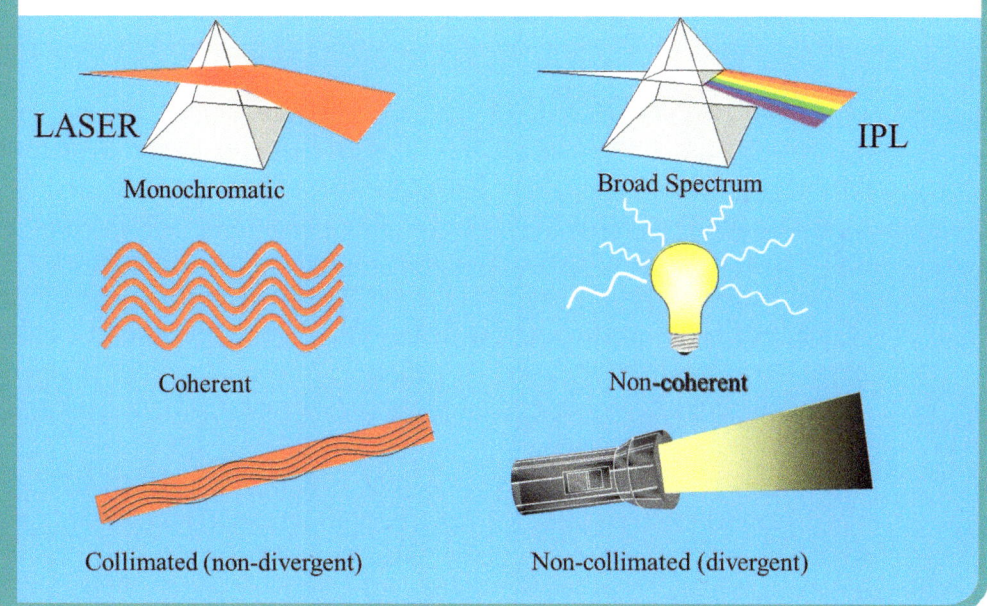

Skin Rejuvenation (including reduction of fine lines, wrinkles, and discoloration)

Skin rejuvenation is a vague term used to describe improving the overall appearance of the skin. Rejuvenation can include anything from giving the skin a glow, to reducing skin discolorations, or diminishing the appearance of fine lines and wrinkles. Given the ambiguous nature of the phrase "skin rejuvenation," there are several treatments available through skin care professionals and physicians that can improve the skin's appearance. This is where a thorough consultation and the provider's knowledge of services come together to determine the best possible course of treatment. Anyone with aging skin concerns is a candidate for rejuvenation of some sort; laser and light treatments provide an exceptional outlet, because multiple concerns are often able to be addressed in a single treatment. Although certain lasers better target specific conditions, most treatments offer multiple benefits.

For example, a middle-aged patient may seek treatment for broken capillaries, pigmentation, and fine lines. Although some light therapies are more focused at a specific target, they will generally help with all of these conditions. If a patient were to come in only concerned with wrinkles and sagging skin, then resurfacing lasers and/or skin tightening treatments would likely be the first consideration.

> Given the ambiguous nature of the phrase "skin rejuvenation," there are several treatments available through skin care professionals and physicians that can improve the skin's appearance. This is where a thorough consultation and the provider's knowledge of services come together to determine the best possible course of treatment.

Tissue Interaction

There are four interactions of light with human tissue, whether the light in question is laser light or intense pulsed light.

Absorption of light causing heating of the chromophore (pigment, blood, water, ink) is the only interaction that will affect the target.

Reflection of light can be caused by dense objects, such as jewelry or within the skin or bones.

Scattering of light is caused by large molecules such as dermal proteins.

Transmission through transparent tissue. In cases of light, where absorption does not take place, no heat is produced, which accounts for why many tissues and structures remain safe.

Reduction of Vascular Lesions:

A vascular lesion is a condition presenting as a red or purple appearance on the skin caused by the disruption of blood vessels, whether superficial or deep.[4] Examples include spider veins, telangiectasia, port wine stains, poikiloderma, and varicose veins.

In the treatment of vascular lesions, energy from the light is absorbed by the red blood cells, and the resulting heat is transferred to the wall of the blood vessel to destroy it. During treatment the vessel may completely disappear or may appear darker before the collapsed vessel is removed by the body. When treatment settings are correct, little energy is dissipated to the surrounding tissue, leaving it uninjured, and thus the skin surface remains unharmed. When treating red blood vessels or telangiectasias, significant results are often achieved. This entails the redness that exists as a patient's primary concern. As a rule of thumb, patients should expect to undergo three to four treatments, each separated by three to four week intervals, in order to receive the optimal result. It is rare for a telangiectatic vessel to remain beyond such a series of treatments, although on occasion this may occur. If the vessel does not respond to light therapy, a specialist may recommend cautery or an injection with a *sclerosing* agent, a medication that shrinks blood vessels.

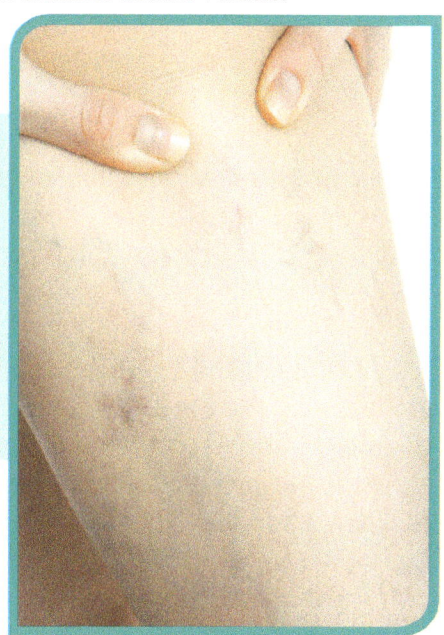

The treatment of dense vascularity associated with port wine stains should be left to the experienced physician. Longer wavelengths are better suited for deep vascular lesions such as telangiectasias, spider veins, port wine stains, angiomas, and **vericose veins**.

Depending on the type of treatment and target area, the vascular lesion may be traced with a beam of light or the energy can be delivered over the entire area. When treating multiple vessels, especially on the face, the entire area is commonly treated following the treatment of individual lesions. In the treatment of varicose veins, the provider typically uses a small spot size to deliver energy precisely to the vein. This can be painful but the use of additional cooling is questioned, as enough heat needs to be delivered for effective treatment.

Reducing Pigmentation:
During the pretreatment evaluation, the patient's natural skin color is taken into consideration. In general, a greater contrast between the patient's base skin color and the existing dyschromia, or discoloration, will result in a better outcome. For example, pigmentation on a patient with Fitzpatrick skin type II will be more visible

than the same pigmentation on skin type V due to the contrast in color. As discussed earlier, the light seeks out pigment, and those with darker complexions will likely absorb some of the light in the surrounding tissues. For this reason, patients must not present with a tan or use self-tanning creams for at least three weeks prior to treatment.

Hyperpigmentation can be caused by several influences, as described in Chapter 11. Light-based treatments such as laser and IPL are used to target melanin for dark brown discolorations. Conditions treated with light energy include solar letigines, actinic keratosis, UV damage, melasma, and birthmarks. Care must be taken when choosing the appropriate device and treatment settings to be used. If the patient is prone to pigmentation, too much heat can result in more discoloration. This is commonly seen in cases of melasma. At one time, visible light lasers and IPL seemed to be the treatment of choice, but there have been reports that the heat produced overstimulates the sensitive skin leading to more pigmentation than there was to begin with.

During treatment for pigmentation, the area must be watched diligently. Some areas may have dense, deeper melanin and could result in burns. (The provider should educate the patient on the importance of communication and to let them know that if there is a stronger sensation of heat in one area opposed to others, they need to be vocal about it.) The dense pigmented lesion is broken up into smaller fragments and removed by the body. Multiple studies

> The lasers that are attracted to melanin are capable of treating photo-damage, solar lentigines, melasma, birth marks, and pigmented hair. Caution should be used when using lasers to treat melasma, as current studies demonstrate that the condition could potentially return with increased severity.

have proven the effectiveness and safety of visible light lasers and/or IPL treatments for pigmentation, which is reflected in the high patient satisfaction rates with these types of systems.[5] When treating pigment issues, managing patient expectations is important. While skin discolorations that have been present since childhood may lighten, they will not do so as significantly as sun-induced brown spots. Finally, it should be reiterated that multiple treatments are recommended to achieve significant results in all cases of pigmentation.

Because the energy emitted in these treatments is attracted to dark pigmentation, patients with darker skin tones or tanned skin are not good candidates. Theoretically, they are at risk for skin injury resulting in a temporary skin color change that leaves the site of application either significantly darker than before, or possibly much lighter (hypopigmentation). However, at a physician's discretion, even these individuals may benefit from treatments by adjusting the laser settings to meet the needs of their skin type. This is yet another reason why thorough knowledge of the Fitzpatrick scale is essential for any provider.

Following treatment for hyperpigmentation, the treated area may appear darker for approximately one week before it begins to lighten. This is when a skin care specialist can perform an exfoliation treatment to enhance the results of the procedure. Typically by the second week, the treated area begins to lighten significantly. The treating physician may recommend that the patient receive dermaplaning, microdermabrasion, or chemical peels between treatments to slough away the pigmented areas on the surface of the skin, either of which may be performed seven to 10 days post-treatment. Three to five treatments separated by four- to six-week intervals are usually recommended. The final results are impressive, and patients are delighted that they no longer must wear makeup to cover up the pigmented spots.

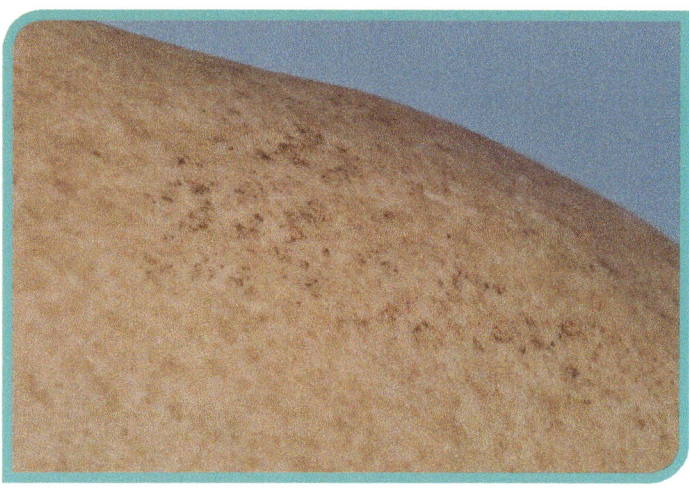
Darkened pigment in skin following laser treatment

Laser Hair Reduction

The term most often associated with this treatment type is *laser hair removal*, but this is a misnomer. *Reduction* is correct, as the intent of the treatment is not irreversible removal but rather a significant and stable loss of hair occurring for a duration longer than the normal hair growth cycle. Lasers in the near infrared range—namely Alexandrite (755 nm), Diode (810 nm), and Nd:YAG (1,064 nm)—are most commonly used for laser hair reduction, although the use of lasers with shorter wavelengths and IPL may show improvement as well. It is common for device reps to tout that the technology they use will treat everything. Although that may be true to a certain extent it is well-known that specific wavelengths are more beneficial for particular targets. When it comes to IPL especially, the range of light offers the ability to treat multiple targets effectively; although in the case of laser hair reduction, the light used in IPL is most often not strong enough to produce enough heat to destroy the hair follicle. For this reason, if IPL is used for hair reduction the patient must understand that it will likely take more than the typical number of treatments for optimal results.

Laser hair reduction procedures are rapidly increasing in popularity. Similar to skin rejuvenation procedures, the best outcomes are observed in patients with a higher contrast between hair color and skin tone (i.e., dark hair and light skin). Laser light is attracted to the pigment in the follicle, which then absorbs the light and converts it to heat. On the basis of energy delivered and the amount of time in which it is delivered, the target or chromophore is heated with the goal being selective photothermolysis. Unfortunately, since lighter hair lacks the target pigment these lasers are attracted to, the treatment becomes less effective and in some cases altogether ineffective. No reliable method for permanently reducing gray or blond hairs exists at this time, and there is only modest success with red hair.

Recommended Intervals for Laser Hair Reduction

Facial hair: 4 weeks

Underarms, bikini, back: 6 weeks

Extremities; legs and arms: 8 weeks

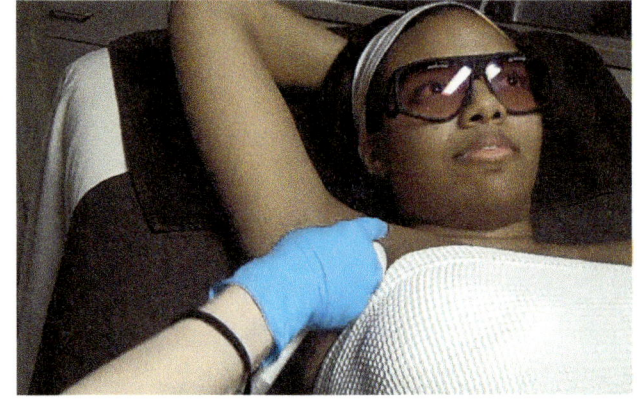

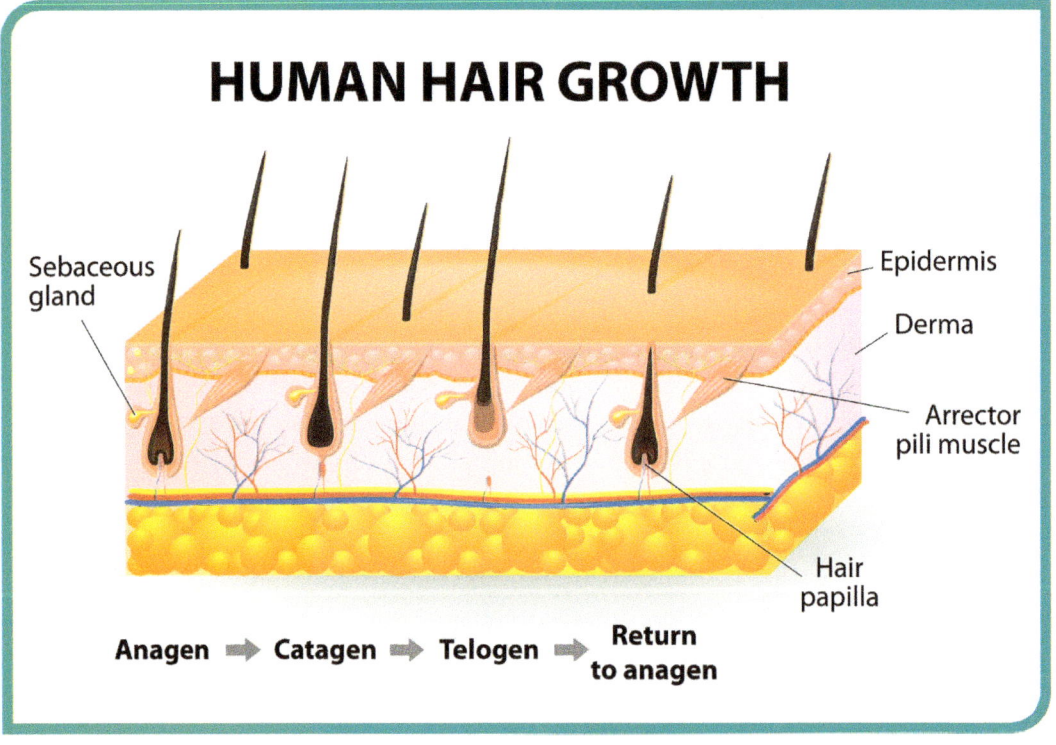

HUMAN HAIR GROWTH

Anagen → Catagen → Telogen → Return to anagen

Lasers only affect the hairs that are in the anagen stage (i.e., the active growth stage). This is why multiple treatments are needed. The hair on the face is in the anagen stage about 70% of the time, while hair on other areas of the body may be in this stage as little as 30% of the time. Due to this timeline, there needs to be proper spacing between laser treatments, and it may take several months or even years to achieve a desired result.

Frequency of Treatment: Permanency varies, and patients should be averted from the expectation that each and every hair will be removed, even after multiple treatments. However, the remaining hair is often thin and sparse. Most individuals consider this a successful outcome, and if desired may continue to follow up for yearly or bi-yearly touch-up regimens.

For safe and effective results, the area marked for reduction should be shaved within 24 hours before treatment. Why—because the laser will be attracted to the hair above the skin's surface *before* reaching the hair follicle below. This surface hair can also burn and/or singe the surface of the skin as it is heated superficially, opposed to deep in the dermis where the target of energy should be focused. By shaving first, there will only be a potential stub of subsurface hair allowing the energy to be absorbed where it is needed in the hair bulge and bulb.

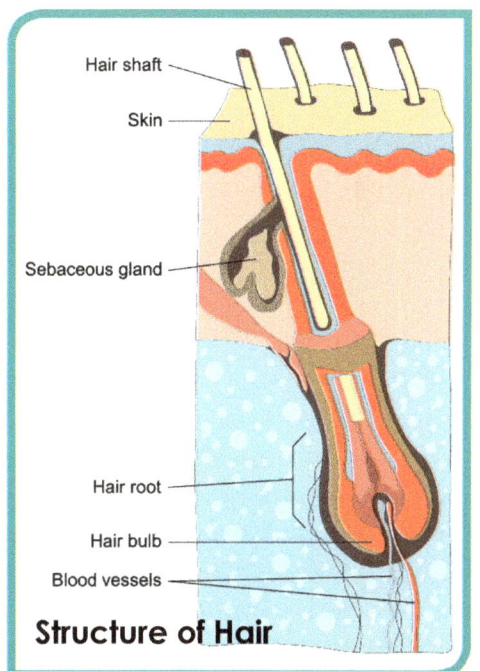

Structure of Hair

Waxing and tweezing are not recommended for at least six weeks prior to the procedure, as this will remove the entire hair shaft along the deep-seated hair follicle, which is precisely what the laser targets. If the client waxes and tweezes before laser hair removal, it will not result in a satisfactory outcome because the targets will be removed.

By four weeks post-treatment, most patients can expect to see ~ 25% reduction in hair volume, especially in areas that tend to have faster growing hair such as the bikini area or face. In some areas, such as the back or leg, where hair grows more slowly, it may take up to eight weeks to see that amount of hair reduction.[5]

General Treatment Scenario for LHR, VLL, and IPL: Remember that all creams, lotions, and deodorants must be removed from the skin before treatment; the skin must be clean and dry. Fragranced lotions or deodorants

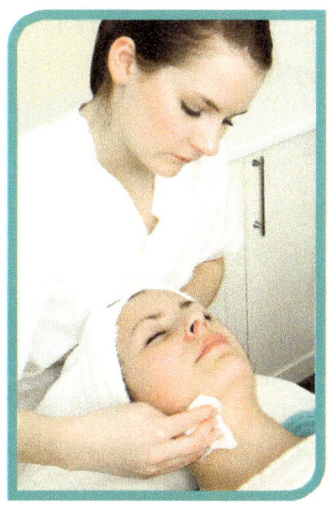

may be flammable; applying a laser over these can result in burns (**pictured**). Any open sores or skin irritations (dermatitis) are contraindications for treatment. The presence of acne, however, does *not* preclude treatment. In fact, there may even be an improvement in the acne lesions.

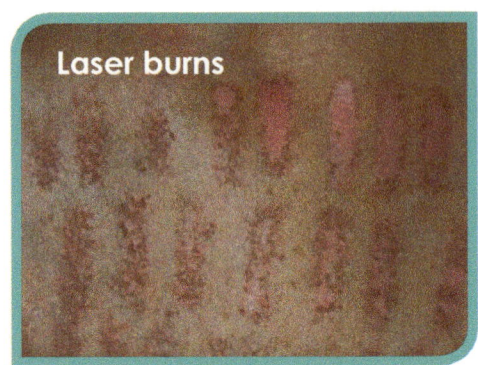
Laser burns

Immediately preceding a light therapy treatment, all makeup and moisturizers must be thoroughly removed from the area. A topical anesthetic is generally not needed and is, in fact, best avoided, because it may affect the efficacy of the laser/IPL treatment by reducing the visible appearance of vascular lesions. Topical anesthetics can function as vasoconstrictors, which narrow the blood vessels and constrict the muscular wall of the skin, thus, any appearance of lesions would be mitigated, or made smaller and possibly unnoticeable. After the skin has been cleansed, a cool water-based gel is commonly placed on the skin, although some of the newer laser devices do not require gel. This facilitates movement of the hand piece and may have additional cooling effects. Devices may also be used to pump cool air against the skin to alleviate discomfort during the treatment; many hand pieces also have a cooling tip to aid in further reduction of discomfort. It is important to protect the epidermis, which each of the aforementioned techniques suggests. Some laser energy will be scattered as it penetrates the superficial skin, and it may be absorbed by competing chromophores in the epidermis and superficial dermis. This absorption results in heat, and it is crucial that these structures are protected so that they are not inadvertently damaged.

The patient is placed in a comfortable position, with the area to be treated exposed and level. Photos of the treatment area should be taken at each visit so that the improvement can be documented and monitored. Protective goggles, chosen according to the wavelength that will be employed, must be provided for everyone in the treatment room to prevent eye injury.

Laser settings are chosen dependent on the client's Fitzpatrick skin type, as well as the color, density, and perceived depth of the target. Manufacturers will have specific parameters for their individual devices and most contain a simple interface in which the

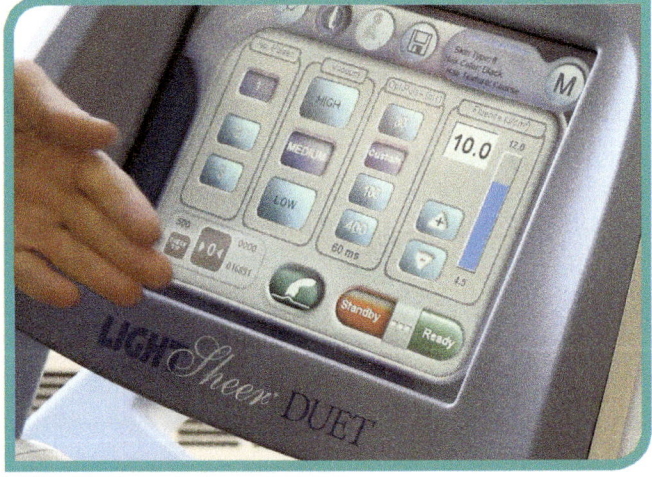
Most devices have an easy-to-use interface, like this one.

technician may enter patient information, whereby the machine generates a safe setting. It is extremely important that all laser providers have a thorough understanding of lasers and tissue interaction regardless of the ease of equipment.

Laser and light therapy treatments are generally quick. A full face skin rejuvenation typically takes 20 minutes, while an entire back or leg for laser hair reduction may take over an hour, depending on the device. Pain is subjective and varies from patient to patient, but is typically minimal. Many say that it feels like a light rubber band snap. There are certain factors, including hormones, medical conditions and medications, that can affect pain sensation. If the patient is particularly sensitive, discomfort may be alleviated with the use of topical numbing creams or additional cooling mechanisms, although with advancements in pursuing comfortable laser technology, topical numbing cream is rarely required.

Post-Treatment Side Effects: The skin may become slightly irritated, aesthetically mimicking a sun burn. An aloe gel or cream may relieve the discomfort, and most people report improvement within hours. Rarely, folliculitis, a red bump-like rash, may occur. This happens when the area of the hair follicle becomes inflamed (swollen and raised). It usually resolves within 24 hours, but if it is bothersome, the physician may prescribe a steroid cream.

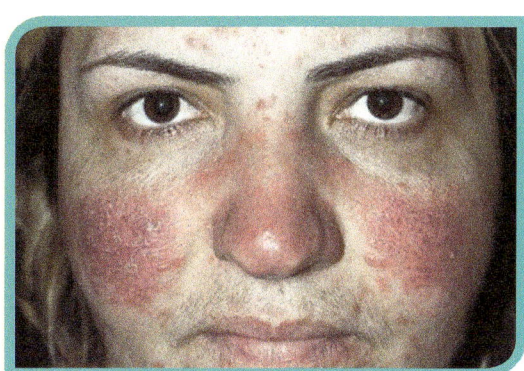

Post-treatment Side Effect: Burns

Laser Hair Reduction

Before

After

Between treatments, it is, as always, important for the client to wear sunscreen, as the treated area may now be more sensitive to the sun and vulnerable to hyperpigmentation. Conversely, although rare and pertaining more to those with darker skin types, a permanent hypopigmented spot, meaning a white spot, may occur; this is likewise a result of excessive sun damage.

> ## Post-treatment Effects
> **Laser hair reduction**, *may present with* folliculitis, or a red, bump-like rash.
>
> **Vascular lesions**, *may present* as a lesion that disappears or becomes darker during treatment; a gray-tone may also be seen.
>
> **Pigmentation**, *may present* with pigmented lesions often becoming darker before they become lighter.

Tattoo Removal

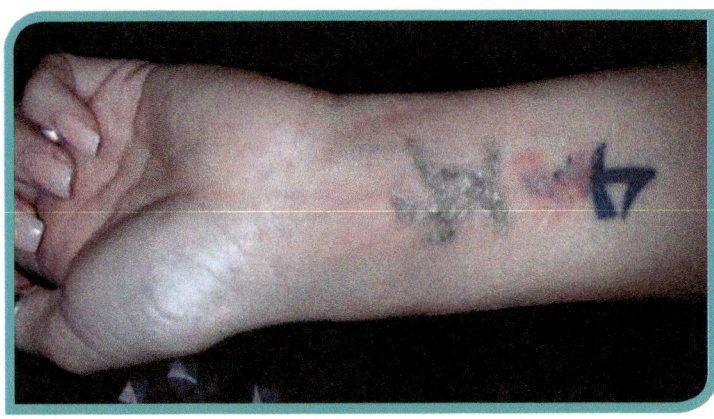

Potential side effect from tattoo removal

While tattoos have become commonplace in society as a means of self-expression, it is not *un*common for people to change their minds about what they want to express. Tattoo remorse leaves a person in an awkward position. Unlike buyer's remorse, tattoos are non-refundable. Accordingly, there has been a growing demand for tattoo removal. As long as methods of ink penetration have been developed, methods for its reversal have never been far behind. Some such removal methods have included the abrasive usage of sandpaper in conjunction with force, dermabrasion, TCA peels, and excision.[6] Although removal has evolved, it still does not exist without some discomfort.

What makes tattoo removal lasers unique is that most deliver energy in nanoseconds (billionths of a second), as opposed to milliseconds, a technology that is referred to as "Q-switched" or quality-switched. This rapid delivery of light energy works by breaking down or fragmenting the ink, a process known as *photomechanical destruction*. This fast pulse width (shorter pulse width = higher energy) also reduces the ability of the surrounding tissue to absorb the energy, providing a safer treatment.

As the short pulse-width of the Q-switched lasers made an impact on laser tattoo removal,[7] the creation of an even faster pulse width was developed. The most recent technology, recognized for its extraordinary results on tattoo removal, is the Picosure laser by Cynosure, which functions at a 755 nm wavelength. This device delivers energy in picoseconds, one-trillionth of a second, making it three times faster than Q-switched technology.

> **Photo-thermal**, *meaning* use of a light source to heat up and destroy a target.
>
> **Photo-chemical**, *meaning* use of a light to activate a chemical to destroy a target.
>
> **Photo-mechanical**, *meaning* use of a light energy to mechanically breakdown a target.

You can't always judge a tattoo by its color. Although a case for tattoo removal may appear to be straightforward and a treatment plan laid out accordingly, many tattoo artists mix white with a more dominant color to create unique shading. While this results in a visibly pleasing tattoo, it also results in less effective removal. White pigment alters the chemical makeup of the ink, and thus it is unable to be targeted in the same way that a pure color would be. Remember: the light is attracted to color. The age of the tattoo must also be taken into consideration; tattoos lighten over time and the lack of pigment may make it more difficult to treat. Like other laser therapies, the depth, density, and size of the target must be taken into account to properly choose the wavelength and settings. The usage of multiple colors in tattooing may result in the need for treatment with different lasers with varying wavelengths. Similarly, as treatments start to show results, colors need to be reevaluated prior to treatment choice.

Suggested Tattoo Removal Wavelengths, by Color:

KTP (532 nm) in the green light spectrum targets red, orange, and yellow.

Ruby (694 nm) in the red light spectrum targets green, dark blue, and black.

Alexandrite (755 nm) in the red light spectrum targets greens and blues.

Nd:YAG (1,064 nm) in the infrared spectrum targets black and dark blues, and is safer for dark skin types.

Laser Tattoo Removal Treatment:

The goal of tattoo removal treatments is still selective photothermolysis, but opposed to destroying the target with heat, the quick burst of heat is used to photo-mechanically break up the targeted ink. The broken up particles of ink are removed by the body just as it would remove other foreign particles. The skin will likely show a raised area of white skin by the high level of heat and possible pin-point bleeding caused by the mechanical impact of the laser. The skin typically becomes scabbed and heals over within two weeks. Multiple treatments are needed, commonly recommended at six-week intervals to allow the body to remove ink particles and heal itself.

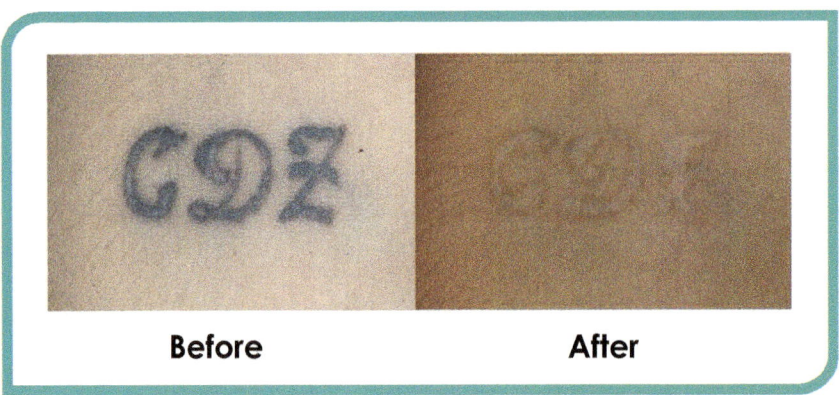

Before   After

Despite the fact that this is not considered an ablative laser treatment, post-care is more involved than typical non-ablative treatments. Namely, immediately following treatment, an occlusive agent is liberally applied to the treatment area. The agent should be continuously applied for a minimum of three days. The area should be cleaned with a gentle cleanser at least twice per day and the occlusive re-applied. If the area is located in a position that has the potential for friction with any clothing or accessories, it should be further covered with a sterile dressing to avoid contamination in the event that the agent is rubbed off. Once this stage has been bypassed, a regimen of continuous sunscreen must be used on the compromised skin.

Even more so than other non-ablative treatments, patient expectations must be diligently managed. The amount of energy required for complete removal of the color(s) may leave the patient at a higher risk for scarring. Conversely, in order to avoid leaving a scar, it is likely that the result is, while not exactly a clean slate, a much lighter and ill-defined version of what the initial image was. This allows for the patient to either more effortlessly cover what remains, or transform it into an alternate image with more ease.

For more on lasers for acne, I refer the reader back to Chapter 9.

References
1. CR Taylor and R Anderson, Ineffective treatment of refractory melasma and postinflammatory hyperpigmentation by Q-switched Ruby laser, *J Dermatologic Surg Oncol*, 20 (9) 592-597 (1994).
2. WP Baugh and WD Kucaba, Non-ablative phototherapy for Acne vulgaris using the KTP 532 nm laser, *Derm Surg*, 31 (10), 1290-1296 (2005).
3. NS Sadick, Update on non-ablative light therapy for rejuvenation: A review, *Lasers in Surg Medicine*, 32 (2), 120-128 (2003).
4. TP Habif, *Clinical Dermatology*, Philadelphia: Elsevier Church Livingstone (2009).
5. U Blume et al, Physiology of the vellus hair follicle: Hair growth and sebum excretion, *Brit J Dermatol*, 124, 21-28 (1991).
6. EF Bernstein, Laser Tattoo Removal, *Semin Plast Surg*, 21(3), 175-192 (2007).
7. SK Kilmer and RR Anderson, Clinical use of Q-switched Ruby and Q-switched Nd:YAG (1064 nm and 562 nm) lasers for treatment of tattoos, *J Dermatol Surg Oncol*, 19(4), 330-8 (1993).

CHAPTER 20

Laser Resurfacing: Ablative, Non-ablative & Fractionated

In this Chapter:
- Defining "Ablative"
- Continuous and Fractionated Ablative Lasers
- Pre-, During, and Post-Treatment
- Non-ablative Fractionated Resurfacing

Laser resurfacing is most commonly used to treat fine lines, wrinkles, large pores, acne scarring, and to produce skin tightening. As stated in the chemical peel section of Chapter 13, removing the outer layers of the skin creates a wound response, resulting in collagen production that ultimately strengthens the structure of the dermis. Similar to VLL and IPL discussed in the previous chapter, pigment and some vascular lesions will be removed by the heat created. Although resurfacing treatments are considered more aggressive due to the associated downtime; when a patient's ultimate goal is to improve their skin texture and to simultaneously tighten the skin, this type of laser treatment is typically considered first.

Skin resurfacing with lasers can range from superficial to deep, with several points in between. In this chapter, we will go over laser resurfacing, starting with the earliest development of the traditional ablative CO_2 laser, which left patients with a considerable amount of downtime during recovery, before moving on to recent devices, notably fractionated lasers, which allow for a much quicker healing time and a lower chance of side effects. As traditional CO_2 lasers are rarely used anymore, it is important to know where the new innovative technologies stemmed from.

Defining "Ablative"
As laser light is directed at a specific target or chromophore, resurfacing lasers are attracted to water in the skin. *Ablative* lasers heat this water to a boiling point, thus *vaporizing* skin cells. In *non-ablative* resurfacing, the water within the skin is heated, causing coagulation (the clotting of small vessels that supply nutrients to the skin),

which will eventually lead to the *desquamation* of skin cells—in other words, the natural removal (peeling) of these cells by the body.

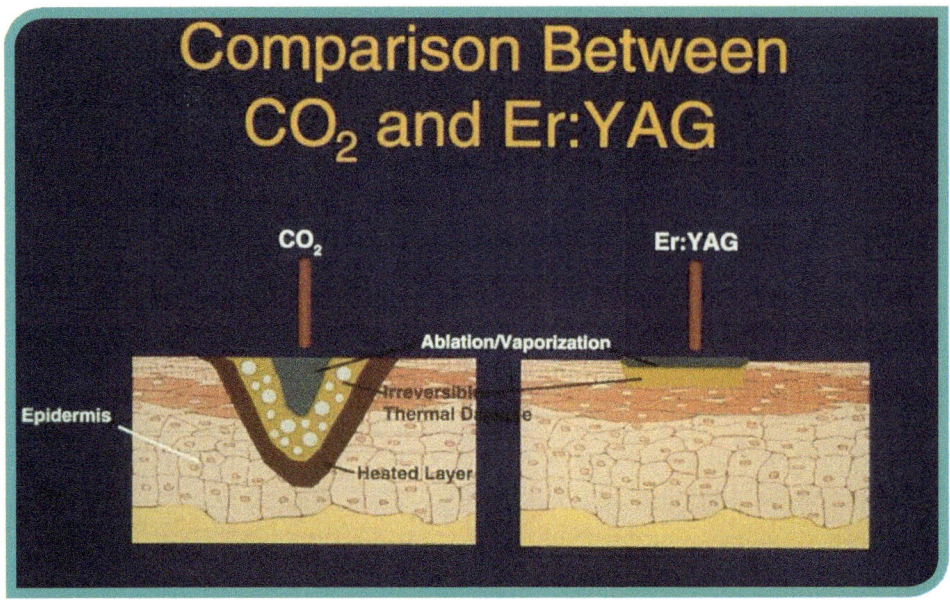

The most commonly used wavelengths for ablative laser treatments are the Er:YAG (2,940 nm) and CO_2 (10,600 nm). A rough contrast of the effect of the two laser types is **pictured**.

The application of ablative lasers results in a "controlled burn," which is limited to the outer layers of the skin. This is considered ablative because the outer layers of skin are being destroyed or "ablated." If the treatment is aggressive, the underlying skin is left raw, uncovered, and unprotected. The skin typically becomes erythematous (red) and weepy following the procedure. It is important that the patient agree to post-treatment instructions. As the wound heals, new skin regenerates and new collagen is laid down in a more orderly fashion. This ultimately results in a thickening of the dermis and the epidermis. Damaged tissues are removed, and sun-induced pigmentation is greatly reduced.

Continuous and Fractionated Ablative Lasers
The Carbon Dioxide Laser
In the early 1990s, the carbon dioxide (CO_2) laser was the most popular laser for skin resurfacing. This laser uses a long wavelength of infrared light (10,600 nm), which is absorbed by the water in the skin, causing the destruction to the outer layers of the skin.

During this ablative therapy, the layers of the epidermis and the dermis are vaporized down to the level of the upper reticular dermis. Heat travels locally in a controlled manner to the deeper dermal reticular layers. The generated heat changes the shape of dermal protein such as collagen, which shrinks as it tightens. This is usually a one-time procedure and is one of the most aggressive treatments for rejuvenating aged and photo-damaged skin. Although the occurrence of adverse effects is higher with a more aggressive laser treatment, most patients ultimately appreciate how their new skin appears the way it did decades earlier.

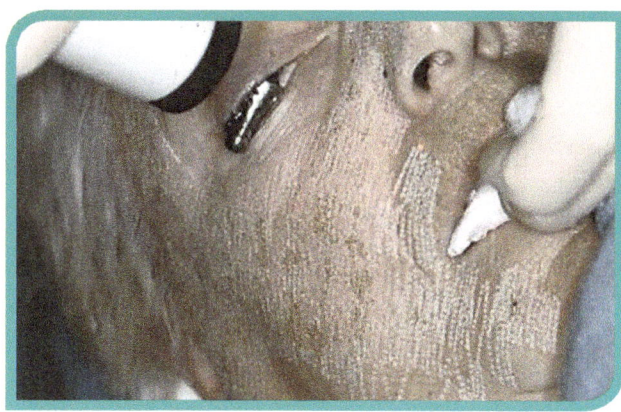

Carbon Dioxide (CO_2) Laser

The major problem with traditional CO_2 laser treatments, however, is the extended recovery time needed. Some patients appear "red" or "pink" for several months, and some develop areas of hypopigmentation; this has been seen in approximately 20% of reporting patients when multiple passes of the CO_2 laser were performed.[1,2] In the end, the extended recovery needed for this treatment, in addition to the substantial risk for complications such as hypopigmentation and scarring, has resulted in this type of deep ablative therapy falling off the radar of most providers, in deference to less problematic options that offer quicker recovery.

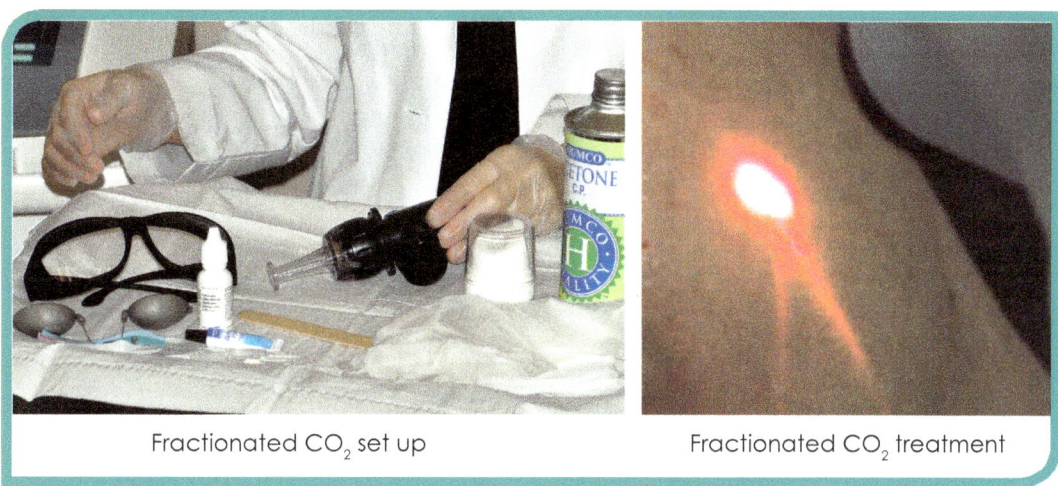

Fractionated CO_2 set up

Fractionated CO_2 treatment

Ablative Erbium:YAG Laser Resurfacing (2,940 nm)

Yet another option for ablative resurfacing without the lengthy downtime of traditional CO_2 is an ablative Erbium laser (Er:YAG). This laser's results are produced via the emission of a shorter wavelength (2,940 nm) than traditional CO_2. By production of energy in the mid-infrared invisible light spectrum, the energy emitted is 10 to 16 times more efficiently absorbed by water in the skin than the CO_2 wavelength.[3] Due to the resulting optimal absorption, the targeted tissue is instantly vaporized, which renders the surrounding skin barely affected. An additional benefit is that the Er:YAG does not singe the skin like traditional CO_2, which results in a more comfortable procedure and an enhanced degree of precision and control by the provider. Due to the depth

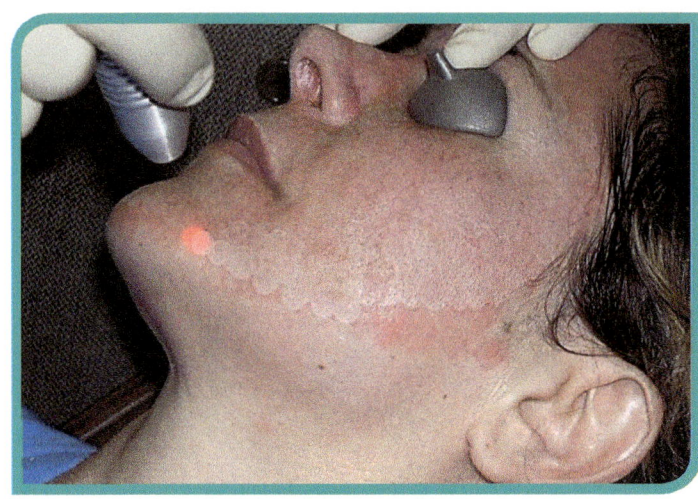

Erbium: YAG Laser Resurfacing

of removal being only a few microns thick with each pass, the healing process is diminished to as little as one week. The higher safety profile of Er:YAG lasers allows the clinician to treat patients with darker skin colors (Fitzpatrick IV, V, and VI).

Ablative Fractionated Lasers

One of the largest breakthroughs in facial rejuvenation treatments in the past two decades is the advent of fractionated laser resurfacing. The laser beam is fractionated by a distinctive difractionated micro-lens, resulting in an even distribution of focused energy. As opposed to completely destroying the entire protective layer of the skin, the goal when using this type of laser is to ablate equally spaced portions

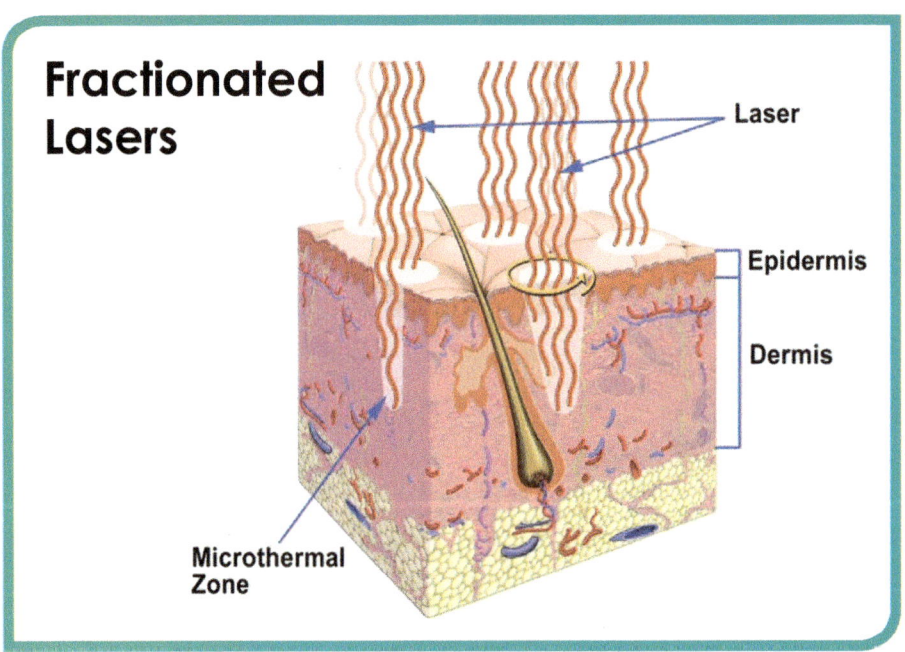

of the skin in order to expedite the healing process, while subsequently stimulating collagen. The ability to leave small portions of untreated, intact skin behind results in rapid re-epithelialization, fewer complications, and more consistent results.

The Fraxel fractionated CO_2 laser was the first of its kind to receive US Food and Drug Administration (FDA) approval for treating melasma, pigmented lesions, periorbital rhytids, and soft tissue coagulation. Many people simply ask for a "Fraxel" treatment due to the popular name, similar to how people ask for Kleenex when they mean tissue.

Who is a Candidate for Ablative Resurfacing?

While traditionally ablative lasers were only recommended for Fitzpatrick skin types I, II, and III, the fractionated CO_2 and Er:YAG lasers can be used (to a certain degree and with discretion) on all skin types. Patients requesting treatment typically do so in the pursuit of diminishing etched-in wrinkles and photo-damage. Due to the essential role of manufacturing new skin, candidates should have the ability to heal properly, thus those with a history of developing large hypertrophic scars or keloids are not candidates for this procedure. Although varying in scope, there is downtime associated with each resurfacing procedure, and a patient's schedule should be considered accordingly. Finally, the follow-up care is highly important, so patients should be diligent with post-treatment compliance.

Contraindications for Ablative Resurfacing: Darker skin tones: Fitzpatrick skin types IV through VI, dependent on the modality chosen • Those who scar easily or anyone prone to keloid scars • Smokers, those using nicotine patches, and even those in proximity to secondhand smoke can have altered healing, because smoke is a vasoconstrictor • Those with an active herpes infection • Those prone to herpetic outbreaks can take antivirals as prescribed by their physician • Pregnancy • Accutane use within a calendar year of proposed treatment.

Sample Fractional Ablative Resurfacing Guidelines

Prior to the Procedure:
- Patient must avoid sun exposure and self-tanning products for four weeks prior to the procedure.
- Depending on medical history, additional pre-treatment instructions may be recommended by the physician.

Immediately Following the Procedure:
- The provider will apply the recommended occlusive ointment.
- Cool compresses may be applied as needed.
- Direct sunlight must be avoided.
- If glasses are worn, placing a piece of gauze between the bridge of the nose and the glasses will help avoid irritation to the treated area.
- A skin care professional will go over a post-treatment skin care regimen.
- Strenuous exercise should be avoided until cleared by the healthcare provider.

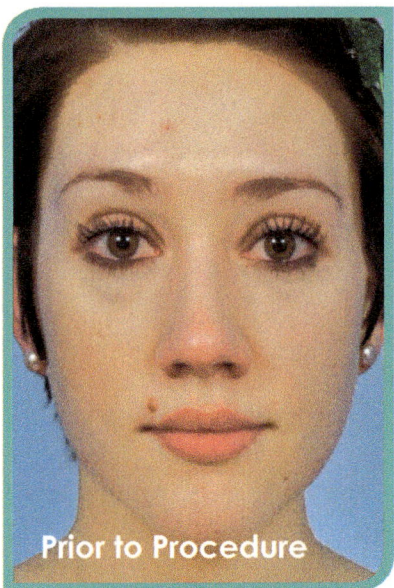
Prior to Procedure

First 2–4 Hours Following the Procedure:
- An analgesic may be recommended for discomfort as needed.
- Direct application of ice should be avoided, but cool compresses may be used.
- A fan may be used to help with the cooling process.
- Keep treated areas covered/ "glossed" with the recommended occlusive ointment for up to four days post-procedure.

First Night Following the Procedure:
- To reduce swelling the patient should sleep on their back with the head slightly elevated (continue this every night until swelling subsides).
- A clean towel free of dander or fragrance should be laid over the pillow.
- If there is irritation in the eyes, an eye lubricant recommended by the provider may be used.
- Try to avoid environmental irritants during the healing process (i.e. dust, dirt, sun, hairspray, makeup, perfumes).

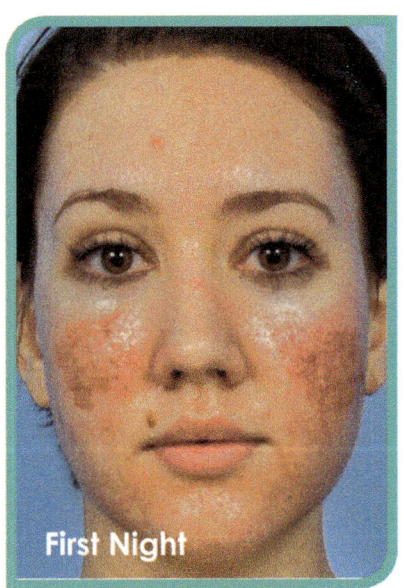
First Night

Laser Resurfacing: Ablative, Non-ablative & Fractionated

Day 2:
- The face should be washed three to four times daily with a gentle cleanser and tepid water.
- Itching (particularly along the jaw-line) tends to begin on this day—the area should not be scratched.
- Extra occlusive ointments or cool compresses can be applied as needed.
- Oral antihistamines can be used to reduce the itch if there are no contraindications.
- Picking or scratching the area must be avoided, as this could result in infection, scarring, and a longer recovery period.

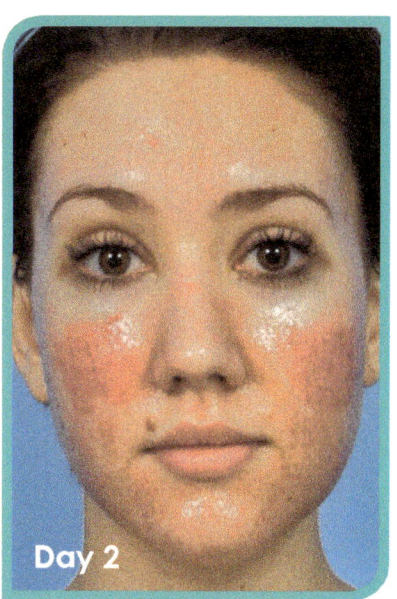
Day 2

Day 3:
- The face should be washed three to four times daily with a gentle cleanser and tepid water.
- Itching may persist; an anti-histamine may be taken as needed.
- The central aspect of the face will typically begin to exfoliate on day 3, leaving behind soft pink tissue. Care must be taken during this stage.

Days 4–7
- A non-occlusive moisturizer can be used along with an occlusive agent to spot treat the drier areas.
- Recommended products may consist of hyaluronic acid, vitamin B5,

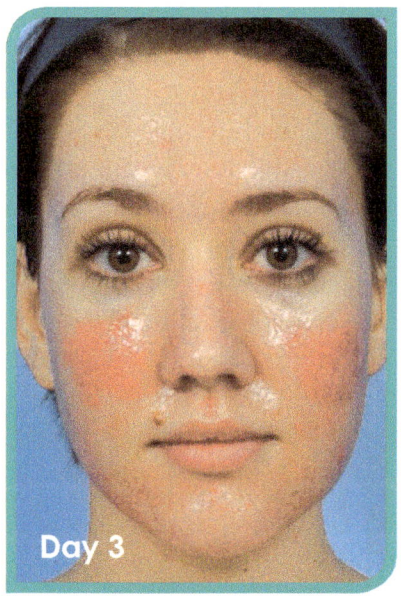
Day 3

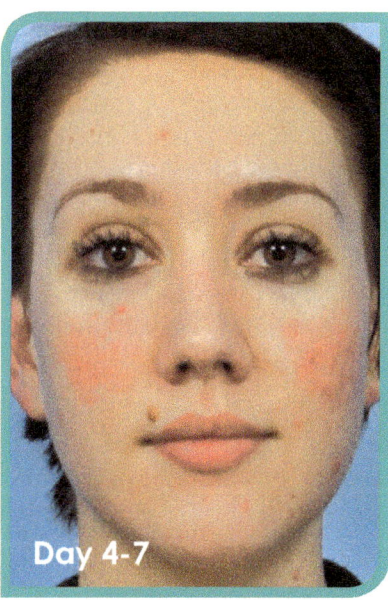
Day 4-7

L-ascorbic acid, vitamin E, beta glucan, niacinamide, growth factors, and pigment lighteners to reduce pigmentation.
- A zinc-oxide based sunscreen (SPF 30+) is necessary when there is any chance of sun exposure.

Day 7+
- The patient should return to the office approximately one week following the procedure for a check-up. At this appointment, a long-term skin care regimen will be put in place to enhance and maintain results. As long as the treated area is healed, the new regimen may begin immediately.
- Regular exercise may be introduced at this time.
- A zinc-oxide based sunscreen should be applied continuously.
- Excess sun exposure must be avoided for at least four weeks. A hat or clothing should be used to protect the treated areas.
- Mineral makeup may be introduced at this time.

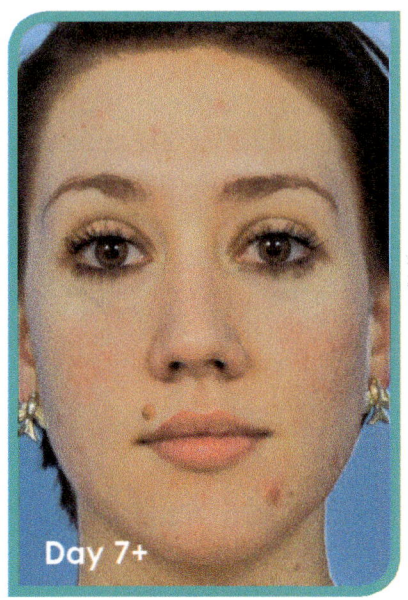

Off the Face Procedures (neck, chest and hands):
Follow the instructions under "DAYS 2 and 3" above for up to five days. These treatment areas occasionally require a longer healing period, depending on the treatment settings.

The Treatments

For patients undergoing any ablative laser treatment, the skin may benefit from pre-treatment with exfoliation and cell metabolism stimulators (retinols) or mild chemical peeling treatments with glycolic or salicylic acid. There is some evidence that pre-treatment with Retin-A may even shorten the recovery time by creating a more effective response to the injury by the pre-sensitization of dermal cells.

Superficial exfoliation treatments are typically performed at least two to six weeks prior to the laser treatment. For pigmentation concerns, pre-treating with skin lightening agents beforehand will further optimize results. It is imperative that for the immediate two to three days preceding the treatment, topical retinoids and alpha hydroxy acid products are discontinued.

Before Treatment
With any ablative treatment, the patient is typically put on a course of antibiotics as

well as anti-virals in order to reduce the risk of infection. Antibiotics are used to cover Gram-positive bacteria such as staphylococcus and streptococcus. Oftentimes an antifungal is added to the regimen prophylactically against a potential fungal infection (yeast) which may result as an unintended consequence of the high antibacterial consumption. If a patient has ever presented with any type of the herpes virus, an anti-viral medication should always be prescribed. Furthermore, if a patient presents with active herpes in the treatment area, treatment must be delayed to avoid spreading the virus.

Due to the painful nature of its application, traditional CO_2 laser treatment often requires general anesthesia. Therefore, traditional CO_2 laser treatment is typically performed in an operating room (OR). Fractionated CO_2 and Er:YAG treatment is, however, easily performed in a clinical setting, although patients undergoing surgery may opt for these procedures. While some level of discomfort still exists, patients are commonly prescribed medication to ease any discomfort or anxiety prior to the procedure.

In order to sterilize the area, treatment begins with the cleansing of the skin with alcohol or acetone. Once cleansed, a topical anesthetic may be applied to the skin, although many providers choose to forego this step. If used, the anesthetic must be cleaned off thoroughly (with alcohol) prior to beginning the laser treatment; if the skin is not properly cleansed, it may result in deep dermal burns. The provider, patient, and anyone in the treatment room must wear appropriate eye protection, and a plume evacuator must be used. Most facilities utilize an aggressive cold burst of air simultaneously with treatment, to offset discomfort.

During Treatment

Due to the "all or nothing" nature of the traditional CO_2 laser, precision on the part of the physician is paramount. Usually, two passes are performed, the first to remove the superficial epidermis, which then becomes a layer of

> It is important that the physician leave the reticular dermis intact. Injury to the reticular dermis can lead to scar formation.

charred ash that is wiped off the face, leaving the papillary dermis (outermost layer of the dermis) exposed, and the second to further stimulate collagen formation. It is important that the physician leave the reticular dermis intact. Injury to the reticular dermis can lead to scar formation. During fractionated CO_2 and ER:YAG treatments, only one pass is necessary due to their differing mechanism of action.

After Treatment

Post-care for all three of these lasers—CO_2, Fractionated CO_2 and Er:YAG—is similar, despite the fact that the more aggressive the treatment, the longer protective measures, including medications and occlusive agents, are put in place. A thick layer of occlusive ointment is immediately applied, and the patient is instructed to avoid direct sun exposure to the face for at least four weeks following the treatment. The patient may use a cool compress or take an analgesic as directed by the physician for discomfort.

Proper care of the skin is imperative in the initial weeks after treatment; the skin is going through a reparative phase and needs to be cared for as such. For traditional CO_2 in particular, the first week of post-treatment care is intense; it involves frequent debriding of the dried serum that is formed by the combination of puss and the applied ointment. The patient is instructed to gently wipe the emollient off the face with tepid tap water on a 4×4 gauze pad three to four times per day to accelerate healing. After the face has been cleansed, the patient is instructed to place a fresh thick layer of the ointment back on the face, as re-epithelization occurs faster in a moist environment.[4]

To decrease the risk for infection, it is crucial that the patient does not contaminate the skin. Cleansing the face and reapplying an occlusive agent must be done using aseptic techniques. There can be no "double dipping" of an applicator or the patient's fingers into the container of emollient. Patients should receive detailed post-treatment instructions that stipulate the use of only clean gauze pads and new applicators with each product application. Any area of skin that is not healing properly (e.g., an ulcerated lesion) must be addressed and treated immediately by the physician. After the epithelium has regenerated, which can be anywhere from three days with the fractionated CO_2 to two weeks with traditional CO_2, the infection risk is significantly lowered.

During this first week after treatment, collagen, elastin, and hyaluronic acids, the building blocks of the skin, are laid down. As the collagen remodels itself, its layers become more orderly in their arrangement, without the solar-damaged material that is common to photo-aged skin. The "new" skin will be tighter and have a more youthful appearance.[5]

Once the ointment is no longer necessary, the treated skin may appear dry and flaky. The farther out from treatment the patient becomes, the more noticeable the glowing new skin will appear. The newly generated skin is highly sensitive and care must be taken to protect it. Hence, the necessity of constantly wearing sunscreen.

Topical mineral makeup is allowed seven days to two weeks after the procedure, once the skin has re-epithelized. Over the next six months, as the skin continues to remodel itself, patients should be closely consulted on their skin care regimen. If the skin is cared for properly, the dermis will thicken, and fine rhytids (wrinkles), lentigines (pigmented areas), and telangiectasias (small dilated red blood vessels) should drastically improve.

Potential Complications
With any of these procedures, there is a risk for post-inflammatory hyperpigmentation, an increase in the natural color of the skin caused by inflammation. Typically presenting anywhere from three to 20 weeks post-treatment, it is most common

in darker skin types and those who have picked at any blemishes or neglected to follow their post-care instructions. If hyperpigmentation does occur, products with skin lightening ingredients are often prescribed such as hydroquinone 2% to 4%, which is applied once daily. (Other ingredients are listed in Chapter 27.) Hyperpigmentation almost universally resolves on its own. However, it can take many months, so patience and reassurance must be communicated to the patient.

> Hyperpigmentation almost universally resolves on its own. However, it can take many months, so patience and reassurance must be communicated to the patient.

During follow-up visits, it is important that all providers be aware of the signs and symptoms of an infection. A bacterial infection is generally associated with significant redness, purulence, and pustules (pimples). A fungal infection is characterized by a central area of raised erythematous patches with surrounding satellite lesions and intense itchiness. A viral infection is commonly identified by weeping vesicles (serum-filled blisters); these vesicles may look surprisingly like chicken pox. If an infection occurs, a culture may be necessary for the physician to determine the cause. If an infection is suspected, all products that the patient has been using on the skin (e.g. applicators and occlusive agents) must be replaced to avoid further contamination.

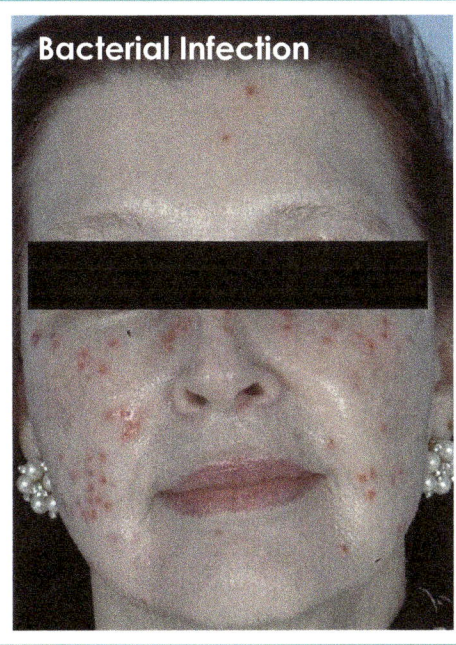
Bacterial Infection

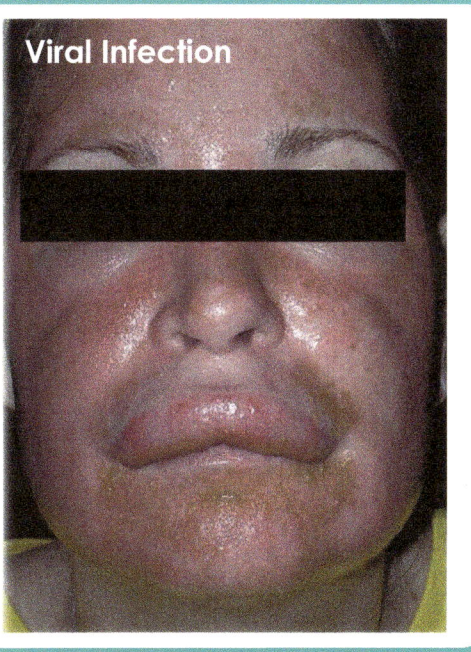
Viral Infection

With the most aggressive treatment (traditional CO_2), many patients experience significant erythema that can last for months. The skin is thin and hyperemic (increased blood flow in the tissue). Persistent, intense erythema may necessitate a topical steroid medication to reduce inflammation. For approximately two to four weeks after the procedure, product recommendations given to the patient must be very specific. Products low in botanicals with limited preservatives are recommended, as irritating substances will exacerbate conditions. No exfoliating agents or devices are recommended. Agents such as topical hyaluronic acid and occlusive emollients are preferred. To prevent sun exposure, a zinc-oxide based sunscreen should be used continuously.

A rare, but potential long-term complication may take the form of hypopigmented streaks and patches (areas with loss of skin color), which are due to damage to the melanocytes (epidermal cells that synthesize melanin) and dermal scarring. Long-term complications usually occur later in the heal-

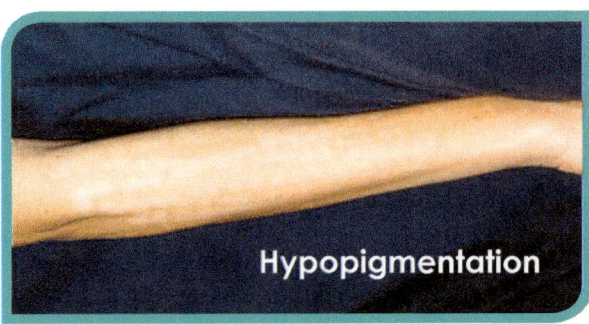
Hypopigmentation

ing cycle, many months after the treatment was performed, and can be difficult to improve. Although incidences of hypopigmentation are high with traditional CO_2, it is not as common with the fractionated CO_2 or Erbium lasers.

Complimenting Ablative Treatments with Skin Care
During the ensuing six-month healing time, the skin will need attentive care. Most patients will be interested in learning about how to care for and protect their "new" rejuvenated skin, and they will be motivated to work with the skin care professional to keep the skin in a healthy state.

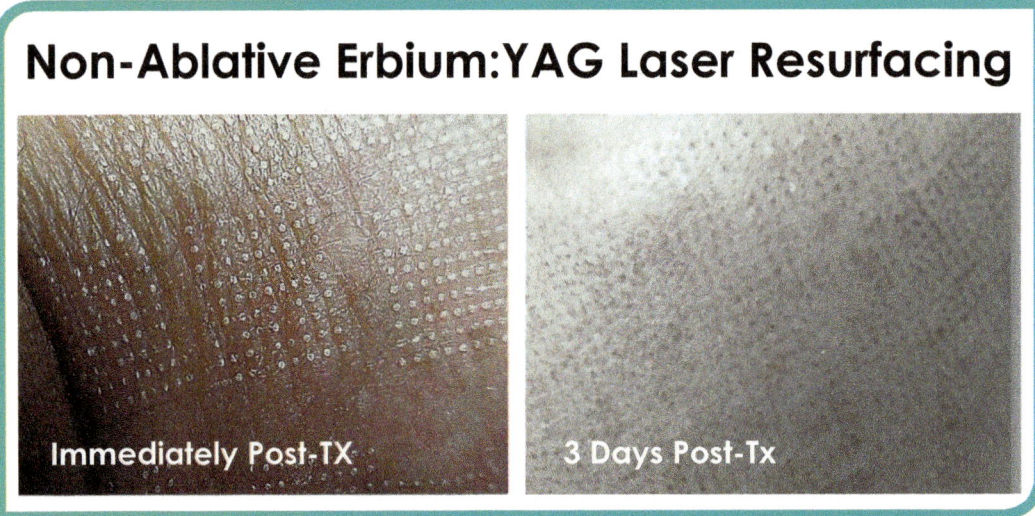
Non-Ablative Erbium:YAG Laser Resurfacing
Immediately Post-TX
3 Days Post-Tx

The *Non-Ablative* Fractionated Resurfacing Laser

This is where it can get even more confusing. There are non-ablative lasers that are still used for skin resurfacing. In this case, the light energy *heats up* portions of the skin as opposed to ablating (or removing) them. There are numerous non-ablative lasers available with different wavelengths, pulse modes, pulse widths, and light delivery. As with all aesthetic treatments, it can be hard to decipher which is best for your practice.

One example is the fractionated Er:YAG (2,940 nm) laser, which was specifically developed to rival the dramatic results of fractional ablative techniques along with more rapid healing, increased comfort, with lowered risk of side effects than resurfacing ablative lasers. The laser can be adjusted to fit the desired aggressiveness of the treatment, the patient's response, and the skin's sensitivity. Rapid epithelization is typically induced within 24 hours. There is considerable skin protection when using this laser due to its non-ablative nature, reducing the risk of scarring and heat-related complications. The results have been reliable and predictable.[6] Treatments produce minimal discomfort and anesthesia is not required. Erythema and edema rarely last more than two days. Complete healing is achieved quickly, and there is comparatively negligible downtime. A series of three to five treatments performed at intervals of three to four weeks are recommended to maximize benefits.

After the laser treatment series is complete, the skin's texture and discolorations generally improve. The efficacy of the treatment is comparable, if not superior, to other modalities used for hyperpigmentation.

Complimentary Skin Care Products

Gentle cleanser with anti-inflammatory properties

Antioxidant serum to promote healing and fight free radicals

Hyaluronic acid adds hydration for a better healing environment

Vitamin B5 has wound-healing properties

Peptides, stem cells, or growth factors stimulate and support collagen growth

Zinc-oxide based sunscreen at least SPF 30 for UV protection

Pre- and Post-treatment Skin Care

The skin care provider frequently takes care of these patients both before and after the laser procedure. Patients may undergo a series of chemical peels or microdermabrasion before requesting a slightly more aggressive treatment without the downtime of ablative resurfacing. A series of chemical peels with good skin care at least four weeks prior to non-ablative resurfacing provides the best results. About three days following this procedure, the skin shows a crusted dark pixelated pattern; this is a normal part of the cell turnover that is taking place. The skin care professional can offer dermaplaning or microdermabrasion seven to 10 days after the treatment to enhance results and remove the superficial pigment that has surfaced. Patients often see an immediate result following exfoliation and are excited about the healthy looking skin underneath. As with all treatments, the use of antioxidants and sunscreens are essential to protect results, and the use of topical retinoids will assist the cellular turnover.

Choosing the Right Resurfacing Treatment: If the patient says, "I have a long weekend and I can take four days off," then the laser's energy (fluence) can be increased to allow for deeper penetration. Patients can expect redness and possible weeping of the skin for three days. The higher the energy setting, the deeper the laser will penetrate, and the more heat that is generated in the dermis. Collagen formation is also increased

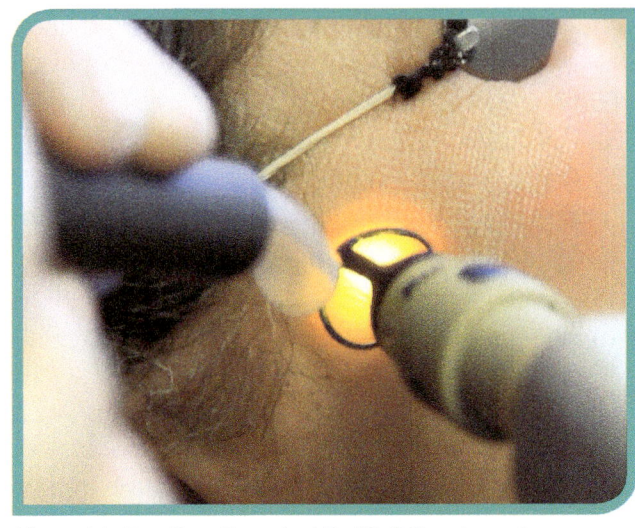

Non-ablative Fractionated Er: YAG Treatment

Fractionated Ablative CO_2 Treatment

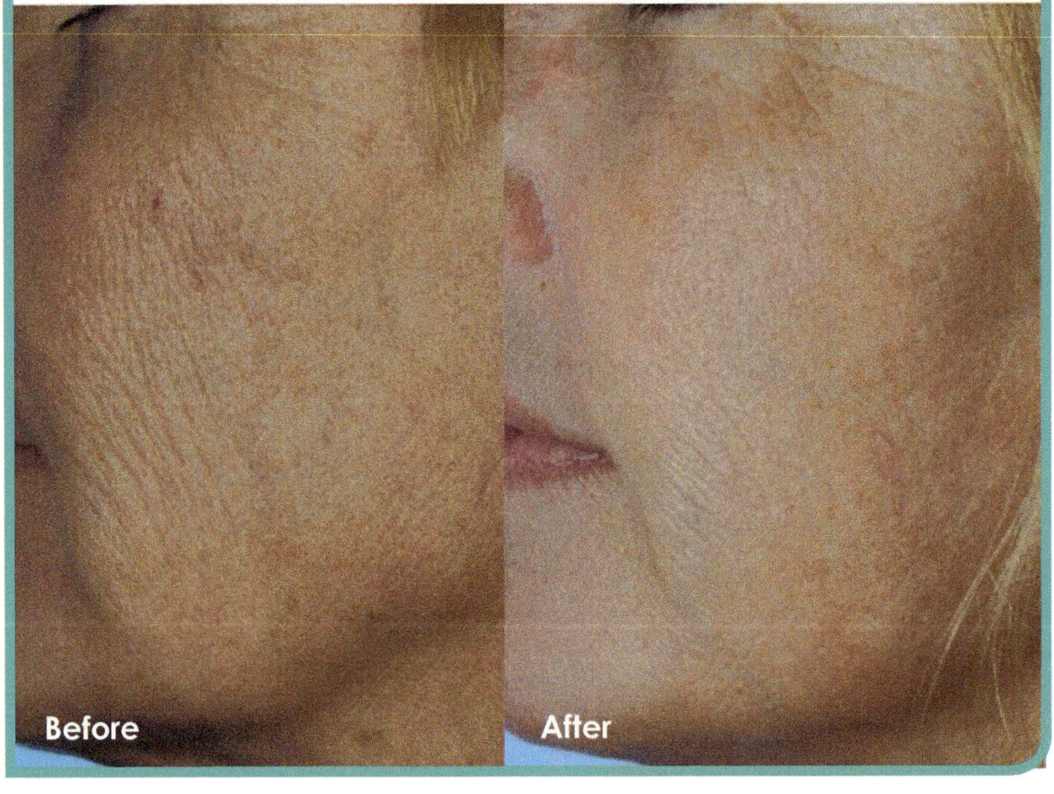

Before

After

at a higher energy setting. With deeper treatments, better results can be achieved and fewer treatments are needed to achieve these results. This is where the provider's expertise really comes into play by taking the patient's lifestyle, personality type, and skin condition into account. To recommend one type of treatment to every patient would be a disservice to all patients.

For patients who are serious about attaining significant improvement in the appearance of their skin, the laser's energy settings can be adjusted to a higher

> For more aggressive treatments the skin must be healthy and able to respond to the type of wound such treatments typically generate. As stated several times before, the goal is to create a wound response and if the skin cannot respond in a healthy way, treatment can cause more damage than good.

SCENARIO: Making the Right Recommendation

Patient comes in wanting the strongest laser treatment available at your practice. She says her skin can handle it because it is tough. After a simple visual evaluation, you realize that what she means by tough is really severely sun-damaged skin. She says she uses a gentle cleanser and a sunscreen she gets from the drugstore, but only for the past couple of months. She was a smoker but quit a year ago, and has only had spa facials in the past. She is ready and willing to pay any price to get the results she is looking for but wants a treatment that day.

What could be done:
The provider can see this as a great opportunity to help this patient get rid of all that damaged skin and to start fresh, and therefore offers an ablative laser treatment and post-laser skin care kit.

What should be done:
The provider should explain that with the cumulative amount of sun-damage present, the skin may not respond to such a deep wound. Optimal results would be achieved not with invasive laser treatment but rather with a skin care regimen and superficial exfoliation to prep the skin and observe how it responds. This does not mean that she cannot get an ablative laser procedure eventually, but she must first take the right steps to ensure that her skin is capable of repairing itself, in order to provide safe, optimal results.

setting. Although this greatly increases the benefits, it also results in significantly more redness and downtime. At higher levels, there is also more discomfort involved, so patients generally request a topical anesthetic for the procedure. These patients can expect gradual improvement in the fine lines and wrinkles over a three- to six-month period. However, even in today's society, in which people desire quick results, not many patients request a deep treatment. More often, a series of non-ablative treatments is preferred.

Patients are constantly seeking out new and exciting ways to rejuvenate the skin. Laser recommendations were at one time at the exclusive discretion of physicians. Direct to consumer marketing from laser device companies has increased patient awareness on technologies that are available, in conjunction with a more widespread application of aesthetic laser technology. It is not uncommon for a patient to call multiple practices and not only ask for a specific type of laser treatment but to also ask for a device by name. Unfortunately, the patient doesn't always know what is best for his/her skin and may be chasing a treatment that would not be optimal for them. Again, this is where patient education comes into play, not just by the providers but also by support staff. Support staff should be able to discuss technologies used in their practice confidently with potential patients. Understanding laser and light therapy and its effects on the skin may take some reviewing, but is essential for anyone working in aesthetics, regardless of his/her position or the treatment setting.

SCENARIO: Giving Sound Advice

A client comes in for the following skin care treatments on a consistent basis: monthly facials, sporadic peels, and some visible light laser treatment for stubborn hyperpigmentation. He is compliant with post-treatment instructions, uses recommended products, protects his skin from the sun, and is otherwise healthy. He is still concerned with some pigmented lesions, sebaceous hyperplasia, large pores, and moderate lines but does not want any downtime.

What could be done:
The same treatments, which still improve his skin texture over time, though without significant improvement.

What should be done:
Talk to him about a stronger procedure and discuss how it could really boost what he has already been doing for his skin. Don't talk him into a treatment he doesn't want, but explain the pros and cons of a non-ablative laser resurfacing procedure to start.

References

1. RJ Schwartz et al, Long-term assessment of CO_2 facial laser resurfacing: Aesthetic results and complications, *Plast Reconstr Surg*, 103, 592-601 (1999).
2. CS Nanni and TS Alster, Complications of carbon dioxide laser resurfacing: An evaluation of 500 patients, *Dermatol Surg*, 24, 315-320 (1998).
3. TS Alster and S Kohn,. Dermatologic lasers: Three decades of progress, *Intl J Dermatol*, 31, 601-10 (1992).
4. JW Little et al, Effect of aquaphor ointment on wound healing, *J Dent Res*, 51, 1672-1674 (1972).
5. ANB Kauvar and RG Geronemus, Histology of laser resurfacing, *Derm Clinics*, 15, 459-467 (1997).
6. DH Sliney, Laser safety, *Laser Surg Med*, 16, 215-25 (1995).

Part 5 Review Questions

1) Which of the following is **not** necessary prior to initializing a safe treatment room?

    a) Protective laser goggles for all those present in the treatment room

    b) Payment from the patient for the procedure

    c) Cleansing the intended treatment area

    d) Placing sign on door to inform others the laser is in use

2) The benefits of an inherent chill tip in the LASER/IPL hand piece is to?

    a) Protect the sweat glands from overheating

    b) Protect the epidermis from thermal injury

    c) Protect the provider's hand from injury

    d) Protect the laser from overheating

3) The amount of time between treatment intervals for laser hair reduction are based on?

    a) The patient's schedule

    b) The medical office's schedule

    c) The phase of hair growth

    d) The color of the hair

4) In which of the following scenarios is treatment with laser hair reduction contra-indicated?

    a) Non-lactating mothers

    b) Patients with blonde hair

    c) Patients with open sores or other skin irritations

    d) Patients taking hormone replacement therapy (HRT)

5) If you have difficulty or are uncertain of the treatment parameters, you should?

    a) Proceed with the manufacturer's suggested treatment settings

    b) Consult your user manual

    c) Not treat the patient

    d) Treat the patient at a low and safe but possibly ineffective setting

6) In laser hair reduction, the laser energy is absorbed by the _____ in the hair follicle before it is converted to heat and damages the follicle.

   a) Water
   b) Pigment
   c) Sebum
   d) Sweat

7) Energy in lasers is measured in _____.

   a) Nanometers
   b) Infrared
   c) Joules
   d) Wavelengths

8) The _____ is the duration of energy delivered during laser treatments.

   a) Chromophore
   b) Fluence
   c) Joules
   d) Pulse width

9) In laser hair removal, only the hairs in the _____ stage will be targeted.

   a) Anagen
   b) Catagen
   c) Telogen
   d) All of the Above

10) In an IPL (Intense Pulsed Light) treatment, the light is absorbed by _____ in the skin.

    a) Sebum
    b) Color (dyschromias)
    c) Keratin
    d) Suderiferous glands

Review Questions

11) What form of energy is released to destroy chromophores in laser treatments?

   a) Thermal
   b) Nuclear
   c) Electrical
   d) All of the above

12) With laser hair removal, results are obtained when the contrast is greater between the skin and the color of the chromophore.

   a) True
   b) False

13) What does the "A" in LASER stand for?

   a) Applied
   b) Amplification
   c) Altered
   d) Aligned

14) What is the fluence in a laser?

   a) Measure of energy delivered
   b) Duration of energy delivered
   c) Deepness of energy delivered
   d) Target of laser energy

15) In ablative laser treatments, what is the target of light energy?

   a) Sebum
   b) Blood
   c) Water
   d) Melanin

16) Intense pulse light (IPL) is another name for a laser.

   a) True
   b) False

17) Increasing pulse width and decreasing energy delivered allows for safer treatment of:

   a) Patients with fair skin
   b) Patients with tanned skin or darker skin
   c) Pregnant patients
   d) Patients with psoriasis

18) Acceptable post-treatment recommendations for IPL treatments include all of the following except:

   a) Application of aloe
   b) Applying an ice pack to the treatment area
   c) Tanning booth
   d) Use of sunscreen

19) What type of laser treatments leave portions of healthy skin behind for quicker healing?

   a) Fractionated Lasers
   b) Visible light Lasers
   c) IPL
   d) Ablative lasers

20) Immediately following treatment with ablative lasers, patients should apply recommended _____ often.

   a) Makeup
   b) Retinol
   c) Occlusive agent
   d) Alpha Hydroxy Acid

21) Laser lights are monochromatic because they are compromised of only one wavelength or color of the light spectrum?

   a) True
   b) False

22) What is NOT an indication of visible light lasers or IPL (non-ablative)?

   a) Skin rejuvenation
   b) Reduce pigmentation
   c) Hair removal
   d) Resurfacing

23) Electromagnetic spectrum is made up of light energy only.

   a) True
   b) False

24) Visible light that produces color is present between which wavelengths?

   a) 5,000–15,000 nm
   b) 400–700 nm
   c) 750–2,000 nm
   d) 190–390 nm

25) What is the term used for selecting the right amount of energy to destroy the target but not the surrounding tissues?

   a) Pulse width
   b) Tissue interaction
   c) Thermal relaxation time
   d) Selective photothermolysis

PART 6

Complementing Medical Procedures with Skin Care

AESTHETICS EXPOSED
MASTERING SKIN CARE IN A MEDICAL SETTING AND BEYOND

CHAPTER 21

Neurotoxins

In this Chapter:
- Neurotoxins—What are they and are they safe?
- Cosmetic Use of Neurotoxins
- Pre- and Post-treatment Expectations
- Potential Complications
- Who Should *Not* Have Neurotoxin Treatments
- Inanimation: The Common Concern
- What Kind of Maintenance is Needed?
- Neurotoxins and Skin Care

What are Neurotoxins?
Cosmetic neurotoxins are purified proteins derived from the bacterium *Clostridium botulinum*, and although technically defined as poisons, they have significant medical benefits. The negative effects of the botulinum toxin were first recognized in 1895 when three Europeans developed a fatal, progressive paralysis after eating raw meat. Tests found that the meat was tainted with a microbe which was later isolated by E. Van Ermengem, who called the bacterium *Bacillus botulinus*. In the 1950s, it was suggested that this poison could be of therapeutic benefit in treating hyperfunctional muscle activity.[1] For decades, people feared contracting the same lethal *botulism* from injections that is acquired by consuming improperly stored canned foods infected with the botulinum toxin. However, physicians have been using neurotoxins for more than 25 years in ophthalmologic practice to treat *blepharospasm* and *strabismus*.

The cosmetic benefits of neurotoxins were first realized in the late 1980s with those plagued with blepharospasm, a condition of uncontrollable blinking. Slowly, more formal trials began to be run on the benefits of isolating and weakening specific muscles using the toxin.[2] Subsequently, in the early 1990s, a husband-and-wife team, Jean and Alastair Carruthers, an ophthalmologist and a dermatologist, respectively, recognized the wrinkle-reducing benefits of using neurotoxins for glabellar frown lines between the eyes. Their observation began experimentation into the safe and effective use of neurotoxins in cosmetic treatments.[3]

When used in the small doses necessary for therapeutic and cosmetic procedures, neurotoxins have a solid safety profile.[4] While it may seem counterintuitive to use a poison to improve one's appearance, it is important to remember that many modern synthetic medications, herbs, vitamins, and minerals have adverse effects if taken in dosages larger than those recommended. In fact, according to the American Society for Aesthetic Plastic Surgery, neurotoxin injections to the face have remained the most popular nonsurgical cosmetic procedures performed since the early 2000s.[5]

Cosmetic Use of Neurotoxins

Neurotoxins are used to temporarily paralyze the muscles of the face in order to treat the worsening of wrinkles. Primarily composed of a polypeptide chain, the neurotoxin is, in essence, an enzyme that acts on one of the fusion proteins at the neuromuscular junction. This ultimately results in the inhibition of acetylcholine release, which is essential in the transmission of nerve impulses.[6] When nerve impulses are blocked, the targeted muscles are unable to contract. Although Botox* was the first, there are currently three FDA approved cosmetic neurotoxins on the market, each manufactured by large well-known pharmaceutical companies. The approved neurotoxins include Botox (Allergan), Dysport (Valeant), and Xeomin (Merz Aesthetics).

> Neurotoxins are used to temporarily paralyze the muscles of the face in order to treat the worsening of wrinkles.

Botox was first approved by the FDA in April 2002 for the treatment of the frown lines between the eyebrows. With aggressive direct-to-consumer marketing by Allergan, Botox was thrust into the public sector and remarkable popularity followed. Prior to the Allergan campaign, the average consumer was relatively unaware of the potential cosmetic uses of neurotoxins. Studies quickly followed, and off-label usage continues to steadily expand.

> There were approximately 6.1 million Botox procedures reported in 2012 in America, making it the number one minimally invasive cosmetic procedure across all age groups.*
>
> *2012 Plastic Surgery Statistics Report by the American Society of Plastic Surgeons

While all three brands of neurotoxins are more similar than they are different, they do vary in size and weight, which provides consumers with more decision making power. The main difference among the neurotoxins is the shape and density of the protein structures surrounding the products. Hence, each brand is technically a different strain of the toxin; Dysport is *abobotulinumtoxinA*, Botox is *onabotulinumtoxinA* and Xeomin is *incobotulinumtoxinA*.

---

*BOTOX is a registered trademark of Allergan, Inc. Irvine, CA. ® and ™ marks owned by Allergan, Inc.

Despite the fact that they are all FDA approved to prevent dynamic glabellar muscle movement, more commonly they are used off-label to treat other dynamic facial muscles. On-label usage refers to treating a patient in a manner by which the product is approved by the FDA. Off-label treatment uses a product that may be FDA approved, but in an area or manner that is not necessarily approved by the FDA. It is important to note that this does not necessarily mean that it has the FDA's disapproval; it could just be that a new use has been observed and full trials and testing have not yet been completed. An example of this would be Botox's initial FDA approval for usage in the procerus muscle for treatment of glabellar rhytides between the eyes. Once its efficacy was recognized, for years physicians were using the same technique and dosage of the product to treat a patient's crow's feet in order to address wrinkles protruding from the sides of the eyes. It was only recently that this area was added as an "on-label" treatment by the FDA.

Cosmetic Uses of Neurotoxins

On-label and off-label common cosmetic uses:

- Reduce the heavy horizontal creases in the forehead
- Reduce the furrow between the eyebrows
- Flatten deep forehead wrinkles
- Smooth out the crow's feet area around the eyes
- Reduce fine lines and wrinkles around the mouth and nose
- Improve the appearance of the thick muscle bands of the neck

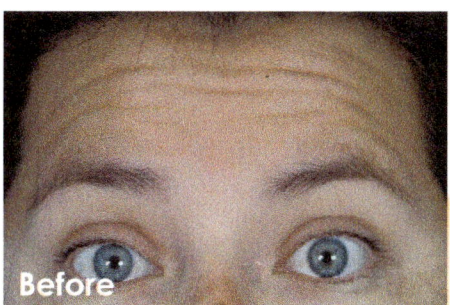 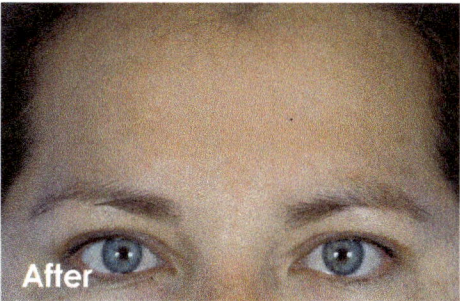

Before and after treatment with botulinum toxin A

Patients and providers may have their own preferences on which toxin they believe works best. The most common feedback has been that Xeomin and Dysport provide patients with a softer look due to their smaller protein structures, while the larger protein of Botox tends to better satisfy patients seeking little to no muscular movement. While there is no scientific evidence to suggest that one brand is universally superior to another, Dysport does present results more rapidly than the others. The average time for Dysport to kick in is typically two to three days, whereas it is five to seven days for the others.[7] As with pharmaceutical usage, each person's individual metabolism and body chemistry will render a degree of variance in the results, despite having identical treatment.

Despite their initial (and still widely perceived as primary) application, the aesthetic use of neurotoxins is no longer constrained to wrinkle reduction. In skilled hands, they are used to improve the shape and balance of one's facial features. For example, off-label, neurotoxins are utilized to widen the aperture of the eyes to make them appear "more open." This can achieve a more awake and lively disposition. The brows can also be elevated giving the eyes a more inviting appearance.[8]

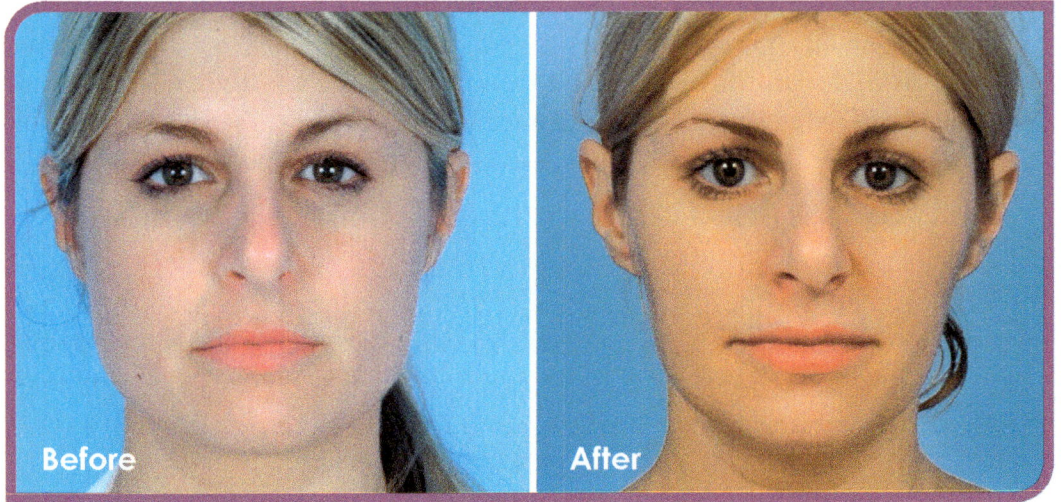

Before and after botulinum toxin treatment to narrow the jawline and "open" the eyes.

Botox can also be used to narrow the jawline. Bulky jawlines are historically characteristic of males and are often times developed over time through the grinding or clenching of one's teeth. These actions are analogous to working out any muscle in the body, in this case, the masseters. The more they are utilized, the larger they become. The usage of neurotoxins in moderation to the belly of the masseter muscles makes it possible to gradually reduce their size, resulting in a more feminine curvature of the jaw. The ability of the neurotoxin to have such a powerful functional effect on this joint has stemmed a plethora of academic articles around the topic of tempmandibular (TMJ) joint problems. Accordingly, the number of dentists using neruotoxins on patients has dramatically increased as well.[9]

Botox is also sought after to address a specific presentation of dimpling in the chin. When the lines or dimples around the chin are superficial enough, neurotoxins improve the appearance by being injected into the mentalis muscle. When this muscle relaxes, the dimples appear to be smoothed out. The types of dimpling that this is able to correct need to be assessed on a case by case basis by a medical professional. When indentations are too deep, as is the case with most lines on the face, the relaxation of the muscle alone may not be enough and filler may be needed to give a more desirable result.

Many current or former smokers and avid straw users are also coming in to reap the benefits of neurotoxins around the mouth to improve fine vertical lines, often referred to as "smoker's lines." This is a new technique and one that is approached with a very light hand. The goal is to decrease movement in the orbicularis oris muscles just enough to cease the movement that creates the wrinkles, but not so much that everyday function becomes inhibited. Results are enhanced when this is done in conjunction with a filler to define the vermillion borders, which also pull the lines apart around the mouth.

Botox is also FDA approved to treat hyperhidrosis, which is a condition characterized by excessive sweating of the axilla, hands, feet, or scalp.[8] This condition has extremely awkward social and professional ramifications. Aside from the potential smell, oftentimes clothing becomes ruined from perspiration stains. The superficial injection of neurotoxins into the hands, feet, underarms, or less commonly, the scalp can help assuage or prevent excessive sweating. The results last six to 12 months, and patients are generally very satisfied.

During Treatment

Each patient should receive a treatment tailored to address their individual concerns. In order to best assess the treatment area, the medical provider may ask the patient to forcibly and repeatedly contract their facial muscles, which will show the optimal places for injection. For example, frowning will pronounce the corrugator muscle, located approximately behind the eyebrows, and the physician determines not only where to place the neurotoxin injection, but also how many units should be administered. Once the treatment field is established, the injections take only minutes. The patient will receive a series of small injections into the desired treatment area. Although pain is always subjective, the needle used is typically around a 30 gauge, which is extremely small and rarely found to be painful.

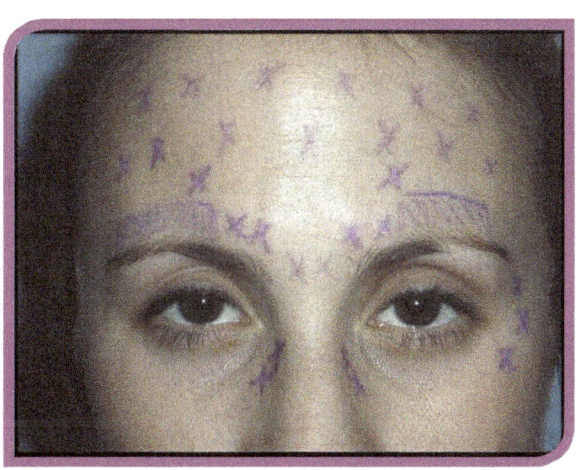

21 points of injection; note the shaded area of avoidance above the eyebrows.

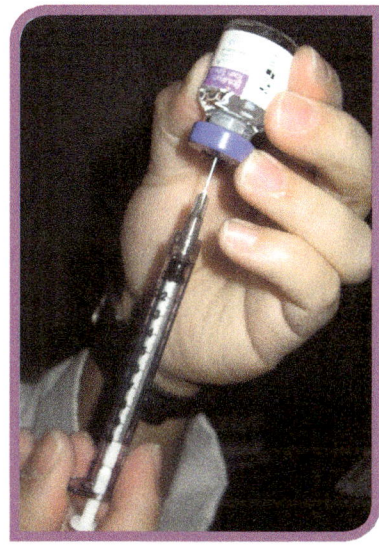

> ## Non-cosmetic Uses for Botox
> - Migraine headaches
> - Hyperhidrosis (excessive sweating)
> - Urinary incontinence
> - A form of stuttering known as *spasmodic dysphonia* (a voice disorder characterized by involuntary movements of one or more muscles of the larynx during speech)
>
>
>

After the injections, an ice pack may be applied for a few minutes to the site of injection in order to reduce the possibility of swelling or bruising. Most patients can expect only a mild, barely noticeable area of erythema and edema at the treatment site. The erythema normally resolves within a few hours.

Post-treatment

Potential adverse effects of neurotoxin injections include bruising, numbness, or headache.

- Bruising is more likely to occur if the patient is taking blood-thinning prescription medications. As a preventative measure, patients should be presented with fact sheets on medications and other products that may be contraindicative to treatment; such sheets should further spell out how long such medications/products should be discontinued prior to treatment. Other substances that thin the blood include aspirin and non-steroidal anti-inflammatory medications, vitamin E, fish oil, herbs such as gingko biloba, and other plant substances, including ginger and evening primrose oil.

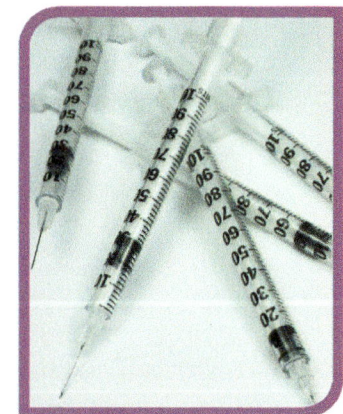

- Numbness at the injection site is rare, and when it does occur, it is likely caused by the local anesthesia that can potentially be used at the treatment site rather than by the neurotoxin itself.
- Occasionally, a headache may develop post-treatment. However, this is generally localized and lasts only a few hours. A dull headache could last up to five days.

At one time, patients were told to avoid manipulating or massaging the treatment area because it was thought that it might increase the chance that the neurotoxin could migrate to another area of the face. Patients were also instructed to avoid exercise, bending over, or lying down for four to six hours post-treatment because theoretically, these actions could cause the neurotoxin to migrate from the treatment area. A trend then also surfaced of patients being instructed to intermittently contract the muscles of the treated area in an attempt to increase the muscle's absorption of the toxin for a more effective treatment. However, after years of widespread practice and application, each of these methods has turned out to be unfounded. In fact, most patients are instructed to go about their normal activities after treatment because doing so appears not to significantly affect the results of treatment.

Potential Complications and Contraindications for Neurotoxin Treatment

As with the introduction of anything foreign into the body, there is always the possibility of complications and reactions. However, it is important to note that many of the side effects listed on the toxin's medication guide have been reported at dosages much higher than the typical dosage used in facial wrinkle improvement. One potential side effect could occur in the unlikely event that the neurotoxin injection migrates, resulting in a temporary ptosis (drooping or asymmetry) of the eyelids. This is rare and occurs in less than 1% of patients treated by experienced physicians. If left untreated it usually resolves on its own in two to six weeks, during which time the cosmetic benefits of the treatment are evident. Although unlikely, it is possible that ptosis could take up to three months to resolve. This example illustrates the importance of only having trained medical providers perform these treatments.

> Injections should be avoided one centimeter above the midpupillary line in order to prevent eyelid ptosis.

Fortunately, neurotoxin procedures remain low risk, and when used in proscribed dosages, toxicity and paralysis that would affect the whole body (systemic effects) are essentially unheard of and are rarely a consideration. One would have to withstand more than 280 times the typical

> Patients with muscular or nerve disorders or an underlying neurologic disease should not undergo neurotoxin treatments, as the effects specific to this group are at present unstudied.

treatment dosage to begin to see adverse effects. What's more, neurotoxins appear to only act locally.[10]

Patients with muscular or nerve disorders or an underlying neurologic disease should not undergo neurotoxin treatments, as the effects specific to this group are at present unstudied. Although rare, some individuals are allergic to saline or albumin, which are substances used in the production of neurotoxins. It is also inadvisable to undergo a neurotoxin treatment when taking *aminoglycosides,* a type of antibiotic. (These antibiotics are not typically used in outpatient settings.) Although no evidence exists that neurotoxins are harmful to pregnant or nursing women, until additional safety studies are done, pregnant or nursing patients should not be treated. A physician should ask questions about the patient's health to ensure that there are no contraindications to treatment. Finally, as previously mentioned, each of the three neurotoxins are a slightly different strain of the toxin. When pairing a patient to a specific type of neurotoxin, it is important to ask if they have a milk allergy. If the answer is 'yes', the patient should not be treated with Dysport and a note should be made in their file. Dysport contains trace amounts of cow milk proteins, and thus should be avoided by those with a true allergy.[11]

Results

Depending on the neurotoxin used, results can be seen as soon as one day, or up to two weeks, post-treatment. The benefits of the treatment typically last three to four months. The skin looks rejuvenated with decreased lines and wrinkles due to the underlying musculature's inability to make certain expressions. A lack of frowning tends to be the most noticeable effect when the product is injected in the glabellar area. This dramatic softening of "frown lines" provides the patient with a much softer and friendly appearance, making the effects even more rewarding. Although the scientific proof is not yet available, some patients who have undergone multiple treatments say they see longer-lasting benefits.

Occasionally, patients have what is known as an *incomplete response,* meaning that the result is slightly asymmetric, uneven, or simply does not meet their expectations. This is why patients should always be encouraged to return to the physician's office for a follow-up appointment two weeks after the initial treatment. Particularly with new patients, it is always easier to start with subtle dosing and add more to achieve a more satisfying result. Each person's anatomy is different and none are perfectly symmetrical. It is possible that one side may need more than the other to achieve an even or similar result. It is also possible that the neurotoxin is not as potent as it should be. A neurotoxin must be activated by a trained medical professional with the correct amount of saline or albumin, and must be used according to prescribed instructions.

Inanimation: The Common Concern

When neurotoxins first became available as a cosmetic treatment, many patients wanted to completely erase forehead wrinkles and the frown lines between the eyebrows. To erase these lines, a calculated amount of toxin was required and it had to be properly placed so that it inhibited facial muscle response. Some concern arose regarding the face's resulting inability to express emotions such as anger, concern, or alertness; before long, some people began to fear that the neurotoxin would make them look emotionally "flat," even though the treatment affected only the top third of the face. On the flip side, there are plenty of patients who come into the office requesting a "shellacked" look. In other words, a "frozen" appearance, no movement at all.

Most people want the benefit of having wrinkles softened, and they prefer to look refreshed and relaxed, but they do not want to lose the ability to show their full range of reactions and emotions. Patients are also increasingly seeking treatments that are less obvious to the casual eye, those that do not sacrifice the option of returning to a baseline appearance. This is why many medical professionals agree 'the more the merrier' when it comes to large companies each creating their own unique neurotoxin. The goal of any provider is to ensure their patients leave happy and to make them feel like an essential part of their own treatment plan, which is simply great customer service.

Whether the patient's preference is subtlety or noticeable change, it is important to note that, if there ever is any loss of the range of facial expression, the situation is only temporary. Within three to six months, communication between the nerve and the muscle is re-established and is back to baseline. It is also important to remember that results vary from person to person. It is obvious that a person with deep wrinkles and furrows is going to have a somewhat different outcome than would a young person with only fine lines after receiving a single treatment.

What Maintenance is Needed?

After three to four months, most people will see that normal facial movement is returning or that they resemble their look before receiving treatment; i.e., the return of the wrinkles and frown lines of an aging skin. At that point, the patient may choose to repeat the treatment. In a minority of people, treatment results last up to six months. At the other end of the spectrum, treatment results may last less than three months. This is yet another testament to the variation of people and their metabolisms.

There have been some questions raised regarding a patient's ability to develop an immunity to neurotoxins over time. Facing this concern, in 1997, the manufacturers of Botox (Allergan) altered the concentration of the albumin protein in Botox.[10] This changed the composition enough that the body ceased production of antibodies against it. If the body were to produce antibodies against the drug, then theoretically it would be neutralized and ineffective; to date, this has not been shown clinically. Yet, over time, muscles treated with a neurotoxin will thin or atrophy from lack of use. This is similar to what happens if you fracture a bone in your arm and immobilize it in a cast while it heals. When the cast is removed, your arm will be thinner from muscle atrophy, but with time and use, the muscle will come back to its original size and strength.

For example, if a woman has deep-set creases between the brows at baseline and she continued receiving injections for one or two years, after this time the deep creases may not return after each treatment wears off. So, although we generally speak of neurotoxins as a temporary solution for wrinkles, we have noticed that over time, wrinkles tend to dissipate. Although we haven't yet clarified why neurotoxins have this cumulative benefit, it appears to be so.

Skin Care and Neurotoxins

There are many ways that aesthetic providers can enhance a patient's results both prior to and following neurotoxin treatment by bundling the treatment with a skin care regimen. Before any injection, the skin must be thoroughly cleansed; this is a great starting point to educate the patient on the importance of caring for the skin even after the treatment is completed. As the provider begins the treatment, an esthetician or medical assistant often remains in the room, not only to functionally assist, but also to help build a rapport with the patient and, essentially, the practice. The assistant does anything from sweeping obstructing hair to the side, holding a nervous hand, or proactively preventing a bruise by administering firm pressure on an injection site.

> When trying to convert patients to a beneficial skin care regimen, it is also the perfect time to introduce an antioxidant and sunscreen into their regimen, while educating the patient on the importance of protecting their skin and preventing further damage as a way to protect their investment.

Following treatment, if directed by the physician, the skin care provider can apply product(s) to protect the skin and decrease the chance or duration of a bruise. Topical or oral vitamin K oxide products are often the gold standard for bruise prevention. However, if oral supplements are chosen, it is recommended that the patient begin taking them up to a week *before* receiving injections, in order to maximize their results. When trying to convert patients to a beneficial skin care regimen, it is also the perfect time to introduce an antioxidant and sunscreen into their regimen, while educating the patient on the importance of protecting their skin and preventing further damage as a way to protect their investment. Camouflage makeup can be performed at this time, if the patient feels that it is necessary in order to make them able to return to their busy schedule. The patient should also be aware that neurotoxins will help to reduce the appearance of fine lines and wrinkles by altering muscle contraction for a period of time, but will not change the overall appearance of the skin—thus no uneven texture, discolorations, or scarring.

> The patient should also be aware that neurotoxins will help to reduce the appearance of fine lines and wrinkles by altering muscle contraction for a period of time, but will not change the overall appearance of the skin—thus no uneven texture, discolorations, or scarring.

There are several skin care treatments that will enhance the patient's overall appearance by complimenting the results of the neurotoxin. Exfoliating services, for example, will leave the skin with a smooth, rejuvenated appearance. When introducing skin care treatments, the question often arises as to how long to wait between neurotoxin and facial treatments, respectively. There should be no significant amount of time needed between superficial skin care treatments and neurotoxin treatment. Any skin care treatment that does not need to remain on for a protracted period of time can be done immediately before neurotoxin injection. If the neurotoxin is done first, then it is best to wait 48 hours before conducting skin care treatments, on the slight chance that the skin could be a little sore from the injections. As for radio frequency, ultrasound, or iontophoresis, waiting two weeks post-injection is typically deemed safe.

Skin Care Products to Compliment Neurotoxin Treatment

Argirilene is a peptide known for its ability to slow down muscle contraction over time; it is often recommended as an adjunct product to those that receive neurotoxins. However, it must be noted that this ingredient should not be compared to medications, including Botox; it is illegal to compare a cosmetic with a pharmaceutical drug.

Further product types of potential benefit include:

- Retinols, AHAs, or BHA to stimulate cell turnover
- Hyaluronic acid and vitamin B5 for hydration
- Collagen stimulators, including peptides and growth factors
- Antioxidants
- Sunscreen

References

1. AB Scott, Development of botulinum toxin therapy, *Dermatol Clin*, 22, 131-133 (2004).
2. A Carruthers, Botulinum toxin type A: History and current cosmetic use in the upper face, *Dis Mon*, 48(5), 299-322 (2002).
3. JD Carruthers and JA Carruthers, Treatment of glabellar frown lines with C. botulinum-A extoxin, *J Derm Surg Oncol*, 18(1), 17-21 (1992).
4. SK Gershon et al, Adverse events reported with cosmetic use of botulinum toxin A, *Pharmacoepidemiol Drug Safety*, 10 (Suppl.), S135-6 (2001).
5. American Society for Aesthetic Plastic Surgery Profile Survey 2010, accessed on Mar 7, 2014, at: *www.surgery.org/sites/default/files/Stats2010_1.pdf*.
6. EJ Schantz and EA Johnson, Botulinum toxin: The story of its development for the treatment of human disease, *Perspect Biol Med*, 40(3), 317-27 (1997); *and* J Albanese, Discussion of unique properties of botulinum toxins, *Toxicon*, 54(5), 702-8 (2009).
7. G Monheit et al, A randomized, double-blind, placebo-controlled study of botulinum toxin type A for the treatment of glabellar lines: Determination of optimal dose, *Derm Surg*, 33(Suppl 1), S51-59 (2007).
8. SH Dayan et al, Botulinum toxin A can positively impact first impression, *Derm Surg*, 34 (Suppl 1), S40-47 (2008).
9. LE Costa, The dentist, Botox, and injectable fillers, *J Esthetic Restor Dentistry*, 26(1), 1-4 (2014).
10. Product Information Package Insert (71390US12J), Allergan Inc., Irvine, Calif. (2002).
11. Dysport Prescription Information, Ipsen Biopharmaceuticals, Inc. (March 2012).

CHAPTER 22

Soft Tissue Fillers

In this Chapter:
- How Soft Tissue Fillers Work
- Indications for Cosmetic Facial Fillers
- Hyaluronic Acid Fillers
- Other Commonly Used Facial Fillers
- Complementing Fillers with Skin Care

Fillers and How They Work: An Overview

Since 1998, there has been a shift in the way aesthetic surgeons approach facial rejuvenation. Increased emphasis has been placed on non-surgical volume enhancement for achieving a youthful appearance. Accordingly, there has been a significant increase in the number of filler products reaching the market that are designed for such corrections. Quick, reliable results, minimal downtime, and the ability to complete these treatments in the office with minimal and effective anesthetic techniques have fueled the surge of growth for filler treatments. Although optimal results may not be seen for two weeks, the initial volume replacement is immediate.

The process of aging, although different for each person, tends to be methodic in its ultimate progression. Understanding the steps in this process is vital to attaining optimal results when performing facial rejuvenation procedures. As time progresses, the first substance to break down is fat. As fat degrades, volume is subsequently lost. This process is similar to the loss of collagen and elastin within the skin, which becomes depleted over time. A decrease of volume in conjunction with loss of elasticity are textbook signs of aging, which, fortunately, can now be addressed. Accentuated by full cheeks and curves in youth, the aged face becomes framed by bony contours wrapped with thin skin. As the facial features in the cheek area drop, many patients begin to notice deeper nasolabial folds (NLF) or smile lines. Oftentimes, it is actually the augmentation of the cheek area that is best able to restore a more youthful look without the hollowing or smile lines. However, there are no steadfast rules that will work for everyone, and much of the degree of improvement relies upon the skin quality of the patient. Ideally, achieving non-surgical rejuvenation is the desired treatment plan, but for older or sun-damaged individuals with thin skin and volume loss, surgical intervention may be the recommended treatment. Surgery often involves tightly retracting the skin in order to reverse the laxity that time has wrought. If additional volume is desired, facial fillers can then be used to achieve the same results that a non-surgical candidate may desire. Of course, most patients would rather not go under the knife, but it is imperative that the medical provider gives realistic expectations, whether of a surgical or non-surgical nature, or the patient may end up dissatisfied.

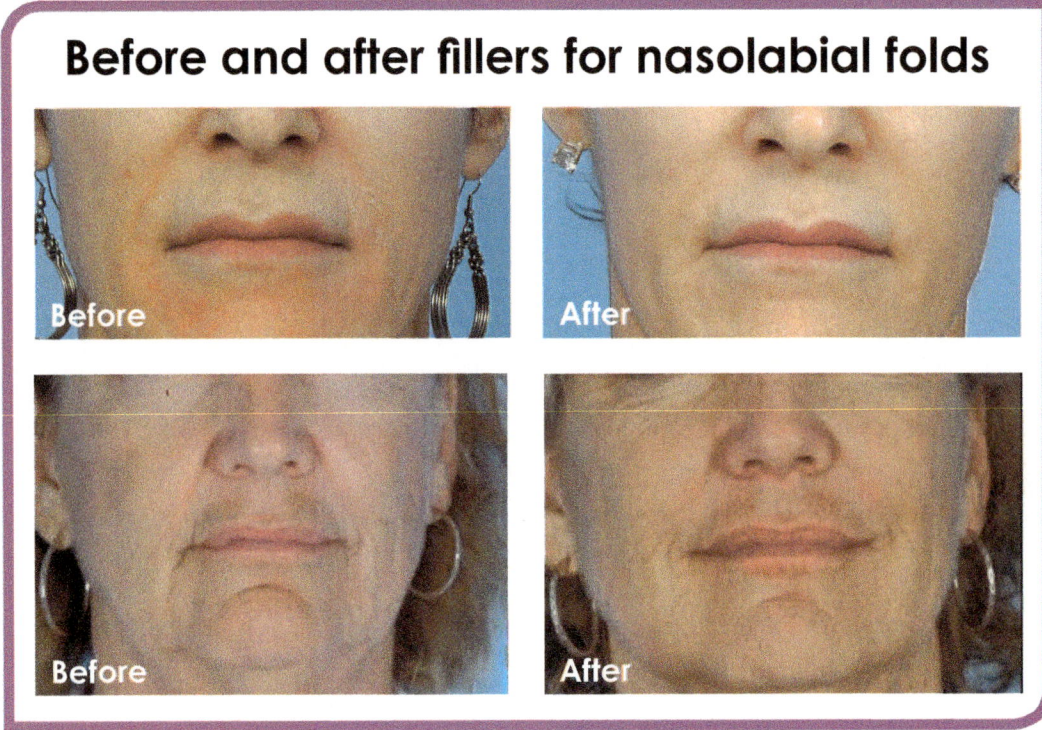

Replenishing facial volume or augmenting a surgical procedure with filler technologies has become commonplace in cosmetic medicine. Injectable fillers (therapeutic materials for soft-tissue augmentation) have provided medical professionals with a plethora of possibilities to treat all manner of concerns related to volume loss. The creation of new fillers is constant, and one is not superior to any other. Each filler has a different viscosity, which allows medical providers to discuss numerous treatment possibilities with patients. For example, if a patient comes in wanting to replace volume in their cheeks that has been lost with time, take care of the smoker's lines above their lips, *and* fill in some of the superficial lines that resemble dimples in the chin area, up to three *different* fillers may be used on the same patient. The tailoring of the treatment to each patient results in a greater confidence between patient and provider, because the patient has an active role in their own experience. Best of all, filler treatments are performed with little to no downtime and with nominal potential risks when compared to those associated with surgery.

Facial fillers are highly versatile tools for volume replacement and provide results that may last months, or even years, depending on the product used and the patient's metabolism. Fillers have the ability to displace wrinkles, plump lips, even out the jawline to improve jowls, and fill in hollows under the eyes and the cheeks, resulting in a more youthful appearance. Slightly less common, but highly successful usage includes filler for facial lipoatrophy (fat loss or "hollowing" of the face, as **pictured** before and after treatment via cannulas, or tubes inserted under the skin to deliver the correct dose to the correct location) and filling in areas of depressed scarring. In a similarly artistic usage, filler can be used to alter the shape of the nose to a limited extent, without a patient requiring surgery. Due to the level of artistry that this requires, the importance of the medical provider having a concrete understanding of each filler and how it works becomes even more apparent.

> Fillers have the ability to displace wrinkles, plump lips, even out the jawline to improve jowls, and fill in hollows under the eyes and the cheeks, resulting in a more youthful appearance.

Fillers Using Cannulas

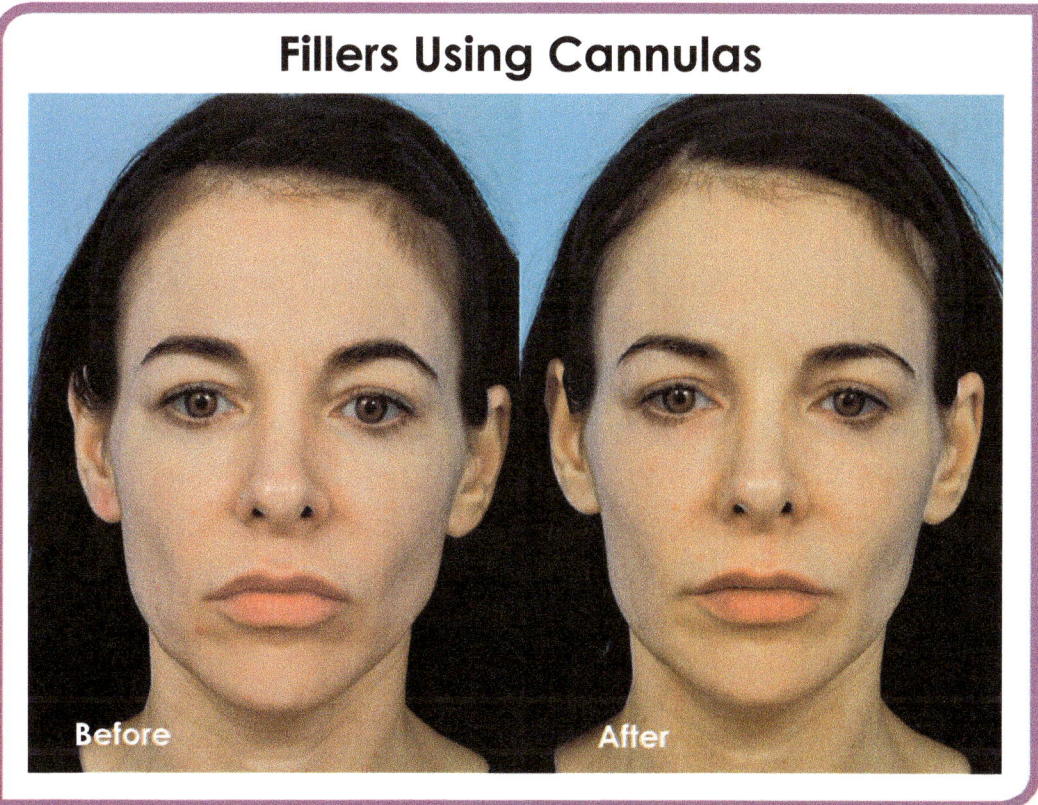

Before — After

Each case must be assessed on an individual basis, but there are some general characteristics that certain categories of fillers share. Due to their similarity of chemical composition, fillers in general tend to have similar side effects, preferred treatment areas, and associated injection techniques. The following compiled information is by no means a replacement for a treatment guide, but can be used to gain an understanding of the more common treatment options available.

Hyaluronic Acid (HA) Fillers

Hyaluronic fillers are the most commonly requested filler type due to their popularity (word of mouth is a powerful sales tool) and high safety profile. It also helps that the keystone of most of their marketing relies on educating the consumer that

Something to Consider…

If two patients with small or thin lips come in desiring enhancement, but one only wants a minimal correction while the other wants voluptuous lips, a provider should not use the same product on both. While a hyaluronic acid may be used in each scenario, the patient desiring smaller lips would want one that is less hydrophilic and thus draws less water to the area, creating less noticeable volume. The accompanying pictures show, **at top**, the results of Juvederm injections into the lips, and, **at bottom**, the effect of Restalyn to "line the lips."

Before and after hyaluronic acid treatment

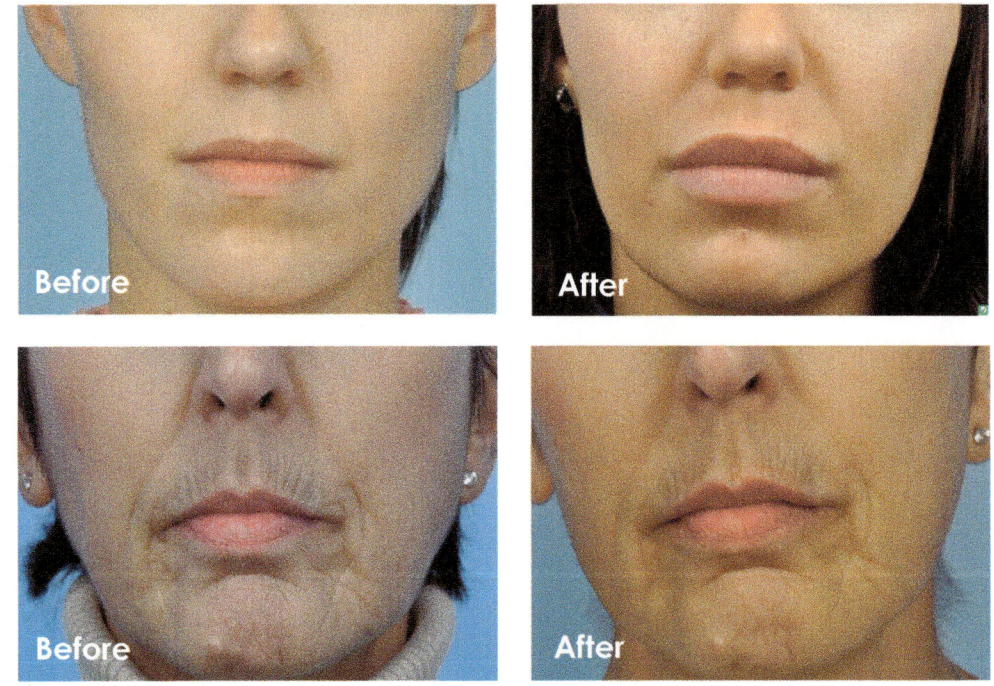

Courtesy of Selika Gutierrez-Borst MS, RN

hyaluronic acid is something that is already naturally occurring in the human body. This substance is found throughout the complex networks of connective tissue and skin. Hyaluronic acid fillers are hydrophilic, meaning they contain molecules that bind to water. There are varying properties to each filler and some may be more hydrophilic than others.

An added reason for physician and patient gravitation towards hyaluronic acids is due to their ability to be reversed. If a patient is unsatisfied, or if a complication arises, an enzyme called hyaluronidase can be injected to quickly and efficiently dissolve the product and return the patient back to their pre-treatment state. There are very few side effects associated with hyaluronidase, and minimal discomfort is typically reported.

Of the available hyaluronic acid fillers (see sidebar for a quick list), Restylane (Medicis) was the first to receive FDA cosmetic approval, which it did in December 2003, to correct moderate-to-severe facial wrinkles and folds such as nasolabial folds.

Hyaluronic Acid Fillers Currently at Market

- Juvederm Ultra
- Juvederm Ultra Plus
- Juvederm Ultra Plus XC
- Juvederm Ultra XC
- Juvederm VOLUMA
- Restylane
- Perlane
- Belotero

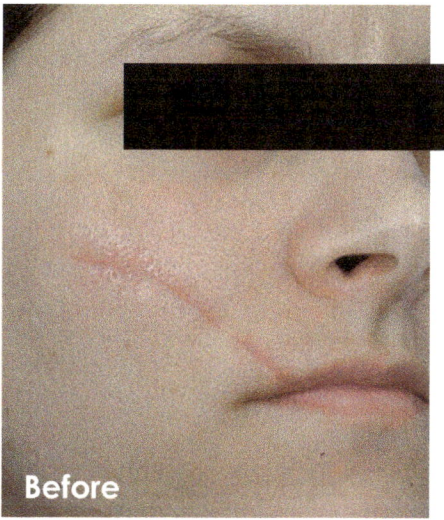
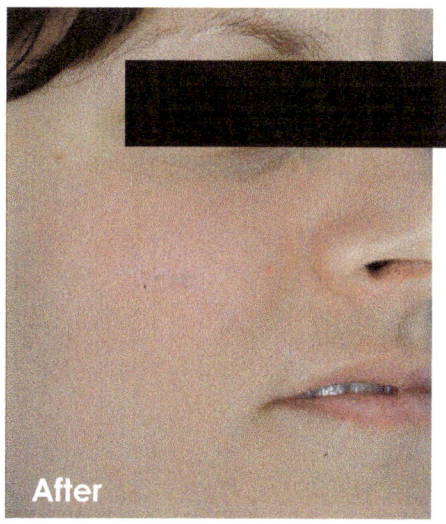

HA filler for scar reversion (before and after).

Calcium Hydroxylapatite

In December of 2006, the FDA approved Radiesse (Merz Aesthetics [formerly Bioform Medical]) for the correction of wrinkles and folds such as nasolabial folds, and for the correction of facial lipoatrophy as a result of HIV disease. Radiesse is composed of calcium hydroxylapatite microspheres, ingredients that can be found in human bone and tooth tissue. Radiesse has an excellent safety profile and stimulates almost no foreign-body reaction.[1]

Before and after filler to reshape the nose

After implantation, this product is slightly moldable, but due to its high viscosity, it will quickly maintain its structure. Additionally, the same amount of volume will go further than that demonstrated by HAs; in other words, less volume of calcium hydroxylapatite is needed to fill the same defect, when compared with the amount required of hyaluronic acid. However, calcium hydroxylapatite is not recommended for lip augmentation because the product could leave an unnatural looking stiff lip.

Collagen Products

Cosmoderm and Cosmoplast (both Allergan) are human-derived bioengineered collagen implants; Zyplast and Zyderm (also Allergan) are their bovine-derived counterparts. These were the very first collagen implants to get FDA approval in 1983. As of 2010, Allergan discontinued their manufacturing of collagen injectables. What's more, Johnson & Johnson also discontinued manufacture of their porcine collagen product, Evolence. Complications with collagen injections, while rare, have been reported. The report of most concern medically has been potential vascular necrosis (death of soft tissue secondary to blockage of blood vessels) after collagen injection in the glabellar area.[2,3] Longevity of the product has also not been particularly promising, and these products have the potential to leave behind a bumpy irregular appearance on the skin. Essentially, the original train of thought was that using a substance that has high similarities to human collagen makeup would be most efficient. However, as science has evolved, the continued scientific tweaking of hyaluronic acids has created superior products. It is important for aesthetic providers to be aware of the wide range of potential products that may be present in treatment areas, as in some instances it may alter their suggestions.

Silicone Treatment Options

Despite lacking FDA approval for cosmetic use in the United States, silicone is used off-label by some practitioners. Silicone has a history shrouded in controversy and perhaps has been unfairly criminalized.[4] Said distain mostly comes from the overdone poster women of plastic surgery centered in Silicone Valley. Other assumptions come from negative reports of silicone breast implants rupturing and causing harm to patients. However, the way the product is administered differs vastly in these cases. Currently, the two brands most commonly used off-label are Silikon 1000 (Alcon) and AdatoSil 5000 (Bausch & Lomb Inc.). Although a benefit of the product is that its chemical makeup renders it smooth to the touch, providers have reported that silicone has a tendency to be more difficult than other fillers to administer. Reports of serious potential complications have included granulomas (a tumor-like mass or nodule), surface deformities, lymph vessel blockage, rosacea-like reactions, migration, embolism, and even blindness.[5-9] Other reports have conversely indicated long-term effective and safe experiences with silicone.[10-12]

Small droplets of silicone, called microdroplets, may provide the best aesthetic results for correcting fine lines, wrinkles, and post-acne scarring. Under-correction and multiple treatments spaced two to three months apart are recommended, as the droplets continue to be coated with the patient's own collagen for up to three months post-treatment.[13]

> Long-term risks of hypersensitivity reactions and scarring, which can occur years later, remain a concern for silicone fillers.

Artefill

Artefill (Artes) is polymethylmethacrylate microspheres surrounded by bovine collagen. This filler agent was approved by the FDA for cosmetic use in 2006; it was originally marketed in Europe and Canada as Artecoll. Because it has a bovine collagen component, an allergy skin test is needed before treatment.[14] The bovine collagen is replaced within three months by host connective tissue, which results in the Artefill beads providing permanent correction. After seven months, there are few differences between the collagen fibers around the implant and those of the surrounding connective tissue.[15] One study reports patient satisfaction with this procedure to be 89%.[16] A Canadian study that followed patients who had been treated with Artecoll for up for 34 months post-treatment reported a patient satisfaction rate of 85%. The mean number of treatments needed for favorable augmentation has been reported to be two to four. The complication rate was 7%, with nodule formation in the lip being the most commonly reported complication.[17]

Artefill results are permanent but are very technique-sensitive and must be done by experienced clinicians. Multiple treatments are probably best, with the clinician paying particular care when placing the microspheres around or in the lips where nodule formation is more likely.

Sculptra

Poly-L-lactic acid (trade name: Sculptra [Valeant]) provides for a semi-permanent correction and was FDA approved in 2004 for use in cases of facial lipoatrophy (loss of subcutaneous fat) caused by HIV infection. Sculptra works by adding volume to the face and the product is reported to remain in the area of injection for approximately 18 months.

In 1999, Sculptra was formulated into a filler and marketed under the name *New Fill* in Europe. Sculptra works by stimulating collagen formation, thereby increasing the dermal thickness of the skin. Results are gradual and require multiple treatments to attain optimal correction.

Before its approval by the FDA, more than 250 persons with HIV were treated with Sculptra, and the results were relatively positive with minimal adverse events.[18] Increased skin thickness was noted.[19,20] Palpable but non-visible nodules were noted in 6% of patients in one study, but these were not seen as bothersome.[21] As is the case with most things, you get what you pay for, and the same is true with Sculptra. While it does reside at a higher price point than other fillers, many patients who have happily been receiving the same filler treatments for years find it worth the price in order to transition to a longer-lasting filler. Sculptra is generally recommended to healthy patients for an average of three injections, lasting up to two years apart when addressing most facial wrinkles.

Fat Transfer

Fat transfer is the process whereby fat is taken (harvested) from one area of the body and moved to another area. It is an abundant product with no risk for immunologic rejection, and recent advances in preparing, harvesting, and injecting fat have made for longer-lasting and more predictable results.[22-26] Fat transfer as a volume correction technique is becoming increasingly popular among many cosmetic physicians as a means of achieving natural facial rejuvenation.

Substantial skill is required for good and consistent results and there is a significant learning curve to the procedure. However, if done well, fat is an excellent filler material. Post-treatment edema and bruising, as well as donor-site harvesting, make this option less enticing as an office-based procedure. Still, it does have its place in the aesthetic market. One myth that physicians should be sure to debunk when meeting with patients is that any treatment lasts forever, and this is no exception to that rule. While using one's own fat to increase volume should outlast the injection of dermal fillers, once the fat is placed into a new spot, it will still go through the natural process of aging, which means it too will degrade once more.

Which Method to Use and When: The Patient

Determining which filler to use on a patient by patient basis depends more on the individual patient than on the product. For the physician to determine which filler to use, the following series of questions is useful:

Soft Tissue Fillers

> A physician's determination of which filler to use on a patient by patient basis depends more on the patient than on the product.

- **Does the patient want a treatment that is permanent or reversible?**
  Although a temporary filler may be recommended, there are some patients who insist on being treated with permanent filler. If the patient is an appropriate candidate, he/she must be ready to accept the potential for a long-term complication. Additionally, the correction that a person desires at one age may not be appreciated a decade later. In contrast, other patients are just becoming introduced to fillers and only want to "test the waters." They often want a product that is either reversible or will be reabsorbed within six months. In cases like this, recommending a hyaluronic acid product is best.

- **Is the patient undergoing simultaneous surgery?**
  For the patient who is undergoing simultaneous surgery, fat transfer makes the most sense. It is abundant and easy to harvest while the patient is under anesthesia. A sterile, controlled environment is assured. Additionally, because a fat transfer usually involves more downtime than an in-office filler, you can recommend a fat transfer to a client undergoing surgery because they already expect at least one week of recovery time.

- **What is the patient's age?**
  Older individuals tend to have a milder immune response to a foreign body injection than do younger patients. Therefore, a permanent product, which might cause an intense inflammatory response in a younger individual, is more appropriate to offer to an older person. Also, in the unlikely event that an unforeseen complication requiring skin excision occurs—it would be easier to camouflage a scar in the creases of an older patient's face than it would be to cover it in the mildly to unblemished thicker skin of a younger patient.

- **Is the skin thick or thin?**
  Thick skin tends to better accept the deep semi-permanent fillers, resulting in better outcomes and greater longevity. Thin skin can get lumpy with thicker products. Which product to use often depends on the treatment area. Frequently, the clinician can use two or three different products on the same patient in one sitting.

- **What did patient satisfaction with previous fillers look like?**
  If a patient has been happy with their current filler, there is generally no reason to switch unless there is a significant cosmetic or safety advantage to using a different product. If they were satisfied with their previous outcome then it is best to use the same filler.

Best Candidates for Permanent Fillers

1. Patients with mature skin
2. Patients with lighter skin types (Fitzpatrick I–III)
3. Patients with thicker skin
4. Patients with deep-etched lines
5. Patients with no history of allergies
6. Patients who have had fillers in the past and have been happy with the results

Potential Complications for Fillers

- Bruising:
  - Patients are asked to discontinue any medications or supplements that can increase the chance of bleeding, including non-steroidal anti-inflammatory drugs, aspirin, platelet inhibitors, anticoagulants, vitamin E, gingko biloba, ginseng, garlic, or other herbal remedies seven to 14 days before treatment.
  - Patients prone to bruising are often recommended a topical vitamin K oxide product to use for a week before and a week after treatment.
- Swelling, pain, or tenderness in the area:
  - This usually subsides within a few hours to a few days.
- Hypersensitivity reactions: Extremely low risk; since our bodies already contain hyaluronic acid; the risk is approximately 1 in 5,000.[27]

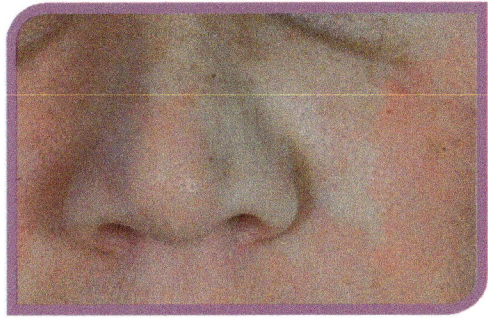
Blanching resulting from filler treatment

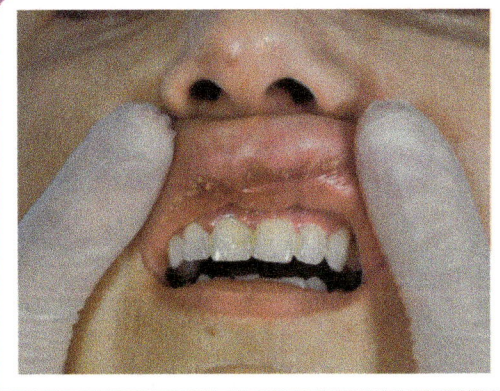 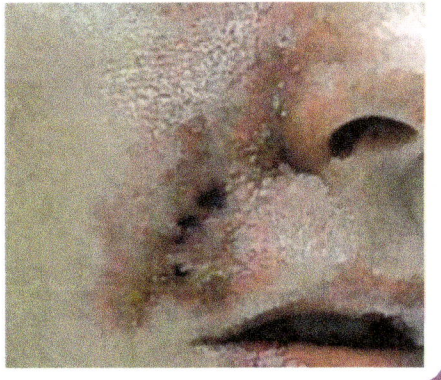
Necrosis resulting from complications in filler treatment

- Infection: Although unlikely, a bacterial, fungal, or viral infection can occur, but proper sanitation in the office will reduce this risk. If patients are prone to cold sores, anti-virals should be used if injections are done around the mouth.
- Post-injection lumps: These will generally smooth out over time, but the lumps can be massaged; if hyaluronic filler was used, hyaluronidase can be used to reverse it.

> ## Common Treatment Areas for Facial Fillers
> 1. Nasolabial Folds
> 2. Lips (usually only hyaluronic fillers)
> 3. Periocular (around the eyes)
> 4. Mentolabial Sulcus (the area between the chin and lower lip)
> 5. Oral Commissure Grooves (marionette lines)
> 6. Pre-jowl
> 7. Cheeks
> 8. Scars

Optimal Correction

Patient satisfaction immediately following a filler treatment has much to do with how the patient's expectations were managed before treatment commenced. Depending on which type of filler was used, the provider may have chosen to under-correct, with the working knowledge that the product will absorb water and plump the area. Although the patient may be optimally corrected once this happens over the next few days, they may initially feel disappointed, as they do not see a complete correction of their concern. There is also the other scenario where some fillers tend to produce edema immediately, resulting in what may appear to be over-correction. However, as the edema diminishes and the filler settles in, the patient should become satisfied. The key is listening to the patient's concerns, being honest and realistic about their desired result, and walking them through each step of the process from choosing the type of filler all the way through their post-treatment care regimen.

Complementing Fillers with Skin Care

Skin care is a foolproof way for a patient to protect the investment they just made to improve their appearance. Like neurotoxins, fillers won't address the appearance of the outer layers of skin, nor will they prevent other age-related pigment or laxity issues.

During the period of time where the patient's skin is being cleansed before treatment, it is an opportunity for the patient to look into a hand mirror and express what their concerns are as far as the medical treatment is concerned. However, with the skin already cleansed, there should be no makeup concealing imperfections, and some of the concerns that are revealed may have much to do with the outer

These are examples of how skin care can be matched to a patient's filler treatment.

The subject in the **top image** received the following skin care regimen post-filler:

- Pigment lightening cream
- Vitamins C and E serum
- Exfoliant
- Hydrating agents
- Sunscreen

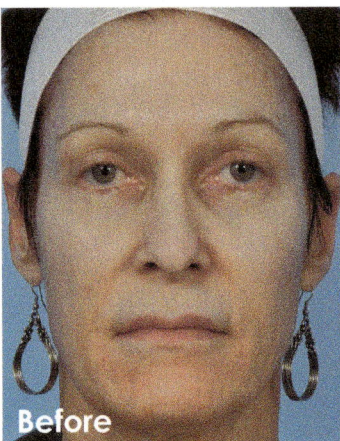
Before

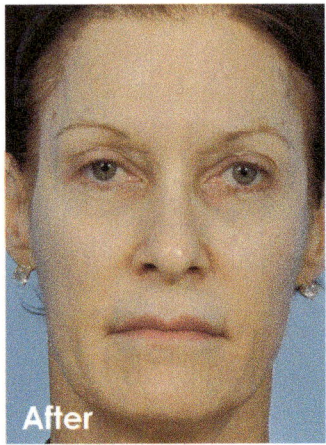
After

The subject in the **bottom image** received the following skin care regimen post-filler and post-IPL treatment:

- Topical antioxidants
- Peptides
- Skin lightening cream

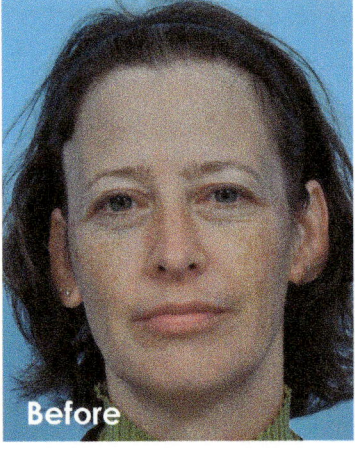
Before

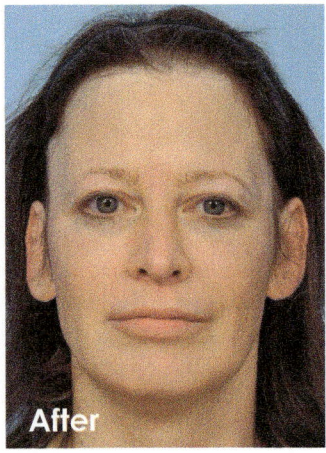
After

As can be seen, the application of these topical products, carefully chosen for each individual patient's skin type and treatment, have yielded significant results that have rendered their respective skins smoother and more supple.

texture or color of the skin, as well. Using this methodology not only gives the patient a more in-depth consult, it also allows the patient a way to further improve his/her new look while fighting other irregularities on the skin.

Complimenting filler results can be done easily with skin care. Exfoliating services, for example, will leave the skin with a smooth, rejuvenated appearance. When introducing skin care treatments, the question often arises as to how long to wait between fillers and facial treatments. There should be no significant amount of time needed between superficial skin care treatments and filler treatments. It is, however, generally recommended that skin care treatments be done at least one week before fillers and two weeks following. It is not that a superficial treatment cannot be done immediately before a filler, but certain treatments, including ultrasound, radio frequency, or even chemical peels, can result in some swelling. If the skin is swollen, it may not be as easy for the physician to assess where and how much filler to inject.

References
1. RS Narins et al, A randomized, double-blind, multicenter comparison of the efficacy and tolerability of Restylane versus Zyplast for the correction of nasolabial folds, *Dermatol Surg*, 29, 588-595 (2003).
2. PM Friedman et al, Safety data of injectable non-animal stabilized hyaluronic acid gel for soft tissue augmentation, *Dermatol Surg*, 28, 491-494 (2002).
3. KW Broder and S Cohen, An overview of permanent and semipermanent fillers, *Plast Reconstr Surg*, 118(suppl), 7s-14s (2006)
4. TL Tzikas, Evaluation of Radiance FN: Soft tissue filler for facial soft tissue augmentation, *Arch Facial Plast Surg*, 6, 234-239 (2004).
5. CW Hanke et al, Abscess formation and local necrosis after treatment with Zyderm and Zyplast collagen implant, *J Am Acad Dermatol*, 25, 319-326 (1991).
6. F Delustro et al, Reaction to injectable collagen: Results in animal models and clinical use, *Plast Reconst Surg*, 79(4), 581-94 (1987).
7. *Laws of Nevada*, Section 1, Chapter 202 of NRS, March 14, 1973.
8. A Bon, Serious long-term complications following silicone injection of the face, *Arch Derm*, 18, 286-287 (1993).
9. C Delage et al, Mammary silicone granuloma, *Arch Derm*, 108,104-107 (1973).
10. W Travis et al, Silicone granulomas: Report of three cases and review of the literature, *Hum Pathol*, 16, 19-27 (1985).
11. D Hexsel et al, Liquid injectable silicone history mechanism of action indications technique and complications, *Semin Cut Med Surg*, 22, 107-114 (2003).
12. SS Jacinto, Ten-year experience using injectable silicone oil for soft tissue augmentation in the Philippines, *Derm Surg*, 31, 1550-1554 (2005).
13. RC Webster et al, Injectable silicone for soft tissue augmentation, *Arch Otol*, 112(3), 290-296 (1986).
14. DS Orentreich, Liquid injectable silicone: Technique for soft tissue augmentation, *Clin Plast Surg*, 27, 595-612 (2000).

15. JG Barnett and CR Barnett, Treatment of acne scars with liquid silicone injections: 30-year perspective, *Derm Surg*, 31, 1542-1549 (2005).
16. D Duffy, Complications of fillers: An overview, *Derm Surg*, 31, 1626-1633 (2005).
17. RA Ersek and AA Beisnag, Bioplastique: A new textured copolymer microparticle promise permanence in soft tissue augmentation, *Plast Reconst Surg*, 33, 693-702 (1991).
18. SR Cohen and RE Holmes, Artecoll: A long-lasting injectable wrinkle filler material: Report of a controlled, randomized, multicenter clinical trial of 251 subjects, *Plas Reconstr Surg*, 114, 964-976 (2004).
19. PJ Nicolau, Long-lasting and permanent fillers: Biomaterial influence over host tissue response, *Plast Reconstr Surg*, 119, 2271-2286 (2007).
20. G Lemperle et al, PMMA microspheres (Artecoll) for long-lasting correction of wrinkles: Refinements and statistical results, *Aesth Plas Surg*, 22, 356-365 (1998).
21. A Bagal et al, Clinical experience with PMMA microspheres (Artecoll) for soft tissue augmentation, *Arch Fac Plas*, 9(4),275-280 (2007).
22. P Englehard et al, Safety of Sculptra: A review of clinical trial data, *J Cosmet Laser Ther*, 7, 201-205 (2005).
23. GJ Moyle et al, A randomized open label study of immediate versus delayed polylactic acid injection of the cosmetic management of facial lipoatrophy in person of with HIV infection, *HIV Med*, 5, 82-87 (2004).
24. MA Valantin et al, Polylactic acid of implants (New Fill) to correct facial lipoatrophy in HIV affected patients: Results of the open label study VEGA, *AIDS*, 17, 2471-2477 (2003).
25. PKM Englehard, *Safety and Efficacy of New Fill in the Treatments of HIV Associated Lipoatrophy of the Face*, presented at the XIV International AIDS Conference, Barcelona Spain, Jul 7-12, 2002.
26. A Goldman et al, Hyaluronic acid dermal fillers: Safety and efficacy for the treatment of wrinkles, aging skin, body sculpturing and medical conditions, *Clinical Medicine Reviews in Therapeutics*, 3 (2011).
27. RC Beljaards et al, New fill for skin augmentation a new filler or failure? *Derm Surg*, 142, 329-334 (2006).
28. SR Coleman, Facial reconstruction with lipostructure, *Clin Plas Surg*, 24, 347-367 (1997).
29. RE Amar, Microinfiltration of the fat cells of the face or reconstruction of the tissue with grafts of fat tissue, *Ann Chirp Last Aesthet*, 44, 593-608 (1999).
30. J Guerrerosantos et al, Long-term survival of free fat grafts in muscle: An experimental study in rats, *Aesthetic Plast Surg*, 20, 403-408 (1996).
31. RJ Rohrich et al, In search of improved fat transfer viability: A quantitative analysis of the role of centrifugation and harvest site, *Plast Reconstr Surg*, 113, 391-395 (2004).
32. PP Narini et al, Repeated exposure to silicone gel can induce delayed hypersensitivity, *Plast Reconstr Surg*, 96, 371-380 (1995).

CHAPTER 23

Facial Cosmetic Surgery

In this Chapter:
- Cosmetic Surgical Procedures
    - Rhytidectomy, Rhinoplasty, Septoplasty, Blepharoplasty
- Patient Expectations
- Possible Side Effects and Complications to Treatment
- Skin Care and Surgery

Cosmetic Surgical Procedures: An Overview

Aesthetic cosmetic surgery emerged in the mid-19th century. In the early 20th century, surgeons vastly increased their use of this trade, notably with regard to wounded soldiers who required reparation of facial deformities resulting from duty and/or combat in World War II. Even then, though performed out of necessity, cosmetic surgery was highly controversial, and to date remains equally scrutinized in some sectors of the medical profession. Though there will always be room for critics, studies have surfaced that indicate the "look good, feel good" philosophy associated with cosmetic surgery holds true. As one enhances their appearance, their self-esteem tends to reflect such a change. True enhancement should leave the patient looking subtly refreshed, not drastically changed. The most successful cosmetic surgical results seem as though no "work" was done at all. When a person receives compliments from friends and family on looking well-rested or otherwise invigorated, though they cannot put their finger on why, cosmetic surgery has fulfilled its purpose.

Regardless of position, all support staff of a cosmetic surgeon must at least have a basic understanding of the most commonly performed procedures. This knowledge should consist of the actual procedures, potential side effects, and patient experiences. The aesthetic providers must have even more knowledge, as they will be working with the patients firsthand, both before and after procedures. In this chapter, information on commonly performed cosmetic surgery procedures, including patient experiences, will be discussed. This is general information, and surgeons may use different techniques or methods. The chapter should be used as a guide for information and expectations; when obtaining a job with a surgeon, it is the responsibility of both the practice and provider to ensure that individual practices are learned.

Facelift (Rhytidectomy)

A facelift, technically termed a *rhytidectomy*, is performed to improve the appearance of the skin by eliminating sagging and the presentment of wrinkles. During this procedure, incisions are placed where they will garner the least amount of visibility, which is typically along the hairline, the front of the ear, around and behind the ear, and along the hairline of the back of the neck. As the name implies, patients are seeking to pull the skin taut, or "lift" it, from the lower part of the face and neck. Minor differences exist in the types of facelift presently offered. The standard has become the superficial muscular aponeurotic system (SMAS) lift. Others are simply small variations of the SMAS procedure.

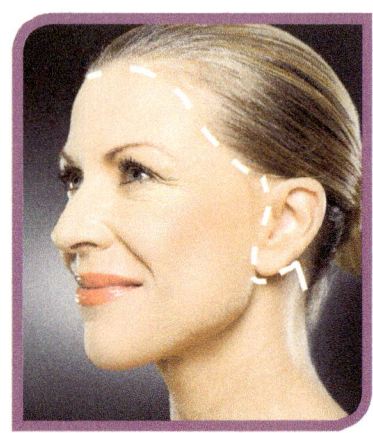

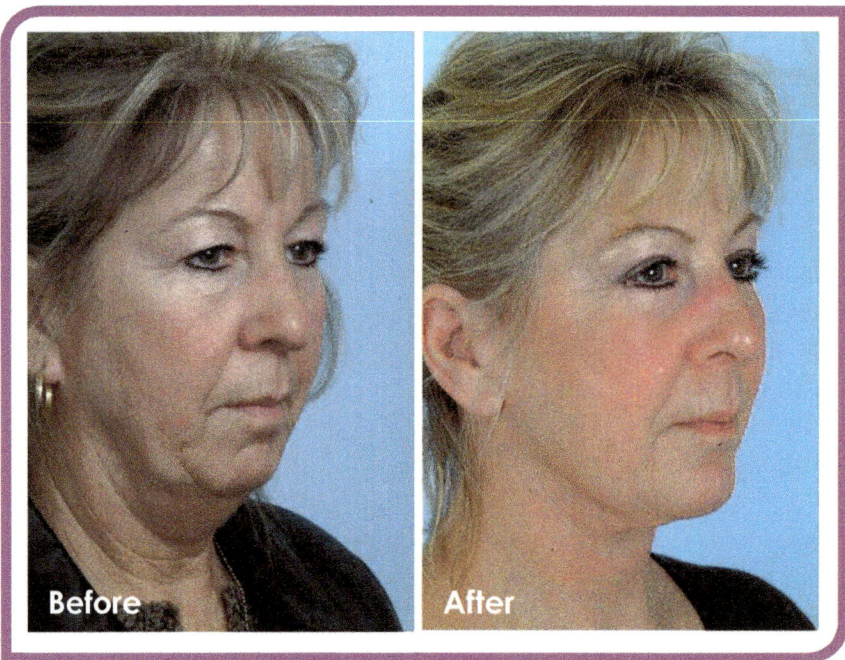

Pre-and Post-operative rhytidectomy

The SMAS is the blanket of tissue enveloping the muscle that lies directly beneath the skin. In an SMAS lift, the incision is made and the skin is separated from the fat and muscle of the face. The SMAS is then lifted and stretched, with any excess skin trimmed or folded over itself. Finally, the skin is re-draped and trimmed without pulling the skin to prevent a "plastic" or "pulled" effect. This procedure diminishes sagging in the neck and lower face including the jaw, but does not affect the nasolabial folds or sagging in the cheek area. Many patients will refer to this as a "mini-lift." A more involved version of the SMAS lift has also been developed where the initial partitioning of the skin and muscle is extended to include the nose and mouth areas. This allows the surgeon to pull any sagging skin that is exhibited in these areas as well.

There are variations to this procedure, but it is the opinion of many that if a facelift is sought, doing a mini-lift will not do justice. A mini-lift procedure is less invasive, involving a smaller incision and work area. This "weekend face-lift" targets primarily jowls and neck skin that shows loss of elasticity. It is requires less down time but is also less dramatic. Underlying muscles and tissues are then tightened. Because this is a smaller area and incision, the recovery time is shorter.

A major misconception about this surgery is that the results are permanent. This is not strictly true. Gravity will continue to work on the freshly pulled skin just as it did prior to the procedure. However, as compared to annually plumping those wrinkles with fillers, the investment in a facelift lasts much longer. Results may last anywhere from five to 12 years, depending on how well the tissue is cared for and maintained—in other words, dependent on the patient's post-surgical skin care regimen.

Rhinoplasty

Rhinoplasty is a cosmetic surgery procedure used to address a wide variety of concerns with regards to the nose and nasal region. This procedure is often as much practical as it is voluntary. The physical appearance of the nose may be secondary to a more bothersome functional issue for the patient. During reconstruction of the septum to allow for more easy nasal respiration, the aesthetics may be altered as well. This is referred to as a functional nasal septal reconstruction (FNSR). Depending on the individual's desire, the surgeon can aesthetically narrow or widen the bridge; manipulate the bone and/or cartilage to reshape, chisel, or file bones that create a hump; cut and suture nostrils that flare; and trim excess cartilage at the tip to shorten the shape of the nose.

There are two basic forms of rhinoplasty: *open* and *closed*. Open rhinoplasty requires an incision in the columella to expose the entire structure of the nose. It is more commonly performed than closed rhinoplasty, and even for the most seasoned plastic surgeon, this method may be required for complex procedures. This affords the surgeon more room to operate and better vision of his surgical field without the use of endoscopes (surgical cameras), which are required for closed procedures. During surgery, the surgeon will separate the skin from its bone and cartilage support structure. The framework of the nose is then reshaped to the desired form. Shape can be altered by removing or reshaping bone, cartilage, or skin. The remaining skin is then reapplied over this new framework. If the procedure requires adding to the structure of the nose, the donated bone, cartilage, or skin may come from an alternate site on the patient's body or from a synthetic source. The procedure typically takes three hours to complete, and the patient is left with external stitches running along the base of the nasal columella (the vertical strip of tissue seperating the nostrils) that will be removed one week post-surgery. There are also numerous dissolvable sutures that remain scattered within the nose. These, of course, dissipate on their own over time.

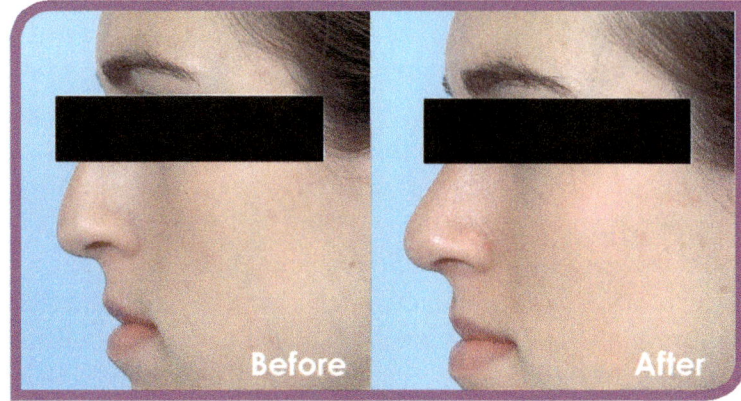

Pre-and Post-operative rhinoplasty

Open rhinoplasty is performed by making a small incision in the columella, (the vertical strip of tissue separating the nostrils); the skin is then pulled back so the surgeon can see the entire structure of the nose.

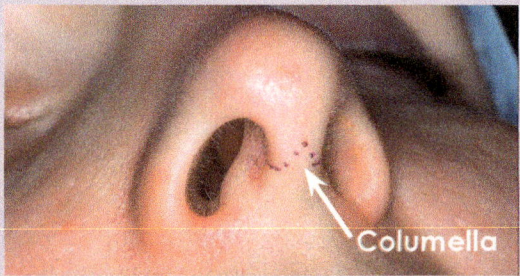

Closed rhinoplasty is a specialty that is done with all incisions made inside the nasal cavity, opposed to cutting the columella.

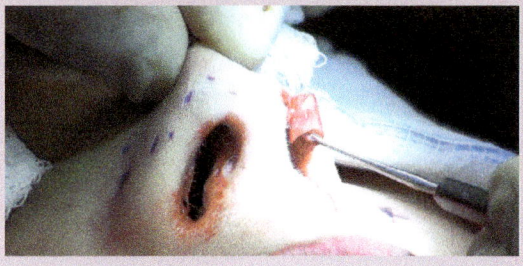

Structure of the Nose

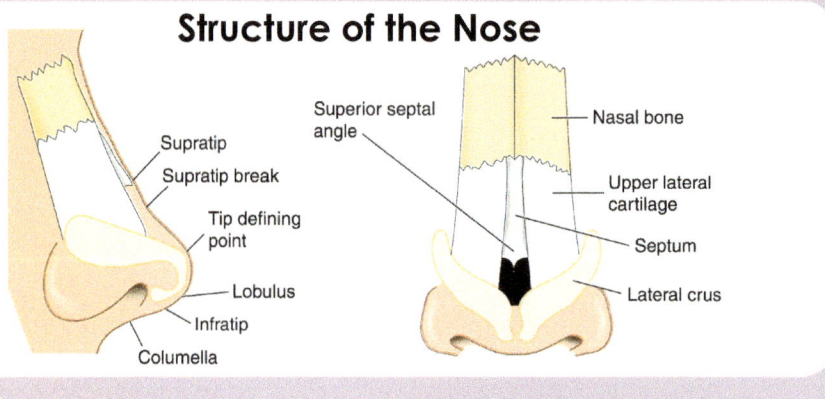

Facial Cosmetic Surgery

Internal or closed rhinoplasty requires a higher degree of specialty and involves making all incisions within the nasal cavity. This is preferred for less-complicated cases, but aims to achieve the same results as open surgery. The benefits of a closed rhinoplasty include a shorter surgical time and absence of external sutures along the nasal columella. However, the possible placement of splints or synthetic and/or cartilaginous grafts remain the same.

Septoplasty

Septoplasty is a procedure that, unlike rhinoplasty, is performed solely to correct a deviated septum. The septum is the area that separates the nostrils and is comprised of bone and cartilage. When the septum is not straight, it is considered deviated, and may cause an obstruction of a person's ability to breathe, which can lead to problems such as snoring or sleep apnea. A deviated septum may be congenital or possibly caused by forceful contact made to the nose. Septoplasty is more likely to be covered by a patient's health insurance, particularly when the condition begins to impact one's daily life, because it is a procedure considered more "medically justified" than rhinoplasty, which is considered more cosmetic in nature.

Blepharoplasty (Eyelid Surgery)

Blepharoplasty (**pictured**), reshaping the eyes, is the most commonly sought out procedure for those concerned with signs of aging. It is well-known that due to the lack of support structure in the skin around the eyes, they are often the first area to show visible signs of aging. Many patients who seek this procedure either have pockets of fat in the lower eyes or heavy skin on or over the eyelids that may even threaten to obstruct their sight. There are many treatments and products claiming to remove "puffiness" without surgery; as there are modalities to remove actual puffiness caused by fluid retention, there is no product that can topically remove the area of fat. The removing of tissue and fat beneath the eyes can only be done through surgical procedures. (This will be discussed in Chapter 28.) Heavy eyelids is a top concern when seeking blepharoplasty; like bags under the eyes, the severity and cause of heavy lids plays a large role when choosing a treatment path. There are several tightening procedures that will be discussed in the next section; however, for

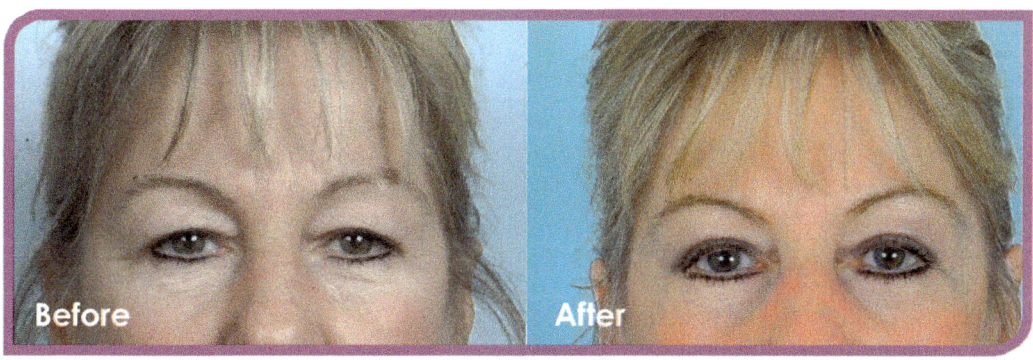

severe laxity, especially in the case of obstructed vision, surgical procedures must be done to remove excess tissue.

Blepharoplasty procedures are intended to reshape the upper and/or lower eyelid by removing and/or repositioning the excess tissue and fat and by reinforcing the surrounding muscles and tendons, which reduces the appearance of under-eye wrinkles and crow's feet (see **illustration** of fatty deposits in the eye area). Blepharoplasty is done with transcutaneous incisions (i.e., through the skin) made externally along the natural skin lines of the eyelids, such as the creases of the upper lids and below the lashes of the lower lids in order to prevent visible scarring. A second option for the procedure is defined as *transconjunctival*, meaning the incisions are made from the inside surface of the upper or lower eyelid. Transcutaneous procedures are generally used only when fat, muscle, and/or skin needs to be removed in addition to being repositioned.

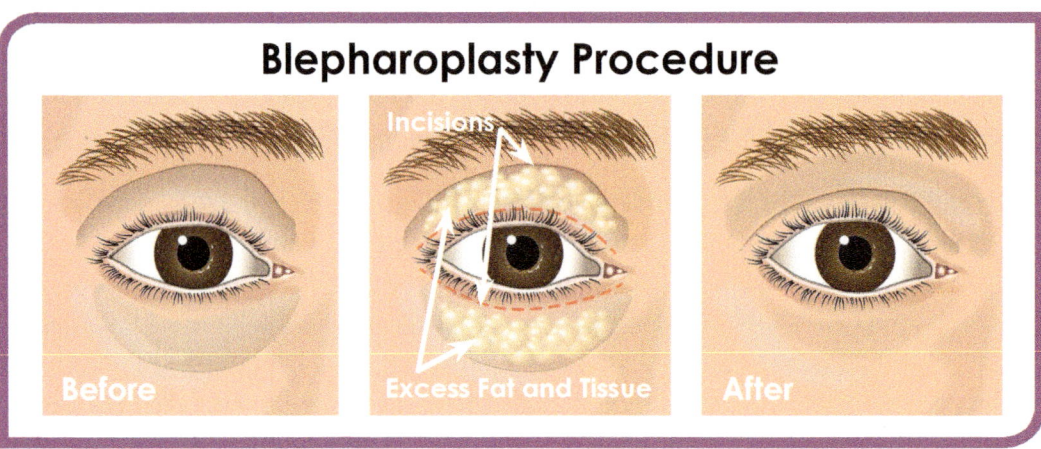

Post-surgical Expectations

The patient requires someone to attend them for at least the first 24 hours immediately following surgery to monitor and assist with anything they are unable to manage physically. It is not unusual for a person to feel weak following the administration of an anesthetic, or following any type of operation; this usually resolves within a few days. Bending over or lifting anything over 10 pounds should be avoided, as this could draw more blood to the head and aggravate swelling, raise blood pressure, and even increase the chance of a hemorrhage. The patient's body temperature may rise as high as 100°F following surgery. This rise may result from mild dehydration; therefore, the patient should try to increase water intake post-surgery. If there is a persistent fever above 100°F, the patient's physician should be notified. Also, if a hemorrhage or heavy uncontrollable amount of bleeding occurs, the patient should lie down, elevate the head, apply cold compresses to the area, and their treating physician should be contacted immediately. Prior to leaving the surgical center, a medical provider will reiterate that some amount of post-surgical bleeding is normal and will further stipulate when to seek medical attention in the case of excessive bleeding.

Facial Cosmetic Surgery

The amount of swelling during recovery varies for each patient, and it is common for the swelling to be uneven between the two sides of the site of surgery. This is one of the biggest challenges for patients to grasp. It is important for the physician as well as support staff to explain this thoroughly before the procedure and make sure the patient understands. Patients are often so excited to see their new look that they seem to forget this possible complication and become upset with and often blame the surgeon. This is especially common with rhinoplasty; when the bandage is first removed, the nose will likely appear larger and the tip may be turned up a bit. This is due to operative swelling over the nose and upper lip. This swelling will subside to a large extent within one week; however, it will take up to one year for all of the swelling to disappear and for the client's nose to reach its final contour. The thicker and

SCENARIO: Advising the Surgical Patient

It is Julie's first time visiting your practice. She has come to you seeking to remove dark, puffy circles around her eyes. She has made an appointment with you but will also be seen by the MD, as it is her first appointment.

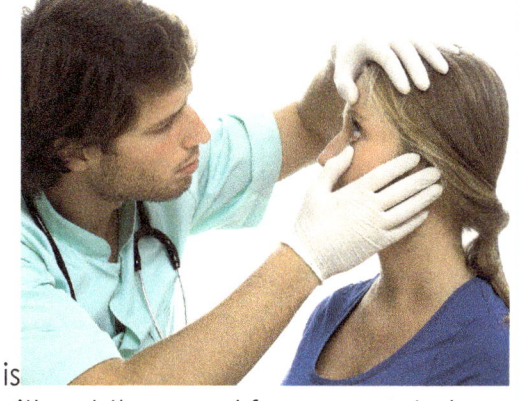

Patient: "I am seeking treatment for the bags under my eyes. I heard about product XYZ, that it is the newest treatment available without the need for surgery. I also have crow's feet and would like to see that improved as well."

What could happen:
Provider (without examining the area): "Yes, I see what you are talking about, and we do have that product available. I would also like to recommend micro-needling to reduce the lines around your eyes."

What should happen:
Provider (while examining the skin under the eyes): "I do see that you have some puffiness in this area. Although the eye cream is effective for mild edema around the eyes caused by water retention and decreased circulation, it seems as though a medical procedure to remove and tighten excess tissue would be best for your concerns. Let me get Dr. Smith and let him examine more thoroughly. Together we can develop a plan to best address your concerns."

oilier the skin, the longer it takes for the swelling to subside. The upper lip also may appear stiff for a while, and the tip of the nose may sometimes feel numb, but this likewise eventually dissipates.

> **TIP:** Many surgeons choose to employ skin care professionals as a liaison between pre-and post-surgical care. To effectively introduce the importance of skin care, a complimentary post-surgical treatment by the skin care provider, such as manual lymphatic drainage to reduce swelling, may be included with the cost of surgery. These will be discussed in more detail in the next chapter.

To reduce the chance of swelling, physicians often recommend keeping the head elevated or upright as much as possible after surgery, and this includes sleeping with the head tilted at a 45-degree angle for at least two weeks. The use of a cold, dry compress, such as a bag of frozen peas, may also be recommended for the first 48 hours immediately following surgery.

Although subjective, there tends to be minimal pain following surgery; however, the individual may experience a tight sensation and pressure as a result of the post-operative swelling that occurs. This may seem worse at night or when the person is in a reclined position. A pain reliever may be prescribed to reduce any postoperative pain, although most patients do not find this necessary. The patient should be informed not to take aspirin or non-steroidal anti-inflammatory drugs including Motrin and Advil, both of which are forms of ibuprofen, or Nuprin, as these products can thin the blood, causing excess bleeding.

It is not uncommon for areas of the face, neck and ears to sometimes feel weak or numb following rhytidectomy, as does the nose following rhinoplasty. Sometimes unusual sensations such as tingling may occur as normal feeling returns. This can range from hypersensitivity to localized pain. The skin of the face also may feel tight for a time after surgery. All of these symptoms are normal and typically subside within a few weeks.

It is also not unusual for an individual to go through a period of mild depression post-surgery. Inform the patient that if this happens, it is a temporary condition that will subside shortly. Some patients seem to think that changing a part of themselves that they deem unattractive will somehow change their life immediately. Their impatience or disappointment on this score should be expected, and addressed with patience, concern, and reassurance.

Consider the following example: A 19-year-old patient comes in and complains that her large nose has prevented her from feeling confident, resulting in being generally shy, having few friends, and absolutely no prospects of romance. In her mind, the moment her nose is altered, she will gain confidence, be more outgoing, present a more attractive image, and meet more people. The skin care professional must be sensitive to such reactive emotions; they are far from uncommon. As we all know, a state of confidence can affect outward appearance, but it is not as simple as that. It takes time to grow, just as the post-operative swelling takes time subside.

Visible post-surgery effects: Discoloration around the eyes, or the appearance of having "black-eyes," is more common in blepharoplasty and rhytidectomy, but can also result from rhinoplasty. If there is discoloration, the patient should be reassured that it will likely resolve within a week to 10 days. It rarely persists beyond this point and, regardless, is not permanent. Topical vitamin K oxide or the ingestion of Arnica, which is not itself vitamin K but is commonly used, may be useful in the prevention of bruising. Recently, other nutritional supplements have been touted as being beneficial for prepping the body for surgery as well as promoting healing. Specifically, the brand Standard Process manufactures supplements called Multizyme and Cyruta, which are both offered to patients before and after surgery for the relief of swelling and inflammation. There is also a fairly new topical gel pad from Cearna that utilizes topical Arnica as a means to reduce post-operative bruising and swelling. High satisfaction rates by providers and patients have been reported.

Thinning hair may occur in areas adjacent to the suture lines in the temple, top of the head, or behind the ear following rhytidectomy. This is due to a temporary shock phase to the hair follicle. The new hair shaft will return, but may it may take a few months before it is visible. There is a supplement on the market, Viviscal (Lifes2good), which comes in a professional strength that many physicians are now recommending to patients who have had hair loss, whether traumatic or age-related. The extracts in the supplements help to stimulate the follicle and new growth may be observed as quickly as a couple months.

And then there is the issue of scars. After all of the stitches have been removed, the incision lines beneath them will appear as a deep pink coloration. There will be varying amounts of swelling in and around the lines themselves. Eventually, however, the pink will pale, the firmness of the incision line will soften and become less noticeable, and the individual's native skin tone will resolve. Individual results vary, but it takes approximately one year for incision lines to completely heal. Silicone-based topical products, in topical gels, creams, or occlusive sheets are often recommended to prevent and reduce scarring. Silicones are known for their wound-healing capabilities through supplying a protective coating for the skin to repair itself more efficiently. The use of these products post-surgery should only be used following clearance from the surgeon.

Product Recommendations

Surgical procedures to reduce the signs of aging do not last indefinitely. Some patients think that by getting a procedure such as a facelift, they will not need to care for the skin following surgery with the same attention that would be required had there been no procedure at all. This is simply not true. A supportive skin care regimen before and after surgery will provide the best possible outcomes. Protection from UV and other harmful external factors should be the first consideration, as the skin will be in a compromised position. Antioxidants and sunscreens are a must. Sunscreens will provide initial protection, reducing the chance of side effects including post-inflammatory hyperpigmentation and scarring. Antioxidants will fight off additional free radicals to maintain skin health during this time. Hydrating agents, including hyaluronic acid and vitamin B5, should be used to help the skin heal itself. The skin heals better in a moist environment, and during healing the body is working hard to replace lost proteins including glycosaminoglycans, the ground substance surrounding matrix proteins. Products used to promote collagen growth will also prove beneficial. Ingredients including peptides, stem cells, and growth factors help to provide support for tissue growth. The use of these products should enhance results as well as maintain them. While surgical procedures change structures of the face, they do nothing for skin texture or color. The use of products that assist with cellular turnover including retinol and AHAs will not only stimulate increased cellular renewal but will also even skin tone and texture to provide an even better result than surgery alone.

Office Visits: The first office visit should be one week following surgery. At this appointment, any sutures requiring removal will be taken out, and for rhinoplasty the external splint will be removed.

Removing the Dressing: A pressure dressing will be applied following rhytidectomy; this remains in place until it is removed by the physician the following morning.

Stages of Wound Healing

- **Stage One: Inflammatory** (occurs immediately)
  Swelling and redness occur during this stage. The body introduces white blood cells into the site of incision to fight infection. Platelets clot to stop bleeding.

- **Stage Two: Proliferative phase** (three to five days)
  Fibroblasts are introduced in this stage. These leave behind webs of collagen and start the contraction process. Collagen is established quickly and its occurrence may be haphazard, especially if the skin is not kept moist.

- **Stage Three: Remodeling Phase**
  (one to six weeks; up to two years to complete)
  The exterior of the wound is healed. Collagen is constantly reorganizing under the skin. If the collagen is not laid down correctly, scars can form. It is important to care for the skin during this time, keeping it well hydrated and applying sunscreen.

Patient Instructions

There are general instructions given to patients post-surgery, although these bear differences depending on the type and details of the procedure. (Please see Appendix B for a sample post-operative instruction sheet.) The patient must avoid hitting, bumping, or applying excess pressure to the area of surgery for at least one month post-procedure. Light physical activity including light walking and swimming must be avoided for at least two weeks, and strenuous activity including running and weight-lifting for at least four weeks. When the patient may return to work depends on the type of surgery, the amount of physical activity the job requires, and the level of public contact that the job involves, in addition to the amount of swelling and discoloration that has developed.

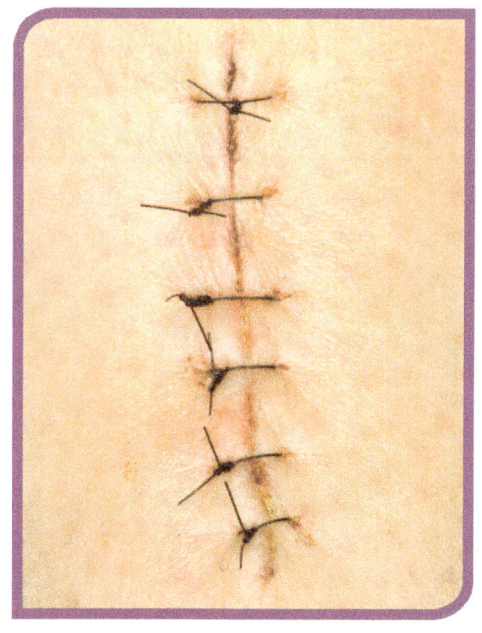

Excess sun exposure should be avoided for four months. The skin is constantly remodeling, ridding itself of damaged collagen and replacing it with healthy collagen in the course of the healing process. Knowing how UV exposure affects healthy skin, it is even more important to protect skin during the healing phase. The chance of hyperpigmentation, collagen degradation, and scarring is heightened at this time. Patients should use a broad-spectrum sunscreen of at least SPF 30 on a daily basis, regardless of weather. (UV rays are not stopped by cloud-cover or any other "overcast" conditions.) Physical sunscreen containing zinc oxide can be applied over any dissolvable suture areas once the sutures have dissipated. Following rhinoplasty, a zinc-oxide based sunscreen should be reapplied to the nose every two hours if there is direct sun exposure.

If there are dissolvable sutures, they should be cleaned two to four times each day with hydrogen peroxide, and covered with the recommended occlusive agent over the stitches (e.g. Aquaphor, Vaseline). Hydrogen peroxide is a disinfectant; it is most commonly used to treat inflammation and fight bacteria. Cleaning sutures and making sure the incisions are occluded or sealed ensures less likelihood of complications or infection. This will keep the stitches and crust soft and thus more comfortable. For all procedures that result in dissolvable or non-dissolvable sutures, at least two weeks should be allowed before resuming use of topical makeup over the healed areas.

Post-rhinoplasty, the patient must avoid getting the nasal dressing wet. If the tape or splint becomes wet, they must pat it dry, not rub or swipe it dry. Typically at a one week follow-up appointment, a provider will use adhesive remover to take it off safely. If the bandage becomes loose before that time, the physician should be notified immediately. The patient should not blow their nose for two weeks after surgery or until instructed to do so. This type of force has the potential to cause bleeding from any existing surgical facial incisions. Avoid rubbing incision points with tissues or handkerchiefs. Not only will this aggravate the swelling, but it can cause infection, bleeding, or dislodge any scaffolding a physician has placed. Dried mucous or a crust may form in or around incision sites. This area should be kept clean by using hydrogen peroxide on cotton-tipped swabs.

Patient must avoid getting the nasal dressing wet.

Patients undergoing cosmetic surgical procedures could use extra support from providers. There are often many questions pertaining to side effects and post-surgical instructions. It is vital that the surgeon's support staff be knowledgeable on any procedures offered/performed by the physician.

The next chapter will go over the pre- and post-operative treatments that the trained skin care professional can do to enhance results safely.

CHAPTER 24

Pre- and Post-surgical Treatment: MLD and Camouflage Makeup

In this Chapter:
- Pre- and Post-operative Care
- Manual Lymphatic Drainage
- Cosmetic Camouflage and Coverage by Condition

Pre- and Post-operative Care

Many aesthetic providers fail to recognize the psychological benefits associated with offering pre- and post-operative treatments. The ultimate goal is not only to make patients look better, but to make them feel better. Going through any surgical procedure may be nerve-wracking, and the decision to undergo elective cosmetic surgery can be particularly emotional. Patients tend to feel more at ease when there are relationships built with multiple staff members they can rely on. Although the patient coordinator is typically the primary contact between the practice and the patient, the aesthetic provider may play an equally important role. It is essential that this member of the team have a thorough understanding of surgical procedures along with an exceptional bedside manner. The more positive the rapport, the better the patient's experience will be. Regular skin care appointments before and after treatment will allow the aesthetic provider a continued chance to reaffirm the patient's satisfaction.

Along with the psychological benefits, there are healing benefits as well. Although there are several treatments and products that can enhance a patient's outcome, a staple treatment has always been manual lymphatic drainage.[1]

> When working for a plastic surgeon or dermatologist, it is in the provider's best interest to observe procedures to gain a sense of what patients experience with each procedure.

Manual Lymphatic Drainage

Manual lymphatic drainage (MLD) is a procedure intended to improve the circulation of lymph throughout the body in order to induce relaxation, reduce edema, and improve specific conditions when directed by a physician. This massage technique was originally founded by Emil Vodder, PhD, and his wife Estrid. The Vodders were both physical therapists in Cannes, France, in the 1930s. During this time, the majority of their patients came from Northern Europe where damp climate was pretty much a constant. As they were treating patients with chronic colds, they noticed a correlation with upper respiratory conditions and swollen lymph nodes. After researching the lymphatic system at great length, the Vodders developed a light, rhythmic massage technique consisting of stretching movements to stimulate lymph flow throughout the body.[2] In 1936, this technique started to become recognized by the medical community when the Vodders presented their findings to the public at a health and beauty congress in Paris. Since then, many physicians, lymphologists, and other researchers have come up with their own techniques for stimulating the lymphatic system, most of which involve many of the same basic principles used in the Vodder method.

Knowing the lymphatic system's functions and components is necessary to mastering MLD treatment. **The lymphatic system is a vital component of the immune system, serving three main functions: to maintain fluid balance by the removal of excess fluids from body tissues; to absorb fats and transport them to blood; and to protect the body against disease.** The lymphatic system consists of a complex network of lymphoid organs including lymph nodes (**pictured**), lymph ducts, lymphatic tissues, lymph capillaries, and lymph vessels that produce and transport lymph fluid from tissues throughout the circulatory system. This system doesn't have a pump like the circulatory system, and may slow down for a variety of reasons, such as poor lifestyle choices, injuries, or autoimmune disorders. These conditions can result in swollen lymph nodes, edema, poor circulation, illness, and disease.

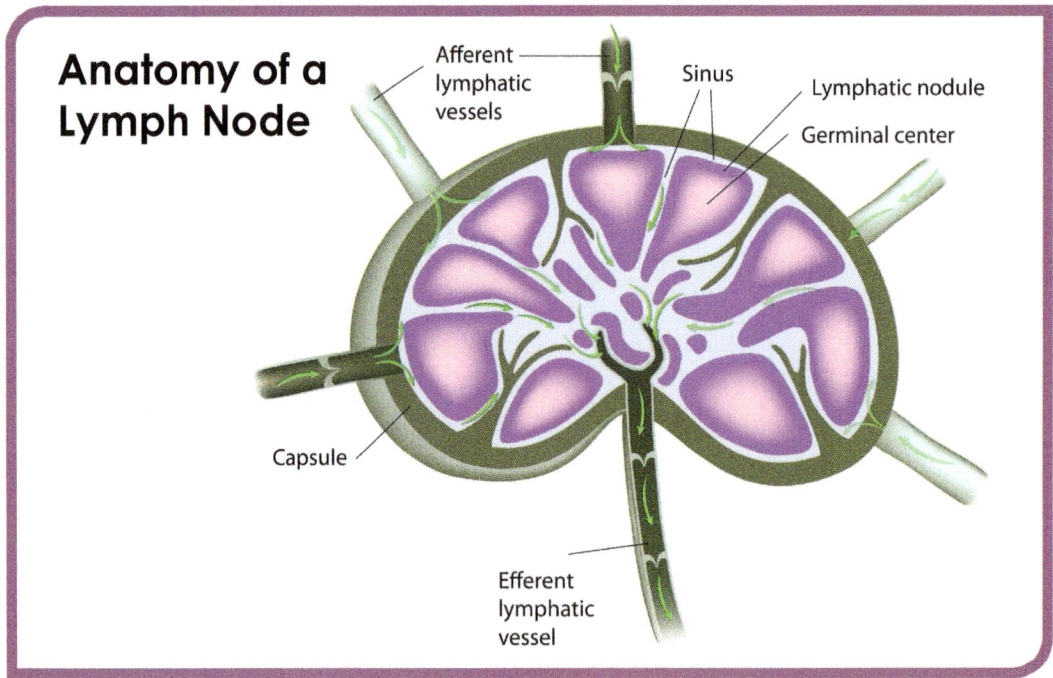

Anatomy of a Lymph Node

Afferent lymphatic vessels
Sinus
Lymphatic nodule
Germinal center
Capsule
Efferent lymphatic vessel

The Vodder Method

The Vodder method of MLD consists of four massage techniques: stationary circles, pumping, scooping, and rotary movements. These movements are the building blocks to performing MLD.

- *Stationary circles* are light movements, done with flat fingers moving in the same spot, or in continuous spirals; they are used primarily for the face and neck.

- The *pumping technique* is done with the therapist's palms facing downward with thumb and fingers together, moving the skin in an ovular motion. In performance, the wrist moves like a hinge.

- The *scooping action* involves the palms facing upward and the wrist rotating in a corkscrew-like motion. In this technique, the pressure is on the inward part of the stroke, but releases so as to impart no pressure at all coming out of the movement.

- The *rotary technique* is for relatively flat areas of the skin and uses a variety of movements. The wrist moves up and down. As it moves down, the motion is from out to in, while the thumb makes circular movements and the palm lies on the skin moving in a spiral fashion. This is during the "pressure" part. During the "pressure-less" part of this technique, the wrist is raised and the four fingers are spread apart as the thumb glides inward.

These techniques are done slowly and methodically, approximately five to seven times at each location. (It takes at least this much time to get lymph moving.) Performing MLD is not as easy it seems. Patience is required to accurately and effectively move lymph.

The Technique

Manual lymphatic drainage massage is not ordinary massage of the skin and muscles; it differs due to the lymphatic system's position directly beneath the skin. The pressure is extremely light—softer than the weight of a quarter; this is a technique that most technicians must acclimate themselves to via considerable training. Massage for therapeutic purposes is primarily focused on pressure and stimulation, and with MLD if the pressure is too hard the lymph system will likely not be affected.

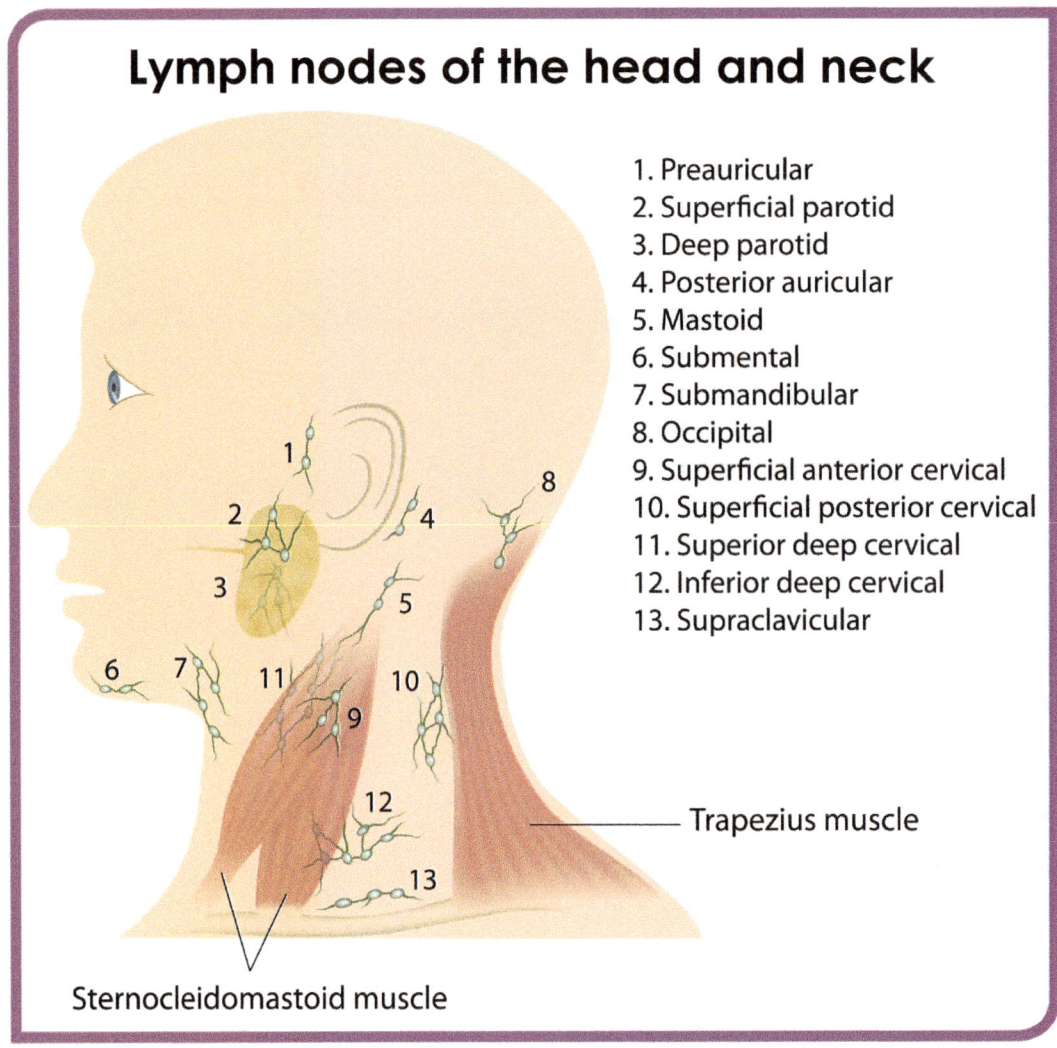

Lymph nodes of the head and neck

1. Preauricular
2. Superficial parotid
3. Deep parotid
4. Posterior auricular
5. Mastoid
6. Submental
7. Submandibular
8. Occipital
9. Superficial anterior cervical
10. Superficial posterior cervical
11. Superior deep cervical
12. Inferior deep cervical
13. Supraclavicular

Trapezius muscle

Sternocleidomastoid muscle

When MLD is performed, all movements must be made in the direction of lymphatic flow, which in turn collects in the right lymphatic duct and the thoracic duct—these both drain lymph into the circulatory system at the right and left subclavian veins. These veins are present at the base of the neck below the clavicles. During MLD, it is of best practice to use light rhythmic movements on the ducts to initiate the drainage of any stagnant lymph back into the circulatory system.

Pre- and Post-surgical Treatment: MLD and Camouflage Makeup

This is followed by movements at the sites where lymph nodes lie. The lymph nodes filter bacteria and foreign material out of lymph and expose it to lymphocytes and macrophages—cells that fight off and engulf bacteria. Movements include smooth, circular, pump-like strokes. On average, the human body has at least 600 lymph nodes, and about one-third of these are found in the face and neck.[3] After manipulating the lymph nodes, effleurage movements toward the thoracic and right lymphatic ducts can be performed to help encourage lymphatic flow through the lymph nodes and eventually back into the circulatory system. When performing MLD, it is important move lymph in the right direction. Watersheds are areas of demarcation that serve as a guide for the direction of lymph flow. If these lines are crossed, the treatment could be ineffective. Following the effleurage movements, the areas where lymph nodes lie are stimulated again, finishing with pumping and draining movements back at the base of the neck where the lymphatic ducts exist.

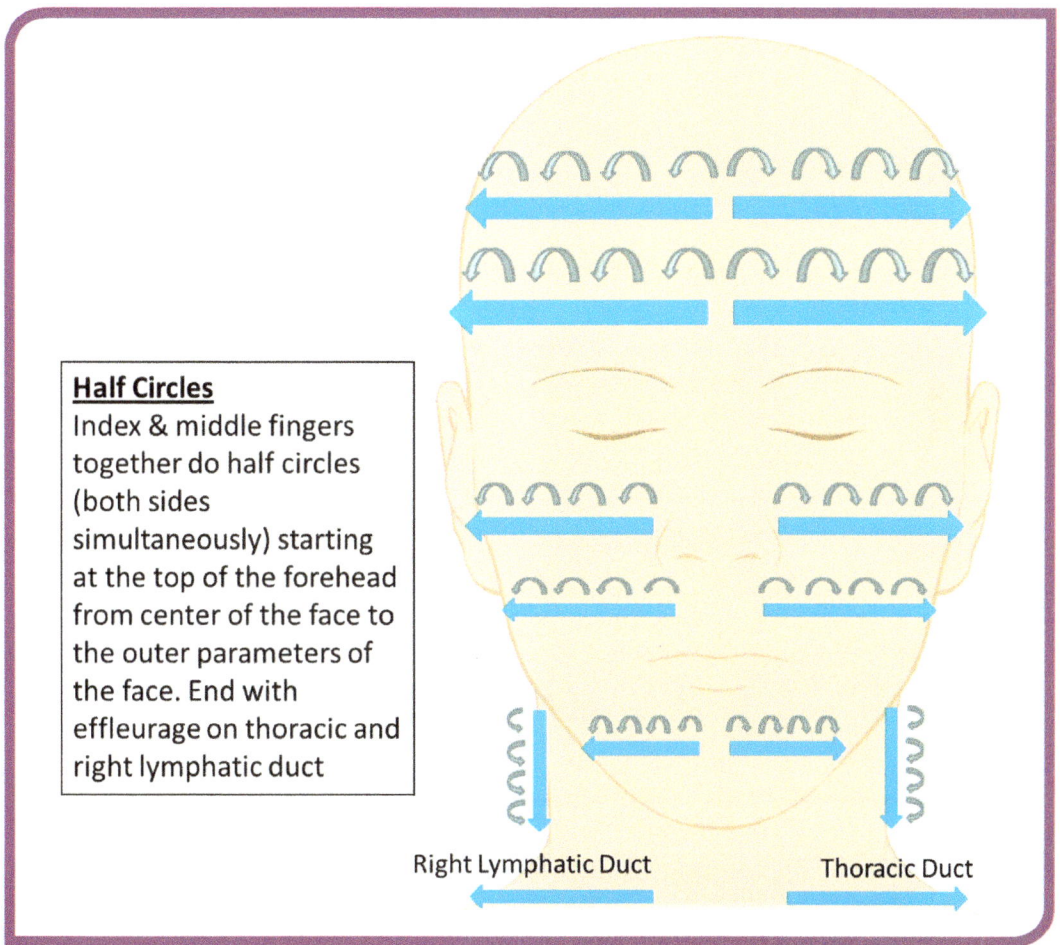

Half Circles
Index & middle fingers together do half circles (both sides simultaneously) starting at the top of the forehead from center of the face to the outer parameters of the face. End with effleurage on thoracic and right lymphatic duct

Necessary Training
Skin care professionals who wish to offer MLD should complete a thorough hands-on training at a respected educational center to assure that the movements and

pressure are performed correctly. Practitioners must also be educated thoroughly on all indications and contraindications to ensure client safety. Although it is simply a massage technique, it can cause serious adverse effects on certain medical conditions, including heart disease, autoimmune disorders, and cancer.

Trained professionals who plan on using this technique pre- and post-operatively must have an in-depth understanding of surgical procedures. Complications could arise if the provider doesn't understand what the patient will experience during the stages of wound healing (as shown in Chapter 23) and how to recognize potential complications. Skin care professionals must check regulations in their practicing state; some state boards consider manual lymphatic drainage to be a practice of medicine and their regulations will reflect that fact.

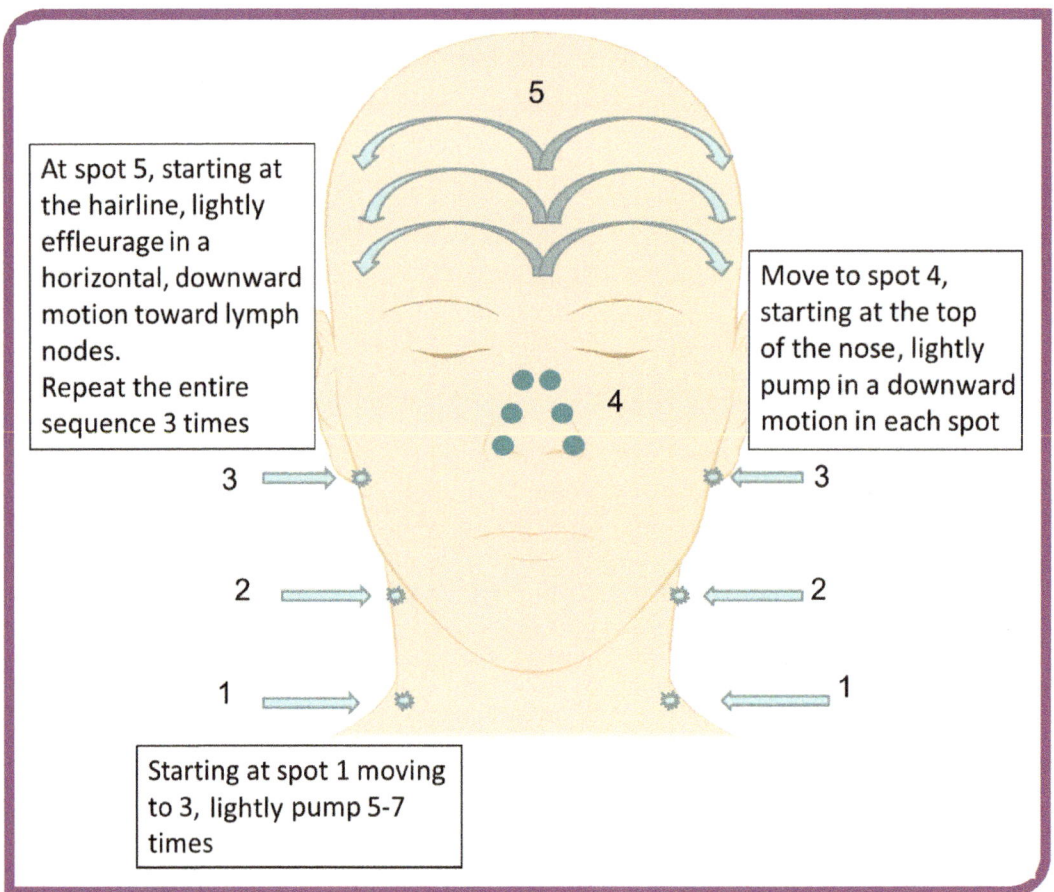

Further Potential Benefits of MLD

MLD is beneficial for other skin conditions as well. Considering the fact that the lymphatic fluid takes potentially harmful substances out of the body, if it is not circulated properly bacteria can build up in the skin. MLD techniques can be incorporated into a variety of facial treatments, as long as there are no contraindications. In cases of sensitive, inflamed skin, including grades III or IV acne and/or rosacea,

MLD can, and perhaps should, take the place of traditional stimulating massage techniques. Over-stimulating inflamed skin can exacerbate the problem, while MLD aids in the maintenance of healthy skin by removing the application of damaging substances from the skin. There is, at the time of this writing, an absence of clinical studies showing these benefits, as the quantifiable results of such studies would be hard to measure or justify. However, I have seen great improvement firsthand in my professional capacity.

Another popular use for this technique is to reduce puffiness in the face or eye area, as this can be caused from a buildup of lymph fluid.[4]

General contraindications for MLD include but are not limited to:
- Cancer or history of cancer
- Current infection anywhere in the body
- Heart problems
- Autoimmune disorders
- Bleeding disorders
- Any medical conditions must be cleared by the treating physician; if the lymphatic system is stimulated during illness, then that illness could potentially spread to other areas of the body.

In Practice...
As the eyes are the first to show visible signs of aging, it is a common concern for most. A specialized eye treatment using MLD can be an add-on for many procedures.

Looking Beyond MLD
Although MLD massage is the most common of the pre- and post-surgical treatments, there are other devices used in skin care that can promote healing. Ultrasound is recognized for its ability to stimulate circulation and induce lymphatic drainage to decrease swelling.[5] Microcurrent and LED are both known for stimulating ATP, an important energy source in cells that plays a role in healing and regeneration. The methodologies of how these devices work in the skin will be laid out in detail in Part 7.

Cosmetic Camouflage
Cosmetic camouflage is the application of makeup to conceal, color, or contour irregularities of the face or body. Makeup used for camouflaging are typically creams or powders with more pigment than cosmetic makeup. Concealers used for camouflaging are typically more dense and opaque to fully hide imperfections.

Makeup consists of cream-based, liquid or powder concealers, liquid foundation, and more commonly loose or pressed mineral powders. Mineral makeup is often used in the medical setting. Pure minerals have anti-inflammatory properties and natural sun-protective qualities. Along the course of working toward the goal of making the aesthetic patient feel better about herself, basic knowledge of camouflaging techniques is necessary. Common side effects following more aggressive surgical procedures include bruising, erythema, and

pigmentation. Patients are more likely to undergo these procedures if they know there is a way to conceal the inevitable side effects afterward. In the treatment of discolored lesions, it is common for the lesions to appear darker before they improve. The treatment of certain skin conditions can be a long process, and the skin care professional's ability to help patients feel more confident during this period of recovery will result in a higher rate of satisfaction, along with a renewed level of trust between patient and provider.

In Practice...

To ensure a makeup is of pure mineral origin, add a small amount to water; if the makeup floats to the top, it is composed of pure minerals. If it does not float to the top, then there may be additional ingredients in the product.

Camouflage makeup may also be used for highlighting and contouring to change the balance of the facial structures. This is a detailed skill set that can be beneficial, because patients may not realize the breadth of options available to them; they may think that covering over flaws is their only option. Specialized makeup training centers have courses specific to this type of camouflaging technique. It is best to start with an understanding of color to hide imperfections and from there develop precise application techniques.

The first step, regardless of the area to be concealed, is to choose the right base color for the patient. Knowing the patient's color undertone is necessary to find the right color. Undertones are typically warm tones or cool tones, yet some people are neutral and either tone can be used. Warm tones have a softer hue, or more depth to the pigment, while cooler colors tend to be bold and defined. A person who is best suited for cooler colors generally has pink undertones in their skin and/or less pigment. Someone who is olive-skinned or with more pigment tends to be have more yellow undertones. Once the undertone is determined, the color choice should be easy, as many companies now have base makeup categorized as warm, cool, or neutral. Pick two or three colors that could match the client, apply vertical lines down the side of the face to the neck, and the matching color should, upon application, disappear in to the skin.

Chose the right base color for the patient.

Once the base color is established, it is time to examine the face for areas of discoloration. To camouflage specific colors, it is advisable to use the opposite color on the color wheel (**pictured**). For example, to camouflage discolorations that are blue (for example, bruising or under-eye circles), use an orange-based concealer; for red (vascular lesions, inflamed acne), use a green-based concealer; for yellow (the end of the bruise or sallow skin tone), use a pink or purple-based concealer; and for purple (under-eye circles, bruising, vascular disorders), use a yellow-based concealer.

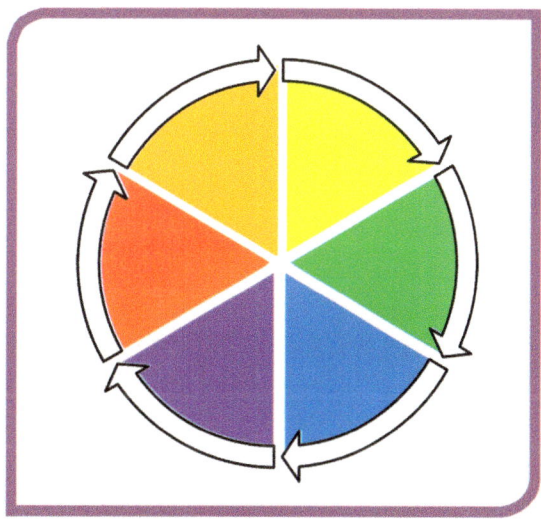

Before treating patients post-operatively, the provider must ensure that any and all wounds have healed and that the physician has given the patient clearance to resume makeup use. Bruising is a common side effect following surgical procedure and filler injections. When concealing bruises, the coloration often changes as the healing process progresses; typically what begins as a deep blue color often ends in a yellowish tone before disappearing. For this reason, a makeup palette, such as the one **pictured**, containing multiple colors, orange, yellow, purple and natural, will be most beneficial to send the patient home with so they can hide the discoloration through each stage of healing. When dealing with postoperative patients, sanitary practices and cleanliness are always of primary concern to prevent any chance of infection.

Advising the Patient
If a patient wishes to determine their own undertone, warm or cool, suggest that they find a piece of silver fabric and a piece of gold fabric. Then have them stand in front of a mirror in natural light, and hold each piece of fabric next to their face, one at a time, and make a comparison. If the silver makes their face light up, the patient is most likely cool toned. If the gold makes them look more vibrant, the patient is probably warm toned.

In Practice...
It is best to select the appropriate base and concealer shades before the patient's surgery. This prevents being distracted by any discoloration caused by the procedure itself, and provides an accurate baseline color that the patient would consider to be normal.

Camouflaging Discolorations
- Blue: use an orange-based concealer
- Red: use a green-based concealer
- Yellow: use a pink or purple-based concealer
- Purple: use a yellow-based concealer

An easy way to remember these color pairs:
- Chicago Bears: blue and orange
- Easter: yellow and purple (or pink)
- Christmas: red and green

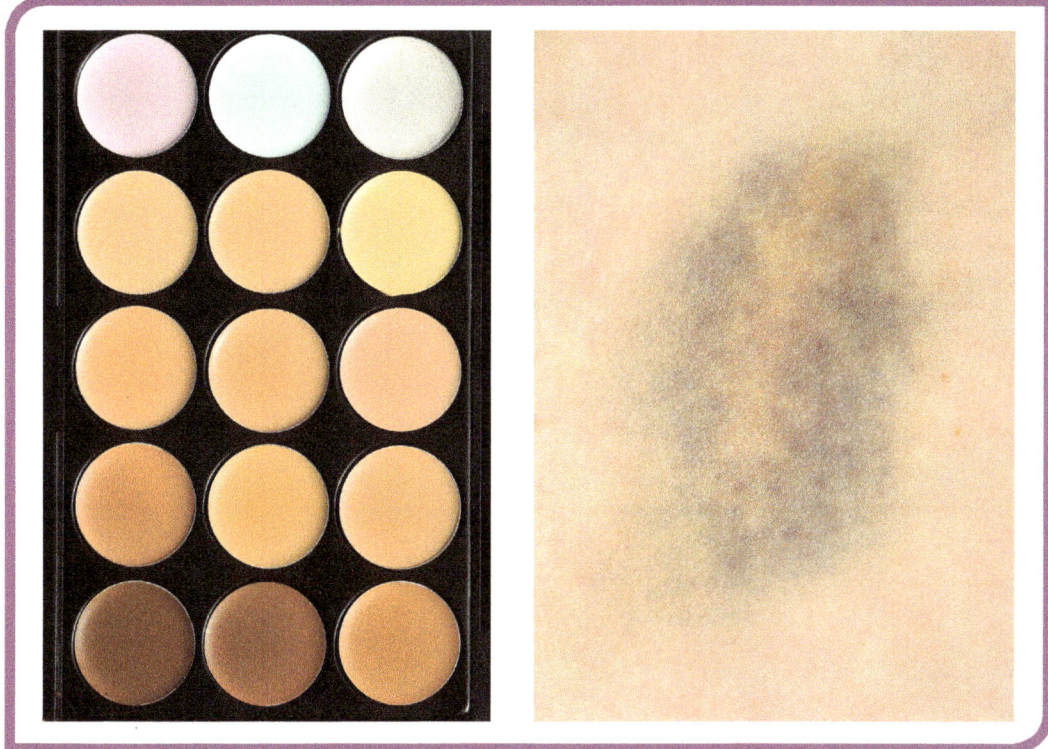

A makeup palette is useful for concealment of bruises.

Rosacea/Erythema

The best way to overcome the embarrassing redness associated with a rosacea flare-up is with mineral makeup. The minerals help neutralize redness while reflecting light away from imperfections, resulting in more natural looking skin. Minerals not only help cover up the symptoms of rosacea, but may also help calm the irritations associated with the condition. Zinc oxide and titanium dioxide, commonly used in mineral makeup, have anti-inflammatory properties and natural sun-protecting qualities.

> **Whitewashing** the face consists of applying a heavy layer of a shade of makeup lighter than the patient's natural skin color to completely cover any underlying issues.

To camouflage rosacea symptoms, the skin should first be thoroughly cleansed and moisturized before selecting the correct color base shade, which will either be warm or cool. Start by whitewashing the face or applying a shade of makeup lighter than the natural skin color in light downward strokes. Once the lightened area has dried, re-evaluate whether another layer is needed depending on whether the redness is still apparent. A yellow shade of makeup is best to hide more extreme redness. After this, apply the pre-chosen color to the rest of the face, bearing in mind the client's preferences.

Acne

Patients with acne may see improvement in the condition by simply switching to mineral makeup. Pure minerals will be free of fragrance and irritating dyes that can lead to acne breakouts. The natural anti-inflammatory properties of minerals often help reduce the severity and frequency of treatments. Mineral makeup is also non-comedogenic, meaning it does not contribute to forming blackheads or pimples, and doesn't support bacteria.

Start by cleansing and lightly moisturizing the client's face. Next, with a sponge, apply a thin layer of a *primer*—a makeup base that provides a smooth finish to the skin; this will help smooth out the skin and control oil production to help keep makeup in place. Using a camouflage brush, apply and blend a thin layer of yellow- or green-based concealer over all red areas. Let dry and repeat if necessary. Apply an appropriate base powder to the entire face using light downward strokes. Finish by adding a bronzer to "warm up" the face.

Discoloration Under Eyes

Dark circles under the eyes tend to have a gray, blue, or purple tinge, and therefore easily show through most makeup bases. The eye area also has few to no sebaceous glands—these are the glands in the dermis of the skin that produce and secrete sebum—and therefore, it is important to use a moisturizing product first to prevent a dehydrated look, showing more pronounced lines. Puffiness and dark circles can be masked by using the following simple concealing technique: Begin by select-

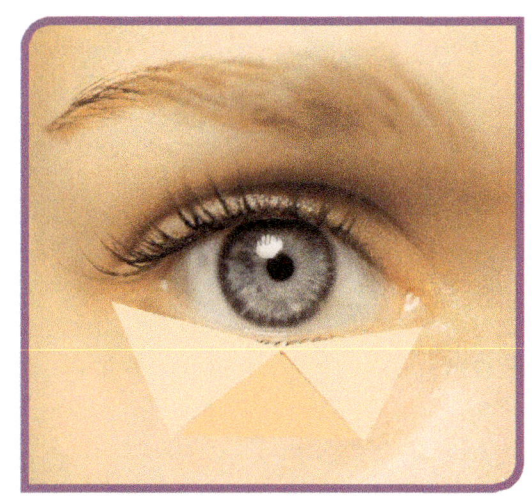
Dark undereye circle concealing technique

ing the appropriate color for your client's skin tone. Pick a concealer shade that is slightly darker than the natural color of the skin and draw a triangle pointed directly under the iris. Then fill in the triangle. Use the lighter shade to draw two inverted triangles on each side and, again, fill in. Blend the three together gently with a stippling motion, and finish with the appropriate matching powder on top.

Hyperpigmentation

Begin with a clean and moisturized face. Apply a thin layer of primer. For clients with oily skin, it is preferable to use a yellow-based primer; for clients with dryer skin, you may need a primer with a pink undertone. First, try applying just the mineral base alone. If you find that this is not enough to give complete coverage, apply a concealer with an orange undertone to the dark spots. Be sure to stay within the boundaries of the spots and feather outward to blend. Next, you can roll-press a mineral-based powder that matches the client's natural skin tone. Blend with a bronzer to combat any ashiness or gray cast that may occur.

> ## Application Techniques
> - *Stippling:* Gently rolling a brush or makeup sponge from one side to another in a quick motion.
> - *Roll Press:* Pressing a makeup sponge or pad in a rolling motion slowly and evenly to apply a heavy layer of color.
> - *Blending:* Lightly patting a brush or sponge until different colors blend together.

Hypopigmentation
Apply a makeup base, again using the whitewashing technique, to cleansed and moisturized skin, focusing on the lighter areas. Allow this makeup base to dry before adding concealer to the light spots. When dry, feather the edges with outward strokes. Brush over the entire area with a matching base shade, and roll-press to set it. Remove any excess makeup with a powder brush.

Scarring
Indented scars create a shadow. To minimize this shadow, apply a shade of concealer *lighter* than the patient's skin color directly onto the center of the scar with a small brush. Do not blend. Next, outline the perimeter of the scar with a *darker shade* of concealer. Roll-press a matched base to finish the look. It is also helpful to powder the rest of the area with the same base color.

Raised scars should be done the opposite of indented scars. A concealer *darker than* the natural skin shade should be applied to the center of the scar, and a concealer *lighter than* the natural skin shade should be applied around it. Do not blend. Finally, apply the appropriate color base that has been matched to the natural skin tone over it.

In Conclusion…
MLD and camouflage makeup are both specialized treatments that can add value to a career in cosmetic medicine. Plastic surgeons that hire support staff to solely care for their patients before and after surgery want to provide a complete experience. Patients appreciate the nurturing and extra attention provided, leading to a strong patient base and multiple referrals.

Although MLD and camouflage makeup are most commonly associated with cosmetic surgery, the benefits reach much further than that. Both of these treatments prove beneficial for inflamed skin conditions, including rosacea and acne. It is important to reduce inflammation by stimulating lymphatic flow, and it is equally important to help the patient feel better while undergoing treatments.

Camouflage makeup or makeup in general completes the treatment of a skin care provider. The essential goal of any skin care treatment is to improve the appearance of the skin, and makeup, in essence, does just that.

> ## SCENARIO: Helping Your Client Decide
>
> A client comes in for acne treatment. Her skin is red and inflamed. After devoting an hour to treating her skin and developing an entire skin care program tailored to help this client attain her goals, she asks what you can do to help her conceal breakouts during treatments. You do not specialize in makeup, and therefore choose not to carry it as a product offering. You recommend that she get a makeup of pure mineral origin, explaining the importance and benefits of mineral makeups. She goes to the cosmetic counter and purchases the first thing that says mineral. It may not be a pure mineral base and it did not do her justice, because she likely has no idea what color to choose or even how to apply it.
>
> **So what happened here?** The client who just left your office feeling amazing is now either feeling misled by a salesperson, or confused as to why your recommendation of makeup type is not yielding the results you assured her she could expect.
>
> Correcting this situation is as easy as explaining the difference between pure mineral makeups and those that simply have a mineral base, and also going further in your treatment by assessing the client's skin tone and making a specific recommendation for what shade of makeup the client should be looking for.

References

1. AA Mottura, Face lift postoperative recovery, *Aesthetic Plast Surg*, 26 (3), 172-180 (2002); accessed on Feb 21, 2014, at: *www.ncbi.nlm.nih.gov/pubmed/12140694*.
2. H Wittlinger, et al, The history of Dr. Vodder and evolution of combined decongestive therapy, *LymphLink*, 24(2) 1-2 (2012).
3. K Premkumar, *The Massage Connection: Anatomy and Physiology*, Philadelphia: Lippincourt, Williams & Wilkins (2004).
4. G Szolnoky et al, Manual lymph drainage efficiently reduces post-operative facial swelling and discomfort after removal of impacted third molars, *Lymphology*, 40, 138-142 (2007).
5. I Hashish et al, Anti-inflammatory effects of ultrasound therapy: Evidence for a major placebo effect, *Br J Rheumator*, 25, 77-81 (1986).

Part 6 Review Questions

1) What is the most commonly used facial filling agent?

    a) Fat

    b) Hyaluronic acid

    c) Cartilage

    d) Calcium hydroxylapetite

2) Calcium hydroxylapetite, the ingredient in the facial filler Radiesse, is also found in what areas of the human body?

    a) Nails and cartilage

    b) The skin and joints

    c) The hands and feet

    d) Bones and teeth

3) Why are bovine collagen products not commonly used anymore?

    a) Longevity is disappointing

    b) They can leave a bumpy irregular appearance on the skin

    c) The client needs skin testing for allergic reactions before being treated

    d) All of the above

4) Which method of volume replacement is most commonly used during a surgical procedure?

    a) Restylane

    b) Radiesse

    c) Sculptra

    d) Fat transfer

5) Neurotoxins are a purified protein toxin that blocks communication between the _____ and the _____ .

    a) Muscles, skin

    b) Nerves, epidermis

    c) Blood flow, joints

    d) Muscles, nerves

6) When were the beneficial side effects of neurotoxins in facial cosmetics first recognized?

   a) The late 1960s
   b) The late 1970s
   c) The late 1980s
   d) The late 1990s

7) Besides reducing fine lines and wrinkles, what non-cosmetic uses do neurotoxins possess?

   a) Addressing blepharospasm
   b) Alleviating migraine headaches
   c) Reduce excess sweating
   d) All of the above

8) When neurotoxins are used *on-label*, what improvements can a patient expect to see?

   a) Reduction of the creases between the eyebrows
   b) More volume in the face
   c) A tightening of loose skin
   d) A smaller jawline

9) What can the patient expect during a neurotoxin treatment?

   a) The patient will receive a series of small injections
   b) The patient is put under general anesthesia before receiving a series of injections
   c) The patient receives one large injection into the forehead
   d) The neurotoxin is applied topically and left on the skin for thirty minutes

10) How long does it usually take for the effects of Botox to take place after the treatment?

    a) Right away
    b) The next day
    c) Up to 7 days
    d) One month

Review Questions

11) How long does Dysport last?

    a) Two months
    b) Three to four months
    c) Six to nine months
    d) One year

12) Where is the incision made during an open rhinoplasty?

    a) The septum
    b) The columella
    c) The tip
    d) The right nostril

13) What is the name of the procedure done to correct a deviated septum?

    a) Septoplasty
    b) Septum revision
    c) Rhinoplasty
    d) Cartilage shaping

14) What should dried mucous or crust around the nose and nostrils be cleaned with?

    a) Glycolic cleanser
    b) Saline spray
    c) Hydrogen peroxide
    d) Alcohol

15) How long should patients receiving rhytidectomy expect results to last?

    a) Five to 12 Years
    b) 15 years
    c) Two years
    d) Forever

16) To minimize swelling after rhytidectomy, now long should the patient keep their head elevated while sleeping?

   a) One week
   b) Three to five days
   c) Two months
   d) Two to four weeks

17) Where are the incisions made for transconjunctival blepharoplasty?

   a) The inside surface of the upper or lower eyelid
   b) The outside surface of the upper or lower eyelid
   c) Around the lash line of the upper and lower eyelids
   d) In the crease of the upper and lower eyelids

18) Who was the founder of MLD?

   a) Johan Georg Mezger
   b) Dr. Vodder
   c) Tokujiro Namikoshi
   d) Pehr Henrik Ling

19) What is Manual Lymph Drainage?

   a) MLD is a process to improve the circulation of lymph through the body to stimulate the body's immune response. Using the hands in a soft stretching fashion, movements are applied in a circular, pumplike or in scooping strokes.
   b) MLD is a very firm pressured massage of the skin and muscles.
   c) MLD is used in light rhythmic movements on the ducts to drain stagnant lymph back into the cardiovascular system.
   d) MLD is a massage which uses effleurage movements away from the thoracic and right lymphatic ducts.

20) What are the names of the two main ducts that lymph flows through?

   a) The right and left subclavian veins
   b) The right lymphatic duct and the thoracic duct
   c) Tear ducts and salivary ducts
   d) The superficial temporal vein and the lingual vein

21) When is MLD contraindicated?

   a) Malignant tumors
   b) Infection
   c) Heart problems
   d) All of the above

22) Why is mineral makeup most often used in a medical setting?

   a) It has anti-inflammatory properties
   b) It has sun protection properties
   c) Pure minerals do not support bacteria
   d) All of the above

23) For rosacea clients, after determining the color tone, what's the next step?

   a) Apply the makeup base
   b) Apply concealer to the entire face
   c) Add bronzer to warm up the face
   d) Whitewashing the face

24) How can puffiness and dark circles under the eyes be concealed with camouflage makeup?

   a) Whitewash the entire area under the eyes, followed by the appropriate base color
   b) Pick a concealer shade that is slightly lighter than the natural color of the skin, and draw a triangle directly under the iris. Then, fill in the triangle. Use the darker shade to draw two inverted triangles on each side, and again, fill in. Blend the three together gently, and finish with appropriate powder on top.
   c) Pick a concealer shade that is slightly darker than the natural color of the skin, and draw a triangle directly under the iris. Then, fill in the triangle. Use the lighter shade to draw two inverted triangles on each side, and again, fill in. Blend the three together gently, and finish with appropriate powder on top.
   d) Camouflage makeup cannot help dark circles and puffiness

25) What is your goal when camouflaging indented scars?

   a) Apply the darker shade of concealer directly onto the scar while outlining the perimeter of the scar with a lighter shade of concealer

   b) Apply the lighter shade of concealer directly onto the scar while outlining the perimeter of the scar with a darker shade of concealer

   c) Apply a yellow-based concealer to the entire scar

   d) Apply a cool foundation to the area several times

PART 7

Innovative Skin Rejuvenation Techniques

AESTHETICS EXPOSED
MASTERING SKIN CARE IN A MEDICAL SETTING AND BEYOND

CHAPTER 25

Five Steps to Making a SMART Purchase

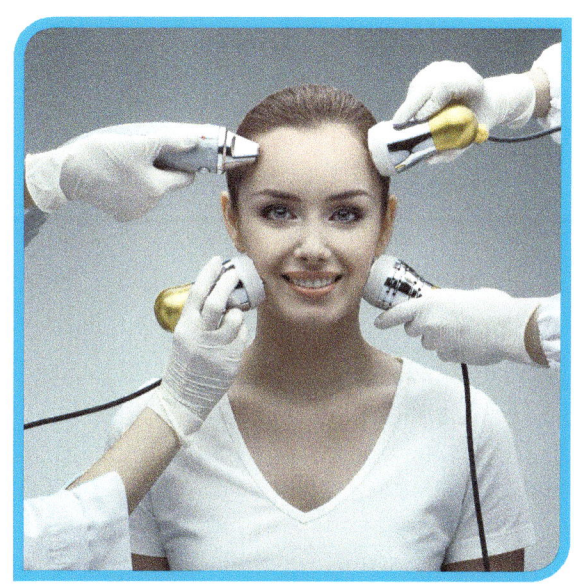

In this Chapter:
- Safety
- Maintenance
- Affirmation
- Research
- Takeaway

Aesthetic providers are constantly inundated with new products, treatments, and devices, all claiming to be the next best thing for their patients. Each product company boasts superior ingredients, quicker results, and longer lasting effects. Aggressive million-dollar advertising campaigns along with savvy businessmen and women hustle these products through flashy words with well-articulated catchphrases. Products today are introduced with fantastic testimonial photos, celebrity endorsements, grandiose claims for instant youth, and case studies that are meant to qualify as scientific evidence of the product's effectiveness. Yet, too often we fall prey to the idea of a new "miracle treatment" before finding out the supporting science. It is important to do your own research and determine the efficacy of the products and services you provide. Prematurely endorsing an ineffective or unproven product can be damaging to your reputation—and your business.

In light of that, here are the *Five Steps to Making a SMART Purchase: Safety, Maintenance, Affirmation, Research,* and *Takeaway (ROI).*

1. Safety
The margin of safety with topical skin products available to the consumer typically does not pose an *immediate* concern. Adverse events occurring secondary to a topical skin product usually only occur after continued use. In contrast, using a powerful heat- or electric-emitting device can cause an immediate adverse reaction and/or

permanent damage. Additional scrutiny is prudent prior to endorsing or using the "latest and greatest" new device. First of all, *make sure that your license allows you to operate the device that is being presented.* Assuming that it is legal, make sure the device is FDA approved. This alone doesn't mean caution isn't necessary; there are many devices that have been FDA approved that show little or no benefit and can actually cause more harm than good.

If you decide to purchase a particular device or invest in a product line, make sure it is from a reputable manufacturer. With the rise in online sales, it is common for consumers of any product to search for cheaper prices on the Web. Although it is enticing to save money—potentially thousands of dollars when it comes to medical equipment—the buyer must *be aware and beware* that many of these "discounted" devices are used and it cannot be known or verified how the previous owner cared for them. Any device could have *been* new but stored for many years in an environment detrimental to the machine's upkeep, such as a humid area that could compromise the machine's functionality or have caused a breakdown in the integrity of its parts.

The same goes for skin care products. It is not worth taking a chance by buying outside the direct manufacturer just because it may be less expensive. These products could be expired, stored incorrectly, used and resealed, or something other than what they are labeled. **Besides being unsafe, the purchase and use of off-manufacturer materials hurts the product industry as a whole.** These products may have been stolen or given as samples. Either way, just as we want our clients to buy from us, we need to respect the company working hard to provide us with safe, effective products to offer.

Ensure that the manufacturer provides you with information on *its* product specifically, not just similar technology; just because one type of technology is deemed safe, it does not mean any or all comparable products are as well. **The manufacturer should offer proper training on the use of its devices; if the company selling a product or device doesn't ensure safe use by their providers, then safety may not be important to them on the whole—and what does that tell you?** Even if the device seems easy to use, there is always a chance of complications. Bottom line: Devices and products should be procured only from reputable sources, and those sources should be ready and willing to educate the provider on safe usage.

2. Maintenance

Whether it is a new product or device, or something that has been on the market for a long period of time, ensure that the manufacturer or company of sale will make itself available to you after you've purchased. When it comes to skin care products, it is especially important to have product representatives who are available following the initial sale. **Representatives should be accessible for follow-up orders and continued education, as well as product and sales support.** Since product representatives often have an ongoing sales commission as part of their compensation package, it is typically easy to find a reputable company with a great support team, because it behooves these sales reps to build strong ties with their customers.

But while product representatives have good reason to support their accounts and help market for continued sales, laser salesmen, on the other hand, are known for their "love them and leave them" approach. Many medical devices have a hefty price tag and may not have consumables that require regular replacing (i.e., parts or disposable aspects of the device as a whole). A rep may come into your practice several times promising that the investment you would be making will be paid off easily, and that he/she will be available to help market the service using this device. Unfortunately, after the check is signed, the rep may suddenly have no time to help promote the service; once the device is sold, the rep has nothing more to gain. Don't get me wrong—some do keep to their word, especially those from larger, more reputable companies. In fact, some companies now provide marketing plans with the sales of their equipment. This is another top consideration in choosing the right company to work with; ongoing marketing support with this type of "big sticker" purchase is a must.

3. Affirmation

Any new product you are considering offering to your clients should be compared against similar products that have been tried in the past. Is it a similar formulation to a product that was introduced last year? If so, what type of results did you or your colleagues see? Were there any complications reported? *Looking to the past will often help you predict the future.* For example, retinols have a proven track record of effectiveness in reversing the signs of aging skin; therefore, a product containing retinol would likely hold more weight than a newly introduced product containing "Vitamin X." *However, just because a product is similar to an established therapeutic does not guarantee its potency.* **There are many factors in a product's delivery system that will determine its effectiveness, including the correct pH, concentration of the active ingredient(s), and the right vehicle to carry the active(s) into the skin.** There are also manufacturers who may add or subtract ingredients or utilize less efficacious forms of the active agent in attempts to cut expenses. These differences make for uncertain effects.

> Looking to the past will often help you predict the future.

The same goes for devices; technology that has been proven effective will likely be further utilized; for example, lasers for skin rejuvenation, radio frequency and ultrasound for skin tightening, and skin needling for collagen induction. Although these modalities are used often for effective, safe treatments in aesthetics, each device must have its own studies and clinical science to qualify and support it. On the other hand, if a product is continuously verified as ineffective, then why use it?

Think back to those weight loss machines from the 1950s on which a person would stand with a vibrating belt wrapped around the waist that was promised to "magically" melt inches away, or the electrical mask that would transmit pulses to give you an "instant face lift." Obviously these devices did not measure up to the extravagant claims they made, but the important lesson is that over the past 40+ years, new versions of these old gimmicks have continued to surface. **Just because the packaging or name changes, doesn't mean the results will!**

> Do your diligence, and remember your purchasing power is just that, power.

4. Research

It is the job of the provider to research the safety and efficacy of any product or service considered for use on clients. There are plenty of resources accessible through the Internet, including user and patient reviews. It is also helpful to get in contact with peers who have experience with the equipment or product line in question to receive feedback from a trusted source. Representatives should have clinical studies, scientific evidence, and before and after pictures made available. **It is important to be skeptical of boasted research and advertised testimonials. Read reports carefully and critically examine presented photographs.** Research studies claimed by manufacturers may be in-house projects, conducted by paid investigators. Rarely are these papers submitted to peer-reviewed medical journals. Ask for a copy of the study, so you can examine it yourself. If the company chooses not to provide one, you should be hesitant before going any further.

Similar to informational materials, photographs intended to demonstrate improvements are notorious for being less than truthful. There are many tricks for fooling the eye that would fool even the most knowledgeable aesthetic provider. However, a critically trained eye will recognize that post-treatment photographs are often taken at different angles and different light exposures. This can have a very dramatic effect on the perceived color and texture of the skin. As a professional in the industry, it is your job to do your homework and investigate any products you consider recommending to your clients.

5. Takeaway (ROI)

Regardless of a product's potential significance to aesthetics, it would be an unwise decision to purchase any product that will not increase your business's revenue in one way or another. **Of course, it is the skin care provider's first priority to make clients feel better about themselves; however, having an expensive product that provides short-term results would not be beneficial to anyone.** There are devices available that, although effective to a certain extent, are not worth the cost to the practice and, ultimately, to the client. First and foremost, disposables must be taken into consideration. Get information *before the purchase* on the cost of maintenance, disposables, warranties, and repairs. Having this information available ahead of time is important for determining your potential return on investment (ROI).

Consider this cautionary tale: I recently gave an in-office training on a laser device. The company in question spent almost $100,000 on a used machine, but the owner didn't realize that there was an additional and perpetual cost of $8 for a disposable tip, which would be needed for each client. Such an unintended cost, the owner quickly realized, would greatly affect the perceived profits from all laser treatments. Another aspect to be aware of when determining a purchase's ROI, particularly for the purchase of equipment and/or devices, is whether there is local competition on "daily deal" websites. If there are other practices in your area that offer a given treatment with the same device you have considered purchasing, this may bring down the perceived value of your practice offering the same treatment. This issue has, in fact, become of such concern to manufacturers that some have started taking steps to maintain device value—which, in turn, protects treatment value. Purchasers are being asked to sign agreements to *not* promote services that use the manufacturer's products on daily deal sites. After all, if another provider decides that high local competition due to such Web-based offers will make purchasing a given device a non-starter, then the manufacturer loses a sale.

As a purchaser, you must always be aware of the bottom line. What will help grow your business? What will help strengthen your present client base and offer you opportunities to attain an even larger clientele? What will you be able to take away from making a purchase?

Summary

If you are considering adopting a new product line or service, be certain you fully understand the treatment you are considering. **Remember your clients seek your expertise because they trust that you know what is best.** If you are not certain or are skeptical of a new product's claim, consult with those who have already used the product or with colleagues in whom you trust. Read all that you can on the product/device and then ask for guidance from those you deem to be knowledgeable. Bottom line: When it comes to the boasted claims of the next hot treatment, it is your job to investigate and your responsibility to not take advertisements and claims at face value.

Remember the SMART purchasing method: Safety, Maintenance, Affirmation, Research, and Takeaway (ROI).

The rest of this section will take a look at the latest devices and innovative ingredients used for skin rejuvenation.

CHAPTER 26

Devices: From Tightening to Rejuvenation, from Medical to Spa

In this Chapter:
- Medical / Skin Tightening Devices
    - Radio Frequency
    - Ultrasound
- Spa/ Skin Rejuvenation Devices
    - Microcurrent
    - LED Light Emitting Diodes

Skin tightening is one of the most sought-after treatments for those over age 45. As the skin continues to age and be exposed to environmental stress, it begins to sag, mainly in the jowls, neck, and eye area. There are several devices and treatments available that claim the ability to produce results that rival those of surgery. In the past, deep chemical peels and ablative lasers were the primary choices to tighten the skin by removing its outer layers, thus resulting in a wound response to stimulate collagen production. As discussed, these procedures are still used today, particularly for those who have additional textural and pigmentation issues. However, those who are solely seeking skin tightening with minimal downtime are moving toward non-ablative treatments. While visible light lasers and IPL are beneficial treatments (covered in Part 5 of this book), this section will outline current, cutting-edge skin tightening devices including radio frequency, ultrasound, LED, and microcurrent.

Radio Frequency
Radio frequency (RF) has quickly become one of the most popular treatments for skin tightening. RF devices emit energy in the form of electromagnetic waves that go through a conversion to create heat. (For a review of the electromagnetic spectrum, see Chapter 18.) These waves heat up the dermis, stimulating collagen and ultimately resulting in skin tightening. RF treatments are most commonly used for patients whose main concerns are sagging skin, fine lines, and premature aging. The use of

RF devices for fat reduction and skin tightening on the body are also becoming highly sought-after treatments.

How RF Works

Radio frequency treatments appear to be best suited for patients with early signs of aging such as wrinkles and skin laxity characterized as mild-to-moderate. Results are optimal when there is a commitment from the patient to adhere to a treatment schedule and at-home skin care regimen. The use of antioxidants, sunscreens and retinoids will further support the rebuilding of collagen. Unlike laser and IPL, the heat used in RF treatment is non-specific, and therefore the procedure can be performed on all Fitzpatrick skin types.

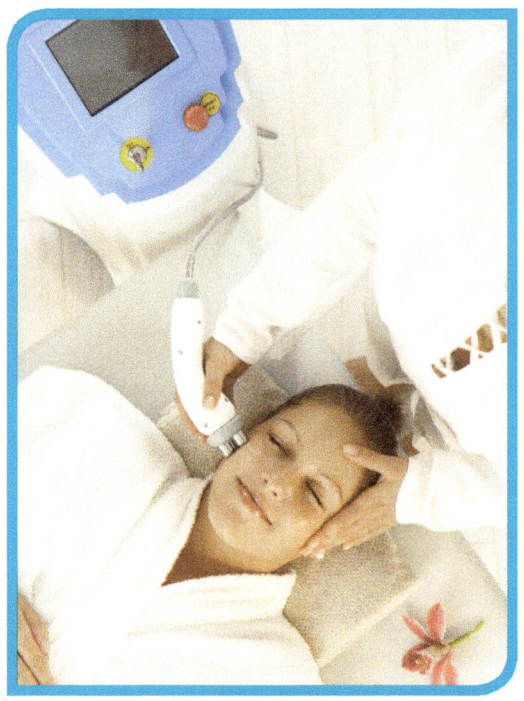

The function of RF is to deliver just enough energy to create a wound healing response to denature damaged collagen and promote collagen remodeling.[1] *As with all treatments, the skin must have the ability to heal the wound in order to avoid injury.* Many devices use radio frequency alone to heat the water content of the skin to an optimal temperature of 40–45°C (104–115°F), dependent on specific protocol. Some patients report visible improvement after one treatment, but in most cases multiple treatments are necessary. Although a tightening response may be immediately evident to the patient, it is often due to initial inflammation, and the true tightening will become evident in about four to six weeks, with likely continuation over the next three to 12 months.[2-4] Each case varies and is highly dependent

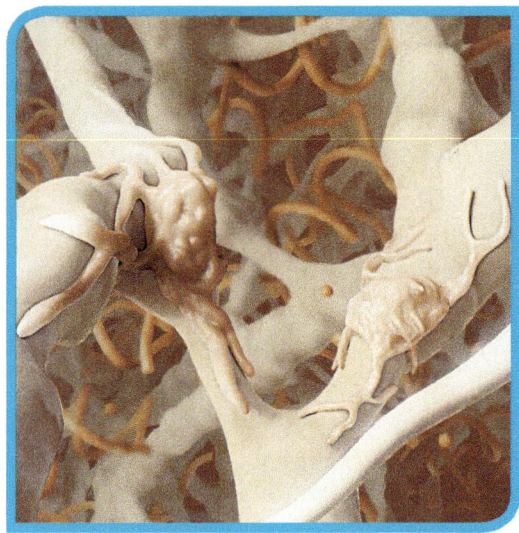

RF treatment affects the collagen elastin matrix.

> As with all treatments, the skin must have the ability to heal the wound in order to avoid injury.

upon protocols and individual patient response. The degree of tightening is progressive and subtle, which makes it difficult for patients to see results over a period of time. Before and after pictures should be taken between treatments as a matter of good practice; as an additional benefit, patients are often presently surprised seeing the results side by side. Repetitive treatments and patient cooperation with consistent home care are essential; this must be discussed thoroughly in the consultation. Over time, the newly formed collagen will reduce the appearance of fine lines and wrinkles as well as tighten the skin.

> Repetitive treatments and patient cooperation with consistent home care are essential; this must be discussed thoroughly in the consultation.

The first RF devices developed were not pain-free, and physicians would either use a topical anesthetic or prescribe medications to alleviate discomfort. These methods of reducing discomfort are no longer recommended, as the patient's feedback on heat response is often needed to reduce the chance of epidermal burns. Additionally, the development of present-day RF devices has rendered several of these treatments essentially pain-free.

Radio Frequency Devices
Thermage Thermacool (Solta Technologies) was the first FDA approved unipolar radio frequency tightening device in the United States. Unipolar devices have no direct target; therefore, the energy is directed at a grounding pad that is attached to the client, prior to the treatment. This allows the energy to be delivered deep into the dermis, as it is attracted to the grounding pad, commonly placed on the client's back. Although unipolar devices consistently show great results, more recent devices utilize *bipolar* RF energy. Bipolar RF devices use the same mechanisms of heat delivery as unipolar models, but have added polarized magnets, eliminating the need for a grounding pad. The bipolar current focuses the RF energy through two strategically placed electrodes on the tip of the hand piece. This provides a specific target of heat within the hand piece, giving the provider a more precise area on which to focus the energy. Varying hand piece sizes also allow for concentrated heat, specific to a given surface area. For example, the area around the eyes would require a smaller hand piece due to the size of the treatment zone, while a larger area on the body would need a larger hand piece to maintain the desired temperature in order to create a response. In essence, more advanced systems with larger surface areas and targeted energy allow the sensation and action of the heat to be evenly distributed in the treatment area, resulting in a more comfortable experience.

Recently, RF devices new to the market are being developed with specialized features. Some manufacturers use fractionated energy, similar to those discussed in Part 5 on lasers, leaving portions of the skin untreated. One fractionated radio frequency device from Syneron called the E-Matrix, uses the focused energy to create sublative resurfacing. Sublative resurfacing is the heating up of portions of the skin *beneath* the surface without removing the superficial layers. The ReFirm from Syneron uses bipolar RF along with light energy to more effectively heat targets. The Alluma from Lumenis is used with a vacuum attachment for the dual purpose of bringing the electrodes closer to the dermal tissue in order to diminish the required energy emitted as well as distract sensory nerves from full heat sensation. EndyMed is a company that has taken it a step further by utilizing multiple electrodes, known as multi-polar technology, as opposed to one or two electrodes which most other devices employ. This provides the advantage of focused heating similar to bipolar but with multiple targets and deeper energy flow. The EndyMed device also has added safety benefits that include a censored feedback mechanism and automatic shut-off when the electrodes are not in full contact with the skin.

> Unlike IPL and visual light lasers where the light energy is attracted to color, RF energy is not color specific and can be used safely regardless of pigment.

Some of the contraindications for radio frequency treatments include pregnancy or nursing, due to the fact that as with most other aesthetic treatments, the side effects are unknown. Wounds or infection on the skin, including herpetic breakouts; because RF is stimulating and could result in spreading of a bacteria or virus, those prone to herpetic breakouts may be put on medication to reduce the chance of an outbreak. Any skin disease or medical condition that could result in poor-healing, e.g., diabetes, auto-immune disorders, or skin cancer. Finally, being that radio frequency delivers energy through electrical currents, it cannot be performed on anyone with an implantable electrical device such as a pacemaker or defibrillator; it could potentially interfere with the current used in these necessary devices.

Radio Frequency Treatment
During an RF treatment, patients are reclined in a relaxed position. Jewelry is removed, and the skin is cleansed of all makeup and products, followed by a thorough degreasing with alcohol. When a unipolar device is used, the provider will likely place the grounding pad on the patient's back. The pad, in effect, completes the electric current and deters it from flowing uncontrollably toward the rest of the body. However, as previously stated, with bipolar devices no grounding pad is needed. Many RF treatment protocols call for a conductive gel or oil to be applied to the skin's surface to ease movement of the hand piece. The hand piece must remain in complete contact with the skin or an arch of energy can be produced resulting in a

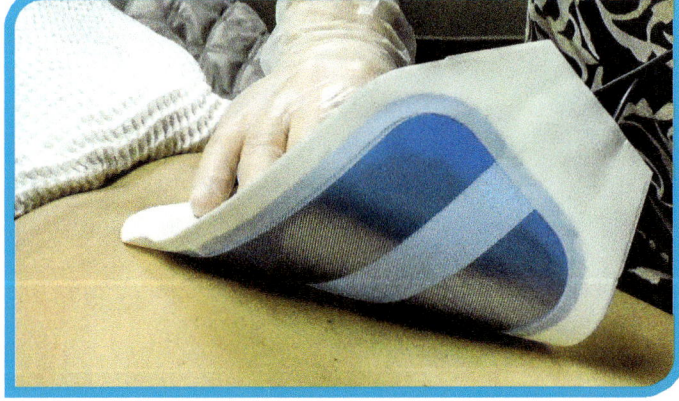

The grounding pad is used to complete the electric current.

shock and/or burn on the skin. This can be difficult at times, as patients tend to jump when the heat starts to build to the target temperature of 105–115°F. The provider's initial reaction may be to quickly remove the device, which could ultimately cause a burn. Some of the newer devices have been developed with a sensor to automatically stop the current any time the applicator is not in full contact with the skin.

During early adoption of this procedure, protocols were developed with high energy settings geared to maximize collagen denaturation. However, the process was painful, dissatisfying, and complications were frequent.[5] Today, standardized protocols have been identified that use lower energy settings but multiple passes. These protocols result in collagen contraction and tightening that are as effective as, if not more than, those of higher energy settings with fewer passes. Lower energy settings also equate to less risk of complications or heat-induced injury.

A swift hand, along with consistent temperature monitoring on the part of the technician, is required. Energy delivered needs to successfully penetrate to the subcutaneous fat layers while not damaging the superficial structures of the skin. Advocates recommend that heating be emphasized over anchoring points in the neck (i.e., over the mastoid) and then continue in the direction of maximum lift of the skin.

Post-treatment Expectations

Due to the epidermis remaining intact, clients experience no downtime and may immediately return to their regular schedule. Edema and erythema are rarely present, but if they occur, it typically resolves within hours and rarely extends beyond a day or two. There is, of course, the risk of localized superficial burns on the skin if the device does not remain in direct contact with the skin.

Although rare, high-energy RF treatments may cause damage, including the potential for fat necrosis, skin color changes, and scar formation. These severe complications are often caused by a lack of temperature monitoring by the provider. Although some of the newer devices have the capability to measure skin temperature, many still require a separate temperature gauge (**pictured**). With new technology and currently recommended lower settings, these complications are rare.

In order to maximize wound response and promote collagen production, anti-inflammatory agents are not recommended.

Patients often ask how long treatment will last. As with any treatment, cosmetic or medical, results vary and what works on one person may not work on another. However,

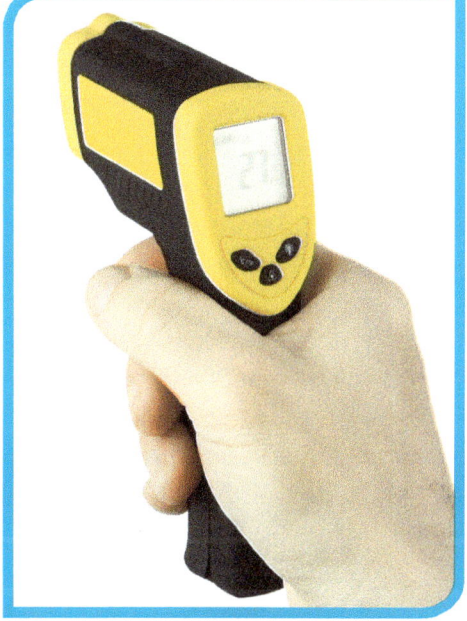

RF Temperature Gauge

most patients require a maintenance treatment every six to 12 months, especially in those with increased laxity. If less than ideal candidates are chosen (i.e., those with severe loss of elasticity that are better candidates for a surgical procedure), they may not experience satisfactory results.

The most prominent adverse event with noninvasive skin tightening procedures is patient dissatisfaction. It is important that patient expectations be managed appropriately and that the procedure be reasonably priced. **Exaggerated definitions of "nonsurgical face-lifting" may leave patients with the impression that such treatments can replace a surgical procedure.** While objective skin tightening is frequently reported, patients expecting a surgical-type result will be disappointed. It is recommended that if a cosmetic device does not reliably achieve a patient satisfaction rate of 90% or higher, the procedure should not be offered. Anything less than 90% may lead to a wearing down of the cosmetic practice and professional's reputation.

Ultrasound

Ultrasound technology is another modality used in a medical setting for skin tightening. It is most commonly associated with monitoring fetuses during pregnancy, and is also widely used in medicine to diagnose underlying medical conditions that might otherwise not be discovered. It is also used in physical therapy for musculoskeletal ailments. Ultrasound's application for skin rejuvenation was discovered in association with its use for stimulating wound repair in poorly healing skin. Specifically, research has shown that the treatment can stimulate fibroblast proliferation and increase circulation at the wound site, thereby increasing the speed at which the wound heals.[6] The ability to stimulate fibroblasts makes it an ideal treatment for skin rejuvenation.

Ultrasound technology uses high frequency sound waves of at least 20,000 Hz* for therapeutic or imaging purposes. (These sound waves are undetectable to the human ear.) The physiological benefits of ultrasound are categorized as *thermal, heat-producing* and *non-thermal, not producing heat*. Thermally, ultrasound waves can cause local tissues to heat up to a range of 104–115°F (40–45°C), which seems to be the optimal temperature range for stimulating collagen production. Ultrasound also increases localized blood flow, allowing the skin to better repair itself.[7] The increase in blood flow allows more nutrients to be circulated, as well as stimulation of the lymphatic system to begin engulfing and removing impurities.

The *non-thermal* nature of ultrasound acts to create microscopic bubbles through vibrations produced by sound waves, known as *cavitation*. The cavitation also works on tissue fluids that act to increase the cell membrane's permeability and calcium intake. In its entirety, the process of cavitation promotes wound repair and collagen production.[8]

---

*Hertz (Hz) is a unit of frequency measured as 1 cycle per second.

Traditional Ultrasound Treatment

Traditional ultrasound uses a rapidly oscillating probe (**pictured**) to create sound waves that are conducted to the epidermal skin tissues through a water-based gel. During this pain-free process, the depth of penetration may be changed by altering the frequency of the oscillations: the higher the frequency, the less penetrating the waves. For example, wavelengths in the 1 MHz** range can extend deeply to muscle and bones, increasing the risk of local tissue damage if not performed correctly. However, in the 3 MHz range, the ultrasound waves remain at a more superficial level, and the risk of tissue damage is not as great. Many ultrasound devices used for skin rejuvenation also deliver medicinal products through the skin by way of a process known as *phonophoresis*. Animal studies have shown that ultrasound may deliver significant levels of hydrocortisone, certain antiviral agents, and even aspirin.

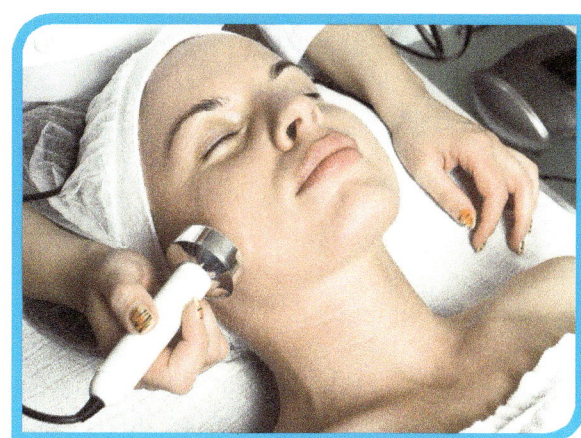

Traditional ultrasound oscillating probe creates sound waves that carry through the skin's epidermal tissue.

Low-level ultrasound remains popular because there is no downtime and takes only minutes. Clients often describe it as a warm soothing massage and are able to immediately reapply makeup and resume their schedules. After treatment, clients see an immediate tightening and glow to their skin, making it ideal before an important event. This method of ultrasound therapy is also beneficial before and after facial surgery, as it accelerates the healing process by reducing inflammation and swelling. For optimal results with cosmetic surgical procedures, it is recommended that ultrasound treatments be done two weeks before surgery and three weeks after surgery at two-week intervals until swelling subsides.

Contraindications for ultrasound treatments include cancer, or history of cancer; because ultrasound induces circulation, it simultaneously stimulates the lymphatic system.
As with any treatment utilizing a form of energy, it cannot be performed on anyone that is pregnant, and should not be done on anyone with implanted medical devices. Ultrasound should not be performed inside the infraorbital rim of the eye, over the spinal cord, or over the thyroid.

**Megahertz (MHz) refers to the number of oscillations; the lower the number, the deeper the penetration.

Micro-focused Ultrasound

The use of micro-focused ultrasound was introduced in 2009 to deliver heat to deep subdermal connective tissue in *focused* zones.[9] Ultherapy (Ulthera Inc.) is FDA approved to lift the skin on the neck, chin and brow. This treatment varies greatly from the previously discussed method for skin rejuvenation with ultrasonic waves. The mechanical energy produced from the sound waves in Ultherapy bypasses the epidermis and papillary layer of the dermis, producing small micro-thermal lesions deep in the reticular layer of the dermis and hypodermis (subcutaneous). This type of ultrasound reaches deeper than other skin tightening modalities with the target of energy being the superficial muscular aponecrotic system, or SMAS, the area where the majority of tightening has the ability to occur in the skin. The SMAS is the blanket of highly organized fibers that connects and efficiently distributes forces between the skin and muscles of the face; due to its connective properties, it is highly comprised of collagen and elastin. Another unique feature of Ultherapy is that it uses the imaging benefits of ultrasound technology to ensure correct focal points in each patient. Therefore, the provider can see precisely where the energy will be focused.

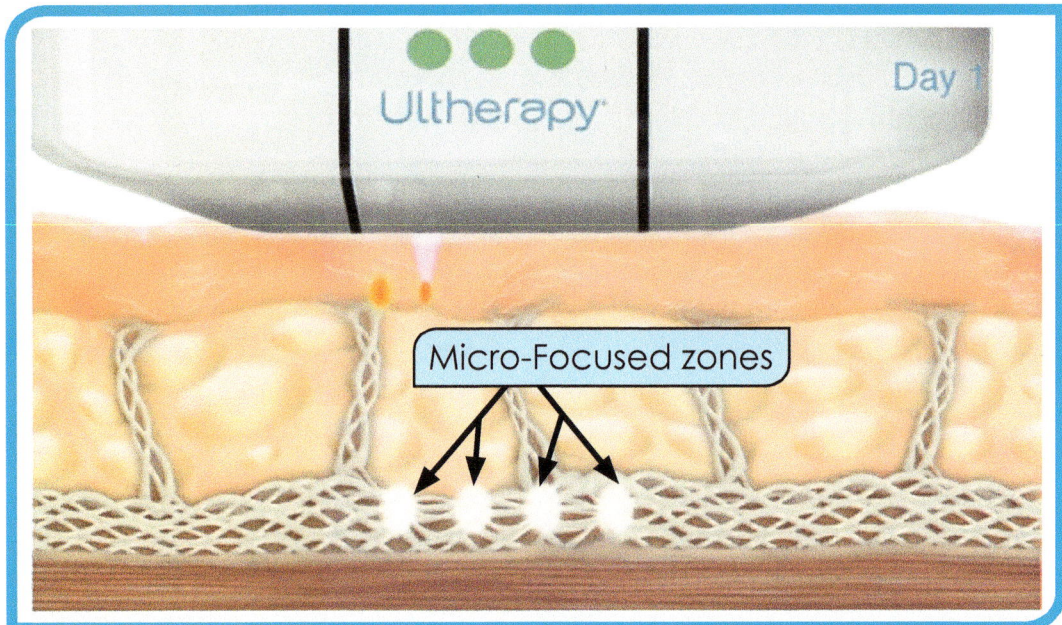

Treatment Expectations

The treatment itself takes 45–60 minutes. The area to be treated is cleansed and degreased with alcohol. Specific protocols may call for treatment grids to be drawn according to manufacturer standards with a surgical marking crayon on the area. This allows the provider to administer a specific amount of passes per area. Ultrasound gel is then applied to the area, and the treatment commences. Treatments with micro-focused ultrasound differ from the warmth felt from lower frequency ultrasound devices used for cumulative skin rejuvenation and healing. Although pain is subjective, many patients describe it as uncomfortable. A significant amount of heat is produced when the energy is focused to the deep subdermal connective tissue. Patients being treated with the Ultherapy device are commonly prescribed a small dose of anti-anxiety or pain medication prior to treatment.

Immediately following treatment, the skin typically appears flushed and cold compresses can be used; the redness usually subsides within a couple of hours. There is no downtime with this procedure, but side effects may include erythema, edema, PIH, wheals, bruising, and sensitized or numb skin. Motor nerve paresis or weakness of the nerves, not to be confused with paralysis which refers to complete loss of movement, and transient dyesthesia or moving numbness, are more serious complications that could occur.

Claims suggest that one of the primary benefits of such a treatment is that optimal results may be achieved after only one treatment as opposed to several with lower-level ultrasound and the majority of radio frequency-based procedures. Radio frequency and ultrasound skin tightening devices are considered medical treatments because they are meant to structurally change the proteins in the skin. The use of these modalities is often delegated by the physician to trained support staff. It is important to abide by specific regulations for each type of device used. For instance, in some states ultrasound may only be used by a medical professional or ultrasound technician. When realistic expectations are given and protocols are strictly followed, these devices provide patients with yet another alternative to surgery for skin tightening. It is not uncommon for those receiving skin tightening procedures to eventually seek out surgery or even those receiving surgery to follow up with skin tightening, in order to enhance and prolong results.

LED and Microcurrent

The influx of medical devices has subsequently triggered a rise in the use of non-medical treatment options. While such treatments typically emit less energy, they still have the potential to positively affect select skin conditions and/or maintain results from previously mentioned cosmetic medical treatments. Some of the more popular skin rejuvenation devices used by skin care professionals and clients alike are light emitting diodes (LED) and microcurrent.

Light Emitting Diodes / LED

LED, commonly referred to simply as *light therapy*, produces low levels of light energy.[10] Similar to the process by which plant life coverts light energy into chemical energy through photosynthesis, LED devices generate a type of energy necessary for the repair and regeneration of human cells. Although LED uses light, it provides significantly less energy than laser or IPL therapies, and does

> Although LED uses light, it provides significantly less energy than laser or IPL therapies, and does not produce a measurable amount of heat.

not produce a measurable amount of heat. This limited thermal effect makes it safer for use in non-medical treatment settings and also for client at-home use.

Simply put, a light emitting diode is a type of semiconductor that converts electrical energy into light energy that is released in the form of photons (bundles of light energy). The body's cells have the ability to absorb photons and convert them to the form of energy that cells use to carry out normal functions. This form of energy is called adenosine triphosphate, or ATP. **As we age, we produce less ATP, which inhibits cells from performing at peak function.** In this way, ATP is a little like the fuel in your car; without it, your car can't go very far. ATP is necessary to power metabolic processes, synthesize DNA and RNA, repair and regenerate cell components, and foster cell proliferation. In addition to building proteins like collagen and elastin, ATP is critical to maintaining homeostasis for cell stability and the facilitation of healing.

LED, like lasers, uses specific wavelengths of the light spectrum to target areas within the skin and stimulate particular responses in the body. LED is used widely in skin care by estheticians and physicians alike since it has demonstrated effective results with certain skin conditions. **The most common uses for LED include acne reduction, controlling inflammation, increasing skin circulation, and stimulating collagen production in the skin.**

The Origins of LED Light Therapy

To fully appreciate the credibility of LED, it's important to be familiar with the study conducted by Dr. Harry T. Whelan of the Medical College of Wisconsin (Milwaukee) in conjunction with NASA's Space Product Development Program at the Marshall Space Flight Center.[11,12] The original focus of this study was on plant growth in space using LED to induce photosynthesis, but was later adapted to the potentially beneficial effect of LED therapy on cancer patients. During the 1990s, NASA-sponsored research determined that an LED system could provide the necessary wavelengths and intensities to produce photosynthesis and grow plants in space. NASA subsequently discovered that LEDs could address astronaut health by maintaining strong cell growth, preventing bone and muscle loss, and boosting the body's ability to heal wounds. Biologists learned that cells exposed to near-infrared LED light grow and heal 150% to 200% faster. The Astroculture3 plant growth chamber was successful, and has subsequently flown on numerous space shuttle missions.[13]

Since that time LED has been developed and used in the treatment of many medical conditions including pain and inflammation, jaundice, radiation induced dermatitis, actinic keratosis, oral mucositis in cancer patients, certain brain and liver cancers, diabetic retinopathy and neuropathy, and certain skin cancers.

There are several forms of LED light, each corresponding to a wavelength range on the spectrum.

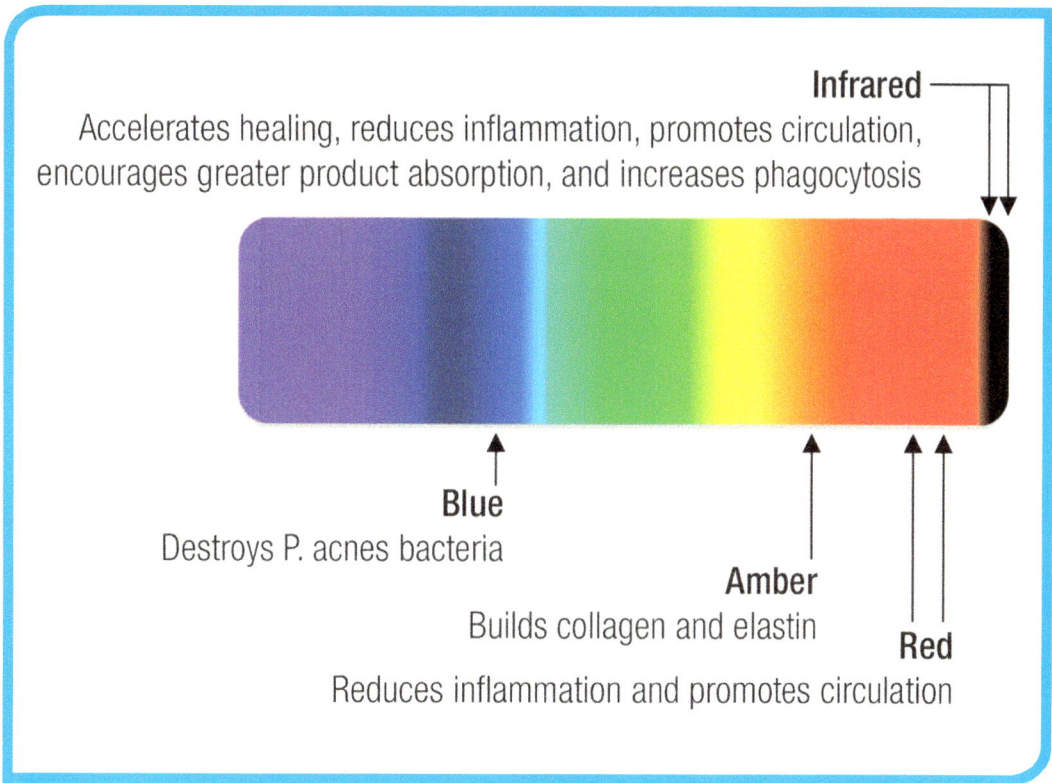

Blue Light: Blue LED light, in the 405–430 nm range, is known for its ability to reduce acne without side effects or irritation common to other treatments. As previously established, *P. acnes* bacteria form proteins called porphyrins. When porphyrins are exposed to specific wavelengths of light, particularly those in the blue to red portion of the spectrum, they produce a singlet oxygen molecule which in turn destroys the *P. acnes* bacteria.

Blue LED is often used in dermatology with a treatment known as photodynamic therapy for acne clients. Photodynamic therapy is a treatment where the use of a photo-sensitizing agent is applied to the skin before the use of light therapy so that the skin reacts more effectively to the light source (This is discussed further in Part 5 of this book).

Amber Light: Light in the yellow to orange, or amber, portion of the light spectrum, in the 585–595 nm range, penetrates deep into the skin, reaching the dermis. This light is commonly used for anti-aging treatments due to its ability to stimulate fibroblasts to produce collagen and increase circulation. It also aids in the reduction of MMPs (matrix metalloproteinases), which are enzymes responsible for protein destruction, thus preventing loss of elasticity. Amber light is also FDA approved to reduce wrinkles.

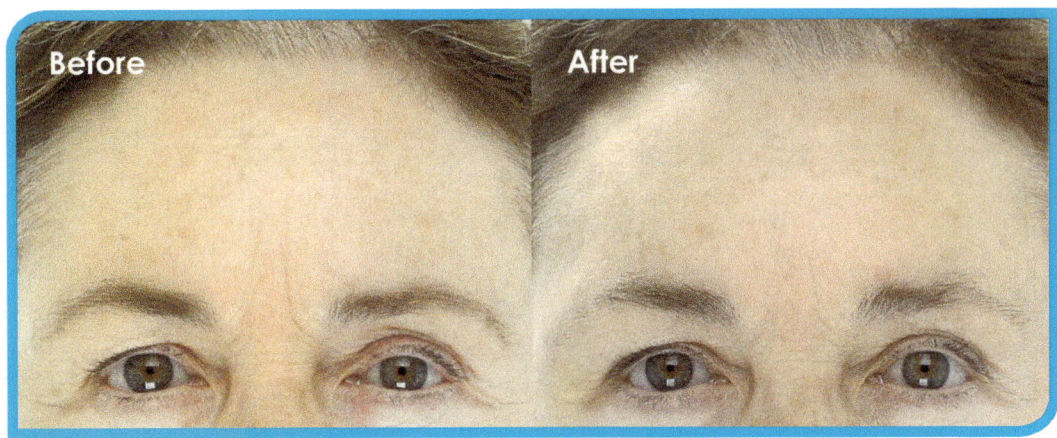

Amber LED for anti-aging treatment, 3 min at each area, 5 days per week for 8 weeks; images courtesy of LightStim LED.

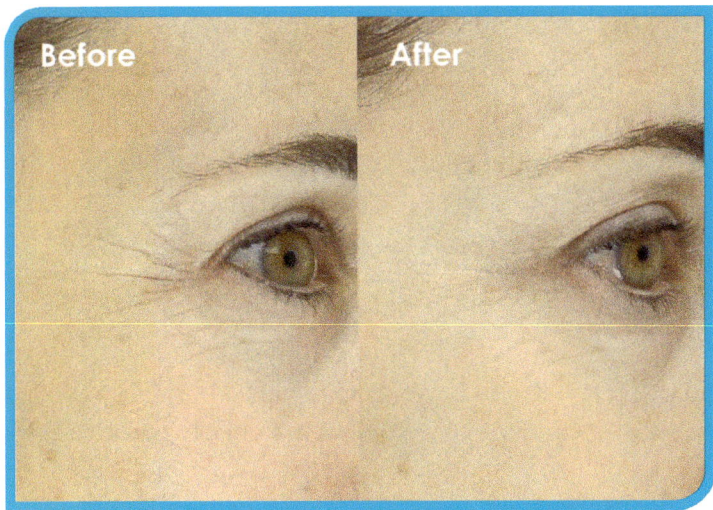

Wrinkle reduction using amber LED; 3 min at each area, 5 days per week for 8 weeks; images courtesy Lightstim LED.

Red Light: Red light, in the 660 nm range, is known for its capability to reduce inflammation and improve circulation. All skin conditions can be triggered by inflammation, making red LED beneficial for anyone without any contraindications to the treatment. Light in the red range is widely used for rosacea due to its anti-inflammatory properties, its ability to kill bacteria and increase skin density, making overactive blood vessels less apparent. Red LED light is FDA approval for the reduction of pain and to aid wound healing.

Infrared Light: Infrared (above 700 nm) accelerates healing, reduces inflammation, promotes circulation, and encourages greater product absorption in the skin. This increased circulation accelerates the body's healing process by delivering oxygen and nutrients to tissues in need of repair, while the reduced inflammation helps to naturally relieve pain. Infrared light is commonly used in physical therapy to relieve pain and is also beneficial in cosmetic medicine to reduce bruising.

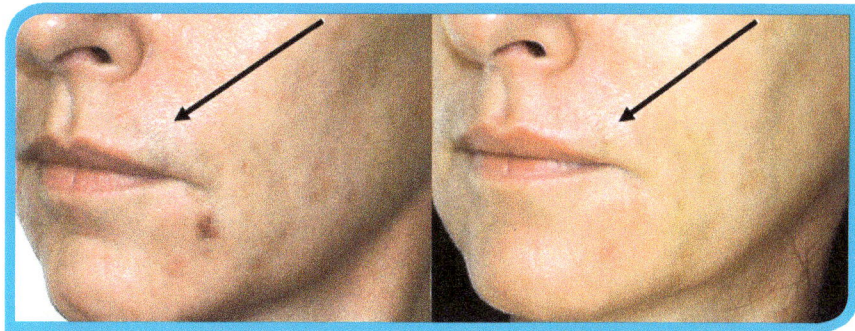

Infrared LED for bruising before and after 3 days of treatment at 45 min per session; images courtesy of Lightstim LED.

Green Light: Green LED (525 nm) is used to reduce hyperpigmentation, although there are not many clinical studies as of this writing that exist for this application.

There are also some LED devices available that have multiple colors/wavelengths of light energy. One in particular is a mix of blue and red, making it appropriate for cases of acne and rosacea.[14]

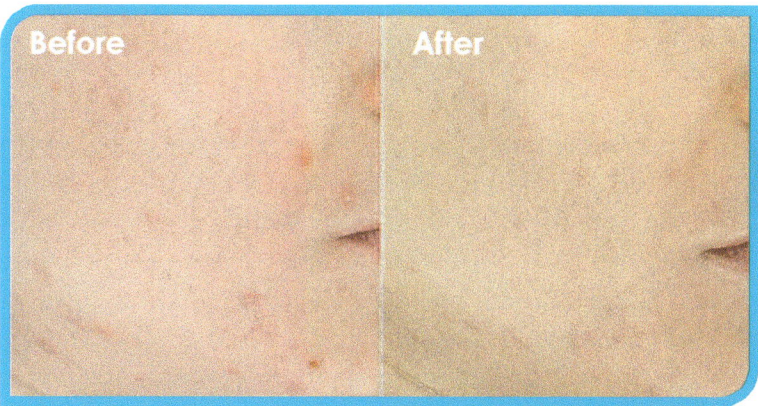

Before/After; A combination of blue and red LED light for a treatment period of 5 mins per area, 5 days per week for 4 weeks; images courtesy of LightStim LED.

Protocol for LED Treatments: In-office LED treatments should take place twice weekly for approximately four weeks. The treatment is simple, as it simply consists of cleansing the skin thoroughly, applying a transparent topical serum, applying eye covers, and placing a panel light over the area to be treated for 20 minutes. The treatment serum is chosen depending on the client's concerns; for example, a hyaluronic acid serum for hydration or a peptide serum for anti-aging. For products to penetrate more effectively, a superficial mechanical exfoliation like a scrub, microdermabrasion, or dermaplaning can be applied prior to application. It is not recommended to use any products with color in them, due to the fact that the colorant may get in the way of the light penetrating the skin. Chemical peeling agents must also be avoided prior to treatment; because the light can penetrate product, excess inflammation leading to burns could occur.

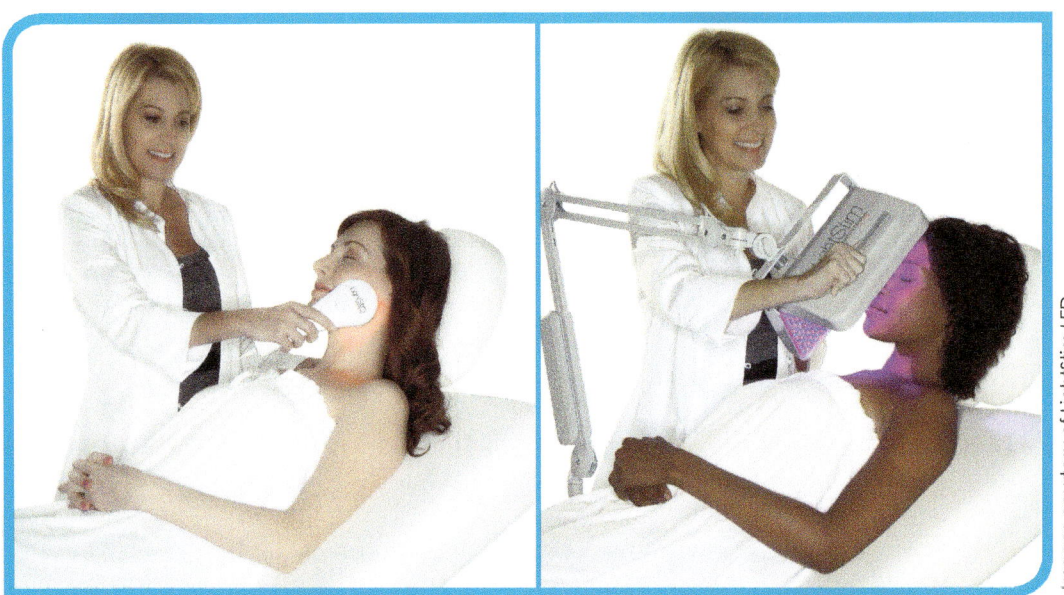

Hand-held LED, used by provider or client   Panel light LED, used by providers in-office

The process is very relaxing, as light therapy in general is shown to improve the mood. Unlike lasers and IPL, there is very little heat, making it a comfortable treatment. The only complaint I have had is the light being bright on the eyes, which can easily be avoided by placing cotton eye pads under protective goggles. Following the light application, recommended products and sunscreen should be applied.

LED in the red and infrared range can also be used post-procedure to speed healing and reduce recovery time. The light helps to diminish bruising and to reduce pain and discomfort. It is most commonly used in an aesthetic practice for post-surgical recovery, after lasers or IPL, and even following injections (neurotoxins and fillers). Post-surgical LED application should only be considered at least three days out, and then only with the treating physician's clearance. Following injections and non-ablative laser treatments, LED can be applied immediately to reduce the chance of bruising. Recently, LED has been used immediately following micro-needling to support the wound healing process, with much success.

Those who choose home-based devices should use them at least five days per week for the first eight weeks, or until desired results are achieved. This is typically followed by a maintenance plan of at least three days per week. Similar to the professional protocol, the skin is cleansed, a physical exfoliant may be used, and a topical serum recommended by the provider is applied, followed by the light placement. The handheld lights cover a much smaller area, therefore the client must be educated on light placement and timing per area. Most protocols consist of application three to five minutes per area, dependent on the skin condition, the light used, and the client's skin type.

LED At-home Hand-held Device.

Indications for LED Light Therapy

- Visible signs of aging
- Acne
- Rosacea
- Hyperpigmentation
- Reduce inflammation
- Increase circulation
- Minimize appearance of pores
- Increase skin density
- Better product absorption
- Accelerated healing
- Prevention of environmental damage

Contraindications for LED Light Therapy

- Light sensitivities
- History of phototoxic reactions
- Taking photosensitizing drugs
- Cancer or epilepsy
- Accutane use within six months of proposed treatment
- Malignant melanoma, or any potentially cancerous lesions
- Any serious health conditions or pregnancy require approval from a physician

Microcurrent

Microcurrent, popular in many medical offices as well as salons and day spas, is low level electrotherapy that helps to tone the muscles beneath the skin as well as increase blood circulation to yield a more youthful appearance. Opposite of neurotoxins which stop muscle movement to improve the appearance of aged skin, the intent of microcurrent is to "retrain" the muscles while strengthening them with repeated movements. Think of it essentially as a workout for facial muscles.

Microcurrent treatments are most effective in a medical office when packaged with other more invasive services to perfect the client's results.

Throughout the human body there are naturally occurring electric currents that aid in repair and regeneration. These currents can essentially turn on a process in the body similar to the way that electricity from a wall socket can turn on a light or radio. Microcurrent mimics a very low level of electrical energy to stimulate the body's tissues for rejuvenation, healing, or repair. Similar to LED, electric current works on adenosine tri-phosphate (ATP) to stimulate overall cellular activity.

Microcurrent further works to "retrain" muscles by stimulating muscle fibers at specific points. The application was originally developed for patients with Bell's palsy, a condition where nerve damage affects the muscles on one side of the face, causing drooping. To extend the "workout" metaphor a bit further, consider the fact that a single day's workout does not bring immediate body transformation; much the same, the idea with microcurrent is to retrain the muscles while strengthening them with *repeated treatments*.

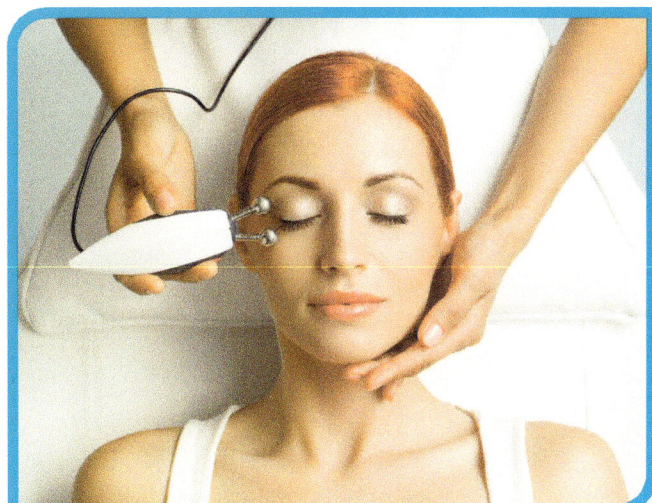

Microcurrent mimics a very low level of electrical energy to stimulate the body's tissues for rejuvenation, healing, or repair.

What is ATP?

Adenosine tri-phosphate is the basic source of energy that is synthesized from nutrients through the process of cellular respiration. Biological processes including tissue repair, collagen and elastin synthesis are dependent on ATP. Mitochondria, which produce cellular energy, oxidize nutrients in order to create ATP through the process of cellular respiration. ATP is essential for all active metabolic processes and its end function is dependent upon which type of enzyme it binds to. Ultimately, ATP fuels cell activity leading to further collagen and elastin production.

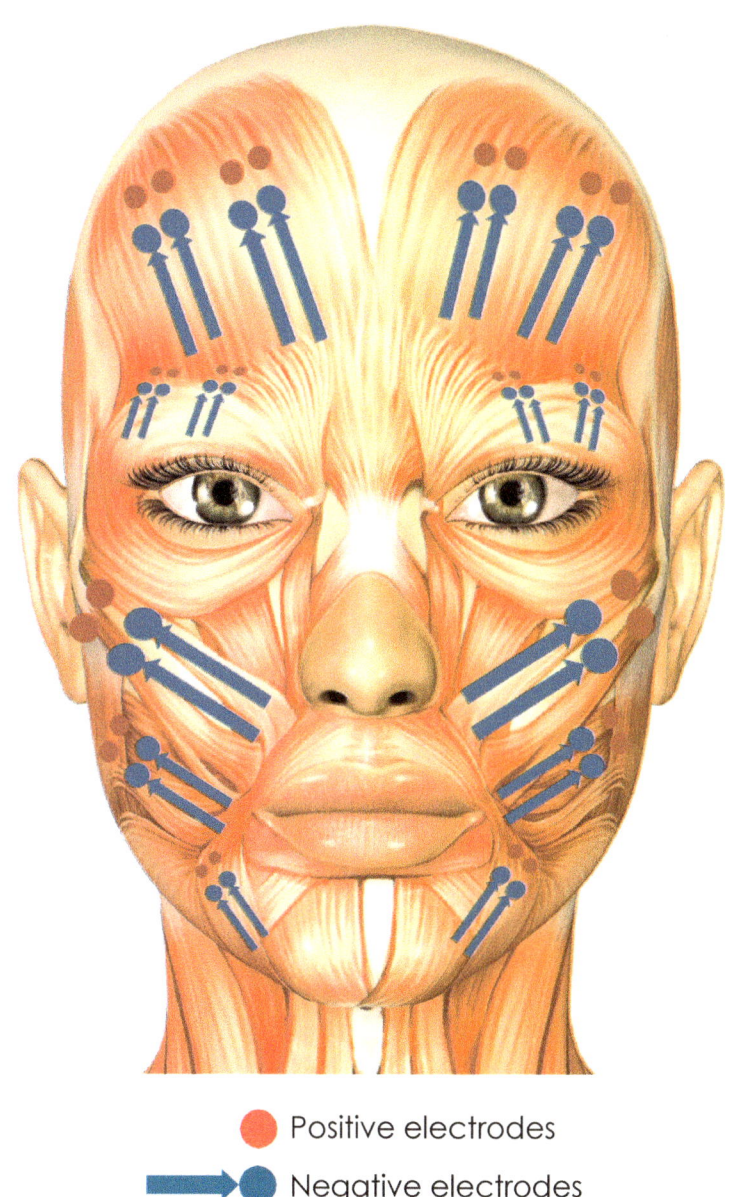

● Positive electrodes
➡️● Negative electrodes

Diagram of a Microcurrent Treatment

Sample diagram of a microcurrent treatment. The red circles indicate the area to place the positive electrodes that would remain stationary. The blue arrows indicate the direction that the negative electrodes should be moved until they reach the areas of the blue circles. Note: Movements are made from origin of the muscles to insertion.

Indications for microcurrent treatment include:
- Reducing the appearance of fine lines and wrinkles
- Cumulative skin tightening
- To increase circulation
- Collagen stimulation

Contraindications for microcurrent treatments include: pregnancy or nursing, medical conditions that can compromise wound healing, and implanted devices like pacemakers or defibrillators. It is important to remember that with any device that uses a form of energy, extra diligence must be taken when reviewing medical conditions. Similarly, inflamed skin conditions should not be treated with any device that creates stimulation.

Some patients say they see some skin tightening immediately after a microcurrent treatment, but the problem is that although there is instant gratification, these results often lose effectiveness within a couple of days. Devices used by skin care professionals typically have more energy and are more intense treatments focused on working the muscles. Microcurrent treatments vary, but the majority of in-office devices have two hand pieces—a stationary electrode with positive energy and a mobile electrode with negative energy. The probes are placed methodically to work muscles from origin to insertion, effectively retraining muscles.

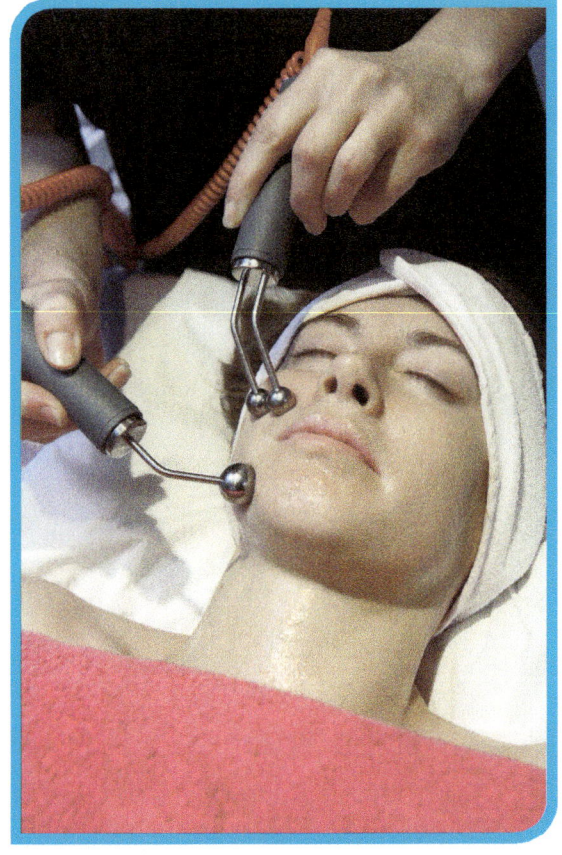

The development of retail microcurrent devices has helped clients keep up the effects of in-office treatments at home. Devices sold for home use should be viewed as maintenance that works to improve circulation and cellular function. Treatments performed at home should be used three to five days per week for optimal results.

It is important to give clients realistic expectations with any of these devices. *As always, under-promise and over-deliver.* Like other treatments used for skin rejuvenation, results are dependent on the individual according to their genetic makeup, overall health, and post-treatment care. These treatments have been proven to show results; however, with microcurrent and LED, clients must be ready and willing to invest the time in the office and at home for optimal results. If dramatic changes are sought, radio frequency or ultrasound are often employed, followed by the lower energy modalities to enhance and maintain the effects. In the next chapter we will go over product formulations and breakthrough ingredients to further support these treatments.

References

1. BD Zelickson et al, Histological and ultrastructural evaluation of the effects of a radio frequency-based non-ablative dermal remodeling device: A pilot study, *Arch Dermatol*, 140(2), 204-209 (2004).
2. R Fitzpatrick et al, Multicenter study of noninvasive radio frequency for periorbital tissue tightening, *Lasers Surg Med*, 33, 232-242 (2003).
3. DJ Narins and RS Narins, Non-surgical radio frequency facelift, *J Drugs Dermatol*, 2, 495-500 (2003).
4. TS Alster and E Tanzi, Improvement of neck and cheek laxity with a non-ablative radio frequency device: A lifting experience, *Dermatol Surg*, 30(4 Part 1), 503-507 (2004).
5. BA Bassichis et al, Use of a non-ablative radio frequency device to rejuvenate the upper one-third of the face, *Otolaryngol Head Neck Surg*, 130, 397-406 (2004).
6. SL Michlovitz, ed, *Thermal Agents in Rehabilitation*, 2nd ed, Philadelphia: FA Davis, Co. (1990).
7. LC Kolth et al, eds, *Wound Healing: Alternatives in Management*, 2nd ed, Philadelphia: FA David, Co. (1995).
8. LD Johns, Non-thermal effects of therapeutic ultrasound: The frequency resonance hypothesis, *J Athl Train*, 37(3), 293-299 (2002).
9. JL Macgregor and EL Tanzi, Microfocused ultrasound for skin tightening, *Semin Cutan Med Surg*, 32, 18-25 (2013).
10. D Barolet, Light-emitting diodes (LEDs) in dermatology, *Semin Cutan Med Surg*, 27, 227-238 (2008).
11. H Whelan, Light emitting diodes bring relief to young cancer patients: A study, accessed on Mar 25, 2014, at: *www.nasa.gov/vision/earth/technologies/led_treatment.html*, originally posted Nov 26, 2003.
12. M Braukus and J Berg, NASA light-emitting diode technology brings relief in clinical trials, accessed on Mar 25, 2014, at: *www.nasa.gov/home/hqnews/2003/nov/HQ_03366_clinical_trials.html*, originally posted on Nov 13, 2003.
13. LED device illuminates new path to healing, accessed on Mar 25, 2014, at: *www.sti.nasa.gov/tto/Spinoff2008/hm_3.html*, originally posted 2008.
14. DJ Goldberg and BA Russel, Combination blue and red LED phototherapy in the treatment of mild to severe Acne vulgaris, *J Cosm Laser Therapy*, 8(2), 71-75 (2006).

CHAPTER 27

Effective Formulations and Breakthrough Ingredients

In this Chapter:
- How Products Penetrate the Skin
- Tips for Product Penetration
- Product Formulations
- Popular Ingredients and Their Uses

Skin care products are essential to the practice of aesthetics. Results for any cosmetic treatment will be compromised if the skin is not nourished and protected properly. This can be, in some ways, related to health. Just as the rest of the body needs nutrients to maintain health, so does the skin. With all of the product lines available claiming to have the next "miracle" ingredient, it can be difficult to decide which products will be best for your practice. **Remember: To maintain a successful practice, client satisfaction is a necessity. It is important to choose a line of products that offers a variety of ingredients to target multiple skin conditions and that each product provides the results it claims.** This chapter will address some of the terms commonly used in the cosmetic industry and their meanings, as well as how to deal with controversial ingredients. The basics of product formulations including how active ingredients penetrate the skin will also be discussed, followed by an overview of commonly used ingredients.

The term "cosmeceutical" was made popular in 1980 by world-renowned dermatologist Dr. Albert Kligman, who discovered Tretinoin, though today the term is commonly used for marketing purposes to describe a product that is a *cosmetic*, but has *pharmaceutical-like* ingredients. At one time, the use of this term was afforded a more profound meaning. Today, the influx of product lines claiming to be "cosmeceuticals" has eliminated some of the credibility the term once had; moreover, the

term is not recognized by the FDA (see sidebar). Pharmaceuticals are used for medicinal purposes and must have FDA approval before being available for purchase. Cosmetics are intended for beautifying and do not need FDA approval to reach market. So the issue here is clear: a product that simply beautifies cannot be marketed in the same manner as products with a pharmaceutical effect. Some companies also use the term "medical grade" in their product descriptions and claims, though this is a misleading misnomer because if a product was medical then it would be available only by prescription.

It is important for professionals as well as consumers to recognize ingredients used in products. **The International Nomenclature for Cosmetic Ingredients (INCI) is the standard used to ensure consistency by using uniform scientific names for ingredients used in cosmetics.** It also confirms that cosmetic ingredients are consistently listed from product to product and in order of predominance. Legally, ingredients that are present in products at amounts exceeding 1% must be listed in order of predominance by weight, in descending order. Ingredients in products that are less than 1% must be listed at the end but can be done so in any order.

> The FDA Ruling on "cosmeceuticals," rendered on February 24, 2000, stipulates that while the Federal Food, Drug, and Cosmetic Act (FD&C Act) does not recognize the term "cosmeceutical," the cosmetic industry uses this word to refer to cosmetic products that have medicinal or drug-like benefits. The FD&C Act defines drugs as those products that cure, treat, mitigate or prevent disease, or that affect the structure or function of the human body. While drugs are subject to review and approval process by the FDA, cosmetics are not approved by the FDA prior to sale. If a product has drug properties, it must be approved as a drug.

Chirality

"Chirally correct" is a phrase used to describe the correct *form* of ingredients. Essentially, opposing molecules are mirror images of each other; there are right-handed versions (D) and left-handed versions (L). Just as a right hand would not fit into a left-hand glove and vice versa, the same goes for an ingredient. For instance, L-ascorbic acid is a commonly used form of vitamin C. D-ascorbic acid, which is the former chemical's right-handed version, would not work in the same way and would conversely be a potential irritant. The ingredients used in any product composition must be in the chirally correct form in order to penetrate effectively without causing irritation. Some product lines use the fact that their product is chirally correct as a marketing tool; when using a reputable skin care line, the ingredients contained should all be chirally correct, regardless if that fact is advertised or not. If there is ever uncertainty, it doesn't hurt to ask.

Formulation Basics and Commonly Used Claims

There are two basic types of ingredients in product formulations: **active** and **inactive** ingredients. **Active ingredients are used to create a change within the skin. Inactive ingredients are included to support and/or deliver the actives appropriately.** Common inactive ingredients used in skin care formulations are preservatives, occlusives, stabilizers, buffers, and preservatives. These are meant to deliver the active as well as create the look, feel, and smell of the product—to create its aesthetic qualities. The way a product is formulated is more important than one may think; it involves a large amount of chemistry. There is an old wives' tale that if a vitamin E capsule that is meant for internal use (ingestion) is opened and rubbed on the skin it will reduce aging and heal the skin. This is in some part true, because vitamin E oil can work as a protectant and occlusive, meaning that it will aid the skin to heal itself. However, a formulation designed to be taken internally will likely not penetrate the skin, since it is meant to be released in a much lower pH in the stomach. Some

ingredients are not small enough to penetrate the skin, others cannot be stabilized, and there are many combinations that don't work together. It is important to work with a reputable company that has scientific evidence and provides education on their particular products.

There are several terms that pop up with regard to claims made for products that can be misleading. The term "hypoallergenic," quite a common term in topical products, requires testing by the FDA in order to back up claims describing products with a low chance of allergic reaction; however, this doesn't mean there is no chance of allergies. Many people who easily react to products are unaware that their symptoms are more of a sensitivity than an allergy. That being said, it cannot be guaranteed that the use of a hypoallergenic product will come without any reaction for every person. Conversely, the term "non-comedogenic" can be used in product descriptions without FDA required testing. Non-comedogenic products suggest that the product does not contain common comedone-causing ingredients such as heavy oils. For the same reason that not every hypoallergenic product will be completely void of potential reactions, products that are non-comedogenic do not always leave a patient without clogged pores.

In order to maintain the stability, color, and texture of a product, there are typically additives that must be included. Although they are not the active ingredients, they still become incorporated into the skin's surface. Additionally, most products, unless noted as preservative-free, contain some sort of preservative to prevent the harmful growth of bacteria within the product over time. The take-home message for sensitive patients and their providers is to always read the ingredient list in its entirety. The products listed first are presented in the highest percentage within the product, but even those towards the end need consideration.

Active Ingredients
- Create changes in the appearance of the skin

Inactive Ingredients
- Ingredients that stabilize the active and make the product cosmetically elegant

Natural, Synthetic, and Organic

Natural ingredients/products are derived from natural sources, as opposed to being synthetically produced in a lab. **The term "natural" is not regulated, meaning a company can state that their product is "natural," even if the product in question contains only a very small amount of a natural substance.** Furthermore, just because a product is "natural," it does not necessarily follow that the product is better than a synthetic or man-made alternative. There are many substances in nature—substances that would qualify as "natural"—that are not good for you, the simplest example of which being tobacco. **In fact, broken down to its simplest form, an ingredient**

created in a laboratory would be no different than one derived from natural sources. And what's more, synthetic ingredients, due to their process of manufacture, are often subject to more rigorous testing for purity and stability before being added to skin care formulations.

Organic ingredients are grown without the use of pesticides or other harmful chemicals and they are not genetically modified. The United States Department of Agriculture (USDA) regulates the use of organic substances. A product must contain at least 95% organic ingredients in order to be labeled as *certified organic*. In order for a product to be labeled *made with organic ingredients*, the product must contain at least 70% organic ingredients. Some companies will claim to be organic even if there is only one organic ingredient, so *always* look for the USDA label. And remember that although organic products have a reduced risk of affects by removing harmful chemicals, these ingredients can still cause irritation.

Product Penetration

It is well-known by now that the main function of the stratum corneum is to protect the organs inside our bodies. This layer holds moisture in and keeps microorganisms and chemicals out. Therefore, for products to reach the area in which they are needed, applying them topically is not the only consideration. The active ingredients meant to make a change in the skin need to find a way through this barrier in order to be effective. This is why other modalities, including micro-needling, LED, ultrasound, and iontophoresis, may be used to assist this penetration.

Molecular size is important with regard to active ingredients; the smaller the molecule, the more easily the product penetrates the skin. Highly lipophilic substances (readily dissolving or combining with lipids) that also have hydrophilic characteristics (readily dissolving or combining with water) penetrate the best, though solids can penetrate if they are able to dissolve in the stratum corneum. If a vehicle is used, penetration power is also related to the ability of the ingredient to part from its vehicle once in the targeted area of the skin. Other permeability factors include the chemical structure of the product; there are ingredients that are simply not structured in a way that can actually penetrate the epidermis, regardless of penetration route.

There are different routes of penetration for molecules. *Transcellular* describes a route directly through the cells of the skin that works for very small lipophilic and hydrophilic molecules, which have the ability to enter cell membranes. *Intercellular* describes a route between the cells of the skin that is the most efficient means for very small lipophilic substances to enter the skin. The intercellular spaces are very narrow (20–2,000 nm) and are composed mostly of ceramides, cholesterol, and long-chain fatty acids. The *transfollicular* route is used for larger molecules and polar molecules, such as water. The sebaceous glands reach depths between 0.2–0.5 mm and are connected to hair follicles. Sebum and water or large molecules do not mix well, which allows for these particles to flow away from the sebum and towards the follicle for eventual delivery.

Tips for Product Penetration: A product will penetrate a moist area better than it will a dry area. Therefore, to increase a product's penetration the skin must be moist upon application. It seems to be a habit of most people that after cleansing the face, they dry it with a towel before applying their skin care products; leaving some water behind will actually help the product penetrate the skin more effectively. Stimulating and heating the tissue also helps to increase absorption; commonly used methods are massage, steam, galvanic (direct-current electricity), and ultrasound. Facials commonly employ at least one of these methods, making it the perfect time to apply active products to the client's skin.

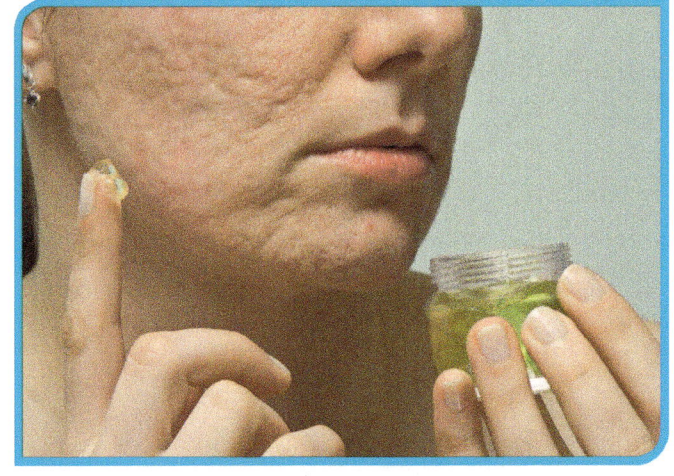

Exfoliating, also done in facial treatments, aids product penetration by removing a portion of the dead skin cells, making it easier to move past the barrier. One last tip is to apply water-based products before oil-based products. The lipid-soluble products will help to carry the water-soluble into the skin.

Of the techniques previously discussed in this book, micro-needling is becoming a top treatment of choice to assist with product penetration. As discussed, micro-needling creates micro-channels in the skin that typically remain open up to an hour following the treatment, making it an optimum time to receive active ingredients. Once the products have been applied, locking them in helps them reach their full delivery potential. Occluding the skin, using a thick mask or cover to completely cover the skin, also helps increase penetration. The thought here is that by blocking the area, the path of least resistance is for the ingredients to be absorbed by the skin.

Product Penetration: A Summary

- Factors affecting penetration
    - Concentration of active ingredient in vehicle
    - Quantity applied to a given surface area
    - Modification of active by other substances
    - How thick the stratum corneum is
- Application
    - Thinnest to thickest
    - Clear to most color
    - Water-soluble products first
    - Apply product to cover entire face
    - Not too much; shouldn't feel sticky
    - Match products to treat all skin conditions
- Tips for penetration
    - Moisten the skin
    - Stimulate and heat the tissue
    - Exfoliate first
    - Apply water-based products before oil-based products
    - Occlude the skin

- Different routes of penetration
    - Transcellular
        - Through the cells
        - Very small lipophilic and hydrophilic molecules pass through cell membranes
    - Intercelluar
        - Between the cells
        - If the active is lipophilic and very small it will penetrate this way
    - Transfollicular
        - Larger molecules and polar molecules (water)

This is commonly seen with the use of topical anesthetics. It is often recommended to occlude the skin with plastic wrap for the topical to absorb faster and work more effectively.

Inactive Ingredients

Preservatives are used to limit microbial growth, including bacteria, molds, and yeast. Preservatives in cosmetics should provide a reasonable shelf life, and be non-irritating and compatible with the other ingredients in the product. Cosmetic products that contain preservatives will have some disinfectant properties. They work effectively against a wide range of organisms over long periods of time, as opposed to antiseptics and astringents that work quickly and powerfully against specific organisms.

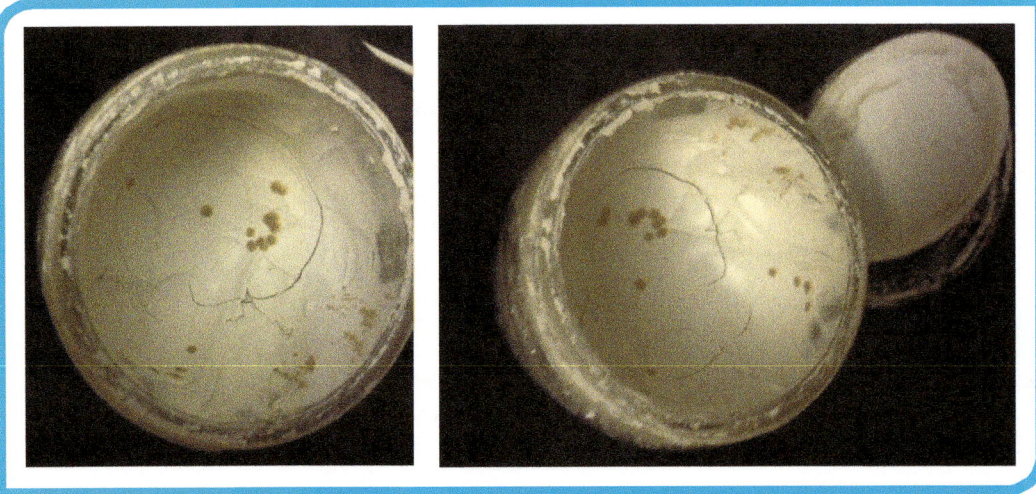

Do not put fingers directly into the product container; doing so may cause mold to develop in the product, as shown.

Products that are not preserved adequately can be harmful. If a preservative is not used, cosmetics can become contaminated during manufacturing or consumer use. **The risks associated with the use of preservatives (which can be harmful in large amounts) must be weighed against not using them (which can also lead to harm).** Recently, manufacturers have begun to use more natural preservatives, such as antioxidants and milk enzymes. Self-pressurized containers also help preserve products without the negative associations that can be tied to chemical preservatives. Many commonly used preservatives can cause allergic reactions, and some may be toxic in large amounts. The best ways to preserve products are to tighten and secure the lids. Avoid contamination by using a utensil instead of fingers to remove product, and be sure to wash your hands prior to product use. Signs of product contamination include a bad odor, a darkening or change in the product color, and visible microbes.

Examples of commonly used preservatives include: alcohol, dimethylol dimethyl

(DMDM) *hydantoin, diazolidinyl urea, sorbic acid, phenoxyethanol, imidazolidinyl urea, and parabens including: methylparaben, ethylparaben, propylparaben, butylparaben, and isobutylparaben.*

The majority of controversy surrounding the use of preservatives in products has to do with the use of parabens. Although the skin does a great job of keeping external or environmental aggressors out, we know that substances can still penetrate, otherwise we would not use topical products. Parabens are one of the most widely used preservatives, due to their effectiveness against bacteria, fungus, mold, and yeast. The cause behind concerns over their use comes from the level of parabens found in cancerous breast tissue. A study published in 2004 detected parabens in breast tumors.[1] Although the findings of parabens in cancerous breast tissue is no doubt concerning, there has yet to be a detailed study on the level of parabens in healthy breast tissue, leaving open the potential that all breast tissue, cancerous or not, may have the same level of parabens. As clinical data on the effect of parabens is still being researched, it is up to the provider to determine whether they are comfortable offering products that contain parabens. But even more importantly, it is the needs and well-being of the client that ultimately shape this decision. The *Cosmetic Ingredient Review* (CIR) reviewed the safety of methylparaben, propylparaben, and butylparaben in 1984, and concluded they were safe for use in cosmetic products at levels up to 25%.[2] Typically parabens are used at levels ranging from 0.01–0.3%. At present, the FDA believes that there is no reason for consumers to be concerned about the use of cosmetics containing parabens. However, the agency will continue to evaluate new data in this area.[3] If the FDA determines that a health hazard exists, the agency will advise the industry and the public, and will consider its legal options under the authority of the FD&C Act in protecting the health and welfare of consumers.

> As clinical data on the effect of parabens is still being researched, it is up to the provider to determine whether they are comfortable offering products that contain parabens. But even more importantly, it is the needs and well-being of the client that ultimately shape this decision.

> Signs of product contamination include a bad odor, a darkening or change in the product color, and visible microbes. The best ways to preserve products are to tighten and secure the lids. Avoid contamination by using a utensil instead of fingers to remove product, and hands should be washed prior to use.

Emollients are commonly used to soften, smooth, and soothe the skin. Many emollients are multifunctional and create an occlusive barrier preventing dehydration.

Examples: acetylated lanolin, apricot kernel oil, cyclomethicone, diisocetyl adipate, glycerin, isopropyl palmitate, ulan, steareth-4 stearate, lanolin, petrolatum, polyethylene glycol, propylene glycol-dioctanoate, caprylic-capric-linoleic triglyceride.

Examples of natural emollients: grapeseed oil, sweet almond oil, castor oil, sunflower oil, safflower oil, coconut oil, palm oil, jojoba oil, soy wax, beeswax, jojoba wax.

SCENARIO: Addressing Client Concerns

Provider: "I would like to recommend this product for the pigmented areas of your skin."
Client: "I see this product has parabens in it, and I've heard they can be linked to cancer."

What Could Happen
Provider: "Don't worry. Nothing has been 100% proven as to whether that's true. I use this product myself and it's great. There is nothing to be worried about."
The problem: You must validate the client's concerns, and if there is any hesitation at all, the product should not be recommended. Period. It can also be a sensitive subject for some, a family member may have cancer and just the thought of something potentially cancerous can be upsetting.

What Should Happen
Provider: "I completely understand. It can be scary choosing products with possible links to cancer. Let me recommend you another product that also works very well, but does not have parabens, or other controversial ingredients in it. How does that sound?"

Emulsifiers are ingredients used to mix water and oil. Oil-in-water emulsions are oils that are suspended in a continuous water phase. Because they penetrate the skin easily and don't feel greasy, they are the most popular formulations. Water-in-oil emulsions will contain small droplets of water in a continuous oil base. Emulsions are a breeding ground for bacteria and fungus, which makes the use of preservatives necessary. There are more than 1,000 emulsifiers available.

Examples: beeswax, ceteareth 20, glycerol stearate, polysorbate 60, stearyl alcohol, ceteth 6/20, monoethanolamine (MEA), laureth sulfate, sorbitan 7/palmitate, emulsifying wax, stearic acid, lanolin.

Stabilizers are added to products to prevent an emulsion from fluctuating.
Examples: magnesium aluminum silicate, glyceryl stearate, xanthan gum.

Humectants are used for moisture absorption and retention in the skin. In cosmetics, propylene glycol has been described as the most common moisturizing vehicle other than water.

Examples: hyaluronic acid, acetamide monoethanolamine (MEA), glycerin, propylene glycol, sorbitol, sodium pyrrolidine carboxylic acid (PCA).

Solvents are substances, usually liquids, used in cosmetics to dissolve or dispense other substances. A commonly used solvent such as ethanol or alcohol has the ability to dry out skin, causing redness or flaking. Solvents also have harsh smells associated with them that can irritate mucous membranes.

Examples: ethanol, glycerin (glycerol), isopropyl myristate, polyethylene glycol (PEG), mineral oil (white oil), castor oil, alcohol, acetone, propylene glycol.

Colorants are used in many cosmetics to enhance the appeal of the product. Dyes or pigments of vegetable, animal, or mineral origin do not need to be certified for use. Vegetable origins include beet powder, grape skin extract, caramel, and beta carotene. Common dyes from animal origins include cochineal extract, which is extracted from the dried bodies of insects. Among the natural colors are *alkanet, annatto, carotene, chlorophyll, saffron,* and *tumeric*. Mineral pigments are most commonly used today, especially in wellness centers and medical settings. Minerals are colored or white chemical compounds that have anti-inflammatory and protective properties. Minerals also do not support the growth of bacteria, which makes products containing them highly recommended following procedures that can compromise the skin. Examples include: *aluminum powder, iron oxides, titanium dioxide,* and *zinc oxides.*

> There are at present 35 colorants that are FDA approved. FD&C colorants are synthetic colors permitted for use in food, drugs and cosmetics. If, however, a colorant is allowed only in drugs and cosmetics, it will be designated as D&C; for example, D&C Blue No. 1, D&C Yellow No. 10, D&C Red No. 30.

Fragrance is the most common cause of allergic reaction to products. In the United States, many product companies don't even list the source of their products' fragrances. It's just listed as "fragrance" or "parfum" on the label. The professional should understand that even though a product may be labeled as "fragrance-free," it can still contain botanical extracts that are used for other purposes and can still cause irritation to the skin. Many people will be turned off to a product that contains fragrance; however, more needs to be considered. What is little known is that "fragrance-free" products typically contain a masking ingredient, because many formulations exude an unattractive or unpleasant odor without the addition of a fragrance. A minute amount of a natural fragrance may make the product much more tolerable. This can be very confusing to consumers who have sensitive skin. Essential oils are derived from different parts of plants but aren't considered fragrances, per se. Also, animal exudates like musk and ambergris may be used without being considered fragrances.

Suspending agents are used to create the desired feel of a product, whether thick or thin, heavy or light, smooth or rough.
Examples: acrylates copolymer, bentonite, carbomer, cetyl alcohol, glyceryl stearate, lauramide DEA and propylene glycol stearate, xanthan gum, cellulose gum, guar gum.

Occlusives can be used as skin conditioners, emollients, protectants, and lubricants. Silicones are most commonly used and studied for their use in scar reduction. Silicones occlude the surface of the skin, making them useful during healing; the protected skin is given the ability to heal itself. They may also be used as antifoaming agents.
Examples: petrolatum, shea butter, zinc, titanium dioxide, squalane, silicones (dimethicone and cyclomethicone), simethicone, octamethyl cyclotetrasiloxane.

Buffers are used to adjust or maintain the pH of a product. Buffers can be any aqueous solution that stabilizes, resists, or minimizes changes in the pH when an acid or a base is added.
Examples: acetic acid, potassium dihydrogen, tromethamine phosphate, citric acid, triethanolamine.

> Buffers are commonly employed when dealing with chemicals and acids, such as non-buffered glycolic acid. Providers tend to think buffered products aren't as effective, but having a product with a controlled pH is a good thing in some cases.

Surfactants are common to cleansers. They are added to products to remove dirt, oil, and debris. The amount used determines how much of their target is removed.
Examples: sodium laureth sulfate, sodium lauryl sulfate, disodium lauryl sulfosuccinate, ammonium lauryl sulfate, cocoamphocarboxyglynate, cocamidopropylbetaine, alpha-olefin sulfonate, decylpolyglucoside.

Lubricants reduce friction and add "slip" to products. These are commonly used in massage creams and lotions to more easily manipulate the skin.
Examples: petrolatum, hyaluronic acid, dimethicone, cyclomethicone.

Vehicles are used to carry active ingredients into the skin. They can be thought of as "vehicles" to get somewhere that is not easily accessible. But more importantly, an active ingredient must be able to part from its vehicle upon reaching its destination, just as a person would need to get out of his car.

Liposomes are an example of a vehicle; these particles can encapsulate active ingredients to carry to easily penetrate the skin.

ACTIVE INGREDIENTS

Cellular turnover ingredients are used to decrease the buildup of dead skin cells and trigger the production of new, healthy cells.

Retinoids are naturally occurring derivatives of beta-carotene that affect the growth of epithelial cells, prevent and reduce comedones, increase cellular turnover, and decrease the buildup of follicular epithelial cells. Retinoids are beneficial for treating acne, psoriasis, photoaging, wrinkles, and actinic keratosis. One way to explain them is as "skin normalizers," i.e., they increase the normal functions of the skin, making them beneficial for all skin types and conditions.

- **Tretinoin / retinoic acid:** First used topically for acne, Retin-A was discovered to have anti-aging properties, and to date is among the most clinically studied ingredients available. While it can be irritating, it is the only chemical to be clinically proven and accepted by the FDA as an anti-aging ingredient.
- **Retinol / vitamin A** is most commonly used in cosmeceuticals, where it has a lower chance of side effects than Tretinoin, though it must be formulated correctly to enter the skin and convert to retinoic acid in order to be effective.
- **Retinyl palmitate** is an artificially stabilized form of vitamin A, often used in over-the-counter products with other active ingredients.
- **Retinaldehyde** is a modified form of vitamin A, closest to retinoic acid. It shows low irritation but is also less active.
- **Tazarotene** is used for psoriasis and acne.
- **Adalpene:** Approved for acne in 1996, adalpene has low irritation and is also effective against keratosis pilaris, a rash that can be mistaken for acne.

Alpha hydroxy acids (AHAs) are well-known for their exfoliating properties. AHAs are water-soluble substances that work between the cells to dissolve desmosomes, protein structures that hold the skin cells together, to create cell proliferation.

- **Glycolic acid** is an exfoliant derived from sugar cane that helps to break down intercellular structures. It has the smallest molecular size of all AHAs and has been shown to strengthen collagen fibers. It can be used as a degreasing agent.
- **Lactic acid** is an AHA found naturally in milk and sugars that is commonly used in skin care products and in peels. It has hydrating and skin lightening properties. It is gentler than glycolic acid and is found naturally in the skin.
- **Malic acid** is found naturally in apples. It has exfoliating, brightening, and hydrating properties.

- **Mandelic acid** comes from bitter almonds. It has skin lightening and hydrating properties.
- **Tartaric acid**, derived from grapes, is only mildly effective.
- **Citric acid**, derived from citrus fruits, is not very powerful on its own, but works quite well with other exfoliants.

Beta hydroxy acids (BHAs) are lipid-soluble exfoliants, good for oily skin and acne.
- **Salicylic acid** is a lipid-soluble exfoliating agent, which makes it ideal for oily skin. It is commonly used in skin care products for acne in concentrations of 2–5% and as a peel in 20–30% concentrations. Salicylic acid also has antibacterial and anti-inflammatory properties.
- **Lipohydroxy acid (LHA)** is in the same family as salicylic acid; it is also lipid-soluble, anti-bacterial, and anti-inflammatory, making it a great choice for acne. It attracts to oil more than salicylic acid but doesn't penetrate as deep.

Poly hydroxy acids (PHAs) are one of the newer exfoliating ingredients being used today. They have been shown to be as effective as alpha hydroxy acids with less irritation and more moisturizing properties.
- **Gluconolactone** is a PHA that works as an antioxidant and anti-inflammatory agent. It is effective in acne and rosacea formulations due to its ability to mildly exfoliate sensitive skin.

Antioxidants are used to fight off free radicals that cause oxidative stress. Antioxidants should be incorporated into each skin care routine for maintenance and protection. There are countless antioxidant ingredients available, and many products use them in combination. Antioxidants must be stabilized and have the ability to penetrate the skin to be effective.
- **Caffeine** increases the effectiveness of sunscreens by fighting UV induced free radicals and working to force damaged cells into apoptosis (programmed cell death needed to prevent damaged cells from replicating).
- **Aminoguanadine** is used for its strong ability to fight advanced glycation end products.
- **Ferulic acid** is a potent plant-based antioxidant; when used with 15% vitamin C and 1% vitamin E, it doubles photo-protection, protects from oxidative stress, and may be useful for protection against photoaging and reducing the potential for skin cancer.
- **Alpha lipoic acid,** also known as *thioctic acid,* is a lipid- and water-soluble antioxidant, making it easily accepted by the skin. It is promoted to repair protein damage. It also has been shown to enhance the effects of vitamin C and E and to control inflammation.
- **Ubiquinone** (coenzyme Q10) is a lipid-soluble antioxidant that helps protect against intrinsic and extrinsic aging. It is also said to produce energy for

cellular vitality and help stabilize cell membranes. It brings oxygen to mitochondria ("power plants" of cells) to increase cellular energy.
- **Idebenone** is a powerful antioxidant used to repair photo-damage and prevent signs of aging by capturing and neutralizing free radicals caused by environmental stress.
- **Vitamin C:** It is easy for the skin to become deficient in vitamin C because the skin is the last organ in line to receive vitamin C when taken internally. It is used first for other body functions and organs, so very little is actually afforded to the skin. The use of topical vitamin C provides antioxidant protection and helps protect against UV damage; there are several forms of vitamin C, below are the most commonly use forms:
  - **L-ascorbic acid** is the most commonly used water-soluble form of vitamin C. It must be formulated with better than 10% concentration and at a pH below 3.5 to be effective. L-ascorbic acid also has skin lightening properties and is shown to strengthen collagen fibers.
  - **L- ascorbyl palmitate** is less potent than L-ascorbic acid but more stable.
  - **Magnesium ascorbyl phosphate (MAP)** is a stable and potent form of vitamin C with skin lightening abilities.
- **Resveratrol** is found mostly in grape skin. It is a potent antioxidant, controls inflammation, and acts as an MMPi, preventing the breakdown of proteins. It is the primary antioxidant present in red wine.
- **Silymarin (milk thistle)** is used to reduce the effects of toxins in the cells, stimulate protein synthesis, and protect DNA from UV radiation. Helps neutralize free radicals that cause cellular inflammation and lead to aging skin.
- **D-Boldine** is found in the boldo tree native to Chile. It has anti-inflammatory and antioxidant properties by preventing peroxidation (degradation of lipids).
- **L-Arginine** is found in almonds, leafy vegetables, and walnuts. It acts as an antioxidant and is used in skin care products promoting wound repair.
- **L-Cysteine** is found in liver and pumpkins. A sulfur amino acid, it is an amazing anti-inflammatory ingredient and antioxidant, and has also been used to help regulate melanin production.
- **Spin Traps PBN, Phenyl-Butyl-Nitrone** holds onto damaging free radicals and turns them into nourishment for cellular growth when used with a vitamin C serum. When used with non-lipid forms of vitamin A or beta-carotene, it helps protect oxygen molecules.
- **Lycopene** is found in guava, rosehip, tomatoes, and watermelon, and is one of the most effective carotenoids for protecting the crucial parts of a cell, including DNA.
- **Copper:** An essential trace mineral present in every cell in the body, copper has been shown to stimulate collagen, elastin, and glycosaminoglycans. As an antioxidant, copper breaks down free radicals. It is often used in wound healing preparations.

- **Zinc** speeds up the repair process during wound healing. It is an anti-inflammatory and antioxidant. It is most often used in acne preparations. The benefits of taking it internally for skin health have already received much recent attention.

Skin Lighteners work, for the most part, by stopping the action of tyrosinase, the enzyme triggered in the melanogenesis process that forms melanin. Some lighteners work on other parts of this process.

- **Hydroquinone** is the only ingredient FDA approved as a skin lightener; it is naturally found in berries, tea, and coffee. It is very effective but has risks if overused. It is used in prescription products at 4% and above, and in OTC products at 2%. This product must be used in a regimen that is six weeks on and six weeks off, in order to prevent side effects including ochronosis (a blue-black mark on the skin) or hypopigmentation. The use of this ingredient is controversial; however, the FDA considers the product safe when used correctly.
- **Azelaic acid** lightens pigment by inhibiting the enzyme tyrosinase. It also has antibacterial properties and is commonly used for the treatment of rosacea. This is a good lightening agent for those with acne who are prone to post-inflammatory hyperpigmentation due to its lightening and antibacterial properties.
- **Kojic acid** works as a tyrosinase inhibitor. It is derived from fungi as a by-product of the fermentation process. Usually made in concentrations of 1–4%, kojic acid can be an irritant to the skin, causing contact dermatitis, therefore a patch test should be done prior to use.
- **Licorice extract** is an effective tyrosinase inhibitor with no cytotoxicity. It is usually used in combination with other skin lighteners. It has been shown to be more effective than hydroquinone with fewer adverse effects.
- **Paper mulberry** is a tyrosinase inhibitor. It is not very strong compared with other agents but shows a very low risk of irritation and is effective with other lightening ingredients.
- **Ellagic acid** is found in fruits like pomegranate and red raspberry. Ellagic acid has skin lightening properties and is a powerful antioxidant that can boost sun protection when used in conjunction with vitamin C.
- **Glycyrrhiza glabra extract (Licorice extract)** is a melanogenesis inhibitor and anti-inflammatory agent. Often used in conjunction with other lightening ingredients for pigment, it is also beneficial for acne.
- **Bearberry/Arbutin** inhibits tyrosinase activity and evens existing skin tone. May also be used as an antioxidant and skin conditioner. Often used in conjunction with other lightening agents.
- **Phytic acid** occurs naturally in brans, cereals, and seeds. Works as a skin lightening agent by blocking oxidation in the melanogenesis process.

- **Phyllanthus emblica**, from the emblica tree, is a highly stable source of ascorbic acid. It provides antioxidant properties and may protect DNA. It is also an effective tyrosinase inhibitor.

Collagen Support ingredients include growth factors, stem cells, and peptides. Growth factors are essentially messenger proteins between living cells.

- **Human growth factors** are obtained from controversial sources; some include processed skin proteins taken from aborted fetuses, originally used for burn victims and ulcers or human fibroblast conditioned media.
- **Animal:** *Crypthompalous aspersa*, an active glycosaminoglycan secretion generated by snails during times of stress can regenerate damaged structures of the animal's skin in less than 48 hours.[4] Via a patented process, snails are stimulated and their secretions are collected. No harm is done to the snails during this process. Secretions are then filtered for purity and tested for consistency.[5,6] These actives were first experimentally adapted to human subjects suffering from radiation-induced dermatitis due to the fallout of the Chernobyl nuclear disaster in 1986, and have subsequently been tested and used in Europe for more than 15 years to regenerate skin damaged by radiation therapy.
- **Plant:** N6-furfuryladenine (Kinetin) is a plant hormone that protects the skin from free radical damage. It also has been shown to be an excellent alternative to retinoids, because it increases cellular turnover without the irritation and sensitivity associated with retinoid use.
- **Synthetic:** Rholigopeptide-1/ EGF (epidermal growth factor) growth factors are developed in a lab to be identical to EGFs found in human skin. A powerful antioxidant that reduces inflammation associated with wound healing, they are designed to enhance epidermal growth and keratinization,

Peptides are short chains of amino acid sequences that make up larger proteins. Small chain peptides stimulate repair, enhance collagen production without irritation, and preserve barrier function.

- **Signal peptides** encourage fibroblasts to increase production of collagen while decreasing the breakdown of existing collagen.
- **Neurotransmitter peptides** limit muscle contraction, and thus are said to mimic the effects of botulinum toxin.
- **Carrier peptides** stabilize and deliver trace elements necessary for wound healing and enzymatic processes; examples include tripeptide GHK and palmitoyl tripeptide-8.
- **Palmitoyl pentapeptide** (at market under the trade name Matrixyl) has effects comparable to retinol without the irritation, and is known for its regenerative properties. It stimulates collagen I, III, and IV, increases skin thickness, and strengthens the epidermal/dermal junction (EDJ), collagen, elastin, and GAGs.
- **Palmitoyl tripeptide-38** (at market under the trade name Matrixyl synthe'6) is the newest generation of Matrixyl, said to have the similar but more advanced properties than palmitoyl pentapeptide.
- **Palmitoyl tetrapeptide** (at market under the trade name Rigin) mimics DHEA and controls the production of chemical messengers that cause inflammation in the skin.
- **Acetyl hexapeptide-8** (at market under the trade name Argireline) works to relax facial muscle contractions that lead to "expression lines." It is commonly used in products that are said to decrease muscle activity by interfering with the release of catecholamine, a neurotransmitter which causes muscle contractions.

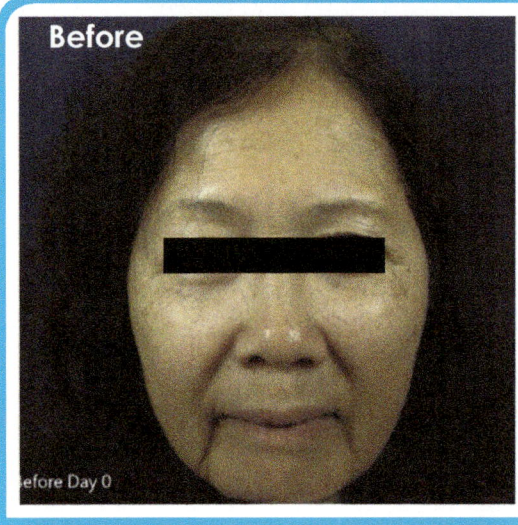
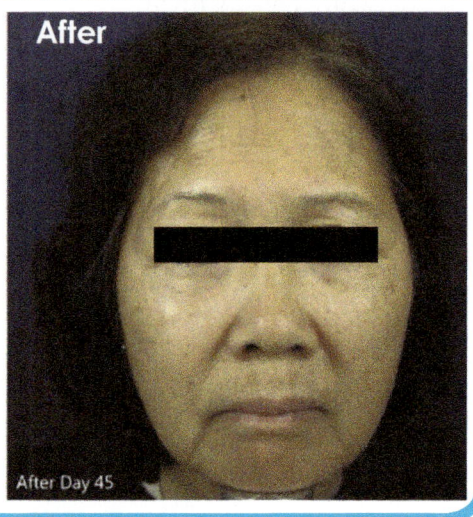

The patient used a daily regiment of Tensage Intensive Serum 40 (containing *Crypthampalous aspersa*) twice daily as "Tensage Advanced Cream" for 45 days as well as a non-treatment cleanser and sunscreen.
Photos courtesy of Tess Mauricio, MD; provided by Biopelle

- **TGF Beta-1** is used in skin care products to stimulate collagen and elastin production and speed up wound healing. It has superior anti-inflammatory properties.

Stem Cells are capable of renewing and triggering needed cells, stimulating cellular turnover, and boosting collagen production. They are what is known as *pluripotent* meaning they can repair every type of cell in the body.
- **Grape seed,** or *Vitis vinifera*: Studies dating back more than a decade suggest that grape seeds are known to contain anti-inflammatory properties to prevent skin aging by scavenging oxygen free radicals and inhibiting UV radiation-induced activity.
- **Sheep placenta or *ovine placenta extract*:** Ethically harvested from sheep raised on farms in New Zealand, this extract is rich in nutrients and proteins that stimulate cell growth. Stem Cell Beauty Innovations, the company that developed O-placenta, states that clinical studies are forthcoming.
- **Lilac** stem cells have anti-inflammatory and antioxidant properties. Most commonly used for its benefits on acne.
- **Swiss Apple** was first studied in 18th century Switzerland. Presently, it is used to increase the longevity of skin cells, preserving a youthful appearance.
- **Edelweiss** has strong antioxidant properties and fights off the breakdown of dermal proteins including collagen and hyaluronic acid.

Anti-inflammatory/Protective
- **Aminoguanadine** is used in anti-aging products as an antioxidant and to inhibit glycation (cross-linking of collagen due to glucose binding to proteins).
- **Fumaric acid:** An essential ingredient for plant life, it is crucial for the completion of the Krebs cycle, which supplies plant cells with energy for growth and respiration. Fumaric acid is often used in the treatment of psoriasis and to stimulate circulation.
- **L-Proline** is predominately taken from animal sources and is a major component of the collagen protein. It is most effective when applied topically with vitamin C. Proline aids in the synthesis and retention of collagen.
- **Niacinamide** is a water-soluble form of niacin/vitamin B3 commonly used to fight photoaging. It reduces transepidermal water loss. Its anti-inflammatory and sebum controlling effects reduce acne severity.

- **Vitamin B5 (Panthenol)** is a water-soluble, stable, and low-molecular weight known to help with tissue repair. Deeply hydrates the stratum corneum and is an effective anti-inflammatory.

Antibacterial

- **Azelaic acid** is effective in fighting breakouts because of its bactericidal and antimicrobial properties. Great for acne and rosacea, and is also used as a tyrosinase inhibitor; it brightens complexions. Normalizes keratinization in the skin.
- **Benzoyl peroxide** brings oxygen to the skin, having a positive effect on acne, since *P. acnes* cannot live in an oxygen-rich environment. It can be irritating if over-used and may cause hyperpigmentation; care should be taken on darker skinned patients. Most often used as a spot treatment in 5–10% formulations or as a cleanser.
- **Bakuchiol** has anti-inflammatory and antibacterial properties. Commonly used to treat acne and as an antioxidant to fight the signs of aging.

Hydrators/Moisture Binders

- **Hyaluronic acid** is a naturally occurring carbohydrate (polysaccharide) found in the space between the cells in our skin. It plays an important role in tissue hydration, lubrication, and cellular function. It holds more water than any other natural substance. The amount of hyaluronic acid a person has decreases with age and is correlated with wrinkling, which is the reason why many products that fight the signs of aging use this ingredient. It also provides an excellent environment for the growth of new cells and healing after peeling treatments.
- **L-lysine:** Found mostly in red meat, poultry and milk, L-lysine is an essential amino acid that cannot be produced by the body. It prevents glycation and nourishes the skin.
- **Squalene** is the main constituent of sebum and has been shown to have a beneficial effect in managing dermatitis. It also presents as an extract from the Aizame shark and is present in olive oil. It is used in expensive beauty products as an effective moisturizer.
- **Avocado oil** is an organic lipid used as an antioxidant to condition the surface of sun-damaged and wrinkled skin.

Healing

- **Centella asiatica/Gotu kola** is used in anti-aging products and for scarring. It stimulates skin repair, improves circulation, and boosts collagen production.
- **L-glycine:** Found in high concentrations in the connective and skin tissues, it is great for promoting the healing of wounded tissues.
- **Vitamin K oxide** helps strengthen broken capillaries (but cannot repair them). It is an anti-inflammatory that reduces redness. It is most often used to treat under-eye circles and in medical offices to prevent bruising.

- **DHEA-Ascorbate:** Dehydroepiandrosterone, or DHEA, is an adrenal gland hormone, and when paired with ascorbate, or vitamin C, it is used topically to enhance wound healing and cellular growth.
- **DMAE (Dimethylaminoethanol):** Found in cold water fish such as salmon, DMAE is used in products that promote firming and tightening of facial and neck skin. With continued use, it may help strengthen and stabilize cells' plasma membrane for a more defined and youthful appearance.

Botanicals are derived from plants and are free of synthetic chemicals. Some may provide more benefits than active agents created in laboratory. Many botanicals must undergo chemical processing to make them better able to be used in formulations. (Remember: Just because it is natural, does not mean it is better.)

Common botanicals include: *papaya*, an enzyme used in wound healing and scar cream; *echinacea*, the largest selling herb in the United States and an antiseptic and antioxidant; *tea tree essential oil*, which is applicable for acne and other antimicrobial means; *soy*, which increases skin thickness and collagen production; *pycnogenol*, an antioxidant that works well with vitamin C; *green tea*, an antioxidant and anti-inflammatory that is good for acne; and *prickly pear*, which is soothing and provides a protective coating upon application.

The Bottom Line ...

Choosing the right support products is essential to success, whether esthetic or medical. **Product choices can make or break a practice.** Regardless of the skill and knowledge a provider has, if a device or product does not live up to its claims, it will eventually catch up to you and wind up costing the practice in terms of customer satisfaction and retention. With any treatment or product offered, there should be at least 90% satisfaction from clients. If a product or device is chosen and doesn't deliver, it is important to the success of the practice that it be discontinued and the manufacturer be informed. Remember that a happy client typically tells one person about a good experience, but an unhappy client will tell ten.

> It is better to put the effort in and choose products using the SMART method than to constantly change equipment and/or products.

There will always be new technology that is touted as the latest and greatest, but this does not mean that your product offerings need to be updated every time something new comes out. In fact, it is better to put the effort in and choose products using the SMART method than to constantly change equipment and/or products. Clients may get upset when they are told that a particular product is the best available for their skin only to come back the following month and find that the product they have come to trust has been replaced, because now there is something "better." Of course this may happen on occasion, and certainly in cases of less-than-successful products, but constantly changing what is offered may have clients questioning the provider's dependability. Once treatments and products are established, it is time to put all of this knowledge into motion with business-building techniques, which will be the topic of the next section of this book.

References
1. D Darbre, Concentrations of parabens in human breast tumours, *J Applied Toxicol*, 24(1), 5-13 (2004).
2. *JACT* 3(5), 147-209 (1984).
3. FDA Report on Cosmetic Product Ingredients and Parabens, posted Oct 31, 2007, to: *www.fda.gov/cosmetics/productsingredients/ingredients/ucm128042.htm*, accessed Apr 2, 2014.
4. MJ Tribo-Boixareu et al, Clinical and histological efficacy of a secretion of the mollusk *Cryptomphalus aspersa* in the treatment of cutaneous photoaging, *J Cosm Derm*, 22(5), 247-252 (2009).
5. RF Abad, Treatment of experimental radio dermatitis with a regenerative glucoproteic mucopolysaccharide complex, *Dermatol Cosmet*, 9, 53-57 (1999).
6. A Brieva et al, Molecular basis for the regenerative properties of a secretion of the mollusk *Cryptomphalus aspersa*, *Skin Pharmacol Physiol*, 21, 15-22 (2008).

CHAPTER 28

Focusing on the Eyes

In this Chapter:
- Prevention
- Fine Lines and Wrinkles
- Under-eye Circles: Causes and Treatments
- Lashes

The eyes are known as the focal points of beauty on the face. Almond-shaped eyes, with the outside corner sitting slightly higher than the inside corner, have since antiquity been an idealized form of beauty. Eyes are also perceived to be more inviting when they are symmetrical and large. Many women have caught on to how important playing up their eyes can be, but unfortunately this is often the first area of the face to show signs of aging. The rapid aging that occurs in the ocular area is due to differences between the skin surrounding the eyes and that of other areas of the face. The skin around the eyes is typically 0.2 mm thick compared to other areas of the face that are thicker than 1.0 mm; this thinner skin makes it easier to see imperfections, including dark circles, puffiness, fine lines, and wrinkles.

Prevention

The delicate eye area should be protected through preventative measures, the most important of which is the use of sun protection. There are not many eye products available that contain sunscreen and due to the higher chance of sensitivities in this area, ingredients must be chosen carefully. A simple formula containing zinc oxide tends to be the best option, as chemical sunscreens are known for their potential skin irritation. The use of UVA/UVB protective sunglasses should also be recommended for optimal protection. Those individuals who have light-sensitive eyes are forced to wear sunglasses on a regular basis and this typically results in a more youthful appearing eye area.

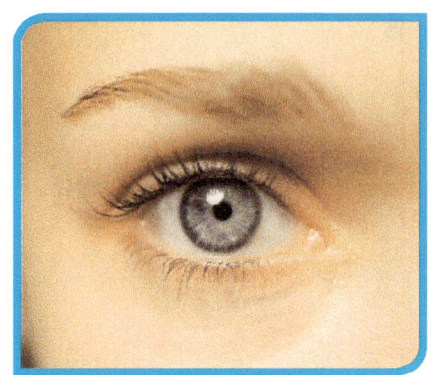

Another means of preventing the signs of aging around the eyes is to keep them moisturized. The eye area has far fewer sebaceous glands compared to other areas of the skin; therefore, more moisture is needed topically to prevent fine lines and wrinkles produced from dehydration. The difference in structure and function of this skin is the reason that a separate product for the eyes is typically needed. When choosing products to protect the eye area, the use of antioxidants should also be incorporated. As stated in the last section, antioxidants are important for all skin types to protect against further damage and that includes the skin around the eyes. Some common ingredients used in eye creams include hyaluronic acid, ceramides, peptides, caffeine, vitamin K, and vitamin C.

Fine Lines and Wrinkles

Once wrinkles have set in, more advanced topical products can be added. Products containing peptides that protect and produce collagen and elastin are often chosen due to the low chance of irritation associated with their use. Mild retinol products may also be called upon to address fine lines on the outer perimeter of the eyes, referred to as crow's feet. As with the use of any retinol, it is something that should be slowly built up as far as application tolerance is concerned, in order to avoid drying out the skin and causing irritation. As discussed earlier, retinols work by stimulating cellular turnover, which produces rapid exfoliation and can lead to sensitized skin. When retinols are used, it is absolutely vital that a sunscreen is constantly being applied to the area

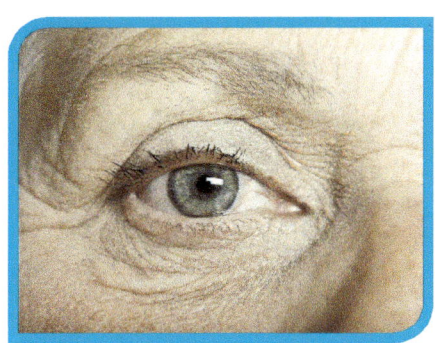

When retinols are used, it is absolutely vital that a sunscreen is constantly being applied to the area of use during the daytime.

of use during the daytime. It is also important for the client to follow instructions carefully; including not applying the product inside the infraorbital rim and building up tolerance by using the product only twice per week to start.

For those who want to speed up the process and enhance results for fine lines and wrinkles around the eye area, radio frequency or ultrasound are often considered. Since these two modalities are used for skin tightening and collagen production, it only makes sense that the eye area can benefit from their use as well. Of course, protocols and settings will differ due to the differences in the skin, but they both have shown great results. Similarly, microcurrent, which can help to retrain the muscles around the eyes, and LED to increase circulation may also be used. As mentioned earlier, these are not one-time solutions; multiple treatments should be expected, and more often than not maintenance treatments are required.

The eyes also begin to lose their youthful, firm appearance and start to sag before other areas of the face. When the eyelids begin to droop, it is clinically referred to as *ptosis*, and oftentimes the only means of correction is surgical, resulting in a blepharoplasty (surgery to reshape the eyes). Luckily, if preventative measures are taken, less invasive procedures, including skin tightening and neurotoxin treatment, can provide results. The use of neurotoxins has the ability to reduce the appearance of crow's feet around the eyes by temporarily disrupting muscle contraction in the area. Neurotoxins also have the ability to open the eyes with specific injection points beneath the tail of the brow to provide a more awake and inviting appearance, providing double benefit for its use in the eye area.

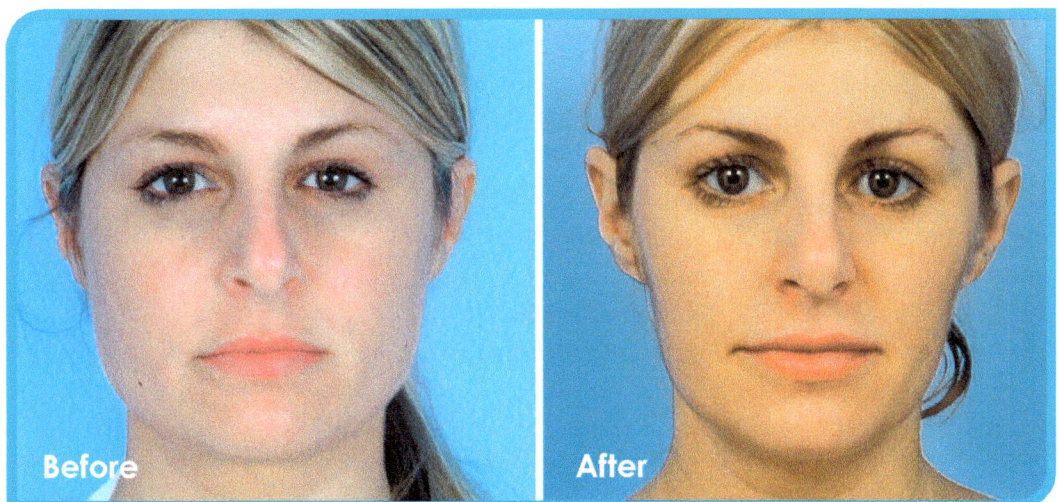

Neurotoxin treatment to "open" the eyes (and "thin" the jawline).

Dark Circles

Other top concerns for the eye area are puffiness and the appearance of dark circles. More often than not, these are two different culprits but can occur together. Dark circles can appear for several reasons, mainly hyperpigmentation, vascularity (blood pooling), and shadowing (see callout for quick breakdown). Dark circles are often genetically inherited in darker skin types. As with other areas of pigmentation, the eyes can get darker with inflammation including sun exposure and frequent rubbing of the eyes, often seen in those with allergies. There is no real treatment for inherited dark circles, although some improvement can be seen with skin lightening products, chemical exfoliation, and laser treatments, similar to that seen with other pigment issues.

> **Potential Causes of Dark Circles under the Eyes**
> - Pooling of blood
>   - Lack of sleep, allergies, vascularity
> - Hyperpigmentation
>   - Genetics, sun-induced, post-inflammatory
> - Shadowing
>   - Hollowing of subcutaneous fat, genetics

Another cause for dark circles is collections of blood beneath the delicate skin of the eye. This can be caused by genetics or triggered by allergies, and is correlated to the leakage of blood from small capillaries. The pooled blood is more noticeable around the eyes due to the thinner skin; furthermore, as skin ages it loses fat that may have once concealed the vessels. When pooled blood alone is suspected, products rich in vitamin K have the potential to help reduce the collection of blood by breaking up the small clots. This is not surprising, as these clots share many similarities to bruising, for which vitamin K is also recommended. Vitamin K rich foods (e.g., green leafy vegetables) may also help combat less severe circles. Vitamin K naturally strengthens blood vessel walls, which prevents leakage, minimizes inflammation, and promotes optimal blood circulation.

One, not so obvious, cause of dark circles, is shadowing that can occur from hollowing around the eyes. As discussed, a major contributing factor to aged skin is the loss of subcutaneous fat, which is even more apparent in the eye area. Medical professionals can reduce this shadowing with the use of soft tissue fillers; this technique requires much skill and is typically done by an injection specialist. Fillers often last at least nine months, making them a good option for those who are not ready for a surgical procedure. If a client is not ready for any medical procedure, the use of camouflage makeup seems to be the next best thing. Highlighting the shadowed areas and contouring the area around the hollow can make a big difference. (See Chapter 24 on camouflage makeup for a specialized technique.)

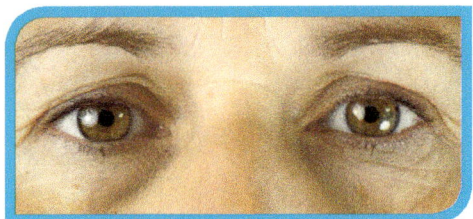

Hollowing is caused by shadows beneath the eye area.

One underlying cause of both bags and dark circles under the eyes during allergy season is the histamine response that an allergen causes the body to elicit. Although responses may vary, the most common manifestations include excess edema on or around the site at which the allergen has entered. For many, seasonal allergies invade the body through the respiratory system, which is located right by the facial sinus cavities. When the elicited edema sets in, the pressure can cause capillaries to enlarge and/or burst,

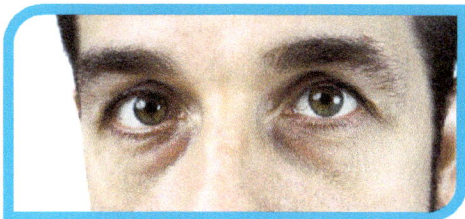

Dark circles with edema can be caused by allergies.

which is why on a day with a high allergen count, a person may look like they have not slept. If allergens are the suspected culprit, an antihistamine may be recommended to diminish the edema.

Moderate to severe puffiness or bags under the eyes are most commonly caused by excess fat. For this reason, the eyes should be analyzed thoroughly, instead of giving false hope that a topical treatment or simply getting a good night's sleep may work. **It is unfortunate that cosmetic retailers and some skin care providers inadvertently sell eye creams promising to reduce the pockets surrounding the eyes without considering the condition's cause. When a collection of fat is the cause, surgery is the only option for resolution.** Mild puffiness can be caused by allergies, lack of sleep, or water retention, these conditions can be improved with the use of topical products, especially those that contain caffeine. Regardless of the severity,

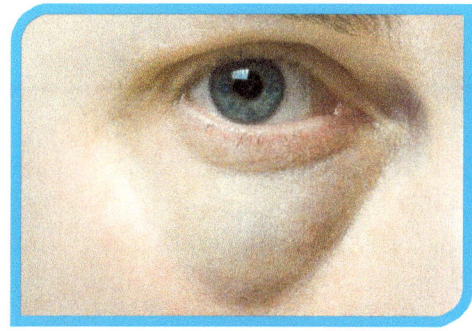

Puffiness is most commonly caused by excess fat around the eyes.

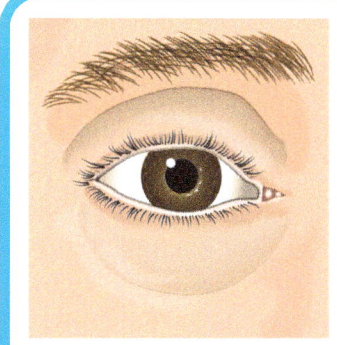 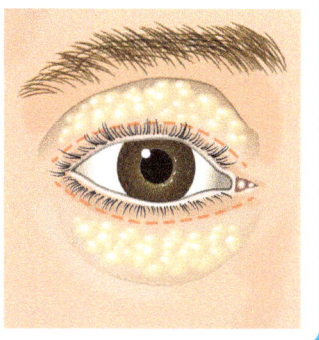

Accumulation of fat may be removed surgically.

swelling under the eyes should be examined by a clinical provider before product or treatment regimens are suggested.

The most recent breakthrough when it comes to improving the appearance of the eyes is a product called Strateris, which launched at the American Academy of Dermatology meeting in March 2014. Strateris is a two-step application of a polymeric film that, when applied to the under eye area, compresses bags and, within an hour, has the ability to completely conceal them. The film acts similar to a shrink wrap, some are even calling it "Spanx for the eyes." Although the solution only lasts a day, it is certainly favorable for someone who doesn't mind applying the product regularly, or those that want to look refreshed on special occasions. As the product just launched, there is sure to be much more advancement when it comes to this "miracle" product.

Lashes

In the last five years, there has been increased focus on the lashes as a way of drawing attention to the eyes. It is common to hear women say that they will not leave the house without first applying mascara. As cosmetic lash enhancing products have made their way in the cosmetic field, a prescription product was likewise developed. Perhaps the most innovative product to come out for enhancement of the eyes is a bimatoprost solution 0.03% for eyelashes (trade name: Latisse [Allergan]). Previously marketed under the trade name Lumigan, it was originally developed to address issues associated with glaucoma. However, while the precise molecular pathway remains unclear, bimatoprost-induced eyelash growth is believed to occur by three mechanisms: a prolonged growth phase of the hair cycle, resulting in longer lashes; stimulating the resting follicles, resulting in thicker/fuller lashes; and increasing melanin synthesis, resulting in darker hair pigmentation. The end result is longer, thicker, darker lashes that will draw more attention to the eyes.

Many patients are afraid that Latisse will cause pigment changes in the eye. While this is a possible side effect that must be stated, since the ingredient used in Latisse was the same used for Lumigan, there is a distinct difference in how the two compounds are administered. Lumigan was placed directly in the eye, whereas Latisse is placed along the lashline of the upper eyelid; at present, there have been no reported eye pigmentation changes associated with its use. Other possible side effects are pigment changes or hair growth on areas of the skin where the product is applied, and an itching sensation or redness. Results are typically seen after six to eight weeks of nightly use. When the medication is stopped, the lashes may return to their normal state; therefore, it is commonly recommended to use the product at least two to three times per week to maintain its effect.

Another method for obtaining long lashes is the use of lash extensions. Extensions can be a good option when applied by a reputable, experienced provider and cared for at home by the client. At one time, lash extensions were considered more harmful than beneficial, due to the ingredients in the adhesive solutions used. This procedure has come a long way, and there are now safer ingredients that have a lower chance of irritation and complications. It is still important that providers have proper training and use them with caution, as adverse effects are always a concern, as is the method of application. If applied incorrectly, natural lashes can become harmed and even result in lash loss. On the other hand, when properly applied, extensions are a good method for immediate eye enhancement. Touch-up treatments are typically recommended every three weeks, due to the lashes' natural hair growth cycle.

Eyes have the potential to be the most attractive thing about a person; thus, enhancing what one already has should be the focal point of any treatment. Studies have shown that dilated pupils make a female more attractive to a male, and pupil dilation in return indicates a reciprocated attraction. This may be the reason that many men prefer blue eyes; dilated pupils are easier to see since there is more contrast. Methods for enhancing and maintaining the youthful appearance of the eyes should be available in any aesthetic practice. If it is an overall improvement in beauty that is being sought, then making the eyes more attractive will go a long way.

Part 7 Review Questions

1) Why are radio frequency techniques becoming more popular than ablative laser resurfacing for the use of skin tightening?

    a) There is a healing period with ablative lasers

    b) Patients see immediate improvement with radio frequency

    c) Patients find radio frequency treatments to be less invasive

    d) All of the above

2) Why is it important to not lose contact with a client's skin while performing a radio frequency treatment?

    a) The treatment won't be as effective

    b) It will immediately result in a scar

    c) The device could break

    d) It can burn the epidermis of the skin

3) Why is it best to perform low energy radio frequency treatments?

    a) To make the client come in for more treatments

    b) To prevent fat necrosis, skin color changes, and scar formation

    c) To achieve a more effective treatment

    d) To alleviate any pain in the procedure

4) How does ultrasound for skin rejuvenation work?

    a) Ultrasound delivers radio frequency to the dermis of the skin

    b) Ultrasound uses a rapidly oscillating probe to create sound waves

    c) Ultrasound delivers UV light to the epidermis of the skin

    d) Ultrasound delivers visible light to fibroblasts within the skin

5) Ultrasound can deliver medicinal products through the skin by way of a process known as _____.

    a) Cavitation

    b) Phonophoresis

    c) Oscillating waves

    d) Inflammation

6) When is ultrasound indicated?

   a) To rejuvenate skin
   b) To reduce edema
   c) To penetrate products
   d) All of the above

7) What is one of the ways to enhance product penetration?

   a) Apply oil-based products before water-based products
   b) When applying several products, always apply thickest to thinnest
   c) Apply the product as sparingly as possible
   d) Stimulate or heat the tissue

8) What are the two basic types of ingredients used in skin care formulations?

   a) Active and inactive
   b) Occlusive and non-occlusive
   c) Gels and moisturizers
   d) Antioxidants and peptides

9) What ingredients are commonly added to limit microbial growth including bacteria, molds, and yeast?

   a) Solvents
   b) Stabilizers
   c) Preservatives
   d) Emollients

10) What type of ingredient is used to alter or maintain the pH of a product?

    a) Occlusives
    b) Buffers
    c) Tyrosinase inhibitors
    d) Vehicles

11) Which of the following is *not* known as a skin lightening ingredient?

    a) Hydroquinone
    b) Kojic acid
    c) Arbutin
    d) Argirilene

12) Which lipid- and water-soluble antioxidant has been shown to enhance the effects of vitamin C and vitamin E?

   a) Alpha lipoic acid
   b) Bearberry
   c) Coenzyme Q10
   d) Matrixyl

13) What is the ingredient used in many anti-aging products promoted to slow down muscle contractions, thus preventing wrinkles?

   a) Argirilene
   b) L-ascorbic acid
   c) Hyaluronic acid
   d) Glutathione

14) Which ingredient is commonly used topically to prevent bruising and eliminate dark circles under the eyes?

   a) Vitamin A
   b) Vitamin C
   c) Vitamin E
   d) Vitamin K

15) Radio frequency treatment is best suited for which skin condition?

   a) Aging
   b) Hyperpigmentation
   c) Rosacea
   d) Grade IV acne

16) Ultrasound for skin rejuvenation stimulates collagen thermally when tissues are heated up to:

   a) 88–98°F
   b) 93–103°F
   c) 115–125°F
   d) 104–113°F

Review Questions

17) What area of the face is commonly the first to show signs of aging?

   a) Eyes
   b) Nose
   c) Chin
   d) Jowls

18) Red light LED is commonly used to:

   a) Reduce hyperpigmentation
   b) Remove dead skin cells
   c) Reduce inflammation
   d) Tighten the skin

19) Microcurrent and LED work to stimulate energy within the cells through stimulating the production of _____.

   a) ATP
   b) MMPs
   c) mitochondria
   d) sebum

20) To reduce puffiness under the eyes caused by fat deposits, the patient should be referred to a physician for _____.

   a) A diet
   b) Eye cream
   c) Chemical peels
   d) Blepheroplasty

21) What is the most common cause of allergic reactions to products?

   a) Fragrance
   b) Colorants
   c) Stabilizers
   d) Humectants

22) What type of ingredient used in cosmetics is derived from grapeseed, sheep placenta, and Swiss apple?

   a) Stem cells
   b) Peptides
   c) Antioxidants
   d) AHAs

23) Ingredients with antibacterial properties are:

   a) Azelaic acid
   b) Benzoyl peroxide
   c) Bakuchiol
   d) All of the above

24) Dark circles around the eye can be caused by:

   a) Genetics
   b) Pooling of blood
   c) Shadow created by hollowing out under the eyes
   d) All of the above

25) Which layer needs to be heated up via radio frequency waves to stimulate collagen, resulting in skin tightening?

   a) Epidermis
   b) Dermis
   c) Subcutaneous
   d) All of the above

PART 8

The Road to Success: Skin to Win

AESTHETICS EXPOSED
MASTERING SKIN CARE IN A MEDICAL SETTING AND BEYOND

CHAPTER 29

Landing Your Dream Job

In this Chapter:
- Choosing Your Career Path
- Finding Opportunities
- Networking
- Internships
- Resumes
- Interviews

All of the effort you exert in your business life should be geared towards the *career* you desire. There is a big difference between a job and a career. **Most people think of a job as necessary to make a living, while a career is something that also provides personal gratification.** I have been training estheticians to work in a medical setting for more than eight years and can now consistently predict which students will be offered significant opportunities and which may not. I can with equal certainty foresee who will be motivated enough to capitalize upon those opportunities. After all, that is what opens the door from a job to a career. Nothing in life comes easy and hard work truly does pay off. The most important thing to consider is that the most respect gained is often earned when no one is watching; determination does not go unnoticed.

> Determination does not go unnoticed.

Choosing your Career Path

One positive aspect about working in the aesthetic industry is the multitude of career paths that exist. There are several options available that go beyond performing skin care services in a salon, spa, or medical office. Performing services is often the most sought-out aspect of the industry, providing the opportunity to put forth the knowledge gained by directly working with clients. This is often the first goal for an esthetician and can be highly rewarding both personally and financially. But many providers like to explore other aspects of the business over time. While one may love being in that area of work at first, some look for a change after several years. The long hours, many of which are spent standing rather than seated, have the ability to become physically taxing over time. Other opportunities include working as a product representative, an educator, a patient coordinator or manager, an assistant in a medical office, as a member of marketing for a skin care company, or in product development, to name just a few. To take it even further, some professionals return for advanced education to work in product development or clinical research for aesthetic products. Be sure the decision you make, whatever it is, is because you genuinely receive satisfaction from the services you provide, that it will keep you motivated, and that it provides room for education and growth. One may think they need to have a specific title, or make a certain amount of money to be fulfilled, but find themselves doing something completely different and loving it. **While some people choose compensation as a primary purpose, although it may provide instant gratification, it may not be fulfilling in the long term.** Like everything else, if it makes *you* happy that's all that really matters.

Aesthetic Career Options

- Spa setting
  - Focus is on relaxation and immediate gratification
- Medical setting
  - Results driven treatments
  - Possibly assisting physician
- Product representative
  - Sales
  - Educating purchasers on products
- Educator
  - Undergraduate teacher
  - Post-graduate educator
  - Product or device educator
- Manager or director
  - Mentor staff members
  - Develop and implement goals

If you are unsure which path might fit you best, explore several options. Regardless of which path is ultimately chosen, experience in other areas will always prove beneficial. For example, an esthetician directly out of school may begin working at a practice, and for the first time be in direct control of treatment formulations and tailoring products to meet a client's expectations. While helping the client is rewarding, a deeper interest in the creation of the products might lead the esthetician to pursue a career with a skin care company in research and development.

Landing Your Dream Job

Once an inclination towards a particular career path sets in, it is important to do in-depth research on every aspect that may come with it. Find out exactly what the job entails, including the degree of responsibility, the average working hours, and any additional/continuing education needed. Just like learning a foreign language, the best way of grasping any career path's requirements is completely immersing yourself in the field. This can be done through interning in a setting where you may ultimately want to be hired or at least one that shares similarities to it. Many professionals are happy to mentor someone, particularly because they receive the added benefit of extra help around the office. When an opportunity to intern arises use it wisely, demonstrate you work ethic and proved subtle suggestions on how you could benefit the practice. If you do get the opportunity to intern, use this time to demonstrate your work ethic and desire to contribute. Let every person in the office see the passion you have for your career. We continuously provide interns with opportunities at our medical skin care center. The first question to often come about is "Are you hiring?" Most of the time we are not hiring; however, we have a great group of companies that complement each other well, and once someone gets hired, they don't leave. That being said, each person who has been hired in the last year in our office once began as an intern: an esthetician, two medical assistants, an education coordinator, a laser technician, and a receptionist, each of whom took our advanced esthetic courses and further evolved through their internship experiences. This gave the intern an exclusive look into the operations of our office and gave staff members the opportunity to see potential staff members work ethic.

Finding Opportunities

Once your career path is chosen, finding the perfect job can be an ambitious undertaking and should not be taken lightly. Of course, the ultimate goal is to arrive at work each day with great coworkers, filled with excitement to make clients feel better about themselves. This certainly exists, but it is important to keep in mind that there may also be disgruntled clients, frustrated coworkers, and, all-in-all, less than perfect days, regardless of the place of employment. Remembering what drives your passion in the field should be enough to push past any obstacles that may occur. It is, however, equally important to remember that if a certain setting or office does not fulfill your passion within a fair trial period, it is perfectly acceptable to move on in pursuit of that perfect fit. *All experiences, whether positive or negative, provide an opportunity for learning and growth.*

> Just like learning a foreign language, the best way of grasping any career path's requirements is completely immersing yourself in the field.

> To a vast extent, people determine their own destiny and when one is passionate about what they do, it will drive their success.

Finding a job is a job in itself and needs to be taken seriously. No matter what roadblocks the journey may throw at you, maintaining motivation is critical to landing a job offer that suits you. To a vast extent, people determine their own destiny and when one is passionate about what they do, it will drive their success.

Networking is one of the most overlooked avenues through which solid employment opportunities present themselves. I have personally witnessed determined estheticians who have capitalized upon networking events, resulting in extraordinary employment opportunities. As with everything, hard work will pay off; it requires time to investigate and to remain current on relevant networking and industry events. Educational workshops and tradeshows provide particularly abundant prospects. Although they often have an air of excitement and fun surrounding them, professionalism should always be taken seriously. You never know when an opportunity may present itself—and never forget someone is always watching. There is no longer the limitation of specific weekends or fees for special events in order to network; it is an activity that can now be performed at all times with the creation of websites such as LinkedIn. It should go without  saying the necessity of maintaining professional appearances at all times on public profile sites, just as you would in person.

The internet is, of course, the most popular method used for seeking out job openings in general. Several websites have surfaced that make the job hunt easier. However, desirable opportunities are typically capitalized upon quickly. One way to stay ahead of the competition is to set up accounts for such websites to receive email alerts for new postings relevant to your career choices. Consistent monitoring of your personal pages where such notifications are received is essential.

Resume

When seeking a position, it is essential to have a professional resume; in most cases it will most likely be your "first impression." This is the first thing a hiring manager will see, as everything is done electronically these days. With that said, it must be a true representation of your abilities, but also be direct and to the point. Also, it must be free of mistakes, such as misspellings. (You might be surprised just how easy it is to overlook such simple things as misspelled words.) **If care is not taken to put together a one-page document to represent your work, how could the company trust that you will put necessary detail into your work? This is especially true when it comes to a position in a medical setting; documentation cannot be taken lightly and if not not done appropriately could lead to serious reprecussions.**

The look of the resume should be clean, concise, and consistent; detailed specifics should be saved for the interview. A professional summary, stating skills and what you can bring to the table, should be on the top. Use words that pertain to the position you are seeking. If you are looking for a job in the medical field, ensure that anything showing medical education or experience is noted. A list of relevant experiences should follow the professional summary, unless you are a recent graduate. Be sure to only list three to four relevant jobs to the position you are applying for. Jobs should be listed in reverse chronological order; this means that topping the list is your most current job. This is followed by education, also listed in reverse chronological order. Be sure to consistently use active voice throughout as well, i.e. use action words.

Pictures, scented paper, or bright colors are not appropriate; you must come across as a professional. Unnecessary information, including babysitting, high school accomplishments, or irrelevant hobbies should be left out. Your name, phone number, address, and professional e-mail address should be at the very top. Note: Professional email addresses should include a name and maybe some numbers, unacceptable emails are ihatemyex@google.com, Ilovemycats@msn.com, or anything else irrelevant and unprofessional. It is worth taking the time out to create a new professional email account. Typical examples would be your **first.last name** or **first initial.last name**. Read and re-read your resume, and ask as many people as possible to read it as well. Look for spelling, grammar, or consistency errors. Even one small mistake may discredit you. Moreover, while your resume can be polished into finality, your cover letter must be tailored specifically to each position of which you are applying.

Interviews

If your resume makes the right impression, an interview will be the next step. Dressing the part for the job you desire is critical, regardless of the job you are applying for. For example, as a medical assistant your daily work attire will likely be a medical scrub uniform, but to the interview you should still dress in business attire. Needless to say, wear a clean, ironed suit and make sure that hair and makeup are neatly and conservatively worn. Before beginning the interview, be sure to have a solid grasp of what your perceived strengths are and why they would make you an asset to the practice you are applying to. Be prepared to answer a multitude of questions.

The most detrimental thing you can do for an interview is come ill-prepared. The person conducting the interview will most likely ask you questions ranging from your employment history, to what your current understanding is of the company you are applying for, and how you see yourself as an asset there. This means do your homework. If it is a surgeon's office, research his/her specialty, the school the surgeon graduated from, his/her years in business, what professional associations he/she are involved in, and what services are offered in the practice. Also, spend time thinking about how you would answer common interview questions such as "Tell me a little bit about yourself," and "Why do you think you are a good candidate for this position?" **You want to sound polished, yet unrehearsed, and most importantly, honest.**

You may also be asked why you left jobs in the past and why you want to work for this new company. Be comfortable with your resume inside and out. Be prepared with factual stories to illustrate experiences or attributes on your resume. It may be helpful to have someone you know conduct a mock interview with you, or practice responses in front of a mirror—it may feel silly, but you will be better prepared for an actual interview this way.

At the end of the interview, if the interviewer asks if you have any questions, always try to have at least one or two to ask. Asking relevant questions shows the interviewer that you are truly interested. Some questions you may want ask include: "What qualities are you looking for in an employee?" or "Is there room for growth in this position?" Do not bring up compensation, benefits, or time off during the first interview; save these questions for if and when you are offered a position. However, you should be prepared to answer questions about these things if the interviewer asks about your expectations in these areas. Before leaving the interview, inquire what their timeline is and when you should expect to hear back. Send a personalized, hand-written thank you note that day. If you have an email address, it is also appropriate to send a thank you email.

It can be a lot of work to find a great job that suits you well, but if you are prepared and persistent, opportunities will present themselves. As scientist Louis Pasteur once said, "Chance favors the prepared." Remember that the most important thing is to remain professional at all times, exude confidence but remain humble, and keep trying until you have succeeded.

SCENARIO: Job Interview Do's and Don'ts

What could happen:
Interviewee (dressed in leggings and a sweater): "Hello, thank you for seeing me."
Manager: "Tell me a little bit about yourself. What would make you a good fit for Beyond Beauty Medical Spa?"
Interviewee: "Um. I think I could be really good with customers after I finish school and get some practice. I like waxing a lot."
Manager: "Why did you leave your last position?"
Interviewee: "It wasn't a good fit. My boss couldn't handle her staff, and then school started, so I decided to focus full-time on that."
Manager: "What would make you an asset here?"
Interviewee: "I'm a fast learner and I don't care how much you pay me. I want to get better at everything and I think I can learn how to here."
Manager: "Do you have any questions for me?"
Interviewee: "Is there vacation pay?"

What should happen:
Interviewee (wearing a suit): "Hello, thank you for seeing me today."
Manager: "Tell me a little bit about yourself. What would make you a good fit for Beyond Beauty Medical Spa?"
Interviewee: "I work well with clients and am confident that I could retain a significant portion within my first year here. In addition, my waxing services are excellent and I am confident that I can convert those clients to skin care services given the opportunity."
Manager: "Why did you leave your last position?"
Interviewee: "I realized once school began that I wanted to focus 100 percent of my energy on learning and wouldn't be able to do that if I were still working."
Manager: "What would make you an asset here?"
Interviewee: "I am passionate about the skin and making clients feel better about themselves. Being new to this industry, I know that you can't start at the top, but I have heard nothing but great things about this practice and would be happy for an opportunity to show you what I can bring to this position. Being new to this industry, I know that you can't start at the top, but I'm excited to get my start here!"
Manager: "Do you have any questions for me?"
Interviewee: "Yes. I am very passionate about my career; do you foresee any opportunities to grow in this position?"

CHAPTER 30

Easy and Efficient Business Building

In this Chapter:
- Accountability
- Extending Your Knowledge
- Networking and Social Media
- Setting Goals

Once you have obtained the job you want, the next step is to build your business. Many aesthetic providers falsely believe that once a job is attained, their appointment books will be miraculously full. Although this can be the case in some established settings, the majority of the time it is the responsibility of the provider to build and maintain a successful following. This doesn't mean it will *all* be on you, as most companies have a management team and many also offer marketing help. Ultimately though, it is the provider's responsibility to ensure continued success. These business-building techniques can be applied to any setting, but are particularly applicable to a cosmetic medical practice.

Accountability

One of the easiest ways to build a clientele is to simply be available. It is all too common to hear skin care professionals state, "I don't understand why I'm not busy, everyone else in the office is busy all day." The same person complaining is the one who assumes they should not be working unless they are treating clients. First of all, that should be a sign that the individual is not motivated for the practice. If the rest of the practice is busy, then this activity level should be taken advantage of. **Your time must be used wisely; ask other providers if you can shadow them during the day.** Just being in the room with patients of the medical practice can dramatically increase business. Patients visiting the practice are already looking for aesthetic recommendations; it couldn't be any easier. Providing recommendations to enhance and maintain their treatments will give maximum satisfaction to the patients.

We did an in-office study at True Skin Care Center in which 100 patients were cleansed with an oscillating cleansing brush prior to their injection appointment. We then took a control group of 100 patients who were simply cleansed with facial wipes by the medical assistants. Subsequent analysis showed that the group pre-cleansed by a skin care professional with the oscillating brush opposed to the group cleaned with facial wipes spent an average of $75 more in retail purchases. Our conclusion was that if a practice were to have a skin care professional cleanse 10 patients per day prior to their medical treatment, it could result in an increase in sales of $195,000 per annum. That is a significant amount of money for a practice, and the higher the revenue, the higher salaries can become. The bottom line is *understand your surroundings and get to know the physician(s), staff members, and current patients of the practice.*

Another great benefit to shadowing the physician is that doing so can be a tremendous learning experience. What better way to learn every aspect of cosmetic medicine, than being able to witness procedures and patient reactions first-hand?

Extending Your Knowledge

It is of course important to be knowledgeable on the services you offer, but it is equally important to share that knowledge with staff members, clients, and patients of the practice. **Every staff member, from the receptionist to the physician, must be educated on all skin care services offered.** The optimal way to do this would be to provide them each the opportunity to receive services themselves. This gives each staff member who has contact with clients an opportunity to speak to their own experiences, which makes it more personal than simply reading from a script. Another way to share your knowledge with staff is to offer in-services. An in-service can be a fun meeting before or after work where employees take turns educating the others on a particular treatment of interest.

As knowledge of treatments and products becomes available, share it with current and potential clients as well. An education center with takeaways for the clients is a great start. To save time and ensure consistency, it can be the same topic presented to the staff. These takeaways can be put in a particular area where the clients can pick and choose what they prefer to read about. Some topics can include: "Combating Dry Skin from Winter Weather," "The Truths and Myths of Chemical Peels," and "The Power of Peptides in Skin Care." These are fun reading materials as opposed to the typical product brochures that many cosmetic offices carry. Providing these materials also shows that the practice cares about education and relating both personally and professionally to clients in order to provide a comfortable, optimal experience.

Networking and Social Media

Just as you used networking to come up with a position, it is equally important to network on a continuous basis to maintain consistent growth of your database. Seek out events in which you can meet potential clients; think outside the box. Reach out to businesses where people go to promote their health and appearance. Health clubs, yoga centers, nutrition centers, and hair salons are good places to start. Ask about hosting a joint event to increase business on both sides or to set up a cross-referral program by simply having educational material in each other's offices. Other places to network are women's groups or associations. Although the increase in men receiving aesthetic services has risen, women tend to be more open to discussing beauty treatments in social settings. These associations may be open to a presentation on "Why protecting the skin is important," or "Maintaining a youthful appearance through healthy aging."

Social media is another form of networking that gives you the ability to market yourself with no cost and to do so at any given time. Regular postings to blogs and discussion sites that pertain to your field, at least once per week, are necessary to gain and maintain visibility. Once a following has been achieved, use it to your advantage. Social media is particularly useful when trying to fill a slow day or rebuild your schedule after clients have canceled. If your day isn't completely booked, offer incentives to those who book that day. For example, on a Monday: "Start the week with fresh skin! All chemical peel appointments today receive a complimentary eye treatment valued at $35.00." Expand on the post and make it educational; for example, informative pieces or blogs are a nice way of boosting

consumer interest and involvement. Track the changes in your schedule throughout the promotional period and use the information to choose the special that draws the most interest, as it can become a regular offering in the future. There is nothing to lose with free forms of advertisement at your disposal.

Setting Goals

Goals are often provided by employers of larger companies—but regardless, set your own goals to stay motivated. Think about other commonly made goals including getting in shape or losing weight. To be successful, one can't just workout or eat healthy when the opportunity presents itself; there are goals to maintain daily or weekly. This type of accountability should be brought into every aspect of your life. Examples of goals in a medical setting could be to convert two patients from the medical side to skin care each day; this can be done by simply making yourself available during clinic times, as discussed above. Other goals could be to book three new consults a week or sell a specific dollar amount of retail monthly. Set and execute goals that will build a strong, steady clientele.

There are several ways to build clientele in an aesthetic setting; these are introductory methods with no overhead that can jumpstart your business. Marketing doesn't always cost money, but it does take care and dedication to maximize your potential. Remember to be accountable, continue to network, share your knowledge, and set goals for continued success.

CHAPTER 31

Retail: Educating vs. Selling

In this Chapter:
- Success is More Than Money
- Client Characteristics
- Addressing Challenges

Retailing is an important part of an aesthetic provider's job in order to be successful. When I say "success," I am not referring to that which is solely, or even primarily based on income; rather, it is based on the ultimate goal of making the client happy, which eventually leads to monetary success. As stated in earlier chapters, a client will not get optimal results if they are not doing their part in caring for their skin at home. Home care recommendations should be made for each and every client that comes through the door, regardless of the treatment. The line of retail products you offer ties directly into those recommendations—but how do you go about securing both the sale *and* the confidence of your client in what recommendations you are making to them?

First of all, unless you are a salesperson, the term "selling" should be taken out of your vocabulary. When I started working as an esthetician 18 years ago, I took a position at a high-end day spa. I was so excited and couldn't wait to start treating clients. My first day of work, I was given my expectations as an employee. These expectations had nothing to do with making clients feel better or, so far as I could tell, about improving their skin. They were sales goals. I was given service and retail quotas that had to be met to keep my position in the company. I went home that day extremely upset, thinking I had made a horrible decision by becoming an esthetician. I was very shy and hated anything that had to do with sales. I felt that I was taking advantage of clients by upgrading their service or recommending products. For the first three months, I struggled with this and barely sold anything. It was a big wake-up call when clients would come in upset, after spending over an hour with me discussing their skin, and I didn't offer advice on treatment follow-ups or product recommendations. Other clients were equally upset that their friends, while treated by another esthetician, had received the "ultimate anti-aging facial" and an eye treatment while they were not even told it was an option; they just got the basic facial. How could that be? I saved them a lot of money and still provided a great service. I didn't want to seem pushy or "salesy." After all, if they wanted to spend money on products, they would have asked me, right? No, they had no idea these other treatments were even options.

Then—it all started to come together. If I was not telling my clients what the best course of action for their skin would be, then who would? It would most likely be a drugstore cashier or a department store salesperson, selling the same product to each customer regardless of their concerns. They didn't know the detail that I did about my client's skin, about the person I had just spent a long period of time with, discussing their concerns, past treatments and products, what has worked on their skin and what hasn't. Having my clients' best interests at heart, I wanted to ensure that they would gain the benefits they were seeking. I knew the products that our spa carried inside and out, and had studied the ingredients in depth. I decided to change my thinking and use my passion for education to increase clients' knowledge on what was happening to their skin and how to best care for it. *So instead of selling, I simply educated my clients on how I believed they could best address their concerns.* That simple task remained my focus and within the next three months, I had the highest retail in the department--though, according to me, I never *sold* a thing! Not only was I meeting my retail goals, I was helping my clients achieve their goals as well.

Although education is one aspect of it, the delivery matters as well. The best way to educate your clients is to relate to them. Watch body reactions and listen intently to find out each client's buying style. Be observant, and you will notice enough traits to make an assessment of who your client is and then determine the approach you will take to create the sale. The goal is to get to know your client's personality type as quickly as possible.

"Analytical" Characteristics

Analytical clients like detail and organization. They think clearly and will want information delivered with accuracy. This client will likely act methodically and be cautious about purchases. They may be cautious without proven results, before and after photos, clinical studies, or testimonials. These types of information should be delivered in a quick, concise way.

Be factual, accurate, and straightforward. Provide information showing improvements by numbers, and use statistics; for example: "This product has shown an average 68% decrease in fine lines in six weeks." Use educational materials, before and after pictures, and clinical studies. Also, develop a detailed plan with thoroughly written instructions. Educate this client using details that include product ingredients and how they will work on the client's skin conditions.

"Driver" Characteristics

Clients with a driver personality focus on the results. Some examples of how to deliver the results this client seeks would be statements like "98% of people that used this product claimed they saw positive results for their pigmentation." Before and after pictures are also a great tool, because "drivers" tend to be more focused on accepting a challenge, which could be improving the appearance of their skin. This client will likely want to make the final decision. Don't be pushy, but give options; e.g. *"We have a couple of products that work effectively on targeting and reducing pigmentation. One product contains retinol which will stimulate cellular turnover with the addition of lightening agents, sunscreen is mandatory with this product. The other product I would recommend would focus on slowing the production of pigment down while adding antioxidants. Which would you prefer?"* If the client starts talking about what they know from commercials, magazines, other estheticians, and so on, validate their opinions. "Drivers" tend to want the latest and greatest, so focus on new products with new technology and show clinical studies to back them up.

"Amiable" Characteristics

The amiable client is a treat to have. They are typically honest, caring, loyal, and cooperative. This not only helps during the service, but it is easy to trust their compliancy with at-home regimens. You don't need to worry as much if the client will wear sunscreen in the morning following retinol use. This client also tends to be more patient, so when dealing with visible results from product use they will be more understanding that it may take a number of weeks in order to see results.

When purchasing, it may be difficult for them to make decisions. Let this client know about any personal experiences you've had with the products. Example: "My sister used this product, and she was really excited when she saw the reduction in breakouts." Focus on the overall results, both how they will look and ultimately how they will feel. By being more casual as opposed to scientific, it will help build trust through communication. Use customized regimens, not something already put together in a box, but instead: "Here is a system that I customized for you." Loyalty programs are also beneficial, offering clients 10% off any repurchased products, or accrued points based on dollars spent that can be allocated toward services.

"Expressive" Characteristics

Expressive clients are typically going to be excited about a new regimen for their skin. They make a good first impression and often show enthusiasm. If they are happy with a skin care regimen, they are likely to motivate others on the difference it can make. They also talk easily to others, commonly striking up conversations with other clients or staff members.

So far as their buying tendencies are concerned, they want personal recognition, not a lot of details. They will likely love the fancy packaging for a featured product or best-seller. Use materials with media hits or other referrals from clients, staff, and doctors. Provide brochures; this client likes to go through the material again and get motivated to use the products consistently. Ask for their opinion and validate what they know. "Have you tried this new vitamin C serum? I've been getting great feedback. I'd love to get your thoughts." Make sure you have time to talk with this client, as opposed to just giving specifics.

Overcoming Objections

There are several objections commonly heard when it comes to retailing products in an aesthetic setting. It may seem difficult to provide simple answers on the importance of using the products recommended. The following are some tips on how to focus on education while relaying the message that proper product use is vital to results.

Client: "The product I bought at the drug store has vitamin C in it, can I just use that?"
Suggestions: Never "put down" another product; rather, focus on the quality and proven efficacy of the products you are recommending. Show before and after pictures, and discuss what makes you product offering unique. Discuss the differences: There are not only several different forms of ingredients, but, like anything else available for purchase, there are different qualities as well.

Let's use this example: Product ingredients differ in the same sense that cooking ingredients differ. If one were wanting a cheeseburger, there are several options open to you, from cheap fast food to culinary offerings that use higher-quality meats and cheeses.

Client: "I just spent a lot of money on services; can I just use body cream on my face at home?"
Home care is an essential part of results and this should be discussed in the consultation, prior to treatment. If during the consult, the client expresses that they are not interested in caring for their skin at home, then only a noninvasive treatment should be performed. If the client is looking to make a change in their skin, they need to know that up to 80% of results often come from using the correct products on a consistent basis.

Client: "My dermatologist told me that any bar soap is fine for cleansing, it makes no difference."
Provider: "How has that been working for you?"
Client: "My skin feels pretty tight and dry after cleansing."
Provider: "Although many dermatologists incorporate preventive skin care recommendations, some dermatologists focus solely on simply treating the underlying condition with medical recommendations, including medication. If you want something easily accessible and low-cost, go for a gentle cleanser such as Cetaphil. It will not help your skin conditions, but it will also not harm them. It is best to stay away from bar soaps. They can be harsh and drying."

Client: "Everything I use on my skin causes me to breakout. I finally found a system that works."
If the client is using reputable safe products, let him/her know that you will assess the skin regularly to ensure it is still working. If the product is not beneficial give a few samples of products to incorporate into their current regimen and follow up with a phone call in five days to discuss how the product is working on their skin.

Client: "I don't like the consistency of this product. I love Vaseline; it makes my skin feel soft."
Provider: "I understand you have dry skin, so Vaseline probably does feel good following application. It is an occlusive agent that makes the skin feel soft on the outside. To make a change in the skin, though, we need to introduce products that will add moisture to your skin and work on repairing the barrier, which Vaseline does not do. Vaseline works more like a "band-aid" for the real issue."

All of these methods for retailing focus on education; it is not about putting other product lines down or being pushy. When focusing on education, the message comes across clearly and gives the client the opportunity to choose for themselves.

Use your resources. The product companies you're working with should be supportive and supply materials that assist in the educational process. Remember that dedication and accountability will always persevere. Follow guidelines and set goals to achieve and maintain success in your career. Ultimately, your career is what you make of it, so fulfill your dreams.

> Remember that dedication and accountability will always persevere.

SCENARIO: Retailing

What could happen #1:
Provider: "Good afternoon! I see you've found our skin care. That particular product is wonderful for your skin."
Client: "It looks nice, but it's really pricey."
Provider: "Well, it's worth it. There's vitamin E in it."
Client: "Oh, I just get capsules at the drugstore and put them right on my face. And they're only $10."
Provider: "Really? Wow. This product is amazing, but if that works for you, then I can't argue with it!"

What should happen #1:
Provider: "Hi there! You are holding one of my favorite products in your hands. It's absolutely brilliant in reducing fine lines."
Client: "It looks nice, but it's really pricey."
Provider: "It might seem that way, but it's due to the years of research that went into making it so effective. The vitamin E in it is a powerful antioxidant that destroys free radicals, which is so necessary in keeping your skin youthful."
Client: "Oh, I just get the capsules at the drugstore and put them directly on my face. And they're only $10."
Provider: "Good for you! That's a great first step. Unfortunately, those capsules actually won't penetrate your skin or activate any changes like this product will. You may have noticed that your skin doesn't look any different now than when you began using the capsules. With this, you will see it change."
Client: "Wow. Well, I will give it a shot!"

What could happen #2:

Provider: "Hi, how are you?"
Client: "Okay, just had some questions about this retinol product."
Provider: "Sure, go ahead!"
Client: "I've been using XY Retinol from the drugstore but haven't noticed any changes. What makes this different?"
Provider: "It's just so much better. The company that makes this product is really good and they know what they're doing."
Client: "There are two different kinds of retinols, I see. What's the difference?
Provider: "One is stronger than the other. You should probably start with the stronger one to get the quickest results."
Client: "Ok. I might come back. Thank you."

What should happen #2:

Provider: "Hello, how are you today?"
Client: "Okay, I just had some questions about this retinol product."
Provider: "Go ahead! I could talk about retinol all day. It's one of the best ingredients around for renewing your skin."
Client: "Really? I've been using XY Retinol from the drugstore and haven't noticed any changes. What makes this different?"
Provider: "This is clinical strength. You probably haven't noticed any difference in your skin because there's such a low percentage of retinol in XY Retinol, whereas here it is pure retinol. What it does is stimulate cell regeneration and build collagen to diminish the appearance of fine lines, as well as pore size. If you've noticed that your skin tone is uneven, this helps correct that as well."
Client: "Wow! I had no idea it was supposed to do all that. Now, I see there are two strengths of retinols. What's the difference?"
Provider: "The first one you see is about half the strength of the other. I'd recommend you start with that until you build a tolerance. If your skin were extremely thick, I might recommend beginning with the stronger retinol, but I think you'll see a big difference with this, and you will be very happy with the condition of your skin."
Client: "Okay, wonderful! Thank you so much for your help."

What could happen #3:
Client: "Excuse me, could you help me?"
Provider: "Of course. What can I do for you?"
Client: "I just was wondering which soap you'd recommend."
Provider: "For your face?"
Client: "Yes. I just saw my dermatologist, and he said that soap and water is fine."
Provider: "Really? I would actually recommend a gel cleanser or even a creamy face wash if you're on the dry side."
Client: "I'd rather follow my dermatologist's advice. Could you please tell me which soap would be best for my face?"
Provider (sighing): "Okay."

What should happen #3:
Provider: "Good afternoon! What a beautiful day!"
Client: "Yes it is. I'm actually in a bit of a rush. Could you point out where your face soaps are?"
Provider: "I sure could, but may I ask why you're looking at soaps instead of creamy cleansers or gels?"
Client: "My dermatologist said soap and water is fine."
Provider: "I'd never come between a client and her dermatologist, but if I could offer you some advice, based on my experience, it would be this: if you use soap on your face, you'll either be back here or in your dermatologist's office, wondering why your face feels so dry and flaky."

Client: "Seriously? What do you know that my dermatologist doesn't?"
Provider: "We both know that soap and water is 'fine' for washing your face, but using a product with soothing ingredients and a pH necessary for your particular skin type is far better than just 'fine' and will actually be beneficial. I know you're pressed for time, but if you'll give me five minutes and your skin concerns, I'm certain we can find a cleanser that's perfect for you."
Client: "You convinced me! Okay. Thank you!"

Retail: Educating vs. Selling

What could happen #4:
Provider: "How are you today?"
Client: "Good, thanks. I don't know what to do. Everything I use makes me break out."
Provider: "Your skin looks fine to me! But what are you using now?"
Client: "Oh, I'm just wearing a lot of makeup. I've tried everything, and none of it works."
Provider: "Why don't you try this serum? It works for everyone."
Client: "Tried it. It broke me out."
Provider: "Oh, that's weird. It usually works for everybody. Why don't you try it again? Maybe in conjunction with other products, it won't break you out this time."
Client: "No thanks. I really just want to find something that works. Maybe I'll just look around for a while."

What should happen #4:
Provider: "How are you today?"
Client: "Good thanks. I don't know what to do. Everything I use makes me break out."
Provider: "I understand trying multiple products can be frustrating. Will you allow me to ask you some questions about your skin so we can get you on a path to better skin care? I am confident that the right products used in conjunction with each other will help alleviate these breakouts."
Client: "Absolutely. I will do anything!"
Provider: "Okay, then let's get started!"

What could happen #5:
Provider: "Good morning, how are you today?"
Client: "Oh, I'm fine, just looking at these moisturizers. My daughter told me I should get something new, but I like Vaseline."
Provider: "You mean you use Vaseline as your primary moisturizer on your face?"
Client: "Yes. I like it because it makes my skin feel so soft."
Provider: "You should use this cream. It's way better than Vaseline and it's a real moisturizer. Plus, it'll make you look younger."
Client: "I don't know. Maybe I'll think about it. Thanks."

What should happen #5:
Provider: "Good morning, how are you today?"
Client: "Oh, I'm fine, just looking at these moisturizers. My daughter told me I should get something new, but I like Vaseline."
Provider: "Is that so? What do you like about it?"
Client: "It makes my skin feel really soft."
Provider: "I see. Now, I think Vaseline is great for a lot of things, but keep in mind it is just petrolatum. It is strictly a barrier. I could recommend several moisturizers which would enrich, protect, revive and soften your skin! Feel this one, for example. If soft is what you're after, soft is definitely what you'll get."
Client: "Ooh, and it smells good, too. Could you show me some of the others you mentioned?"
Provider: "Of course."

CHAPTER 32

Tools for Client Retention

In this Chapter:
- Before, During, and After the Appointment
- Tips for Client Retention

Exceptional customer service is the cornerstone of success for any business or individual provider. The adage "*The customer is always right*" has withstood time, and for good reason. Most people are familiar with the basic skills of customer service. However, survival in the aesthetics business is dependent on mastering it. **It is a fact that any service provider without customers will have no business, so you must treat each client as if they are your one and only.** If clients are not happy, success cannot be achieved. Multiple businesses are in competition for the same clientele, so it is critical to take measures to define yourself within the pack and to separate and elevate yourself from the rest. This entails not only mastering your own trade, but also maintaining excellent customer service at all times. The cosmetic industry is continually growing, and there are new salons, day spas, med spas, and cosmetic medical practices that offer skin care treatments popping up every day. You must go above and beyond to set yourself apart from your competition.

Before the Appointment

Customer service starts at the client's first call to your office right up to the follow-up. The receptionist's actions during the initial phone call are typically the first impression of your practice. This may seem out of your control—that the language and tone of voice of a single person carries such significance—but you must accept the fact that your business is ultimately dependent on it. If you see or hear of any actions that may be deterring clients from making appointments, management must be notified; one simple disservice by any staff member could result in the loss of a client that worked hard to gain. On that note, it is helpful to get clients excited before they even come in for their appointment. This can be done by sending out information about the services you offer, in particular the treatment that they booked the appointment for. **A simple card or letter saying "We look forward to meeting you. Here is some information we thought you would find helpful before your appointment" shows the client that they are valuable.** This overture will help secure the appointment and portray true professionalism. This may also conjure up additional questions that the client had previously forgotten to ask over the phone, and they will likely appreciate having a hard copy of the information to review prior to their visit. For example, if someone books an appointment for a chemical peel, send them information on what the treatment entails, how they should prepare for the appointment, and what they may expect to experience afterward. You can also add before and after pictures and testimonials of previous patients. This can be sent through the mail or even e-mail, so there is no cost to the practice.

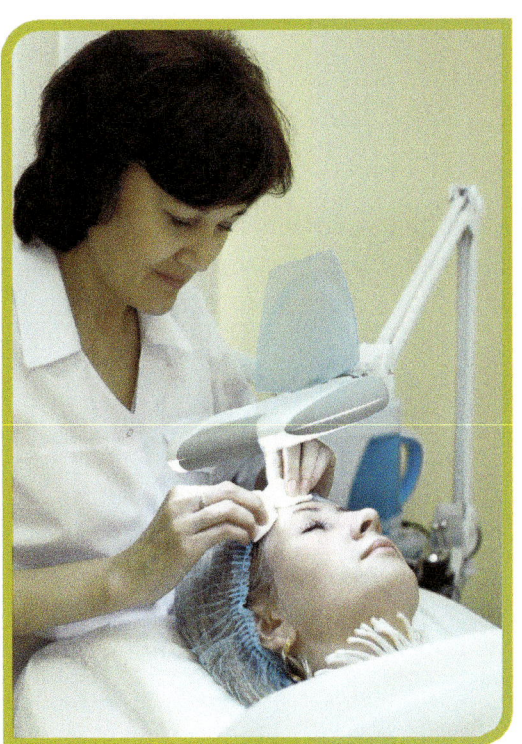

During the Appointment

When the client comes in for a first-time appointment, take a few minutes to introduce yourself and offer a brief tour of the office to boost the client's comfort level. Keep in mind, first-time clients can be easily overwhelmed by a busy office. Make it your goal to earn and maintain their trust and loyalty by comforting them from the minute they walk in the door. After bringing the client back to the treatment room, a thorough consultation must be done. This is the most crucial part of the treatment. (I refer you back to Part 2 for more in-depth discussion of consultation techniques.) The consult provides an opportunity to build a relationship with the client and find out what *their* concerns are. A successful business is based on making clients happy; this can only be done if you fully understand what their end goals are. Involve the client in making decisions on their treatment plan; this communication will ensure that a relationship is built and expectations are managed. **When expectations are discussed, it is crucial that as a provider you always "under-promise" and "over-deliver."** Exude confidence in your skills when building a relationship with a client.

As you begin treatment, keep the client's well-being in mind at all times. Leave communication devices aside, and do not talk about your personal life or the horrible day you had. Explain each step of the treatment as it is performed. This provides an opportunity to educate the client and make him/her feel involved. Be detailed; if applying a chemical peel, describe that it may burn or itch as it is being applied.

Prompt the client to let you know if there is any discomfort during the treatment. The client should constantly have your devoted attention. After all, this is their time; they are paying for your service. For instance, while the client is steaming or masking, it is common practice for an esthetician to step out of the treatment room. Again, you must go above and beyond, the competition is fierce. During this time, instead of leaving the room, perform a shoulder, neck, or hand massage. This also goes for shorter treatments such as microdermabrasion and chemical exfoliation. Just because they are quick, result-oriented services does not mean there isn't room for relaxation. This small action is one of those little steps that will set you apart from your competition, so take advantage of the time you have with the client and always go the extra mile. It is extremely important to make sure the client also leaves with proper post-care instructions. This is an intricate part of customer service because it makes the patient feel well prepared and informed. This type of one-on-one time creates the beginnings of a strong rapport and long-lasting relationship with the client, reassuring them that you are dedicated to their well-being.

If time allows, the experience does not need to end the moment the treatment ends. The application of complimentary touch-up makeup greatly adds to the entire experience. Remember always that you are making the client feel better about him/herself. Some people feel incomplete going into public without makeup on, and some services' post-procedure protocols only allow for the use of mineral makeup.

The ability to read and understand people is the key to operating effectively in your profession. When you clearly understand your client's needs and anticipate them, you put yourself in a better position to become successful through client retention and satisfaction.

By providing this makeup for them, you are ensuring that the client is applying a safe barrier that keeps bacteria out and has natural sun-protective qualities. Clients who are planning on returning to their workplace post-treatment or have social plans will appreciate the fact that they can go about their day without any downtime. Also keep in mind that your client is a walking advertisement for your skill and practice. It is good to have them looking their best when they leave your office.

After the Treatment

The treatment doesn't end as soon as the service ends. Client relationships must continuously be nurtured. Even things that may seem small have the ability to add up. You should personally walk the client up to the front desk to make him/her feel important. Always go out of your way to ensure their comfort. Your receptionist should be instructed to always address clients by their first name along with asking how their experience was and if there is anything else they can help with before checking him/her out will go a long way toward firming up your client's relationship with the practice and will send your client on their way with a sense of positivity and satisfaction. The receptionist should pre-book their next appointment; this is a simple and direct method of client retention. It is extremely important at this time that the client does not feel rushed out of the office. Another helpful tip for customer service is to simply have small candies or cookies at check-out, as this gives them something positive simultaneously with the negative (the bill).

> Client relationships must continuously be nurtured.

Follow-up

Though the client leaves, customer service still continues. What happens during the follow-up speaks directly to how a business sets itself apart and makes its clientele feel special. It is six to seven times harder to bring in a new client than to retain one. Hence, it is critical to ensure current clients continue to return.

> Note that when adding value, it is better to do a gift or an add-on than discounting. This gives the opportunity for clients to experience something new and doesn't affect revenue.

Following a client's initial treatment, it is important to place a follow-up call a few days afterward to see if the client has any questions or concerns. It is not uncommon for those receiving a treatment such as a chemical peel for the first time to be worried about the amount of peeling that occurs. Although this is often discussed thoroughly, some tend to get nervous when it actually happens. The follow-up call can ensure that the client is comfortable and provide the opportunity to reiterate post-treatment instructions. Clients appreciate this extra step to ensure their comfort and well-being. They take such things personally. It is also thoughtful to send a personalized thank you note or card letting them know that you appreciate their business. You can also add in a gift with purchase toward a future appointment. *Note that when adding value, it is better to do a gift or an add-on than discounting. This gives the opportunity for clients to experience something new and doesn't affect revenue.* Furthermore, providing a gift for a friend is a simple way to get them talking about you and garner more business. Sending holiday cards and birthday cards are additional ways to foster this new relationship. These cards should be personalized to further secure the relationship. Again: the client will take such things *personally*. Small samples or add-on services could also be included in these acts of kindness.

Customer service does not take much additional time or effort. To be a successful provider, you must have your client's best interest at heart and this extra attention to detail will help show that. Following these simple steps will provide you with satisfied clientele, which eventually will translate into a striving business. Harvard Business School teaches that selling to a current customer has a conversion probability of 1 in 2, while marketing to a new client has a mere 1 in 16 chance of resulting in a purchase, therefore retention is perhaps the most crucial aspect of the business of your practice.

> ## Tips for Retaining Clientele
>
> Try using this mnemonic aid to remember it's all about the **CLIENT**: **C**onsult, **L**isten, **I**nform, **E**xecute, **N**urture and **T**hank.
>
> **Consult**: Proper consulting is the first step to building a relationship with the client. This is the *"make it or break it"* stage. You will determine the client's personality type (according to Chapter 6), go over anything questionable on client intake forms, and determine what the client's needs are. Without a proper consult, you cannot give an effective treatment.
>
> **Listen:** Listen closely to what your client has to say. You need to fully understand their needs and concerns to provide the proper treatment. Ask as many questions as you can. Find out how they care for their skin at home, what treatments they have had in the past and their motivation for coming to see you. **Do not tell them what you want for their skin; let them tell you what they want.** For instance, an individual may come in and complain of pigmentation on their skin, when you as an esthetician notice that they have deep lines that are much more obvious and, to your mind, of more direct concern. BUT: If the pigment is the main concern … then treat the pigment. You can also suggest treatments that will soften the lines, but let the client know that everything you are doing will address her primary concern.
>
> *continued on next page*

Inform: Every client should know exactly what their options are concerning the care of their skin. As you know, most clients can benefit from a variety of treatments. Take the time to explain each service that you think would be beneficial to them. This will give him/her the impression that they are making the final decision, and it illustrates to them also that you are taking the time to give them what they really want. Every step of each service should be explained thoroughly before and during the treatment. They need to know that if you are doing a chemical peel, they will feel it, as opposed to just putting something on the face that may cause some irritation. Explain thoroughly what they should expect from the treatment and how to care for it after. Be specific; clients appreciate detailed information on how treatments and products actually work on the skin.

Execute: Execute a plan to treat your client's skin that is consistent with their conditions, their budget, and the time they have available. To keep the client returning you need to let them know when to come back and how often. You also need to develop a plan for them to care for their skin at home. We all know that the client will get much better results if they are using the proper skin care to compliment in-office treatments. **Go through a schedule with them. If you don't have a plan to treat their skin, they will go somewhere that cares enough to develop a plan.** Schedule the next couple of appointments before they leave the office. Once appointments are set there is a much higher chance that the client will return on a regular basis.

Nurture: Always ensure that the client feels important. Let each and every client know that you really care about their needs, especially in the case of pre- and post-operative treatments. This can be a very traumatic time for some people and part of your job as an esthetic provider is to care for the patient before and after surgery. Make sure they know that they can count on you if there are any questions or
concerns. **You are their advocate.** Follow-up phone calls should be made within two days following all treatments. This will show them that you will be there if needed.

Thank: Make sure your clients know you appreciate them. Every new patient should receive a thank you card saying that you appreciate their business. Offering a discount for their next treatment can also help ensure they will be back for another visit.

Tools for Client Retention

You also want to thank clients who have been loyal for a long time. You can have client appreciation days where you offer free treatments for them and a friend; this will also give you the opportunity to acquire more clients. Every so often you can add a complimentary service, such as an eyebrow wax. There is very little cost involved and it doesn't take a lot of time; the client will appreciate it and will, like as not, become a regular waxing client. You can also send a small gift, such as a CD of music that you play during their treatments. It will be much appreciated that you thought of them, and it will remind them of you every time they hear the music that is played during their treatments. I've said it before but it is crucial to remember: Clients will take such gestures *personally*.

Remember ... the key to success in the cosmetic industry lies within the CLIENT! If you care for your client's needs, it will pay off in the end.

Part 8 Review

1) A skin care professional should decide their career path according to: _____.

   a) The highest salary
   b) What is most impressive to their friends
   c) Whomever hires them
   d) Where their passion is

2) If an esthetician wants to focus on relaxation and immediate gratification where should they pursue a career?

   a) Medical
   b) Educator
   c) Traditional spa
   d) Product representative

3) To find out exactly what a job entails you should:

   a) Google it
   b) Research only the degree of responsibility needed
   c) Do as much research as possible including responsibilities, hours, and education required
   d) Only ask people who have been estheticians for 10+ years

4) Your resume is important, since it is most often

   a) The only thing needed to get hired
   b) Your "first impression"
   c) Your "last impression"
   d) An introduction to your personality

5) A professional summary stating your skills and what you can bring to the table should be located where in your resume?

   a) On the top
   b) On a separate sheet
   c) Below work history
   d) On the bottom

6) Work history should be arranged in what order in your resume?

   a) Listed from most favorite to least
   b) Listed by length of time with that position
   c) Listed in reverse chronological order
   d) It doesn't matter

7) How should you dress for your interview?

   a) The way you would dress for that job (i.e, scrubs for a medical position)
   b) Business attire
   c) Formal attire
   d) Business casual attire

8) Before your interview you should spend time thinking about:

   a) Everything you need to do before your interview
   b) What questions you may be asked
   c) Not think about it at all and stay calm
   d) Everything you might answer wrong

9) You should ask a few questions towards the end of the *first* interview about:

   a) Benefits
   b) Compensation
   c) The qualities they seek in a potential new hire
   d) Don't ask any questions, let them ask the questions

10) Regarding customer service you should treat each client as if they are your: _____.

    a) Only client
    b) First client
    c) Last client
    d) Best friend

11) If someone books a first-time appointment for a chemical peel you should send them:

   a) Before and after pictures of procedures gone wrong
   b) A personalized handwritten thank you note that day
   c) A list of other services offered
   d) Information on what the treatment entails, and how to prepare for the appointment

12) How much harder is it to bring in a new client than to retain one?

   a) 70%
   b) 10 times
   c) 6–7 times
   d) 40%

13) It is important for the client to leave the office feeling:

   a) Better than last week
   b) Energized
   c) Stressed out but prettier
   d) Relaxed and better about themselves

14) For loyal clients who you want to thank, an add-on service can include:

   a) Lunch for two
   b) Basket of products
   c) Package of treatments purchased
   d) Neck, hand, and décolleté treatments

15) It is the sole responsibility of the _____ to build a clientele.

   a) Marketing director
   b) Business owner
   c) Skin care professional
   d) None of the above, each member plays a role

16) CLIENT stands for

   a) Clean, Lean, Immaculate, Execute, Normal, Tall
   b) Consult, Learn, Inform, Exude, Nurture, Thorough
   c) Consult, Listen, Inform, Execute, Nurture, Thank
   d) Conduct, Listen, Injure, Execute, Nice, Thank

17) When it comes to recommending products:

   a) Don't recommend products unless the client asks
   b) Try to save the client money by only recommending one product per appointment
   c) Be forceful so the client uses only the products you carry
   d) Forget the word retail and focus on education

18) Amiable clients tend to:

   a) Be honest, caring, loyal and cooperative
   b) Make a good first impression as they show enthusiasm
   c) Tend to want the latest and greatest
   d) Be moody, rude, dishonest, and loud

19) Following a treatment, great customer service would include:

   a) Asking the client to tip you
   b) Handing the client their check
   c) Giving free product
   d) Offering to apply mineral makeup

20) What POI is likely to make a first impression on a client?

   a) Greeting them as they walk in the door to your establishment
   b) During the client's initial phone call to the business
   c) Through direct mail
   d) From word of mouth

21) How is it best to train your staff about each service offered?

   a) Give each member a pamphlet with firm instructions to memorize each treatment
   b) Invite every member to experience the treatments for themselves
   c) Have them ask clients about their experiences
   d) It is only important for the providers themselves to be educated on services

22) Why is it important to make sure that the client leaves with proper post-care instructions?

   a) It makes the client feel well-prepared and informed
   b) The client will be sure to make a purchase
   c) The client will be likely to leave sooner with that information instead of waiting around and asking questions
   d) The client won't need to call the office with questions

23) What are the benefits of interning?

   a) The possibility of getting free services
   b) Getting an exclusive look into different career options that are available
   c) You are guaranteed to be hired after interning
   d) It is an easy way to spend your time

24) Where are some places to network?

   a) Social media websites
   b) Trade shows
   c) Educational workshops
   d) All of the above

25) When recommending products, if the client is using a product from the health food store with the same active ingredient, what should you do?

   a) Tell him/her to keep using the product they already have
   b) Point out the bad things about the product he/she is currently using
   c) Explain that there are differences in ingredients and focus on the benefits of the product recommended
   d) Recommend a product that may not be as beneficial, but will not be questioned

Appendix A

Medical Terminology, Recognizing Instruments Used in Aesthetic Medicine, and Anatomy & Skin Physiology

A Guide to Medical Terminology

When working alongside a physician in a medical office, you must understand medical nomenclature, which manifests in several ways. By learning the basics of medical terminology—the prefixes and suffixes pertaining to dermatology and cosmetic surgery, as well as the shorthand abbreviations that are often used both in writing and verbally—you will be in a better position to understand the procedures the physician is performing. Many of these terms are used routinely by estheticians with little knowledge of their derivation. The following is a simple categorical series listing aspects of medical terminology the esthetician should familiarize him/herself with.

Basic Directional Terms

Superior: Structure located towards the head.
Inferior: Structure located towards the feet.
   Example: The chest is superior to the knee.
Anterior: Located towards the front side of the body.
Posterior: Located on the backside of the body.
   Example: The nose is anterior to the back of the skull.
Medial: Structure located more towards the midline.
Lateral: Structure located away from the midline in reference to something else.
   Example: The belly button is medial to the hip bone.
Deep: Something that is away from the surface of the skin.
Superficial: Something that is towards the surface of the skin.
   Example: The epidermis is superficial to the dermis.

Common Prefixes & Suffixes

Prefix	Meaning	Examples
derm	skin	dermabrasion
multi	many	multivitamin
hyper	many	hyperpigmentation
hypo	few	hypopigmentation
poly	many	polysaccharide
epi	upon	epidermis
oligo	few	oligopeptide
a or in	none	inert
iso	equal	isometric
orth	straight	orthodontist
anti	against	antibacterial
sclera/sclero	hard	scleroderma
albin	white	albinism
chlor	green	chlorophyll
cirrih	yellow	cirrhosis
cyan	blue	cyanosis
erythr	red	erythema
melan	black	melanin
leuk	white	leukoderma

Suffix	Meaning	Examples
tomy	incision	tracheotomy
ectomy	removal	appendectomy
stomy	making an opening	colostomy
ose	full of	adipose
oid	likeness, resembling	keloid
gram	record	electrocardiogram
plasty	to form	rhinoplasty
aemia	blood	anemia
itis	inflammation	dermatitis
algia	pain	fibromyalgia
olysis	breakdown	electrolysis
trophy	nourishment	atrophy

Common Abbreviations

Term	Meaning
Bid	Twice a day
Qid	Four times a day
Tid	Three times a day
Qd	Every day
Qod	Every other day
Qam	Every morning
Qpm	Every night
Qhs	At bedtime
Qh	Every hour
q 6 h	Every 6 hours
STAT	Immediately
PRN	As needed
DOB	Date of Birth
c/o	Complains of
Hx/o	History of
Dx	Diagnosis
H & P	History & physical
CC	Chief complaint
y/o or yr o	Years old
BP	Blood pressure
HR	Heart rate
VS	Vital signs
Ht	Height
Wt	Weight
Wnl	Within normal limits
IM	Intramuscular
SQ	Subcutaneous
IV	Intravenous
PO	By mouth
L	Left
R	Right
NPO	Nothing by mouth

Pt	Patient
NKA	No known allergies
NKDA	No known drug allergies

Medication Routes

Term	Meaning
Transdermal	Through the dermis
Subcutaneous	Under the skin
Percutaneous	Through the skin
Sublingual	Under the tongue
Intravenous	Within the vein
Intramuscular	Within the muscle
Oral	By mouth
Rectal	In the rectum

Basic Categories of Surgical/Medical Instruments & Common Uses

Term	Meaning
Suture	To stitch
Cautery	To heat
Excise	To cut out
Debride	To scrape
Lance	To prick
Drain	To remove fluid from

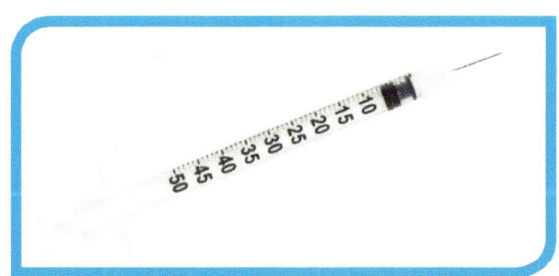

Syringe: A device to inject or withdraw fluid

Appendix A

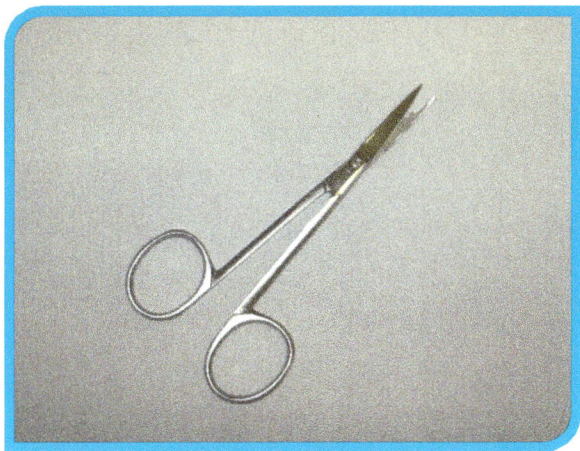
Scissors: Used to cut tissues or supplies

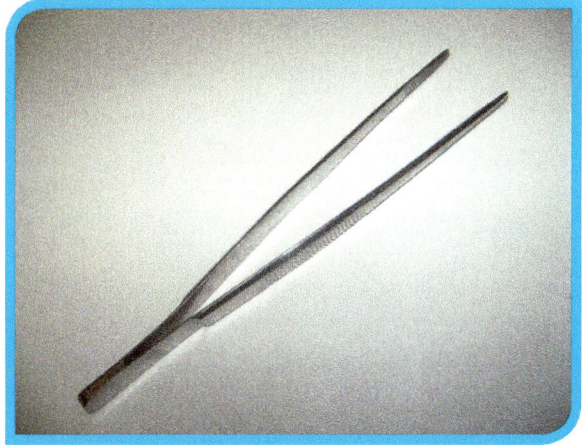
Forceps: Used for grasping, compressing, or holding

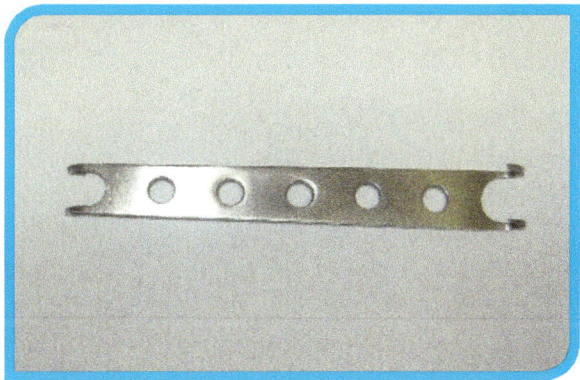
Retractor: Used to hold back or retract

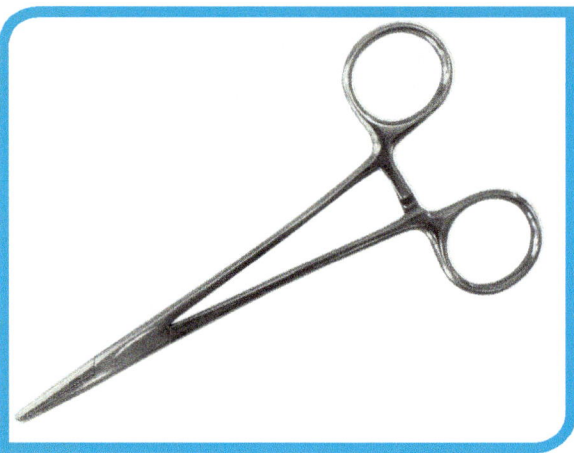

Needle Driver: Used to hold needles attached to sutures

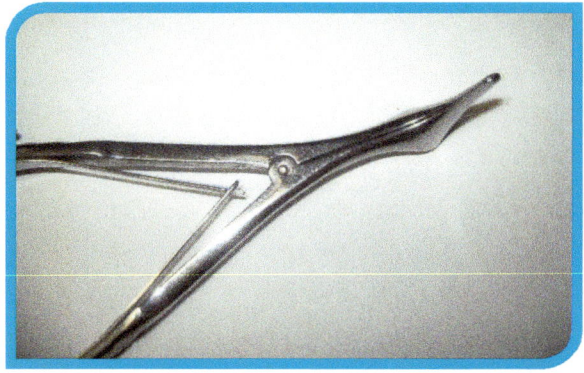

Nasal Speculum: Used to spread nostrils

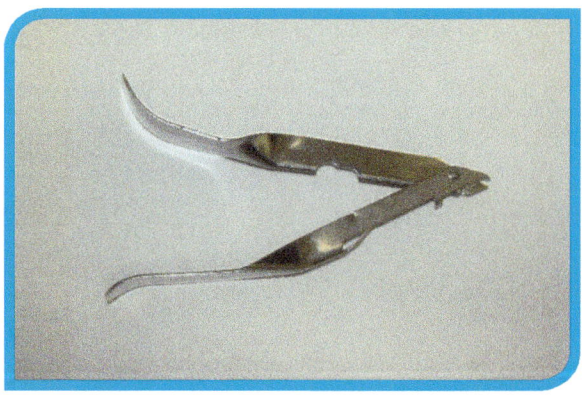

Staple Remover: Used to remove surgical staples

Scalpel: Used to cut or scrape

Anatomy and Skin Physiology

1. **The Main Functions of the Skin**

    Heat regulation: By sweating
    Absorption: Through the acid mantle
    Secretion: Sebum that protects and moisturizes the skin
    Protection: Barrier against invasion of bacteria
    Excretion: Perspiration excretes waste
    Sensation: Through our nerve endings
    The average human body has 2.5 million sweat glands. One square inch of skin has 650 sweat glands, 65 hair follicles, 234 feet of nerves, 57 feet of capillaries, 19,000 sensory cells, 94 sebaceous (oil) glands, 1250 pain receptors, 13 cold and 78 heat receptors, and Langerhans (immune) cells. Human skin is a barrier of protection, but it also can allow substances in.

2. **Layers of the Epidermis and their Functions**

    Stratum corneum (horny layer): Composed of flattened tightly packed keratin
    Stratum lucidum (clear layer): Composed of transparent cells that light can pass through; only present on palms of hands and soles of feet
    Stratum granulosum (granule cell layer): Contain coarse cytoplasmic granules
    Stratum spinosum (prickle cell layer): Composed of polygonal cells; can also be called the spiny layer because of the desmosomes, which are structures that assist in holding cells together
    Stratum germinativum (basal cell layer): Bottom layer composed of basal cells (stem cells)

3. **Layers of the Dermis**

    Papillary layer:
    - Loose collagen

- Blood vessels
- Nerve fibers (Sense of touch)
- Fibrocytes

Reticular layer:
- Fat cells
- Blood vessels
- Lymphatics
- Nerves
- Sebaceous and suderiferous glands
- Fibrous and elastic tissue

Subcutaneous:
- Fatty layer directly below dermis. It gives smoothness and contours to the body.
- The fat is used for energy and acts as a protective cushion for the outer skin.
- Composed of:
  - Fat cells
  - Blood
  - Nerves
  - Lymph supply

4. **Cell Types**
   - Basal cells (Stem Cells)
     - Mother cells that divide to form keratinocytes
     - Sensitive to UV light
   - Langerhan's Cells
     - Clear cells found mainly in the prickle cell layer
     - Microphages used in defense against microorganisms
   - Fibrocytes
     - Main cells in dermis
     - Abundant in papillary, but sparse in reticular
     - Responds to wound injury or stress by producing collagen
   - Keratinocytes
     - Compose most of epidermis
     - They produce keratin that protects skin and underlying tissues
   - Melanocytes
     - Synthesize melanin pigments to protect against UV damage
   - Mast Cells
     - Connective tissue cells that release inflammatory response messages

5. **Desmosomes**
    - Made up of protein
    - Hold cells together
    - Exfoliation can't occur without breaking them apart

6. **Cell Components**
    - *Cell membrane:* Controls passage of materials in and out of the cell; made up of lipids, proteins and carbohydrates; most drugs are lipid-soluble to penetrate the membrane
    - *Nucleus:* DNA and RNA are located here
    - *Lysosomes:* A cell's "garbage disposal"
    - *Ribosomes:* Where translation occurs to make proteins
    - *Centrioles:* Division center of the cell
    - *Golgi apparatus:* Involved in collecting and transporting molecules
    - *Mitochondrian:* Responsible for cellular respiration
    - *Endoplasmic Reticulum:* A transport network

7. **DNA & RNA**
    - Deoxyribonucleic Acid (DNA)
        - Blueprint of all cells that is transported during cell division
        - Codes for the sequence of amino acids in proteins
    - Ribonucleic Acid (RNA)
        - Translator
        - Performs protein synthesis that is directed by the DNA

8. **Suderiferous Glands**
    - Eccrine glands
        - Distributed over the entire body
        - Produce sweat composed of water with various salts
        - Used for body temperature regulation
    - Apocrine Glands
        - Produce sweat that contains fatty materials
        - Mainly present in the armpits and around the genital area
        - Main cause of sweat odor, due to the bacteria that break down the organic compounds in the sweat
        - Emotional stress increases the production of sweat from the apocrine glands

9. **Sebaceous Glands**
    - Primarily in association with hair follicles
    - Also occurs in hairless areas except palms of hands and sole of feet
    - Odorless, but bacterial breakdown can cause odor
    - A mixture of fat and debris of dead fat producing cells

10. Collagen and Elastin
- Collagen:
    - Responsible for skin strength and elasticity
    - It strengthens blood vessels and plays a role in tissue development
    - 80% of skin is Type I
    - Type III is present during wound healing, which later turns to collagen I
- Elastin:
    - Provides elasticity
    - A protein in connective tissue composed of amino acids

11. Main Muscles of Face
- *Frontalis:* Elevates eyebrows
- *Orbicularis Oculi:* Encircles the eye
- *Orbicularis Oris:* Encircles the mouth
- *Zygomaticus major and minor:* Laughing muscles
- *Corrugator:* Frowning muscles
- *Mentales:* Chin muscle

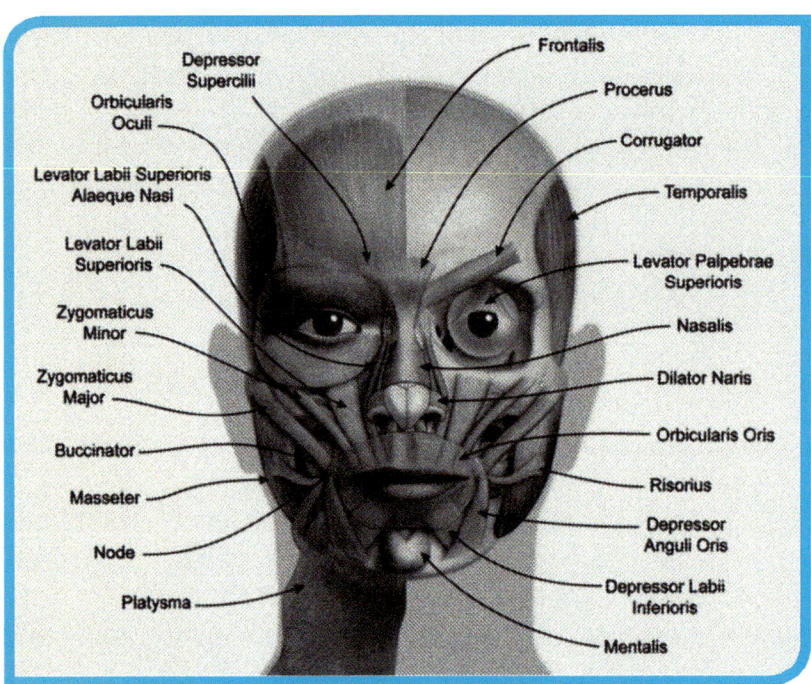

12. Skeletal Bones of the Face
- *Mandible:* Jaw (only U-shaped bone of face)
- *Maxilla:* Forms roof of mouth, houses teeth
- *Frontal bones:* Help form nose and orbit, house frontal sinuses and forehead
- *Nasal bones:* Form nose
- *Zygomatic:* Form cheek bones

13. Biochemistry
- Ionic bonds
    - Giving or taking of electrons
    - Any compound formed by an ionic bond will dissolve
- Covalent bonds
    - Sharing of electrons
    - Most covalent bonds are loosened by water but are not water-soluble
- Free radicals: An unstable molecule trying to stabilize its outer shell
- Antioxidant: Gives needed electrons to the outer shell of the free radical
- pH
    - pH stands for Power of Hydrogen
    - Optimum skin pH is 5.5, but can range from 4.0-7.0
    - pH is important for estheticians for product reaction
- Acids
    - Any substance that breaks apart to release hydrogen ions
    - pH below 7 acidic
- Bases
    - Removes hydrogen ions from a solution
    - pH above 7 alkaline
- Buffers
    - A compound that can stabilize pH by either removing or releasing hydrogen ions; e.g. sodium bicarbonate, Rolaids, Alka-Seltzer
- Proteins
    - Amino acids are building blocks
    - Very sensitive to pH
    - Besides water most plentiful compound in our bodies
    - Proteins can be made water-soluble or fat-soluble by chemical additions
    - Sugars make a protein more hydrophilic
    - Fatty acids make it more hydrophobic
- Carbohydrates
    - Always contain carbon, hydrogen, oxygen
    - Monosaccharides (simple sugars)
    - Disaccharides (lactose and maltose)
    - Polysaccharides (starch, cellulose and glycogen)
- Complex carbohydrates
    - A carbohydrate with another structural component
    - Proteoglycans (carbohydrate and protein): Make up ground substance for cells; e.g. glycosaminoglycans

- Lipids
  - Fats: Serve as energy reserves
  - Phospholipids: Make up a large portion of cell membranes
  - Waxes: Ceramides, protect the skin barrier
  - Steroids: Hormones responsible for many body functions

Appendix B

Standard Operating Procedures (SOPs)

Standard Operating Procedures, more commonly referred to as SOPs, are printed guidelines for any process performed in a medical setting. There should be an SOP to describe in perfect detail tasks as simple as answering phones to those as important as ensuring a patient has the proper consent forms on file. It is pertinent to have a printed copy available on site in the event that a procedure is ever called into question by a higher authority such as the FDA. Examples of a few such procedures are further provided as reference points.

Sample Aesthetic Photo SOP

Complete documentation is essential in medical facilities and photos provide a much better message than words ever could. Taking consistent standardized photos during each appointment allows patients to track their progress, and in the unfortunate event of an adverse reaction, pictures will document the healing process. With the patient's consent, they can also be used for marketing purposes.

Photo Preparation Process

1. Cleanse the client's face to remove makeup.

2. Instruct the patient to remove any jewelry, scarves, glasses, hats, etc., that may obstruct a clean view of the treatment area.

3. Bring the patient into a photo room and instruct the patient to put on a black headband and pull back their hair.

4. Have the patient stand with each foot on the blue lines facing the camera. Inform the patient that you will be giving them instructions on how to position their body towards the camera.

5. Instruct the patient to stand with their palms out (this naturally will straighten their posture). Then instruct them to move their chin up or down and their nose to the left or right; be clear that these small movements will get them in the correct position for the photo.

Photography and Poses

- Use the grid feature on any camera to ensure the Frankfort Plane (imaginary line from tragus to infraorbital rim) is parallel to the floor (as **pictured**)

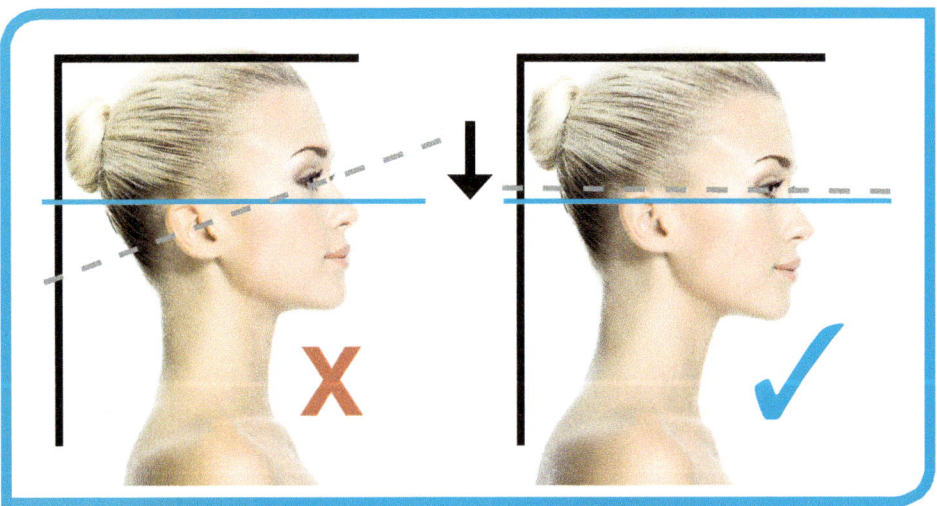

- With full face photos, stand approximately 1.5 m from the patient with the camera in a portrait position. For close-up photos, stand approximately 0.8 m from the patient with the camera in landscape position.
- Ensure the patient has a relaxed expression and that their lips are closed and eyes are open for each photo.
- Give instructions like, "Slowly move your chin down," or "Slowly turn your nose to the left" to achieve the standard poses listed below and **pictured**.

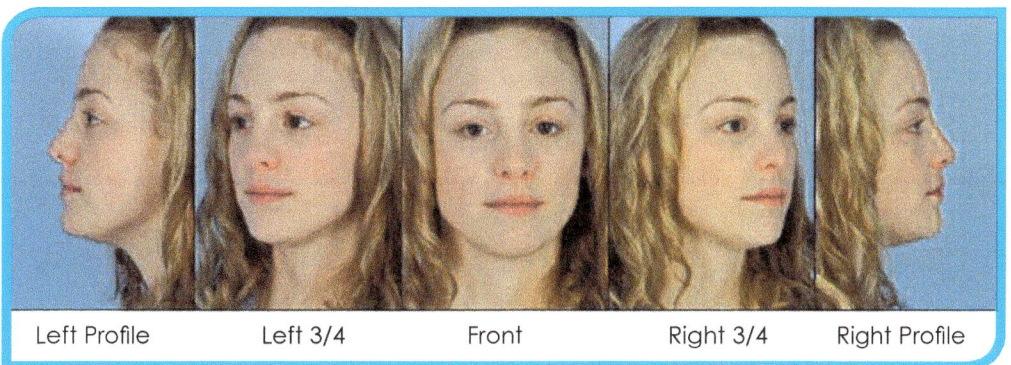

Left Profile   Left 3/4   Front   Right 3/4   Right Profile

Standard Poses (all at 1.5 m)
1. **Frontal**
    a. Make sure the patient doesn't have their chin high or low by checking the Frankfort Plane. For this view, the line on the viewfinder should extend from the right tragus, across both infraorbital rims and across the left tragus. This should be parallel to the floor.

2. **45° Left**
    a. For this view, the tip of the nose should line up with the edge of the cheek.

3. **Left Profile**
    a. For this view, ensure the patient is not rotated to the left or right (*Hint: Look at the eyebrows to see how much of the glabella you see*).

4. **45° Right**
    a. For this view, the tip of the nose should line up with the edge of the cheek.

5. **Right Profile**
    a. For this view, ensure the patient is not rotated to the left or right (*Hint: Look at the eyebrows to see how much of the glabella you see*).

Procedure Specific (all at 0.8 m unless otherwise noted)

1. **Botox (Forehead)**
    a. View 1: Relaxed Pose
    b. View 2: Eyebrows elevated
    c. View 3: Eyebrows furrowed

2. **Botox (Masseters)**
    a. Bottom of photo frame will be patient's chin
    b. View 1: Relaxed Pose
    c. View 2: Jaw clenched

3. **Lips**
    a. View 1: relaxed with lips closed

4. **Rhinoplasty**
    a. Instruct patient to tilt head back as far as possible
    b. The base of the nose should appear just below the glabella

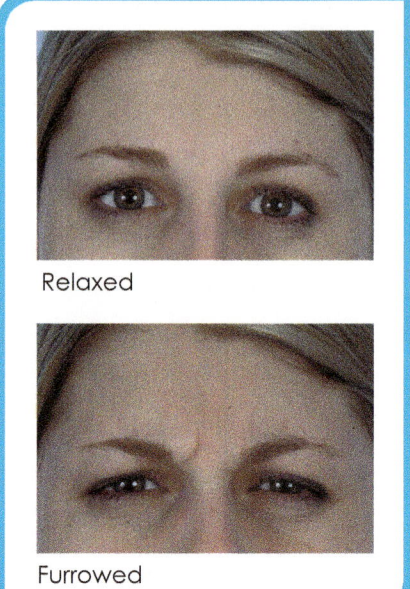

Relaxed

Furrowed

*Please note that the above procedure list is not exhaustive, and critical thinking should be employed when documenting procedural areas outside of what is suggested.

Assisting the Medical Provider

- Once placed into a clinic room, check the patient chart to determine which areas are to be treated and with what type of product or procedure.

- Cleanse the treatment area with a gentle cleanser, and further sterilize by wiping any potential treatment areas with an alcohol or choloroscrub pad.
    - Many times patients are reluctant to be cleansed, as they plan on returning to work and do not want to remove their makeup, but make them aware that this process is necessary in order to prevent any potential bacteria from being poked into the skin along with any penetrating devices or needles during treatment.

- Prepare the clinic area for the medical provider.
    - Set out correctly sized gloves along with pre-mixed treatment product ready to go and laid out in sterile syringes.
    - Any needles should be "hidden" from patient's immediate view in order to maintain a low anxiety level for the patient.

- Once the treatment begins, the assistant should be wearing gloves and have a gauze pad, or "4 x 4," in hand, ready to put pressure on any injection points.
    - Note: Firm pressure inhibits bleeding and aids in reduction of bruise formation.

- While assisting, the left hand should always be used in order to avoid obstruction of the provider's view.

- Once the treatment is done, benzocronium cloths may be used to wipe any excess blood or discoloration.

- When bleeding stops recommended products may be applied.
    - Vitamin K: To ease bruising
    - Vitamin C serum: To support collagen building
    - Vitamin B product: To promote healing and hydration
    - Zinc-oxide based sunscreen: To protect the skin from sun exposure

Sample Pre and Post- Operative Instructions for Patients

The following instructions should be followed closely, except when overruled by specific instructions by your cosmetic surgeon. This is a sample *only*; protocols may differ depending on physician, patient, or surgery.

2 Weeks Prior to Surgery

1. NO aspirin, ibuprofen or naproxen.
    - Tylenol may be taken as directed, if not contraindicated by any current medical condition.
2. Discontinue **all** herbal supplements, whether prescription or over-the-counter.
    - This includes but is not limited to diet pills.
3. **DO NOT** continue taking supplemental doses of vitamin E, although a multi-vitamin that contains a minimal dosage of vitamin E is encouraged.
4. **NO** smoking; this can greatly effect healing.
5. Start taking a multi-vitamin and vitamin C every day and continue taking them through your recovery period.
6. For prescription and over-the-counter medications/supplements, please check with your prescribing provider to see if you are cleared to continue taking your current medications prior to your surgery.

The healthier you are, the quicker your recovery will be!

1 Week Prior to Surgery

1. **DO NOT** drink any alcohol or take any illicit drugs.
2. Please report any signs of a cold or infection (fevers, chills, etc.) to the provider's office immediately.
    - **DO NOT** take any cough or cold medications without permission from the office.
3. Plan ahead. Make the following arrangements, if necessary:
    - Arrange to have an adult friend or family member to take you home from the surgical center on the day of surgery. The patient **WILL NOT** be allowed to leave on their own. A cab or any other form of public transportation is not acceptable.
    - Arrange for a responsible adult to spend the first 24 hours with you. You **CANNOT** be left alone after surgery.

The Night Before Surgery and the Morning of Surgery

1. **DO NOT** eat or drink anything **after midnight the night before your surgery**. If you have any questions regarding these instructions, please feel free to contact our office.
   - This includes but is not limited to gum, candy, mints, coffee and water.
   - You may brush your teeth on the morning of surgery but, again, **DO NOT** drink anything.

2. We encourage you to take a shower on the morning of surgery and wash your face thoroughly with a gentle cleanser.

3. **DO NOT** apply any of the following to your face or hair the morning of surgery: makeup, creams, lotions, serums, hair gels, sprays, perfumes, or powders.

4. **DO NOT** wear your contacts to surgery. If you wear glasses, please be sure to bring them in a case.

5. Wear comfortable, loose fitting clothing that does not require being pulled over your head.
   - A button up or zippered top is best.

6. **DO NOT** wear any jewelry or bring with you any valuables.

7. On arrival, be sure that the operating room staff knows your driver's name and phone number(s) in case they need to be contacted.

8. Please be sure that we have the number of where you can be contacted after surgery. This is very important!

Post-surgery

You must follow instructions from the treating surgeon, as indicated for your specific surgery. Immediately notify the physician with any unusual changes in your condition.

1. You cannot be left alone for the first 24 hours after surgery. The first 24-hour period begins when you are discharged from the surgical facility.

2. The effects of anesthesia can persist for 24 hours. You must exercise extreme caution before engaging in any activity that could be harmful to yourself or others.

3. Drink plenty of fluids to help rid the body of medications used during surgery and to stay hydrated.

4. Eating bland and soft foods for the first day or so is recommended. You must eat more than crackers and juice, otherwise you will continue to feel weak. Also, do not take any of the prescribed medication on an empty stomach, as you may feel uneasy afterward.
5. Please continue to avoid smoking and the use of alcoholic beverages for the next two weeks after surgery for optimal healing results.
6. Take your medications according to the instructions. Your pain medication may make you feel "spacey"; be sure to write down the time these medications are taken or have someone else give them to you.
7. If you experience any generalized itching, rash, wheezing, or tightness in the throat, stop taking all medications and call the office or report to the nearest emergency room immediately, as this may be a sign of a medication allergy.
8. You can expect moderate discomfort after surgery, which should be lessened with the prescribed pain medication. The greatest discomfort is usually during the first 24 hours.
9. After surgery, you may experience constipation from the anesthesia and/or the pain medication. You may take a mild laxative or stool softener to encourage bowel movements.
10. Only participate in minimal activity for the first week. No extreme house cleaning, furniture rearranging, etc. Relax, be pampered, and let your body heal.
11. It is important that you sleep elevated for the first seven days. This requires a pillow under the small of your back, two pillows under your shoulders and head, and a pillow under each elbow. This will help you relax and stay in position.
12. Please remain within a reasonable traveling distance of the office for approximately ten days post-surgery.
13. You may begin to drive approximately five days after surgery. You must be completely off all pain medication prior to operating a vehicle.
14. Make sure to wear a full-spectrum sunscreen with SPF 30 or higher.
15. You may return to work or school when you feel able and are cleared to do so.

Appendix C

Intake Forms, Consents, Checklists & Safety Guidelines

Consent Forms

Securing properly filled-out consent forms is as critical to aesthetic and medical treatment as any other aspect of the procedure. Consents should be comprehensive, addressing the benefits and potential risks of a procedure and also securing permission from the client to perform the treatment and gather photo evidence of the treatment. From both legal and ethical perspectives, consents are essential prior to any treatments being performed.

The following provides examples of photography release forms, HIPPA Privacy Notices, treatment consent, and general product consent. It is important to keep each of these documents updated with regard to any legislation or regulation changes over time.

Record of Authorization for Taking and Publication of Photographs

In connection with the cosmetic or medical services which I am receiving from my provider, I consent that photographs may be taken of me under the following conditions:

- The photographs may be taken only with the consent of my provider, under such conditions and at such time as may be approved by him or her.
- The photographs shall be taken by my provider or by a delegated photographer.

Photographs are necessary for the following:

____ Medical Records Only (Your Patient Chart)

Photographs may be utilized with your consent for the following:

Please review and initial below where appropriate:

____ Medical Related Research, Education or Science.

____ Medical Books, Professional Journals, or Professional Videos.

____ "Practice name" Office Literature, Speaking Engagements, Consultation and Instructional Booklets or for General Information.

____ Public Relation Purposes, including use in Newspapers, Magazines, Brochures and Computer Programs for Public Interest and Information.

Please review and circle below where appropriate:

A. My photographs may be utilized by the office of "Practice Name" for the purposes initialed above and my identity may be made known.

B. My photographs may be utilized by the office of "Practice Name" for the purposes initialed above as long as my identity is *not* made known.

_____ _____
Printed Name of Patient   Date

_____ _____
Patient/Guardian's Signature   Date

_____ _____
Provider's Signature   Date

Appendix C

General Treatment Consent

Consent Form
(Specify Name of Treatment)

I voluntarily ask for treatment of mild to moderate wrinkles utilizing a skin tightening device called X. This device was granted FDA clearance as a skin tightening system for non-ablative treatment of mild to moderate facial rhytids (wrinkles).

Possible Risks
- Your condition may improve if you choose to have this treatment.
- Currently known risks include (list known treatment risks; *for example superficial burns*).
- In addition to the risks or discomforts listed here, there may be other risks that are currently not known.
- Also the risks or discomforts described may occur more often or be more severe than has been seen before.

Possible Benefits
Your symptoms of facial wrinkles may improve while having this treatment.

Subject's Statement of Consent
- I have been told that this is a skin tightening device that utilizes radio frequency.
- To the best of my knowledge, I am not pregnant.
- Receiving this treatment is voluntary.
- I understand that more than one treatment may be required to obtain significant improvement, and despite multiple treatments, the improvements are not permanent.
- I have had an opportunity to ask my provider questions about this procedure and my questions so far have been answered to my satisfaction.
- I understand the treated area may have some discomfort, appear red, and/or irritated areas. The effects can last from minutes to days.
- I have been told what the possible risks and benefits are from receiving this treatment.

_____   _____
Patient Signature   Date

_____   _____
Signature of Provider   Date

HIPAA Notice of Privacy Practices

THIS NOTICE DESCRIBES HOW MEDICAL INFORMATION ABOUT YOU MAY BE USED AND DISCLOSED AND HOW YOU CAN GET ACCESS TO THIS INFORMATION. PLEASE REVIEW IT CAREFULLY.

This Notice of Privacy Practices describes how we may use and disclose your protected health information (PHI) to carry out treatment, payment or health care operations and for other purposes that are permitted or required by law. It also describes your rights to access and control your protected health information. "Protected Health Information" is information about you, including demographic information, that may identify you and that relates to your past, present or future physical or mental health or condition and related health care services.

Uses and Disclosures of Protected Health Information

Your protected health information may be used and disclosed by your physician, our office staff and others outside of our office that are involved in your care and treatment for the purpose of providing health care services to you, to pay your health care bills, to support the operation or procedure of the physician's practice, and any other use required by law.

Treatment: We will use and disclose your protected health information to provide, coordinate, or manage your health care and any related services. This may include, but is not limited to the coordination or management of your health care with a third party. For example, we would disclose your protected health information, as necessary, to a home health agency that provides care to you. Your protected health information may also be provided to a physician to whom you have been referred to ensure that the physician has the necessary information to diagnose or treat you.

Payment: Your protected health information will be used, as needed, to obtain payment for your health care services. For example, obtaining approval for a biopsy may require that your relevant protected health information be disclosed to the health plan to obtain approval for the laboratory services.

Healthcare Operations: We may use or disclose, as-needed, your protected health information in order to support the business activities of your physician's practice. These activities include, but are not limited to, quality assessment activities, employee review activities, training of medical students, and licensing. For example, we may disclose your protected health information to medical school students that see patients at our office. We may also call you by name in the waiting room when your clinician is ready to see you. We may use or disclose your protected health information, as necessary, to contact you to remind you of your appointment.

We may use or disclose your protected health information in the following situations without your authorization. These situations include: as Required By Law, Public Health issues as required by law, Communicable Diseases; Health Oversight; Abuse or Neglect; Food and Drug Administration requirements; Legal Proceedings; Law Enforcement; Research; Criminal Activity; Workers' Compensation; Required Uses and Disclosures. Under the law, we must make disclosures to you and when required by the Secretary of the Department of Health and Human Services to investigate or determine our compliance with the requirements of Section 164.500.

Other Permitted and Required Uses and Disclosures will be made only with your Consent, Authorization, or Opportunity to object, unless required by law.

You may revoke this authorization, at any time, in writing, except to the extent that your physician or the physician's practice has taken an action in reliance on the use or disclosure indicated in the authorization.

Your Rights
Following is a statement of your rights with respect to your protected health information.

You have the right to inspect and copy your protected health information. Under federal law, however, you may not inspect or copy the following records: psychotherapy notes; information compiled in reasonable anticipation of, or use in, a civil, criminal, or administrative action or proceeding, and protected health information that is subject to law that prohibits access to protected health information.

You have the right to request a restriction of your protected health information. This means you may ask us not to use or disclose any part of your protected health information for the purposes of treatment, payment or healthcare operations. You may also request that any part of your protected health information not be disclosed to family members or friends who may be involved in your care or for notification purposes as described in this Notice of Privacy Practices. Your request must state the specific restriction requested and to whom you want the restriction to apply.

Your physician is not required to agree to a restriction that you may request. If your physician believes it is in your best interest to permit use and disclosure of your protected health information, your protected health information will not be restricted. You then have the right to use another Healthcare Professional.

You have the right to request to receive confidential communications from us by alternative means or at an alternative location. You have the right to obtain a paper copy of this notice from us, upon request, even if you have agreed to accept this notice alternatively i.e. electronically.

You may have the right to have your physician amend your protected health information. If we deny your request for amendment, you have the right to file a statement of disagreement with us and we may prepare a rebuttal to your statement and will provide you with a copy of any such rebuttal.

You have the right to receive an accounting of certain disclosures we have made, if any, of your protected health information. We reserve the right to change the terms of this notice and will inform you by mail of any changes. You then have the right to object or withdraw as provided in this notice.

Complaints
You may complain to us or to the Secretary of Health and Human Services if you believe your privacy rights have been violated by us. You may file a complaint with us by notifying our privacy contact of your complaint. **We will not retaliate against you for filing a complaint.**

We are required by law to maintain the privacy of, and provide individuals with, this notice of our legal duties and privacy practices with respect to protected health information.

Signature below is only acknowledgement that you have received this Notice of our Privacy Practices:

_____   _____
Printed Name of Patient/Guardian   Date

_____   _____
Signature of Patient/Guardian   Date

CHECKLISTS (Including Fitzpatrick Worksheet)

Once a patient has consented to a particular treatment, the provider needs to assure that the treatment is safe. This is streamlined by going through a series of checklists such as concomitant medications that may interfere adversely with the treatment or treatment products. A second checklist that is particularly important in skin care is a Fitzpatrick rating. This provides the patient with a numerical baseline skin type, which may be used in safely choosing the correct products and laser settings. Examples of each are as follows.

General Photo-sensitizing Medication Checklist: All medications should be checked prior to any treatment. If uncertain, medical consent must be given before any light-based therapies.

Antibiotics agents:
- Quinolones
- Tetracyclines
- Sulfonamides

Antifungal agents:
- Flucytosine
- Griseofulvin
- Terconazole

Antihistamines agents:
- Diphenhydramine
- Promethazine

Antimalarial agents:
- Quinine
- Chloroquine
- Hydroxychloroquine

Cancer chemotherapy agents:
- 5-fluorouracil
- Vinblastine
- Dacarbazine

Cardiovascular agents:
- Amiodarone
- Nifedipine
- Quinidine
- Diltiazem
- Furosemide
- Thiazides

Antidiabetic agents
- Sulfonylureas

Skin agents:
- Photodynamic therapy for skin cancer
- Paba
- Tretinoin
- Isotretinoin
- Acitretin

Antipsychotic agents:
- Phenothiazines
- Chlorpromazine

General Photo-sensitizing Conditions Checklist

Care must be taken dependent on light source: These conditions can be affected by one or more areas of the light spectrum; therefore medical consent must be given before any light-based therapies.

- Hydroa vacciniforme
- Polymorphic light eruption
- Juvenile spring eruption
- Actinic prurigo
- Solar urticaria
- Chronic actinic dermatitis
- Porphyria cutanea tarda
- Erythropoeitic protoporphyria
- Variegate porphyria
- Lupus erythematosus (especially subacute and systemic forms)
- Dermatomyositis
- Darier's disease
- Rosacea
- Pemphigus
- Atopic dermatitis
- Psoriasis
- Xeroderma pigmentosum
- Bloom syndrome
- Rothmund Thomson syndrome
- Epilepsy

Fitzpatrick Skin Type Worksheet

Name: _____ Date: _____

What is your ethnic background? _____

Score		0	1	2	3	4
	What is the color of your eyes?	Light Blue, Gray or Green	Blue, Gray, or Green	Blue	Dark Brown	Brownish Black
	What is your natural hair color?	Sandy Red	Blond	Chestnut, Dark Blond	Dark Brown	Black
	What is the color of your unexposed skin?	Reddish	Very Pale	Pale with Beige Tint	Light Brown	Dark Brown
	Do you have Freckles on Sun exposed areas?	Many	Several	Few	Incidental	None
	What happens when you stay in the sun to long?	Painful Redness, Blistering, Peeling	Blistering Followed	Burns sometimes followed by Peeling	Rare Burns	Never had Burns
	To what degree do you turn Brown?	Hardly or Not at all	Light color Tan	Reasonable Tan	Tan Very Easily	Turn Dark Brown Quickly
	Do you turn brown several hours after sun exposure?	Never	Seldom	Sometimes	Often	Always
	How does your face respond to the Sun?	Very Sensitive	Sensitive	Normal	Very Resistant	Never had a Problem
	When did you last expose yourself to the sun tanning bed or self-tanning creams?	More than 3 Months ago	2-3 Months ago	1-2 Months ago	Less Than 1 Month ago	Less than 2 Weeks ago
	Do you expose the area to be treated to the sun?	Never	Hardly Ever	Sometimes	Often	Always

Total Score:	Score	Fitzpatrick Skin Type:
_____	0-7	I
	8-16	II
Skin Type:	17-25	III
_____	26-30	IV
	Over 30	V-VI

Laser and Light Therapy Pre-Treatment Checklist

Patient Name: _____ DOB: _____ Date: _____

Allergies: _____

Current Medications: _____

Review Prior to Each Treatment	Yes	No	NA
Any changes in health or skin disorders/conditions			
Any changes in medications or supplements			
Use of medications or over-the-counter supplements that may cause photosensitivity in the time since your last treatment (antibiotics, St John's Wart, etc)			
Pregnant or possibility of pregnancy, postpartum or nursing			
Recent sun-exposure, use of tanning beds or self-tanners			
Inflammatory skin conditions (dermatitis, etc)			
Hx of cold sores, open lacerations or abrasions on the treatment area			
Any recent resurfacing procedures: fraxel, chemical peels, dermabrasion, etc.			
Abnormal photosensitivity (sensitive reaction to sun)			
Use of Retin-A or glycolic acid in the last three days			
Completed at Initial Treatment			
History of vitiligo or psoriasis (koebernizing skin disorder)			
History of keloids or hypertrophic scarring			
Presence of tattoo, permanent makeup, or moles in the treatment area			
Active Systemic Lupus or any active autoimmune disorder			
Uncontrolled Diabetes			
Active Cancer (currently on chemotherapy or radiation)			
Active HIV/ AIDS/ Hepatitis			
Use of oral isotrentinoin (Accutane®) within the past year			

Laser Safety Guideline Checklist

General Contraindications:

- Pregnancy and breast feeding
- Present tan, including self-tanners
- Photo-sensitizing medications
- Medical conditions associated with photo-sensitivity
- Auto-immune disorders
- Cancer
- Diabetics, dependent on laser
- History of keloid scarring (thick dark scarring)
- Open wounds or lesions near the area
- Herpes Simplex (cold sores): We can treat you if a cold sore is not present, as long as you understand that laser can, in some instances, trigger the onset of a cold sore. You may talk to your doctor about taking an anti-viral medication before and after treatments to prevent possible breakouts.
- Epilepsy
- Hepatitis/HIV
- Lymphatic/Immune system disorders
- Steroid Therapy
- Pacemaker
- Raised moles, birthmarks, or any suspicious lesions
- Tattoos including permanent makeup in the area (unless that is the chromophores)
- Patients who are unlikely to follow the post treatment guidelines
- Those with unrealistic expectations

Safety Precautions:

- Laser Eyewear Protection
    - Must be based on specific wavelengths
    - Glasses or goggles of sufficient **optical density most OD 4-8** level of reduction for laser beam i.e. $10^4 = 10,000$ (allows 1/10,000) of the beam through eyewear
    - Must have side shields to protect from peripheral injury and impact
    - Sanitize goggles before use and follow the manufacture procedure for cleaning
    - Must be inspected for cracks, holes, scratches, discoloration, or other damage before and after each procedure
    - Patient goggles with elastic band must fit snugly

- Treatment Room Set-up
    - No flammable materials left visible in the room
    - No reflective materials such as fancy glass vases, chandelier or mirrors should be present
    - Metal implements should be put away, not left on countertops
    - Windows must be covered with the flame retardant material of the appropriate ocular density.
    - Adequate ventilation should be installed to reduce any toxic contaminants or potentially hazardous fumes
    - For ablative procedures a plume evacuator to remove Laser-generated air contaminants (LGAC) is required, as well as filtration masks
    - A fire extinguisher is to be kept nearby rooms during procedures
- During Treatment
    - A sign stating *Danger: Visible and/or invisible laser radiation, avoid eye or skin exposures to direct or scattered radiation* must be put on the door before laser use
    - The door to the laser room should be closed but never locked
    - The laser hand piece must be cleaned according to manufacturer instructions
    - Technician and patient should remove any reflective jewelry
    - Hands must be sanitized before the procedure and gloves are mandatory.
    - The safety-belt for the laser hand-piece must be placed around the wrist for added protection
    - A test patch should be done in each area being treated, waiting the appropriate amount for that skin color
    - While working with laser on different part of the body, you must place the laser machine on standby mode to move to the other side of the body treated area.
    - When operating the laser machine, the hand laser piece should be pointed towards the ground and never look into the distal end of the hand piece

Appendix D

Documentation Practices

When a client comes into the office, the first thing that they will do is fill out a medical history form that should outline their entire prior health and treatment records. Although most patients will diligently and honestly answer each question, it is not uncommon for a certain percentage of your client base to be in a hurry to get treated and fail to disclose important information to the provider, either on purpose or as a simple "mental slip-up." No matter, it is critical that the provider go through each question with the patient once they are in the treatment room. Specifically, any answers that pertain to possible contraindications with treatment options should be clarified. Typically this initial intake form is only filled out during the first visit and will remain on file unless subsequent updates are required. It is important to ask before each visit "Have you had any change in health or medications since your last visit?" Being sure to start on the right foot requires working with the the patient to dig thoroughly through their history by using proper documentation.

General Health History Form

(Circle One) Miss. Ms. Mrs. Mr. Dr.   Date_____

First Name: _____ Middle Initial: ____ Last Name: _____

Address: _____

City: _____ State: _____ Zip: _____

Home Telephone: (____)_____ *Mobile: (____)_____ *Could affect skin condition or treatment choice*

Work Telephone: (____)_____ Occupation: _____

Date of Birth: _____ Age: ____ What is your hereditary background? — *Helps determine Fitzpatrick type*

*Email Address: _____@_____

How would you describe your skin? ❏ Oily ❏ Sensitive ❏ Dry ❏ Normal ❏ Combination

Have you received any of the following procedures?   *Helps you gain a sense of how they view their skin and compare it to your findings*

❏ Chemical Peel   ❏ Facial Ultrasound   ❏ Eyelash/Eyebrow Ti
❏ Microdermabrasion   ❏ Facial   ❏ Waxing
❏ Dermaplaning   ❏ Laser Hair Removal   ❏ Skin Care Products

Other: _____ *Gaining feedback on the client's past experiences with previous treatments will help determine current course of action*

If yes, please explain:_____

_____

Have you used any of the following topical/oral medications?

❏ Accutane®   ❏ Differin®   ❏ Retin-A®   ❏ Avage®
❏ Renova®   ❏ Tazarac®   ❏ Trentinoin   ❏ EpiDuo®
❏ Hydroquinone   ❏ Topical Antibiotics ❏ Alpha Hydroxy Acids   ❏ Ziana®

Other:__ *The use of certain products can sensitize the skin and/or be contraindicated for specific treatments*

Current Medications   **Current Herbal Supplements**
(Include Birth Control and Over The Counter)   **and Vitamins**

1. _____   1. _____
2. _____   2. _____
3. _____   3. _____
4. _____   *Certain medications are contraindicated to treatments or ingredients.*
5. _____
6. _____   6. _____
7. _____   7. _____
8. _____   8. _____

Habits:	Never	Frequency Of Use	# Of Years	Date Late Used
Tobacco		packs/day		
Alcohol		beverages/day		
Caffeine		glasses/day		
Drugs Used:				

Lifestyle may affect different aspects of the skin

Allergies (Food, Latex or Medications) ❏ Yes ❏ No if yes, please list:
_____

Distinguish ALLERGY (shock, hives, & swelling) from ADVERSE REACTION (nausea & upset stomach)

Avoid allergic reactions by ensuring that you are not using any product ingredient to which the client has had a negative reaction.

MEDICAL HISTORY

Have you ever had any of the following conditions?

Condition			Note
Acne	☐ Yes	☐ No	*Determine stage before deciding proper treatment*
Arthritis	☐ Yes	☐ No	*Use caution in massage*
Diabetes	☐ Yes	☐ No	*Be aware of the lack of wound response*
Severe Headache/Migraine	☐ Yes	☐ No	*Fragrance, light therapy may trigger*
Cold Sores/Fever Blisters	☐ Yes	☐ No	*Certain treatments may cause an outbreak*
Seizures	☐ Yes	☐ No	*Light therapies must be avoided*
Cancer	☐ Yes	☐ No	*Skin sensitivity and wound-healing impaired*
Heart Conditions	☐ Yes	☐ No	*Products containing phenol should not be used*
Pacemaker/Metal Implants	☐ Yes	☐ No	*Avoid Radio Frequency/Electrotherapies*
Hepatitis	☐ Yes	☐ No	*Avoid causing a wound response*
Skin Disorder (i.e. Dermatitis)	☐ Yes	☐ No	*If present, don't treat refer to physician*
Hypertrophic scaring (i.e. Keloids)	☐ Yes	☐ No	*Aggressive treatments should be avoided*
Bleeding Disorder (i.e. Anemia)	☐ Yes	☐ No	*Avoid treatments where blood may be drawn*
HIV/AIDS	☐ Yes	☐ No	*Avoid causing a wound response*
Thyroid Disease	☐ Yes	☐ No	*Avoid causing a wound response*
Lupus	☐ Yes	☐ No	*Avoid causing a wound response*

REVIEW OF SYSTEMS

How much water do you consume daily? _____ — *Regular water consumption helps keep the skin hydrated*

How much caffeine do you consume daily? _____ — *Regular caffeine consumption can dehydrate the skin*

Do you currently have a sunburn/windburn or red face? ☐ Yes ☐ No — *Best not to treat for 24 hours*

Are you in the habit of using tanning booths? ☐ Yes ☐ No

Are you pregnant or breast feeding? — *Tanning is not safe and only facials should be done*

Do you wear contact lenses or eyeglasses? ☐ Yes ☐ No — *Beware of contraindications*

Do you have intolerance to heat or cold? ☐ Yes ☐ No

Do you have any other medical concerns that have not been covered in this form? ☐ Yes ☐ No — *Contacts need to be removed for some treatments*

If yes, please explain: *Good insight to help predict treatment sensitivities*

_____

Do you understand that every procedure/ operation is followed by a period of healing before the tissue returns to normal and the final result is apparent? ☐ Yes ☐ No

Do you understand that the objective of any cosmetic procedure is an improvement not perfection? ☐ Yes ☐ No

This is important and should be laid out specifically in individual consents per procedure

_____ _____
Patient Signature   Date

_____ _____
Parent/Guardian Signature (If under the age of 18 years) Date

_____ _____
Health Care Provider Signature Date

Procedural Notes

Once a health history is gathered, each and every treatment must be recorded. Documentation of health care services must be complete for both ethical and legal reasons. The most commonly used form of documentation is called the SOAP approach. SOAP stands for *subjective, objective, assessment*, and *plan*. The subjective covers what the patient comes in feeling or what their personal goal of the treatment session is. The objective aspect is gathered from the provider; this includes an examination of the skin or any conditions that may be notable. The assessment stage is the processing and examination of all the facts presented in order to reach a conclusion. Finally, the plan is what the treatment regimen will consist of and extends beyond not only the current treatment, but also any actions moving forward such as a follow-up skin care regimens that may have been discussed. Below is an example SOAP note, followed by another, modified version of the same note—this one "filled out."

Name: _____ DOB: _____ Date: _____

S: _____

_____

Consent on file for procedure/s being done today: ❏ YES ❏ NO
Pre-Laser Check List completed: ❏ YES ❏ NO

Photographs Taken: ❏ YES ❏ NO
If NO, why: _____ Taken By? Initials: _____
O:
Will treatment be performed today? ❏ YES ❏ NO
If NO, why? _____

Treatment Area(s):		Fitzpatrick Skin Type:
_____		I II III IV V VI
_____		

Hair Color:	Hair Texture:
Blonde/Red	Fine
Light Brown	Coarse
Dark Brown	Dense
Black	

Treatment area cleansed with: Alcohol Other: _____ Patient shaved: ❏ YES ❏ NO/NA
If NO, PT was shaved by: _____

Topical anesthetic applied: ❏ YES ❏ NO If YES, Where: _____ 30% Lidocaine
Other: _____ Time Allotted: _____

Treatment Summary:
Laser Hair Removal treatment performed with:
❏ Alexandrite 755nm ❏ Diode 810nm ❏ Nd:Yag 1064nm

_____
_____
_____
_____
_____

TREATMENT #	Additional Notes:
	_____
	_____
	_____

ALL possible risks and benefits were reviewed with the patient and contact information supplied:
❏ YES ❏ NO If NO, why: _____

Follow Up: _____ Practitioner Signature: _____

Initial consultation performed by: _____ (Medical Provider)

Name: _____ Jane Smith _____ **DOB:** _____ **Date:** _____

S: _____ Pt CC- smile lines and brown spots on forehead _____

Any change in health condition (including current pregnancy or breast-feeding) since completing original demographics form? ☒ NO ☐ YES, explain: _____
Any change in medications since completing original demographics form?
☒ NO ☐ YES, explain: _____

Any Known Allergies? ☐ NO ☒ YES, list: _____ Sulfa, PCN _____

Photographs Taken Today? ☒ YES ☐ NO, please explain: _____ **Taken By? Initials:** _____

O:

+moderate volume loss in the NLF

+mild pigmentation on forehead

A: _____

Consent on file for procedure(s) being performed today? ☒ YES ☐ NO ☐ NA

All risks, benefits and possible limitations of the procedure(s) being performed today were discussed with the patient and all questions were answered.
☒ YES ☐ NO ☐ NA _____

Pre-Laser Check List completed/reviewed: ☒ YES ☐ NO ☐ NA

Treatment Preparation: (Alcohol) Benzalkonium Chloride Betadine Avagard Other: _____

Topical Anesthetic ☐ YES ☒ NO 30% Lidocaine Other: _____ Where: _____ Time Allotted: ___

Nerve Block ☒ YES ☐ NO
(Infraorbital/Mental) Septocaine or (Mepivacaine 3% Plain) 20% Benzacaine Oral Anesthetic

P.

Product:	Quantity:	Application:
Botox		
Dysport		
Restylane/L	2	1 vial to each NLF
Juvederm Ultra/XC		
Juvederm Ultra Plus/XC		
Perlane/L		
Radiesse		
Misc	IPL	1 pass, 1 stack on forehead

Additional Notes: _____ Pt tolerated well . Ice pack was given post-tx _____

Recommended Treatment Plan: _____ Package of 3-5 IPL treatments to the forehead _____

Follow Up: _____ 2 weeks prn _____ **Practitioner Signature:** _____

GLOSSARY

Ablative	Removal of material from the surface of an object by vaporization or other erosive process.
Ablative or hot lasers	Lasers that remove wrinkles by heating water in the skin to a boiling point and vaporizing the skin cell.
Abrade	To rub off; to scrape away.
Absorption	The uptake of a product or substance by a tissue.
Accutane	A trade name for Isotretinoin; a retinoid derived from Vitamin A that inhibits sebaceous gland function and the process of keritinzation. Usually prescribed for severe cases of acne. Its side effects continue to be controversial.
Acetone	A colorless by-product resulting from the oxidation of fats with extreme frying properties. Commonly used as a solvent in nail polish removers and used in aesthetics to remove surface oils or fats before certain medical procedures.
Acetyl Hexapeptide-3	See Argireline.
Acetylated lanolin	A product of the oil glands of sheep that is a natural emulsifier; used in many cosmetics and is highly comedogenic.
Acne	A chronic inflammatory disorder of the sebaceous glands that occurs when hair follicles become clogged with sebum (oil), dead skin cells and bacteria.
Acne Grade I	The mildest form of acne consisting of blackheads and whiteheads with no inflammation.
Acne Grade II	A form of acne mainly consisting of blackheads and whiteheads with few papules and pustules.
Acne Grade III	A form of acne usually consisting of a combination of whiteheads and blackheads along with papules and pustules, consistent with inflammation.
Acne Grade IV	A Severly inflamed form of acne with blackheads, whiteheads, papules, pustules, nodule and/or cysts.
Acne Simplex	Grades I and II acne, consisting mainly of open and closed comodones with little to no inflammation present.
Acne Vulgaris	Grades III and IV acne which are bacterial infections of follicles that are characterized by papules and pustules. There are typically several signs of infections present including soreness, inflammation, pus, and redness.
Actinic keratoses	A common pre-malignant growth on the skin that results from excessive sun exposure. Identified by an irregular border that is usually red-pink in color and scaly. Also known as solar keratoses.
Active ingredients	Ingredients used in product formulations that are meant to carry out an action on the skin.
Active voice	Placing emphasis on the verb or action of a statement.

Add-on service	An additional service not previously discussed in consultation that can benefit client total satisfaction and serve as additional revenue for the skin care center.
Adrenal gland	An endocrine gland positioned slightly above each kidney in the posterior abdomen, each compromised of an outer layer (cortex) and an inner core (medulla).
Adverse effect	A unexpected side-effect of something that is typically harmful or different than the desired outcome.
Aerobic	A state that occurs when molecular oxygen is present.
Aesthetics	The philisophical concerns of beauty, outward corrections, feelings towards art and creation.
Age management medicine	Healthcare focused on the preservation of the quality of life and physical health of the aging population.
Albumin	A water-soluble protein; in the body, it is found in muscle and blood serum or plasma.
Alcohol	A solvent widely used in the cosmetic industry which is a by-product of fermentation of starch, sugar and other carbohydrates. When applied externally, it has antiseptic and disinfectant properties.
Alkanet	An ingredient used in hair oils and other cosmetics that produces a red coloring; it is extracted from an herblike tree root found in Asia and Mediterranean.
Allergan, Inc	A pharmaceutical company most recognized for the neurologic product Botox and Botox Cosmetic.
Allergenic	A substance or an ingredient that potentially could provoke an allergic reaction.
Alpha hydroxy acids (AHAs)	Organic acids that are extracted from naturally occuring sources found in fruits (malic acid, citric acid, tartaric acid), sugar (gycolic acid), bitter almonds (mandelic), and milk (lactic acid). When placed in a skin care product, the normal desquamation (shedding) of the superficial layer of the epidermis results in a healthier texture.
Alpha Lipoic Acid	Also known as thiotic acid, it is lipid- and water-soluble antioxidant making it easily accepted by the skin. It is promoted to repair protein damage, also enhances the effects of vitamin C and E and controls inflammation.
Ambergris	A substance historically used as a preservative in perfumes. Has a wax-like consistency and secreted from sperm whales.
Aminoguanidine	A guanidine derivative found in mushrooms, mussels, and turnip juice, which prevents glycation of cells.
Amphadase	A hyaluronidase enzyme, commonly used to reverse the action of a hyaluronic acid filler.
Amplification	Production of trillions of protons of the same wavelength and direction.
Amplitude	The measurement that describes how tall each wave of a wavelength is.

Anabolic steroids	A steroid hormone that can be used to increase muscle mass. Also used to stimulate appetite or induce male puberty. This type of steroid is associated with masculine properties.
Anaerobic bacteria	Bacteria that cannot live in an oxygen-rich environment.
Anagen stage	The active growth stage of hair.
Androgens	Male hormones responsible for the development of the male reproductive system and secondary male sexual characteristics such as voice depth and facial hair.
Anesthetics	A substance that reduces sensitivity to pain.
Aniline	A coal tar that is considered a poison in its natural state. Its use in such products as hair dyes, medicinals and perfumes is controversial, as it is a potential carcinogen.
Animal exudate	A fluid that has leaked out of an animal's pores, usually as a result of inflammation.
Annatto	A substance extracted from the pulp of the achiote seed, which is found on the achiote tree in the tropical regions of the Americas; used as a food additive or as a red food coloring.
Anovulation	The absence of ovulation during a time in which ovulation is expected.
Antibody	Complex proteins used by the immune system to identify and neutralize pathogenic substances such as bacteria or viruses.
Anticoagulants	A substance that prevents blood from clotting.
Antifibrotic	Inhibiting or reducing fibrotic activity in connective tissue.
Antigen-specific	Referring to molecules that stimulate a specific immune response.
Antihistamines	A substance that works against histamine in the body. Often used to treat allergies.
Antioxidants	A molecule that fights off free radicals to reduce damage due to unstable oxygen. Some examples include vitamin C, vitamin E, and beta-carotene.
Antiseptics	A sanitizing antimicrobial substance that inhibits the growth of mircobes (such as bacteria, viruses, fungi) on the surface of skin.
Apricot kernel oil	An oil derived from the inner portion of the apricot pit. Known for its mosturizing properties and often used in the manufacturing of soap.
Aquaphor	A healing ointment used on dry or irritated skin as a protective skin barrier. It is commonly used for post-laser healing.
Arbutin (Bearberry)	Extracted from the bearberry plant to aid in skin-lightening by stopping the formation of melanin inhibiting tyrosinase.
Argireline	Also known as Acetyl Hexapeptide-3. A chain of 6 amino acids formulated to relax facial muscle contractions that lead to "expression lines." It works by decreasing muscle activity by slowing the release of catecholamine , a neurotransmitter that causes muscle contractions.
Argon laser	Produces wavelengths in the bluegreen spectrum and absorbs melanin and oxyhemoglobin in blood. Often used to treat skin disorders such as hemangiomas, superficial spider viens, and rosacea.

Aromatherapy	The therapeutic use of scents from organic material, typically used in the form of essential oils, to alter a person's phycological state, emotional well-being, or voluntary sensory function.
Artefill	A facial filler using polymethylmethacrylate microspheres surrounded by bovine collagen.
Asphyxiated	In a state of decreased oxygen and increased carbon dioxide in the body.
Aspirin	A medication with anti-clotting properties, often used to reduce pain and/or reduce a fever.
Astringents	A substance that typically results in contstriction of body tissues. Examples include witch hazel and calamine lotion.
Attributes	Particular personal or professional qualities that one possesses.
Autonomic nervous system	The system of nerves comprised of three sub-systems: the sympathetic, parasympathetic and enteric nervous systems.
Aversion Response	Action, such as closing the eye or moving the head to avoid exposure to laser light, typically .025 seconds.
Avocado oil	An oil produced by the avacado. May be used in cosmetics for its mosturizing effects.
Azelaic acid	Lightens pigment by inhibiting the enzyme tyrosinase. It also has antibacterial properties and is commonly used for the treatment of rosacea. This is a good lightening agent for those with acne who are prone to post-inflammatory hyperpigmentation due to its lightening and antibacterial properties.
Bacilli	A class of bacteria comprised of two parts that contain pathogens.
Basal metabolism	The minimum amount of energy required to maintain the body's vital functions.
Base color	The foundational color. Can be considered first or last depending on the application.
B-cells	A group of white blood cells (lymphocytes) that are a key component in the humoral immune response. Their key function is to produce antibodies.
Beam	A collection of rays which may be parallel, divergent, or convergent.
Bearberry extract	A tyrosinase inhibitor used in many skin lightnening agents. Also known as arbutin.
Beet powder	A substance derived from ripe beets. Occasionally used in lipstick.
Benadryl (diphenhydramine)	An anti-histamine often used to treat allergic reactions; however not commonly used today to treat allergies due to its sedative properties.
Benzoyl Peroxide (BPO)	A peroxide often used to treat acne due to its antibacterial effects on the skin. May also be used in hair dyes or teeth-whitening systems.
Beta Carotene	A compound with antioxidant characteristics. Beta carotene can be converted to retinol and subsequently retinoic acid, which can play an important role in the health of skin.
Beta Hydroxy Acids	An organic compound that is also referred to as salicylic acid. Can be used to treat acne or in anti-aging products.

Betacaine	A topical anesthetic, often used during cosmetic procedures, such as injectables or hair removal.
Binge	A behavior done in excess (such as binge eating).
Bioflavonoids	Biologically active compounds found in citrus and other fruits. Often known for their anti-oxidant properties. Also known as flavonoids.
Blackhead	Also called open comedone; a clogged pore with a dark appearance caused form oxidation.
Blepharitis	Inflammation of the eyelids.
Blepharoplasty	Surgery of the upper or lower eyelid to remove excess tissue or alter the eye.
Blepharospasm	An abnormal spasm of the eyelid.
Bloodborne pathogens	Microorganisms in the blood that can result in disease, such as hepatits or HIV.
Body dysmorphic disorder	A mental illness in which an individual is obsessed or overly concerned with one or many aspects of his/her appearance.
Botanical	A substance derived from plants.
Botulism	A paralytic disease that is a result of exposure of the toxin Botulin. The illness is rare, yet often lethal if contracted.
Boundary	A small but healthy separation from your patients' emotional issues.
Buffers	A substance that, when added, alters the pH of a solution.
Butylparaben	A preservative used in cosmetics that also has anti-fungal properties.
Calcium hydroxylapatite	An ingredient found in the popular facial filler Radiesse. It is a constituent of teeth and bone.
Cancer	A class of disease where a group of cells show uncontrolled growth, invade and destroy normal cells, and may spread to other locations in the body.
Caramel	An ingredient commonly used in cosmetics for coloring a product, made from sugar
Carbon Dioxide Laser	A laser that uses a long wavelength (10,600 nanometers), which is attracted to the water in the skin. Often used in aesthetics for resurfacing procedures.
Cardiac arrhythmias	An irregular beating of the heart.
Carotene	A provitamin that can be stored in the liver and then converted to vitamin A when needed.
Castor oil	A clear and thick oil that comes from castor beans that is used as a lubricant.
Catecholamine	A neurotransmitter that causes muscle contractions. Also a hormone that the adrenal gland releases when the body is under stress.
Cauterized	To burn, sear, or freeze tissue.
Cavitation	The microscopic bubbling of blood, lymphatic and tissue fluids.
Cellular immunity	Immunity that activates antigen-specific T-lymphocytes, macrophages and natural killer cells.

Cellulite	A skin condition where subcutaneous fat shows as a dimpled appearance on the epidermis.
Central nervous system	A subdivision of the nervous system, which includes the brain and spinal cord and is responsible for behavior by way of sensory information.
Ceramides	Natural fats in skin that allow it to retain moisture.
Cerebral Palsy	A group of nonprogressive disorders of movement and posture caused by abnormal development of, or damage to, motor control centers of the brain.
Cervical Dystonia	A focal dystonia, or sustained contractions that affect the neck and sometimes the shoulders having symptoms including involuntary contracting of the neck muscles, causing abnormal movements and awkward posture of the head and neck.
Ceteareth 20	An emulsifying wax used in cosmetic products.
Chemical peel	A cosmetic procedure where a specific acid is applied to the face in order to obtain various cosmetic results.
Chloasma	See **Melasma**.
Chlorophyll	A green pigment found in most plants.
Cholesterol	A lipid found in cell membranes, responsible for many body functions.
Chromophore	A colored chemical capable of selective light absorption. Used as a target in laser and light therapy treatments.
Citric acid	A weak acid that is used as a preservative and commonly used as a flavoring agent.
Clindamycin	An antibiotic used to treat anaerobic bacterial infections. Commonly used internally or topically to treat acne.
Coagulation	A disruption of tissue to resulting in a chemical change.
Coenzyme Q10 (Ubiquinone)	Powerful antioxidant that protects and revitalizes skin cells.
Coherent	Having or being on the same path; as in coherent light.
Collagen	Protein fiber produced by fibroblasts which makes up about 70 percent of the dermis.
Collimated	A laser light that is a single wavelength of light which is harnessed, focused and directed.
Colorants	A dye, pigment, ink or similar agent that is used to add or change color in many cosmetics to enhance the appeal of the product to the consumer.
Comedones	Clogged pores caused by a buildup of debris, oil, and dead skin cells. Open comedones are referred to as blackheads; closed comedones are referred to as whiteheads.
Compression wrapping	A method of wrapping the limbs or affected areas, and applying pressure to facilitate lymph movement.
Concierge	A service available to guests that offers detailed customer care and assistance.

Conjunctivitis	Inflammation or redness of the lining of the white part of the eye and the underside of the eyelid. Also known as pink eye.
Consent form	A document including possible complications that can arise from a particular procedure for a patient to sign.
Consultation	A meeting or discussion to evaluate a client's concerns.
Continuous Wave (CW) Laser	A laser in which energy output is constant.
Contouring	Using highlighting and shading to create depth or corrections in a design; in aesthetics in regard to camouflage makeup.
Contraindication	A symptom or condition that gives reason to withold a specific treatment.
Copper	A trace mineral present in every cell in the body; has been shown to stimulate collagen, elastin, and glycosaminoglycans.
Corneocyte adhesion	The bonding together of keratinized cells of the skin; peeling is often required to separate them.
Crepiness	Very fine lines creating uneven texture to the surface of the skin. Often due to dehydration.
Crest	Part of a wave with the greatest magnitude.
Cross-promote	Promoting features and benefits of treatments or products to clients that would coincide with treatment or products the client is currently using.
Curare	A poison that originated from South America.
Customer service	Demonstrating professionalism, care, and tact to achieve customer satisfaction with products or services.
Cyclomethicone	A clear and odorless silicone that is used as a base to blend with fragrance and perfume oils.
Cystic acne	A severe form of acne characterized by cysts.
Cytokines	Signaling proteins used in cellular communication which are secreted by immune cells that have been confronted by pathogen.
Cytotoxicity	Being toxic to cells.
D-alpha-tocopherol	The form of vitamin E that is readily absorbed and accumulated in humans.
D&C	Abbreviation for "Drug and Cosmetic."
Decongestant	A broad classification of medicine that is used to relieve symptoms of nasal congestion.
Deep-plane lift	A surgery procedure where tissue in the mid facial region and the cheekbones is lifted and repositioned.
Degreasing	The process of removing excess bacteria and sebum in preperation for skin resurfacing procedures.
Dehydration	Lack of moisture or water. Can be identified by crepy skin.
Demodex mite	A parasite that lives in or near hair follicles. There is evidence that links this mite to rosacea.
Denature	To change the structure, or nature, of something.

Dendrites	Arms or branches of a cell that extend to carry information to other cells.
Depigmentation	The loss of normal color.
Depilatory	A substance that uses a chemical agent to dissolve the hair shaft at the level of the skin, but does not affect the root or bulb.
Dermabrasion	A cosmetic medical procedure that removes the epidermis and often portions of the papillary dermis through the process of abrasion.
Dermal implanting	Placing of an implant into the skin to alter the appearance of an area by adding volume.
Dermaplaning	The use of a scalpel to gently abrade dead surface skin and vellus hair.
Dermatitis	Inflammation of the skin.
Dermatochalsis	Excessive skin on the eyelid.
Dermatologist	A physician who specializes in the treatment of the skin.
Desmosomes	Hair-like structure made of protein that anchor cells to each other.
Detergent	An agent that is used to cleanse.
DHEA	Dehydroepiandrosterone, a hormone precursor claimed to enhance immunity, memory and neural functioning; used topically in anti-aging formulations.
Diabetes	A metabolic disorder in which high blood glucose levels are present due to low insulin levels.
Diazolidinyl urea	A preservative used in cosmetics to prevent microbial growth.
Differin	A trade name for a medication that is used to treat acne. The active ingredient in this product is adapalene, a derivative of vitamin A.
Diuretics	Any drug that increases the rate at which the body removes excess water through urination.
DMAE	Dimethylaminoethanol, a primary alcohol that helps stabilize cell membranes protecting them from free radical damage, helps expel waste and hold on to valuable skin enhancing nutrients
DNA	Deoxyribonucleic acid (DNA) is a molecule that encodes the genetic instructions used in the development and functioning of all known living organisms and many viruses.
Down time	Brief periods of idle time when activity either slows or ceases. In aesthetics, a period of time the client may not be able to carry about normal activities.
Drainage	Natural flow or forced manipulation of the removal of water or fluids from surface and subsurface areas.
Dramamine (dimenhydrinate)	An anti-nausea medication.
Dry eye syndrome	A disease of the eye that is caused by a decrease in the production of tears.
Dyschromias	Discolorations of the skin, ooften seen as red from vasular or brown from pigmentation.
Ecchymoses	A bruise.

Edema	The increase or acculumation of interstitial fluid, swelling caused by impaired or slow lymphatic (removal) system.
Effleurage	A light stroking massage technique commonly used in manual lymphatic drainage massage techniques.
Elastin	A connective tissue protein that allows body tissue to stretch and return to their orignal state.
Electromagnetic Radiation	The radiated energy created by the motion of waves created from energy in the electromagmetic spectrum.
Electromagnetic spectrum	The range of all possible frequencies of electromagnetic radiation. It refers to the characteristic distribution of electromagnetic radiation emitted or absorbed by a particular object.
Electrolysis	A procedure that deposits electrical energy to each individual hair follicle, thus destroying the follicle through direct current.
Electron	The elementary particle of an atom that orbits the nucleus and pairs with protons to give atoms their nuclear weight.
Ellagic Acid	An antioxidant that is found in many fruits and vegetables; used topically as a skin-lightening agent.
Embolism	The blockage of a blood vessel by a foreign object. It can be caused from a clot, an air bubble, bacteria, etc.
Emission	Molecular process in which energy is released.
Emollients	A substance which softens, smooths and soothes the skin.
Emulsifying wax	A cosmetic ingredient that binds oil and water together.
Emulsion	A mixture of two immiscible substances, like water and oil, with the help of a binder.
Energy (Q)	The capacity for doing work and creating a change of a physical state.
Epidermal Growth Factor—EGF	A growth factor that accelerates skin rejuvenation, proliferation, and differentiation during tissue normal growth/repair.
Epidermis	Outermost layer of the skin that functions to protect and cover the dermis, as well as all organs of the body.
Epithelial cells	Skin cells that create an epithelium membrane.
Epithelium	The protective membrane that surrounds the surface of a cavity, mainly in animals.
Erbium:YAG laser	A laser which produces energy in the mid-infrared portion of the light spectrum; commonly used in resurfacing lasers.
Erythema	Redness of the skin caused by increased blood flow due and dilation of capillaries, often caused by inflammation or infection.
Erythematotelangiectasic rosacea	Type of rosacea noted by flushing that persists for longer than ten minutes, often associated with burning and stinging.
Erythromycin	An antibiotic that is used to treat many different types of bacterial infections including acne.
Essential oils	Oils extracted from plants that are used in perfumes, as flavorings, and in aromatherapy.
Esthetic	The branch of philosophy dealing with beauty.

Ethanol	A commonly used solvent that has the ability to dry out skin causing reddness or flaking.
Evening primrose oil	An oil that is extracted from the seeds of the evening primrose, used topically as an anti-inflammatory.
Exfoliate	A cosmetic technique by which dead skin cells are removed from the face or body.
Extrinsic aging	Aging caused from external factors; such as environment, health, nutrition, sun exposure and stress.
Facelift	A cosmetic surgery procedure that is intended to give a person's face and neck a more youthful appearance by tightening the skin. Also called a rhytidectomy.
Far-infrared	Infrared light found between 5,000–15,000 nm.
FD&C	Abbreviation for "Food, Drug and Cosmetic."
Fibroblast	A type of cell responsible for the production of collagen, which forms the structural framework of connective tissues.
Fibrosis	An increased production of connective tissue.
Fish oil	An oil extracted from fish that is said to be rich in Omega-3 fatty acids.
Fluence	The measure of energy delivered typically J/cm2.
Folliculitis	An infection of the hair follicles characterized by red-ringed papules.
Food and Drug Administration	A United States regulatory agency that oversees the safety of most foods and drugs. Abbreviation is FDA.
Foreign-body reaction	An inflammatory response of the bodies tissues.
Fractionated resurfacing	A skin rejuvenation procedure that uses a difractionated lens, treating only portions of the skin at a time. Commonly used for treating acne scars, photo-damage, sunspots and wrinkles.
Fragrance	A substance used to provide a pleasant odor to a product.
Free radicals	Highly reactive molecules that can cause damage to the body. Triggered by environmental components including sun exposure.
Galvanic	An electrical current procedure that uses cataphoresis and anaphoresis to penetrate products into skin.
Gamma ray	Electromagnetic radiation with wavelengths shorter than approximately one tenth of a nanometer.
Garlic	A plant that has been used as food and as an herbal supplement for its antioxidant properties.
Gas	A substance with the molecular proerty of indefinate expansion such as CO_2, Argon, and Krypton.
Glabella	The smooth area between the eyebrows above the nose.
Glycation	The result of an uncontrolled sugar molecule attacking proteins causing damage to the body.
Glycerin	A cosmetic ingredient that is used as a skin softener, humectant and strong water binder.

Glycogen	Glucose that is stored in the liver or muscle tissue.
Glycolic Acid	An alpha hydroxy acid derived from sugar cane, used as exfoliant that helps to break down intercellular structures. It has the smallest molecular size of all AHAs and has been shown to strengthen collagen fibers. It can be used as a degreasing agent.
Granulomas	A localized nodule found in tissues. May be caused by biological, chemical or physical irritants.
Grape seed	A powerful antioxidant and natural emollient with soothing properties.
Grounding pad	A pad commonly used with monopolar radio frequency energy. It is an inactive electrode attached to the patient to close the circuit to return current.
Growth factors	Any of several substances that affects the growth of a cell or organism.
Growth hormone	A protein hormone that is a major participant in growth and metabolism.
Hemangiomas	A raised lesion on the skin which is a buildup of blood vessels. It is a birthmark sometimes called a strawberry mark.
Hematomas	Bruising as result of internal bleeding; typically injury related. They are not limited to the skin surface, but can also occur in organs and form into welt-like formations.
Hemorrhage	An abnormal flow of blood.
Hepatitis B	A viral infection of the liver. This infection can be acute or chronic. It is transmitted through infected blood or body fluids.
Highlighting	Making an area stand out or protrude forward as in contouring.
HIPAA	An abbreviation for Health Insurance Portability and Accountablility Act.
HIV	An abbreviation for Human Immunodeficiency Virus; causes failure of the human immune system.
Hodgkin's disease	Also known as Hodgkin's lymphoma, a type of cancer derived from lymphocytes (while blood cells). The disease was discovered by Thomas Hodgkin in 1832.
Humectant	An ingredient that attracts water.
Hyaluronic acid	A naturally occurring carbohydrate (polysaccharide) found in the space between the cells in our skin. It plays an important role in tissue hydration, lubrication, and cellular function. It holds more water than any other natural substance. The amount of hyaluronic acid a person has decreases with age and is correlated with wrinkling, which is the reason why many products that fight the signs of aging use this ingredient. It also provides an excellent environment for the growth of new cells and healing after peeling treatments.
Hyaluronidase	An enzyme that is used to break down hyaluronic acid.
Hydrated	To contain water.
Hydrogen peroxide	A liquid that is widely used as a bleaching agent, an oxidizing agent, and as an antiseptic.

Hyperandrogenism	An excessive amounts of androgens in the body.
Hyperemic	Increased and excessive blood in a tissue.
Hyperhidrosis	Condition resulting in excessive sweating primarily on the hands, feet, underarms and groin area.
Hyperkinesis	An abnormal increase of muscular activity.
Hyperpigmentation	Skin dicoloration caused by an overproduction of melanin; an increase in the natural color of the skin.
Hypertrophic scar	An elevated scar with deposits of excessive amounts of collagen.
Hypodermis	The layer of tissue directly below the dermis often noted as the subcutaneous layer that houses the fibroblast, microphage, and adipose cells.
Hypopigmentation	Depletion of melanin or melanocytes causing skin to lack pigment, commonly seen as white patches.
Ibuprofen	A non-steroidal anti-inflammatory drug that may cause thinning of the blood.
Ice-pick scarring	Pitted scars that cause a V-shape in the skin, looking like it was punctured with an ice pick, often caused from severe acne.
Idebenone	A powerful antioxidant used to repair photo-damage and prevent signs of aging by capturing and neutralizing free radicals caused by environmental stress.
Imidazolidinyl urea	A cosmetic preservative used to prevent bacterial growth.
Inactive ingredients	Ingredients that are used to make the product look, feel, and smell better.
Incentive	An enticement offering to encourage a customer response or act from a marketing standpoint.
Inflammation	A physiologic response to tissue damage that is characterized by redness, swelling and pain.
Infrared Radiation	Electromagnetic radiation with wavelengths from 700 nm to 1 mm, commonly used in aesthetic laser procedures
In-office procedures	Procedures performed in a medical office as opposed to a hospital or surgery center.
Intense pulsed light	Light therapy that uses multiple colors of the light spectrum for overall skin rejuvenation. Commonly used to treat skin discolorations and to stimulate collagen.
Interleukine-5 and 6	Chemical messengers that cause inflammation in the skin, which can be major components of aging skin and increased sensitivity.
Interstitial fluid	Extracellular fluid that is made up of interstitial fluid, plasma, and trancellular fluid.
Interview	A formal meeting to discuss professional attributes and answer questions from potential employers.
Infraorbital rim	The area beneath the orbit of the eye, lower part of eye socket.
Intrinsic aging	The skin's natural aging process, from genetics resulting in a loss of subcutaneous fat, a decrease in collagen

Invisible light	Waves on the electromagnetic spectrum not visible by the naked eye such as ultraviolet light or infrared light.
Ionizing	The process of a molecule gaining or losing an electron.
Ions	Active eletrons.
Iron oxide	A red pigment that is used in colorants, adhevises, plastics, and paper.
Joule	A unit of energy (1 joule = 1 watt/second).
Keloids	An overgrowth of fibrous tissue resulting after skin injury, leaving large bulky scars that grow beyond their wounded area.
Keratitis	Inflammation of the cornea.
Kinetin - N6-furfuryladenine	A plant hormone that protects the skin from free radical damage.
Kojic acid	Works as a tyrosinase inhibitor. It is derived from fungi as a by-product of the fermentation process. Usually made in concentrations of 1% to 4%, kojic acid can be an irritant to the skin, causing contact dermatitis, therefore a patch test should be done prior to use.
KTP Laser	Potassium-titanyl-phosphate laser at 532 nm range of light spectrum, commonly used for superficial vascular lesions and pigmentation.
Lactic Acid	An AHA found naturally in milk and sugars that is commonly used in skin care products and in peels. It has hydrating and skin-lightening properties. It is gentler than glycolic acid and is found naturally in the skin.
Langerhans Cells	Cells which help protect the body from foreign substances that want to enter the body; found mainly in the stratum spinosum layer of the skin.
Lanolin	An occlusive moisturizer; may cause allergic contact dermatitis.
L-Arginine	Found in almonds, leafy vegetables, and walnuts. It acts as an antioxidant and is used in skin care products promoting wound repair.
Larynx	The medical term for voice box; it is the organ through which air passes to the lungs. It houses the vocal cords.
L-Ascorbic acid	The most commonly used water-soluble form of vitamin C. It must be formulated with better than 10% concentration and at a pH below 3.5 to be effective. L-ascorbic acid also has skin-lightening properties and is shown to strengthen collagen fibers.
Laser	Acronym for Light Amplification by Stimulated Emission of Radiation.
Laser mediums	Substances in which laser energies can flow.
Laser resurfacing	A resurfacing procedure using a beam of light to dissolve the layers of damaged skin at various levels of penetration; as a result, new skin cells are formed and collagen and elastin are produced. It is used to treat fine lines, wrinkles, hyperpigmentation and to minimize the appearance of scars.
Laser Safety Officer	Individual who has the responsibility and authority to monitor and enforce the control of lasers.

Laureth sulfate	An ingredient used in cosmetics such as shampoo and cleansers; derived from lauryl alcohol, it has foaming action.
L-Carnosine	A substance found in the brain, heart, muscles, and skin; prevents the breakdown of lipids, keeps cell membranes intact and prevents glycosylation.
L-Cysteine	Found in liver and pumpkins. A sulfur amino acid, it is an amazing anti-inflammatory ingredient and antioxidant, and has also been used to help regulate melanin production.
L-Glutathione	An antioxidant naturally found in the body, it strengthens and rebuilds collagen bonds thereby eliminating and preventing wrinkles.
L-Glycine	Found in high concentrations in the connective and skin tissues, it is great for promoting the healing of wounded tissues.
Licorice extract	An effective tyrosinase inhibitor used in many skin care formulations.
Lidocaine	A local anesthetic that is often used in aesthetics as a nerve block to reduce pain.
Light	Potential to be visible or invisible dependent upon wavelength.
Lipoatrophy	A loss of subcutaneous fatty tissue in the body.
Liquid	A substance containing free flowing molecules with a definite weight and volume.
L-Lysine	Found mostly in red meat, poultry and milk, L-lysine is an essential amino acid that cannot be produced by the body. It prevents glycation and nourishes the skin.
Loose Connective Tissue	A thin mesh-like tissue whose functions as a cushion to body organs; located in the skin beneath the dermis and epithelial tissue for the entire body.
L-Proline	A substance predominately taken from animal sources; a major component of the collagen protein, it is most effective when applied topically with vitamin C. Proline aids in the synthesis and retention of collagen.
Lubricant	A substance that reduces friction and adds "slip" to products.
Lunchtime procedures	A cosmetic procedures that take a short amount of time and allows for a client/patient to return to work with no down time.
Lycopene	Found in guava, rosehip, tomatoes, and watermelon, and is one of the most effective carotenoids for protecting the crucial parts of a cell, including DNA.
Lymph	A colorless body fluid that filters the blood and tissues, helping to remove toxins.
Lymph node	Filtering stations composed of adenoid tissue which continually produces white blood cells and whose sole function is to hold back and/or destroy harmful substances and bacteria.
Manual Lymphatic Drainage (MLD)	A procedure using a light pumping technique intended to improve the circulation of lymph throughout the body in order to induce relaxation, reduce edema, remove toxins, and improve specific conditions.

Glossary

Lymphatic system	A network of tissues and organs that primarily consists of lymph vessels, lymph nodes and lymph, helps rid the body of toxins, waste and other unwanted material.
Lymphedema	Fluid retention or accumulation due to a slowed or compromised lymphatic system.
Lymphocyte	A group of white blood cells of lymphoid tissue that participate in immunity.
Lymphoid tissue	A part of the body's immune system that helps protect it from bacteria and other foreign entities.
Lymphologists	Persons who studies and/or works with the lymphatic system.
Macrophages	A type of immune tissue cell that digest cellular bebris and pathogens while stimulating other lymphocytes to respond to pathogen.
Macule	A primary lesion that causes discoloration of the skin. It can appear as flat, round, oval or irrregular shape. An example would be a freckle.
Magnesium aluminum silicate	A substance used as a thickener in cosmetic products.
Malic acid	An alpha hydroxy acid found naturally in apples. It has exfoliating, brightening, and hydrating properties.
Maser	A device for amplifying electromagnetic waves by stimulated emission of radiation.
Masseter	A muscle that assists in the process of chewing.
Mastoid process	The bony prominence of the skull, located at the base of the skull behind the ear.
Maximum Permissible Exposure (MPE)	The maximum level of laser radiation to which a human can be exposed without adverse biological effetcs to the eye or skin.
Medical Esthetician	An esthetician working in the medical field. This is not a title recognized by licensing.
Melanin	Pigment created in melanosome sacs of the stratenum germinativum layer of the epidermis that determines the depth of color in humans, animals, and mammals.
Melanocytes	Epidermal cells that synthesize melanin. Responsible for producing color in the skin.
Melanophages	Immune cells that contain melanin due to ingestion, a process called phagocytosis.
Melanosomes	Organelles which synthesize and store melanin.
Melasma	A dark irregular discoloration of the skin typically found in women with darker skin types, those taking oral contraceptives and pregnancy patients.
Metal	A chemical element or alloy such as gold or copper that serve as diodes of electricity.
Methylparaben	A substance, also known as methyl p-hydroxybenzoate, that has anti-microbial properties and is used as a preservative in cosmetics.
Metronidazole	A chemical used commonly in the treatment of rosacea, as an antibacterial and/or antiprotozoal drug.

Microdermabrasion	A procedure commonly used by estheticians to exfoliate the epidermis of the skin using crystals or a diamond tip and suction simultaneously.
Microwaves	Waves from .01–10 nm of the electromagnetic spectrum used for telecommunication, microwave ovens, and radar technology.
Mineral makeup	Cosmetics primarily composed of pure minerals that are said to be beneficial to skin.
Mineral oil	A mixture of refined hydrocarbons derived from petroleum used in many cosmetic products; has lubricant and protective properties.
Moisturizer	A product used to replenish, protect and balance the moisture of the skin.
Molds	A group of fungi that act as parasites or saprophytes growing on organic substances.
Monochramatic	A grouping only comprised of different shades/tones of one hue.
Monoethanolamine (MEA)	A surfactant that has medium viscosity.
Monounsaturated fats	Fatty acids that have one double band; diets rich in monosaturated fats are healthy.
Motrin	A non-steroidal anti-inflammatory drug that may cause thinning of the blood.
Musk	A brown fetid substance used in perfumes that is extracted from the follicles of a small hornless deer.
Nanometer	A unit that measures the wavelength of light.
Nanosecond	One billionth of a second.
Nasal columella	The vertical strip of tissue separating the nostrils.
Nasolabial folds	The skin folds that run from corners of the nose to the sides of the mouth. Most common area to get injected with soft-tissue fillers.
Near infrared	Infrared light on the electromagnetic spectrum found between 750–2,000 nm.
Neocollagenesis	The process of eliminating damaged collagen and replacing it with healthy collagen
Nervous system	A highly complex frame or network of nerves (neurons) that interconnect while using electrochemical signals or stimuli found within nervous tissue.
Networking	A professional tool used to create new opportunities by cultivating relationships with other professional or like minded individuals.
Neutrophilis	A type of phagocyte that releases cytotoxic cells which is part of the wound healing process.
Nominal Hazard Zone (NHZ)	The zone inside which laser radiation that is direct, reflected, or scattered exceeds the MPE for the laser.
Nonablative	A laser therapy technique in which light penetrates the papilary layer to activate skin renewal without removing the upper layers of skin.
Non-ionizing	Non-dangerous radiation that has enough energy to move atoms in a molecule around or vibrate them, but not enough energy to remove any electrons.

NSAIDs	Nonsteroidal anti-inflammatory drugs.
Nuprin	Trade name for a nonsteroidal anti-inflammatory drug containing ibuprofen.
Nutraceuticals	Nutritional supplements that are used as professional only products.
Obesity	An excess accumulation of body fat.
Ocular rosacea	Type of rosacea with the presence of red, watery, swollen eyes as well as burning, stinging and even blurred vision.
Off-label	A drug legally prescribed to treat a condition other than what is specified and approved of on the label by the FDA.
Omega-3	An essential fatty acid found most conmmonly in fish, green leafy vegetables and supplements.
Oral	Taken by mouth.
OSHA	Occupational Safety and Health Administration; this administration regulates health and saftey in the workplace.
Osteoporosis	A bone disease characterized by fragile or brittle bones.
Over-the-counter	Medication or topical products that can be purchased without a perscription.
Oxyhemoglobin	Bright red arterial blood cells that have been oxygenated in the lungs.
Palmitoyl Pentapeptide	At market under the trade name Matrixyl synthe'6, it is the newest generation of Matrixyl, said to have the similar but more advanced properties than palmitoyl pentapeptide.
Palmitoyl Tetrapeptide	At market under the trade name Rigin, it mimics DHEA and controls the production of chemical messengers that cause inflammation in the skin.
Paper mulberry	A tyrosinase inhibitor. It is not very strong compared with other agents but shows a very low risk of irritation and is effective with other lightening ingredients.
Papules	Solid palpable lesion less than 10 mm in diameter; examples, warts, elevated pimples.
Papulopustular rosacea	Classical rosacea characterized by a red central portion of the face with small papules as well as flushing, episodic inflammation and even chronic edema. There is usually burning and stinging of the skin.
Peyer's patches	Oval elevated patches of closley packed lymph follicles on the mucosa of the small intestine, named after 17th century Swiss anatomist Johann Conrad Peyer.
Perimenopause	The term used to define the timeframe before and after menopause.
Perlane	A hyaluronic based injectable filler from the company Medicis.
Peroxide	An oxygen group that contains a single bond.
Petechia	Small purplish spots on the skin. Small 1–2 mm cause by a local hemmorhage.
Petrolatum	Petroleum jelly, commonly used in cosmetic medicine as a skin protectant.

Phagocytes	Biological white blood cells that ingest and destroy foreign material and substances.
Phenol Acid Peel	A deep chemical peels used to treat sun-damaged skin. Not commonly used anymore due to the potential adverse reactions.
Phenoxyethanol	An oily liquid with antibacterial effects, that is used widely in perfumes and in topical anesthetics.
Phlebitis	Inflammation of veins.
Phonophoresis	The process of penetration of topicals and products into the skin's surface.
Photodynamic therapy	A therapy where medicines are applied to the skin or taken as a pill that will go into the skin and lie dormant until a laser light hits them and turns them "on" at which time they start to work.
Photomechanical	The use of light to mechanically breakdown a chromaphore or target.
Photon	An elementary particle that has 0 mass and charge and a spin of 1.
Photothermal	Using light to heat up and destroy a target.
Phyllanthus emblica	From the emblica tree, it is a highly stable source of ascorbic acid. It provides antioxidant properties and may protect DNA. It is also an effective tyrosinase inhibitor.
Phymatous rosacea	Rosacea characterized with marked skin thickening and irregular surface nodularities leading to rhinophyma, gnathophyma and metophyma. There is also pronounced redness and telangiectasia at this stage.
Picosecond	One trillionth of a second.
Platelets	Cells that circulate and bind together when they recognize damaged blood vessels.
Platysma	Superficial neck muscle used during facial expression.
Poikiloderma	A harmless skin condition that produces areas of physical changes to the skin such as hyperpigmentation and atrophy.
Polycystic ovarian syndrome	An endocrine disease with the primary symptoms being: irregular menses, weight gain and signs of excessive androgenic (masculine) hormones.
Polyethylene glycol	A plastic material that is also a binder and solvent; acts as a softener in cosmetics as well as pharmaceuticals.
Polyhydroxy acids (PHAs)	A newer exfoliating ingredient shown to be as effective as alphahydroxy acids with less irritation and more moisturizing properties.
Poly-L-lactic acid	An acid used as a product that stimulates the skin and increases collagen production. Can be used to treat wrinkles.
Polysaccharide	An organic compound composed of carbon, hydrogen and oxygen. Part of the carbohydrate group.
Polysorbate	An ingredient in cosmetics that acts as an emulsifier and can stabilize oils in water.
Polyunsaturated fat	"Healthy" fat that contains animal and vegetable oils, may lower cholesterol.

Pomegranate extract	A substance that has high levels of polyphenols and is reported to increase sun protection factor power by 20%.
Porphyrins	Group of naturaly occuring organic compounds. A well-known porphyrin is called "heme". It is the pigment found in red blood cells.
Port Wine Stain	A birthmark that is swollen blood vessels creates a deep reddish-purplish discoloration on the skin.
Power	The rate at which energy is emitted, transferred, or received, usually expressed in watts (joules per second).
Pre-book	Setting a future appointment for services prior to customer coming into the skin care center.
Premenopause	The term used to define the timeframe before menopause.
Preservatives	Compounds used in foods or cosmetics that limit microbial growth including bacteria.
Primer	A makeup base that provides a smooth finish to the skin and increases the longevity of makeup wear.
Prism	A clear normally triangular object used for dispersing light into a spectrum or for reflecting rays of light.
Professionalism	A powerful, positive impression that represents a person showing confidence and poise in and out of the workplace.
Propionibacterium acnes	A bacteria that is present on most people's skin but can be linked to acne.
Propylene glycol	One of the most common moisture-carrying ingredients used in cosmetics. It is very permeable and acts as a solvent and moisturizing ingredient.
Propylparaben	A compound widely used as preservatives in cosmetics; also helps kill fungus and bacteria.
Proteins	Organic compounds composed of amino acid chains joined by a chemical bond (peptide bonds).
Pseudofolliculitis barbae	A condition that is characterized by irritation and inflammation of the skin, often due to shaving. Most commonly seen on the face in individuals with eliptical hair.
Psoriasis	A chronic skin disease resulting in red, scaly plaques on the skin.
Ptosis (of the eyelid)	The drooping of the upper eyelid.
Pulse Width/ Pulse Duration	The amount of time specified to deliver light energy.
Pulsed Laser	Laser which delivers energy in single or multiple pulses.
Pumping Technique	A technique that uses slow, rythmic, pump-like moves done with palms of hands facing down and fingers and thumb together; commonly used in manual lymphatic drainage massage.
Purpura	A red or purple skin discoloration, usually as a result of bleeding under the skin.
Pustules	A collection of pus, often formed in sweat glands or hair follicles.

Q-switched Laser	Laser that emits short high power pulses measured in nanoseconds by means of a Q-switch.
Quantum mechanics	A branch of physics which deals with physical phenomena.
Radiant Energy	Laser energy emitted, expressed in joules (J).
Radiant Exposure	Radiant energy per unit area, expressed in joules per square centimeter.
Radiant Power	Laser power emitted, expressed in watts (W).
Radiation	The process in which energy is emitted as particles or waves through a vacuum.
Radiesse	A commonly used facial filler made of calcium hydroxylapeptate.
Radio frequency	Electromagnetic wave frequenciy in the range extending from below 3 kilohertz to about 300 gigahertz and includes frequencies used for communications signals or radar signals.
Radiowaves	Radio waves are longer in length than infrared light on the magnetic spectrum that are 1 mm to 100 klm and travel at the speed of light.
Re-epithelization	Also called wound healing. The gradual restoration of skin over an area that has been disrupted.
Reflection	The bending back of an image caused by dense objects.
Resorcinol	A chemical compound used as an antiseptic and disinfectant; it is also used in ointments to treat skin diseases such as psoriasis and sold in current over-the-counter products to treat acne.
Restylane	A hyaluronic acid based facial filler.
Resume	A descriptive summary of work place skills, employment history, and education that is presented to postential employers.
Resveratrol	Resveratrol is found mostly in grape skin. It is a potent antioxidant, controls inflammation, and acts as an MMPi, preventing the breakdown of proteins. It is the primary antioxidant present in red wine.
Retail	To sell products that generates revenue for a business.
Retain	To keep for future use or acknowledgement.
Revenue	Gross income from products or services of a business.
Rhinophyma	A hyperplasia of the soft tissue of the nose, usually occuring in middle-aged men with stage III rosacea.
Rhinoplasty	A cosmetic surgery procedure to alter the appearance of the nose.
Rhytidectomy	See **Facelift**.
Rhytides	Wrinkles, creases, and lines in the skin.
Right lymphatic duct	One of the two largest lymphatic ducts that collects lymph from the right side of the head, neck, chest and right arm.
Rosacea	A vascular disorder of the skin characterized by flushing, erythema, telangiectasia; presenting flushing and erythema on cheek, forehead, chin, nose area. The cause is unknown and there is no cure.

Rotary technique	A technique used in Manual Lymphatic Drainage. This technique consists of the palms facing skin, while the wrists move in an up and down spiral motion using slight pressure.
Roy G. Biv	A mnemonic device used to remember the color spectrum: R is red, O is orange, Y is yellow, G is green, B is blue, I is indigo, & V is violet.
Scalpel	An instrument commonly used in medical procedures to cut or scrape.
Scattering	Diffusing light or other substances irregularly in many directions.
Sclerotherapy	A compound that induces an inflammatory response; a procedure that uses injections into blood vessels to shrink them.
Scooping technique	A technique used in Manual Lymphatic Drainage. In this technique the palms are moving upward, while wrists are turning back and forth making a shovel like motion.
Sebaceous glands	Glands in the dermis of the skin that produce and secrete sebum.
Sebum	Oil produced by the sebaceous glands.
Selective photothermolysis	The precice amount of heat used to destroy the target without damaging the surrounding tissue.
Selenium	A trace mineral commonly used topically as an antioxidant or to treat fungal infections of the skin.
Senescence	The process of growing old or deteriorating.
Septoplasty	A surgical procedure to correct a deviated septum.
Silymarin (Milk Thistle)	Used to reduce the effects of toxins in the cells, stimulate protein synthesis, and protect DNA from UV radiation. Helps neutralize free radicals that cause cellular inflammation and lead to aging skin.
Sleep apnea	A condition in which breathing stops for more than 10 seconds during sleep.
Slip	To move smoothly.
SMAS	Superficial muscular aponeurotic system, the blanket of muscle that lies directly beneath the skin.
Snoring	An involuntary sound made while sleeping caused by blocking of the passages in the mouth and nose.
Sodium PCA	Sodium pyrrolidone carboxylic acid.
Solar lentigines	Brown spots 1 cm or larger, occurring usually on the face and back of the hands; usually evidence of excessive sunlight exposure.
Solvents	Substances, usually liquids, used in cosmetics to dissolve or dispense other substances.
Somatic nervous system	The system of nerves associated with voluntary or conscious body movement.
Spasmodic dysphonia	A voice disorder characterized by involuntary movements of one or more muscles of the larynx during speech.
Specular reflection	Mirror-like reflection.
Spider veins	Smaller than varicose veins. Vary in color from red to blue. Primarily present on legs and face.

Spin Traps PBN	Nitrone holds onto damaging free radicals and turns them into nourishment for cellular growth when used with a vitamin C serum. When used with non-lipid forms of vitamin A or beta-carotene, it helps protect oxygen molecules.
Spironolactone	A prescription medication used as a steroidal diuretic and androgen reducer.
Squalene	The main constituent of sebum and has been shown to have a beneficial effect in managing dermatitis. It also presents as an extract from the Aizame shark and is present in olive oil. It is used in expensive beauty products as an effective moisturizer.
Squamous cell carcinoma	Abnormal growths of squamous cells that can cause skin cancer in various parts of the body, especially sun exposed skin.
Strabismus	When eyes cannot properly align. This condition is also know as heteropia.
Stationary circles	Feather light circular movements performed with flat fingers in the same spot.
Stimulate	To excite.
Stratum corneum	The horny outer layer of the epidermis, consisting of dead or keratinized cells.
Subcutaneous	The third layer of skin consisting of adipose, fibroblast, and microphage cells, that give support to the integumentary system.
Sulfacetamide	A topical antibiotic that when combined with sulfur inhibits the growth of bacteria and can be used to treat acneic skin.
Suspending agents	Agents used in formulations to keep heavier elemets of fluid products from settling.
Tarsal glands	A special kind of sebaceous gland located at the rim of the eyelids.
Tartaric acid	An alpha hydroxy acid derived from grapes; mildly effective.
Tazorac	A vitamin A based perscription strength cream or gel commonly used for the treatment of acne.
T-cells	A group of white blood cells (lymphocytes) that are a key component in the cell-medited immune response. They are different from other lymphocytes by a special marking on their cell surface.
Telangiectasias	Abnormally dialated superficial capillaries or blood vessels.
Temporal muscles	Muscles over the temples; one of the group of muscles used in mastication.
Testosterone	A steroid hormone from the androgen group. It is the principal male sex hormone derived from cholesterol and is involved in the fromation of acne.
Tetracaine	A topically used local anesthetic.
TEWL	Transepidermal water loss. Measures amount of water that is passed from inside of the body through the epidermal layer of the skin.
TGF Beta-1	Used in skin care products to stimulate collagen and elastin production and speed up wound healing. It has superior anti-inflammatory properties.

Thickeners	Substances that increase the viscosity of products.
Thoracic duct	One of two largest lymphatic duct that collects lymph from the lower limbs, left arm, left side of the head, neck and chest.
Tinnitus	An ailment usually described as a ringing sound in one or both ears without a corresponding external noise.
Tocopherol	See **Vitamin E**.
Trans fats	A type of unsaturated fat with trans-isomer fatty acids, these fats can lead to heart disease.
Transconjunctival blepharoplasty	A procedure to remove fat from the lower eyelid with incisions made from the inner part of the eyelid so there are no external incisions.
Tretinoin cream	The acid form of vitamin A.
Trichloracetic Acid peels (TCA)	A medium depth peel used by physicians in strengths of 25–35% that can pentrate to the papillary layer of the dermis and by estheticians in strengths of 5 -10% to treat the epidermis; this peel is effective for photo-damage, fine lines, wrinkles and pigmentation.
Turmeric	A plant of the ginger family used as a coloring agent.
Tyrosinase inhibitors	Ingredients in skin lightening products to stop the action of tyrosinase (the enzyme that produces pigmentation in the melanogenesis process).
Ubiquinone	A lipid-soluble antioxidant that helps protect against intrinsic and extrinsic aging. It is also said to produce energy for cellular vitality and help stabilize cell membranes. It brings oxygen to mitochondria (cells' "power plants") to increase cellular energy.
Ulcer	Disintegration of epidermis. Possible deeper tissue loss of the dermis and subcutaneous layers.
Ultrasound technology	A cyclic sound pressure with a frequency greater than human hearing that penetrates a medium by generating heat in biological tissue.
Ultraviolet radiation	Electromagnetic radiation with wavelengths from 180–400 nm.
Undertones	The underlying colors found in skin; typically described as neutral, warm or cool.
Ultraviolet Rays	Rays that are outside the spectrum of visible light, making them invisible. They have short wavelengths, ranging from 10–400 nm.
UVA	Ultraviolet A, cause more damage to the dermal layers and are associated with signs of aging such as wrinkles and sun spots. Electromagnetic wavelength ranges from 315–400 nm.
UVC	Ultraviolet C, often referred to as the "cancer causing rays," as they have the potential to continuously replicate additional damaged cells without regulation, leading to the creation of pre-cancerous lesions. Electromagnetic wavelength ranges from 100–280 nm.
Vagus nerve	10th cranial nerve (wandering nerve) responsible for motor functions affecting the neck.
Vellus hair	Also known as peach fuzz, a short fine body hair that grows in most places of the body in both sexes.
Venous	Referring to or vein or blood vessel like.

Vesicles	Serum-filled lesions on or beneath the skin.
Vicryl suture	An absorbable, synthetic suture that holds it strength for about three to four weeks.
Visible light	A combination of multiple colors that are blended together.
Visible radiation	Electromagnetic radiation which is visible to the human eye; wavelengths from 400–700 nm.
Vitamin C	An antioxidant essential for many body functions; also used topically on the skin in age preventing preparations.
Vitamin E	An antioxidant important for many body functions; also used topically on the skin for it's moisturizing properties.
Vitrase	A hyaluronidase, commonly used to reverse the action of a hyaluronic acid filler.
Water	A liquid involved in hydration with a definite volume and weight composed of 2 parts hydrogen and 1 part oxygen commonly stated H_2O.
Watersheds	Dividing lines or borders that determine direction of lymph flows
Watt (W)	Unit of power or radiant flux (1 watt = 1 joule per second).
Wavelength	The distance between two successive points on a periodic wave that have the same phase.
Waxing	A procedure used commonly be estheticians to remove hair with the use of hot wax.
White blood cells	Cells of the body's immune system responsible for fighting infection.
Whitehead	A closed comedone caused by excess sebum and dead skin plugging a follicle.
Whitewashing	Applying a shade of makeup lighter than the natural skin color in light downward strokes when doing camouflage makeup.
Word of mouth	The most effective form of advertisement in the service industry; information on products and services are passed via person to person, ie. passive referral marketing.
Wrinkles	In aesthetics known as rhytides, these are thin wounds or depressions in the skin mostly prematurely formed by extrinsic aging factors such sun exposure and free radical damage.
Xanthan gum	A polysaccharide emulsifier found in food and cosmetics.
X-ray	The second to smallest rays on the electromagnetic spectrum that allow visibility through tissues in the body.
Yeast	Once cell organism that causes fermentation and skin disorders such as fungus.
Zinc	Speeds up the repair process during wound healing. It is an anti-inflammatory and antioxidant. It is most often used in acne preparations. The benefits of taking it internally for skin health have already received much recent attention.

Review Questions Answers Key

AESTHETICS EXPOSED
MASTERING SKIN CARE IN A MEDICAL SETTING AND BEYOND

Part 1: Review Questions

1) The job of an esthetician in a medical setting is to:
   a) Perform medical treatments
   b) Treat medical conditions of the skin
   c) ==Cosmetically enhance the skin==
   d) Take clients from the physician

2) What are the two most common procedures performed by skin care professionals in a medical setting?
   a) ==Chemical peels and microdermabrasion==
   b) Facials and massages
   c) Ultrasound treatments and dermaplaning
   d) Lymphatic drainage massage and facials

3) What are some of the benefits of working with a physician?
   a) Products, procedures, equipment will have scientific validity
   b) The ability to build a strong clientele
   c) You can give medical advice
   d) ==Answers a and b==

4) How can an esthetician help a client to maintain their skin after medical procedures?
   a) ==Educating them on the importance of using the proper products==
   b) Perform medical treatments for the physician
   c) Enhance treatments by applying a deep chemical peel the day of procedure
   d) The esthetician cannot help a client after medical procedures

5) What is the best way to introduce skin care treatments and products to patients?
   a) Ask the patient if they would like a consultation
   b) ==Cleanse the patient's skin before their medical service==
   c) Have the physician come in to sell products after the appointment
   d) Cold call all of the patients of the medical practice

6) What is the most valuable asset of a practice?

   a) Medical supplies
   b) Medical rooms
   c) The spa
   d) **The physician's time**

7) Product use is especially important following invasive treatments (e.g., deep laser resurfacing). If the skin is not cared for properly following deep laser resurfacing treatments which adverse reactions can occur?

   a) Infections
   b) Discoloration
   c) Scarring
   d) **All of the above**

8) What does OSHA stand for?

   a) **Occupational Safety and Health Administration**
   b) Occupational Safety and HIV Administration
   c) Occupational Sharps and Health Administration
   d) Occupational Safety and Hepatitis Administration

9) What are bloodborne pathogens?

   a) Blood
   b) Uncapped needles
   c) Bleach solutions
   d) **Infectious materials in blood that can cause diseases**

10) What type of vaccination should be available from the employer to all employees within ten days of employment?

    a) HIV
    b) Hepatitis A
    c) **Hepatitis B**
    d) Hepatitis C

Review Questions

11) How can the employee prevent an accident from a cut or a stick?

   a) Recap needles
   b) Clean work areas thoroughly with bleach
   c) Wear gloves
   d) **Dispose of sharps immediately**

12) Who should supply all personal protective equipment?

   a) Employees
   b) **Employers**
   c) OSHA
   d) Patients

13) What does HIPAA stand for?

   a) **Health Insurance Portability and Accountability Act**
   b) Health Insurance Preventability and Accountability Act
   c) Health Insurance Portability and Auditing Act
   d) Health Insurance Preventability and Auditing Act

14) What does HIPAA protect?

   a) It protects the practice from insurance fraud
   b) It protects employee records
   c) **It protects patients' medical records and other health information**
   d) It protects physicians' records and other health information

15) Is it appropriate to call a person by their full name in front of others?

   a) **No, patients and clients may be referred to by their first name only**
   b) Yes, it is more professional
   c) Only with new clients
   d) Only on regular clients

16) When using a patient's file, where is it acceptable to place that file?
    a) All patient files must be kept in a secure location
    b) Files should not be left any place where anyone other than an employee can see the names on them
    c) A good rule of thumb is to place all files face down
    d) **All of the above**

17) If you see a patient outside of your office, should you say hello to them?
    a) Yes, as long as you're friendly
    b) **If the client speaks to you first then you may speak to them**
    c) You must never speak to them outside the office
    d) Yes, as long as you're the first to speak

18) Who may own and operate a medical spa in most states?
    a) **A physician**
    b) A physician partnered with an esthetician
    c) Anyone with a business license
    d) A medical esthetician partnered with a physician

19) The prohibition against fee-splitting stems from:
    a) Lawsuits from injured clients
    b) The belief that allowing non-physicians to share in medical revenue could affect client care
    c) It is unethical to pay others for referring business to physicians, who should be concerned more with healing than with revenue
    d) **Both b and c**

20) Which treatments are estheticians allowed to perform in medical spas in all states?
    a) Neurotoxin and fillers
    b) **Superficial treatments**
    c) Laser skin rejuvenation
    d) Micro-needling

Review Questions

21) How can social media be a detriment in medical spa advertising?
    a) Facebook is for a younger generation than those going to a medical spa
    b) Clients may inadvertently violate HIPAA via posts or tweets
    c) Anyone can see the treatments offered at the medical spa
    d) None of the above

22) With the increased popularity of medical spas, what are some issues that have arisen?
    a) Decreased regulation
    b) Criminal prosecution
    c) Fewer violations of local laws
    d) Lack of suspension due to negligence

23) In most states, if a physician is not on-site who may substitute in his or her place?
    a) A trained medical esthetician
    b) A laser technician
    c) A medical assistant
    d) Another medical professional as long as the physician is available by phone

24) Who can benefit from incorporating skin care and cosmetic medicine?
    a) The patient
    b) The practice
    c) The physician
    d) All of the above

25) Who in the practice is ultimately responsible for patient care?
    a) The practice manager
    b) The physician
    c) The insurance company
    d) Whoever provided the service

Part 2: Review Questions

1) Which of the following is most important when treating clients?
    a) Making the client relaxed
    b) ==Making the client feel better==
    c) Making the client look better
    d) Making the client spend money

2) Which male trait suggests a high level of testosterone?
    a) A long neck
    b) Full lips
    c) Small ears
    d) ==A chiseled jaw==

3) What happens to a woman's eyes when she is attracted to someone?
    a) They flutter
    b) She blinks a lot
    c) ==Her pupils dilate==
    d) All of the above

4) What trait, along with physical appearance, can anticipate more positive responses from others?
    a) ==The energy we gain from self-esteem==
    b) The color choices we wear on a daily basis
    c) The vehicle we choose to drive
    d) None of the above

5) Studies show that once a person views his or her face with fewer wrinkles they are less efficient in emoting anger but *will feel more* anger.
    a) True
    b) ==False==

6) Cosmetic enhancements should be:
    a) ==Simple and powerful==
    b) Extravagant and noticeable
    c) Subtle and unique
    d) Obvious and extreme

Review Questions

7) The morals and ethics of mating, marriage, and child-rearing have varied widely based on what factor?

   a) Social status
   b) Culture
   c) Political status
   d) All of the above

8) What are first impressions based on?

   a) Appearance
   b) Self-esteem
   c) Personality
   d) Financial status

9) During a client consultation, what is the most important thing the provider should do?

   a) Tell the client what he/she thinks would be best for them
   b) Tell the client about procedures that they have had done themselves
   c) Understand what the client wants and support their decisions
   d) Sell as many services as possible

10) What should you do with a dissatisfied client?

    a) Dismiss the unhappy client
    b) Address the client's issue head-on
    c) Admit that you are guilty
    d) Avoid the client at all costs

11) What can the provider do for a "Satisfied Sally" to let her know she is appreciated?

    a) Discount the price on all services
    b) Give free products with each treatment
    c) Provide an add-on treatment once in a while
    d) Nothing, she is privileged to be your client

12) Who gets cosmetic procedures?

    a) People who have a lot of money
    b) People with Body Dysmorphic Disorder
    c) People who are overly concerned with their appearance
    d) ==People from all walks of life==

13) Which patient personality type likely comes in knowing the procedure she wants?

    a) Satisfied Sally
    b) Esthetic Shopper Sharon
    c) ==Know-It-All Nancy==
    d) Passive-Aggressive Patty

14) What are some of the signs to look for with Body Dysmorhpic Disorder?

    a) Having anxiety or stress about their looks
    b) Picking at the skin or hair
    c) Frequently looking in the mirror
    d) ==All of the above==

15) What is the first and most essential question to ask every client during the initial consultation, before the treatment?

    a) ==What are your concerns with your skin?==
    b) What treatments have you had in the past?
    c) Do you have any vacations coming up?
    d) Is your skin sensitive?

16) What is the minimum length of time the *initial* consultation should take?

    a) 10 minutes
    b) 25 minutes
    c) ==45 minutes==
    d) 1 hour

17) What information is important to gather from the client during the initial consultation?

   a) Allergies or past allergic reactions
   b) The client's lifestyle and product use
   c) Any medical conditions the client may have
   d) **All of the above**

18) From information gathered during the initial consultation, which client would the esthetician more likely *not* recommend a chemical peel for?

   a) **A client getting family pictures taken a few days post-treatment**
   b) A client who has arranged to have a week off from work post-treatment
   c) A client who received a chemical peel in the past and liked the results
   d) A client who wants results for pigmentation

19) Why is it important to know what home skin care products the client is currently using?

   a) **To ensure the client's products are compatible with in-office treatments**
   b) To ensure the client will only use products bought from your office
   c) To ensure the client discontinues the use of antioxidants for five days before a peeling treatment
   d) To help determine how much money the client is willing to spend on services

20) Why is providing medical history information on an intake form crucial?

   a) To help the esthetician find out as much personal information about the client as possible
   b) **To ensure there are no contraindications to recommended treatments**
   c) To help better educate the esthetician on competing techniques
   d) To recommend medical treatments for medical conditions if it will help the client's skin

21) Why is it important to know the past treatments a client has received?

   a) To help determine what has and has not worked for the client in the past
   b) To ensure enough time has passed since the last treatment
   c) To discuss why treatments you offer are better
   d) **All of the above**

22) When cleansing the skin during analysis what should the technician be feeling for?

   a) Whiteheads
   b) Keratin buildup
   c) Keratosis
   d) All of the above

23) When looking under a Wood's lamp at pigmentation and the pigment appears *lighter,* what is that a sign of?

   a) Infection
   b) Dermal melasma
   c) Scarring
   d) Dry skin

24) When skin is inflamed, which treatments are to be avoided?

   a) Microdermabrasion
   b) Ultrasound
   c) Radio frequency
   d) All of the above

25) Which of the commonly seen skin lesions is caused by an enlarged sebaceous gland?

   a) Milia
   b) Syringoma
   c) Xanthelasma
   d) Sebaceous hyperplasia

Part 3: Review Questions

1) What is acne?

    a) A chronic inflammatory disorder of the capillaries
    b) ==A chronic inflammatory disorder of the sebaceous glands==
    c) A chronic inflammatory disorder of the suderiferous glands
    d) A chronic inflammatory disorder of the skin cells.

2) Which treatment is beneficial for inflamed papules and pustules?

    a) Extractions
    b) ==Salicylic acid peel==
    c) Micro-needling
    d) Microdermabrasion

3) Who is affected by acne?

    a) Teenagers going through puberty
    b) Women going through menopause
    c) Those that don't care for the skin
    d) ==Virtually everyone at some point in their life==

4) What factors can contribute to acne?

    a) Excess sebum
    b) Buildup of dead skin cells
    c) *Propionibacterium acne*
    d) ==All of the above==

5) Which oral medication used to treat acne can cause severe side effects including extremely dry skin, poor wound healing and depression, and needs to be monitored closely?

    a) Minocycline
    b) Spironolactone
    c) ==Isotretinoin (Accutane)==
    d) Aminolevulonic acid

6) What treatment can be used to treat a large painful acneic lesion to reduce inflammation quickly?

   a) Botox injections
   b) Restylane injections
   c) ==Steroid injection==
   d) Photodynamic therapy

7) Which would be the best treatment option for rosacea on a client whose main concern is redness?

   a) ==Intense Pulsed Light (IPL)==
   b) Lactic acid peel
   c) Dermaplaning
   d) Topical antibiotics

8) What is the main characteristic difference between acne vulgaris and papulopustular rosacea?

   a) There is a lack of pustules with rosacea
   b) ==There is a lack of comedones with rosacea==
   c) There is a lack of cysts with rosacea
   d) There is a lack of nodules with rosacea

9) Which medication or treatment is proven to cure rosacea?

   a) Ablative laser treatment
   b) Accutane
   c) Antibiotics
   d) ==Rosacea is not curable==

10) Who is rhinophyma most prevalent in?

    a) ==Middle-aged men==
    b) Middle-aged women
    c) Teenage boys
    d) The elderly

11) What is the beneficial key ingredient someone with rosacea should look for in a sunscreen?

   a) Avobenzone
   b) Benzoyl peroxide
   c) Titianium dioxide
   d) Zinc oxide

12) What are some topical medications used to treat rosacea?

   a) Metronidazole
   b) Sulfacetamide
   c) Clindamycin
   d) All of the above

13) _____ should be avoided during facial treatments on a client with rosacea?

   a) Steam
   b) Facial massage
   c) Ultrasound
   d) All the above

14) What condition of rosacea does ablative laser or dermabrasion treat?

   a) Redness
   b) Capillaries
   c) Telangiectasias
   d) Rhinophyma

15) What is the cause of solar lentigines?

   a) Overexposure to the sun
   b) Inflammation or skin trauma
   c) Hormones
   d) Acne

16) What are solar lentigines?

    a) Old age spots or liver spots
    b) Flat, oval, evenly pigmented macules in areas of chronic sun exposure
    c) Common benign lesions of the skin
    d) **All of the above**

17) What is melasma most often caused from?

    a) Aggressive picking of the skin
    b) **Birth control and hormone replacement therapy**
    c) Harsh product use on the skin
    d) Infection in the body

18) What are treatment options for solar lentigines?

    a) Freezing with liquid nitrogen
    b) Hydroquinone topical agent
    c) Chemical peels
    d) **All of the above**

19) The loss of subcutaneous fat, resulting in volume loss, can be caused by which type of aging?

    a) Intrinsic aging
    b) Extrinsic aging
    c) **Both intrinsic and extrinsic aging**
    d) The skin does not lose subcutaneous fat during aging

20) Which two skin care treatments can be performed 7–10 days following non-ablative laser treatments to reduce superficial pigmentation?

    a) **Dermaplaning and microdermabrasion**
    b) Ultrasound and phenol peels
    c) Lymphatic drainage massage and dermabrasion
    d) Phenol peels and lasers

Review Questions

21) What types of supplements are known to reduce inflammation and even to reverse some of the damage of heart disease?

   a) Antioxidants
   b) Minerals
   c) Vitamin B5
   d) Vitamin B12

22) Which layer of the skin is mostly affected by extrinsic aging?

   a) Dermis
   b) Epidermis
   c) Both A and B
   d) Subcutaneous

23) Extrinsic aging is also called?

   a) Slow aging
   b) Photoaging
   c) Out of town aging
   d) Lipo aggressive-aging

24) A diet rich in sugar ultimately affects the aging of skin and can actually make you look older. Excess sugar can also affect collagen fibers. What is this process called?

   a) Glycation
   b) Collaganese
   c) Elastosis
   d) Wrinkles

25) What does AGE, relating to glycation, stand for?

   a) Advanced Genetics Energy Systems
   b) The intrinsic aging factor index
   c) Abnormal Glycation End Products
   d) Advanced Glycation End Products

Part 4 Review Questions

1) What is *not* one of the benefits of chemical peels?

   a) To refine fine lines
   b) To lighten hyperpigmentation
   c) To exfoliate dead skin cells
   d) ==To add volume to the skin==

2) Which factor will affect the results of a chemical peel?

   a) The percentage of acid in the product
   b) The pH
   c) The amount of acid applied to the skin
   d) ==All of the above==

3) Which peeling treatment needs to be neutralized following the proper application?

   a) ==Glycolic acid==
   b) Salicylic acid
   c) Jessner's peel
   d) TCA peel

4) What is the most commonly used alpha hydroxyl acid (AHA) for people with sensitive skin?

   a) Glycolic acid
   b) ==Lactic acid==
   c) Malic acid
   d) Tartaric acid

5) Which chemical peel is often the first choice for oily and acne skin types?

   a) Glycolic acid
   b) Lactic acid
   c) ==Salicylic acid==
   d) TCA

Review Questions

6) If a client is allergic to aspirin, which chemical peels should not be used?

    a) Glycolic acid, lactic acid
    b) Salicylic acid, Jessner's
    c) Jessner's, TCA
    d) No chemical peels can be used

7) What are some of the post-care instructions given to a client after a peeling treatment?

    a) Avoid excess sun exposure, don't moisturize the skin for three to five days until the peeling has subsided
    b) Avoid activities that cause excess heat in the skin, refrain from using skin lightening agents for two weeks
    c) Avoid excess sun exposure, keep skin well hydrated with a suitable moisturizer
    d) Keep the skin well hydrated, apply heat to the skin every couple of hours for three to five days

8) Describe microdermabrasion.

    a) A technique that involves mechanically exfoliating the upper layers of dead skin cells through a hand piece using suction
    b) A technique that involves mechanically exfoliating the upper layers of dead skin cells with an ablative rotary device
    c) A technique that involves vacuuming layers of dead skin cells through a hand piece
    d) A technique that involves exfoliating the living layers of skin through a hand piece with crystals

9) What are some factors that affect the results of microdermabrasion?

    a) The type of machine used
    b) The condition of the client's skin before the treatment
    c) The flow of crystals and suction strength used
    d) All of the above

10) Which area of the skin should not be treated with microdermabrasion?
    a) **Eyelids**
    b) Hands
    c) Neck
    d) Nose

11) What is an alternate use for microdermabrasion in a medical setting?
    a) To replace the client's moisturizer
    b) To replace the client's exfoliator
    c) **To remove crusted pigmentation seven to 10 days after non-ablative laser treatments**
    d) To remove crusted pigmentation one to two days after ablative laser treatments

12) What is a contraindication to microdermabrasion?
    a) Superficial pigmentation
    b) Presence of blackheads and whiteheads
    c) **Inflamed acne grades III and IV**
    d) The use of antioxidants and pigment lightening products

13) When deciding on the type of microdermabrasion to be used, it is important to know:
    a) The cost of consumables
    b) The warranty on the device
    c) OSHA regulations for sanitation
    d) **All of the above**

14) Define dermaplaning.
    a) Using a scalpel to deeply exfoliate the epidermal layers of the skin down to the dermis
    b) **Using a scalpel to gently abrade the epidermis using light feathering strokes**
    c) Using a whisk-like device to gently abrade the epidermal layers of the skin down to the dermis
    d) Using a whisk-like device to gently abrade the surface of the epidermis using light feathering strokes

Review Questions

15) Which of the following does dermaplaning *not* accomplish?
    a) Removes unwanted vellus facial hair
    b) Lightly exfoliates the skin
    c) Allows other products or treatments to penetrate more effectively
    d) Removes pigmented lesions

16) What is the downtime associated with this dermaplaning?
    a) Two days
    b) One week
    c) Two weeks
    d) There is no downtime

17) When performing dermaplaning, at what angle should the blade be held?
    a) 30° angle
    b) 45° angle
    c) 65° angle
    d) 90° angle

18) Which of the following is a contraindication for dermaplaning?
    a) Fine, vellus hair
    b) Rough surface skin
    c) Inflamed acne
    d) Rosacea

19) What is another name for micro-needling?
    a) Microdermabrasion
    b) Collagen Induction Therapy
    c) Ablative Resurfacing
    d) Epidermal Growth Factor

20) What is not an indication for needling?
    a) Fine lines and wrinkles
    b) Acne scarring
    c) Inflamed acne
    d) Stretch marks

21) Micro-channels on the skin formed by micro-needling stay open for an average of _____.

   a) 10–15 seconds
   b) 10–15 minutes
   c) **1 hour**
   d) 12 hours

22) How many days, on average, does it take following micro-needling for swelling and redness to subside?

   a) 1 day
   b) **3 days**
   c) 1 week
   d) 3 months

23) What stage of wound healing can continue for up to two years?

   a) Inflammatory stage
   b) Proliferative stage
   c) Fibroplastic stage
   d) **Maturative stage**

24) Which method of micro-needling allows for different treatment depths during a single treatment?

   a) Stamping
   b) Rolling
   c) **Automated Needing Device**
   d) The depth cannot be changed during treatment regardless of device

25) Which of the following factors affect the results of micro-needling?

   a) The client's skin condition prior to treatment
   b) The needle gauge
   c) Post-treatment care
   d) **All of the above**

Part 5 Review Questions

1) Which of the following is **not** necessary prior to initializing a safe treatment room?

    a) Protective laser goggles for all those present in the treatment room
    b) Payment from the patient for the procedure
    c) Cleansing the intended treatment area
    d) Placing sign on door to inform others the laser is in use

2) The benefits of an inherent chill tip in the LASER/IPL hand piece is to?

    a) Protect the sweat glands from overheating
    b) Protect the epidermis from thermal injury
    c) Protect the provider's hand from injury
    d) Protect the laser from overheating

3) The amount of time between treatment intervals for laser hair reduction are based on?

    a) The patient's schedule
    b) The medical office's schedule
    c) The phase of hair growth
    d) The color of the hair

4) In which of the following scenarios is treatment with laser hair reduction contraindicated?

    a) Non-lactating mothers
    b) Patients with blonde hair
    c) Patients with open sores or other skin irritations
    d) Patients taking hormone replacement therapy (HRT)

5) If you have difficulty or are uncertain of the treatment parameters, you should:

    a) Proceed with the manufacturer's suggested treatment settings
    b) Consult your user manual
    c) Not treat the patient
    d) Treat the patient at a low and safe but possibly ineffective setting

6) In laser hair reduction, the laser energy is absorbed by the _____ in the hair follicle before it is converted to heat and damages the follicle.

   a) Water
   b) **Pigment**
   c) Sebum
   d) Sweat

7) Energy in lasers is measured in _____.

   a) Nanometers
   b) Infrared
   c) **Joules**
   d) Wavelengths

8) The _____ is the duration of energy delivered during laser treatments.

   a) Chromophore
   b) Fluence
   c) Joules
   d) **Pulse width**

9) In laser hair removal, only the hairs in the _____ stage will be targeted.

   a) **Anagen**
   b) Catagen
   c) Telogen
   d) All of the Above

10) In an IPL (Intense Pulsed Light) treatment, the light is absorbed by _____ in the skin.

    a) Sebum
    b) **Color (dyschromias)**
    c) Keratin
    d) Suderiferous glands

Review Questions

11) What form of energy is released to destroy chromophores in laser treatments?

   a) Thermal
   b) Nuclear
   c) Electrical
   d) All of the above

12) With laser hair removal, results are obtained when the contrast is greater between the skin and the color of the chromophore.

   a) True
   b) False

13) What does the "A" in LASER stand for?

   a) Applied
   b) Amplification
   c) Altered
   d) Aligned

14) What is the fluence in a laser?

   a) Measure of energy delivered
   b) Duration of energy delivered
   c) Deepness of energy delivered
   d) Target of laser energy

15) In ablative laser treatments, what is the target of light energy?

   a) Sebum
   b) Blood
   c) Water
   d) Melanin

16) Intense pulse light (IPL) is another name for a laser.

   a) True
   b) False

17) Increasing pulse width and decreasing energy delivered allows for safer treatment of:

   a) Patients with fair skin
   b) **Patients with tanned skin or darker skin**
   c) Pregnant patients
   d) Patients with psoriasis

18) Acceptable post-treatment recommendations for IPL treatments include all of the following except:

   a) Application of aloe
   b) Applying an ice pack to the treatment area
   c) **Tanning booth**
   d) Use of sunscreen

19) What type of laser treatments leave portions of healthy skin behind for quicker healing?

   a) **Fractionated Lasers**
   b) Visible light Lasers
   c) IPL
   d) Ablative lasers

20) Immediately following treatment with ablative lasers, patients should apply recommended _____ often.

   a) Makeup
   b) Retinol
   c) **Occlusive agent**
   d) Alpha hydroxy acid

21) Laser lights are monochromatic because they are compromised of only one wavelength or color of the light spectrum?

   a) **True**
   b) False

Review Questions

22) What is NOT an indication of visible light lasers or IPL (non-ablative)?
    a) Skin rejuvenation
    b) Reduce pigmentation
    c) Hair removal
    d) Resurfacing

23) Electromagnetic spectrum is made up of light energy only.
    a) True
    b) False

24) Visible light that produces color is present between which wavelengths?
    a) 5,000–15,000 nm
    b) 400–700 nm
    c) 750–2,000 nm
    d) 190–390 nm

25) What is the term used for selecting the right amount of energy to destroy the target but not the surrounding tissues?
    a) Pulse width
    b) Tissue interaction
    c) Thermal relaxation time
    d) Selective photothermolysis

Part 6 Review Questions

1) What is the most commonly used facial filling agent?

   a) Fat
   b) **Hyaluronic acid**
   c) Cartilage
   d) Calcium hydroxylapetite

2) Calcium hydroxylapetite, the ingredient in the facial filler Radiesse, is also found in what areas of the human body?

   a) Nails and cartilage
   b) The skin and joints
   c) The hands and feet
   d) **Bones and teeth**

3) Why are bovine collagen products not commonly used anymore?

   a) Longevity is disappointing
   b) They can leave a bumpy irregular appearance on the skin
   c) The client needs skin testing for allergic reactions before being treated
   d) **All of the above**

4) Which method of volume replacement is most commonly used during a surgical procedure?

   a) Restylane
   b) Radiesse
   c) Sculptra
   d) **Fat transfer**

5) Neurotoxins are a purified protein toxin that blocks communication between the _____ and the _____ .

   a) Muscles, skin
   b) Nerves, epidermis
   c) Blood flow, joints
   d) **Muscles, nerves**

Review Questions

6) When were the beneficial side effects of neurotoxins in facial cosmetics first recognized?
    a) The late 1960s
    b) The late 1970s
    c) ==The late 1980s==
    d) The late 1990s

7) Besides reducing fine lines and wrinkles, what non-cosmetic uses do neurotoxins possess?
    a) Addressing blepharospasm
    b) Alleviating migraine headaches
    c) Reduce excess sweating
    d) ==All of the above==

8) When neurotoxins are used *on-label*, what improvements can a patient expect to see?
    a) ==Reduction of the creases between the eyebrows==
    b) More volume in the face
    c) A tightening of loose skin
    d) A smaller jawline

9) What can the patient expect during a neurotoxin treatment?
    a) ==The patient will receive a series of small injections==
    b) The patient is put under general anesthesia before receiving a series of injections
    c) The patient receives one large injection into the forehead
    d) The neurotoxin is applied topically and left on the skin for thirty minutes

10) How long does it usually take for the effects of Botox to take place after the treatment?
    a) Right away
    b) The next day
    c) ==Up to 7 days==
    d) One month

11) How long does Dysport last?

   a) Two months
   b) **Three to four months**
   c) Six to nine months
   d) One year

12) Where is the incision made during an open rhinoplasty?

   a) The septum
   b) **The columella**
   c) The tip
   d) The right nostril

13) What is the name of the procedure done to correct a deviated septum?

   a) **Septoplasty**
   b) Septum revision
   c) Rhinoplasty
   d) Cartilage shaping

14) What should dried mucous or crust around the nose and nostrils be cleaned with?

   a) Glycolic cleanser
   b) Saline spray
   c) **Hydrogen peroxide**
   d) Alcohol

15) How long should patients receiving rhytidectomy expect results to last?

   a) **Five to 12 Years**
   b) 15 years
   c) Two years
   d) Forever

Review Questions

16) To minimize swelling after rhytidectomy, now long should the patient keep their head elevated while sleeping?

   a) One week
   b) Three to five days
   c) Two months
   d) Two to four weeks

17) Where are the incisions made for transconjunctival blepharoplasty?

   a) The inside surface of the upper or lower eyelid
   b) The outside surface of the upper or lower eyelid
   c) Around the lash line of the upper and lower eyelids
   d) In the crease of the upper and lower eyelids

18) Who was the founder of MLD?

   a) Johan Georg Mezger
   b) Dr. Vodder
   c) Tokujiro Namikoshi
   d) Pehr Henrik Ling

19) What is Manual Lymph Drainage?

   a) MLD is a process to improve the circulation of lymph through the body to stimulate the body's immune response. Using the hands in a soft stretching fashion, movements are applied in a circular, pumplike or in scooping strokes.
   b) MLD is a very firm pressured massage of the skin and muscles.
   c) MLD is used in light rhythmic movements on the ducts to drain stagnant lymph back into the cardiovascular system.
   d) MLD is a massage which uses effleurage movements away from the thoracic and right lymphatic ducts.

20) What are the names of the two main ducts that lymph flows through?

   a) The right and left subclavian veins
   b) The right lymphatic duct and the thoracic duct
   c) Tear ducts and salivary ducts
   d) The superficial temporal vein and the lingual vein

21) When is MLD contraindicated?

   a) Malignant tumors
   b) Infection
   c) Heart problems
   d) ==All of the above==

22) Why is mineral makeup most often used in a medical setting?

   a) It has anti-inflammatory properties
   b) It has sun protection properties
   c) Pure minerals do not support bacteria
   d) ==All of the above==

23) For rosacea clients, after determining the color tone, what's the next step?

   a) Apply the makeup base
   b) Apply concealer to the entire face
   c) Add bronzer to warm up the face
   d) ==Whitewashing the face==

24) How can puffiness and dark circles under the eyes be concealed with camouflage makeup?

   a) Whitewash the entire area under the eyes, followed by the appropriate base color
   b) Pick a concealer shade that is slightly lighter than the natural color of the skin, and draw a triangle directly under the iris. Then, fill in the triangle. Use the darker shade to draw two inverted triangles on each side, and again, fill in. Blend the three together gently, and finish with appropriate powder on top.
   c) ==Pick a concealer shade that is slightly darker than the natural color of the skin, and draw a triangle directly under the iris. Then, fill in the triangle. Use the lighter shade to draw two inverted triangles on each side, and again, fill in. Blend the three together gently, and finish with appropriate powder on top.==
   d) Camouflage makeup cannot help dark circles and puffiness

25) What is your goal when camouflaging indented scars?

   a) Apply the darker shade of concealer directly onto the scar while outlining the perimeter of the scar with a lighter shade of concealer

   b) Apply the lighter shade of concealer directly onto the scar while outlining the perimeter of the scar with a darker shade of concealer

   c) Apply a yellow-based concealer to the entire scar

   d) Apply a cool foundation to the area several times

Part 7 Review Questions

1) Why are radio frequency techniques becoming more popular than ablative laser resurfacing for the use of skin tightening?
   a) There is a healing period with ablative lasers
   b) Patients see immediate improvement with radio frequency
   c) Patients find radio frequency treatments to be less invasive
   d) **All of the above**

2) Why is it important to not lose contact with a client's skin while performing a radio frequency treatment?
   a) The treatment won't be as effective
   b) It will immediately result in a scar
   c) The device could break
   d) **It can burn the epidermis of the skin**

3) Why is it best to perform low energy radio frequency treatments?
   a) To make the client come in for more treatments
   b) **To prevent fat necrosis, skin color changes, and scar formation**
   c) To achieve a more effective treatment
   d) To alleviate any pain in the procedure

4) How does ultrasound for skin rejuvenation work?
   a) **Ultrasound delivers radio frequency to the dermis of the skin**
   b) Ultrasound uses a rapidly oscillating probe to create sound waves
   c) Ultrasound delivers UV light to the epidermis of the skin
   d) Ultrasound delivers visible light to fibroblasts within the skin

5) Ultrasound can deliver medicinal products through the skin by way of a process known as _____.
   a) Cavitation
   b) **Phonophoresis**
   c) Oscillating waves
   d) Inflammation

6) When is ultrasound indicated?

   a) To rejuvenate skin
   b) To reduce edema
   c) To penetrate products
   d) All of the above

7) What is one of the ways to enhance product penetration?

   a) Apply oil-based products before water-based products
   b) When applying several products, always apply thickest to thinnest
   c) Apply the product as sparingly as possible
   d) Stimulate or heat the tissue

8) What are the two basic types of ingredients used in skin care formulations?

   a) Active and inactive
   b) Occlusive and non-occlusive
   c) Gels and moisturizers
   d) Antioxidants and peptides

9) What ingredients are commonly added to limit microbial growth including bacteria, molds, and yeast?

   a) Solvents
   b) Stabilizers
   c) Preservatives
   d) Emollients

10) What type of ingredient is used to alter or maintain the pH of a product?

    a) Occlusives
    b) Buffers
    c) Tyrosinase inhibitors
    d) Vehicles

11) Which of the following is *not* known as a skin lightening ingredient?

    a) Hydroquinone
    b) Kojic acid
    c) Arbutin
    d) Argirilene

12) Which lipid- and water-soluble antioxidant has been shown to enhance the effects of vitamin C and vitamin E?

   a) **Alpha lipoic acid**
   b) Bearberry
   c) Coenzyme Q10
   d) Matrixyl

13) What is the ingredient used in many anti-aging products promoted to slow down muscle contractions, thus preventing wrinkles?

   a) **Argirilene**
   b) L-ascorbic acid
   c) Hyaluronic acid
   d) Glutathione

14) Which ingredient is commonly used topically to prevent bruising and eliminate dark circles under the eyes?

   a) Vitamin A
   b) Vitamin C
   c) Vitamin E
   d) **Vitamin K**

15) Radio frequency treatment is best suited for which skin condition?

   a) **Aging**
   b) Hyperpigmentation
   c) Rosacea
   d) Grade IV acne

16) Ultrasound for skin rejuvenation stimulates collagen thermally when tissues are heated up to:

   a) 88–98°F
   b) 93–103°F
   c) 115–125°F
   d) **104–113°F**

17) What area of the face is commonly the first to show signs of aging?

   a) Eyes
   b) Nose
   c) Chin
   d) Jowls

18) Red light LED is commonly used to:

   a) Reduce hyperpigmentation
   b) Remove dead skin cells
   c) Reduce inflammation
   d) Tighten the skin

19) Microcurrent and LED work to stimulate energy within the cells through stimulating the production of _____.

   a) ATP
   b) MMPs
   c) mitochondria
   d) sebum

20) To reduce puffiness under the eyes caused by fat deposits, the patient should be referred to a physician for _____.

   a) A diet
   b) Eye cream
   c) Chemical peels
   d) Blepheroplasty

21) What is the most common cause of allergic reactions to products?

   a) Fragrance
   b) Colorants
   c) Stabilizers
   d) Humectants

22) What type of ingredient used in cosmetics is derived from grapeseed, sheep placenta, and Swiss apple?

   a) **Stem cells**
   b) Peptides
   c) Antioxidants
   d) AHAs

23) Ingredients with antibacterial properties are:

   a) Azelaic acid
   b) Benzoyl peroxide
   c) Bakuchiol
   d) **All of the above**

24) Dark circles around the eye can be caused by:

   a) Genetics
   b) Pooling of blood
   c) Shadow created by hollowing out under the eyes
   d) **All of the above**

25) Which layer needs to be heated up via radio frequency waves to stimulate collagen, resulting in skin tightening?

   a) Epidermis
   b) **Dermis**
   c) Subcutaneous
   d) All of the above

Part 8 Review

1) A skin care professional should decide their career path according to: _____.

   a) The highest salary
   b) What is most impressive to their friends
   c) Whomever hires them
   d) Where their passion is

2) If an esthetician wants to focus on relaxation and immediate gratification where should they pursue a career?

   a) Medical
   b) Educator
   c) Traditional spa
   d) Product representative

3) To find out exactly what a job entails you should:

   a) Google it
   b) Research only the degree of responsibility needed
   c) Do as much research as possible including responsibilities, hours, and education required
   d) Only ask people who have been estheticians for 10+ years

4) Your resume is important, since it is most often

   a) The only thing needed to get hired
   b) Your "first impression"
   c) Your "last impression"
   d) An introduction to your personality

5) A professional summary stating your skills and what you can bring to the table should be located where in your resume?

   a) On the top
   b) On a separate sheet
   c) Below work history
   d) On the bottom

6) Work history should be arranged in what order in your resume?

   a) Listed from most favorite to least
   b) Listed by length of time with that position
   c) ==Listed in reverse chronological order==
   d) It doesn't matter

7) How should you dress for your interview?

   a) The way you would dress for that job (i.e, scrubs for a medical position)
   b) ==Business attire==
   c) Formal attire
   d) Business casual attire

8) Before your interview you should spend time thinking about:

   a) Everything you need to do before your interview
   b) ==What questions you may be asked==
   c) Not think about it at all and stay calm
   d) Everything you might answer wrong

9) You should ask a few questions towards the end of the *first* interview about:

   a) Benefits
   b) Compensation
   c) ==The qualities they seek in a potential new hire==
   d) Don't ask any questions, let them ask the questions

10) Regarding customer service you should treat each client as if they are your: _____.

    a) ==Only client==
    b) First client
    c) Last client
    d) Best friend

11) If someone books a first-time appointment for a chemical peel you should send them:

   a) Before and after pictures of procedures gone wrong
   b) A personalized handwritten thank you note that day
   c) A list of other services offered
   d) ==Information on what the treatment entails, and how to prepare for the appointment==

12) How much harder is it to bring in a new client than to retain one?

   a) 70%
   b) 10 times
   c) ==6–7 times==
   d) 40%

13) It is important for the client to leave the office feeling:

   a) Better than last week
   b) Energized
   c) Stressed out but prettier
   d) ==Relaxed and better about themselves==

14) For loyal clients who you want to thank, an add-on service can include:

   a) Lunch for two
   b) Basket of products
   c) Package of treatments purchased
   d) ==Neck, hand, and décolleté treatments==

15) It is the sole responsibility of the _____ to build a clientele.

   a) Marketing director
   b) Business owner
   c) Skin care professional
   d) ==None of the above, each member plays a role==

16) CLIENT stands for:

   a) Clean, Lean, Immaculate, Execute, Normal, Tall
   b) Consult, Learn, Inform, Exude, Nurture, Thorough
   c) ==Consult, Listen, Inform, Execute, Nurture, Thank==
   d) Conduct, Listen, Injure, Execute, Nice, Thank

17) When it comes to recommending products:

   a) Don't recommend products unless the client asks
   b) Try to save the client money by only recommending one product per appointment
   c) Be forceful so the client uses only the products you carry
   d) ==Forget the word retail and focus on education==

18) Amiable clients tend to:

   a) ==Be honest, caring, loyal and cooperative==
   b) Make a good first impression as they show enthusiasm
   c) Tend to want the latest and greatest
   d) Be moody, rude, dishonest, and loud

19) Following a treatment, great customer service would include:

   a) Asking the client to tip you
   b) Handing the client their check
   c) Giving free product
   d) ==Offering to apply mineral makeup==

20) What POI is likely to make a first impression on a client?

   a) Greeting them as they walk in the door to your establishment
   b) ==During the client's initial phone call to the business==
   c) Through direct mail
   d) From word of mouth

Review Questions

21) How is it best to train your staff about each service offered?

   a) Give each member a pamphlet with firm instructions to memorize each treatment
   b) ==Invite every member to experience the treatments for themselves==
   c) Have them ask clients about their experiences
   d) It is only important for the providers themselves to be educated on services

22) Why is it important to make sure that the client leaves with proper post-care instructions?

   a) ==It makes the client feel well-prepared and informed==
   b) The client will be sure to make a purchase
   c) The client will be likely to leave sooner with that information instead of waiting around and asking questions
   d) The client won't need to call the office with questions

23) What are the benefits of interning?

   a) The possibility of getting free services
   b) ==Getting an exclusive look into different career options that are available==
   c) You are guaranteed to be hired after interning
   d) It is an easy way to spend your time

24) Where are some places to network?

   a) Social media websites
   b) Trade shows
   c) Educational workshops
   d) ==All of the above==

25) When recommending products, if the client is using a product from the health food store with the same active ingredient, what should you do?

   a) Tell him/her to keep using the product they already have
   b) Point out the bad things about the product he/she is currently using
   c) ==Explain that there are differences in ingredients and focus on the benefits of the product recommended==
   d) Recommend a product that may not be as beneficial, but will not be questioned

Terri A. Wojak, LE

Terri A. Wojak, LE, is a highly sought-after professional with 20 years of experience in the aesthetic industry. She is a respected authority on skin care in a medical setting, education, and business development on multiple levels. Wojak has built 30 individual courses based on skin care in a medical setting, and she has written more than 40 articles for a multitude of industry magazines, including *Skin Inc.,* for which she is a sitting board member. Her book, *Mastering Medical Esthetics*, coauthored with noted facial plastic surgeon Dr. Steven H. Dayan, MD, FACS, debuted in 2009.

A highly requested speaker at skin care seminars, medical conferences, tradeshows, and international aesthetic symposiums, Ms. Wojak has devoted her professional life to aesthetic education, training more than 2,000 estheticians to date. In partnership with Dr. Dayan, she developed True U Esthetics and True U Laser, two corporations focused on providing advanced education for professionals in the aesthetic industry, of which she is education director.

Acknowledgments

I would like to extend a special thank you to Steven H. Dayan, MD FACS for giving me countless opportunities and unending support that encouraged me to pursue my goals. His drive and passion for education continually inspires me.

I greatly appreciate the content contributions and dedicated research hours provided by Tara Davison; thank you for your hard work.

I would like to thank my editor Brian W. Budzynski and Allured Business Media for their diligence in producing this book.

I am grateful for the assistance given by my co-workers at True Skin Care Center and SDmd: Kaitlin Walker, Michelle Whitehall PA-C, Joan Almaguer-Brown, and Melissa Deady.

Thank you to American MedSpa Association for providing content; as well as PCA Skin, Aerolase Lasers, LightStim LED, *Skin Inc.* magazine, Biopelle, and Dermapen for their data and picture contributions.

I wish to acknowledge the help provided by our amazing True U interns, support staff, and peers for their assistance with research, content review, and feedback provided along the way.

Finally, I owe my motivation to my dad who always believed in me, as well as the numerous students that support and encourage me every day.

Index

A

ablative   142-3, 215, 232, 247-9, 251, 253, 255, 257, 259, 261, 263
  defined   247
ablative fractionated laser   188, 192, 247-51, 253, 255-61, 263, 268, 341
ablative laser treatment   60, 146, 244, 254, 261
ablative lasers   63, 78-9, 83-4, 115, 147, 201, 212, 232, 251, 268, 339, 388
ablative resurfacing   202, 249, 251-2, 259
  contraindications   251
  guidelines   252
Accutane   63, 145-6, 164-5, 167, 192, 213, 251, 353
acetic acid   370
acetone   160, 168, 178, 183-4, 255, 369
acetyl hexapeptide-8   376
acetylated lanolin   367
acid peels
  alpha hydroxy   95, 102, 153, 157, 160
  beta hydroxy   95-6, 153, 163
acids   139, 153, 157, 159, 162-4, 169, 177, 199, 370
  acetic   370
  alpha hydroxy   62, 80, 153, 156-7, 170, 176, 184, 371-2
  alpha lipoic   372, 390
  ferulic   372
  fumaric acid   377
  kojic   125, 142-3, 162, 374, 389
  lactic   96, 102, 113-14, 125, 153, 159, 162, 164, 199-200, 371
  lipohydroxy   372
  malic   159, 199, 371
  phytic   125, 142-3, 374
  retinoic   371
  salicylic   80, 82-3, 95-6, 100, 102, 113, 157, 162-6, 169, 199-200, 254, 372
  sodium pyrrolidine carboxylic   368

   sorbic 366
   stearic 368
   tartaric 159, 199, 371
   uric 136
acne 44, 51-2, 68, 74, 77, 80, 84, 93-107, 110-11, 114, 145, 322-3, 371-2, 374, 377-9
   breakouts 93, 98-9, 104, 164, 322
   educating the client 105
   formation 93
   grades 93, 95, 160, 164-5, 167, 183
   inflamed 102, 176, 183, 186, 202-3, 319
   lesions 104-5, 240
   lifestyle triggers 99
   pathogenesis 93
   scarring 167, 170, 191-2, 194, 203, 247
   skin types 199
   treatment 100
     medical 102
     products 100
acne simplex 94-5, 101
acne vulgaris 94-5, 101, 107, 146, 230, 245, 357-8
acrylates copolymer 370
actinic keratoses 117, 122-3
active ingredients 335, 361-5, 370-1, 428
adalpene 100, 371
adenosine tri-phosphate *see* ATP
advanced glycation end products (AGEs) 135, 372
   precursors 135
   prevention 136
aesthetic providers 8, 43, 45, 66, 75, 84, 116, 282, 290, 299, 311, 333, 403
aging 5, 68, 74, 129-31, 133, 135, 137, 139, 144, 148, 223, 285, 303, 381-2, 390-1
   extrinsic 129-31, 148-9, 372
     causes 131
   intrinsic 130-1, 144, 148
     causes 131
aging skin 100, 129, 131, 133-9, 141, 143-4, 149, 170, 234, 281, 298, 335, 373, 377
AHAs *see* alpha hydroxy acids

Index 541

alcohol   102, 112, 160, 168, 183-4, 211-12, 214-15, 255, 327, 342, 346, 366, 369
alkanet   369
Allergan   274, 281, 290, 386
allergen   81, 384-5
allergies   66, 88, 99, 122, 163-5, 194, 280, 294, 362, 384-5
alpha hydroxy acids   62, 78, 80-1, 95, 141-3, 153, 155-7, 159-63, 165, 167-71, 176, 184, 283, 308, 371-2
　citric acid   159, 370, 372
　glycolic acid   157, 159, 171, 199-200, 371
　lactic acid   96, 102, 113-14, 125, 153, 159, 162, 164, 199-200, 371
　malic acid   159, 199, 371
　mandelic acid   159, 371
　tartaric acid   159, 199, 371
alpha hydroxy acid peels   95, 102, 153, 157, 160
　contraindications   160
　indications   160
　post-treatment   162
　protocol   160
　types   157
alpha lipoic acid   372, 390
alpha-olefin sulfonate   370
aluminum powders   369
ambergris   370
American National Standards Institute (ANSI)   207-8
American Society for Aesthetic Plastic Surgery   4, 274
aminoguanadine   136, 372, 377
ammonium lauryl sulfate   370
androgens   96, 98, 104
animal exudates
　ambergris   370
　musk   370
annatto   369
ANSI (American National Standards Institute)   207-8
　classifications of laser safety   208
anti-inflammatory   112, 369, 372-3, 377-9
　aminoguanadine   136, 372, 377

fumaric acid 377
L-Proline 377
niacinamide 95-6, 113, 254, 377
vitamin B5 113, 149, 253, 259, 283, 308, 377
antibacterial 196, 372, 378
  azelaic acid 96, 114, 162, 374, 378, 392
  bakuchiol 95-6, 107, 136, 378, 392
  benzoyl peroxide 52, 96, 101, 114, 147, 378, 392
antibiotics 52, 80, 103, 109, 114, 122, 146, 254-5, 280
antioxidant properties 373-4, 377
antioxidants 88, 105, 113, 133, 136-7, 140-2, 144, 149, 157, 189, 282-3, 308, 372-5, 377-9, 382
  alpha lipoic acid 372, 390
  aminoguanadine 136, 372, 377
  caffeine 372, 382, 385
  copper 373
  D-Boldine 373
  ferulic acid 372
  idebenone 372
  L-Arginine 373
  L-Cysteine 373
  lycopene 140, 373
  magnesium ascorbyl phosphate (MAP) 373
  resveratrol 136, 140-2, 373
  silymarin (milk thistle) 373
  ubiquinone 372
  vitamin C 113, 136, 140-1, 144, 361, 372-4, 377-9, 382, 390, 410
  zinc 140, 370
antiseptics 113, 366, 379
arbutin 125, 162, 374, 389
Argon lasers 230
Artefill 291
aspirin 63, 102, 163-5, 200, 278, 294, 306
atopic dermatitis 81
ATP 317, 348, 354, 391
atrophic scars 84

Index

autoimmune disorders   160, 312, 316-17
Avobenzone   147
avocado oil   378
azelaic acid   96, 114, 162, 374, 378, 392

B
bacteria   82, 93-5, 97, 101-2, 104-6, 111, 229, 316, 342, 349-50, 367-8, 389, 420
bakuchiol   95-6, 107, 136, 378, 392
BDD (Body Dysmorphic Disorder)   56-7, 87
bearberry   125, 374, 390
beeswax   367-8
beet powder   369
bentonite   370
benzoyl peroxide   52, 96, 101, 114, 147, 378, 392
beta carotene   369
beta hydroxy acid
  see BHAs
  lipohydroxy acid   372
  salicylic acid   80, 82-3, 95-6, 100, 102, 113, 157, 162-6, 169, 199-200, 254, 372
beta hydroxy acid peels   95-6, 153, 163
  contraindications   164
  indications   164
  post-treatment   164
BHAs (beta hydroxy acid)   78, 95-6, 141-3, 153, 155-7, 159, 161-3, 165, 167-9, 171, 283, 372
blackheads   93-4, 201, 322
blanching   166-7, 294
blepharoplasty   142-3, 299, 303-4, 307, 383
  post-surgery   304
  procedure   304
  stages of wound healing   187, 189, 308, 316
blood   20-4, 30, 77, 109, 130, 192, 230-1, 234, 267, 278, 304, 306, 312, 383-4, 392
  blood thinners   5, 63, 183, 186
  bloodborne pathogens   19-20, 22, 24, 30
  sugar levels   134-5
blood thinners   5, 63, 183, 186

bloodborne pathogens 19-20, 22, 24, 30
Body Dysmorphic Disorder *see* BDD
botanicals 140, 177, 258, 379
  papaya 95, 379
  prickly pear 379
  soy 139, 379
  tea tree 379
Botox 13-14, 16, 18, 28, 68, 274-8, 281, 284, 326
  complications 279
  FDA approval 274
  inanimation 280
  maintenance 281
  non-cosmetic uses 278
  results 280
  treatment 277
botulinum toxin (Botox) 115-16, 273, 275, 284, 375
BPO *see* benzoyl peroxide
breakouts 44, 68, 98, 100-1, 105-6, 324, 409, 411, 415
bruises 282, 319-21
bruising 63, 278, 292, 294, 307, 318-20, 347, 351-2, 378, 384, 390
buffers 361, 370, 389
  acetic acid 370
  citric acid 159, 370, 372
  potassium dihydrogen 370
  triethanolamine 370
  tromethamine phosphate 370
bulla circumscribed 76
burns 71-2, 122, 127, 176, 183, 213-14, 218, 236, 239-40, 343, 352, 418

C

caffeine 372, 382, 385
calcium hydroxylapatite 290
camouflage makeup 311, 313, 315, 317-19, 321, 323-4, 329-30, 384
  acne 322
  dark circles 322
  hyperpigmentation 322

Index 545

   hypopigmentation 323
   rosacea 321
   scars 323
cancer 75, 123-4, 132-3, 139, 144, 160, 167, 192, 214, 223, 316-17, 345, 353, 368
   basal cell carcinoma 124
   melanoma 124-5
   squamous cell carcinoma 124
cancerous 123, 367-8
   lesions 123
cannulas 287
caprylic-capric-linoleic triglyceride 367
carbomer 370
carotene 369
carrier peptides 376
cartilage 301-3, 325
castor oil 367, 369
cells 60, 103, 117, 120, 123, 130, 136, 139, 154, 192, 248, 315, 364-5, 371-3, 377-8
   mesangial 135
   stem 141-3, 189, 259, 308, 375, 377, 392
cellular turnover 69, 100-1, 105, 113, 134, 142-3, 154, 260, 308, 371, 375, 377, 382, 409
centella asiatica 136, 378
Center for Devices and Radiological Health (CDRH) 207
certified laser safety officer *see* CLSO
cetyl alcohol 370
cheeks 68, 78, 109, 116-17, 285-7, 295
chemical exfoliation 74, 105, 153-5, 157, 159, 161, 163, 165, 167, 169, 171, 384, 419
chemical peels 4-5, 7, 27-9, 45, 60-1, 88, 101-2, 121-2, 142-3, 153, 156-8, 170-1, 199-200, 259, 418
   alpha hydroxy *see* alpha hydroxy acid peels
   beta hydroxy *see* beta hydroxy acid peels
   considerations 157
   deep 155, 170
   depths 155
   history 153
   precautions 157

prepping 157
superficial 50-1, 101, 154, 175, 182-3
TCA (Trichloroacetic Acid) 27, 79, 102, 114, 126, 153, 155-7, 159, 161, 163, 165, 167, 169, 171, 199-200
chemical sunscreens 112, 196, 381
chemicals 50-1, 134, 153, 157, 363, 370
synthetic 379
cherry angioma 79
chlorophyll 369
chromophores 226, 229, 232, 234, 238, 247, 266-7
chronic inflammation 75
CIR (Cosmetic Ingredient Review) 367
circulation 95, 101, 106, 134, 175, 311-12, 317, 328, 344-5, 349-50, 353, 356, 377-8, 383
circulatory system 312, 314-15
citric acid 159, 370, 372
claims 337, 339, 347, 359-60, 362-3, 379
cleansers, gentle 244, 253, 259, 261, 411
cleansing 17, 73, 75, 89, 93, 105, 255-6, 265, 322, 351, 364, 411
client consultation 28, 59, 62, 66-7, 86
client intake form 62, 178, 196, 421
client panel light 352
client retention 417, 419-21, 423
client safety 195, 316
clindamycin 63, 114, 147
clinician 250, 291, 293
CLSO (certified laser safety officer) 207-9, 211
CO_2 laser 78, 212, 247-9, 251, 255-6
traditional 249-50, 256-8
cocamidopropylbetaine 370
cocoamphocarboxyglynate 370
collagen 69, 130-1, 134, 136, 138, 144, 188-9, 229, 248-9, 291, 308, 339-40, 348-9, 354, 375-7
collagen induction therapy 187, 202
collagen production 69, 140, 154, 230, 247, 339, 343-4, 348, 375, 378-9, 383
collagen stimulators 142-3, 283

color 74, 78, 110, 121, 123-4, 127, 214, 216, 223-5, 233, 243-4, 265-9, 317-19, 323-4, 342
  natural 256, 322, 329, 369
colorants 352, 369, 391
  animal 297, 345, 369-70, 375, 377
  FDA approved 369
  mineral origin 369
  natural
    alkanet 369
    annatto 369
    carotene 369
    chlorophyll 369
    saffron 369
    tumeric 369
  vegetable 369
columella 301-2, 327
comedones 69, 94, 101, 110-11, 146, 371
compresses, cool 252-3, 256
concealer 320, 322-3, 329-30
connective tissue 289, 291, 346-7
consultation 6, 9, 28-9, 35, 47-8, 50, 52-3, 57, 59-63, 65-7, 86-8, 127, 234, 341, 418
  BDD (Body Dysmorphic Disorder) 56-7, 87
  purpose 59
contact dermatitis 81, 374
copper 373
cortisone 62
cosmeceuticals 100, 144, 359-60, 371
cosmetic camouflage 317
Cosmetic Ingredient Review (CIR) 367
cosmetic ingredients 360
cosmetic surgery 3, 61, 142-3, 299, 323, 345
cosmetics 3, 45, 78, 224, 283, 303, 343, 359-60, 366-9, 392
Cosmoderm 290
Cosmoplast 290
crow's feet 68, 304-5, 382-3
Crypthompalous aspersa 375

crystals 174, 177, 179, 200
customer service 175, 417, 419-21
cyclomethicone 367, 370

D

D-Boldine 373
dark circles 322, 329, 383-5, 390, 392
dead skin cells 93, 145, 154, 182, 199-200, 364, 371, 391
decylpolyglucoside 370
deep peels 155, 170
dehydrated epidermis 95, 182-3
dehydrated skin 73
dehydroepiandrosterone 378
dermal melasma 89, 119-20
dermaplaning 5, 29, 56, 63, 95, 126, 128, 141-2, 146, 148, 155, 181-3, 185-6, 201-2, 237
  contraindications 183
  indications 183
  protocol 184
  supplies 101, 105, 141, 183-4, 370, 378, 414
dermatologist 3, 123-4, 273, 311, 359, 411, 414
dermis 115, 119-20, 129-30, 133, 149, 156, 167, 170, 175, 182, 201, 230, 247-8, 255-6, 346
DHEA-Ascorbate 378
diazolidinyl urea 366
diet 61, 73, 99, 106, 112, 131, 134-6, 139-40, 149, 391
diisocetyl adipate 367
dimethicone 370
dimethylol dimethyl (DMDM) hydantoin 366
discoloration 8, 30, 117-18, 138, 176, 210, 215, 233, 235-6, 259, 282-3, 307, 309, 319-20, 322
diseases 18, 20-1, 30, 75, 114, 143, 312, 360
disodium lauryl sulfosuccinate 370
DMAE (Dimethylaminoethanol) 379
DNA 133, 135-7, 139, 373-4
drugs 103, 110, 116, 281, 360, 369, 410

dry skin   43, 62, 69, 73, 89, 145, 411
dryness   100, 103, 143, 164-5, 167
Dysport   274-5, 280, 327

E

ears   163, 216, 300, 306-7
Edelweiss   377
edema   81, 259, 278, 295, 311-12, 343, 347, 385, 389
elastin   130-1, 133-6, 138, 191, 256, 285, 346, 348, 373, 376, 382
elastin production   354, 376
electrocautery   78-9, 83
electromagnetic spectrum   219-20, 222, 231, 269, 339
ellagic acid   374
emblica   125, 162
emitting diodes   347-8, 357
emollients   256, 367, 370, 389
  acetylated lanolin   367
  apricot kernel oil   367
  caprylic-capric-linoleic triglyceride   367
  cyclomethicone   367, 370
  diisocetyl adipate   367
  glycerin   73, 367-9
  isopropyl palmitate   367
  lanolin   367-8
  natural
    beeswax   367-8
    castor oil   367, 369
    coconut oil   367
    grapeseed   367
    jojoba oil   367
    jojoba wax   367
    palm oil   367
    safflower oil   367
    soy wax   367
    sunflower oil   367
    sweet almond oil   367

petrolatum   367, 370, 416
polyethylene glycol   367, 369
propylene glycol-dioctanoate   367
steareth-4 stearate   367
ulan   367

emulsifiers
  beeswax   367-8
  emulsifying wax   368
  glycerol stearate   368
  lanolin   367-8
  polysorbate   368
  stearic acid   368
  stearyl 7/palmitate   368

emulsions
  oil-in-water   368
  water-in-oil   368

energy   85, 210, 213, 220, 222, 225-7, 229-30, 233-6, 238-9, 242-4, 249-50, 266-7, 340-3, 345-8, 356
  electrical   348, 354

enzymes   113, 117, 134-7, 139, 141, 154, 274, 289, 349, 354, 374, 379

epidermal layers   201

epidermis   19, 69, 77, 100, 122, 128-9, 133, 154-6, 159, 181-2, 190-1, 201, 240, 248, 388

Erbium: YAG lasers   221, 225, 230-1, 237, 243, 245, 248-51, 255, 259

erythema   69, 81, 109, 127, 166, 195, 223, 259, 278, 318, 343, 347

Erythematotelangiectatic type rosacea (ETR)   110

estheticians   3-10, 13, 15, 17-20, 28-9, 32, 88, 123, 156-7, 165-7, 181, 193, 395-7, 407-9, 424
  advanced training   7, 10, 13, 25, 84, 112, 218, 334, 361, 396, 399, 405, 408, 410-11, 424
  education   7, 10, 13, 25, 84, 112, 218, 334, 361, 396, 399, 405, 408, 410-11, 424
  licensed   7, 175
  medical   6-7, 18, 32
  professionalism   3, 10, 210, 398, 418
  role   17
  supervision   14-15

ETR (Erythematotelangiectatic type rosacea)   110
exercise   61, 99, 135, 139-40, 279
  aerobic   162, 164, 166, 170
exfoliants
  citric acid   159, 370, 372
  gluconolactone   372
  glycolic acid   157, 159, 171, 199-200, 371
  lactic acid   96, 102, 113-14, 125, 153, 159, 162, 164, 199-200, 371
  lipohydroxy acid   372
  malic acid   159, 199, 371
  mandelic acid   159, 371
  salicylic acid   80, 82-3, 95-6, 100, 102, 113, 157, 162-6, 169, 199-200, 254, 372
  tartaric acid   159, 199, 371
  TCA peel   5, 27, 96, 102, 156, 163, 165, 167, 169, 199, 242
exfoliate   162, 173-5, 199, 201-2, 253, 365, 372
exfoliating   17, 126, 173-4, 181, 200, 364, 371
exfoliation   154, 159, 174-5, 254
extract
  cochineal   369
  grape skin   369
  rumex   125
extractions   95, 101, 145, 155, 162
eye area   142, 210, 304, 317, 322, 339, 382-5
eyebrows   274-5, 277, 281, 326
eyelids   109, 112, 180, 201, 279, 303-4, 383
eyes   37-9, 43-4, 72, 74, 110-12, 141-2, 160, 168, 174, 207-11, 274-6, 303, 305, 381-7, 390-2
eyewear   209-10, 215

F

facelift (rhytidectomy)   300-1, 307
facial cosmetic surgery   299, 301, 303, 305, 307, 309
facial fillers   286-7, 295
facial lipoatrophy   287, 290, 292, 298
fat   96, 99, 134-5, 139, 285, 292, 300, 303-4, 312, 325, 384-5
fat transfer   292-3, 325

FDA (Food and Drug Administration) 23, 104, 123, 208, 251, 274-5, 277, 290-2, 334, 346, 349, 359-60, 362, 367, 369
FDA approval 103, 290-1, 350, 359
Federal Food, Drug and Cosmetic Act (FD&C Act) 360
fee-splitting 16-17, 46
ferulic acid 372
filler treatment 294-5
fillers 9, 13-14, 32, 41, 129, 142-3, 276-7, 285-95, 297-8, 301, 352, 384
  Artefill 291
  best candidates 294
  calcium hydroxylapatite 290
  cannulas 287
  collagen 290
  complications 294
  determine which to use 292
  facial 286-7, 295
  fat transfer 292-3, 325
  hyaluronic 288, 295
  hyaluronic acid 288, 295
  Sculptra 292, 298, 325
  silicone 291
  soft tissue 285, 287, 289, 291, 293, 295, 297, 384
  treatment areas 295
fine lines and wrinkles, appearance of 140, 233, 282-3, 341, 356
fingers 299, 313, 366-7
first impression 37, 39-41, 86, 284, 398, 417, 424, 427
Fitzpatrick scale 67, 71, 118, 236
  type I 71
  type II 72
  type III 72
  type IV 70, 72
  type V 72
  type VI 72
Fitzpatrick skin types 127, 167, 188, 251, 340
flushing 66, 109-10, 114-15, 232
follicles 80-1, 100, 102, 162, 182, 186, 232, 237, 266, 307, 364

folliculitis   80, 241-2
Food and Drug Administration *see* FDA
form, client's history   160, 168
formulations   102, 114, 132, 165, 361, 378-9
fractional ablative resurfacing *see* ablative resurfacing
fractionated ablative lasers   247-8
fractionated CO_2 laser   251, 255-6, 258
fragrance   177, 215, 252, 322, 369-70, 391
free radicals   61, 113, 135-6, 144, 259, 372-3, 377, 412
  production of   140
frown lines   274, 280-1
fumaric acid   377

G

genetics   111, 130, 384, 392
Glogau Wrinkle Scale   70
  type I   70
  type II   70
  type III   70
  type IV   70
gloves   22, 24, 212, 214, 216
gluconolactone   372
glutathione   136, 390
glycerin   73, 367-9
glyceryl stearate   368, 370
glycolic acid   157, 159, 171, 199-200, 371
glycolic acid peels   156, 170
  results   159
glycyrrhiza glabra extract   374
goggles   180, 209-11, 215
gotu kola   378
grape seed   139, 377
green tea   96, 136, 140, 379
growth factors   142-3, 189, 254, 259, 283, 375
  animal   375
    crypthompalous aspersa   375

human   375
plant   375
  N6-furfuryladenine   375
synthetic   375

H

hair   18, 37-8, 42, 57, 81, 87, 125, 182, 186, 214, 237, 239, 265-6, 282, 399
hair follicle   80, 217, 237, 239, 241, 266, 307, 364
hair reduction   229-30, 232, 237, 239
hair removal   182, 230, 269
HBV (Hepatitis B virus)   19-20, 23
HBV, vaccination   30
head   37, 252, 304, 306-7, 314, 328
heal   60, 124, 176, 186, 188, 214, 244, 251, 281, 307, 340, 348, 361, 370
healing
  centella asiatica   136, 378
  DHEA-ascorbate   378
  DMAE (Dimethylaminoethanol)   379
  gotu kola   378
  L-glycine   378
  vitamin K   113, 282, 294, 307, 378, 382, 384, 390
health   4-5, 19, 25, 38, 40, 61, 93, 129, 133, 312, 356, 359, 367, 405
health information   25, 31
Health Insurance Portability and Accountability Act *see* HIPAA
healthy skin   5, 8, 93, 129, 137, 141, 154, 268, 309, 317
heart disease   140, 143, 149
heat   101, 112-13, 115, 192, 200, 216, 226-7, 229-30, 232, 234-8, 243-4, 247-8, 339-41, 343-4, 346-8
heating   229, 234, 341-3, 364
Hepatitis   19-21, 30, 214
Hepatitis B virus *see* HBV
Hepatitis C   19, 21, 30
HIPAA (Health Insurance Portability and Accountability Act)   7, 17, 25, 27-8, 31, 33
  guidelines   27
HIV (human immunodeficiency virus)   19-21, 23, 30, 292, 298
hollowing   286-7, 384, 392

home skin care 62, 88, 340
human growth factors 375
human immunodeficiency virus *see* HIV
humectants 112, 368, 391
  acetamide monoethanolamine (MEA) 368
  glycerin 73, 367-9
  hyaluronic acid 73, 95-6, 113, 174, 191, 253, 256, 259, 283, 288-90, 294, 325, 368, 370, 377-8
  propylene glycol 368-9
  sodium pyrrolidine carboxylic acid (PCA) 368
  sorbitol 368
hyaluronic acid fillers 288, 295
hyaluronic fillers, on the market 289
hydrating products 162, 169, 191
hydrators 378
  avocado oil 378
  hyaluronic acid 73, 95-6, 113, 174, 191, 253, 256, 259, 283, 288-90, 294, 325, 368, 370, 377-8
  L-lysine 378
  squalane 370, 378
hydroquinone 125-6, 128, 142, 148, 162, 257, 374, 389
hyperhidrosis 277-8
hyperpigmentation 51, 101, 117, 119, 121, 123, 125-7, 157, 162, 164-5, 167, 236-7, 257, 383-4, 390-1
  actinic keratoses 117, 122-3
  camouflage makeup 322
  cancerous lesions 117, 123
  clinical characteristics 117
  medication 122
  melasma 118
  PIH (post-inflammatory hyperpigmentation) 101, 117, 122, 157, 217, 230, 256, 347, 374
  treatment 125
  ultraviolet exposure 118
hypertrophic scars 84
hypopigmentation 71, 126-7, 131, 170, 216, 218, 236, 249, 258, 323, 374
  camouflage makeup 323

I

idebenone 372
imidazolidinyl urea 366
impetigo 77, 83
incisions 300-4, 308-9, 327-8
infection 21, 23-4, 30, 80, 83, 89, 103, 106, 148, 164, 170, 176, 183, 255-7, 309-10
infectious materials 19-24, 30
inflammation 50-1, 71, 74-5, 94, 96-7, 101, 106, 109-10, 112-13, 117, 121-2, 135-7, 146-7, 216-17, 350
  reducing 96, 114, 140, 345
ingredients 62, 64, 66, 84, 95-6, 100, 102, 113, 118, 126, 142-3, 359-66, 386, 389-90, 392
  active
    alpha hydroxy acids (AHAs) 62, 78, 80-1, 95, 141-3, 153, 155-7, 159-63, 165, 167-71, 176, 184, 283, 308, 371-2
    antibacterial 196, 372, 378
    antioxidants 88, 105, 113, 133, 136-7, 140-2, 144, 149, 157, 189, 282-3, 308, 372-5, 377-9, 382
    BHAs (beta hydroxy acid) 78, 95-6, 141-3, 153, 155-7, 159, 161-3, 165, 167-9, 171, 283, 372
    growth factors 142-3, 189, 254, 259, 283, 375
    hydrators 378
    retinoids 81, 84, 100-1, 103, 114, 125-6, 194, 340, 371, 375
    skin lighteners 125, 374
    stem cells 141-3, 189, 259, 308, 375, 377, 392
  inactive 361-2, 366
    buffers 361, 370, 389
    colorants 352, 369, 391
    emollients 256, 367, 370, 389
    emulsifiers 368
    fragrance 177, 215, 252, 322, 369-70, 391
    humectants 112, 368, 391
    liposomes 371
    lubricants 252, 370
    occlusives 361, 370, 389
    parabens 366-8, 380

    preservatives   177, 361-2, 366, 368, 389
    solvents   369, 389
    stabilizers   140, 361, 368, 389, 391
    surfactants   370
    suspending agents   370
    vehicles   85, 363, 365, 370-1, 389
  natural / organic   363
injections   21, 105, 115, 235, 273, 277-9, 282-3, 292, 295, 298, 326
injury   75, 77, 104, 122, 131, 157, 189, 209, 211, 254-5, 265, 312, 340
intense pulsed light *see* IPL
interview   395, 399-400, 425
IPL (intense pulsed light)   63, 81, 115, 146, 177, 229, 231-7, 239, 241, 243, 245, 247, 266-9, 339-40, 352
iron oxides   369
isopropyl myristate   369
isopropyl palmitate   367
Isotretinoin   52, 63, 78, 96, 100, 103, 145, 160, 176

J

jawline   216, 276, 287, 326
Jessner's peel   68, 96, 102, 126, 153, 155, 157, 159, 161, 163-5, 167, 169, 171, 199-200
  contraindications   165
  indications   165
  post-treatment   165
jojoba wax   367
joules   217, 227, 266
Juvederm injections   288

K

keloid scars   83, 251
keratosis pilaris   81, 163, 175, 371
kojic acid   125, 142-3, 162, 374, 389
KTP (potassium titanyl phosphate) laser   221, 225, 230-1, 243, 245

L

L-arginine 373
L-ascorbic acid 113, 140, 162, 254, 361, 373, 390
L-ascorbyl palmitate 373
L-asorbic acid 125
L-cysteine 373
L-glycine 378
L-lysine 378
L-proline 377
lactic acid 96, 102, 113-14, 125, 153, 159, 162, 164, 199-200, 371
lanolin 367-8
laser 6, 13-16, 18, 78-80, 127-8, 141-3, 207-20, 224-8, 230, 232-4, 236-45, 247-51, 253-5, 257-63, 265-8
  components 219, 224
  devices 209, 211-12, 240, 337
  energy 214, 240, 266-7
  hair reduction 210, 214, 217, 237-8, 241-2, 265-6
  hair removal 4, 13-16, 18, 80, 217, 237, 239, 266-7
  hand piece 212-13, 216
  light 104, 213, 224, 233-4, 237, 247, 268
  mediums 225
  pointer 232
  resurfacing 78, 81, 219, 234, 247, 249, 251, 253, 255, 257, 259, 261, 263
  safety 207-9, 211, 213, 215, 217, 263
  tattoo removal 243, 245
  technicians 14-16, 18, 33, 397
laser-generated air contaminants (LGAC) 212, 215
laser treatment 6, 14, 18, 115, 121-2, 127-8, 141-3, 183, 212-13, 215-17, 226-7, 247-9, 254-5, 261-2, 266-8
  checklist of precautions 215
  contraindications 213
  resurfacing 78, 81, 219, 234, 247, 249, 251, 253, 255, 257, 259, 261, 263
  settings 226-7, 262
  supplies 214
laser treatments
  precautions 215

treatment room setup   215
lasers   79, 114-15, 127, 141-3, 207-9, 211-12, 214, 216-18, 220, 228-34, 236-41, 243-5, 247-50, 259-60, 265-7
  ablative   63, 78-9, 83-4, 115, 147, 201, 212, 232, 251, 268, 339, 388
  ablative fractionated   188, 192, 247-51, 253, 255-61, 263, 268, 341
  ANSI Classifications of Laser Safety   208
  Argon   230
  fractionated   192, 247, 268
  infrared   229, 231
  non-ablative laser   60, 148, 175, 183, 194, 215, 229, 232, 258-9, 262, 352
  safety   207-9, 211, 213, 215, 217, 263
  visible light   229, 232, 236, 262, 268-9, 339
lashes   304, 381, 386-7
lauramide DEA   370
LEDs *see* light-emitting diodes
lesions   67, 74-7, 79, 82, 84, 105, 114, 121, 123-4, 127, 186-7, 213, 235, 242, 318
  elevated   76-7
  palpable   74, 76
  pigmented   124, 126, 131, 161, 202, 242, 251, 262
  primary   76
  raised   77, 122, 186
  secondary   76
LGAC (laser-generated air contaminants)   212, 215
licorice extract   374
licorice root   125, 142-3, 162
light, infrared   231, 248, 350-1
light-based therapies   63, 104
light-emitting diodes (LEDs)   3, 10, 63, 96, 115, 187, 317, 339, 347-54, 356-8, 363, 383, 391
  amber light   349
  blue light   349
  contraindications   353
  forms   348
  green light   351
  indications   353
  infrared light   350

origins   348
protocol   351
red light   221, 350, 391
light energy   132, 219-20, 227, 229, 236, 243, 267, 269, 341-2, 347-8, 351
  effects   227
light physics   219, 221, 223, 225, 227
light skin   237
light spectrum   224, 233, 268, 348-9
  visible   115, 208, 222, 224, 230
light therapy   114-15, 123, 126, 182, 205, 208-9, 228, 230, 234-5, 262, 347-9, 352-3
  safety   207-9, 211, 213, 215, 217, 263
lighten   128, 236-7
lightening ingredients   374
lilac stem cells   377
lipohydroxy acid   372
liposomes   371
lips   37-8, 85, 103, 157, 286, 288, 291, 295
liquid nitrogen   83, 121-3, 148
liquids   22, 224-5, 297, 318, 369
low power lasers, indicating   208
lubricants   252, 370
  cyclomethicone   367, 370
  dimethicone   370
  hyaluronic acid   73, 95-6, 113, 174, 191, 253, 256, 259, 283, 288-90, 294, 325, 368, 370, 377-8
  petrolatum   367, 370, 416
lycopene   140, 373
lymph nodes   124, 314-15
lymphatic drainage, manual   306, 311, 316
lymphatic ducts, right   314-15, 328
lymphatic system   312, 317, 344-5

M

macrophages   135, 315
macule   76
magnesium aluminum silicate   368

magnesium ascorbyl phosphate (MAP) 373
malic acid 159, 199, 371
mandelic acid 159, 371
manual lymphatic drainage 306, 311, 316
  see MLD
  benefits 316
  contraindications 7, 88, 103, 127, 153, 160, 164-5, 167, 173, 186-7, 201-2, 213, 279-80, 316-17, 356
  post-sugery 317
  technique 314
  training 315
  Vodder Method 312-13, 324, 328
massage techniques 311, 313, 316-17
matrix metalloproteinase inhibitors (MMPIs) 137
matrix metalloproteinases (MMPs) 134, 136, 144, 349
medical 7, 13-15, 17-18, 33, 56, 62, 65, 96, 99, 102, 155, 165, 175, 192, 220
  conditions 29, 56, 59, 62, 79, 88, 93, 95, 104, 165, 188, 192, 214, 241, 316-17
  devices 217-18, 335, 347
  facilities 15-17
  offices 19-20, 24, 52, 173, 353-4, 378, 395-6
  practice 4, 6, 14, 27, 29, 68, 403
  procedures 6-8, 15-16, 18, 29, 61, 182-3, 191, 305, 384
  providers 7, 10, 41, 277, 286-7, 304
medical esthetician 6-7, 18, 32
medical spas 13, 17-18, 32-3
  advertising 16
  esthetician in a 18
  social media 16-17, 33, 403, 405
medical treatment 14, 16, 194, 295, 404
medications 5, 52, 63-4, 66, 93, 95-6, 99, 103-4, 106, 112, 114, 122, 146, 213, 230
medicine 3, 8, 15, 18, 40, 132, 316, 344
melanin 117-19, 122, 126, 133, 226, 229-31, 236, 267
  producing 117
melanin production 71, 119, 373
melanocytes 71, 117, 119, 122, 124, 218, 258
melanogenesis process 117-18, 374

melanoma 124-5
  ABC's rule 124
  risk factors 125
melasma 68, 76, 117-18, 121, 126, 128, 148, 236, 251
message 8, 26, 37, 410-11
metronidazole 114, 147
micro-focused ultrasound 346
  treatment 346
micro-needling 7, 32, 50-1, 63, 74-5, 83-4, 95, 141, 145, 183, 187-95, 197, 202-4, 305, 363-4
  contraindications 192
  healing stages 189
  history 187
  indications 192
  methods 188
  post-treatment 195
  pre-treatment 194, 207
  protocol 196
microbial growth 366
microcurrent 317, 339, 347, 353-4, 356, 383, 391
  ATP (adenosine tri-phosphate) 317, 348, 354, 391
  contraindications 356
  indications 356
microdermabrasion 4-6, 29, 60, 63, 75, 89, 95, 126-8, 141, 145, 148, 155-6, 170, 173-7, 200-2
  aluminum oxide crystals 173-4
  contraindications 176
  factors affecting results 177
  indications 175
  micronized diamond-tip 173
  post-treatment 176, 195, 343
  protocol 178
  safety 180
  sodium bicarbonate salts 173
  treatment expectations 153, 173, 176, 346
microdermabrasion machine 177

microdermabrasion treatment   173, 176
migraines   278
milia   78, 89
mineral makeup   106, 254, 318, 321-2, 329, 419, 427
mineral oil   369
minerals   140, 143, 149, 274, 321-2, 324, 369
  aluminum powders   369
  iron oxides   369
  titanium dioxide   321, 369-70
  zinc oxide   112-13, 147, 162, 169, 254, 258-9, 309, 321, 369, 381
MLD (Manual lymphatic drainage)   306, 311, 314-17, 323, 328-9
MMPs   134, 136, 349, 391 *see also* matrix metalloproteinases
  overproduction of   136-7
modified Jessner's   155, 163, 165, 168
moisturizers   74, 101, 106, 141-3, 157, 162, 164, 179, 183, 189, 200, 240, 389, 416
muscle contraction   282-3, 375
muscles   273-4, 276, 278-9, 281-2, 298, 300-1, 304, 314, 325, 328, 345-6, 353-6, 376, 383
musk   370

N

N6-furfuryladenine   375
nasolabial folds   9, 286, 289-90, 295, 297, 301
natural   41, 45, 63, 112, 130-1, 156, 191-2, 292, 320-3, 329, 362, 366-7, 369, 378-9, 387
natural skin color   235, 321
natural skin tone   322-3
neck skin   301, 379
needles   22-4, 188, 190, 195-6, 277
needling   187, 192, 194, 203
needling devices   189-90
neurotoxin injections   274, 277-9, 283
neurotoxin treatment   194, 279-80, 283, 326, 383
neurotoxins   14, 32, 141-3, 273-7, 279-83, 295, 325-6, 352-3, 383
  Botox   13-14, 16, 18, 28, 68, 274-8, 281, 284, 326
  complications   279

complimentary products 283
skin care 282
neurotoxins. cosmetic use 273-4
NHZ (Nominal Hazard Zone) 209-10
niacinamide 95-6, 113, 254, 377
nodule 76, 124, 291
Nominal Hazard Zone (NHZ) 209-10
non-ablative 142-3, 201, 229, 269
non-ablative laser 60, 148, 175, 183, 194, 215, 229, 232, 258-9, 262, 352
nose 24, 39, 43, 56, 109, 111, 117, 122, 142, 157, 160, 162, 301-3, 305-6, 309-10
nostrils 160, 168, 302-3, 327
NPs (nurse practitioners) 7, 14, 16-17
nurse practitioners *see* NPs
nurses 13-16

O

occlusive agents 112, 142-3, 160, 168, 244, 253, 255-7, 268, 411
occlusives 361, 370, 389
  octamethyl cyclotetrasiloxane 370
  shea butter 113, 370
  simethicone 370
  squalane 370, 378
  titanium dioxide 321, 369-70
  zinc 140, 370
occlusives, petrolatum 367, 370, 416
Occupational Safety and Health Administration *see* OSHA
octamethyl cyclotetrasiloxane 370
oil 68, 73-4, 98, 100, 106, 133, 139, 163, 182, 342, 361, 368, 370, 372
  apricot kernel 367
  castor 367, 369
  coconut 367
  grapeseed 367
  jojoba 367
  mineral 369
  palm 367
  safflower 367

sunflower   367
sweet almond   367
tea tree   96, 379
visible   68, 73-4
OSHA
  regulations   20-1, 23-4, 179, 190, 196, 201, 207, 211
  safe handling of needles   23
  sanitation requirements   23
OSHA (Occupational Safety and Health Administration)   7, 19, 21, 23, 30-1, 208, 212
OSHA, handle an exposure   24
OSHA, Personal Protective Equipment (PPE)   22, 24, 31, 212
oxygen   61, 95-6, 101, 117, 134, 136, 141, 350, 372, 378
oxyhemoglobin   115, 226, 229-30

P

palmitoyl pentapeptide   376
palmitoyl tetrapeptide   376
palmitoyl tripeptide-38   376
papaya   95, 379
paper mulberry   374
papule   76
papules   80-2, 94, 113
parabens   366-8, 380
  butylparaben   366-7
  ethylparaben   366
  and the FDA   366-8, 380
  isobutylparaben   366
  methylparaben   366-7
  propylparaben   366-7
PAs (physician assistants)   7, 14, 17
patch   76
patch test   180, 216, 374
patient care   16, 33
patient coordinator   311, 396
patient files   27, 32

patients   7-10, 25-9, 210-18, 234-7, 248-52, 254-63, 275-83, 285-9, 291-5, 297-307, 309-12, 318-24, 326-8, 339-44, 403-4
peeling   74, 156, 163, 165-8, 200, 248, 420
peeling skin   156, 166, 170
peels   51, 60, 100, 102, 133, 153, 155-7, 159, 161-2, 164-70, 185, 371-2
  phenol   148, 170
  timed   160, 163-4
peptides   111, 141-3, 189, 259, 283, 296, 375, 382, 389, 392, 404
  acetyl hexapeptide-8   376
  carrier   376
  neurotransmitter   375
  palmitoyl pentapeptide   376
  palmitoyl tetrapeptide   376
  palmitoyl tripeptide-38   376
  signal   375
  TGF Beta-1   376
permanent fillers   293-4, 298
personal devices   25
Personal Protective Equipment (PPE)   22, 24, 31, 212
personality types   46
pesticides   363
petrolatum   367, 370, 416
pharmaceuticals   359
PHAs (poly hydroxy acids)   372
phenyl-butyl-nitrone   373
photodynamic therapy   104, 123, 230, 349
photons   219, 224-5, 348
phyllanthus emblica   374
physician assistants *see* PAs
physician-owned corporations   15-16
physician supervision   14
physicians   3-10, 13-18, 29, 31-3, 52, 80-1, 103-5, 121-3, 155-7, 213-14, 233-5, 255-7, 304-8, 310-12, 404
phytic acid   125, 142-3, 374
pigment   71, 75, 89, 110, 117-22, 125-8, 130, 218, 230, 234, 236-7, 243, 247, 319, 421
pigment lighteners   126, 142-3, 162, 164, 254

Index

pigment production   121, 409
pigmentation   45, 68, 70, 74-5, 88-9, 122, 125-7, 142, 162, 182, 194, 217, 230, 234-6, 254
  crusted   175, 183, 201
  dermal   119, 175
  superficial   148, 160, 163-5, 201
pigments
  animal   297, 345, 369-70, 375, 377
  mineral origin   369
  vegetable   369
PIH (post-inflammatory hyperpigmentation)   101, 117, 122, 157, 217, 230, 256, 347, 374
pityrosporum follicultis   80
plaque plateau   76
poly hydroxy acids
  see PHAs
  gluconolactone   372
polyethylene glycol   367, 369
polyphenols   136
port wine stain   79, 230, 234-5
post-inflammatory hyperpigmentation see PIH
post-laser skin care kit   261
post-treatment   60, 194, 239, 256, 278-80, 291
post-treatment care instructions   162, 164-5, 169-70
post-treatment instructions   162
potassium dihydrogen   370
potassium titanyl phosphate (KTP) lasers   230
PPE see Personal Protective Equipment
prepping solution   160, 163, 165, 168
preservatives   177, 361-2, 366, 368, 389
  emollients   256, 367, 370, 389
  parabens   366-8, 380
prickly pear   379
products   29-30, 48-9, 100-1, 126, 141-4, 157-9, 162-3, 287-93, 333-7, 359-70, 378-9, 382-6, 396, 407-15, 426-8
  anti-aging   377-8, 390

cosmetic 99, 360, 366-7
hypoallergenic 362
lipid-soluble 163, 364
medicinal 345, 388
oil-based 364-5, 389
oxide 282, 294
petrolatum-based 160, 168
pigment lightening 162, 201
retinol 155, 413
topical skin 333
water-based 364-5, 389
propionibacterium acnes 93, 145
propylene glycol 368-9
propylene glycol-dioctanoate 367
protective eyewear 208-10, 215
proteins 104, 133, 135-6, 226, 275, 347, 373, 375, 377
pseudofolliculitis barbae 80, 164
psoriasis 61, 76-7, 82, 163, 175, 268, 371, 377
puffiness 303, 305, 317, 322, 329, 381, 383, 385, 391
pulse width 210, 217, 227, 243, 259, 266, 269
pure minerals 318, 322, 329
pustules 76-7, 80, 93-4, 113, 145-6, 257

R

radiation 209, 219-20, 222, 348
Radiesse 290
radio frequency (RF) 63, 75, 89, 113, 283, 297, 335, 339-43, 347, 357, 380, 383, 388, 390, 392
  devices 340-1
redness 6, 50, 69, 82, 109-10, 112-14, 127, 146-7, 160, 164-7, 203, 235, 260, 262, 321
registered nurses *see* RNs
regulations 6-7, 10, 13, 18-19, 24-6, 181, 207, 209, 223, 316, 347
rejuvenation 233-4, 245, 339, 341, 343, 345, 347, 349, 351, 353-5, 357
resveratrol 136, 140-2, 373
reticular dermis 190, 255
retinaldehyde 100, 371

retinoic acid (Retin-A) 371
retinoid products 100, 114
retinoids 81, 84, 100-1, 103, 114, 125-6, 194, 340, 371, 375
  adalpene 100, 371
  retinaldehyde 100, 371
  retinoic acid 371
  retinol 78, 95-6, 100, 133, 136, 141-3, 155, 254, 268, 283, 335, 371, 376, 382, 413
  retinyl palmitate 100, 371
  tazarotene 100, 371
  tretinoin 63, 100, 359, 371
retinol 78, 95-6, 100, 133, 136, 141-3, 155, 254, 268, 283, 335, 371, 376, 382, 413
retinyl palmitate 100, 371
RF *see* Radio frequency
rhinophyma 109, 111, 146-7
rhinoplasty 299, 301, 303, 305, 307-8, 327
  closed 301-3
  open 301-2, 327
rhytidectomy 142-3, 299-300, 307, 328
ringworm 83
RNs (registered nurses) 7, 17
ROS (reactive oxygen species) 134-6, 143
rosacea 50-1, 61, 67-8, 109-16, 146-7, 165, 175-6, 191, 193, 202, 224, 230, 232, 316, 350-1
  causes 111
  erythematotelangiectatic 110
  papulopustular 50, 110-11, 146, 192
  phymatous 111, 115
  skin care recommendations 109, 112
  stages 109-10
  triggers 112
Ruby lasers 220, 228, 230

S

safety 7, 24, 71, 126, 196, 209, 217, 236, 298, 333-4, 336-7, 367
safety measures 207-10, 228
saffron 369

sagging skin 130-1, 234, 301, 339
salicylic acid 80, 82-3, 95-6, 100, 102, 113, 157, 162-6, 169, 199-200, 254, 372
salicylic peels 113
saunas 162, 164, 166, 170
scale 67, 70-1, 77, 81, 118, 122, 160-1, 168-9, 236
scalpel 181-4, 201
scarring 30, 89, 101, 106, 109, 126, 166-7, 170, 179, 191, 244, 249, 258-9, 282-3, 307-9
scars 83, 105, 167, 187, 192, 218, 244, 251, 293, 295, 307-8, 323, 330, 388
  atrophic 84
  hypertrophic 84
  indented 323
  keloid 83, 251
Sculptra 292, 298, 325
sebaceous hyperplasia 78, 89, 262
seborrheic dermatitis 82
seborrheic keratoses 82
sebum 75, 93, 95, 162, 266-7, 364, 377-8, 391
  overproduction of 96, 100
self-esteem 40, 43-4, 85-6, 96, 299
sensation, skin 160-2, 168, 306, 341
sensitivity 60, 62, 100-2, 138, 143, 157, 160, 164-5, 167-8, 170, 174, 191, 362, 375, 381
septoplasty 299, 303, 327
septum 301, 303, 327
sharps 22-3, 31
shea butter 113, 370
sheep placenta 377
signal peptides 375
silicones 113, 291, 307, 370
  cyclomethicone 367, 370
  dimethicone 370
silymarin (milk thistle) 373
simethicone 370
skin 49-54, 59-64, 67-71, 73-5, 121-6, 129-40, 156-60, 162-70, 173-84, 254-62, 300-9, 339-53, 361-5, 367-76, 411-16

acne-affected   107
acneic   163
conditioners   370, 374
dead   81, 93, 100, 102, 182, 184
deeper layers of   133, 229
dry   95-6
exfoliation   100, 154, 156
inflamed   53, 101, 316-17
lifestyle effects   133
non-intact   24
oily   74, 95-6, 102, 105, 165, 322, 372
photo-damaged   167, 249
resurfacing   247-8, 258
sensitive   114, 156, 174, 199, 236, 370, 372
sensitized   101-2, 113, 382
superficial layers   119, 132, 136, 174, 185, 187, 223, 229, 341
tanned   214, 236, 268
taut   178, 300
texture   138, 247, 262, 308
skin cancer   123-4, 132-3, 214, 223, 342, 348, 372
skin care   3-5, 7-10, 20, 28-9, 41, 66, 100, 113-14, 123, 157, 162, 258-9, 295-7, 306, 404
skin care formulations   361-2, 389
skin care products   4, 62, 113, 128, 196, 334, 359, 364, 371-3, 376
skin care provider   8-10, 44, 67, 102, 114, 122, 124, 259, 282, 306, 324, 336, 385
skin care provider's role   127
skin care regimen   256, 261, 282, 409
  client's   62
  patient's post-surgical   301
skin care regimen post-filler, following   296
skin care treatment   283, 324
skin color   216-17, 258
  changes   343, 388
skin condition analysis   67, 69, 71, 73, 75, 77, 79, 81, 83
  characteristics   70, 73
  documentation   67

Fitzpatrick Scale   67, 71, 118, 236
hydration   73
primary lesions   76
sebum levels   74
skin age   69
skin types   68
texture   73
skin conditions   51, 61-2, 64, 66-8, 84, 91, 99, 118, 121, 131, 137, 153, 176, 188, 347-8
  inflamed   175, 323, 356
skin disorders   76, 171, 230
skin health   308, 373
skin irritations   240, 265, 382
skin lesions   83, 89, 124
skin lighteners   125, 374
  arbutin   125, 162, 374, 389
  azelaic acid   96, 114, 162, 374, 378, 392
  bearberry   125, 374, 390
  ellagic acid   374
  glycyrrhiza glabra extract   374
  hydroquinone   125-6, 128, 142, 148, 162, 257, 374, 389
  Kojic acid   125, 142-3, 162, 374, 389
  licorice extract   374
  paper mulberry   374
  phyllanthus emblica   374
  phytic acid   125, 142-3, 374
skin lightening   126, 159, 371
  abilities   373
  agents   157, 174, 254, 374
  cream   296
  ingredients   257, 389
  products   68, 118, 121, 384
  properties   371, 373-4
skin needling   187-8, 335
skin reactions   122, 216-17
  patient's   217

skin signaling inflammation   166
skin structure, building healthier   154, 156
skin tone   68, 115, 237, 374, 413
  client's   322, 324
skin types   5, 48-9, 68, 71, 73, 124, 141, 188, 191, 236, 251, 371, 382, 414
  client's   68, 105, 178, 195, 353
  Fitzpatrick   240
  lighter   217, 294
sleep   135, 139, 252, 384-5
SMAS (superficial muscular aponeurotic system)   300, 346
smoking   61, 106, 131, 133-4, 136
social media   16-17, 33, 403, 405
sodium laureth sulfate   370
sodium lauryl sulfate   370
sodium pyrrolidine carboxylic acid (PCA)   368
soft tissue fillers   285, 287, 289, 291, 293, 295, 297, 384
solar lentigines   116-17, 121-2, 147-8, 236
solvents   369, 389
  acetone   160, 168, 178, 183-4, 255, 369
  alcohol   102, 112, 160, 168, 183-4, 211-12, 214-15, 255, 327, 342, 346, 366, 369
  castor oil   367, 369
  ethanol   369
  glycerin   73, 367-9
  isopropyl myristate   369
  mineral oil   369
  polyethylene glycol   367, 369
  propylene glycol   368-9
SOPs (Standard Operating Procedures)   22, 68, 208, 211
sorbic acid   366
sorbitol   368
sound waves   344-6, 388
soy   139, 379
soy wax   367
spas   6, 10, 13, 15-17, 30, 339, 341, 343, 345, 347, 349, 351, 353, 355, 357
spin traps PBN   373
spots, pigmented   67-8, 237

squalane   370, 378
squamous cell carcinoma   124
stabilizers   140, 361, 368, 389, 391
  glyceryl stearate   368, 370
  magnesium aluminum silicate   368
  xanthan gum   368, 370
Standard Operating Procedures *see* SOPs
steam baths   162, 164, 166, 170
steareth-4 stearate   367
stearic acid   368
stearyl 7/palmitate   368
stem cells   141-3, 189, 259, 308, 375, 377, 392
  edelweiss   377
  grape seed   139, 377
  lilac   377
  sheep placenta   377
  swiss apple   377, 392
steroids   63, 82-4, 99, 105
stinging   6, 110-11, 162, 168
stratum corneum   154, 176, 363, 365, 377
stress   44, 57, 61, 87, 93, 99, 106, 111-12, 131, 135-6, 139-40, 375
  oxidative   136, 140, 372
suction   174, 177-8, 180
sulfacetamide   114, 147
sulfur   82, 96
sun   53, 61, 63, 100, 102, 122, 125, 132-3, 139, 147, 215, 223-4, 242, 252, 262
  exposure   71, 106, 112, 117, 125, 131, 133, 136, 177, 194, 216-17, 252, 254, 258
sunlight   116, 132-3
sunscreen   62, 74, 100, 112, 125, 132-3, 136-7, 147, 157, 162, 164, 183-4, 282-3, 308, 381-2
  based   162, 169, 254, 258-9, 309
superficial muscular aponeurotic system *see* SMAS
superficial peels   101-2, 128, 141, 155-7
surfactants   370
  alpha-olefin sulfonate   370
  ammonium lauryl sulfate   370

    cocamidopropylbetaine   370
    cocoamphocarboxyglynate   370
    decylpolyglucoside   370
    disodium lauryl sulfosuccinate   370
    sodium laureth sulfate   370
    sodium lauryl sulfate   370
surgery   195, 219, 286-7, 299, 301, 303, 305-10, 323, 339, 345, 347, 383, 385, 422
surgical procedures   286, 303-4, 307, 311, 316, 325, 344, 384
suspending agents   370
    acrylates copolymer   370
    bentonite   370
    carbomer   370
    cellulose gum   370
    cetyl alcohol   370
    glyceryl stearate   368, 370
    gum   370
    lauramide DEA   370
    propylene glycol stearate   370
    xanthan gum   368, 370
swelling   6, 104, 195, 203, 252, 278, 294, 297, 304-10, 317, 328, 345, 385
Swiss apple   377, 392
syringomas   78, 89

T

tape   211, 309, 334
    laser-safe   210
target chromophore   213, 226-7
tartaric acid   159, 199, 371
tattoos   26, 213, 229-30, 242-3, 245
    removal   192, 213, 226, 229, 242-3
tazarotene   100, 371
TCA (Trichloroacetic Acid) peels   5, 27, 79, 96, 102, 114, 126, 153, 155-7, 159, 161, 163, 165, 167, 169, 171, 199-200, 242
    contraindications   167
    indications   167
    post-treatment   170

protocol   168
tea, green   96, 136, 140, 379
tea tree oil   96, 379
teenagers   93, 96, 107, 145
telangiectasia   109-12, 114, 124, 131, 138, 147, 232, 234-5, 256
telomeres   137, 139, 144
TGF Beta-1   376
therapy, photodynamic   104, 123, 146, 230, 349
thermage thermacool   341
thermal relaxation time *see* TRT (thermal relaxation time)
tinea corporus   83
tingling   162, 164-5, 167, 306
tissues   75, 127, 183, 222, 234, 250-1, 257, 298, 300-1, 303-4, 310, 312, 345, 364-5, 389-90
titanium dioxide   321, 369-70
titianium dioxide   147
topical
  agents   80, 112, 114, 121-2
  products   63, 94, 96, 113, 140, 162, 169, 174, 177, 191, 296, 367, 385
toxin   273-5, 279-81, 373
transcellular   364-5
transepidermal water loss   113, 138, 377
trauma   78, 84, 122
tretinoin   63, 100, 359, 371
trichloroacetic acid *see* TCA
triethanolamine   370
tromethamine phosphate   370
TRT (thermal relaxation time)   227
tumeric   369
tyrosinase   117-18, 374

U

ubiquinone   372
ulan   367
ulcer   77
ultrasound   29, 75, 89, 113, 147-8, 283, 317, 335, 339, 344-6, 357, 363-4, 383, 388-90

contraindications   345
   micro-focused   346
   traditional   345
under-eye circles   319, 378, 381
UV light   118-19, 133, 388
   UVA   132
   UVB   81, 132, 223
   UVC   132, 223

V

vascular lesions   115, 189, 229-30, 232, 234-5, 240, 242, 247, 319
Vaseline   160, 168, 309, 411, 416
vehicles   85, 363, 365, 370-1, 389
   liposomes   371
vellus hair   182, 202
venous lakes   79
vesicle circumscribed   76
visible light   221-4, 231, 269, 388
visible light laser   229, 232, 236, 262, 268-9, 339
vitamin   63, 82, 100, 103, 113, 137, 140-3, 157, 361, 371-4, 377-9, 382, 384, 390, 412
   vitamin A   62, 100, 103, 126, 157, 176, 371, 373, 390
   vitamin B5   113, 149, 253, 259, 283, 308, 377
   vitamin C   113, 136, 140-1, 144, 361, 372-4, 377-9, 382, 390, 410
   vitamin E   63, 113, 140, 254, 278, 294, 361, 372, 390, 412
   vitamin K   113, 282, 294, 307, 378, 382, 384, 390
Vodder Method   312-13, 324, 328

W

warts   67, 76, 82-3, 163
water   24, 62, 73, 113, 174, 191, 226, 231, 234, 247-9, 266-7, 289, 363-5, 368, 414
wavelengths   104, 209-10, 213, 215, 220-6, 229-33, 237, 240, 243, 259, 266, 268-9, 345, 348-9
   longer   209, 221, 224, 230, 232, 235
   multiple   231-3
wheals   77, 347
whiteheads   73, 89, 93-4, 201

Wood's lamp   75, 89, 119-21
wound response, controlled   154, 187-8
wounds   24, 69, 75, 164, 188, 195, 261, 308, 320, 340, 342
   healing   62-3, 140, 145, 165, 187, 189, 203, 263, 308, 316, 373, 375-6, 378-9
   response   62-3, 69, 75, 187-8, 192, 194, 247, 261, 339
wrinkles   41, 43, 69-70, 73, 85, 142-3, 191-2, 233-4, 274-5, 280-3, 290-1, 298, 300-1, 340-1, 381-3
   displace   287

X

xanthan gum   368, 370
xanthelasmas   79, 89
xeomin   274-5

Y

YAG laser *see also* Erbium: YAG laser   221, 225, 230-1, 237, 243, 245, 248-51, 255, 259
   resurfacing   249-50, 258

Z

zinc   140, 370
zinc oxide   112-13, 147, 162, 169, 254, 258-9, 309, 321, 369, 381